KINGDOM COME

Dedicated to
CHRISTOPHER REEVE
who makes us believe
that a man can fly.

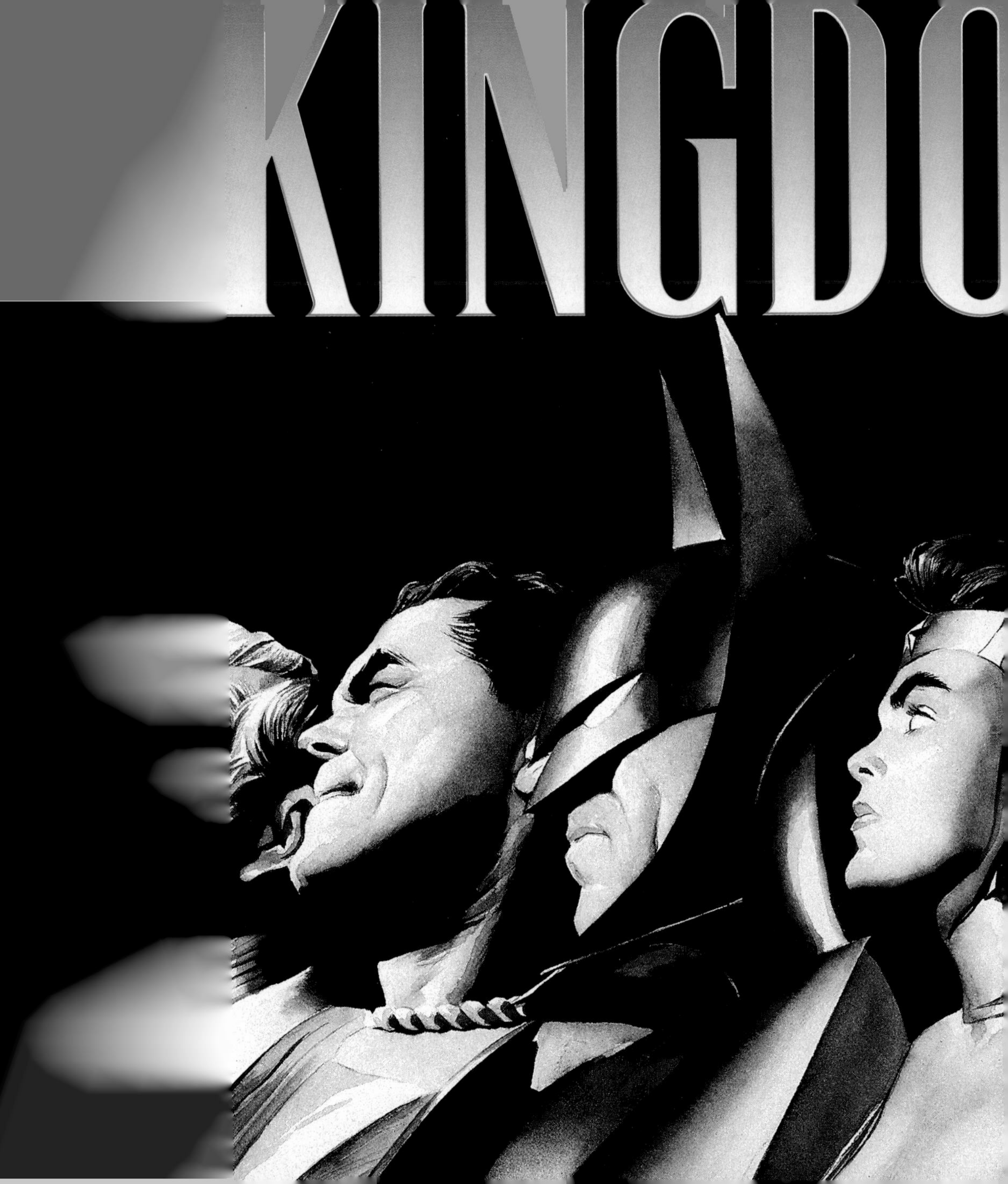
KINGDO

M COME

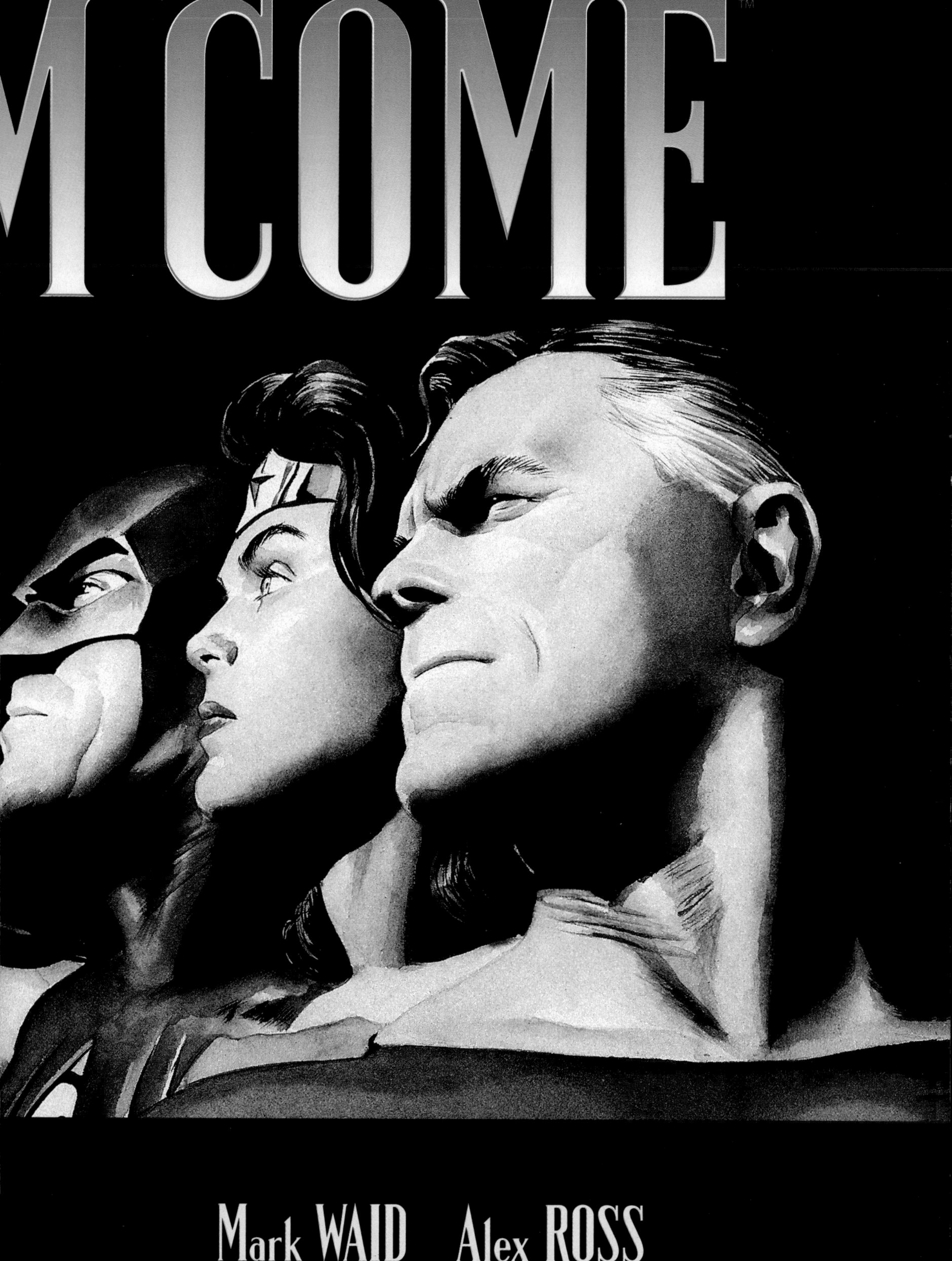

Mark WAID Alex ROSS

TABLE OF CONTENTS

In Elseworlds, heroes are taken from their usual settings and put into strange times and places — some that have existed or might have existed, and others that can't, couldn't or shouldn't exist.

Jenette Kahn
President & Editor-in-Chief

Paul Levitz
Executive Vice President & Publisher

Mike Carlin
VP-Executive Editor

Dan Raspler
Senior Editor & Editor-original miniseries

Bob Kahan
Editor-collected edition

Peter J. Tomasi
Assistant Editor-original miniseries

Jim Spivey
Associate Editor-collected edition

Robbin Brosterman
Senior Art Director

Georg Brewer
VP-Design & Retail Product Development

Richard Bruning
VP-Creative Director

Patrick Caldon
Senior VP-Finance & Operations

Terri Cunningham
VP-Managing Editor

Dan DiDio
VP-Editorial

Joel Ehrlich
Senior VP-Advertising & Promotions

Alison Gill
VP-Manufacturing

Lillian Laserson
VP & General Counsel

Jim Lee
Editorial Director-WildStorm

David McKillips
VP-Advertising

John Nee
VP-Business Development

Cheryl Rubin
VP-Licensing & Merchandising

Bob Wayne
VP-Sales & Marketing

KINGDOM COME
Published by DC Comics. Cover, introduction and additional

DC Comics. 1700 Broadway, New York, New York 10019

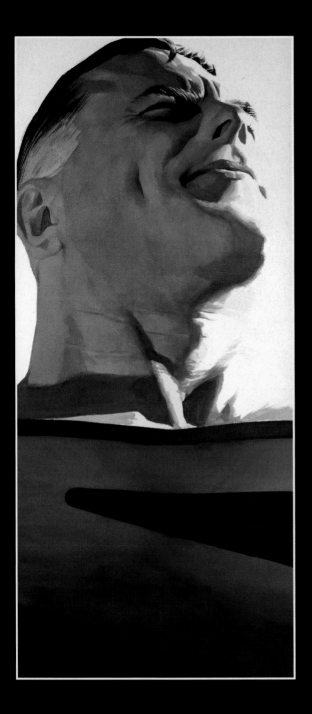

THE NEW BARDS

*An Introduction by
Elliot S. Maggin*

In the waning moments of the twentieth century, the super-hero is Everyman.

Look at the way we live: traveling over the Earth at astounding speeds with unimaginable ease; communicating instantly at will with people in the farthest corners of the globe; engineering economies, driving environmental forces, working wonders. If a person from only a hundred years or so in the past could look in on our lives, that person would suppose that we were not mortals, but gods. He would be bowled over by what the most ordinary among us could do with a car or a light switch or an automatic teller machine. This is the way many of us have always looked upon our super-heroes—as though they were gods. Our person from a lost century would be wrong about us, of course, but no more wrong than we are about our heroes.

In the story that you hold in your hands, Mark Waid and Alex Ross tell us that our proper response to the inexorable march of progress that has brought us to this place and time in the history of civilization is to find a way to confront it responsibly. Not modestly. Not unself-consciously. Not with faith in a power greater than ours to descend from the sky and set things right despite our best efforts to screw up. We have an obligation to know who we are and where we are and what we can do. We have an obligation to understand the ramifications of the things we do, and to choose to do them—or not—with our eyes open.

That is what *Kingdom Come* is about.

As I write this, I am completing

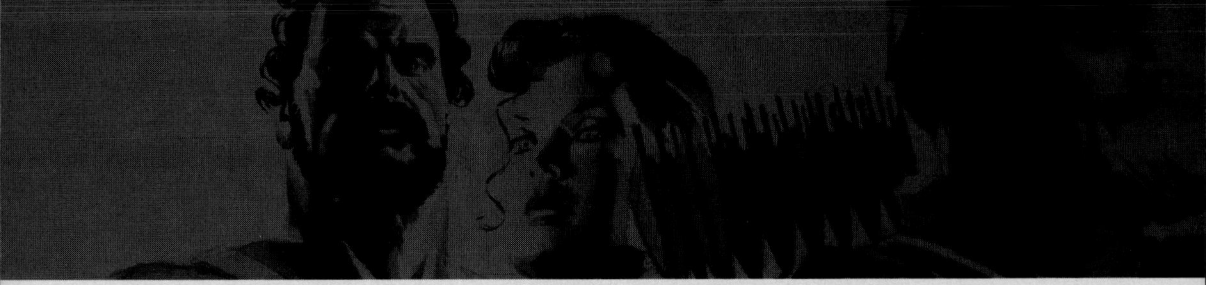

a novel—about a hundred thousand words, one strung after the other without pictures other than the occasional new free-standing illustration by Alex Ross—called *Kingdom Come*. It is an elaboration in prose of the story that follows. In order to write it I, like Mark and Alex, have to believe in heroes. I do. I believe in Superman. For real. I really believe in Wonder Woman, so help me. I believe in Santa Claus. I believe that men have walked on the moon. I believe that every Passover Elijah the prophet comes over for a sip of wine. I believe in metaphors. Metaphors are real. That is why the Scriptures are composed not only of the proverbs and prophecies that Pastor McCay, in the pages that follow, spouts in involuntary reflex; but that is why those Scriptures surround and embrace those pronouncements in stories—the allegories and metaphors—that teach us our values. Here before you is a clash of good against evil, of course, but more than that. There are clashes of judgment, clashes among different interpretations of what is good and of what is justice, and clashes over who is to suffer the wages of the evil born of our best intentions. This is a love story. This is a story of hatred and rage. This is the Iliad. This is the story of how we—we ourselves; you and I—choose to use whatever special powers and abilities we have, when even those powers and abilities are only a little bit beyond those of mortal men. This is a story about truth obscured, justice deferred and the American way distorted in the hands of petty semanticists.

Super-hero stories—whether their vehicle is through comic books or otherwise—are today the most coherent manifestation of the popular unconscious. They're stories not about gods, but about the way humans wish themselves to be; ought, in fact, to be. They're the successors to the stories that once came from the hoe-down and the campfire and the wandering bard. We—all of us—come up with these stories all the time around dorms and carpools and along cafeteria lines at work and at school. Here's one:

I have a friend named Jeph. You know Jeph. I was maybe nineteen or twenty and he was maybe twelve or thirteen and I was a student at this college and Jeph's stepdad was a big muckamuck at the college and stepdad and I made friends. I went over to stepdad's house for dinner one day and Jeph and I got to talking there about our common ground: our mutual love for super-heroes and their stories. We came up with a nifty story over mom and stepdad's dinner table. See, I'd just sold my first comic-book script, a Green Arrow story called "What Can One Man Do?" and I had a problem. I had a meeting soon with Julius Schwartz, the Bard of Bards, to see whether I was a one-trick pony or I could do this sort of thing again. I had to come up with a hit-it-outta-the-park idea for a Superman story or else spend the next three years in law school. I guess I told Jeph a few of my ideas and I guess Jeph told me a few of his. And Jeph came up with this thing he called "Why Must There Be a Superman?" It was about the Guardians of the Universe planting a new idea in Big Blue's head. The idea was that maybe, in his zeal to preserve life and ease the path of the human race, Superman was keeping ordinary everyday good humans from growing on their own. Maybe he was killing the butterfly by helping it out of the chrysalis. Not for sure, but just maybe. That was Jeph's idea.

So I went to Gotham to see the Bard and I had maybe a dozen little germs of ideas packed under my scalp. I'd try this one on him. I'd toss him that one. I'd pitch him another one. Some of them he liked; some of them he didn't. Some of them inspired ideas of the Bard's own; some of them made him snort or snore. By the end of a couple of hours—they were a loud, intense couple of hours, as hours I spent with the Bard of Bards always would be—I was emotionally exhausted and still he wanted to hear more. So I dredged up this idea about what might happen if the Guardians came calling on Superman with the tiniest little criticism of how he was going about his job. Now you're talking fresh stuff, the old man let me know. He got excited. He yanked people in from the hall and made me repeat the idea for them.

I called the story "Must There Be a Superman?" and Saint Curt and Murphy drew it and it made me happy and I put words in Superman's mouth pretty much steadily for the next fifteen years and never went to law school. And I swear I did not have a clue where the idea had come from. Who knows where ideas come from anyway? I didn't remember—still don't remember, in fact, but I believe Jeph—until Jeph told me about his contribution years later. Like twenty or so years later.

Jeph has never suffered, I don't believe, for my inconsiderate oversight, and in fact has always been my friend. He's done well, too. With his buddy Matthew he wrote the first great super-hero movie of the modern period, *Commando* with Arnold Schwarzenegger, and lots of other great stuff. And one day later on I was editor of Jeph's first comic-book series of his own, an eight-issue masterpiece with Tim Sale called *Challengers of the Unknown*. Now he writes for Hollywood and he writes for DC and Marvel and he's happy and he's still my friend, and now I get to make this right too.

Today there are new bards and new stories. Not long ago Mark and Alex went to Gotham to see Dan Raspler—who, it seems to me, was just a smart, ambitious kid last time I saw him and now he's a big muckamuck like Jeph's stepdad—to sell Dan on an idea about what the world would be like if all the super-heroes were to retire and their children, grandchildren and successors generally turn out to be schmucks.

The theme of "Must There Be a Superman?," that icon of another life, is the theme that the new bards of *Kingdom Come* continue. Maybe complete. It is about the time in the lives of Superman, Captain Marvel, Wonder Woman, Batman and the others, when they learn that they are not gods. And it is about the time in their lives when finally they learn that despite their limitations they must be potent and responsible anyway. Now is the time in the life of the human race when all of us need to learn these same things. That is why this story, despite its garish primary-colored clothing, is an important one.

The heroes of fable and fact to whose virtue we all aspire, are not only colorful people leading vivid lives; they traditionally understand the value of human life in all its places and conditions. But real-life heroes, unlike many of the icons we have created, also understand human dignity and human immortality, and these are concepts that are lacking in, for example, Superman's education. Heroes especially need to understand the value of the things of a life: its artifacts, its ideas, its loves. It is the markers you leave along that road that define you. It is the trees a man plants, the children he raises and the stories he tells that signify his life. It is the palaces a people build, the heritage they inspire, the art they create that makes their civilization. I've been trying to tell Superman for years that he mustn't just save lives, he has to spit-polish the real estate too. He's never understood that. He never got it until Mark and Alex told him. They got through to him, finally, and for that I'm proud of them.

In *Kingdom Come*, Mark and Alex draw a dichotomy between the human race and what we call the metahuman race. It is the source of conflict throughout the story. And the story's synthesis is the realization that this distinction is false. As clearly as another hero, Mahatma Gandhi, asserted that he is a Hindu as well as a Muslim—as well as a Christian, a Jew or a Buddhist if that becomes appropriate—so do we learn here that the most ordinary among us are heroes, and the most colorful and vivid among us are quite ordinary and flawed. It is a conclusion to which our new bards lead us as elegantly and precisely as Socrates led us through an argument or Pythagoras led us through a geometric proof.

Even super-heroes need to grow. We know that now. When you read *Kingdom Come*, you will too.

If we were to peek in on the lives of the people of the Earth in generations to come, surely we would think we were gazing upon Olympus. And of course, again, we would be wrong. They are only our children, our grandchildren and our successors who will surely stride the Earth as titans in those days, wearing our own features and our own shortcomings. They are our messengers to that resplendent future. And they will bring with them into their time whatever values and iconography that we have to offer them today. Here in the pages that follow is an admirable start. To cite the sentiment of another old friend whom I miss (And if you travel west anytime, Alan, come find me, will you?): This is an imaginary story...aren't they all?

Elliot S! Maggin
Where the Wind Hits Heavy
New Year's, 1997

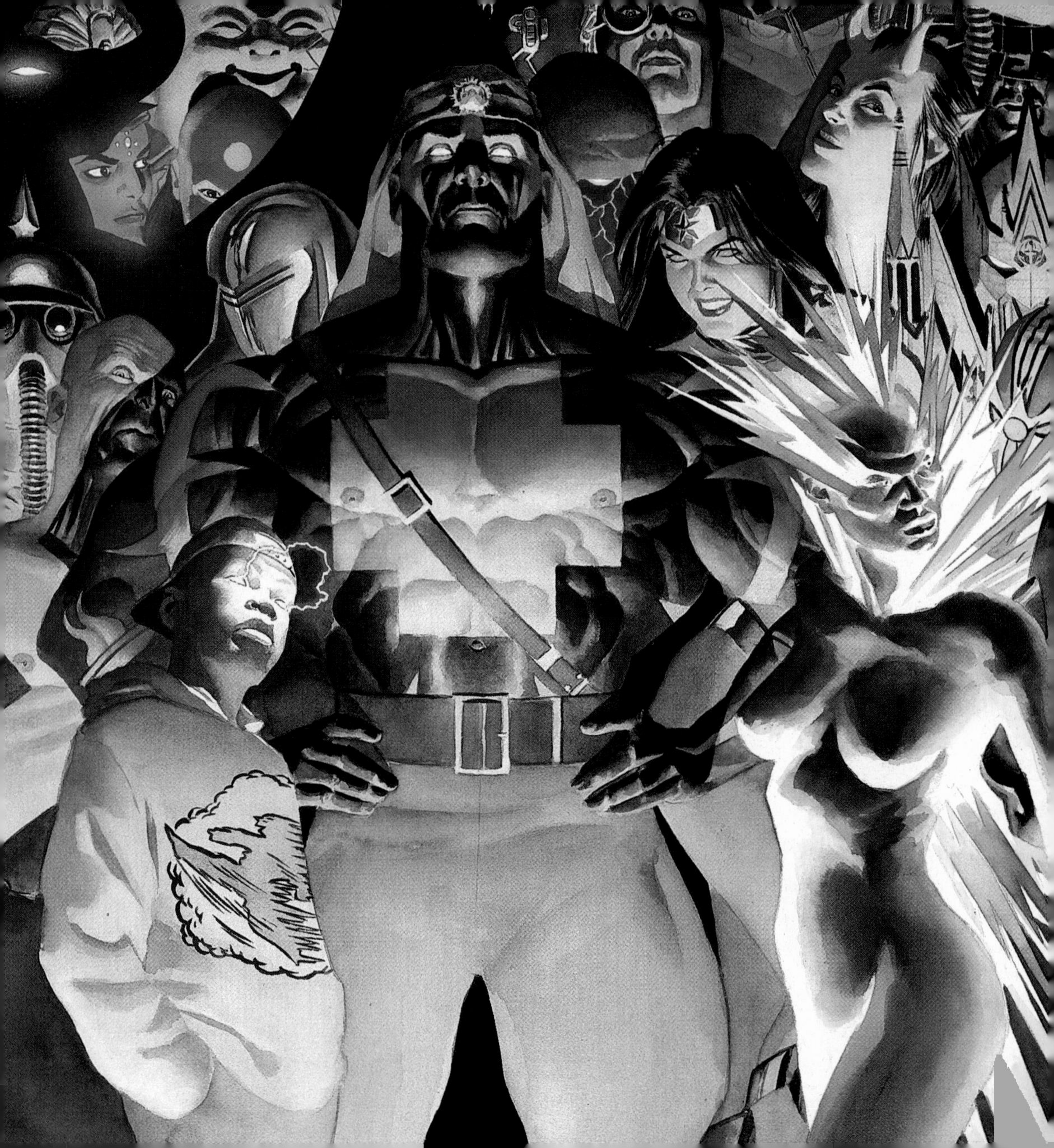

CHAPTER ONE

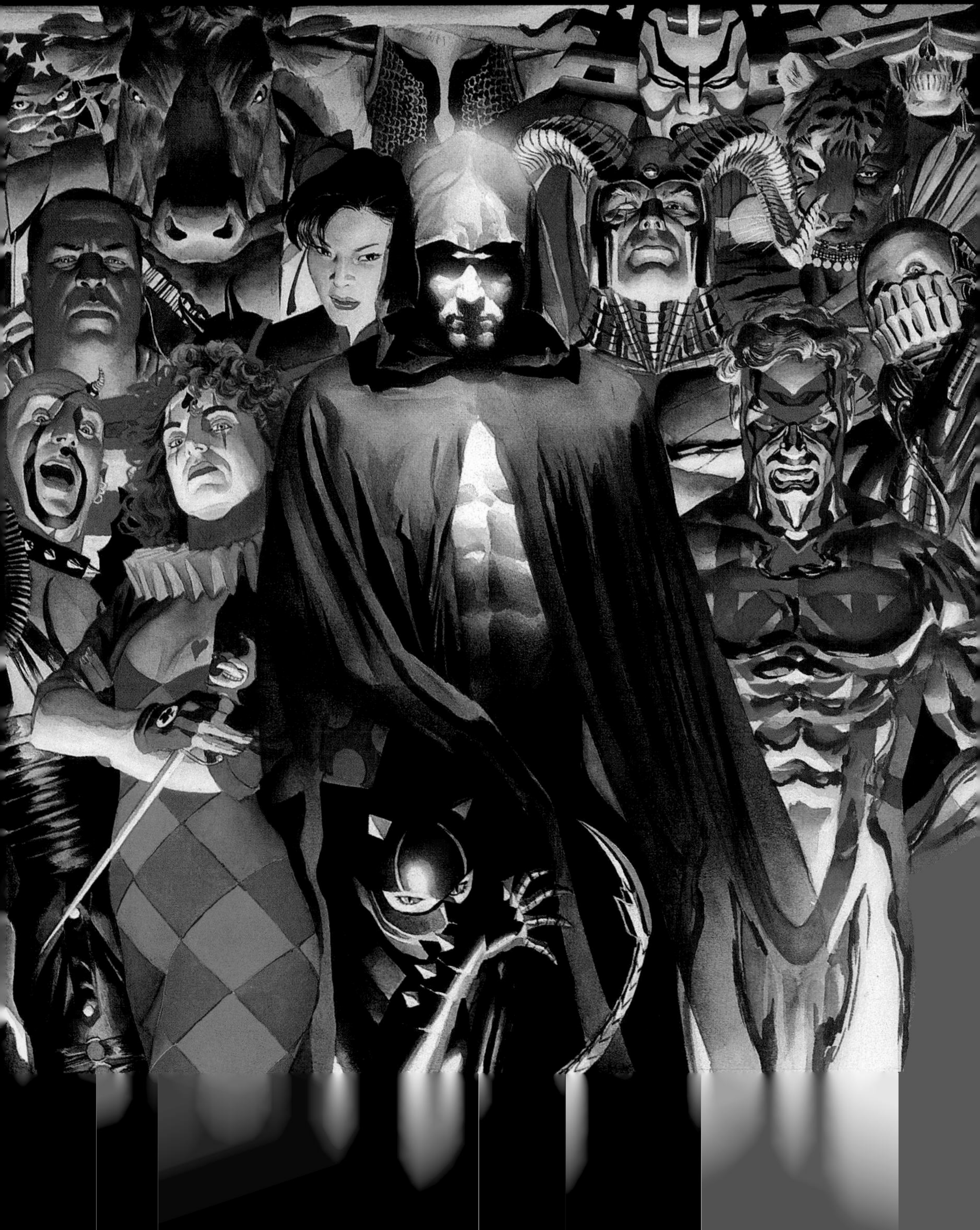

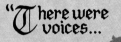

"There were voices...

"...and thunderings, and lightnings...

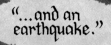

"...and an earthquake."

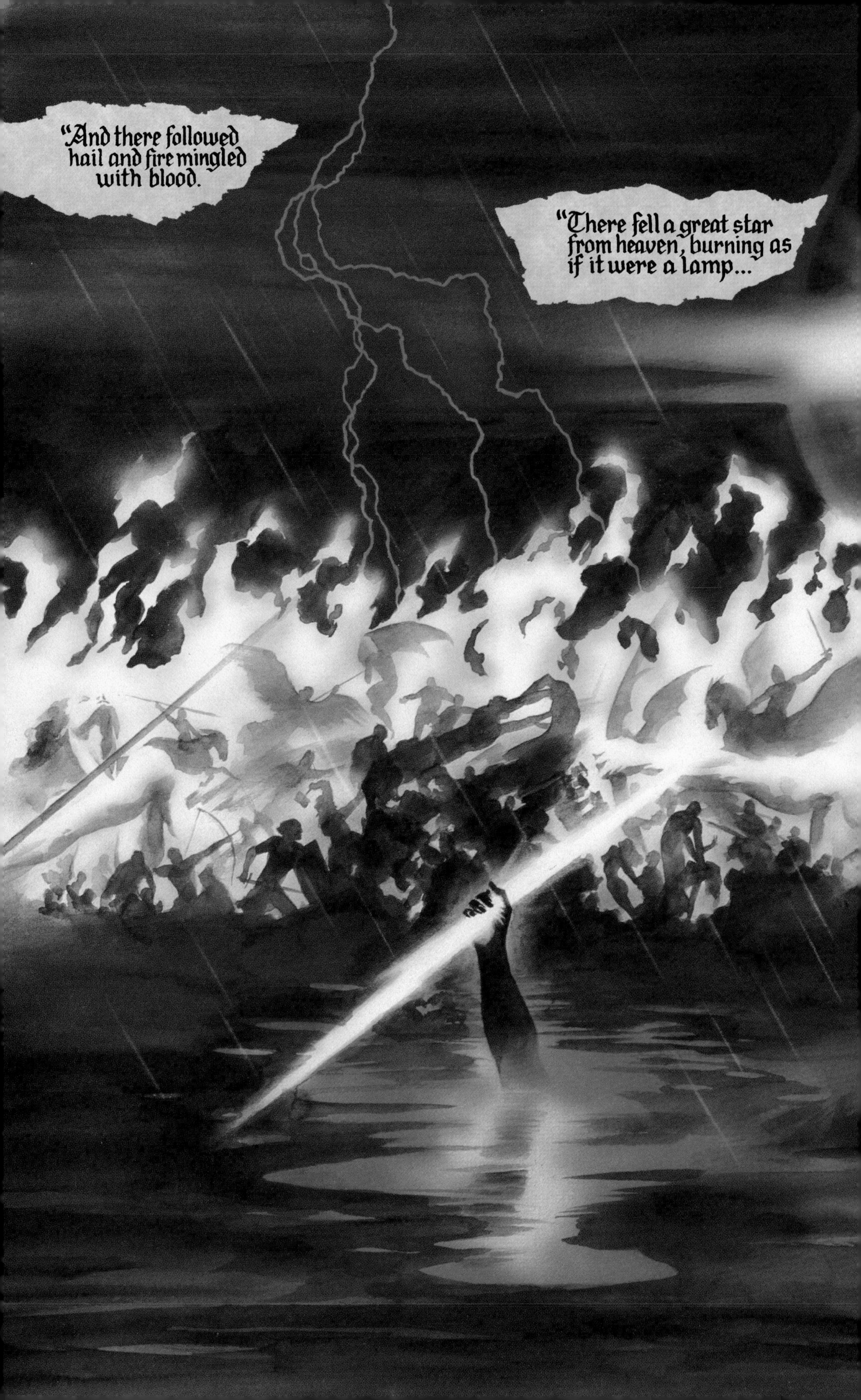
"And there followed hail and fire mingled with blood.
"There fell a great star from heaven, burning as if it were a lamp...

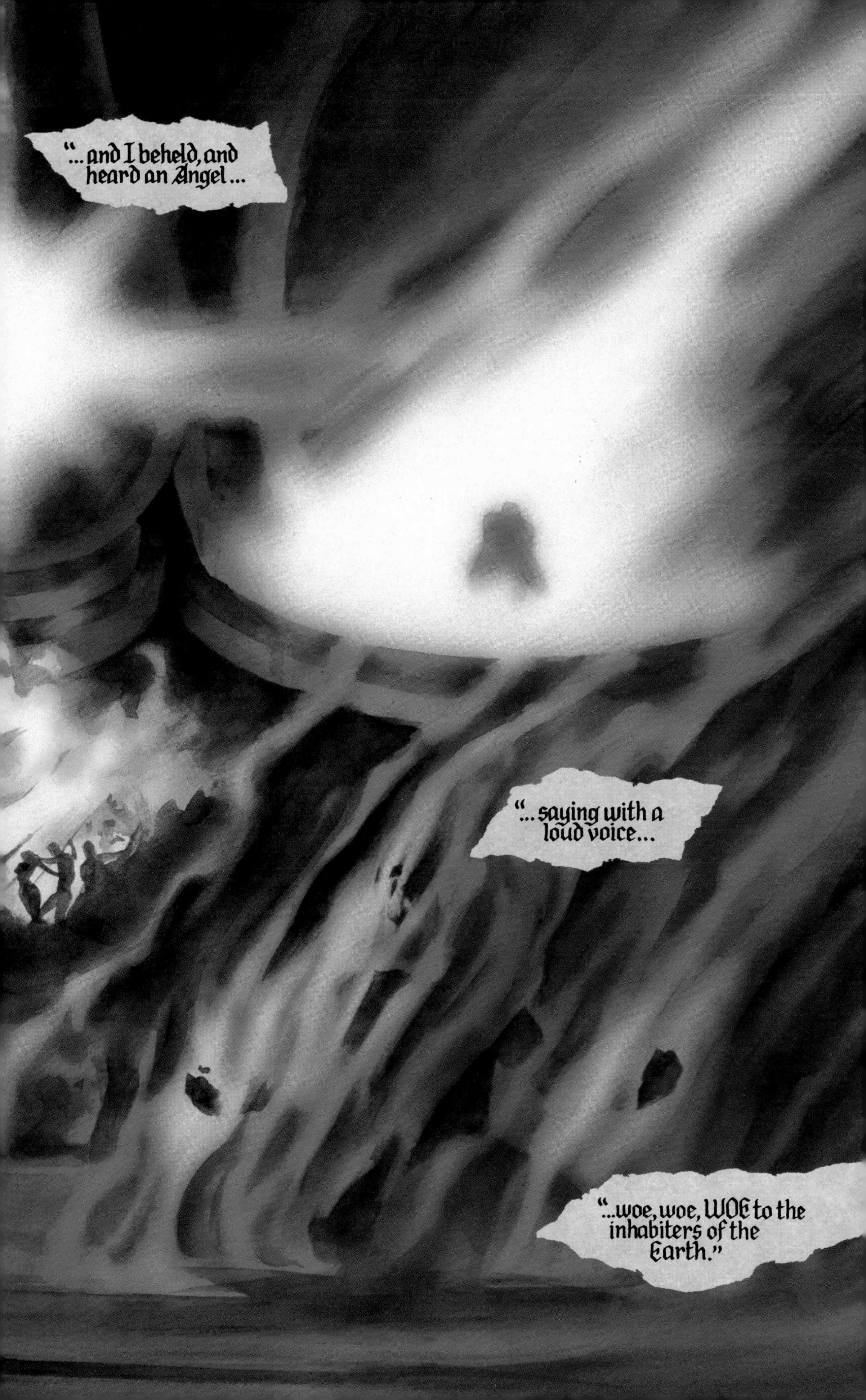
"...and I beheld, and heard an Angel...
"...saying with a loud voice...
"...woe, woe, WOE to the inhabiters of the Earth."

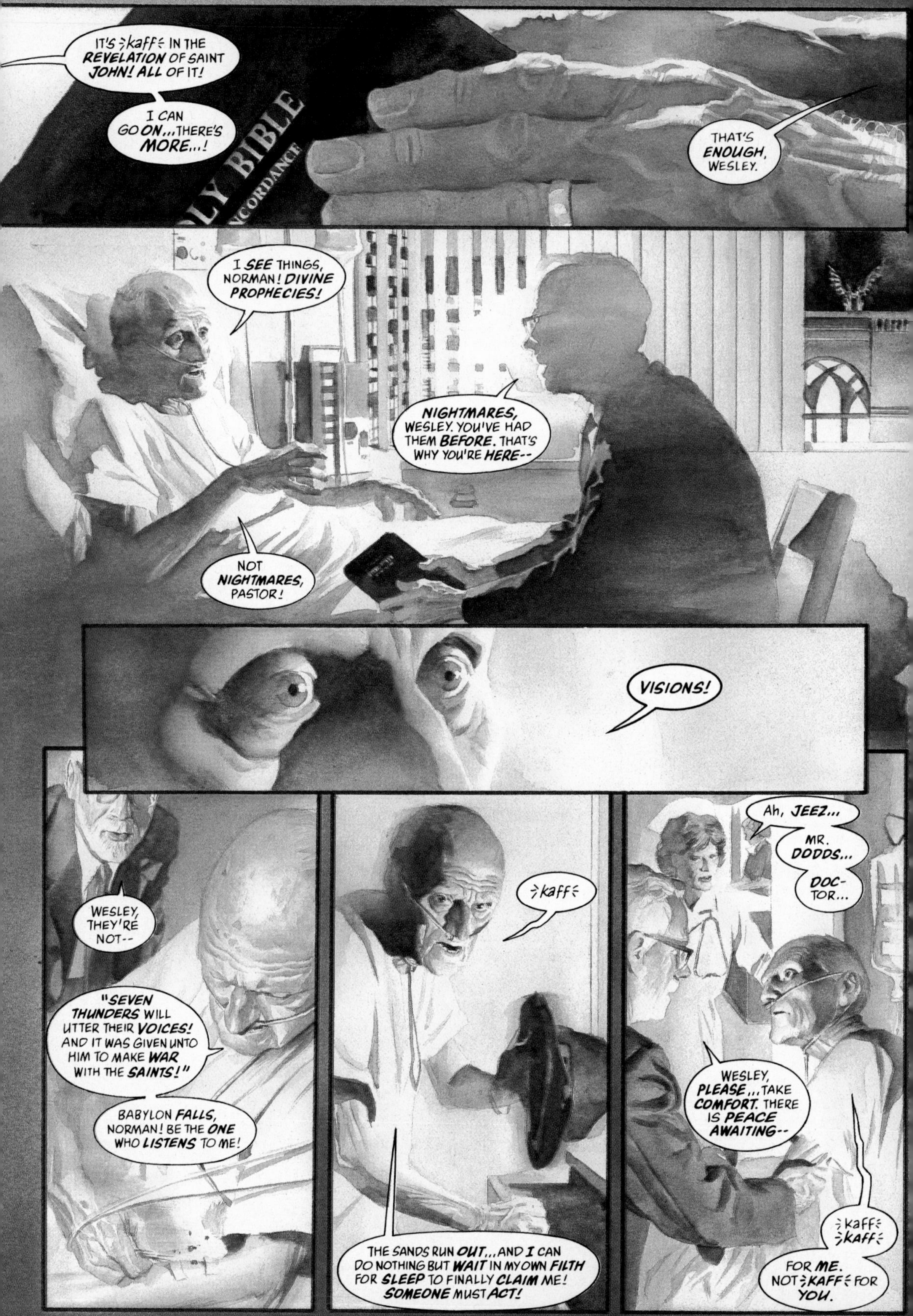
IT'S ⋟kaff⋞ IN THE REVELATION OF SAINT JOHN! ALL OF IT!
I CAN GO ON... THERE'S MORE...!
THAT'S ENOUGH, WESLEY.
I SEE THINGS, NORMAN! DIVINE PROPHECIES!
NIGHTMARES, WESLEY. YOU'VE HAD THEM BEFORE. THAT'S WHY YOU'RE HERE--
NOT NIGHTMARES, PASTOR!
VISIONS!
WESLEY, THEY'RE NOT--
"SEVEN THUNDERS WILL UTTER THEIR VOICES! AND IT WAS GIVEN UNTO HIM TO MAKE WAR WITH THE SAINTS!"
BABYLON FALLS, NORMAN! BE THE ONE WHO LISTENS TO ME!
⋟kaff⋞
THE SANDS RUN OUT... AND I CAN DO NOTHING BUT WAIT IN MY OWN FILTH FOR SLEEP TO FINALLY CLAIM ME! SOMEONE MUST ACT!
Ah, JEEZ...
MR. DODDS...
DOC-TOR...
WESLEY, PLEASE... TAKE COMFORT. THERE IS PEACE AWAITING--
⋟kaff⋞ ⋟kaff⋞
FOR ME. NOT ⋟kaff⋞ FOR YOU.

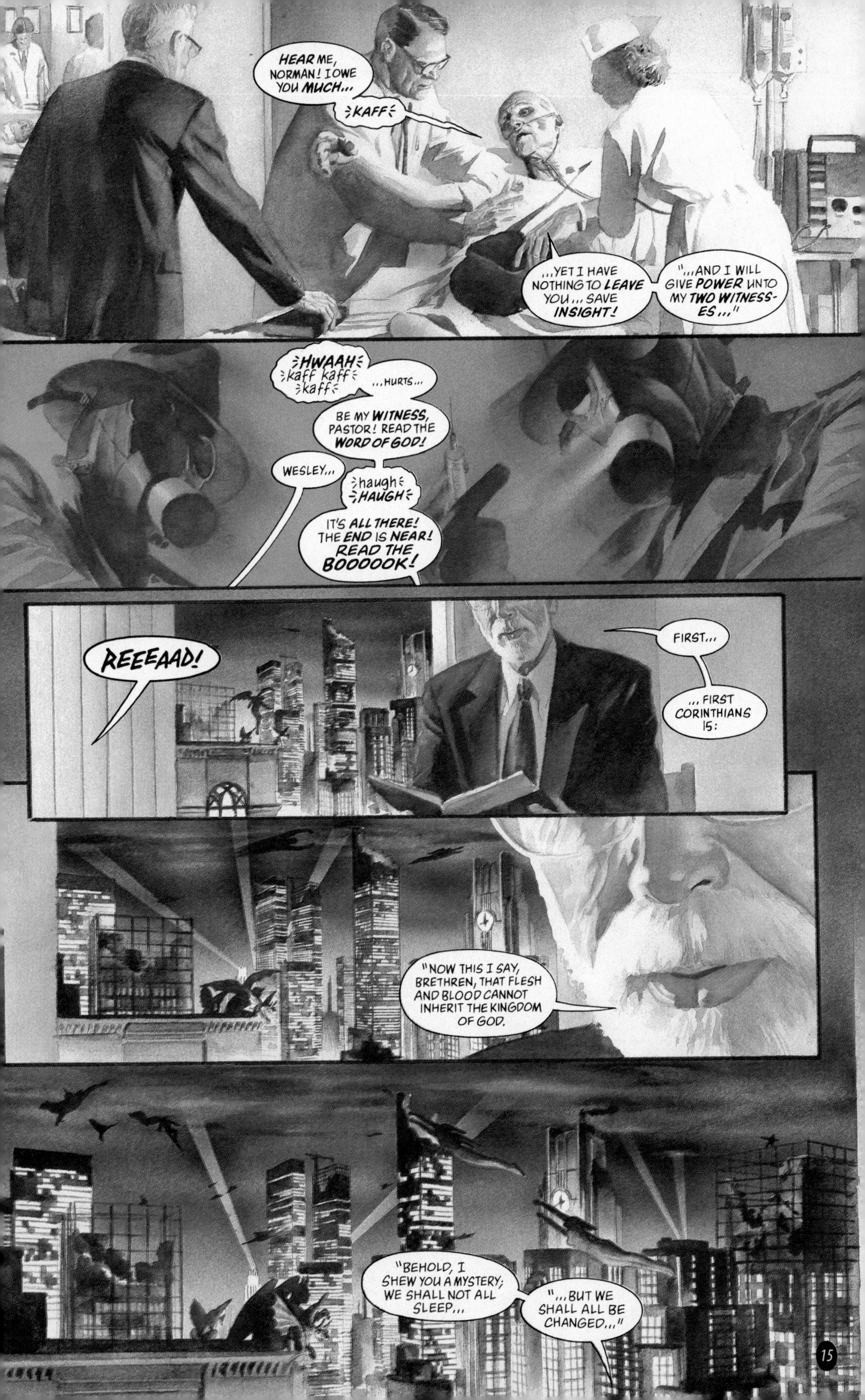
HEAR ME, NORMAN! I OWE YOU MUCH...
KAFF
...YET I HAVE NOTHING TO LEAVE YOU... SAVE INSIGHT!
"...AND I WILL GIVE POWER UNTO MY TWO WITNESS-ES..."
HWAAH kaff kaff kaff
...HURTS...
BE MY WITNESS, PASTOR! READ THE WORD OF GOD!
WESLEY...
haugh HAUGH
IT'S ALL THERE! THE END IS NEAR! READ THE BOOOOOK!
REEEAAD!
FIRST...
...FIRST CORINTHIANS 15:
"NOW THIS I SAY, BRETHREN, THAT FLESH AND BLOOD CANNOT INHERIT THE KINGDOM OF GOD.
"BEHOLD, I SHEW YOU A MYSTERY; WE SHALL NOT ALL SLEEP...
"...BUT WE SHALL ALL BE CHANGED..."

There was **more**, but Wesley never **heard** it.

In the **end**, he was listening to **another** voice... from Lord knows where.

My service was **brief**... his mourners, **few**. My wife and I met Wesley in his **twilight**... and had been the **last** of his **friends**.

He came to our **church** questioning what there was to **believe** in these days. I wish **now** I'd had better **answers**.

The **three** of us shared **many** a **dinner** in this apartment. **Ellen**, God rest her soul, would in **one** moment tease Wesley **mercilessly** about living in the **past**...

...and in the **next**, beg him to spin another tale of his... how did she put it?... his **glory days**.

Sometimes, I wish I'd made more time to listen **with** her. Wes's **stories** were melodies of **wonder**. Back **then**, it seemed, his dreams were of **yesterdays**, not **tomorrows**... of of times **bright**, not **barbaric**.

Once upon a time, he said, he'd called himself the **Sandman**.

DAILY PLANET

U.N. Enacts More Metahuman Censures

Will Censures Curb Metahuman Violence?

91% NO
7% YES
2% UNDECIDED

He was a super-hero.

KLIK

YES
2% UNDECIDED

...man Cens...

You'll excuse the expression.

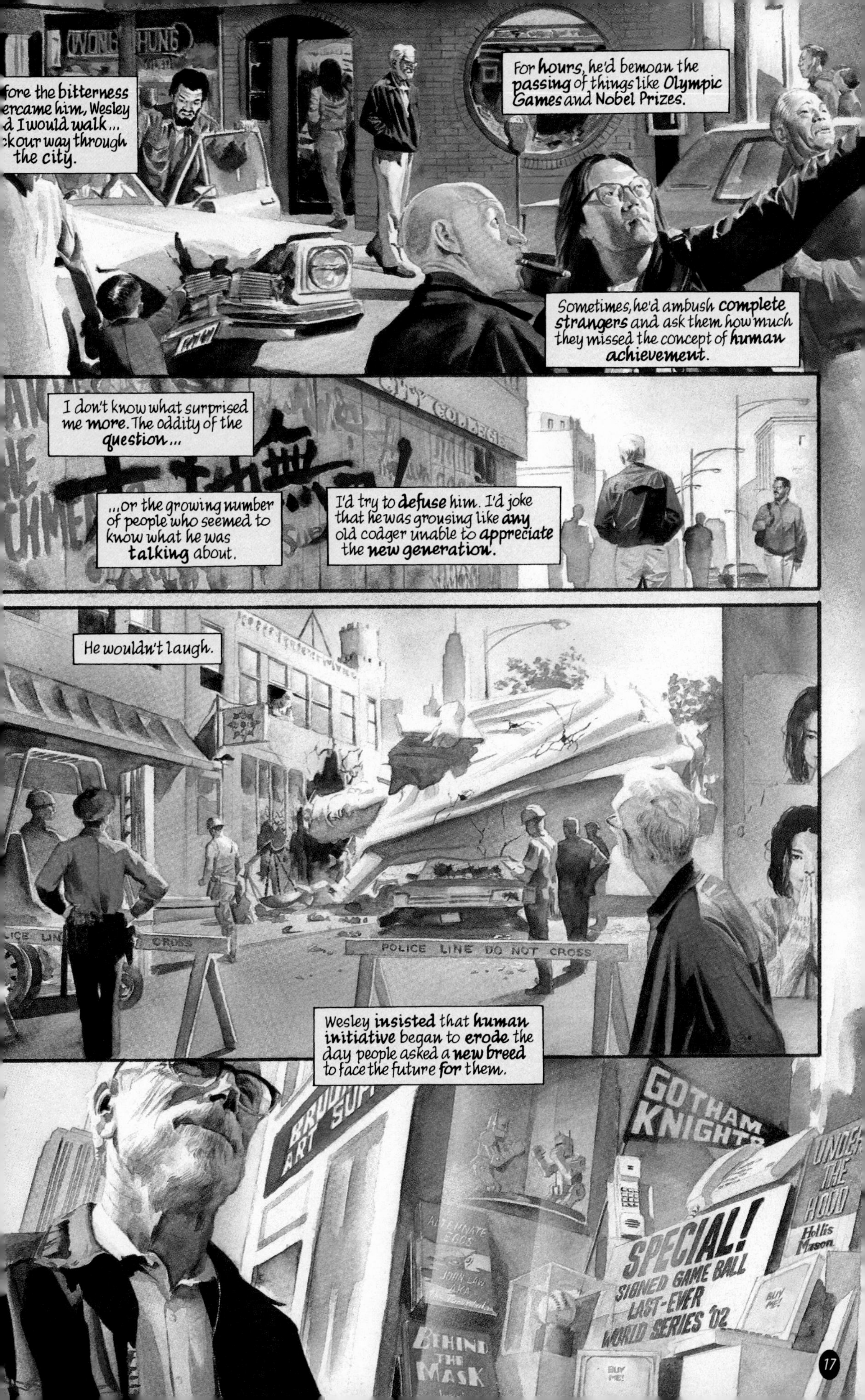

fore the bitterness
ercame him, Wesley
d I would walk...
ck our way through
the city.
For hours, he'd bemoan the passing of things like Olympic Games and Nobel Prizes.
Sometimes, he'd ambush complete strangers and ask them how much they missed the concept of human achievement.
I don't know what surprised me more. The oddity of the question...
...or the growing number of people who seemed to know what he was talking about.
I'd try to defuse him. I'd joke that he was grousing like any old codger unable to appreciate the new generation.
He wouldn't laugh.
POLICE LINE DO NOT CROSS
Wesley insisted that human initiative began to erode the day people asked a new breed to face the future for them.
GOTHAM KNIGHTS
SPECIAL! SIGNED GAME BALL LAST-EVER WORLD SERIES '02
UNDER THE HOOD
Hollis Mason
BEHIND THE MASK
BUY ME!

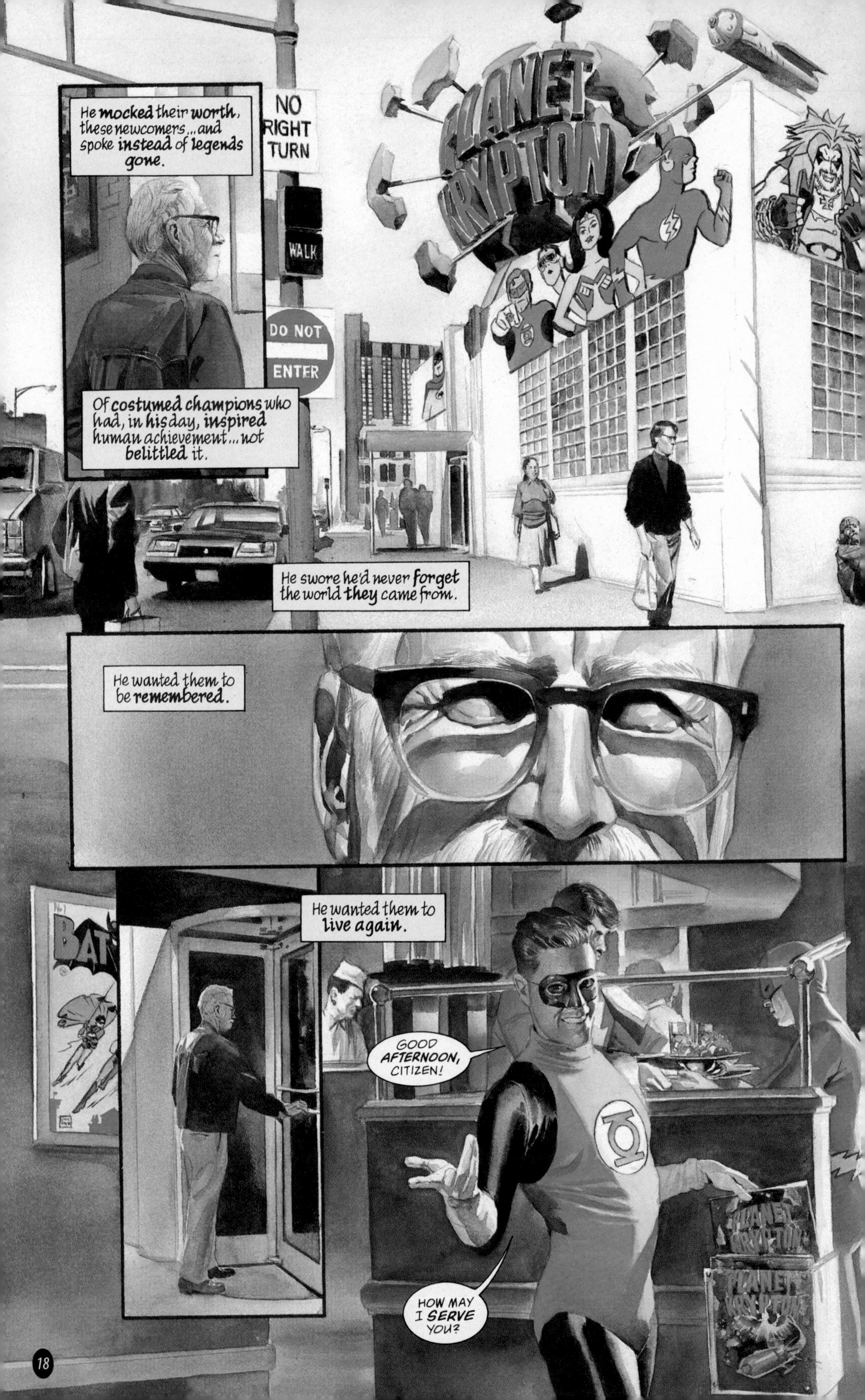
He mocked their worth, these newcomers... and spoke instead of legends gone.
NO RIGHT TURN
WALK
DO NOT ENTER
PLANET KRYPTON
Of costumed champions who had, in his day, inspired human achievement... not belittled it.
He swore he'd never forget the world they came from.
He wanted them to be remembered.
He wanted them to live again.
GOOD AFTERNOON, CITIZEN!
HOW MAY I SERVE YOU?

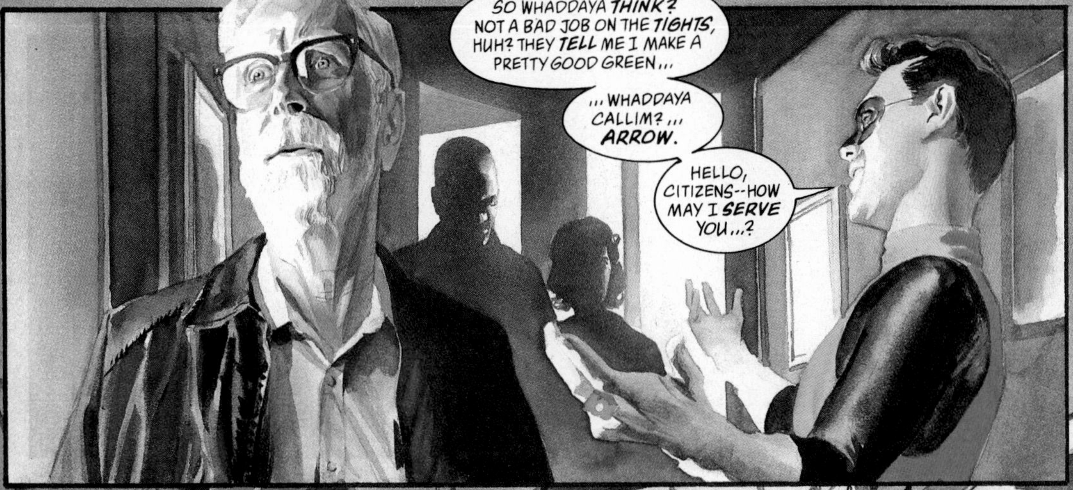
SO WHADDAYA THINK? NOT A BAD JOB ON THE TIGHTS, HUH? THEY TELL ME I MAKE A PRETTY GOOD GREEN,,,
,,, WHADDAYA CALLIM? ,,, ARROW.
HELLO, CITIZENS--HOW MAY I SERVE YOU,,,?

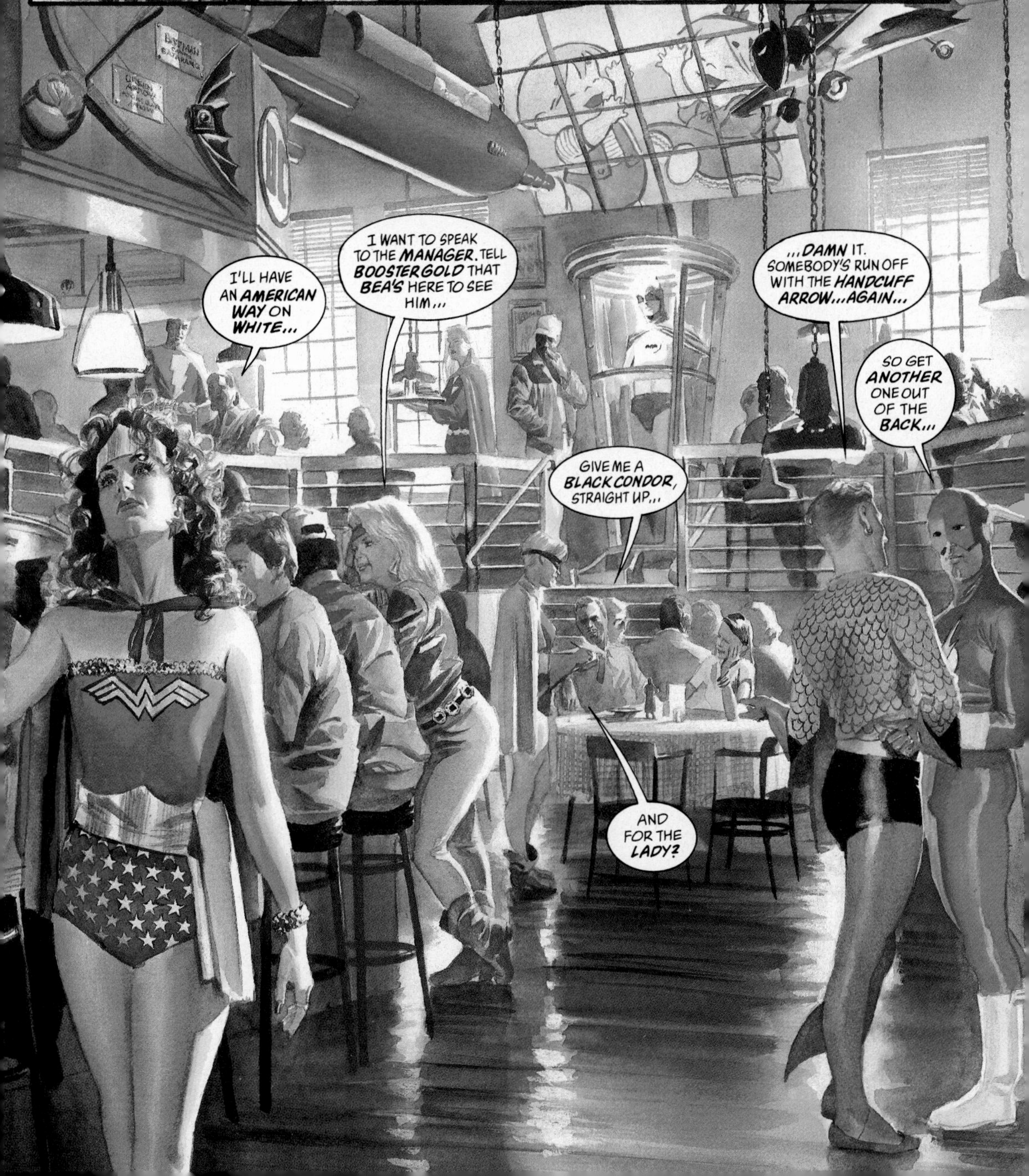
I'LL HAVE AN AMERICAN WAY ON WHITE,,,
I WANT TO SPEAK TO THE MANAGER. TELL BOOSTER GOLD THAT BEA'S HERE TO SEE HIM,,,
,,, DAMN IT. SOMEBODY'S RUN OFF WITH THE HANDCUFF ARROW,,, AGAIN,,,
SO GET ANOTHER ONE OUT OF THE BACK,,,
GIVE ME A BLACK CONDOR, STRAIGHT UP,,,
AND FOR THE LADY?

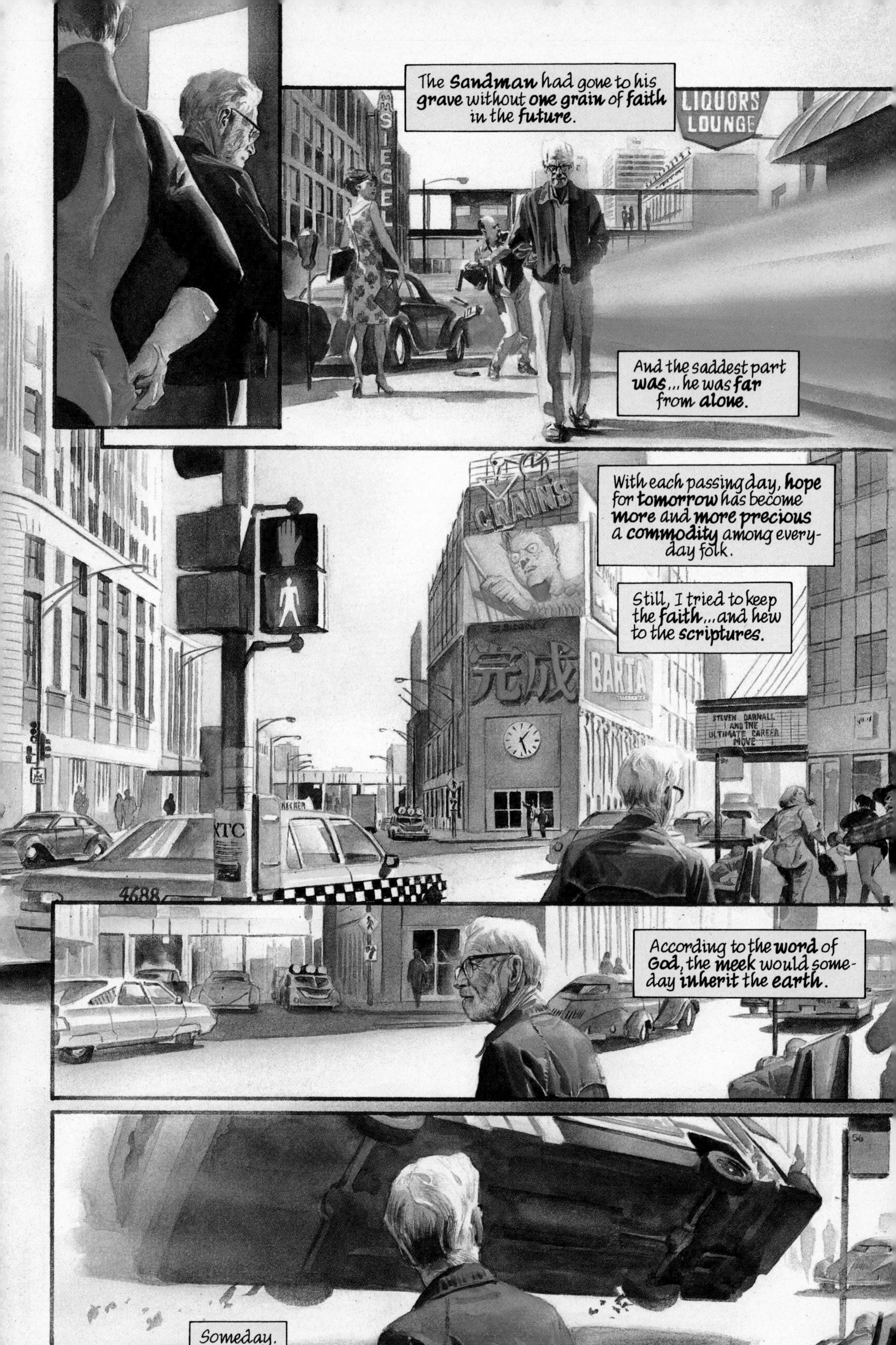
The **Sandman** had gone to his **grave** without **one grain** of **faith** in the **future**.
SIEGEL
LIQUORS LOUNGE
And the saddest part **was**... he was **far** from **alone**.
CRAIN'S
With each passing day, **hope** for **tomorrow** has become **more** and **more precious** a **commodity** among every-day folk.
Still, I tried to keep the **faith**... and hew to the **scriptures**.
完成
BARTA
STEVEN DARNALL AND THE ULTIMATE CAREER MOVE
XTC
4688
According to the **word** of **God**, the **meek** would some-day **inherit** the **earth**.
Someday.

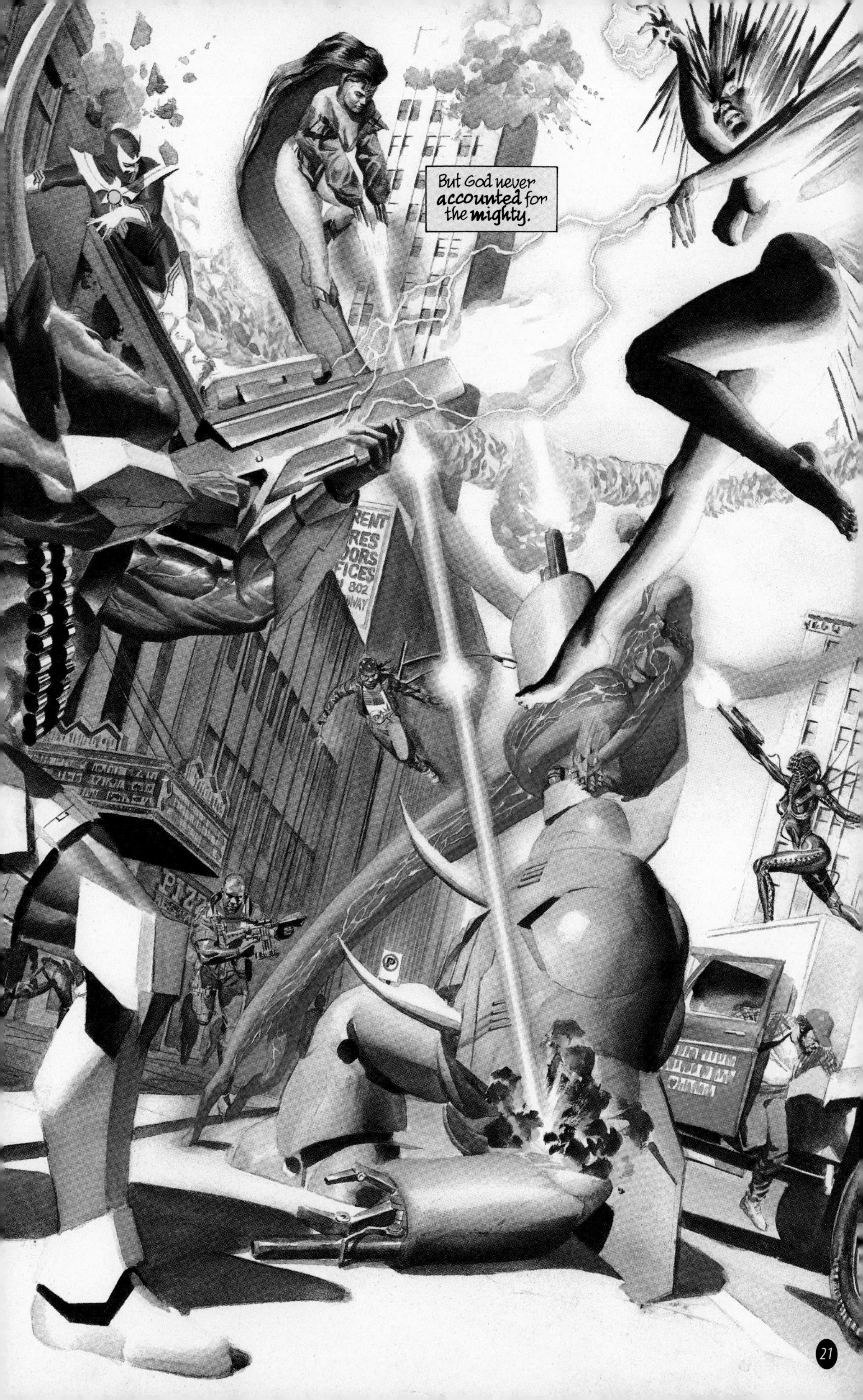
But God never accounted for the mighty.

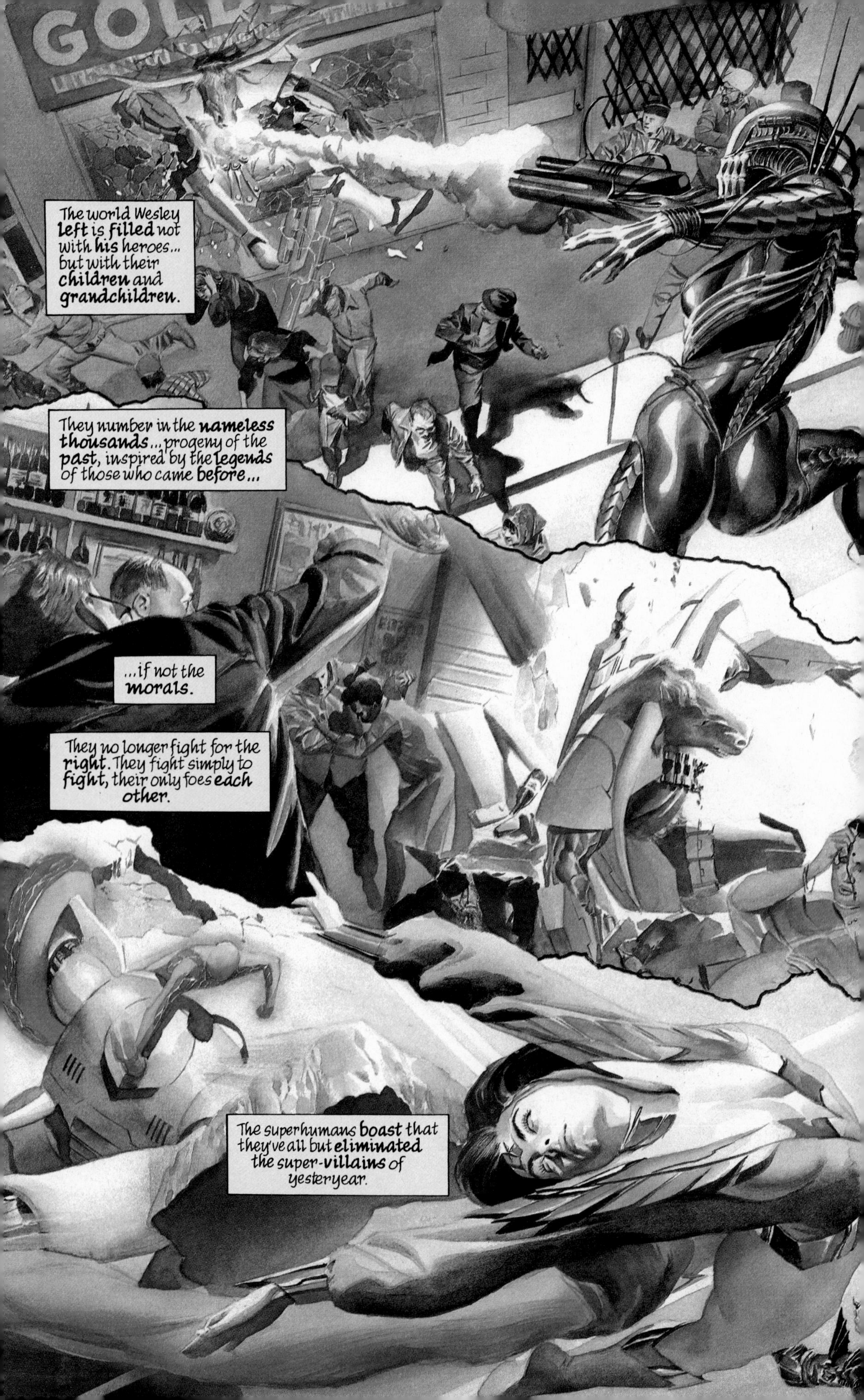
The world Wesley left is filled not with his heroes... but with their children and grandchildren.
They number in the nameless thousands... progeny of the past, inspired by the legends of those who came before...
...if not the morals.
They no longer fight for the right. They fight simply to fight, their only foes each other.
The superhumans boast that they've all but eliminated the super-villains of yesteryear.

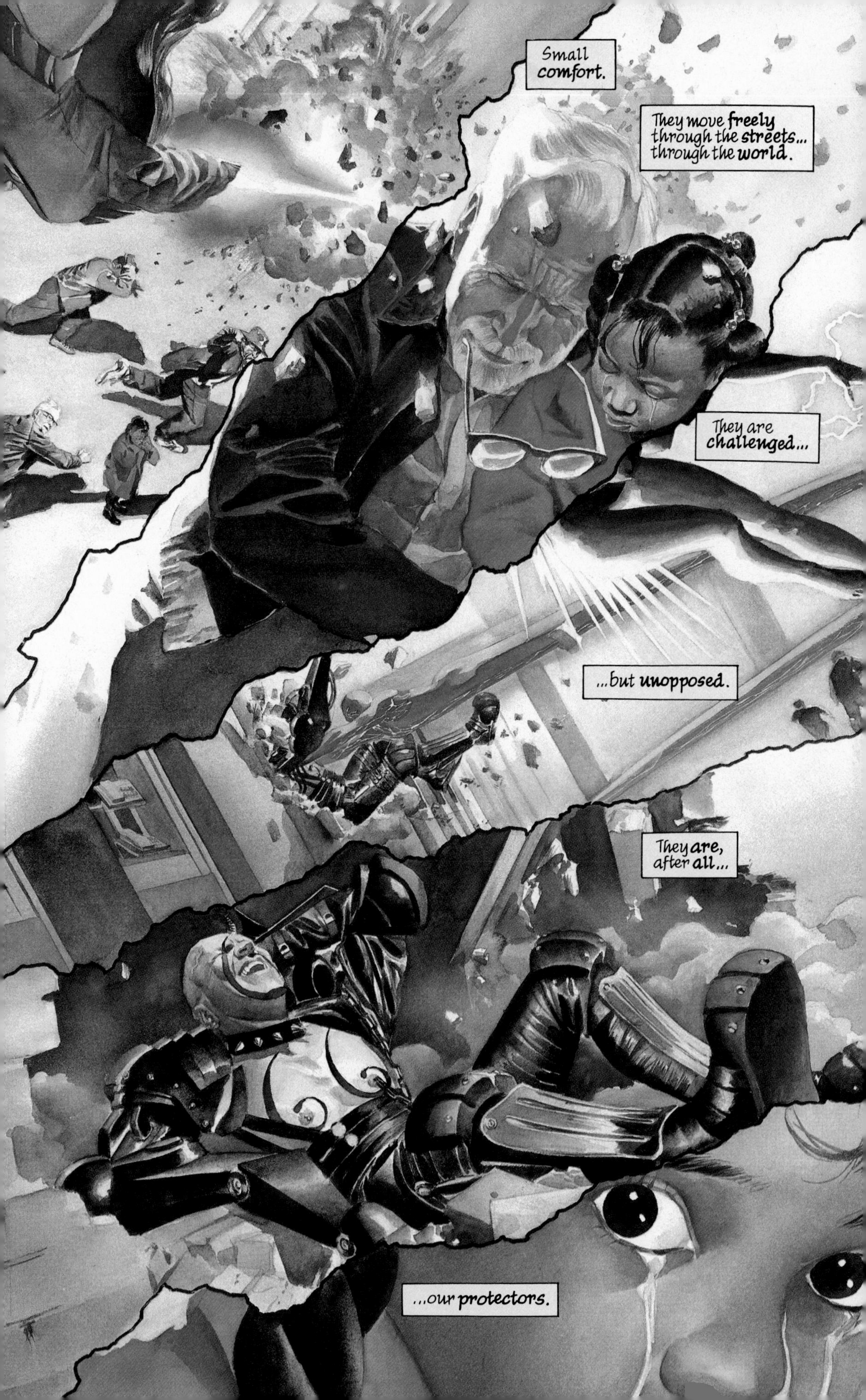
Small comfort.
They move freely through the streets... through the world.
They are challenged...
...but unopposed.
They are, after all...
...our protectors.

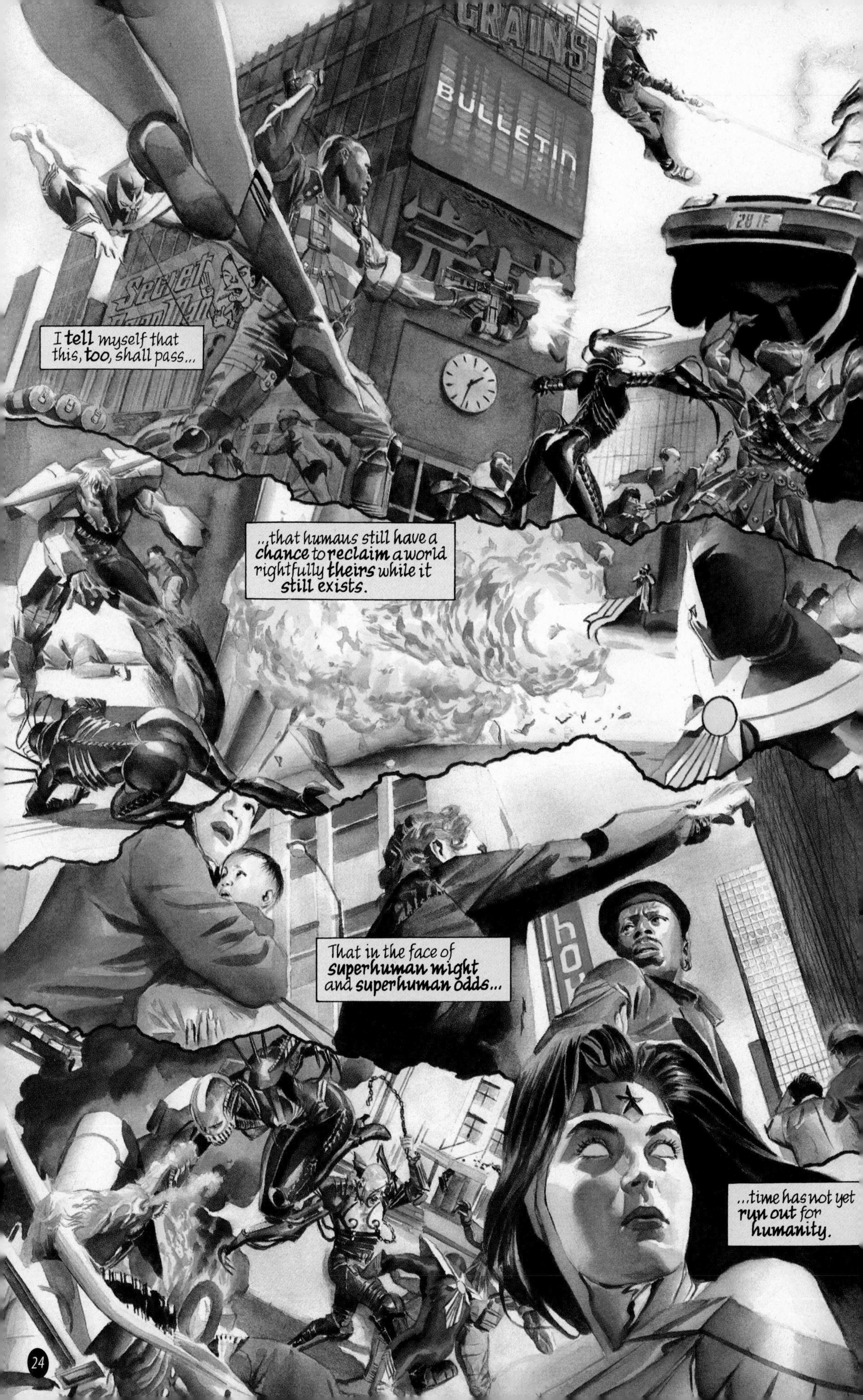
GRAIN'S
BULLETIN
I tell myself that this, too, shall pass...
...that humans still have a chance to reclaim a world rightfully theirs while it still exists.
That in the face of superhuman might and superhuman odds...
...time has not yet run out for humanity.

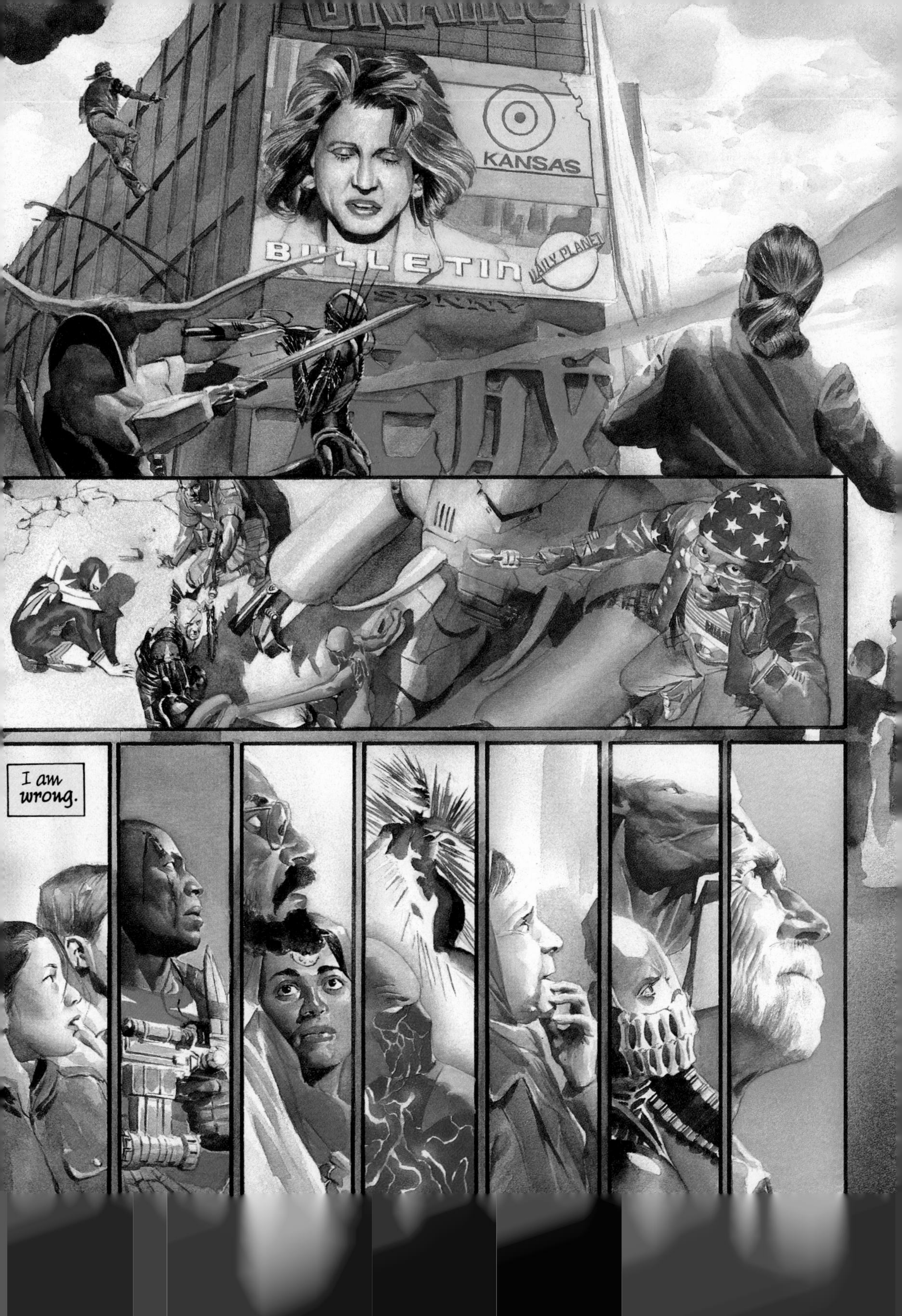
KANSAS
BULLETIN
DAILY PLANET
I am wrong.

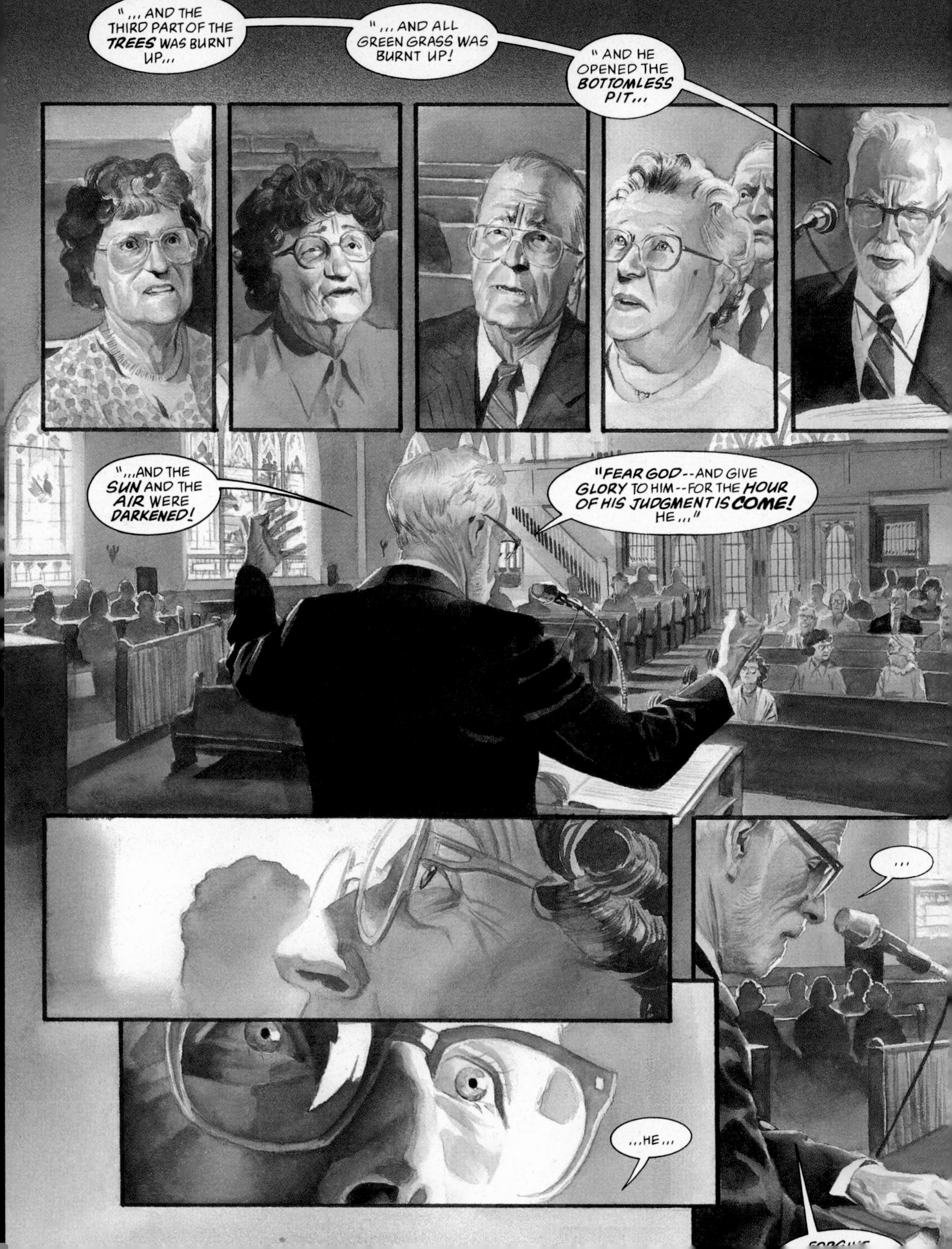
"... AND THE THIRD PART OF THE TREES WAS BURNT UP...
"... AND ALL GREEN GRASS WAS BURNT UP!
" AND HE OPENED THE BOTTOMLESS PIT...
"...AND THE SUN AND THE AIR WERE DARKENED!
"FEAR GOD--AND GIVE GLORY TO HIM--FOR THE HOUR OF HIS JUDGMENT IS COME! HE..."
...HE...
...

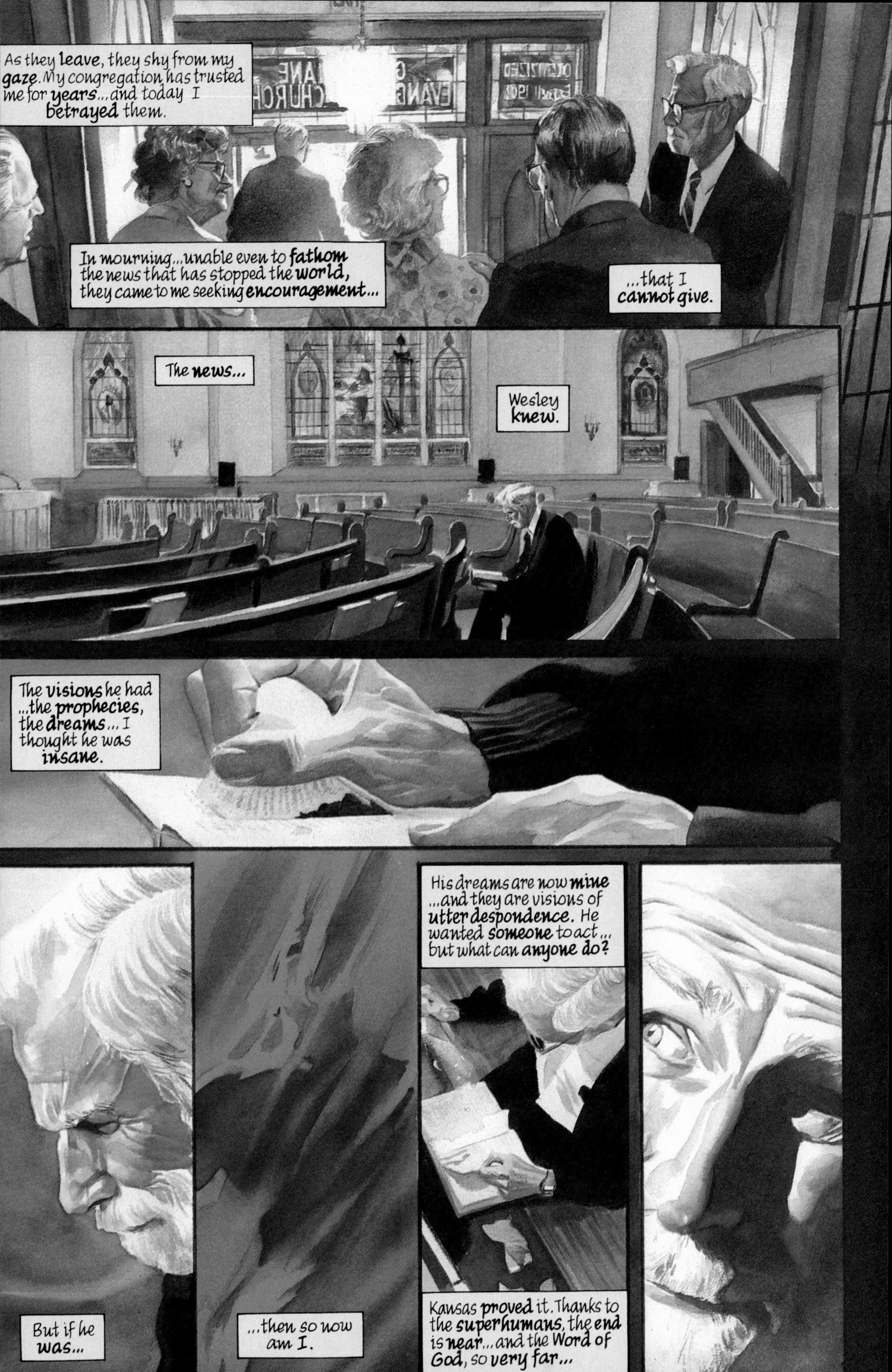
As they leave, they shy from my gaze. My congregation has trusted me for years... and today I betrayed them.
In mourning... unable even to fathom the news that has stopped the world, they came to me seeking encouragement...
...that I cannot give.
The news...
Wesley knew.
The visions he had ...the prophecies, the dreams... I thought he was insane.
But if he was...
...then so now am I.
His dreams are now mine ...and they are visions of utter despondence. He wanted someone to act... but what can anyone do?
Kansas proved it. Thanks to the superhumans, the end is near... and the Word of God, so very far...

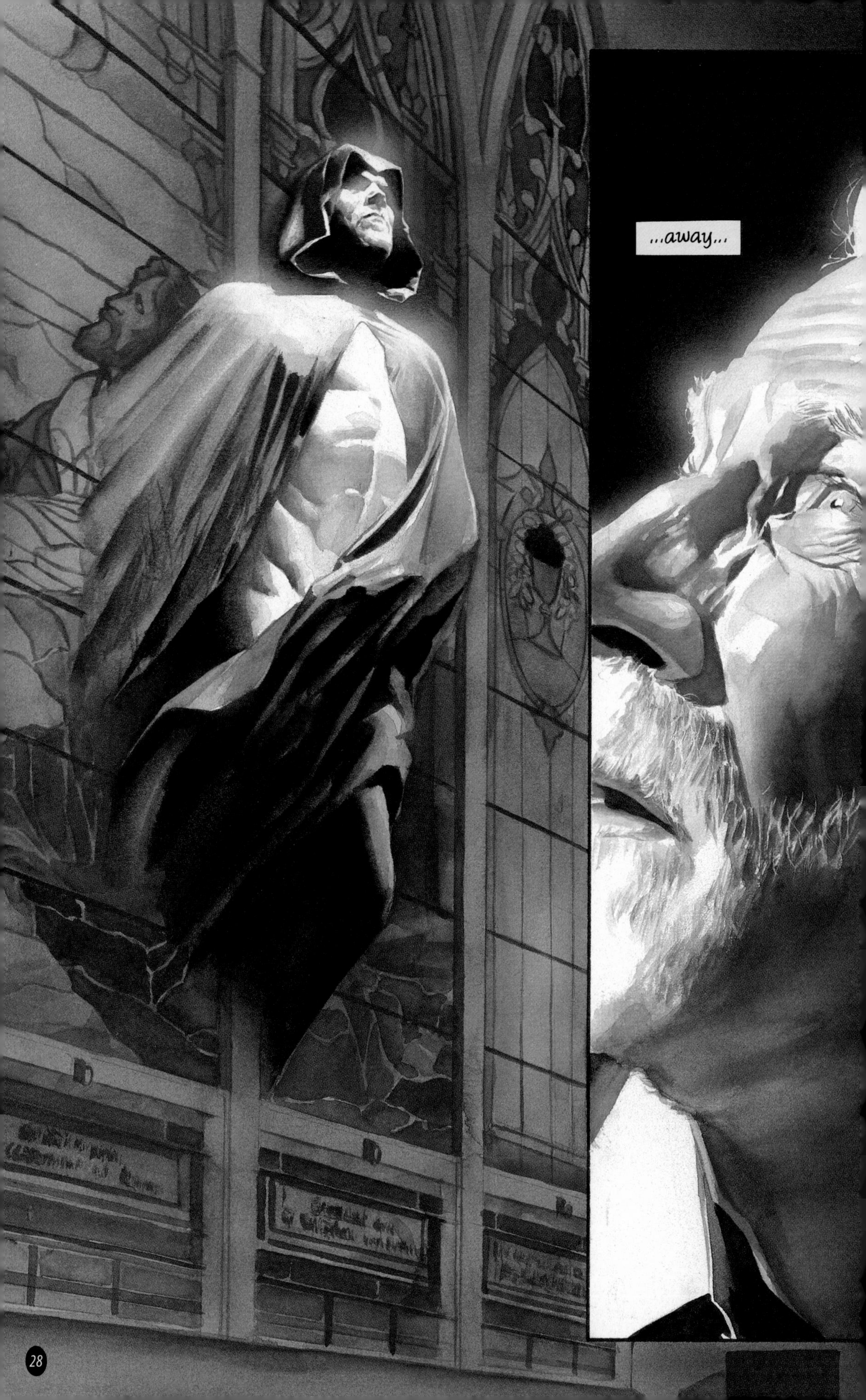
...away...

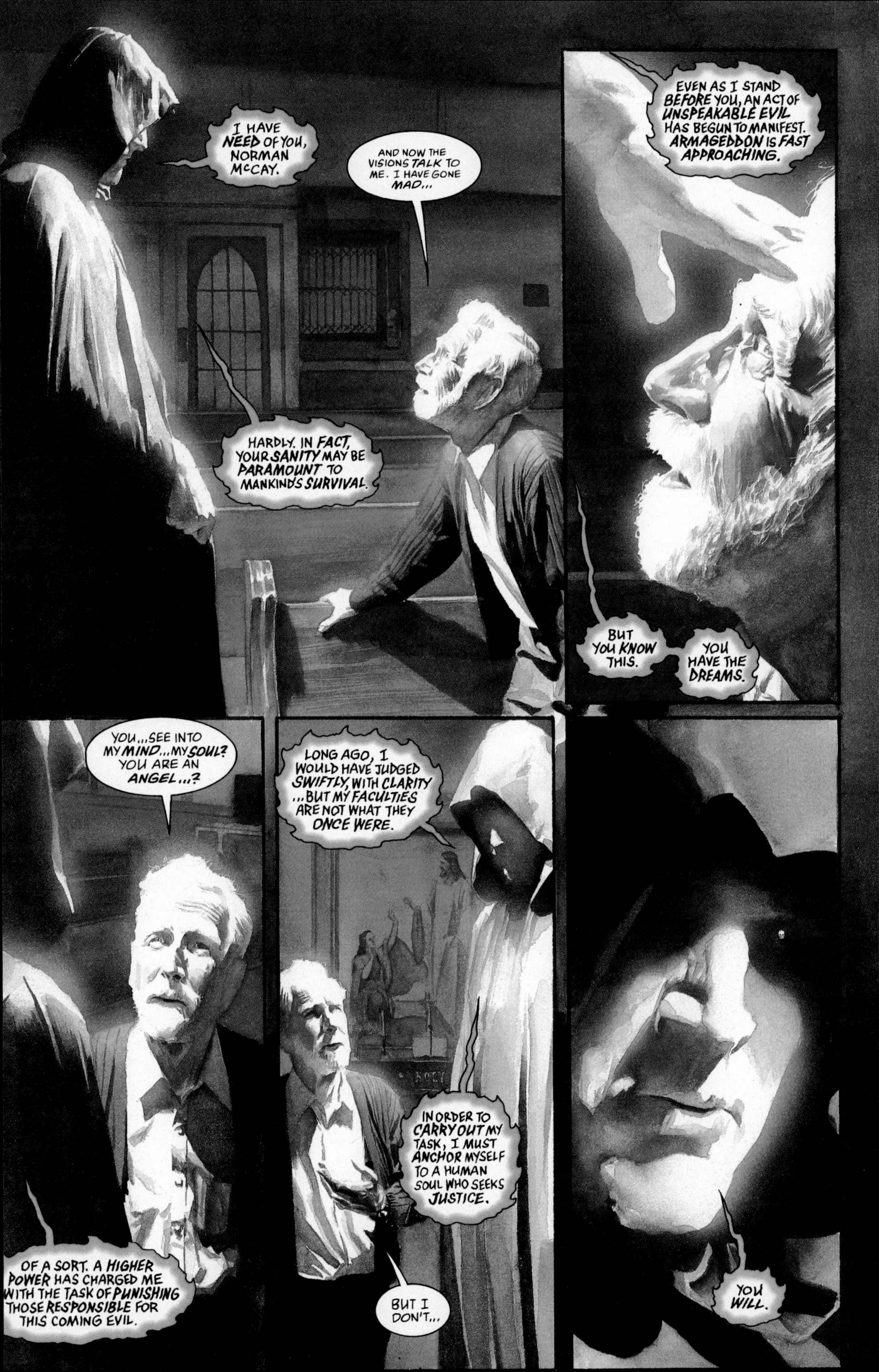

I HAVE NEED OF YOU, NORMAN McCAY.
AND NOW THE VISIONS TALK TO ME. I HAVE GONE MAD...
HARDLY. IN FACT, YOUR SANITY MAY BE PARAMOUNT TO MANKIND'S SURVIVAL.
EVEN AS I STAND BEFORE YOU, AN ACT OF UNSPEAKABLE EVIL HAS BEGUN TO MANIFEST. ARMAGEDDON IS FAST APPROACHING.
BUT YOU KNOW THIS.
YOU HAVE THE DREAMS.
YOU...SEE INTO MY MIND...MY SOUL? YOU ARE AN ANGEL...?
OF A SORT. A HIGHER POWER HAS CHARGED ME WITH THE TASK OF PUNISHING THOSE RESPONSIBLE FOR THIS COMING EVIL.
LONG AGO, I WOULD HAVE JUDGED SWIFTLY, WITH CLARITY ...BUT MY FACULTIES ARE NOT WHAT THEY ONCE WERE.
IN ORDER TO CARRY OUT MY TASK, I MUST ANCHOR MYSELF TO A HUMAN SOUL WHO SEEKS JUSTICE.
BUT I DON'T...
YOU WILL.

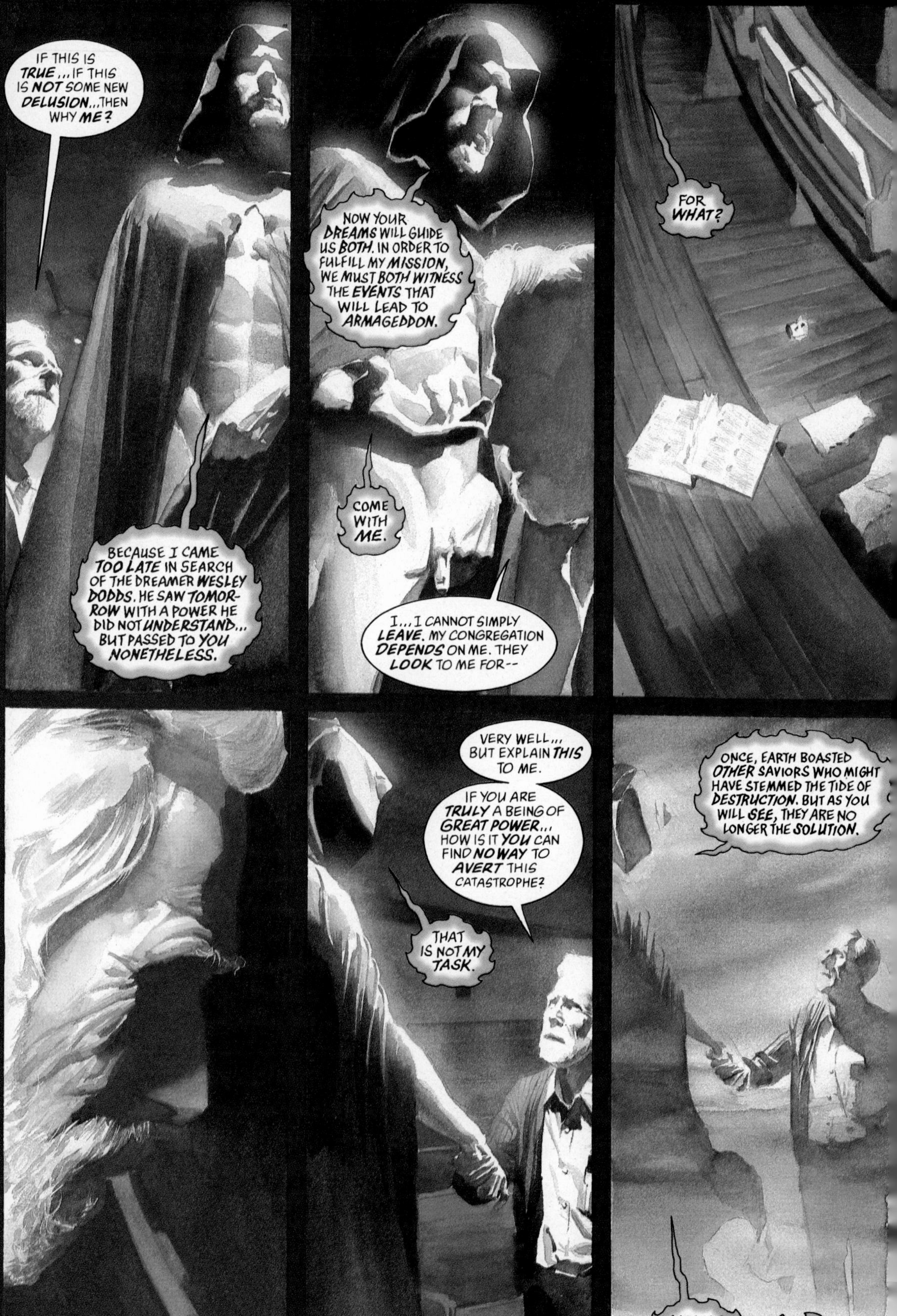
IF THIS IS TRUE... IF THIS IS NOT SOME NEW DELUSION... THEN WHY ME?
BECAUSE I CAME TOO LATE IN SEARCH OF THE DREAMER WESLEY DODDS. HE SAW TOMORROW WITH A POWER HE DID NOT UNDERSTAND... BUT PASSED TO YOU NONETHELESS.
NOW YOUR DREAMS WILL GUIDE US BOTH. IN ORDER TO FULFILL MY MISSION, WE MUST BOTH WITNESS THE EVENTS THAT WILL LEAD TO ARMAGEDDON.
COME WITH ME.
I... I CANNOT SIMPLY LEAVE. MY CONGREGATION DEPENDS ON ME. THEY LOOK TO ME FOR--
FOR WHAT?
VERY WELL... BUT EXPLAIN THIS TO ME.
IF YOU ARE TRULY A BEING OF GREAT POWER... HOW IS IT YOU CAN FIND NO WAY TO AVERT THIS CATASTROPHE?
THAT IS NOT MY TASK.
ONCE, EARTH BOASTED OTHER SAVIORS WHO MIGHT HAVE STEMMED THE TIDE OF DESTRUCTION. BUT AS YOU WILL SEE, THEY ARE NO LONGER THE SOLUTION.
THEY ARE, IN MANY WAYS...
...THE PROBLEM.

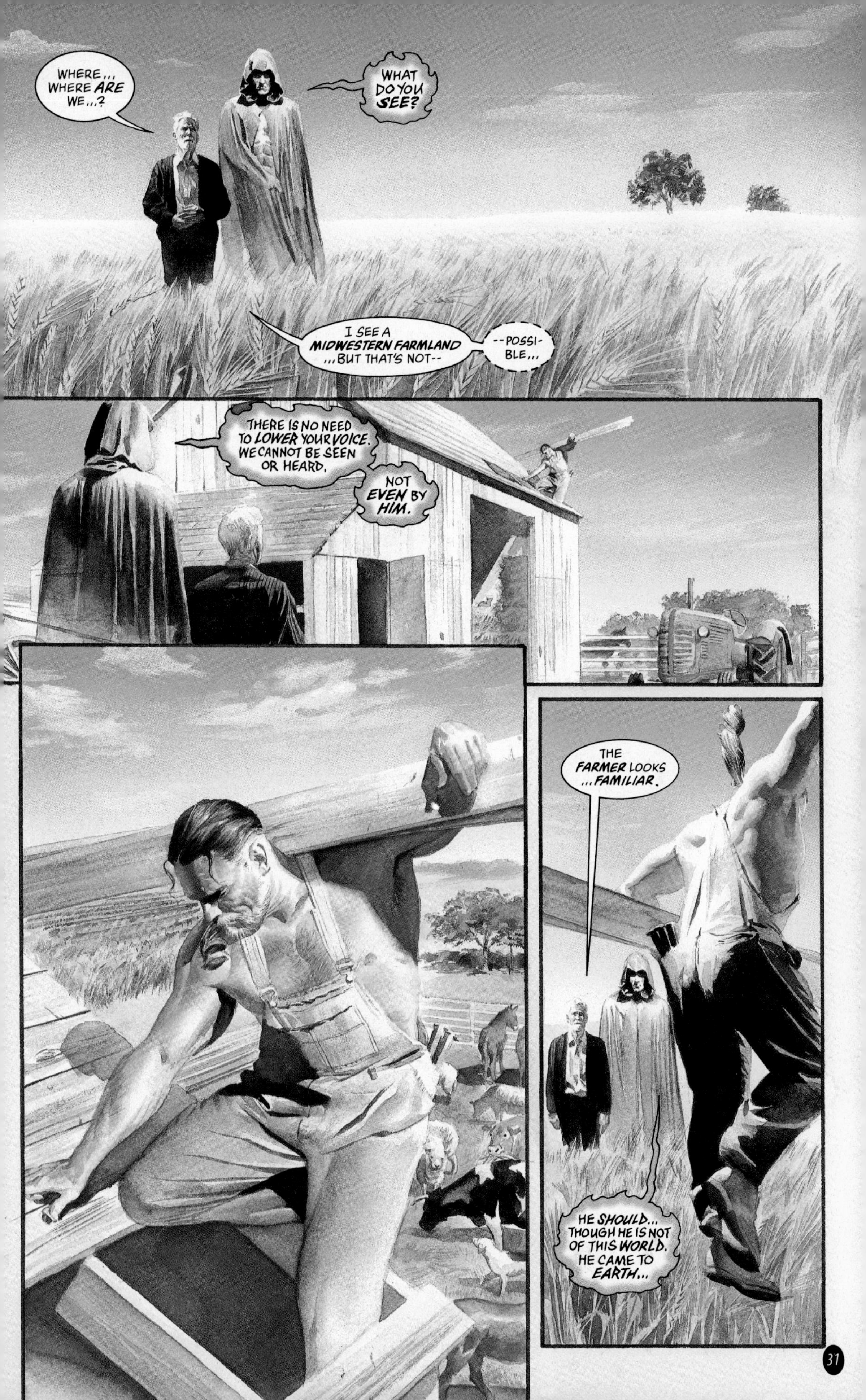
WHERE... WHERE ARE WE...?
WHAT DO YOU SEE?
I SEE A MIDWESTERN FARMLAND ...BUT THAT'S NOT--
--POSSI-BLE...
THERE IS NO NEED TO LOWER YOUR VOICE. WE CANNOT BE SEEN OR HEARD.
NOT EVEN BY HIM.
THE FARMER LOOKS ...FAMILIAR.
HE SHOULD... THOUGH HE IS NOT OF THIS WORLD. HE CAME TO EARTH...

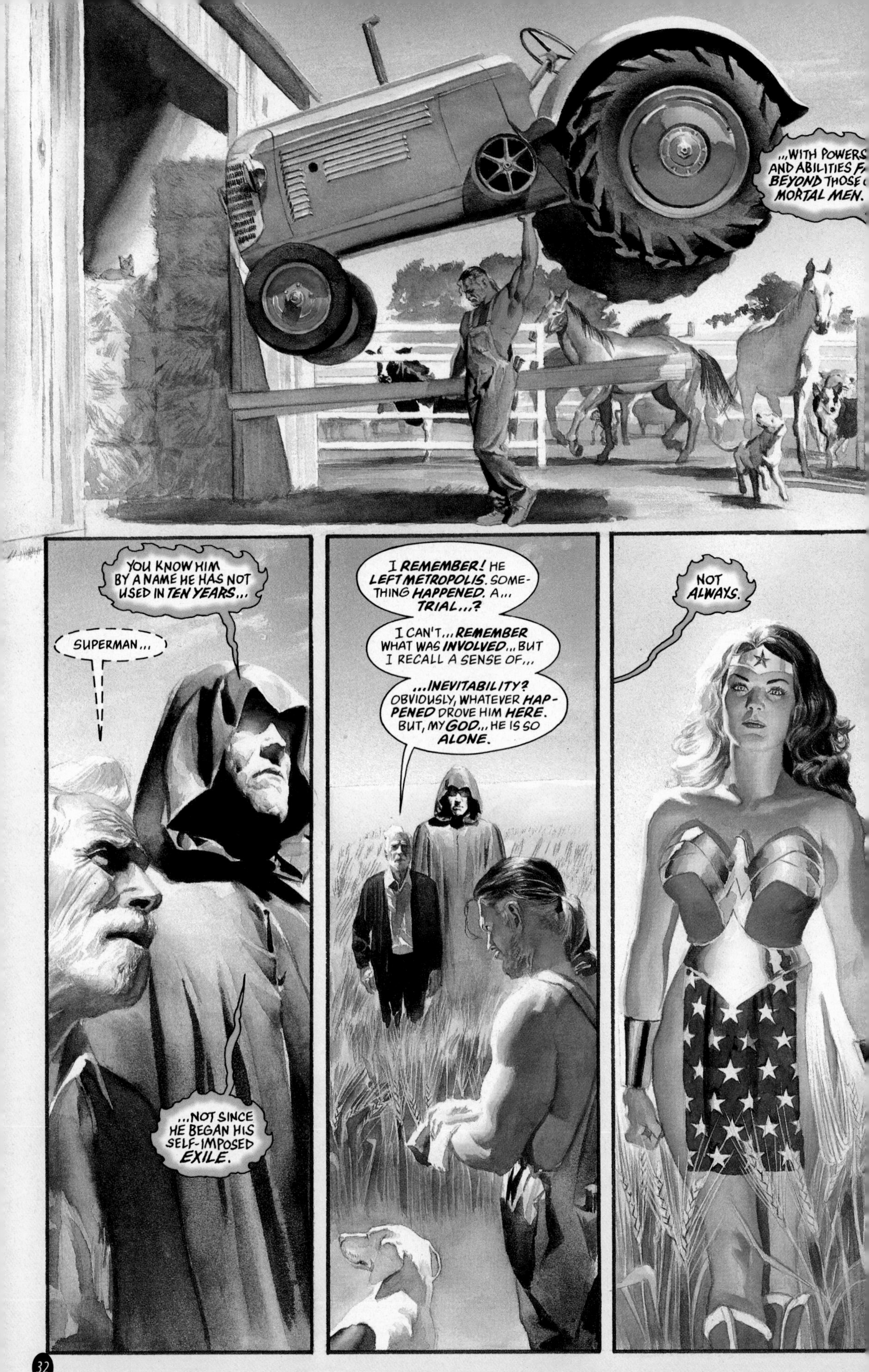
...WITH POWERS AND ABILITIES FA
BEYOND THOSE
MORTAL MEN.
YOU KNOW HIM BY A NAME HE HAS NOT USED IN TEN YEARS...
SUPERMAN...
...NOT SINCE HE BEGAN HIS SELF-IMPOSED EXILE.
I REMEMBER! HE LEFT METROPOLIS. SOMETHING HAPPENED. A... TRIAL...?
I CAN'T... REMEMBER WHAT WAS INVOLVED... BUT I RECALL A SENSE OF...
...INEVITABILITY? OBVIOUSLY, WHATEVER HAPPENED DROVE HIM HERE. BUT, MY GOD... HE IS SO ALONE.
NOT ALWAYS.

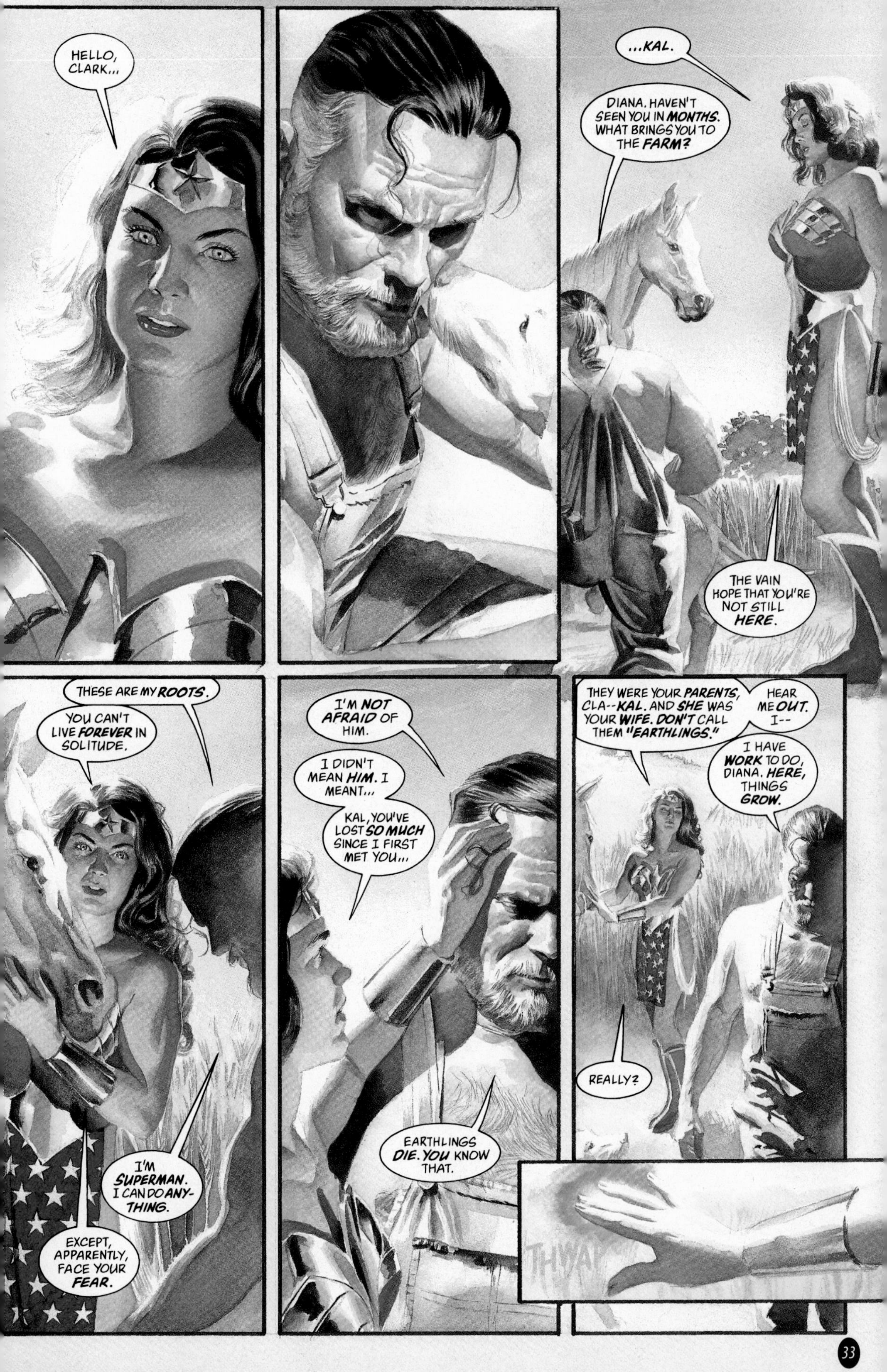
HELLO, CLARK...
...KAL.
DIANA. HAVEN'T SEEN YOU IN MONTHS. WHAT BRINGS YOU TO THE FARM?
THE VAIN HOPE THAT YOU'RE NOT STILL HERE.
THESE ARE MY ROOTS.
YOU CAN'T LIVE FOREVER IN SOLITUDE.
I'M SUPERMAN. I CAN DO ANYTHING.
EXCEPT, APPARENTLY, FACE YOUR FEAR.
I'M NOT AFRAID OF HIM.
I DIDN'T MEAN HIM. I MEANT...
KAL, YOU'VE LOST SO MUCH SINCE I FIRST MET YOU...
EARTHLINGS DIE. YOU KNOW THAT.
THEY WERE YOUR PARENTS, CLA--KAL. AND SHE WAS YOUR WIFE. DON'T CALL THEM "EARTHLINGS."
HEAR ME OUT. I--
I HAVE WORK TO DO, DIANA. HERE, THINGS GROW.
REALLY?
THWAP

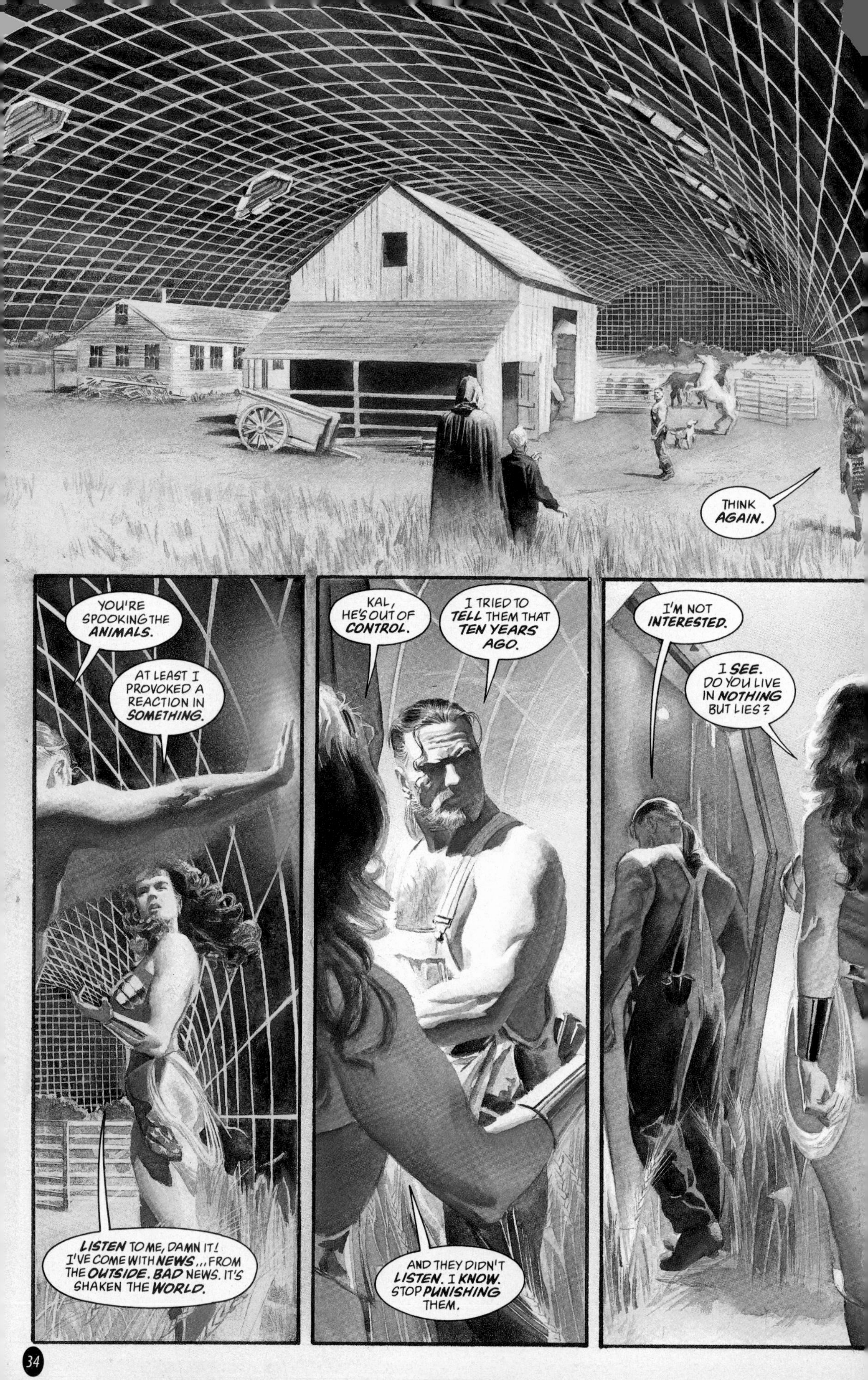
THINK AGAIN.
YOU'RE SPOOKING THE ANIMALS.
AT LEAST I PROVOKED A REACTION IN SOMETHING.
LISTEN TO ME, DAMN IT! I'VE COME WITH NEWS... FROM THE OUTSIDE. BAD NEWS. IT'S SHAKEN THE WORLD.
KAL, HE'S OUT OF CONTROL.
I TRIED TO TELL THEM THAT TEN YEARS AGO.
AND THEY DIDN'T LISTEN. I KNOW. STOP PUNISHING THEM.
I'M NOT INTERESTED.
I SEE. DO YOU LIVE IN NOTHING BUT LIES?

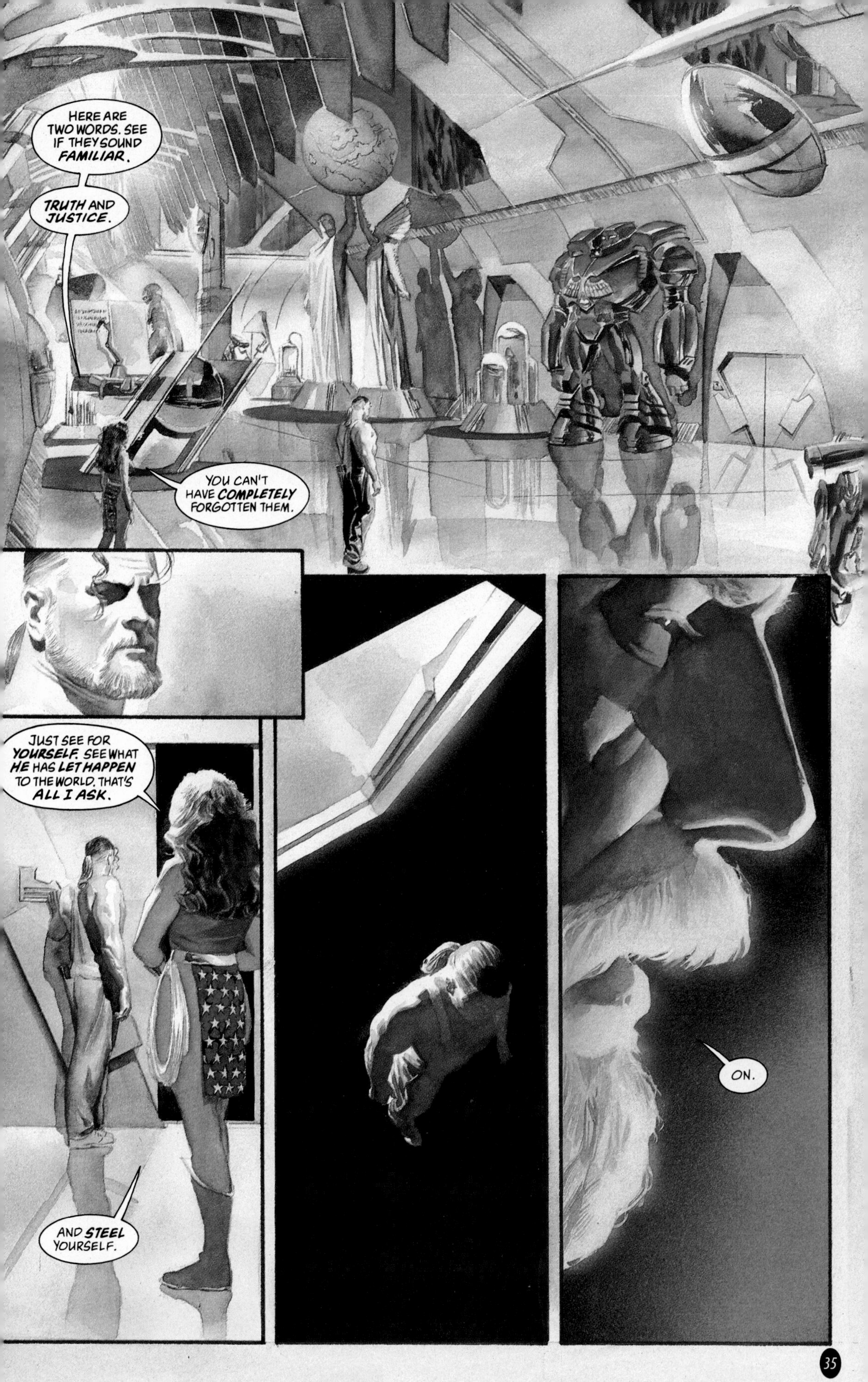
HERE ARE TWO WORDS. SEE IF THEY SOUND FAMILIAR.
TRUTH AND JUSTICE.
YOU CAN'T HAVE COMPLETELY FORGOTTEN THEM.
JUST SEE FOR YOURSELF. SEE WHAT HE HAS LET HAPPEN TO THE WORLD. THAT'S ALL I ASK.
AND STEEL YOURSELF.
ON.

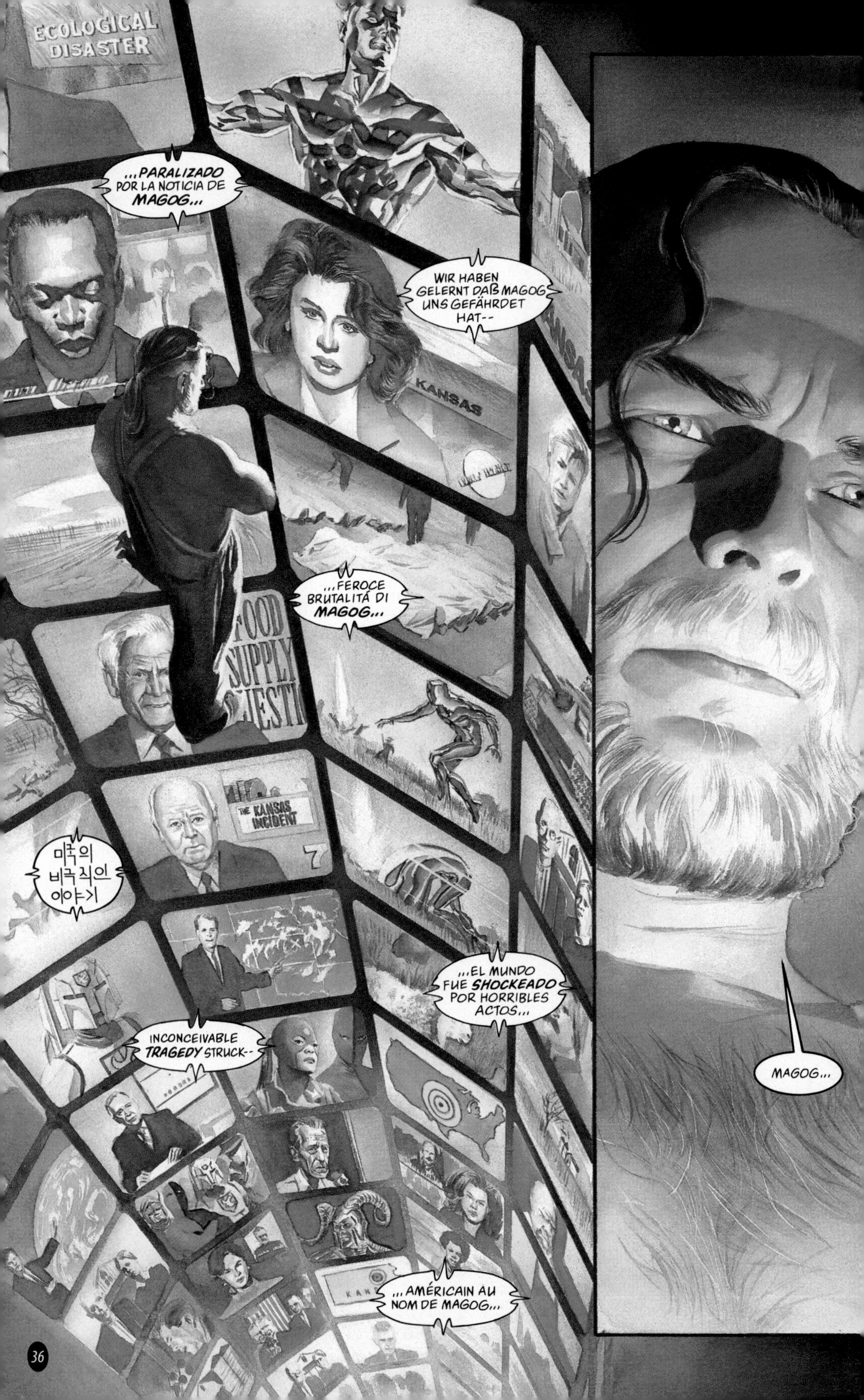
ECOLOGICAL DISASTER
...PARALIZADO POR LA NOTICIA DE MAGOG...
WIR HABEN GELERNT DAß MAGOG UNS GEFÄHRDET HAT--
KANSAS
...FEROCE BRUTALITÀ DI MAGOG...
FOOD SUPPLY
THE KANSAS INCIDENT
미국의 비극적인 이야기
...EL MUNDO FUE SHOCKEADO POR HORRIBLES ACTOS...
INCONCEIVABLE TRAGEDY STRUCK--
MAGOG...
...AMÉRICAIN AU NOM DE MAGOG...

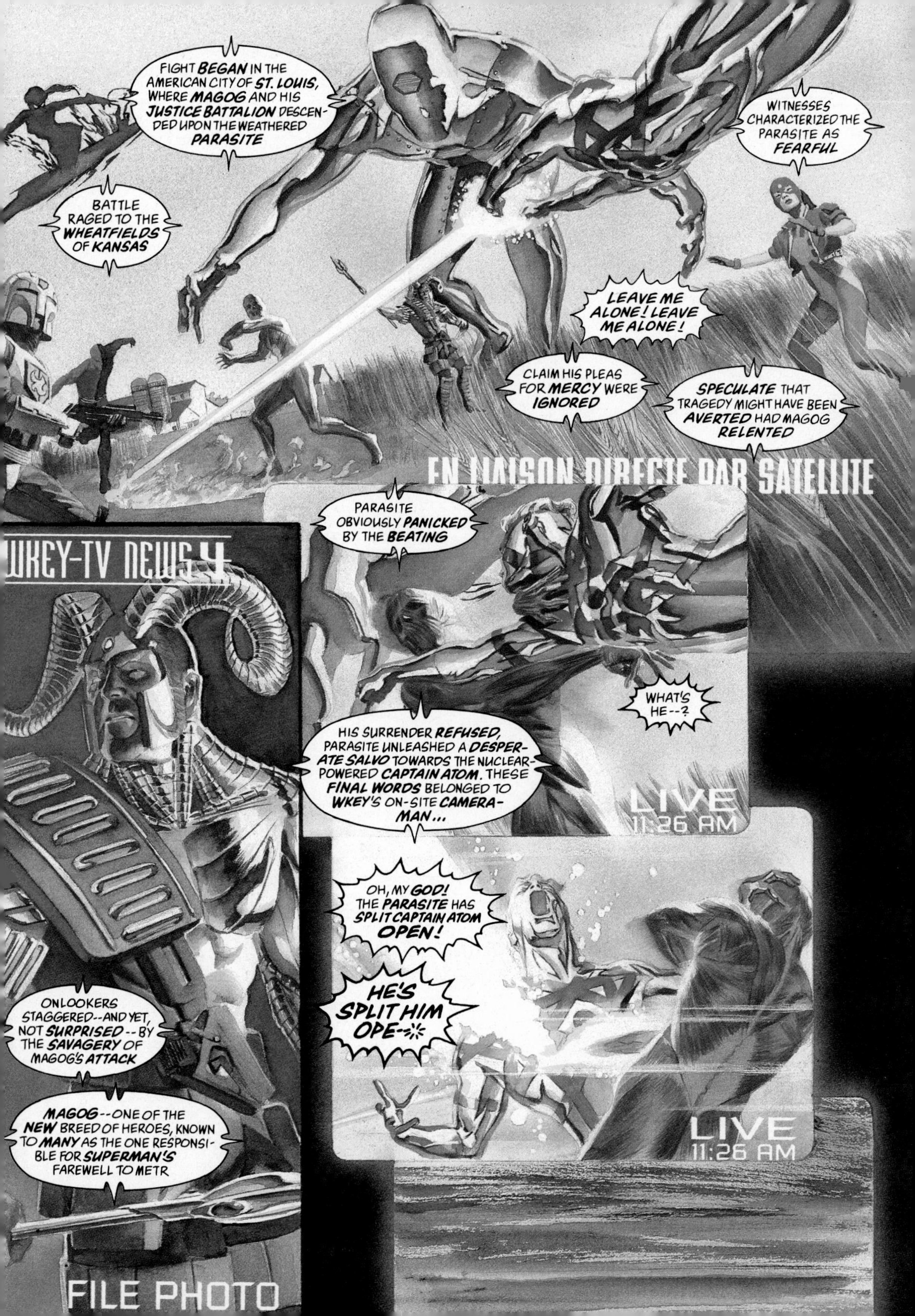
FIGHT BEGAN IN THE AMERICAN CITY OF ST. LOUIS, WHERE MAGOG AND HIS JUSTICE BATTALION DESCENDED UPON THE WEATHERED PARASITE
WITNESSES CHARACTERIZED THE PARASITE AS FEARFUL
BATTLE RAGED TO THE WHEATFIELDS OF KANSAS
LEAVE ME ALONE! LEAVE ME ALONE!
CLAIM HIS PLEAS FOR MERCY WERE IGNORED
SPECULATE THAT TRAGEDY MIGHT HAVE BEEN AVERTED HAD MAGOG RELENTED
EN LIAISON DIRECTE PAR SATELLITE
PARASITE OBVIOUSLY PANICKED BY THE BEATING
WKEY-TV NEWS 4
WHAT'S HE--?
HIS SURRENDER REFUSED, PARASITE UNLEASHED A DESPERATE SALVO TOWARDS THE NUCLEAR-POWERED CAPTAIN ATOM. THESE FINAL WORDS BELONGED TO WKEY'S ON-SITE CAMERAMAN...
LIVE 11:26 AM
OH, MY GOD! THE PARASITE HAS SPLIT CAPTAIN ATOM OPEN!
HE'S SPLIT HIM OPE--
ONLOOKERS STAGGERED--AND YET, NOT SURPRISED--BY THE SAVAGERY OF MAGOG'S ATTACK
LIVE 11:26 AM
MAGOG--ONE OF THE NEW BREED OF HEROES, KNOWN TO MANY AS THE ONE RESPONSIBLE FOR SUPERMAN'S FAREWELL TO METR
FILE PHOTO

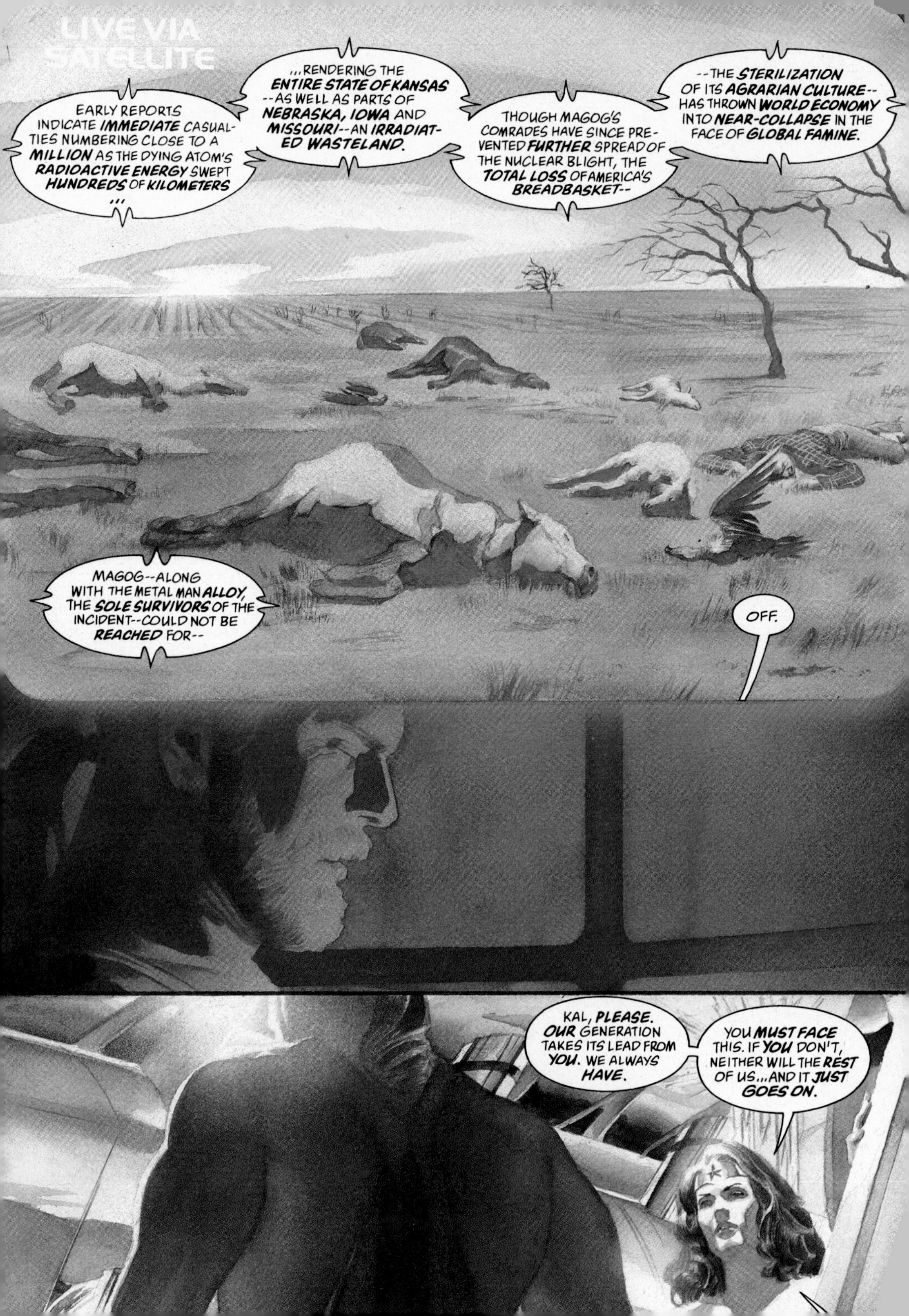
LIVE VIA SATELLITE
EARLY REPORTS INDICATE IMMEDIATE CASUALTIES NUMBERING CLOSE TO A MILLION AS THE DYING ATOM'S RADIOACTIVE ENERGY SWEPT HUNDREDS OF KILOMETERS ...
...RENDERING THE ENTIRE STATE OF KANSAS --AS WELL AS PARTS OF NEBRASKA, IOWA AND MISSOURI--AN IRRADIATED WASTELAND.
THOUGH MAGOG'S COMRADES HAVE SINCE PREVENTED FURTHER SPREAD OF THE NUCLEAR BLIGHT, THE TOTAL LOSS OF AMERICA'S BREADBASKET--
--THE STERILIZATION OF ITS AGRARIAN CULTURE--HAS THROWN WORLD ECONOMY INTO NEAR-COLLAPSE IN THE FACE OF GLOBAL FAMINE.
MAGOG--ALONG WITH THE METAL MAN ALLOY, THE SOLE SURVIVORS OF THE INCIDENT--COULD NOT BE REACHED FOR--
OFF.
KAL, PLEASE. OUR GENERATION TAKES ITS LEAD FROM YOU. WE ALWAYS HAVE.
YOU MUST FACE THIS. IF YOU DON'T, NEITHER WILL THE REST OF US...AND IT JUST GOES ON.

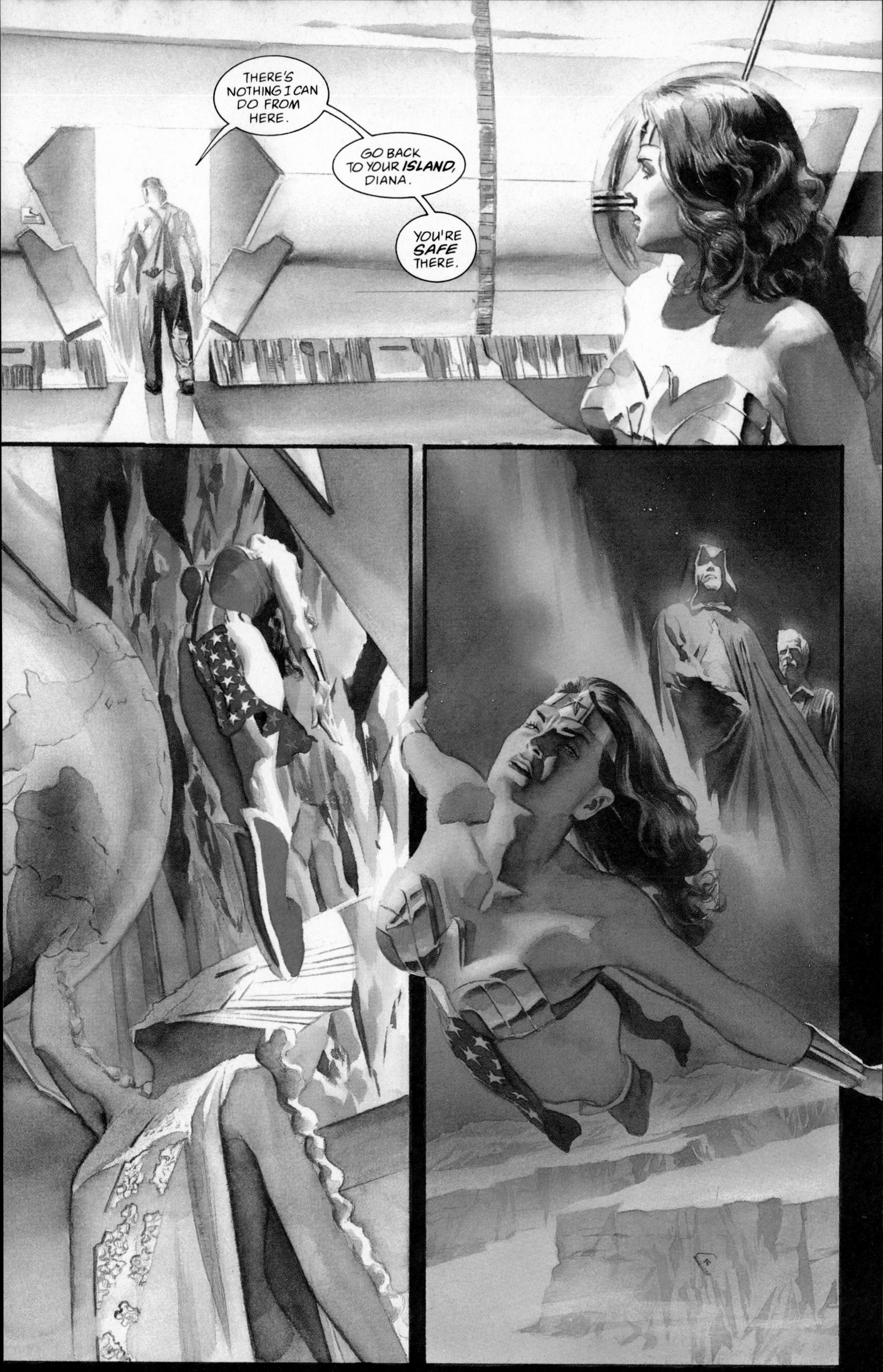
THERE'S NOTHING I CAN DO FROM HERE.
GO BACK TO YOUR ISLAND, DIANA.
YOU'RE SAFE THERE.

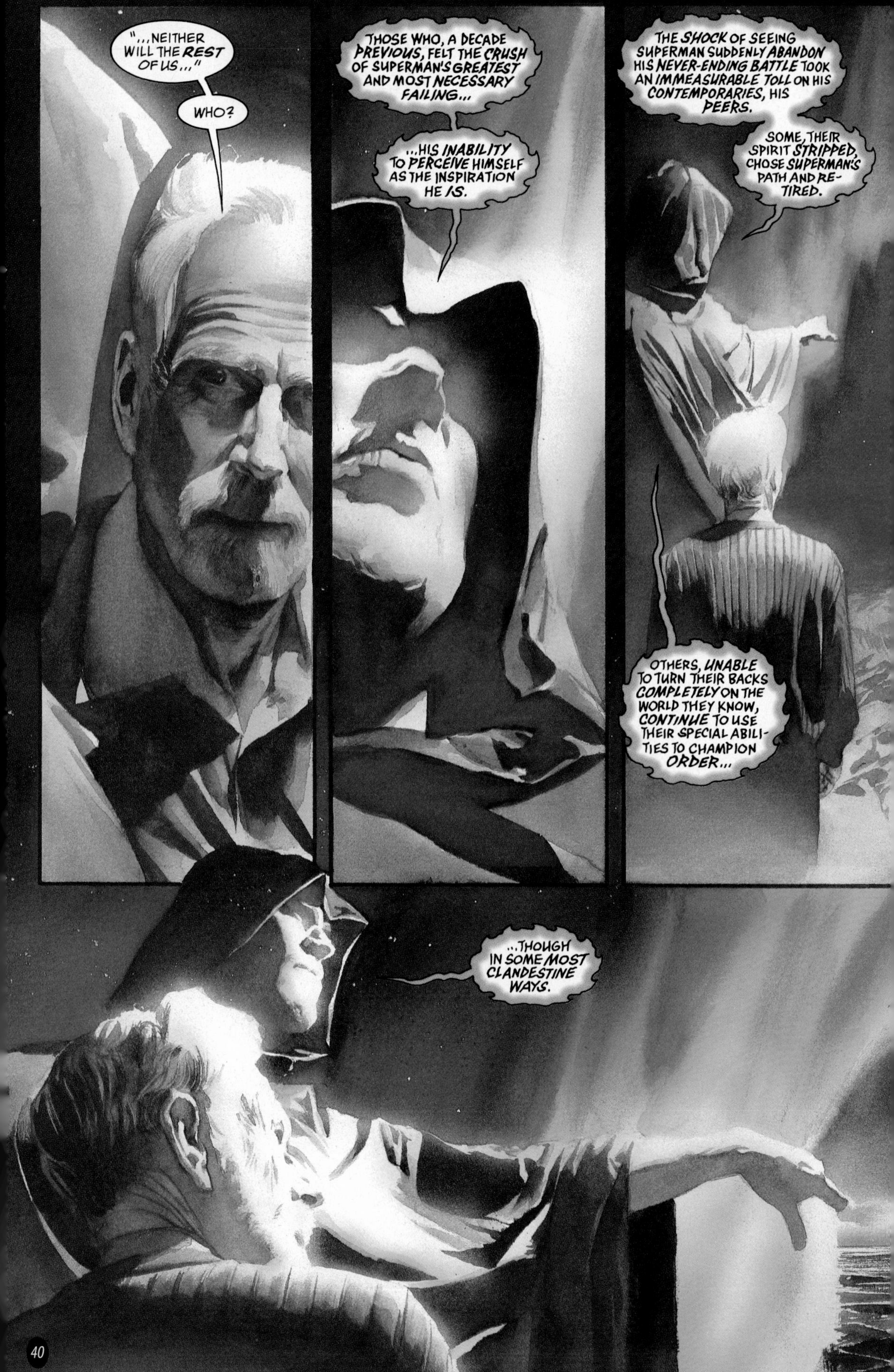
"...NEITHER WILL THE REST OF US..."
WHO?
THOSE WHO, A DECADE PREVIOUS, FELT THE CRUSH OF SUPERMAN'S GREATEST AND MOST NECESSARY FAILING...
...HIS INABILITY TO PERCEIVE HIMSELF AS THE INSPIRATION HE IS.
THE SHOCK OF SEEING SUPERMAN SUDDENLY ABANDON HIS NEVER-ENDING BATTLE TOOK AN IMMEASURABLE TOLL ON HIS CONTEMPORARIES, HIS PEERS.
SOME, THEIR SPIRIT STRIPPED, CHOSE SUPERMAN'S PATH AND RE-TIRED.
OTHERS, UNABLE TO TURN THEIR BACKS COMPLETELY ON THE WORLD THEY KNOW, CONTINUE TO USE THEIR SPECIAL ABILI-TIES TO CHAMPION ORDER...
...THOUGH IN SOME MOST CLANDESTINE WAYS.

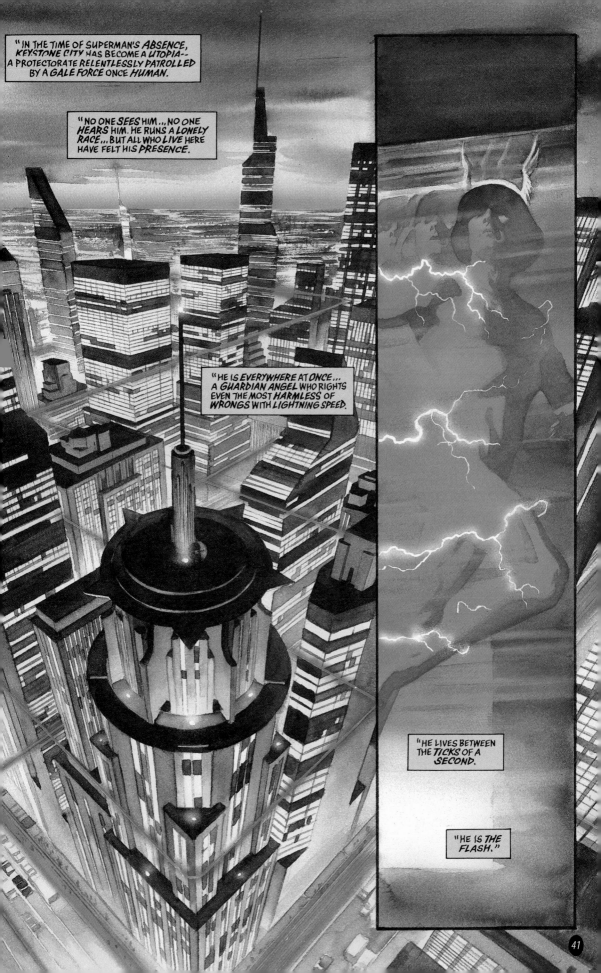

"IN THE TIME OF SUPERMAN'S *ABSENCE,* KEYSTONE CITY HAS BECOME A *UTOPIA*-- A PROTECTORATE RELENTLESSLY PATROLLED BY A *GALE FORCE* ONCE *HUMAN.*

"NO ONE *SEES* HIM ... NO ONE *HEARS* HIM. HE RUNS A *LONELY RACE* ... BUT ALL WHO *LIVE* HERE HAVE FELT HIS *PRESENCE.*

"HE IS *EVERYWHERE* AT *ONCE* ... A *GUARDIAN ANGEL* WHO RIGHTS EVEN THE MOST *HARMLESS* OF *WRONGS* WITH *LIGHTNING SPEED.*

"HE LIVES BETWEEN THE *TICKS* OF A *SECOND.*

"HE IS *THE FLASH.*"

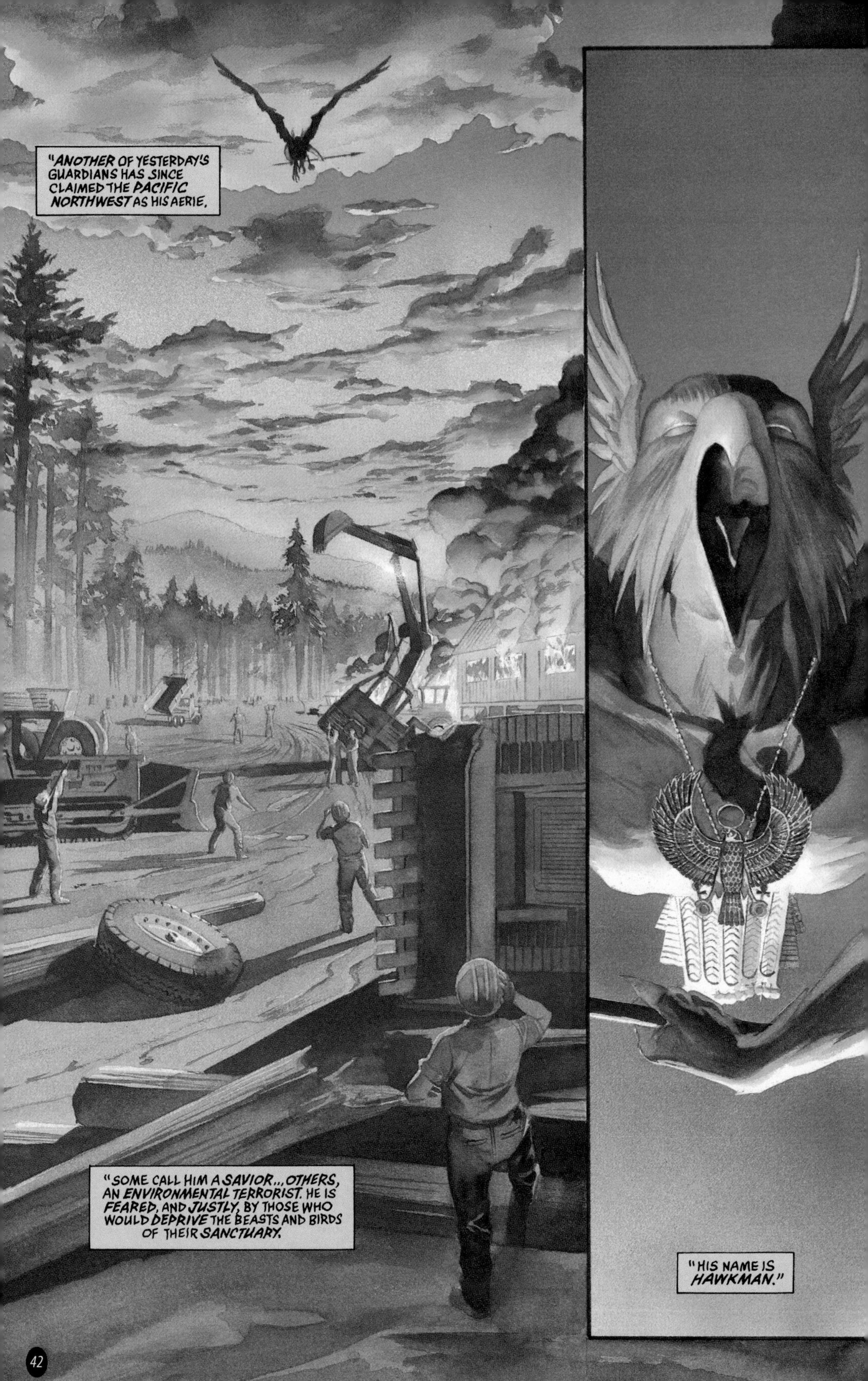
"ANOTHER OF YESTERDAY'S GUARDIANS HAS SINCE CLAIMED THE PACIFIC NORTHWEST AS HIS AERIE.
"SOME CALL HIM A SAVIOR... OTHERS, AN ENVIRONMENTAL TERRORIST. HE IS FEARED, AND JUSTLY, BY THOSE WHO WOULD DEPRIVE THE BEASTS AND BIRDS OF THEIR SANCTUARY.
"HIS NAME IS HAWKMAN."

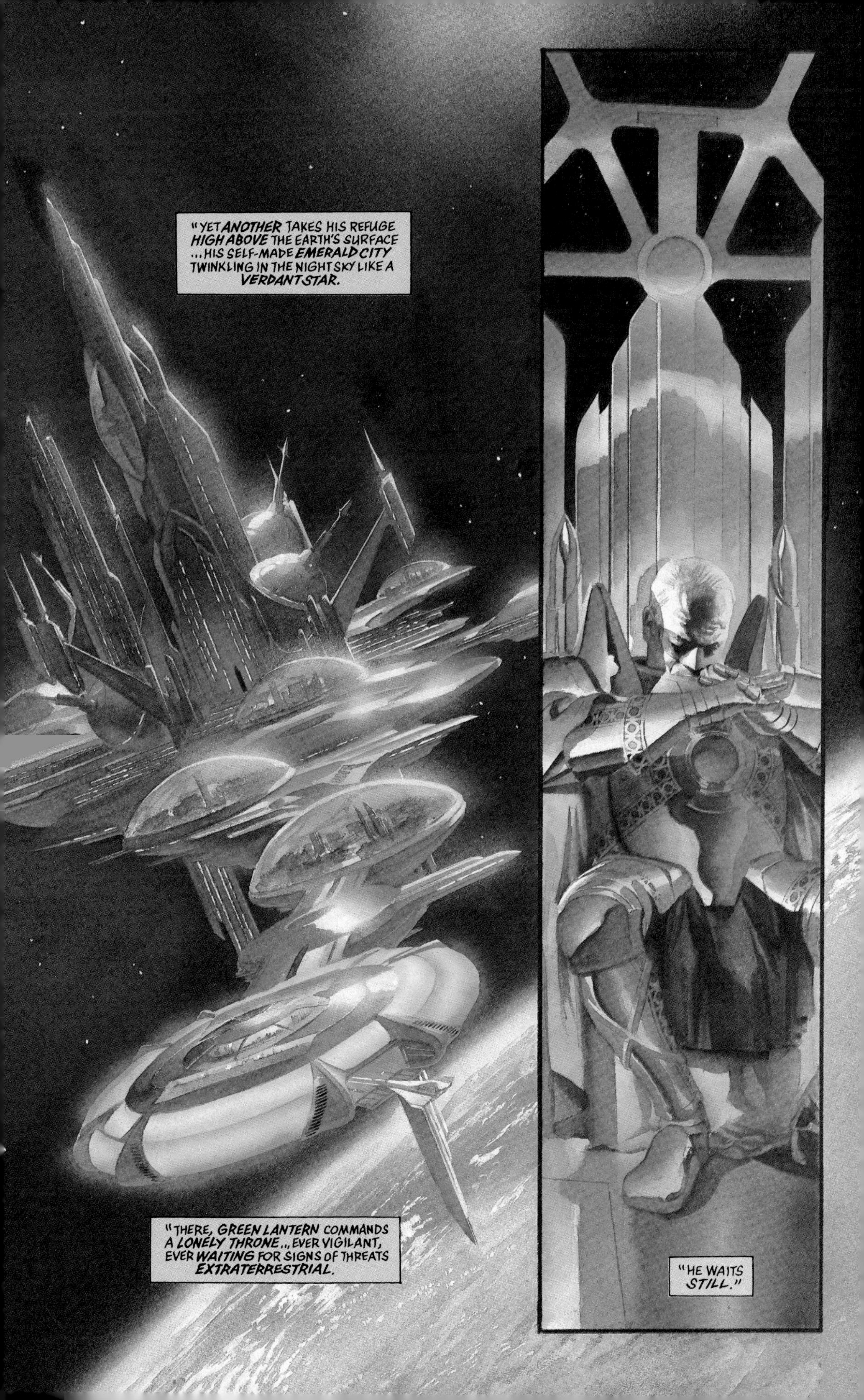
"YET ANOTHER TAKES HIS REFUGE HIGH ABOVE THE EARTH'S SURFACE ...HIS SELF-MADE EMERALD CITY TWINKLING IN THE NIGHT SKY LIKE A VERDANT STAR.
"THERE, GREEN LANTERN COMMANDS A LONELY THRONE... EVER VIGILANT, EVER WAITING FOR SIGNS OF THREATS EXTRATERRESTRIAL.
"HE WAITS STILL."

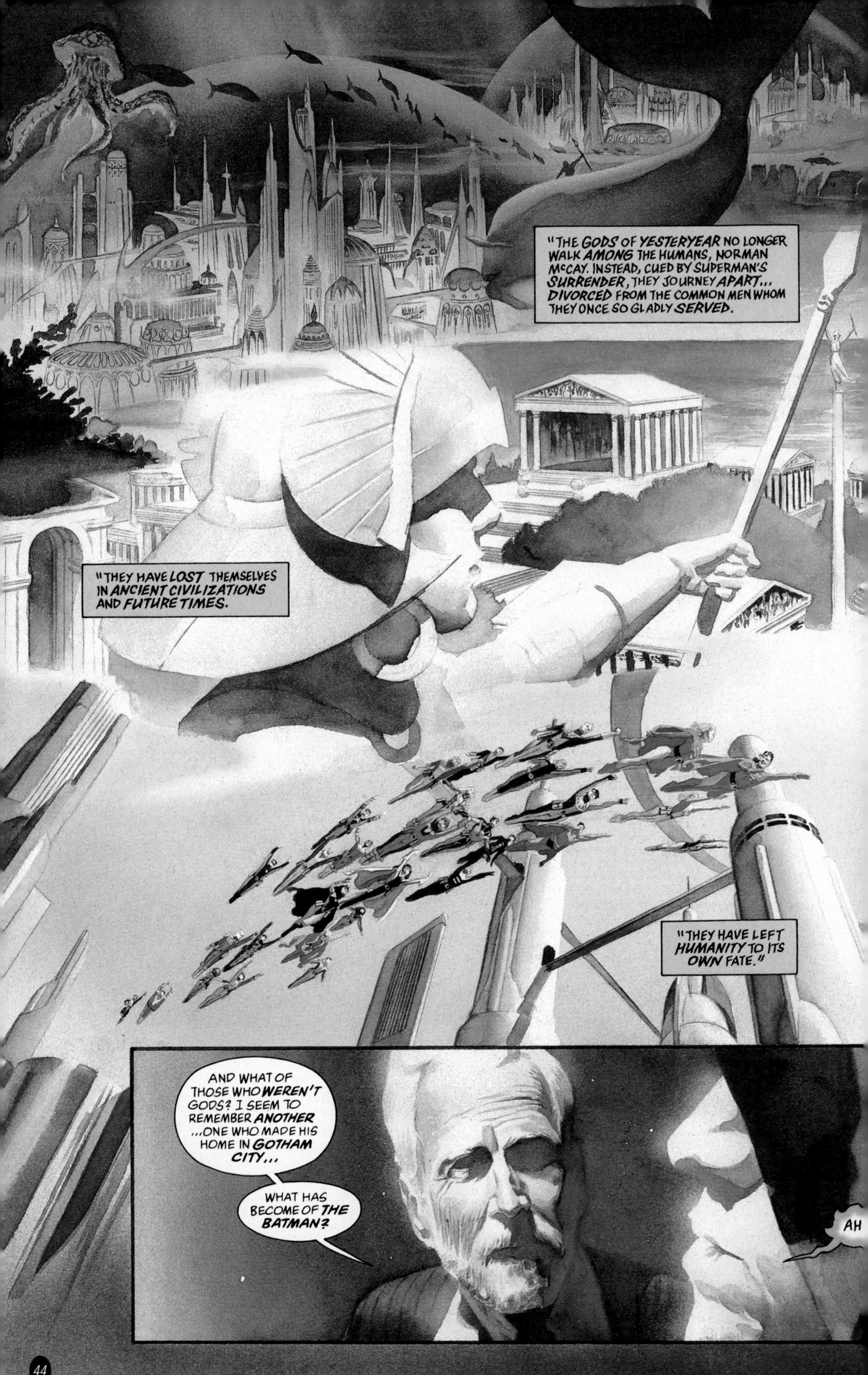

"THE GODS OF YESTERYEAR NO LONGER WALK AMONG THE HUMANS, NORMAN McCAY. INSTEAD, CUED BY SUPERMAN'S SURRENDER, THEY JOURNEY APART... DIVORCED FROM THE COMMON MEN WHOM THEY ONCE SO GLADLY SERVED.
"THEY HAVE LOST THEMSELVES IN ANCIENT CIVILIZATIONS AND FUTURE TIMES.
"THEY HAVE LEFT HUMANITY TO ITS OWN FATE."
AND WHAT OF THOSE WHO WEREN'T GODS? I SEEM TO REMEMBER ANOTHER ...ONE WHO MADE HIS HOME IN GOTHAM CITY...
WHAT HAS BECOME OF THE BATMAN?
AH

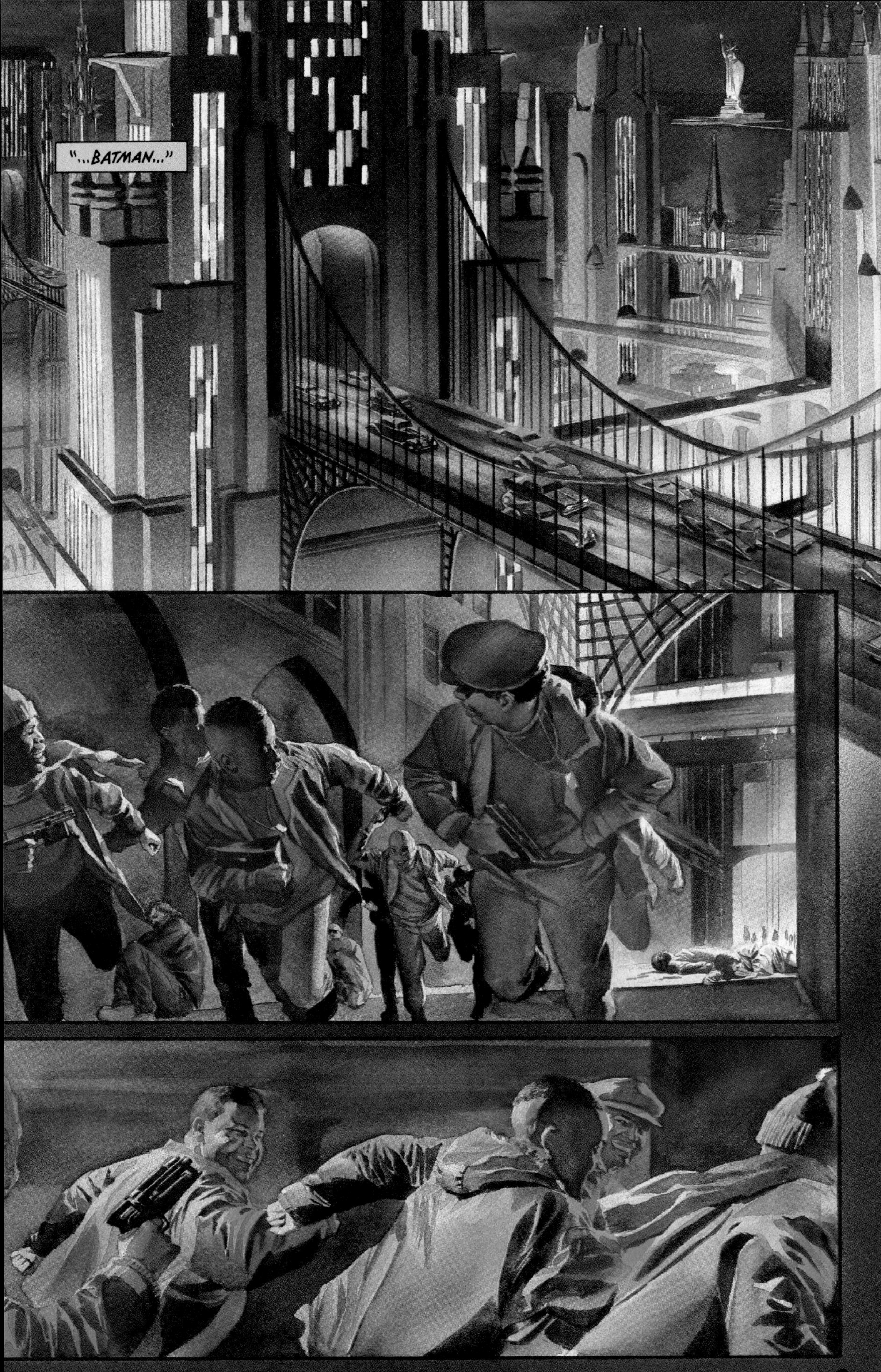
"...BATMAN..."

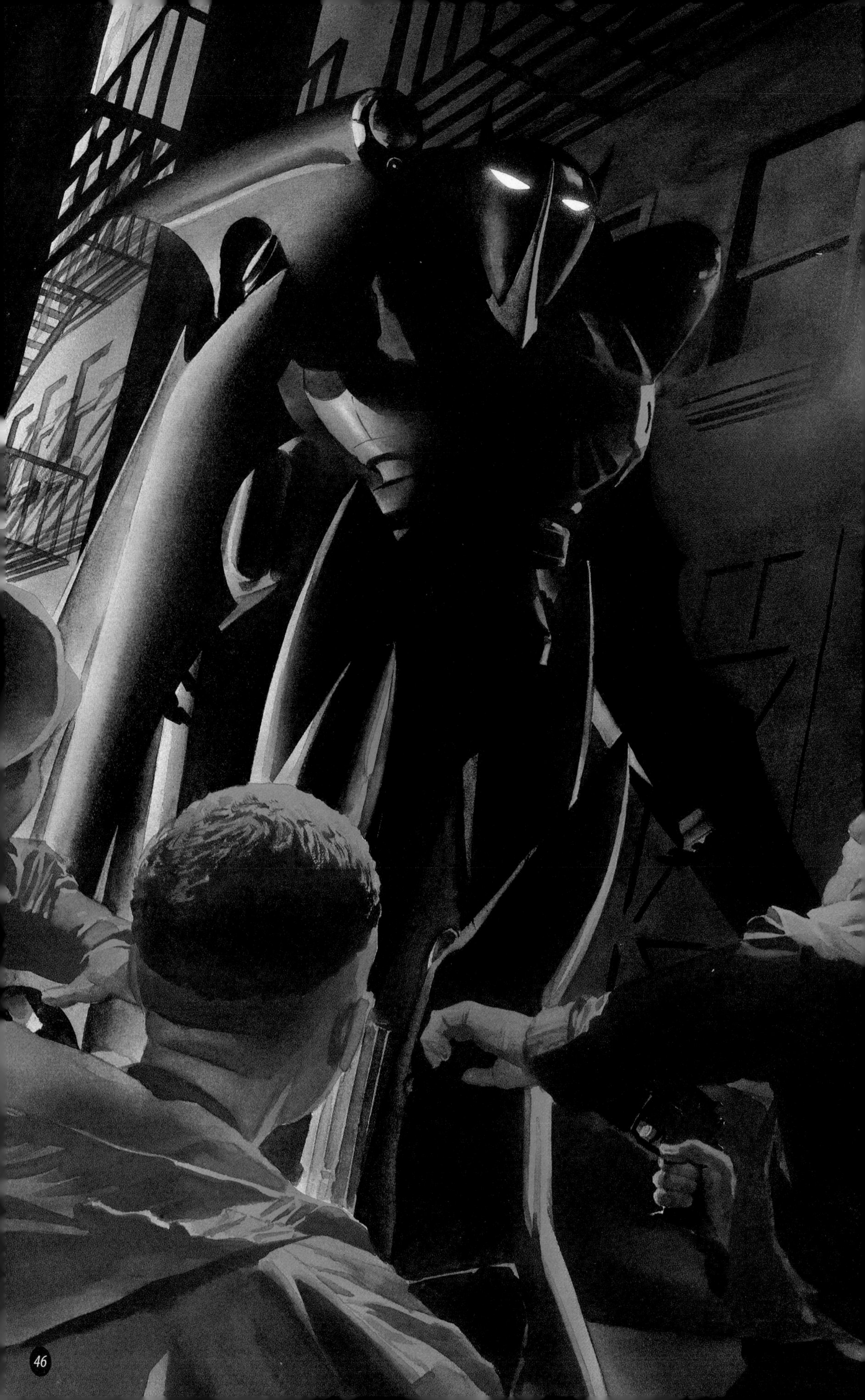

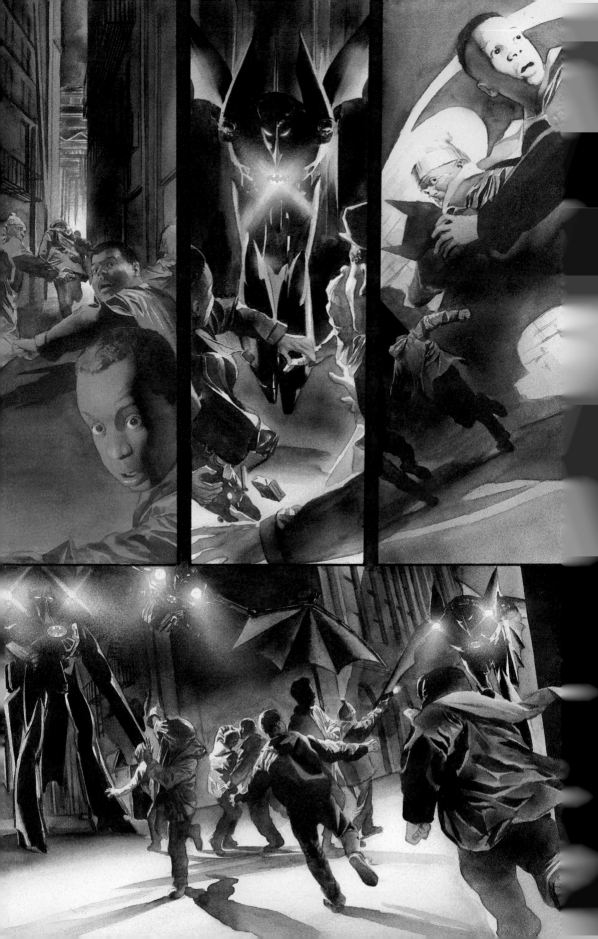

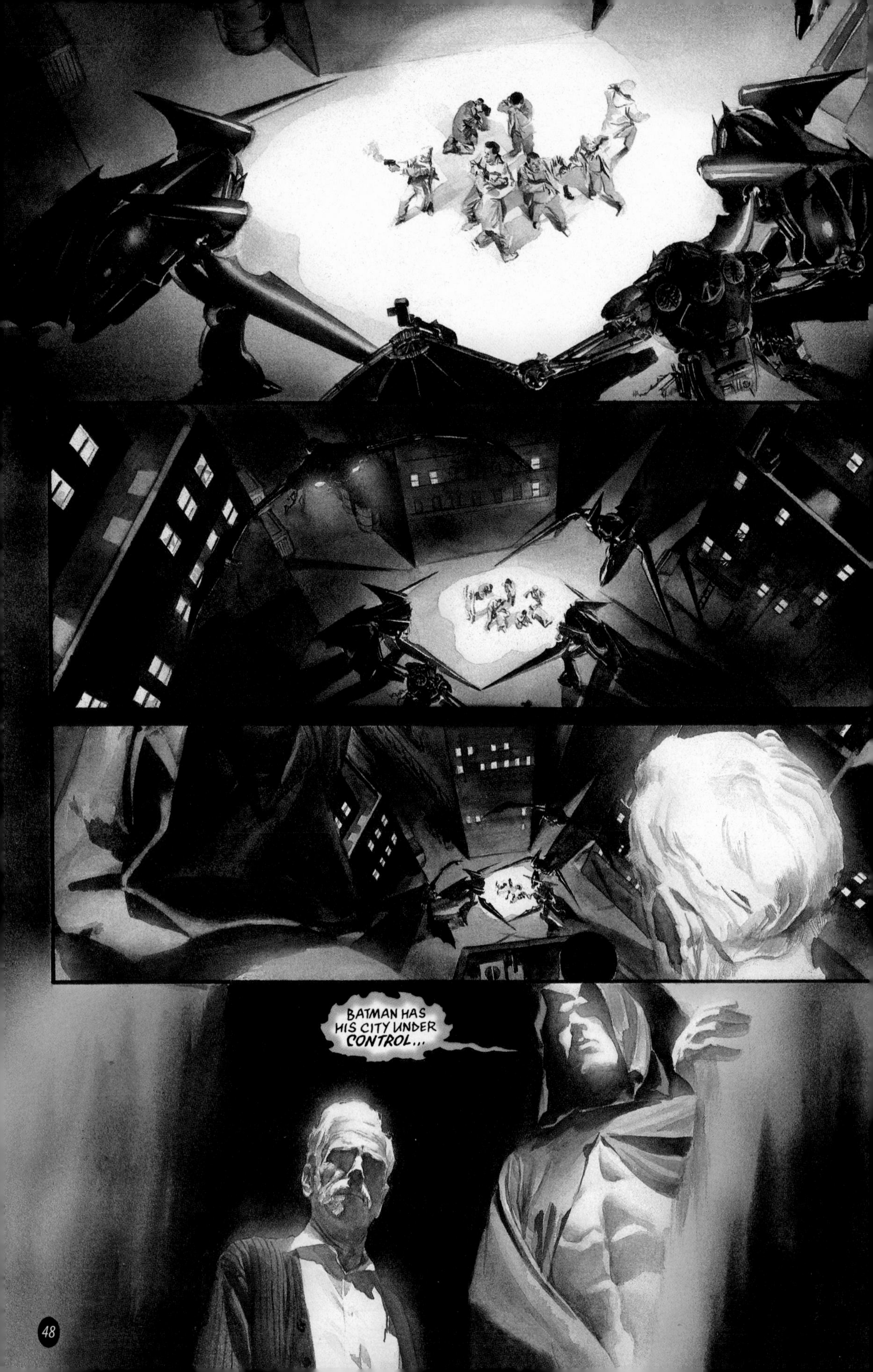
BATMAN HAS HIS CITY UNDER CONTROL...

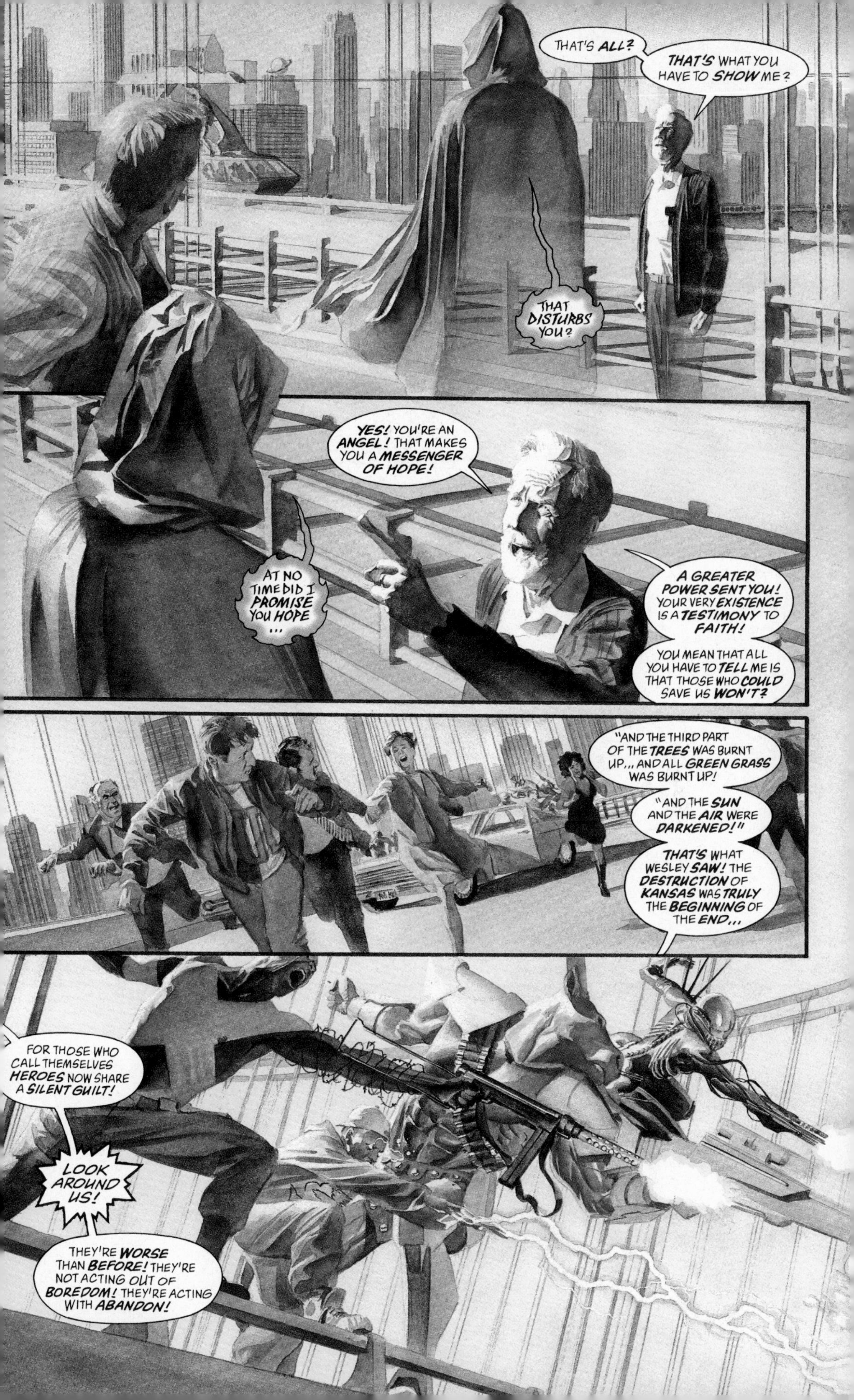
THAT'S ALL?
THAT'S WHAT YOU HAVE TO SHOW ME?
THAT DISTURBS YOU?
YES! YOU'RE AN ANGEL! THAT MAKES YOU A MESSENGER OF HOPE!
AT NO TIME DID I PROMISE YOU HOPE...
A GREATER POWER SENT YOU! YOUR VERY EXISTENCE IS A TESTIMONY TO FAITH!
YOU MEAN THAT ALL YOU HAVE TO TELL ME IS THAT THOSE WHO COULD SAVE US WON'T?
"AND THE THIRD PART OF THE TREES WAS BURNT UP... AND ALL GREEN GRASS WAS BURNT UP!
"AND THE SUN AND THE AIR WERE DARKENED!"
THAT'S WHAT WESLEY SAW! THE DESTRUCTION OF KANSAS WAS TRULY THE BEGINNING OF THE END...
FOR THOSE WHO CALL THEMSELVES HEROES NOW SHARE A SILENT GUILT!
LOOK AROUND US!
THEY'RE WORSE THAN BEFORE! THEY'RE NOT ACTING OUT OF BOREDOM! THEY'RE ACTING WITH ABANDON!

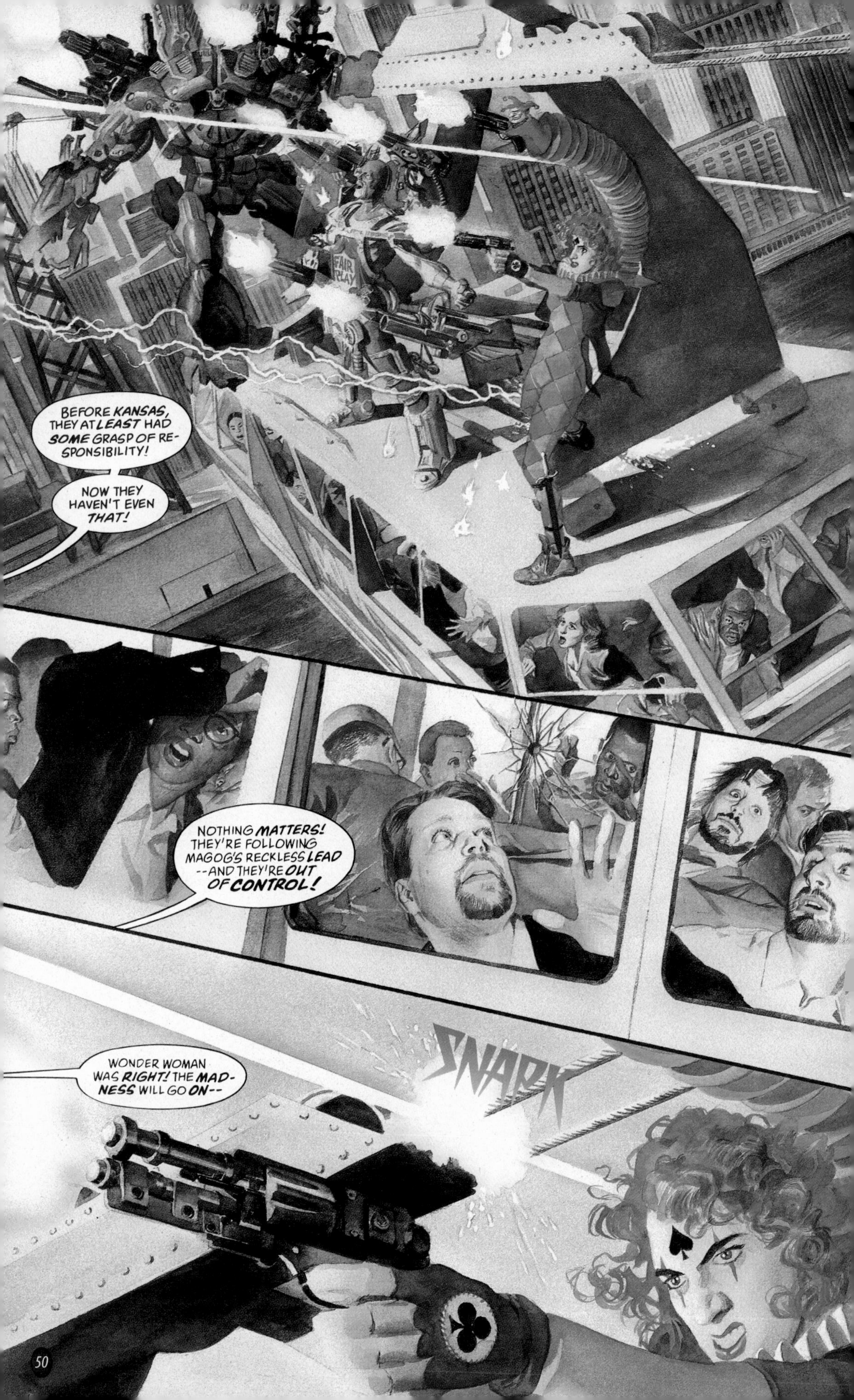
BEFORE KANSAS, THEY AT LEAST HAD SOME GRASP OF RE-SPONSIBILITY!
NOW THEY HAVEN'T EVEN THAT!
FAIR PLAY
NOTHING MATTERS! THEY'RE FOLLOWING MAGOG'S RECKLESS LEAD --AND THEY'RE OUT OF CONTROL!
SNAPK
WONDER WOMAN WAS RIGHT! THE MAD-NESS WILL GO ON--

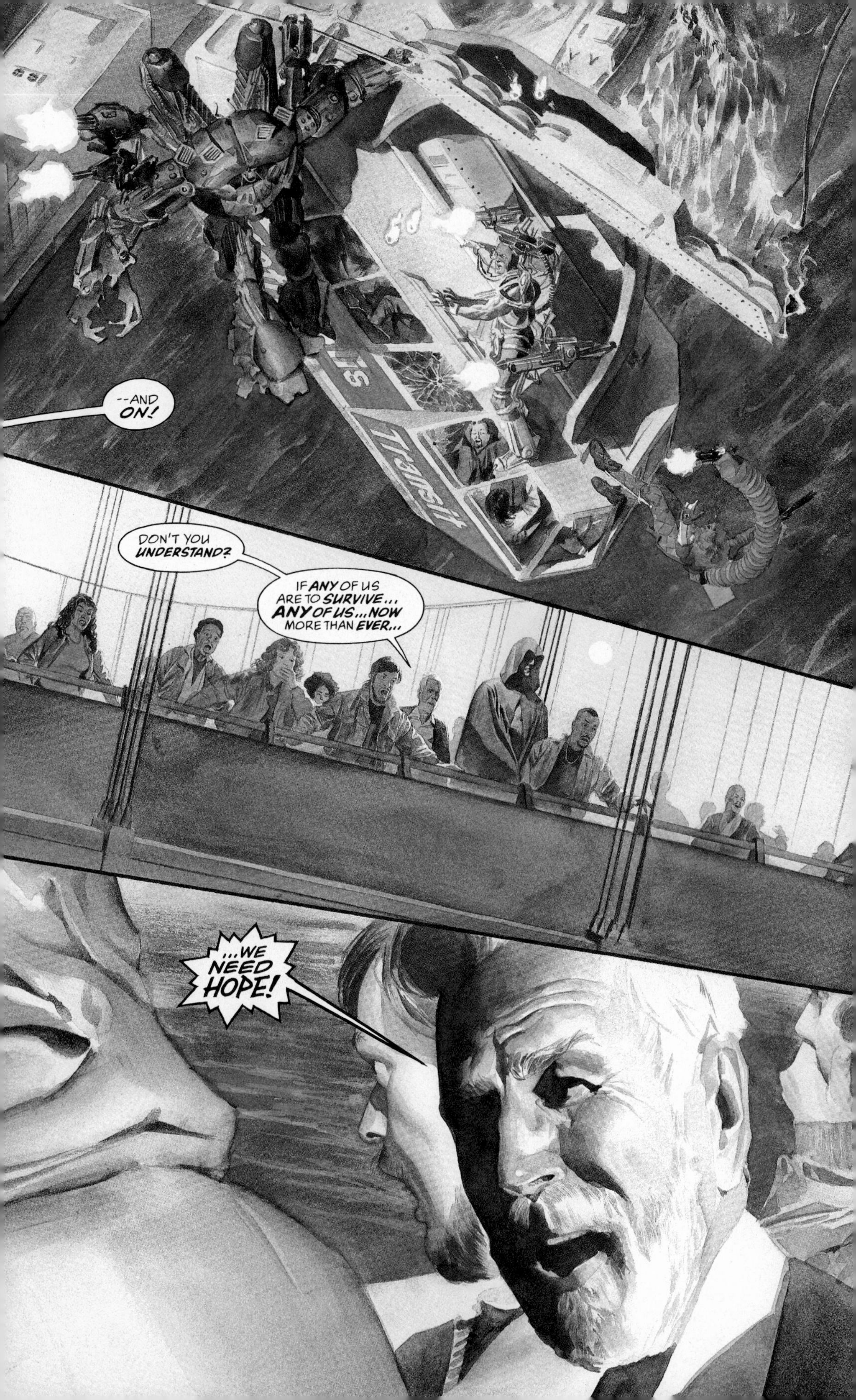
--AND ON!
DON'T YOU UNDERSTAND?
IF ANY OF US ARE TO SURVIVE... ANY OF US...NOW MORE THAN EVER...
...WE NEED HOPE!

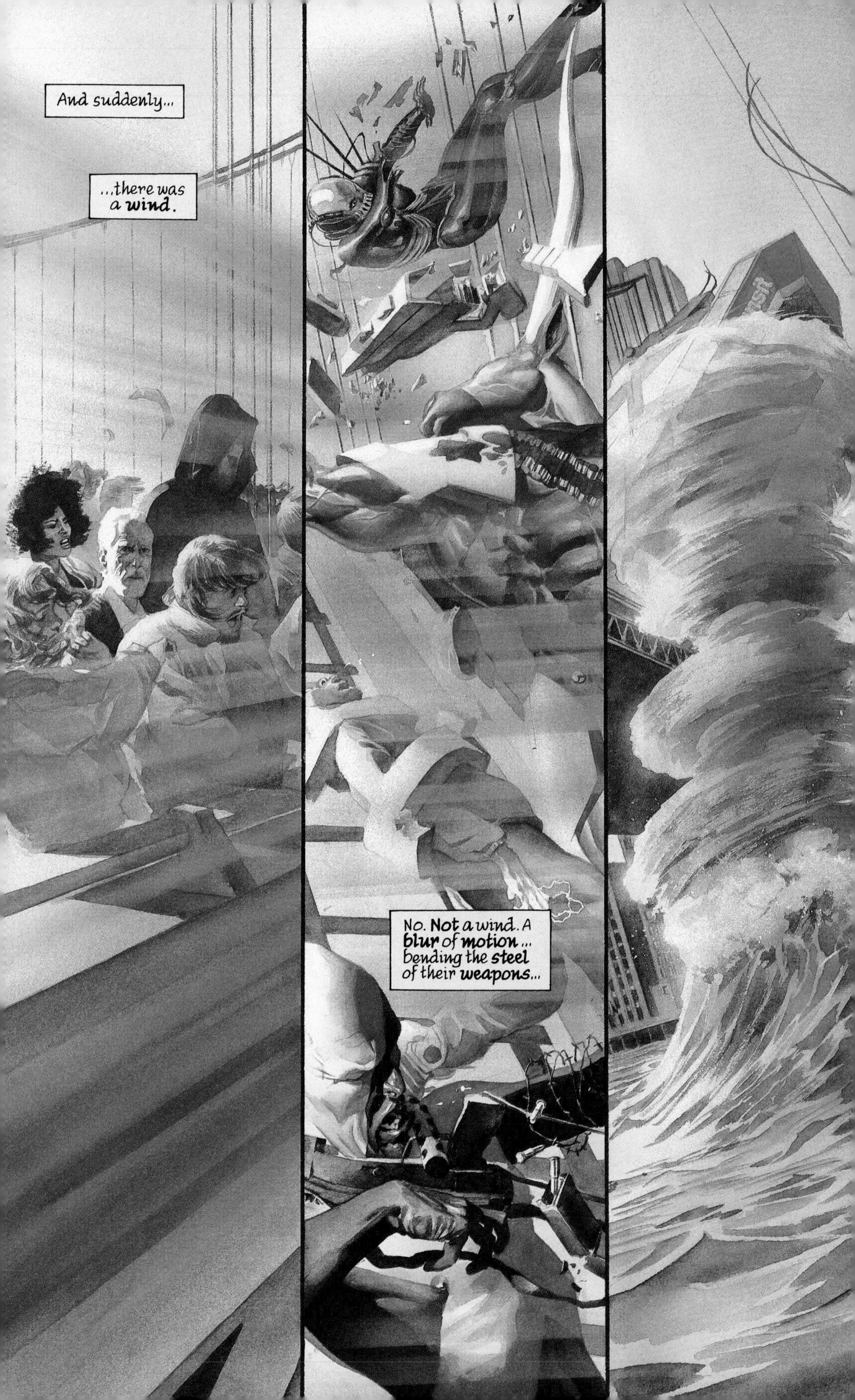
And suddenly...
...there was a **wind**.
No. **Not** a wind. A **blur** of **motion**... bending the **steel** of their **weapons**...

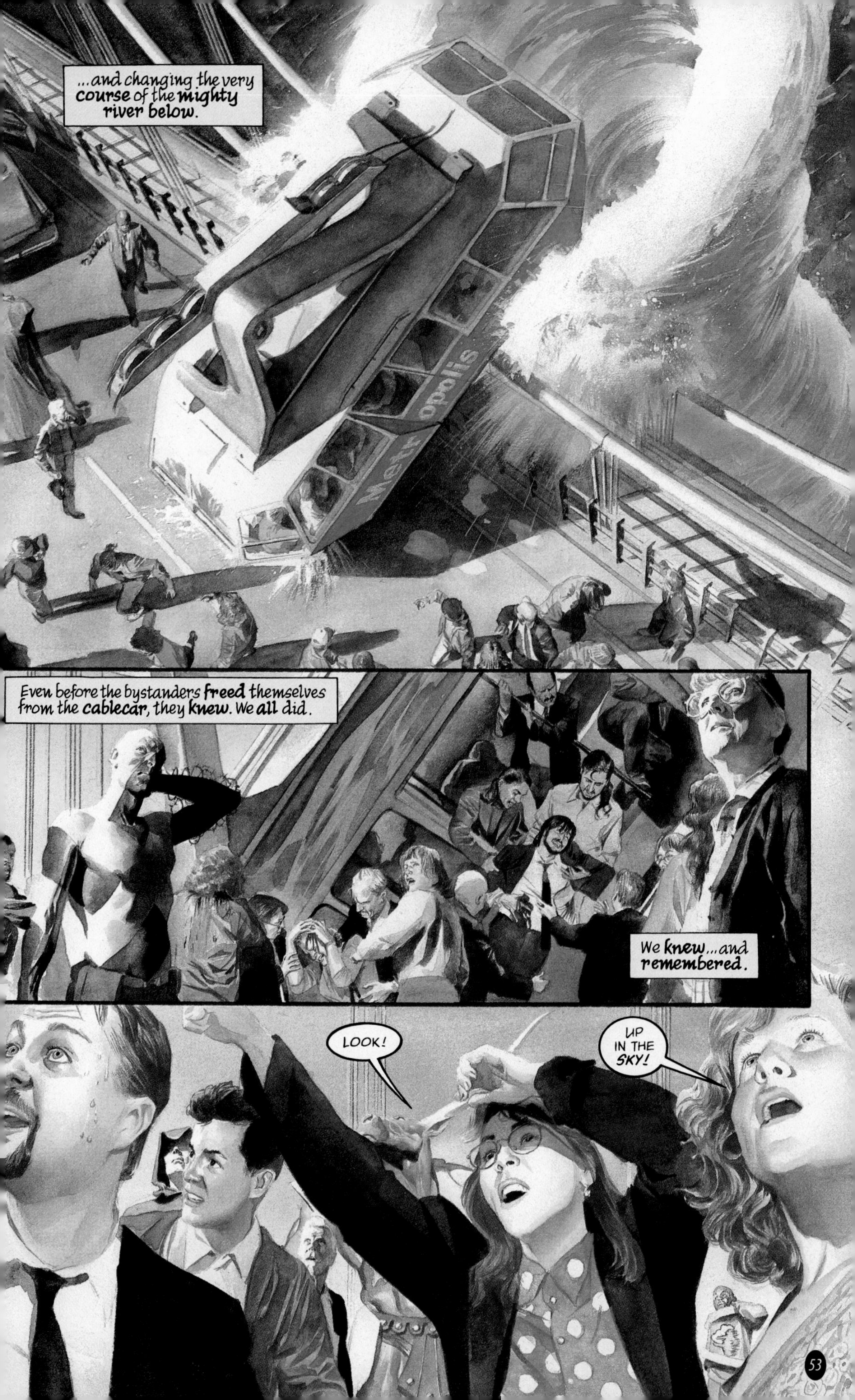
...and changing the very course of the mighty river below.
Metropolis
Even before the bystanders freed themselves from the cablecar, they knew. We all did.
We knew...and remembered.
LOOK!
UP IN THE SKY!

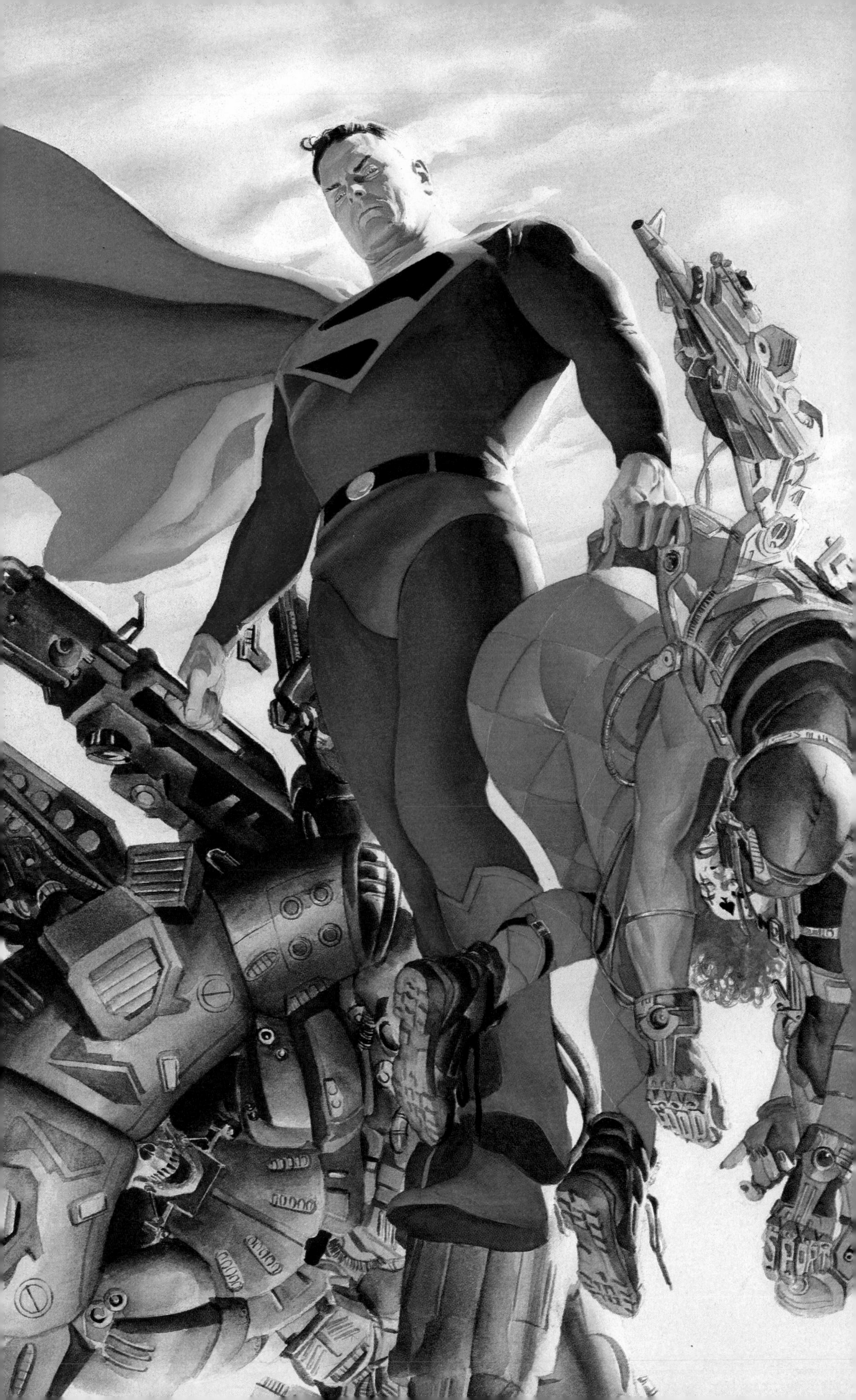

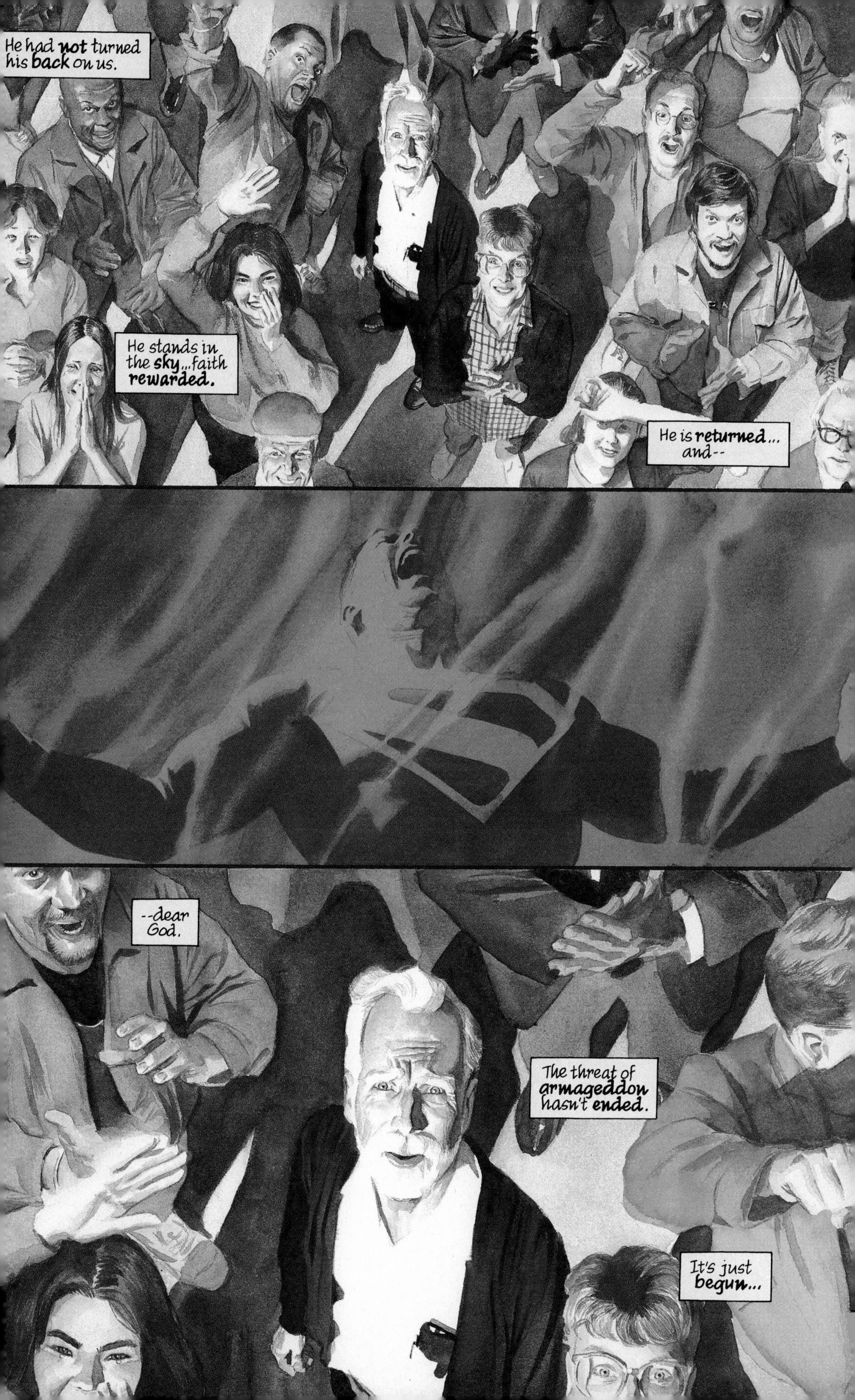
He had not turned his back on us.
He stands in the sky...faith rewarded.
He is returned... and--
--dear God.
The threat of armageddon hasn't ended.
It's just begun...

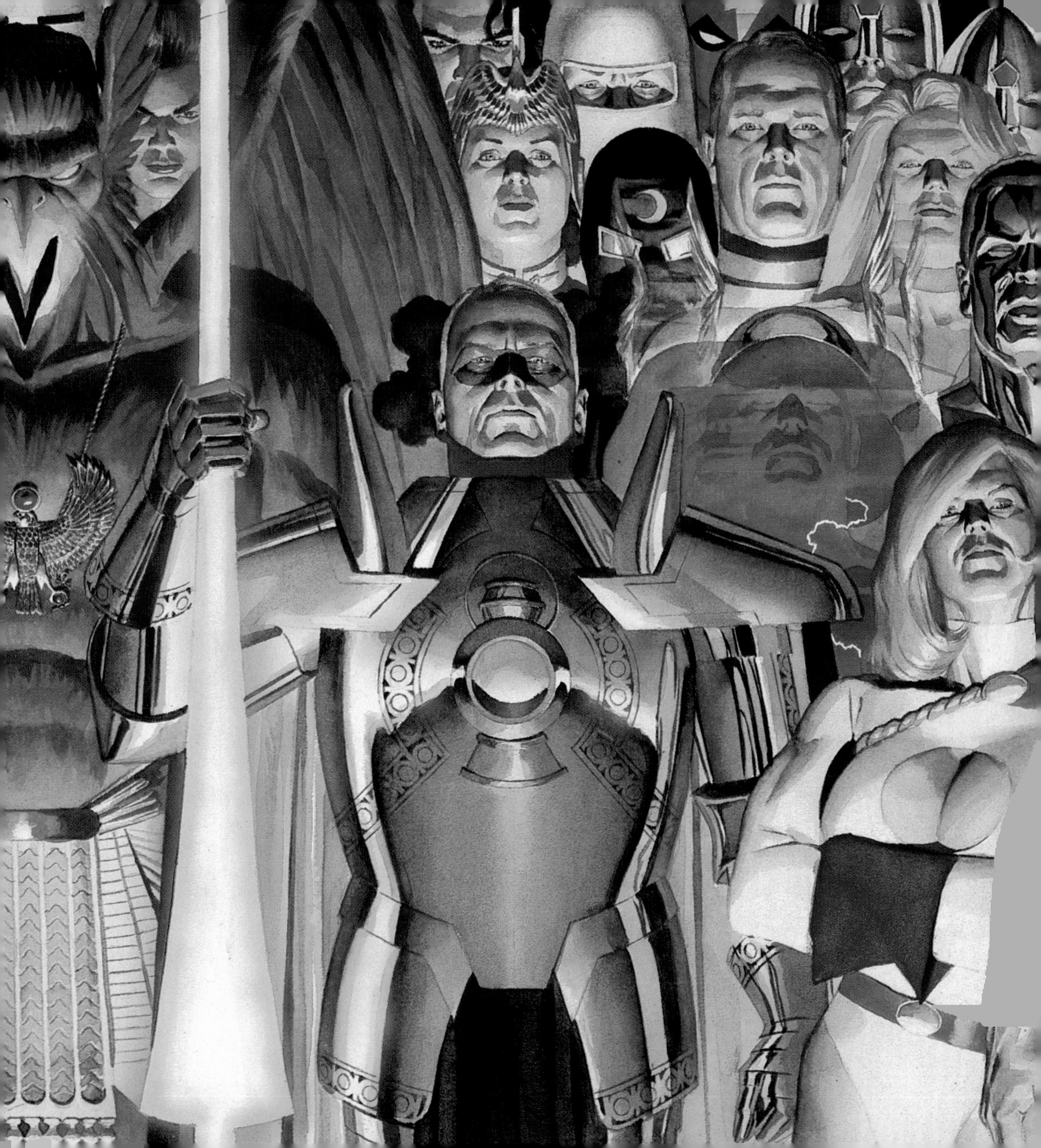

CHAPTER TWO

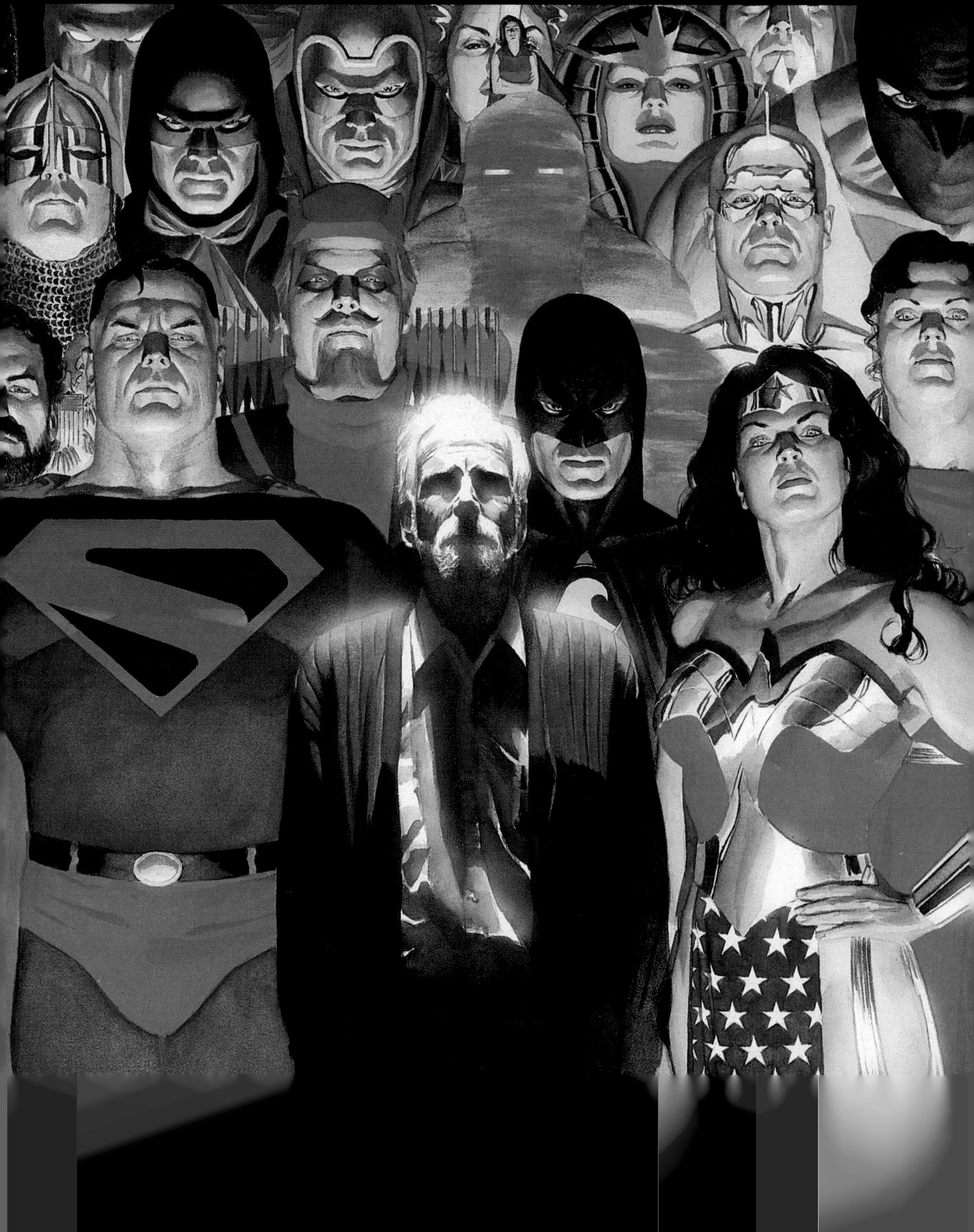

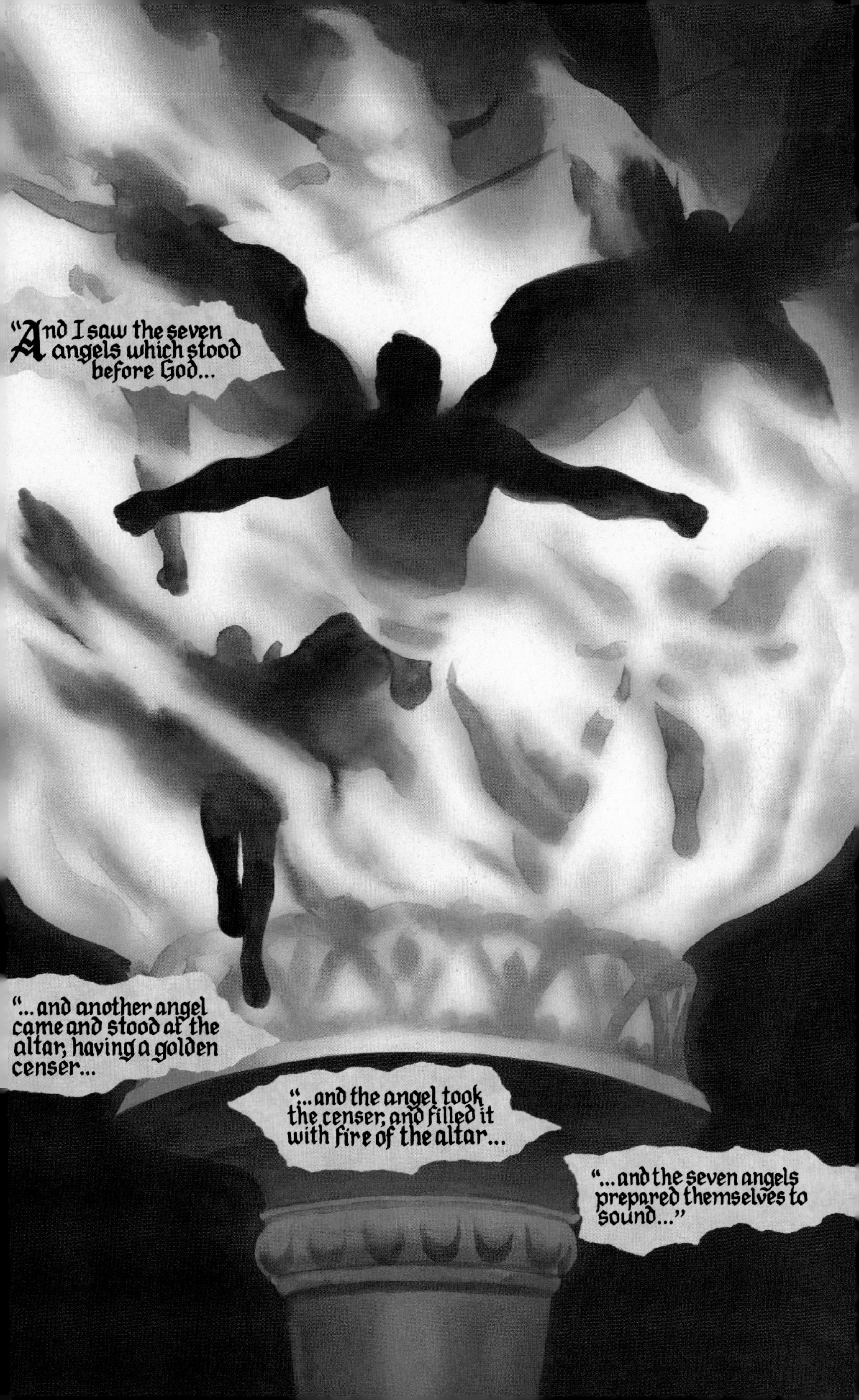
"And I saw the seven angels which stood before God...
"...and another angel came and stood at the altar, having a golden censer...
"...and the angel took the censer, and filled it with fire of the altar...
"...and the seven angels prepared themselves to sound..."

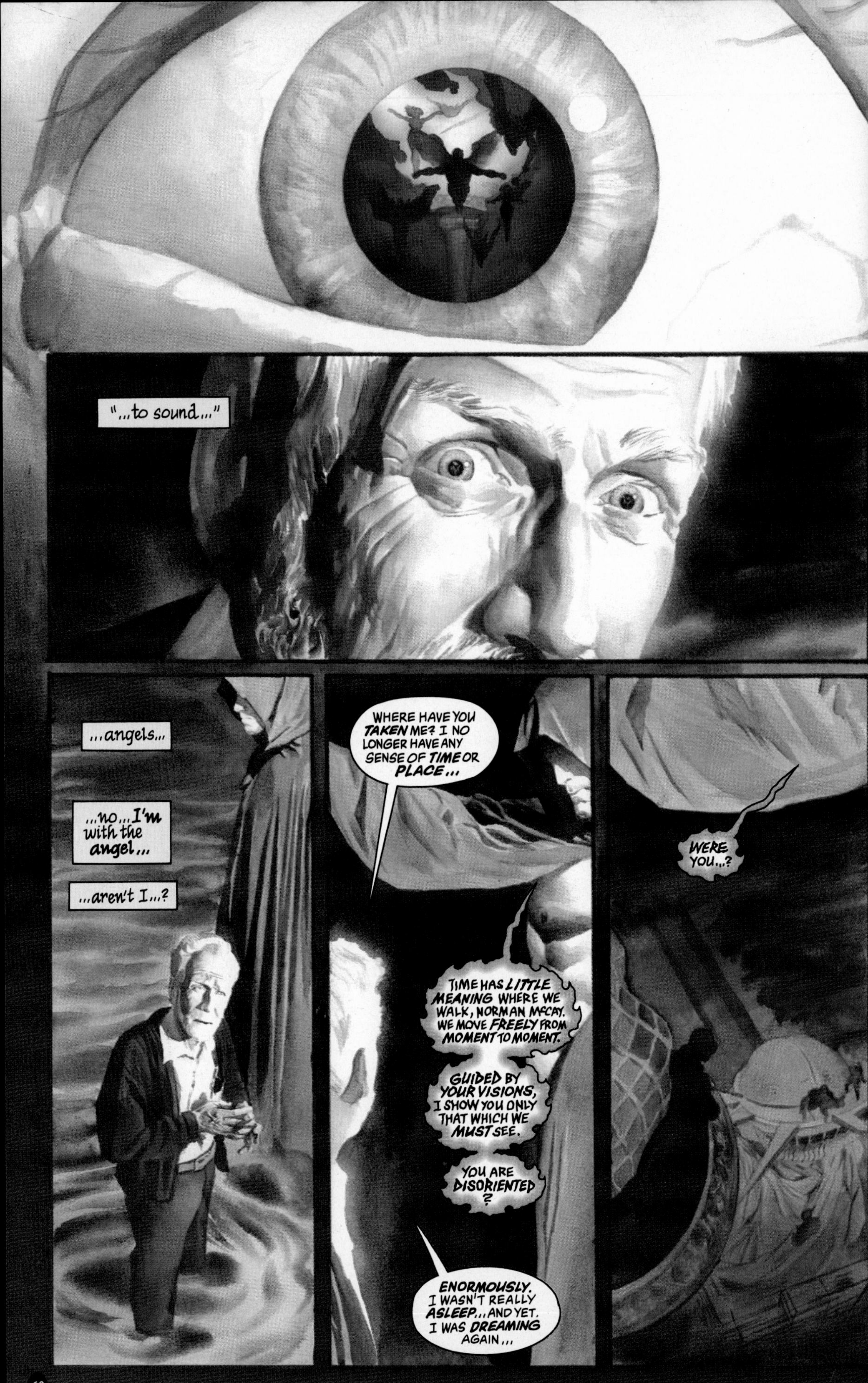
"...to sound..."
...angels...
...no...I'm with the angel...
...aren't I...?
WHERE HAVE YOU TAKEN ME? I NO LONGER HAVE ANY SENSE OF TIME OR PLACE...
TIME HAS LITTLE MEANING WHERE WE WALK, NORMAN McCAY. WE MOVE FREELY FROM MOMENT TO MOMENT.
GUIDED BY YOUR VISIONS, I SHOW YOU ONLY THAT WHICH WE MUST SEE.
YOU ARE DISORIENTED?
ENORMOUSLY. I WASN'T REALLY ASLEEP...AND YET, I WAS DREAMING AGAIN...
WERE YOU...?

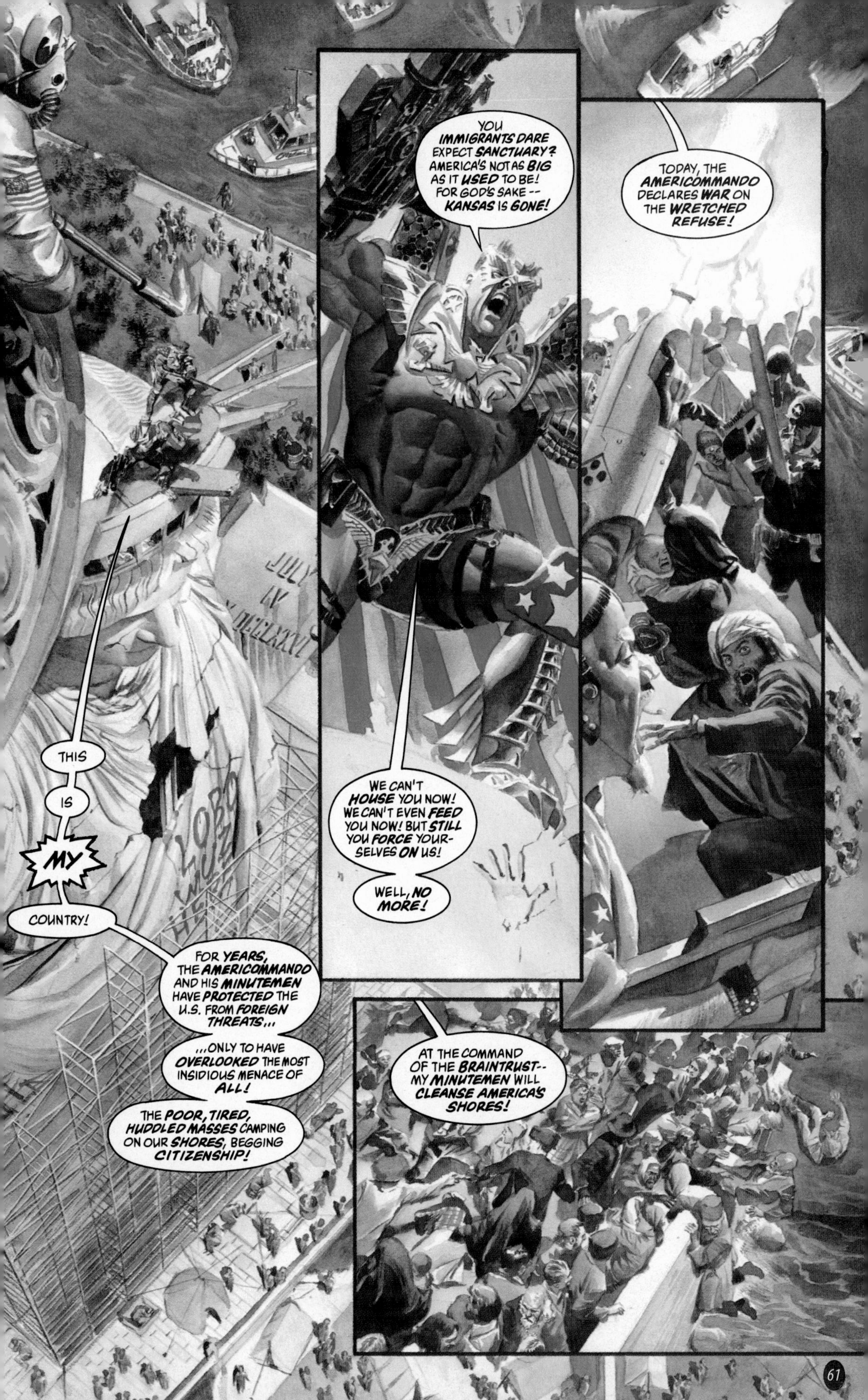

YOU IMMIGRANTS DARE EXPECT SANCTUARY? AMERICA'S NOT AS BIG AS IT USED TO BE! FOR GOD'S SAKE -- KANSAS IS GONE!
TODAY, THE AMERICOMMANDO DECLARES WAR ON THE WRETCHED REFUSE!
THIS
IS
MY
COUNTRY!
WE CAN'T HOUSE YOU NOW! WE CAN'T EVEN FEED YOU NOW! BUT STILL YOU FORCE YOURSELVES ON US!
WELL, NO MORE!
FOR YEARS, THE AMERICOMMANDO AND HIS MINUTEMEN HAVE PROTECTED THE U.S. FROM FOREIGN THREATS...
...ONLY TO HAVE OVERLOOKED THE MOST INSIDIOUS MENACE OF ALL!
THE POOR, TIRED, HUDDLED MASSES CAMPING ON OUR SHORES, BEGGING CITIZENSHIP!
AT THE COMMAND OF THE BRAINTRUST-- MY MINUTEMEN WILL CLEANSE AMERICA'S SHORES!

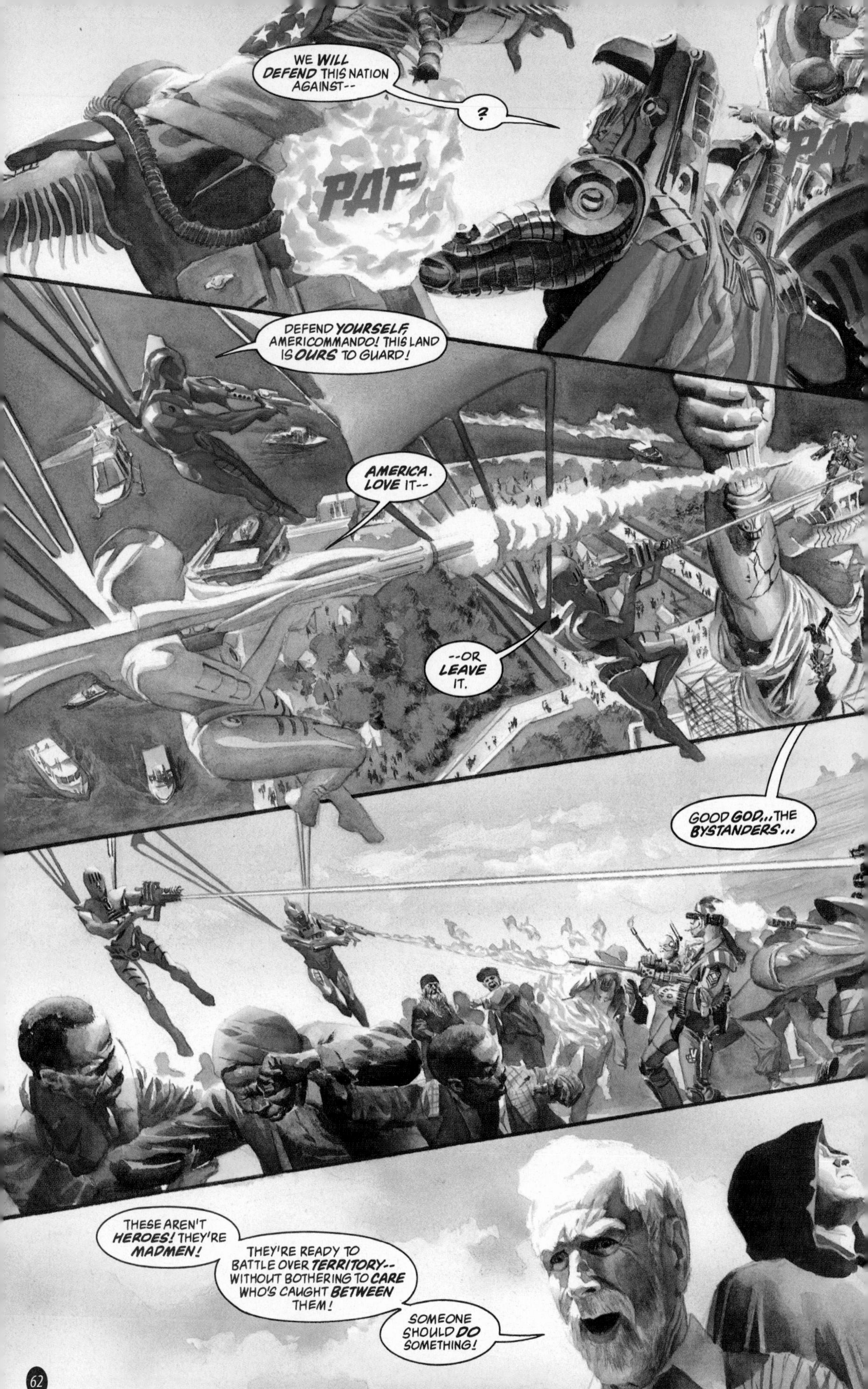
WE WILL DEFEND THIS NATION AGAINST--
?
PAF
PAF
DEFEND YOURSELF, AMERICOMMANDO! THIS LAND IS OURS TO GUARD!
AMERICA. LOVE IT--
--OR LEAVE IT.
GOOD GOD... THE BYSTANDERS...
THESE AREN'T HEROES! THEY'RE MADMEN!
THEY'RE READY TO BATTLE OVER TERRITORY-- WITHOUT BOTHERING TO CARE WHO'S CAUGHT BETWEEN THEM!
SOMEONE SHOULD DO SOMETHING!

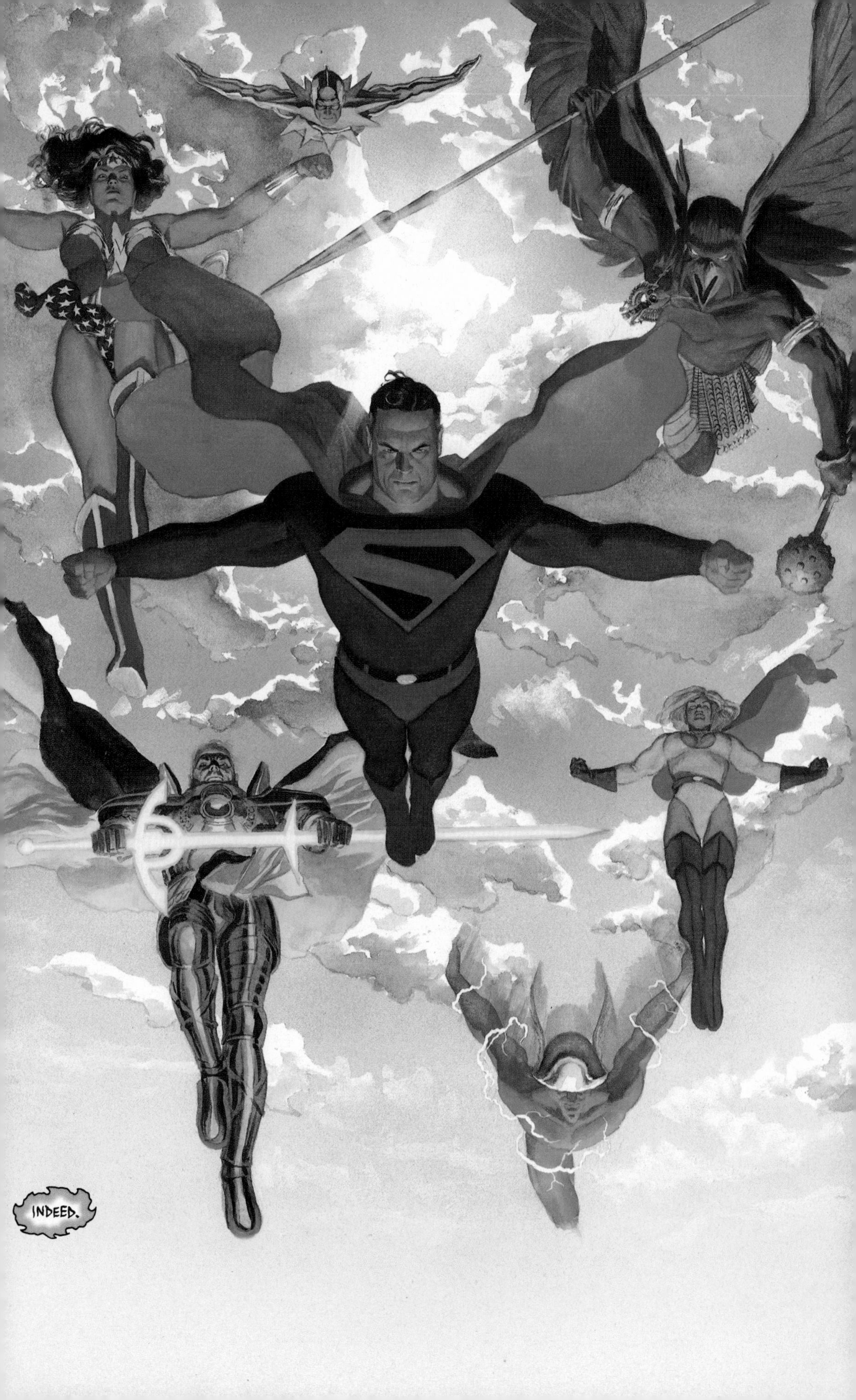
INDEED.

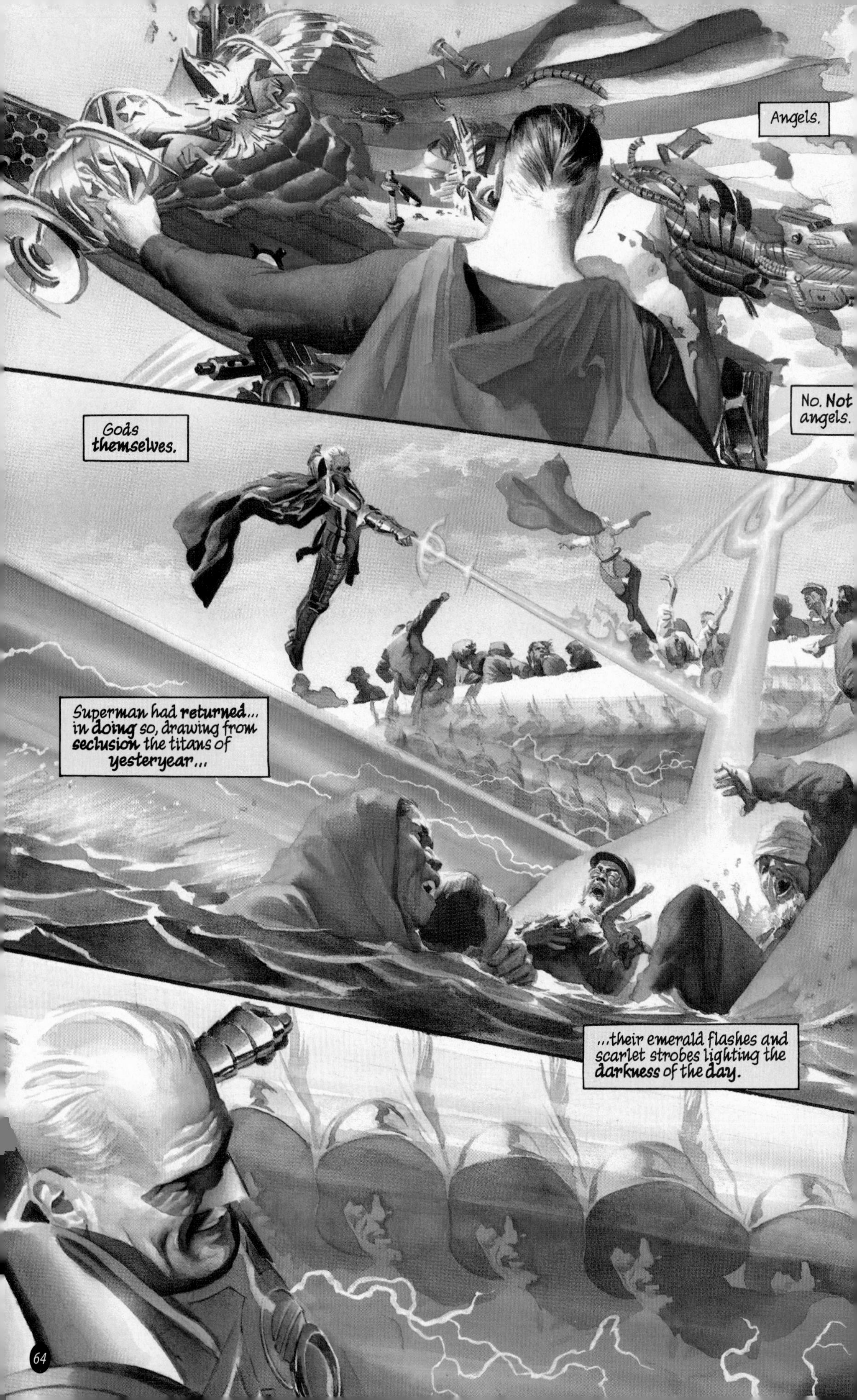
Angels.
No. Not angels.
Gods themselves.
Superman had returned... in doing so, drawing from seclusion the titans of yesteryear...
...their emerald flashes and scarlet strobes lighting the darkness of the day.

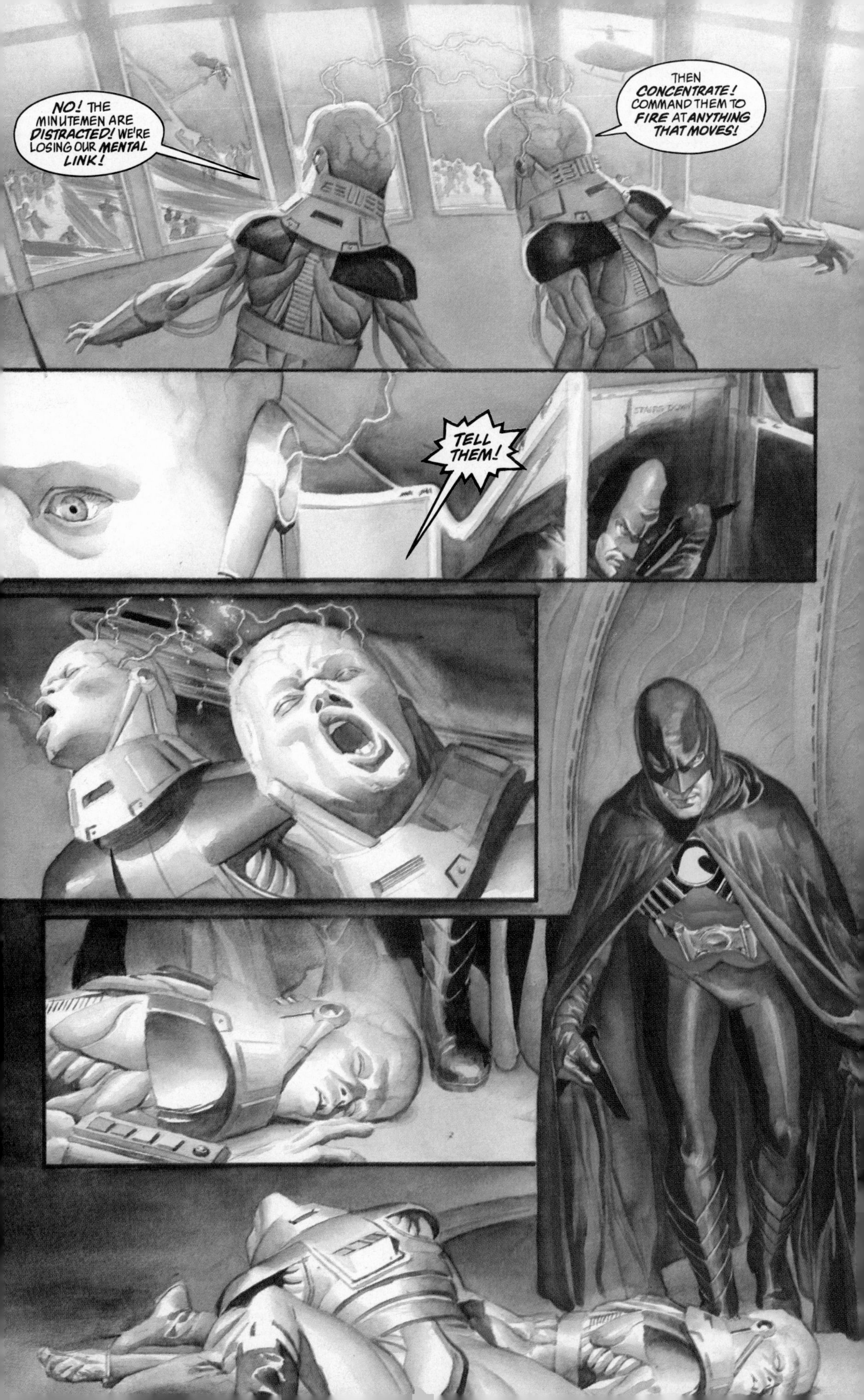
NO! THE MINUTEMEN ARE DISTRACTED! WE'RE LOSING OUR MENTAL LINK!
THEN CONCENTRATE! COMMAND THEM TO FIRE AT ANYTHING THAT MOVES!
TELL THEM!

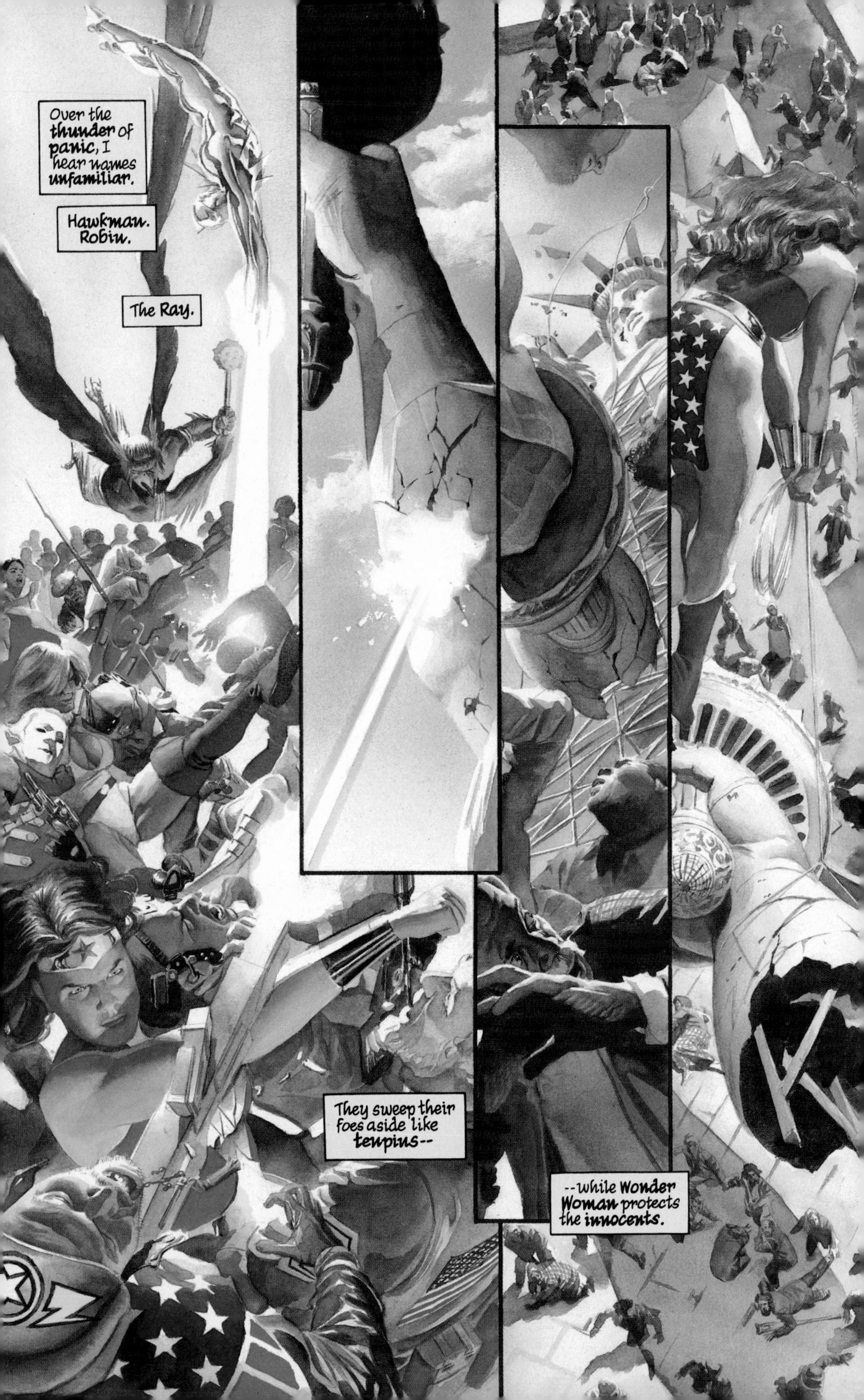
Over the thunder of panic, I hear names unfamiliar.
Hawkman. Robin.
The Ray.
They sweep their foes aside like tenpins--
--while Wonder Woman protects the innocents.

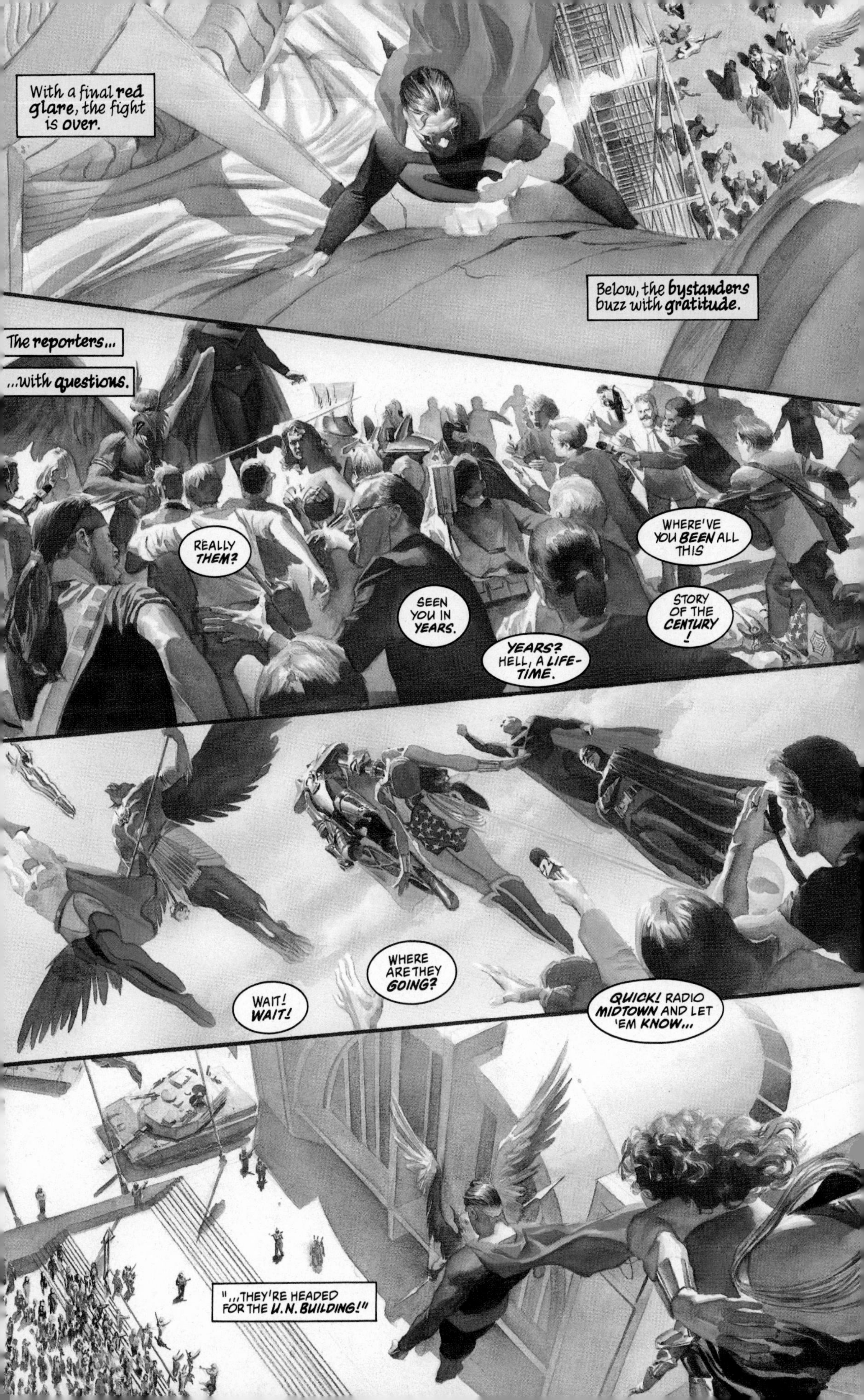
With a final red glare, the fight is over.
Below, the bystanders buzz with gratitude.
The reporters...
...with questions.
REALLY THEM?
WHERE'VE YOU BEEN ALL THIS
SEEN YOU IN YEARS.
YEARS? HELL, A LIFE-TIME.
STORY OF THE CENTURY!
WAIT! WAIT!
WHERE ARE THEY GOING?
QUICK! RADIO MIDTOWN AND LET 'EM KNOW...
"...THEY'RE HEADED FOR THE U.N. BUILDING!"

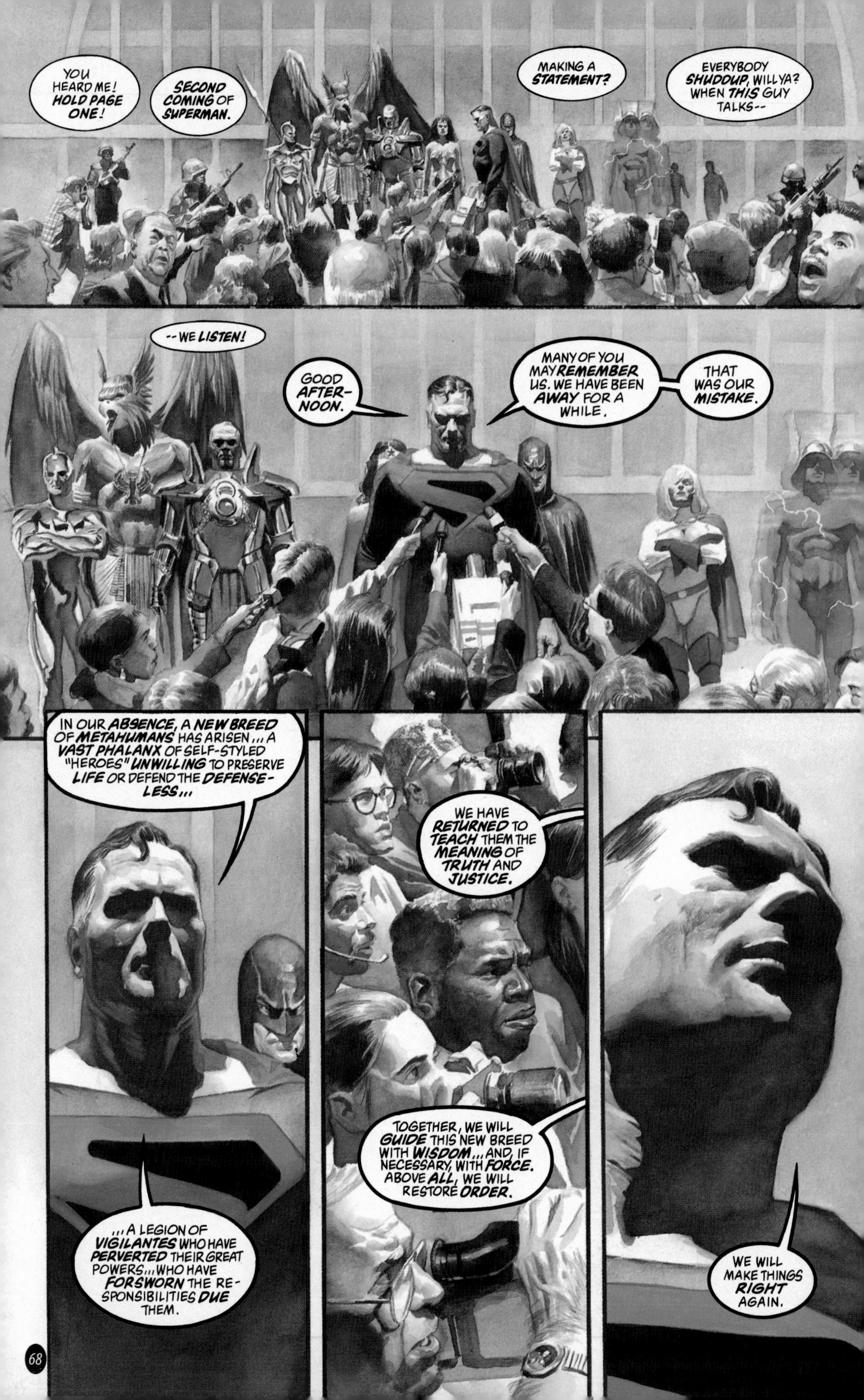
YOU HEARD ME! HOLD PAGE ONE!
SECOND COMING OF SUPERMAN.
MAKING A STATEMENT?
EVERYBODY SHUDDUP, WILLYA? WHEN THIS GUY TALKS--
--WE LISTEN!
GOOD AFTER-NOON.
MANY OF YOU MAY REMEMBER US. WE HAVE BEEN AWAY FOR A WHILE.
THAT WAS OUR MISTAKE.
IN OUR ABSENCE, A NEW BREED OF METAHUMANS HAS ARISEN... A VAST PHALANX OF SELF-STYLED "HEROES" UNWILLING TO PRESERVE LIFE OR DEFEND THE DEFENSE-LESS...
...A LEGION OF VIGILANTES WHO HAVE PERVERTED THEIR GREAT POWERS... WHO HAVE FORSWORN THE RE-SPONSIBILITIES DUE THEM.
WE HAVE RETURNED TO TEACH THEM THE MEANING OF TRUTH AND JUSTICE.
TOGETHER, WE WILL GUIDE THIS NEW BREED WITH WISDOM... AND, IF NECESSARY, WITH FORCE. ABOVE ALL, WE WILL RESTORE ORDER.
WE WILL MAKE THINGS RIGHT AGAIN.

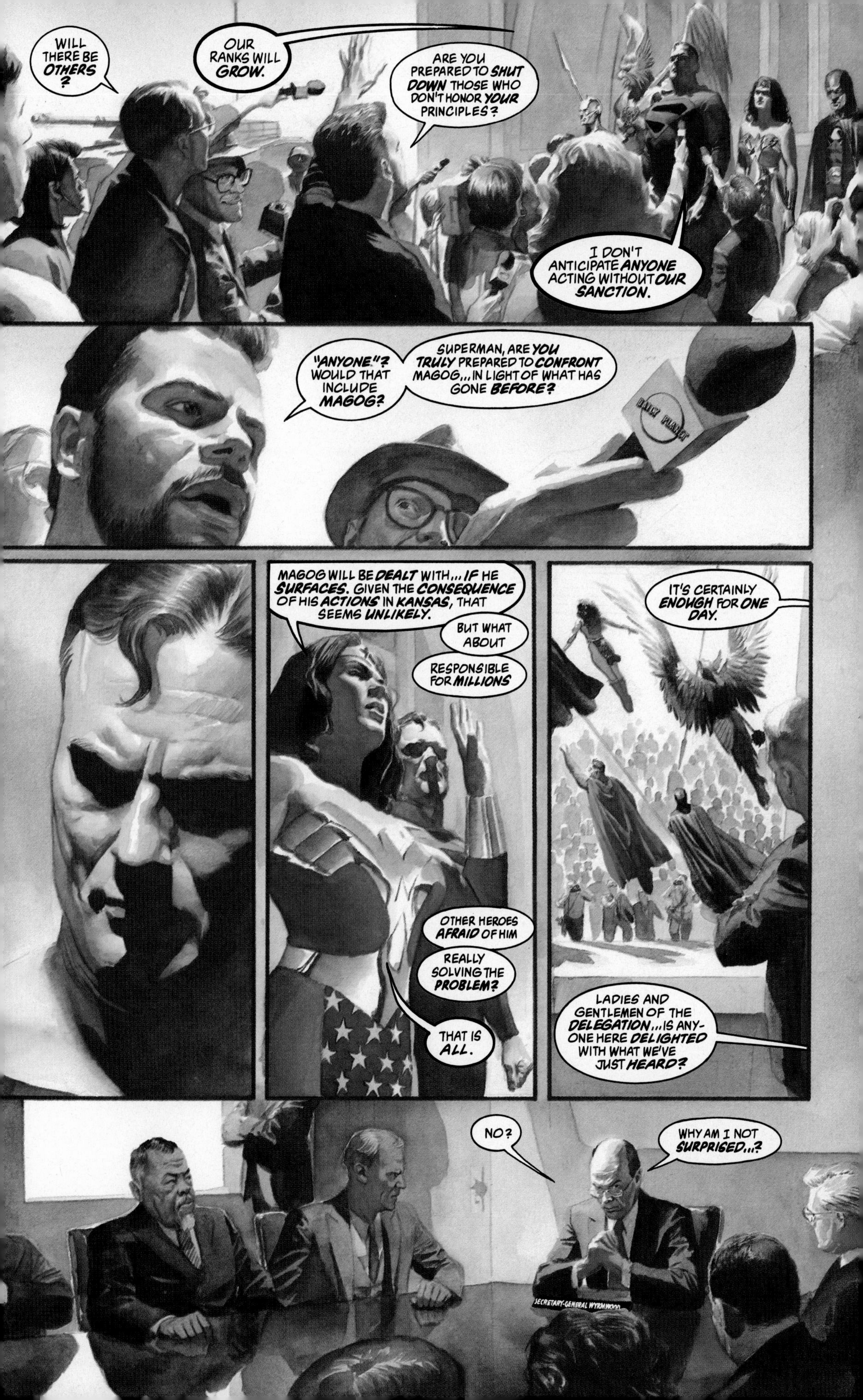
WILL THERE BE OTHERS?
OUR RANKS WILL GROW.
ARE YOU PREPARED TO SHUT DOWN THOSE WHO DON'T HONOR YOUR PRINCIPLES?
I DON'T ANTICIPATE ANYONE ACTING WITHOUT OUR SANCTION.
"ANYONE"? WOULD THAT INCLUDE MAGOG?
SUPERMAN, ARE YOU TRULY PREPARED TO CONFRONT MAGOG... IN LIGHT OF WHAT HAS GONE BEFORE?
DAILY PLANET
MAGOG WILL BE DEALT WITH... IF HE SURFACES. GIVEN THE CONSEQUENCE OF HIS ACTIONS IN KANSAS, THAT SEEMS UNLIKELY.
BUT WHAT ABOUT
RESPONSIBLE FOR MILLIONS
OTHER HEROES AFRAID OF HIM
REALLY SOLVING THE PROBLEM?
THAT IS ALL.
IT'S CERTAINLY ENOUGH FOR ONE DAY.
LADIES AND GENTLEMEN OF THE DELEGATION... IS ANYONE HERE DELIGHTED WITH WHAT WE'VE JUST HEARD?
NO?
WHY AM I NOT SURPRISED...?
SECRETARY-GENERAL WYRMWOOD

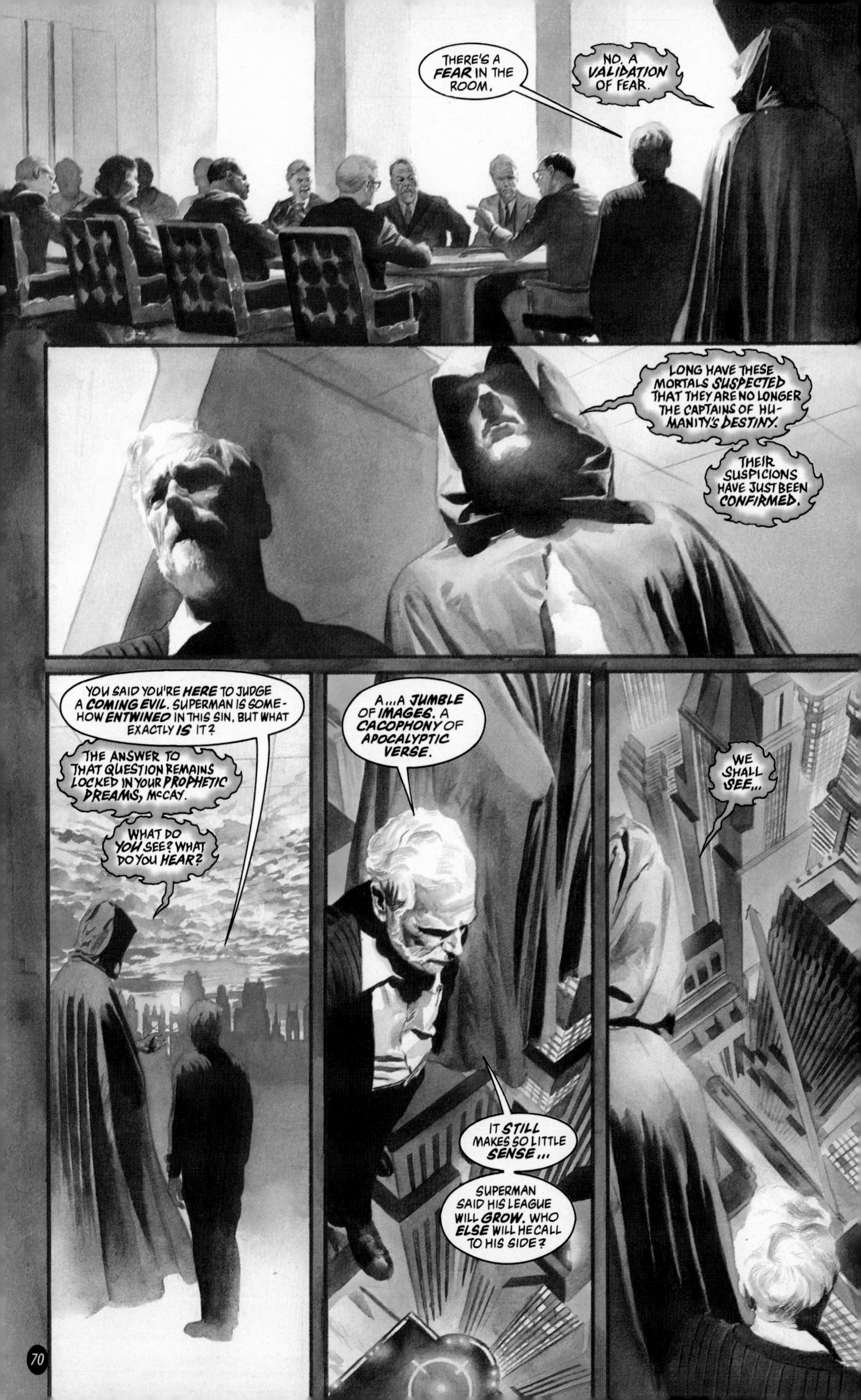
THERE'S A FEAR IN THE ROOM.
NO. A VALIDATION OF FEAR.
LONG HAVE THESE MORTALS SUSPECTED THAT THEY ARE NO LONGER THE CAPTAINS OF HU-MANITY'S DESTINY.
THEIR SUSPICIONS HAVE JUST BEEN CONFIRMED.
YOU SAID YOU'RE HERE TO JUDGE A COMING EVIL. SUPERMAN IS SOME-HOW ENTWINED IN THIS SIN. BUT WHAT EXACTLY IS IT?
THE ANSWER TO THAT QUESTION REMAINS LOCKED IN YOUR PROPHETIC DREAMS, McCAY.
WHAT DO YOU SEE? WHAT DO YOU HEAR?
A...A JUMBLE OF IMAGES. A CACOPHONY OF APOCALYPTIC VERSE.
IT STILL MAKES SO LITTLE SENSE...
SUPERMAN SAID HIS LEAGUE WILL GROW. WHO ELSE WILL HE CALL TO HIS SIDE?
WE SHALL SEE...

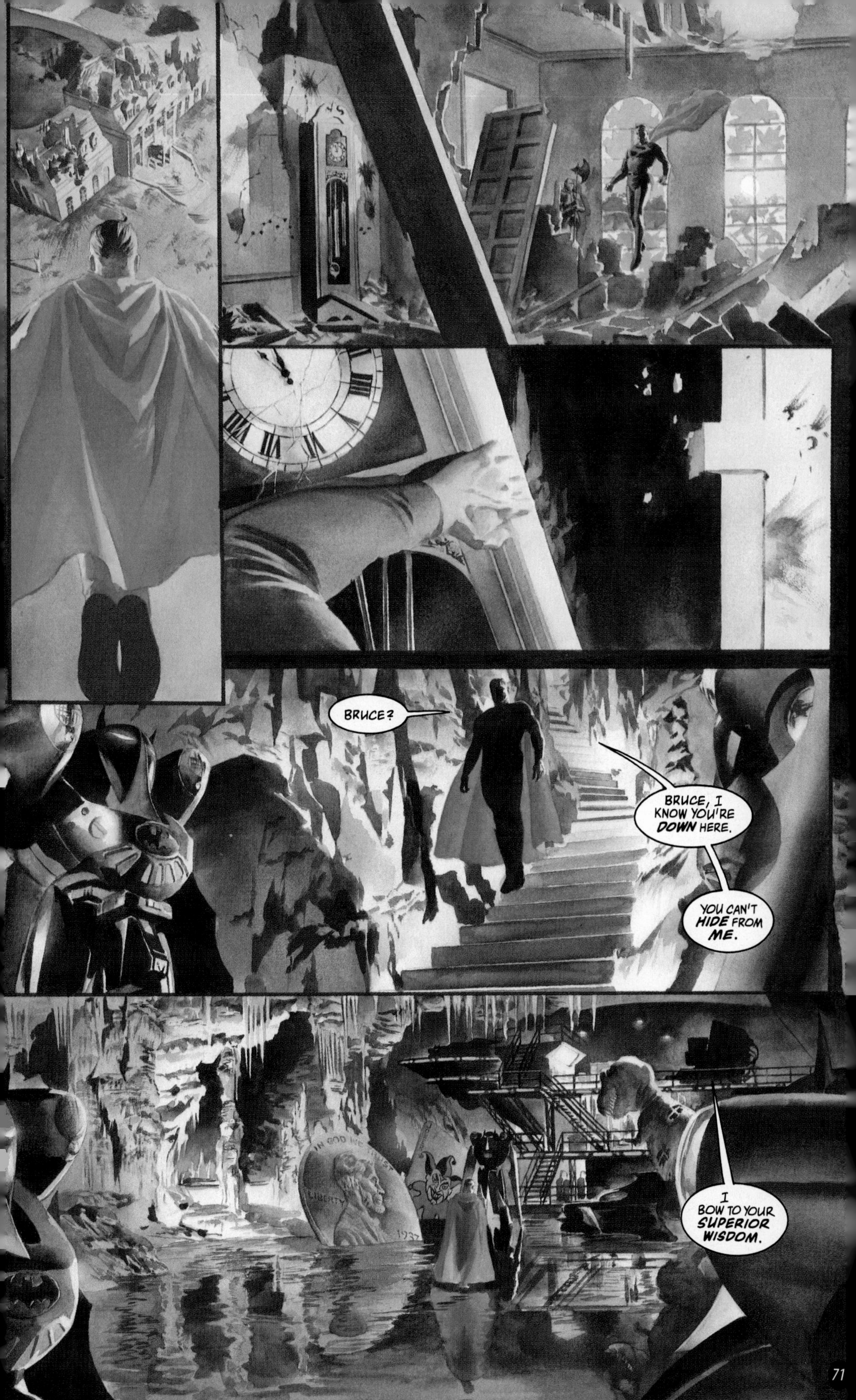
BRUCE?
BRUCE, I KNOW YOU'RE DOWN HERE.
YOU CAN'T HIDE FROM ME.
I BOW TO YOUR SUPERIOR WISDOM.

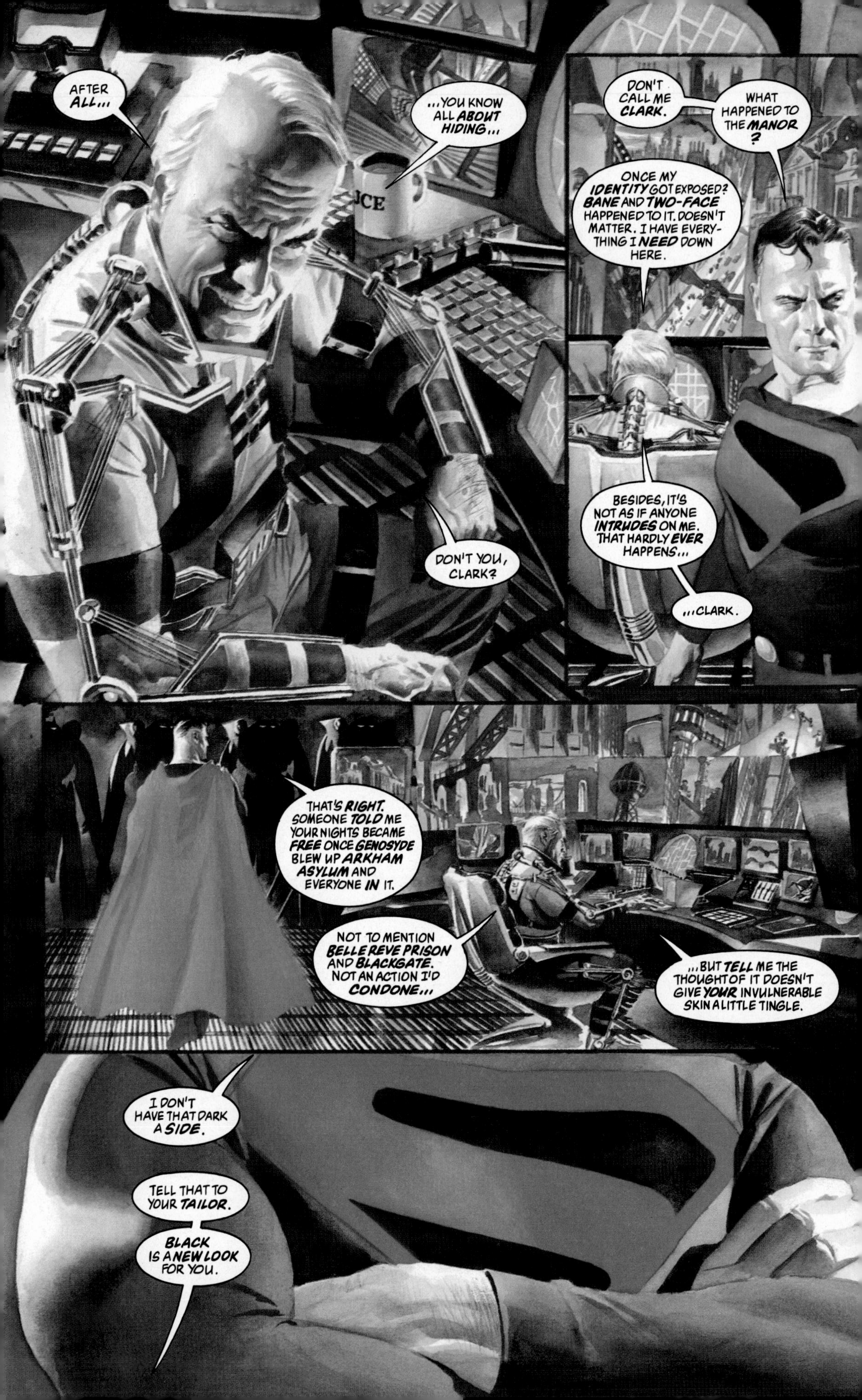
AFTER ALL...
...YOU KNOW ALL ABOUT HIDING...
DON'T YOU, CLARK?
DON'T CALL ME CLARK.
WHAT HAPPENED TO THE MANOR?
ONCE MY IDENTITY GOT EXPOSED? BANE AND TWO-FACE HAPPENED TO IT. DOESN'T MATTER. I HAVE EVERYTHING I NEED DOWN HERE.
BESIDES, IT'S NOT AS IF ANYONE INTRUDES ON ME. THAT HARDLY EVER HAPPENS...
...CLARK.
THAT'S RIGHT. SOMEONE TOLD ME YOUR NIGHTS BECAME FREE ONCE GENOSYDE BLEW UP ARKHAM ASYLUM AND EVERYONE IN IT.
NOT TO MENTION BELLE REVE PRISON AND BLACKGATE. NOT AN ACTION I'D CONDONE...
...BUT TELL ME THE THOUGHT OF IT DOESN'T GIVE YOUR INVULNERABLE SKIN A LITTLE TINGLE.
I DON'T HAVE THAT DARK A SIDE.
TELL THAT TO YOUR TAILOR.
BLACK IS A NEW LOOK FOR YOU.

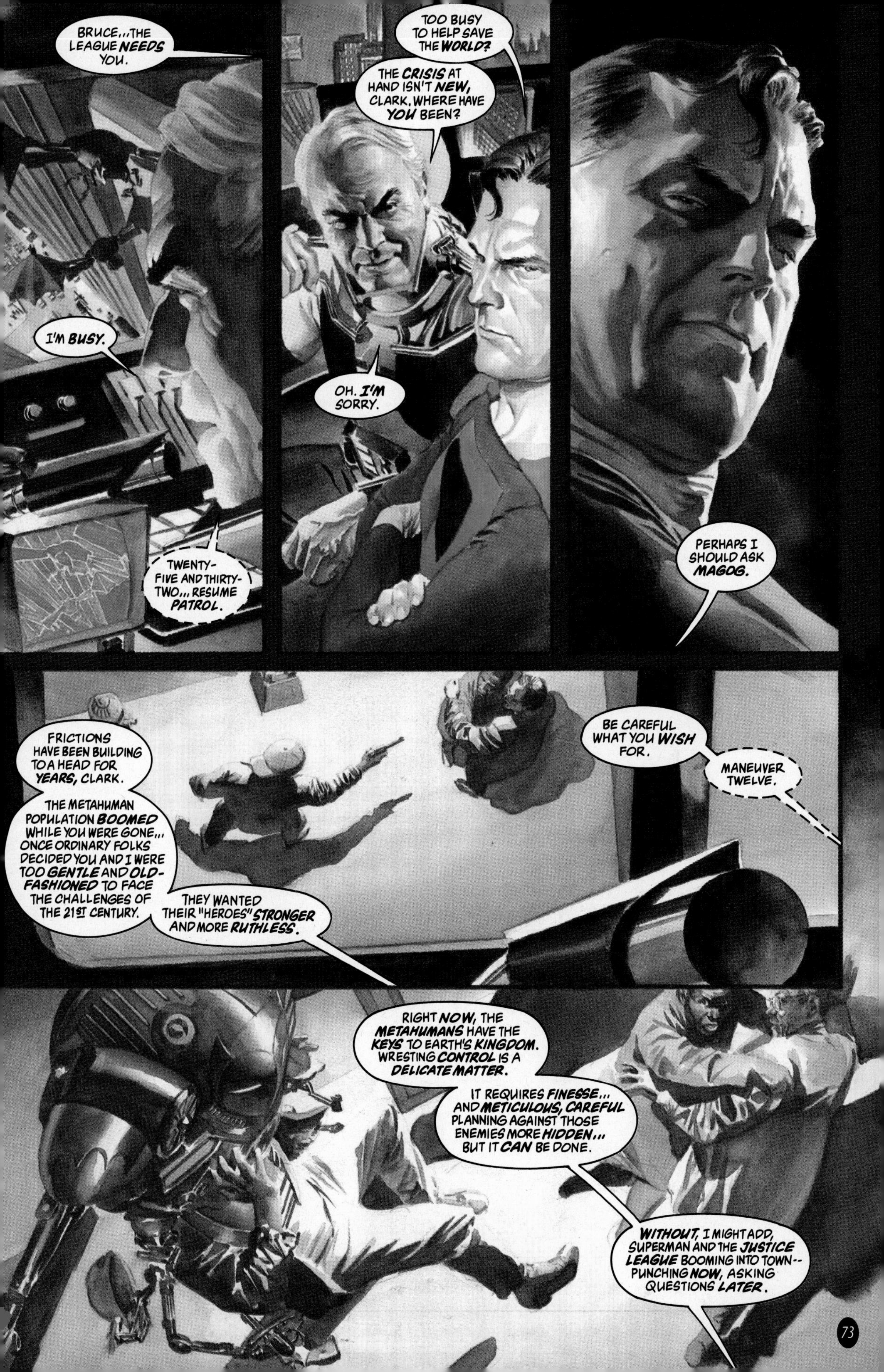

BRUCE... THE LEAGUE NEEDS YOU.
I'M BUSY.
TWENTY-FIVE AND THIRTY-TWO... RESUME PATROL.
TOO BUSY TO HELP SAVE THE WORLD?
THE CRISIS AT HAND ISN'T NEW, CLARK. WHERE HAVE YOU BEEN?
OH. I'M SORRY.
PERHAPS I SHOULD ASK MAGOG.
FRICTIONS HAVE BEEN BUILDING TO A HEAD FOR YEARS, CLARK.
THE METAHUMAN POPULATION BOOMED WHILE YOU WERE GONE... ONCE ORDINARY FOLKS DECIDED YOU AND I WERE TOO GENTLE AND OLD-FASHIONED TO FACE THE CHALLENGES OF THE 21ST CENTURY.
THEY WANTED THEIR "HEROES" STRONGER AND MORE RUTHLESS.
BE CAREFUL WHAT YOU WISH FOR.
MANEUVER TWELVE.
RIGHT NOW, THE METAHUMANS HAVE THE KEYS TO EARTH'S KINGDOM. WRESTING CONTROL IS A DELICATE MATTER.
IT REQUIRES FINESSE... AND METICULOUS, CAREFUL PLANNING AGAINST THOSE ENEMIES MORE HIDDEN... BUT IT CAN BE DONE.
WITHOUT, I MIGHT ADD, SUPERMAN AND THE JUSTICE LEAGUE BOOMING INTO TOWN-- PUNCHING NOW, ASKING QUESTIONS LATER.

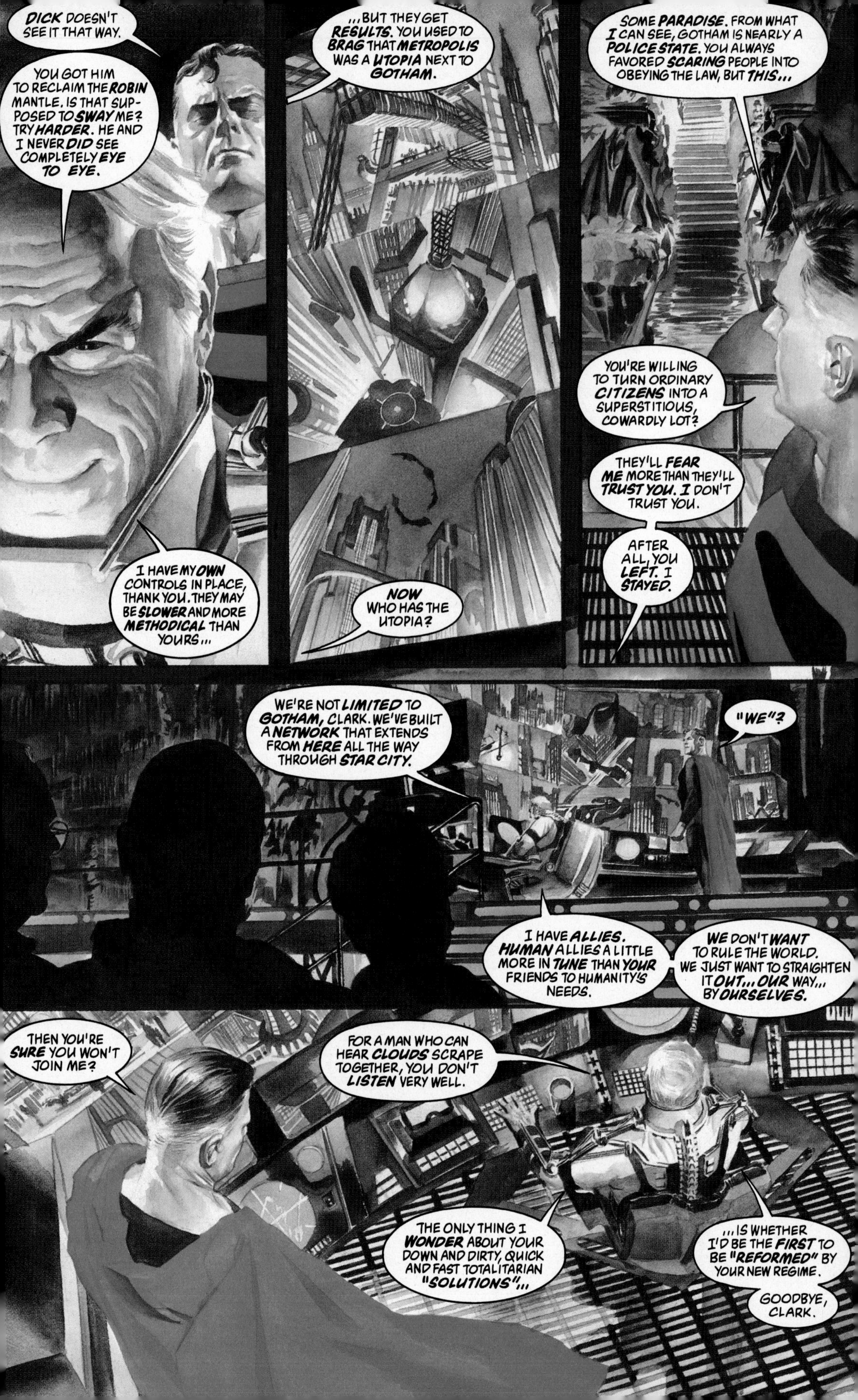
DICK DOESN'T SEE IT THAT WAY.
YOU GOT HIM TO RECLAIM THE ROBIN MANTLE. IS THAT SUPPOSED TO SWAY ME? TRY HARDER. HE AND I NEVER DID SEE COMPLETELY EYE TO EYE.
I HAVE MY OWN CONTROLS IN PLACE, THANK YOU. THEY MAY BE SLOWER AND MORE METHODICAL THAN YOURS...
...BUT THEY GET RESULTS. YOU USED TO BRAG THAT METROPOLIS WAS A UTOPIA NEXT TO GOTHAM.
NOW WHO HAS THE UTOPIA?
SOME PARADISE. FROM WHAT I CAN SEE, GOTHAM IS NEARLY A POLICE STATE. YOU ALWAYS FAVORED SCARING PEOPLE INTO OBEYING THE LAW, BUT THIS...
YOU'RE WILLING TO TURN ORDINARY CITIZENS INTO A SUPERSTITIOUS, COWARDLY LOT?
THEY'LL FEAR ME MORE THAN THEY'LL TRUST YOU. I DON'T TRUST YOU.
AFTER ALL, YOU LEFT. I STAYED.
WE'RE NOT LIMITED TO GOTHAM, CLARK. WE'VE BUILT A NETWORK THAT EXTENDS FROM HERE ALL THE WAY THROUGH STAR CITY.
"WE"?
I HAVE ALLIES. HUMAN ALLIES A LITTLE MORE IN TUNE THAN YOUR FRIENDS TO HUMANITY'S NEEDS.
WE DON'T WANT TO RULE THE WORLD. WE JUST WANT TO STRAIGHTEN IT OUT... OUR WAY... BY OURSELVES.
THEN YOU'RE SURE YOU WON'T JOIN ME?
FOR A MAN WHO CAN HEAR CLOUDS SCRAPE TOGETHER, YOU DON'T LISTEN VERY WELL.
THE ONLY THING I WONDER ABOUT YOUR DOWN AND DIRTY, QUICK AND FAST TOTALITARIAN "SOLUTIONS"...
...IS WHETHER I'D BE THE FIRST TO BE "REFORMED" BY YOUR NEW REGIME.
GOODBYE, CLARK.

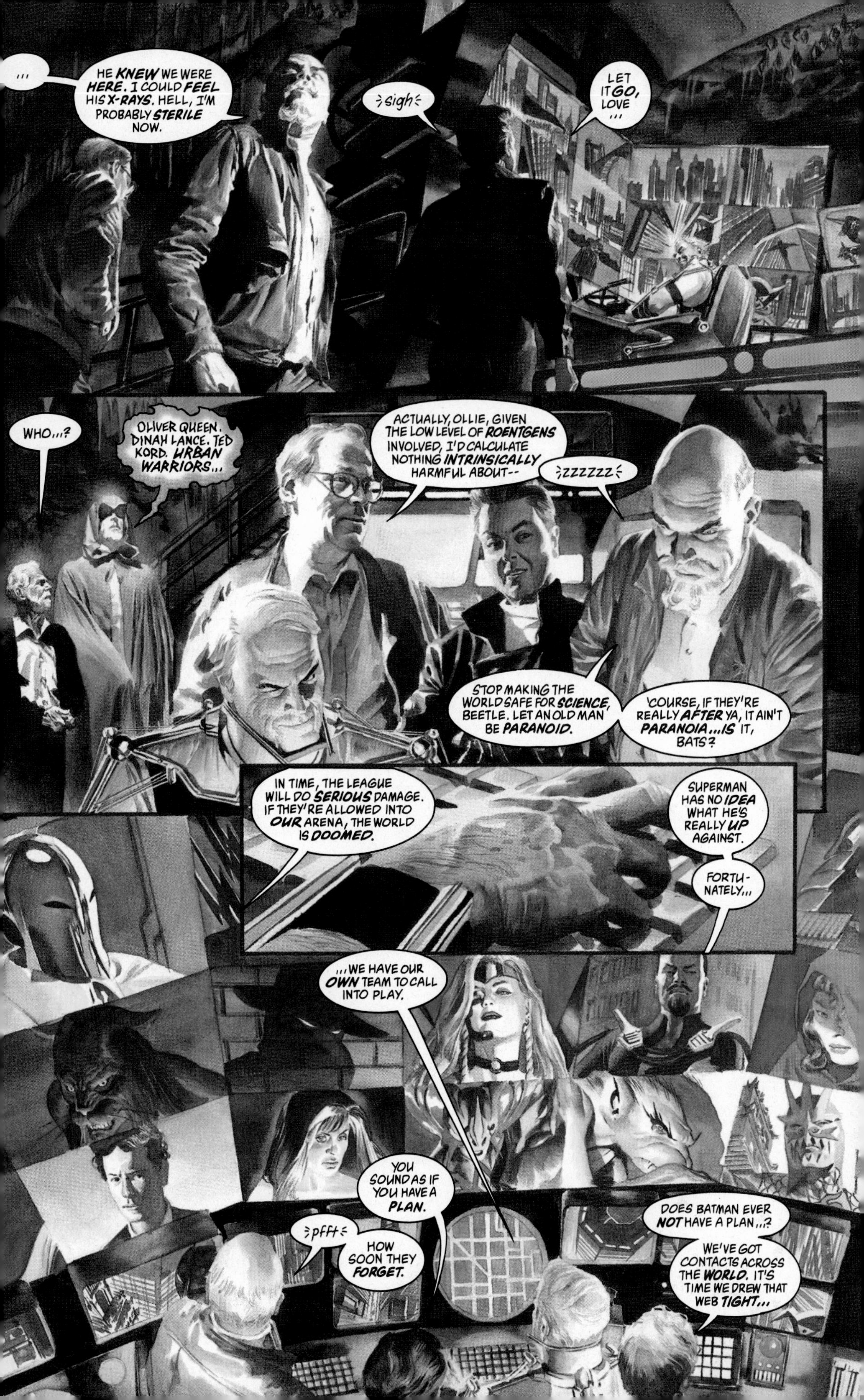
...
HE KNEW WE WERE HERE. I COULD FEEL HIS X-RAYS. HELL, I'M PROBABLY STERILE NOW.
sigh
LET IT GO, LOVE ...
WHO...?
OLIVER QUEEN. DINAH LANCE. TED KORD. URBAN WARRIORS...
ACTUALLY, OLLIE, GIVEN THE LOW LEVEL OF ROENTGENS INVOLVED, I'D CALCULATE NOTHING INTRINSICALLY HARMFUL ABOUT--
ZZZZZZ
STOP MAKING THE WORLD SAFE FOR SCIENCE, BEETLE. LET AN OLD MAN BE PARANOID.
'COURSE, IF THEY'RE REALLY AFTER YA, IT AIN'T PARANOIA...IS IT, BATS?
IN TIME, THE LEAGUE WILL DO SERIOUS DAMAGE. IF THEY'RE ALLOWED INTO OUR ARENA, THE WORLD IS DOOMED.
SUPERMAN HAS NO IDEA WHAT HE'S REALLY UP AGAINST.
FORTU-NATELY...
...WE HAVE OUR OWN TEAM TO CALL INTO PLAY.
YOU SOUND AS IF YOU HAVE A PLAN.
pfft
HOW SOON THEY FORGET.
DOES BATMAN EVER NOT HAVE A PLAN...?
WE'VE GOT CONTACTS ACROSS THE WORLD. IT'S TIME WE DREW THAT WEB TIGHT...

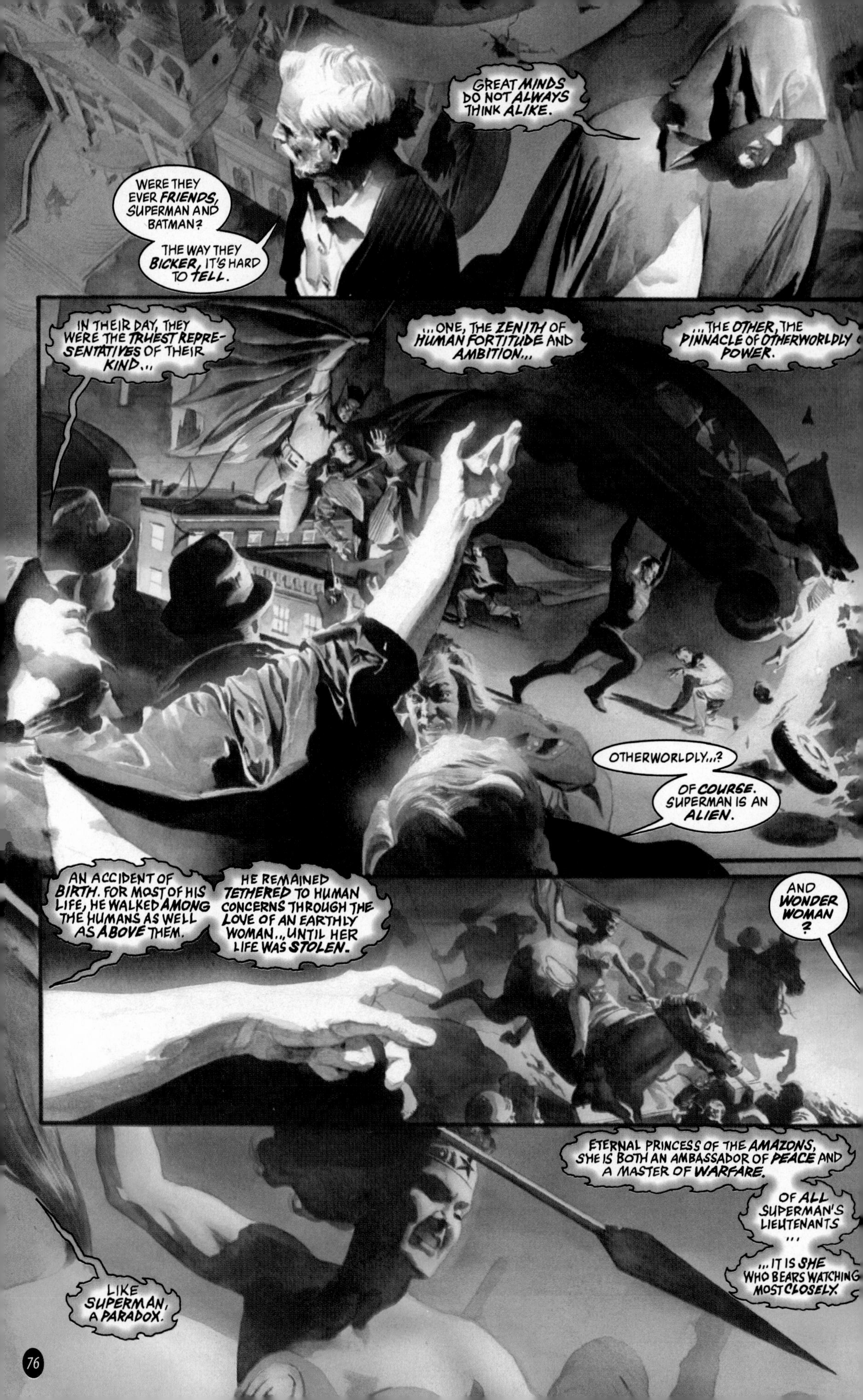
GREAT MINDS DO NOT ALWAYS THINK ALIKE.
WERE THEY EVER FRIENDS, SUPERMAN AND BATMAN?
THE WAY THEY BICKER, IT'S HARD TO TELL.
IN THEIR DAY, THEY WERE THE TRUEST REPRESENTATIVES OF THEIR KIND...
...ONE, THE ZENITH OF HUMAN FORTITUDE AND AMBITION...
...THE OTHER, THE PINNACLE OF OTHERWORLDLY POWER.
OTHERWORLDLY...?
OF COURSE. SUPERMAN IS AN ALIEN.
AN ACCIDENT OF BIRTH. FOR MOST OF HIS LIFE, HE WALKED AMONG THE HUMANS AS WELL AS ABOVE THEM.
HE REMAINED TETHERED TO HUMAN CONCERNS THROUGH THE LOVE OF AN EARTHLY WOMAN... UNTIL HER LIFE WAS STOLEN.
AND WONDER WOMAN?
ETERNAL PRINCESS OF THE AMAZONS, SHE IS BOTH AN AMBASSADOR OF PEACE AND A MASTER OF WARFARE.
OF ALL SUPERMAN'S LIEUTENANTS...
...IT IS SHE WHO BEARS WATCHING MOST CLOSELY.
LIKE SUPERMAN, A PARADOX.

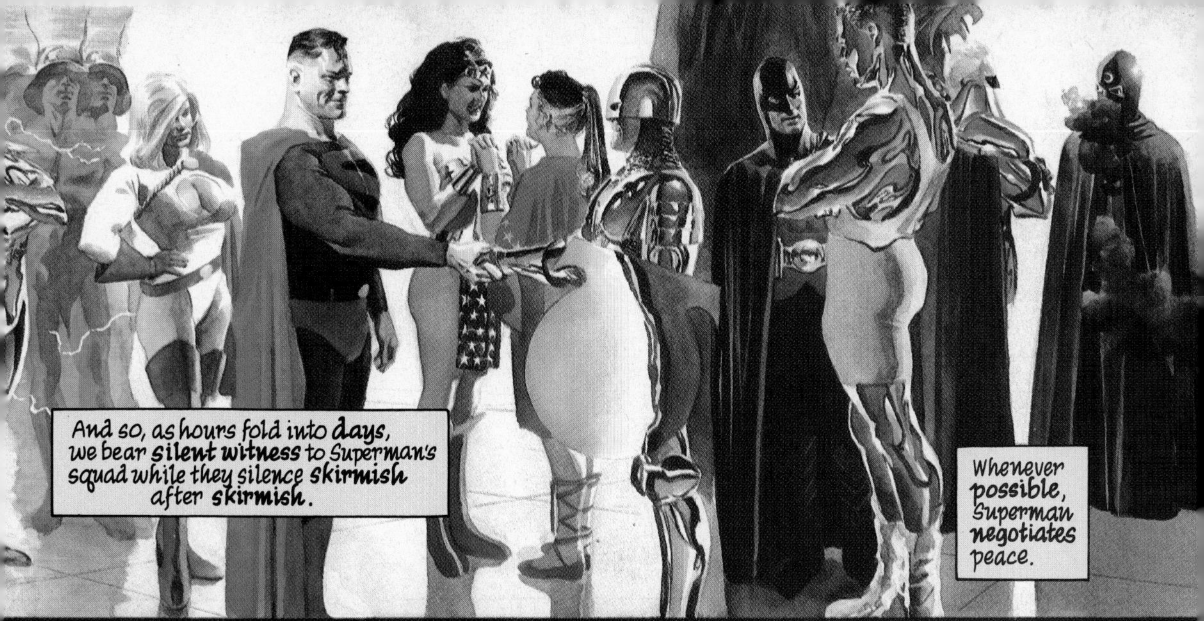

And so, as hours fold into days, we bear silent witness to Superman's squad while they silence skirmish after skirmish.
Whenever possible, Superman negotiates peace.

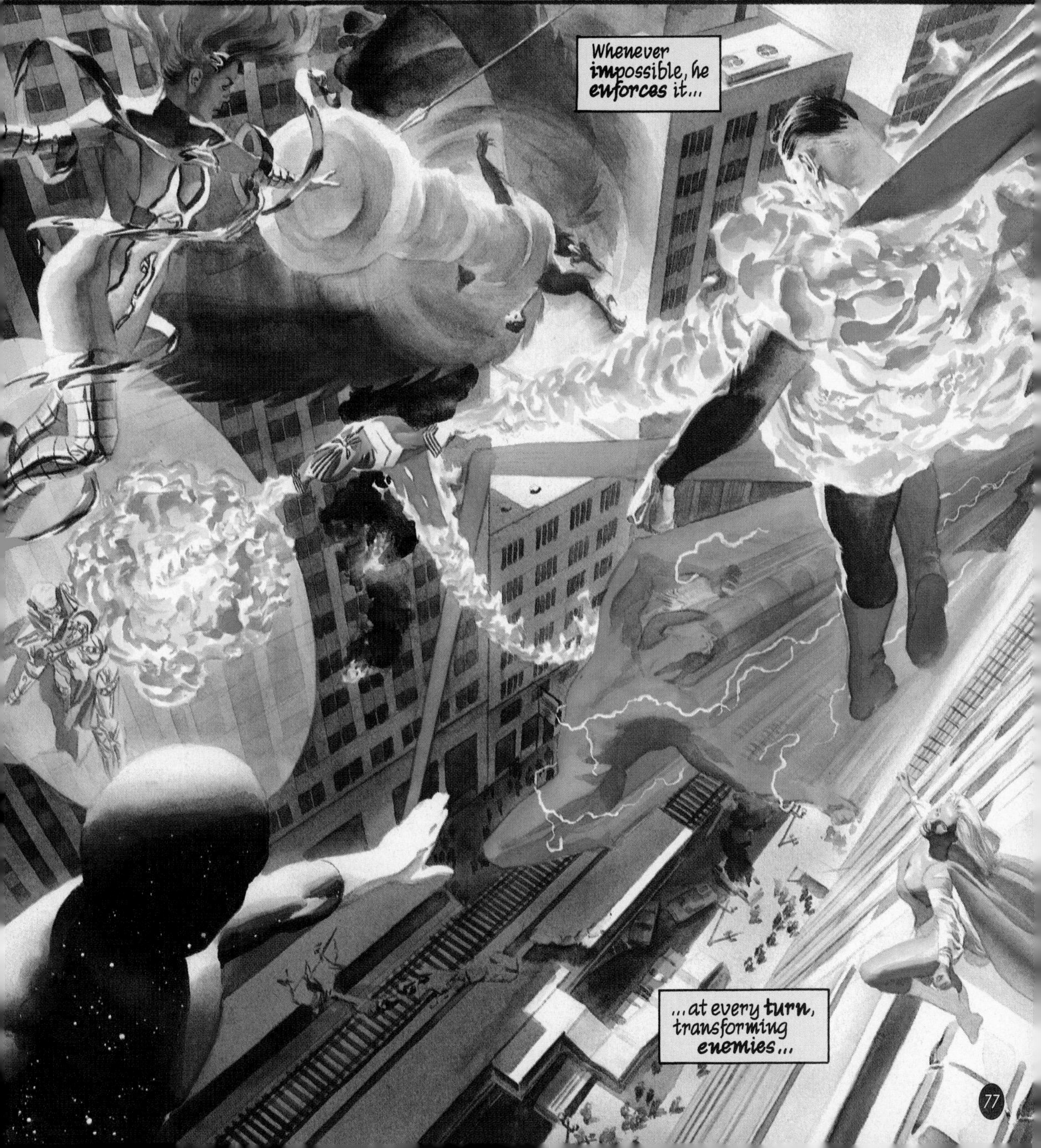

Whenever impossible, he enforces it...
...at every turn, transforming enemies...

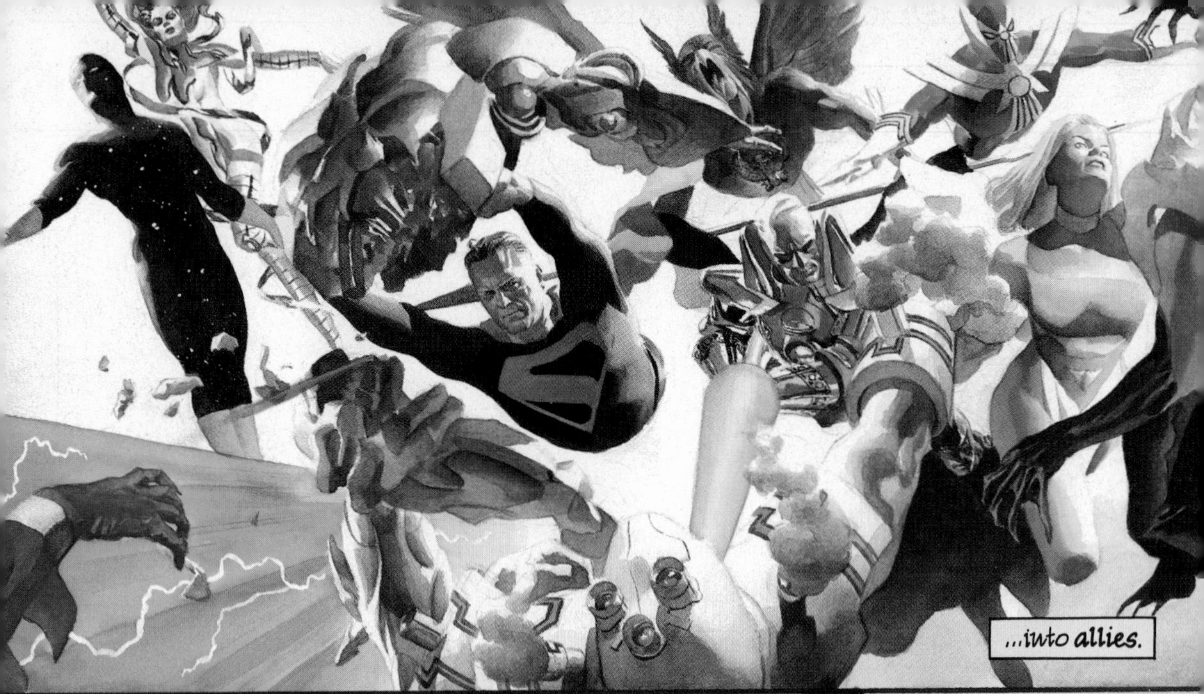
...into allies.

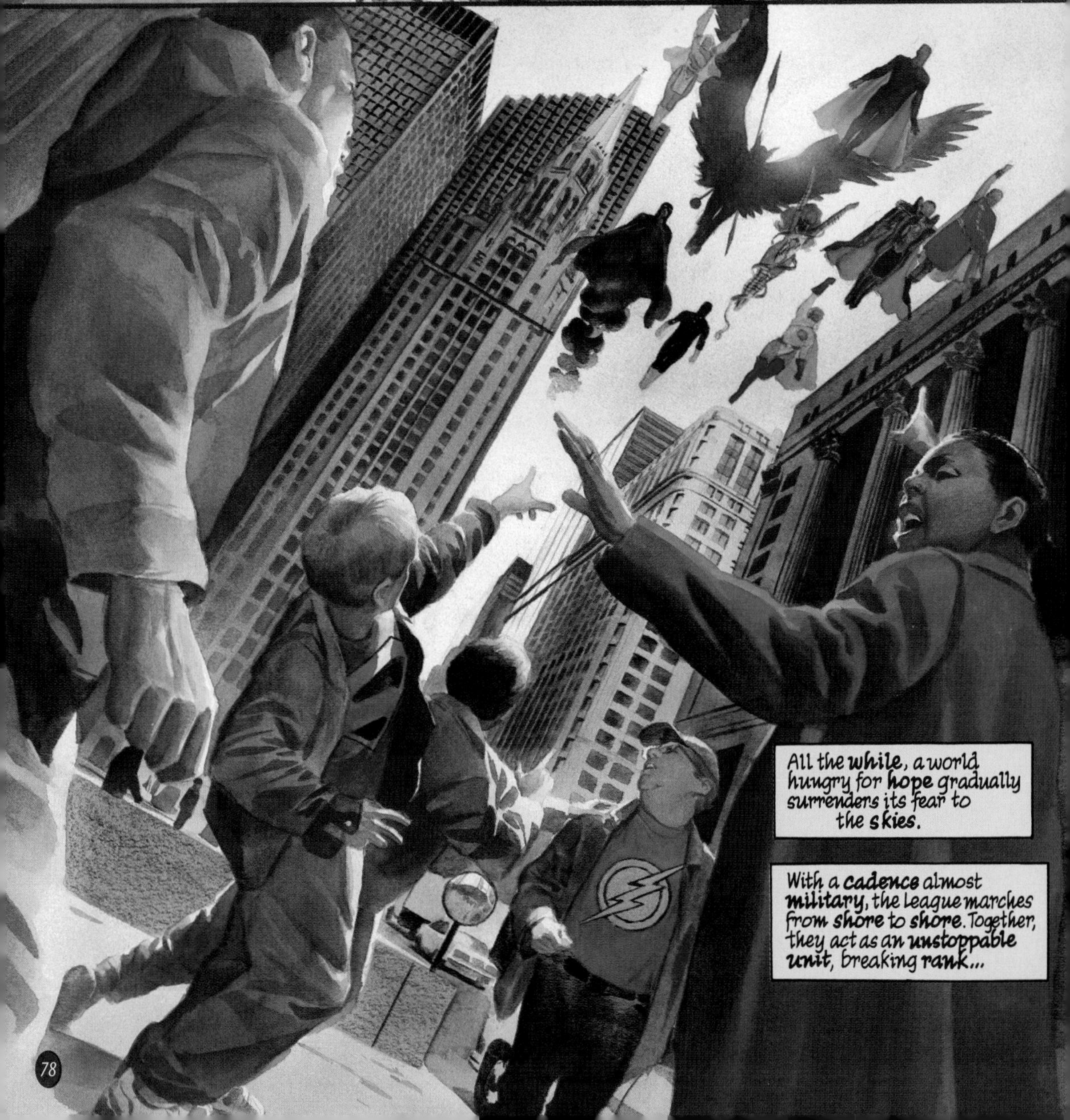
All the while, a world hungry for hope gradually surrenders its fear to the skies.
With a cadence almost military, the League marches from shore to shore. Together, they act as an unstoppable unit, breaking rank...

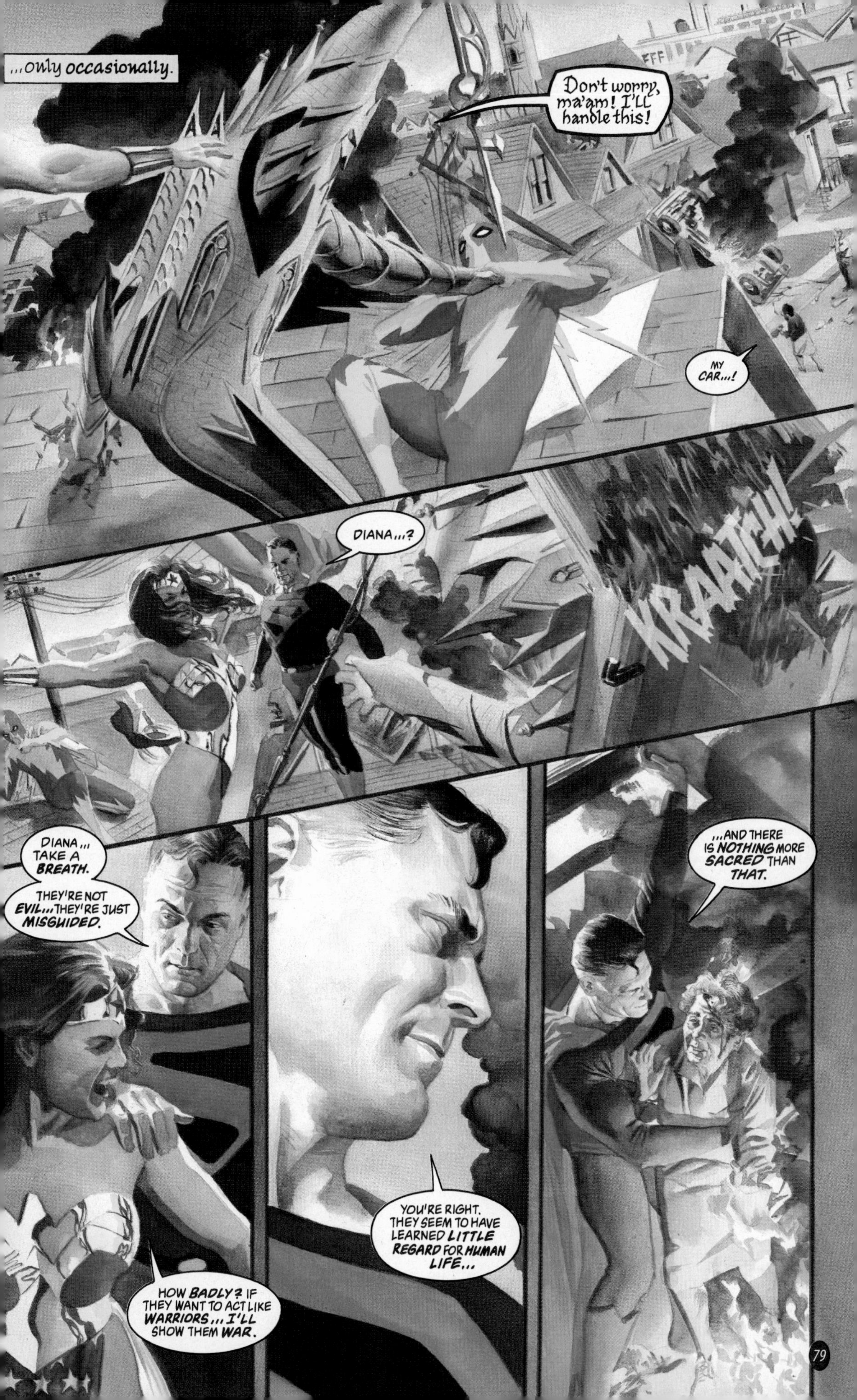
...only occasionally.
Don't worry, ma'am! I'LL handle this!
MY CAR...!
KRAATCH!
DIANA...?
DIANA... TAKE A BREATH.
THEY'RE NOT EVIL... THEY'RE JUST MISGUIDED.
HOW BADLY? IF THEY WANT TO ACT LIKE WARRIORS... I'LL SHOW THEM WAR.
YOU'RE RIGHT. THEY SEEM TO HAVE LEARNED LITTLE REGARD FOR HUMAN LIFE...
...AND THERE IS NOTHING MORE SACRED THAN THAT.

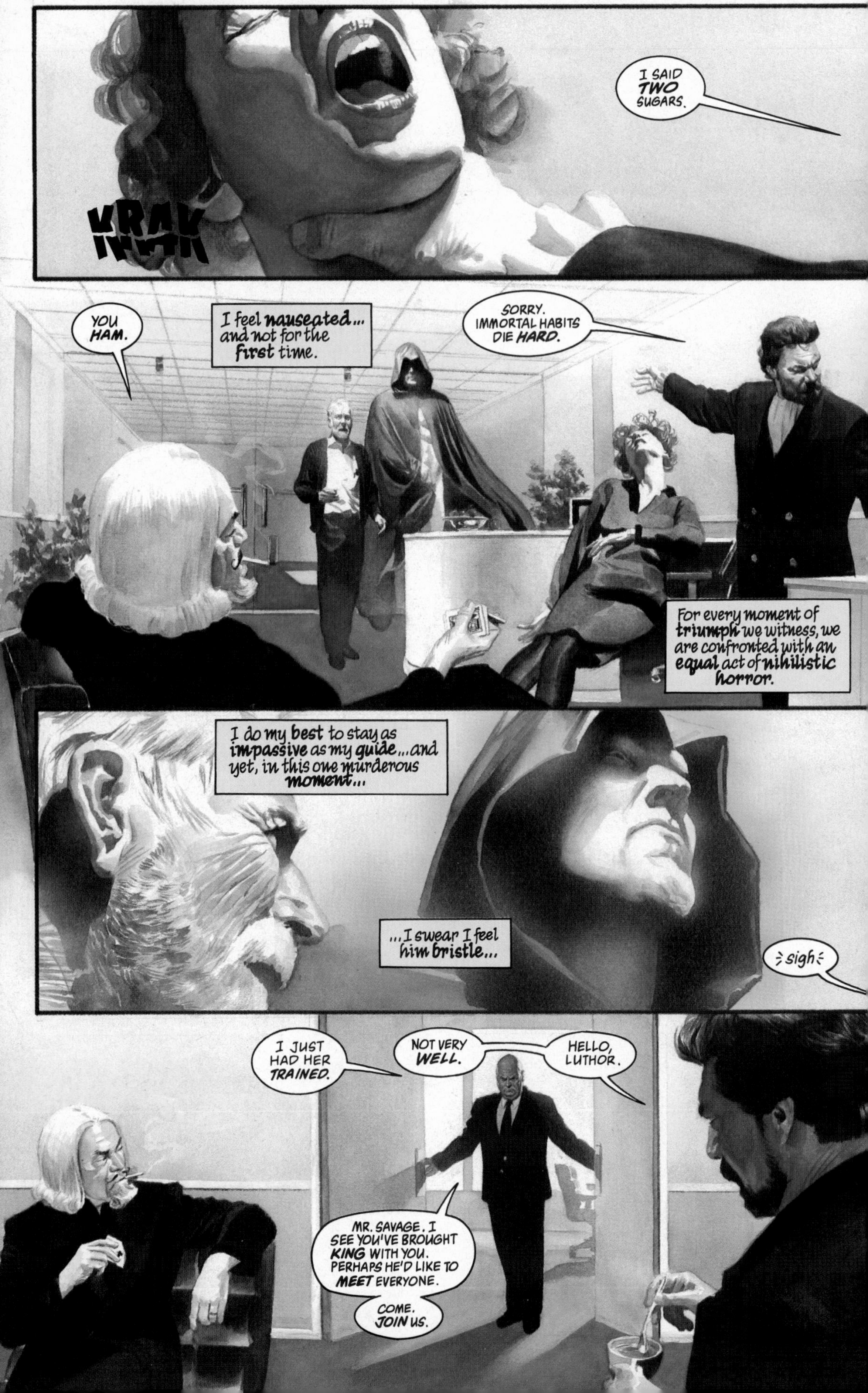
I SAID TWO SUGARS.
KRAK
YOU HAM.
I feel nauseated... and not for the first time.
SORRY. IMMORTAL HABITS DIE HARD.
For every moment of triumph we witness, we are confronted with an equal act of nihilistic horror.
I do my best to stay as impassive as my guide... and yet, in this one murderous moment...
...I swear I feel him bristle...
sigh
I JUST HAD HER TRAINED.
NOT VERY WELL.
HELLO, LUTHOR.
MR. SAVAGE. I SEE YOU'VE BROUGHT KING WITH YOU. PERHAPS HE'D LIKE TO MEET EVERYONE.
COME. JOIN US.

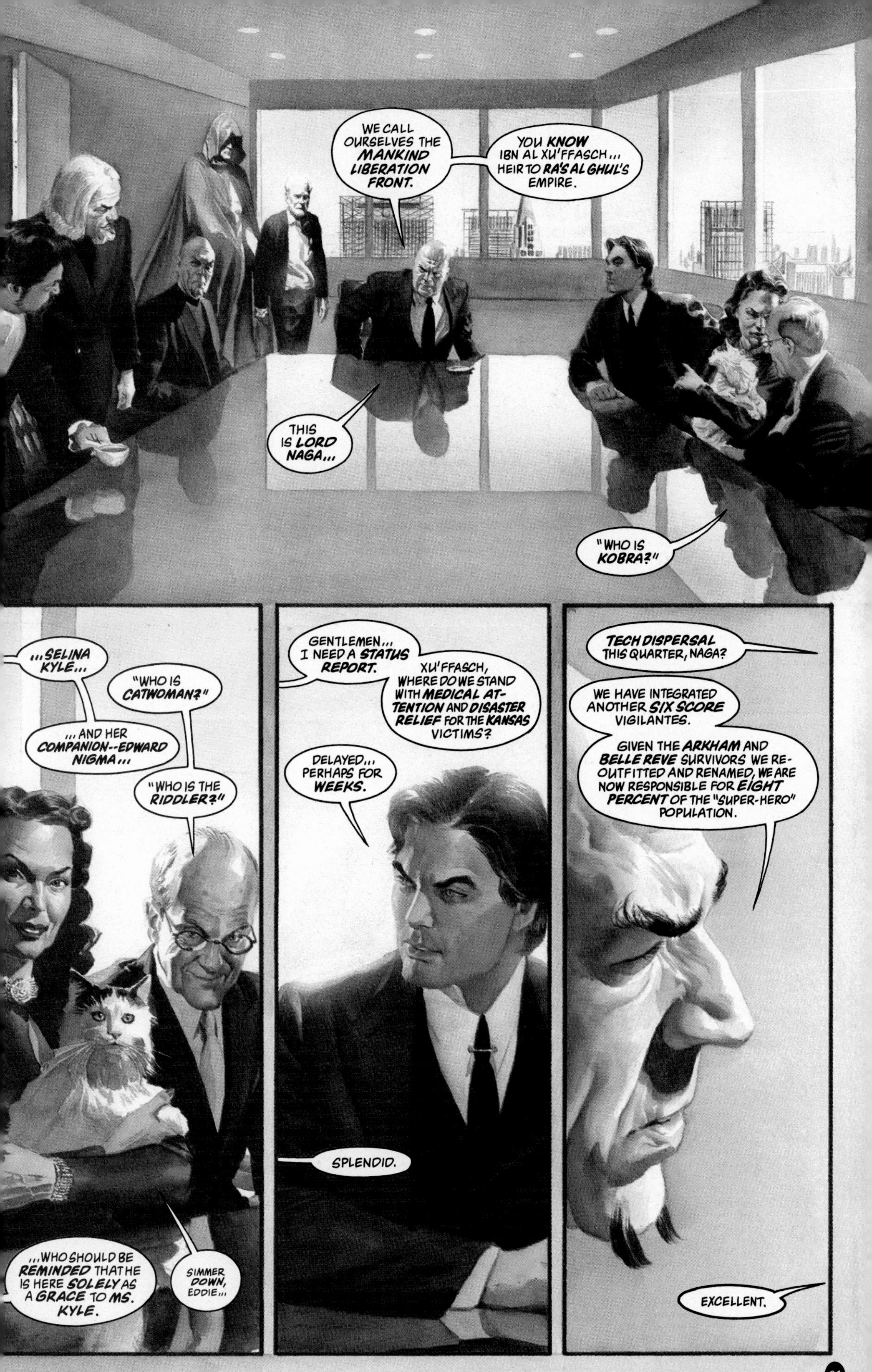

WE CALL OURSELVES THE MANKIND LIBERATION FRONT.
YOU KNOW IBN AL XU'FFASCH... HEIR TO RA'S AL GHUL'S EMPIRE.
THIS IS LORD NAGA...
"WHO IS KOBRA?"
...SELINA KYLE...
"WHO IS CATWOMAN?"
...AND HER COMPANION--EDWARD NIGMA...
"WHO IS THE RIDDLER?"
...WHO SHOULD BE REMINDED THAT HE IS HERE SOLELY AS A GRACE TO MS. KYLE.
SIMMER DOWN, EDDIE...
GENTLEMEN... I NEED A STATUS REPORT.
XU'FFASCH, WHERE DO WE STAND WITH MEDICAL ATTENTION AND DISASTER RELIEF FOR THE KANSAS VICTIMS?
DELAYED... PERHAPS FOR WEEKS.
SPLENDID.
TECH DISPERSAL THIS QUARTER, NAGA?
WE HAVE INTEGRATED ANOTHER SIX SCORE VIGILANTES.
GIVEN THE ARKHAM AND BELLE REVE SURVIVORS WE RE-OUTFITTED AND RENAMED, WE ARE NOW RESPONSIBLE FOR EIGHT PERCENT OF THE "SUPER-HERO" POPULATION.
EXCELLENT.

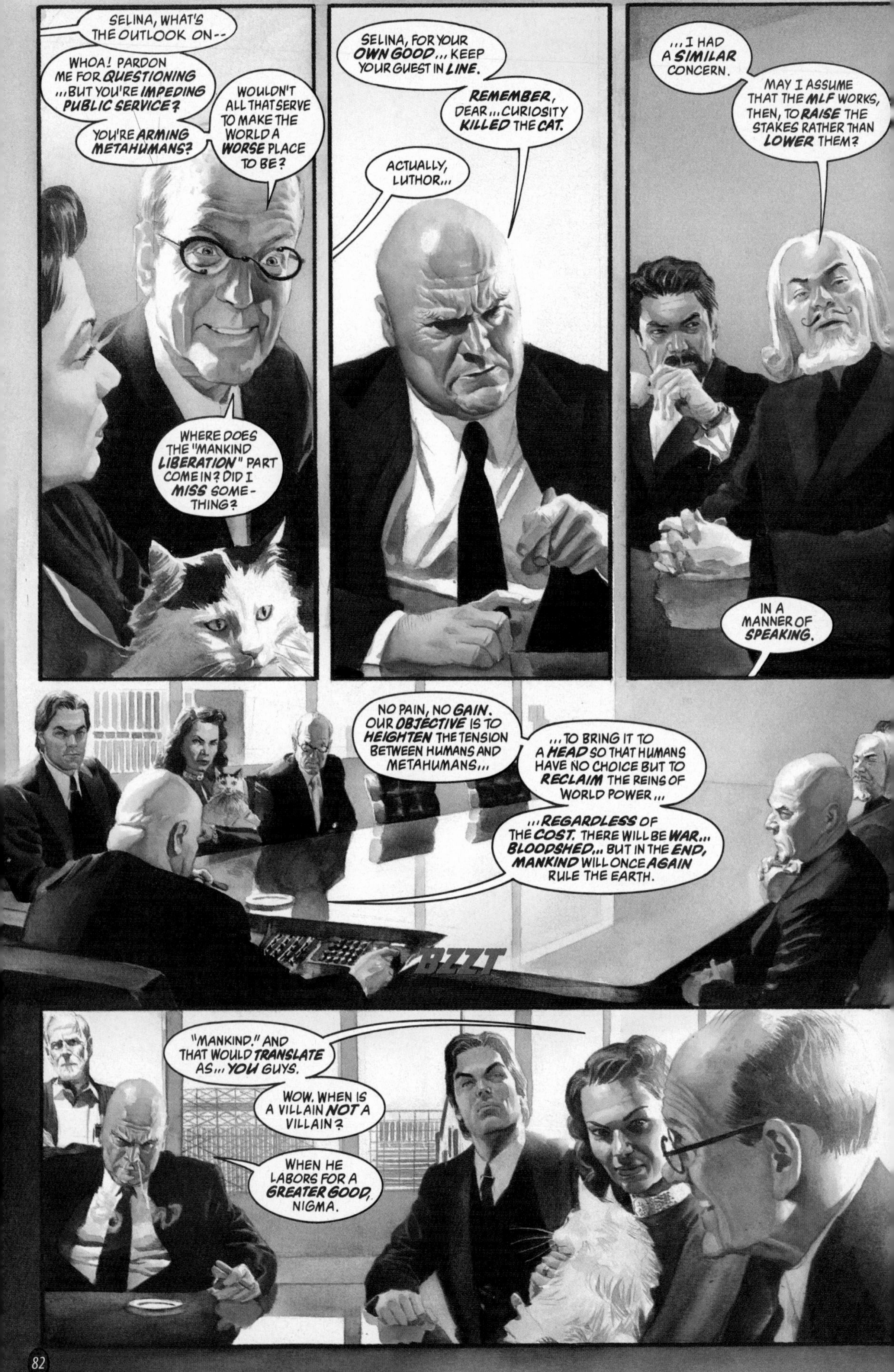
SELINA, WHAT'S THE OUTLOOK ON--
WHOA! PARDON ME FOR QUESTIONING ...BUT YOU'RE IMPEDING PUBLIC SERVICE?
YOU'RE ARMING METAHUMANS?
WOULDN'T ALL THAT SERVE TO MAKE THE WORLD A WORSE PLACE TO BE?
WHERE DOES THE "MANKIND LIBERATION" PART COME IN? DID I MISS SOME-THING?
SELINA, FOR YOUR OWN GOOD... KEEP YOUR GUEST IN LINE.
REMEMBER, DEAR... CURIOSITY KILLED THE CAT.
ACTUALLY, LUTHOR...
...I HAD A SIMILAR CONCERN.
MAY I ASSUME THAT THE MLF WORKS, THEN, TO RAISE THE STAKES RATHER THAN LOWER THEM?
IN A MANNER OF SPEAKING.
NO PAIN, NO GAIN. OUR OBJECTIVE IS TO HEIGHTEN THE TENSION BETWEEN HUMANS AND METAHUMANS...
...TO BRING IT TO A HEAD SO THAT HUMANS HAVE NO CHOICE BUT TO RECLAIM THE REINS OF WORLD POWER...
...REGARDLESS OF THE COST. THERE WILL BE WAR... BLOODSHED... BUT IN THE END, MANKIND WILL ONCE AGAIN RULE THE EARTH.
BZZT
"MANKIND." AND THAT WOULD TRANSLATE AS... YOU GUYS.
WOW. WHEN IS A VILLAIN NOT A VILLAIN?
WHEN HE LABORS FOR A GREATER GOOD, NIGMA.

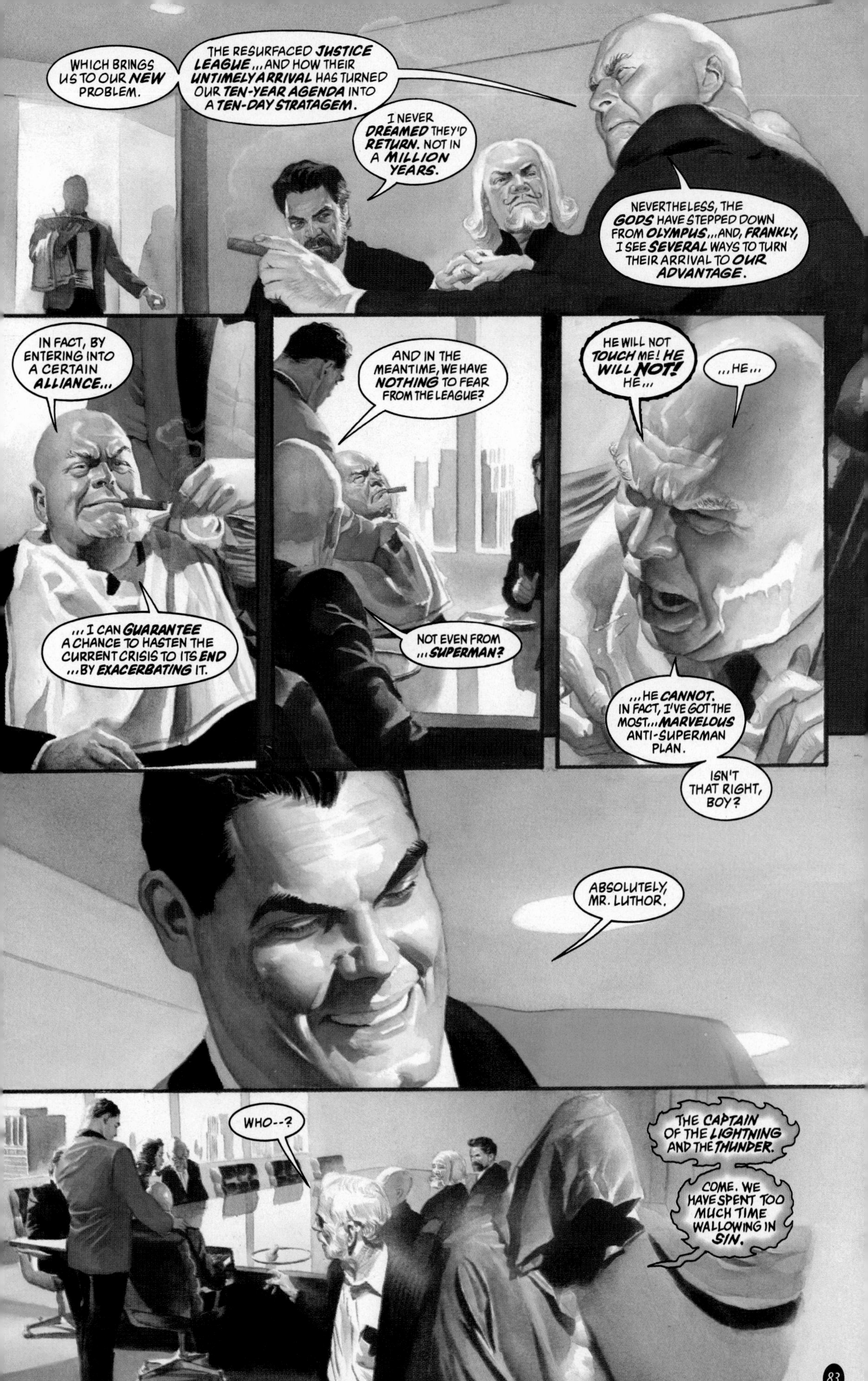
WHICH BRINGS US TO OUR NEW PROBLEM.
THE RESURFACED JUSTICE LEAGUE ... AND HOW THEIR UNTIMELY ARRIVAL HAS TURNED OUR TEN-YEAR AGENDA INTO A TEN-DAY STRATAGEM.
I NEVER DREAMED THEY'D RETURN. NOT IN A MILLION YEARS.
NEVERTHELESS, THE GODS HAVE STEPPED DOWN FROM OLYMPUS ... AND, FRANKLY, I SEE SEVERAL WAYS TO TURN THEIR ARRIVAL TO OUR ADVANTAGE.
IN FACT, BY ENTERING INTO A CERTAIN ALLIANCE...
... I CAN GUARANTEE A CHANCE TO HASTEN THE CURRENT CRISIS TO ITS END ... BY EXACERBATING IT.
AND IN THE MEANTIME, WE HAVE NOTHING TO FEAR FROM THE LEAGUE?
NOT EVEN FROM ... SUPERMAN?
HE WILL NOT TOUCH ME! HE WILL NOT! HE ...
... HE ...
... HE CANNOT. IN FACT, I'VE GOT THE MOST ... MARVELOUS ANTI-SUPERMAN PLAN.
ISN'T THAT RIGHT, BOY?
ABSOLUTELY, MR. LUTHOR.
WHO--?
THE CAPTAIN OF THE LIGHTNING AND THE THUNDER.
COME. WE HAVE SPENT TOO MUCH TIME WALLOWING IN SIN.

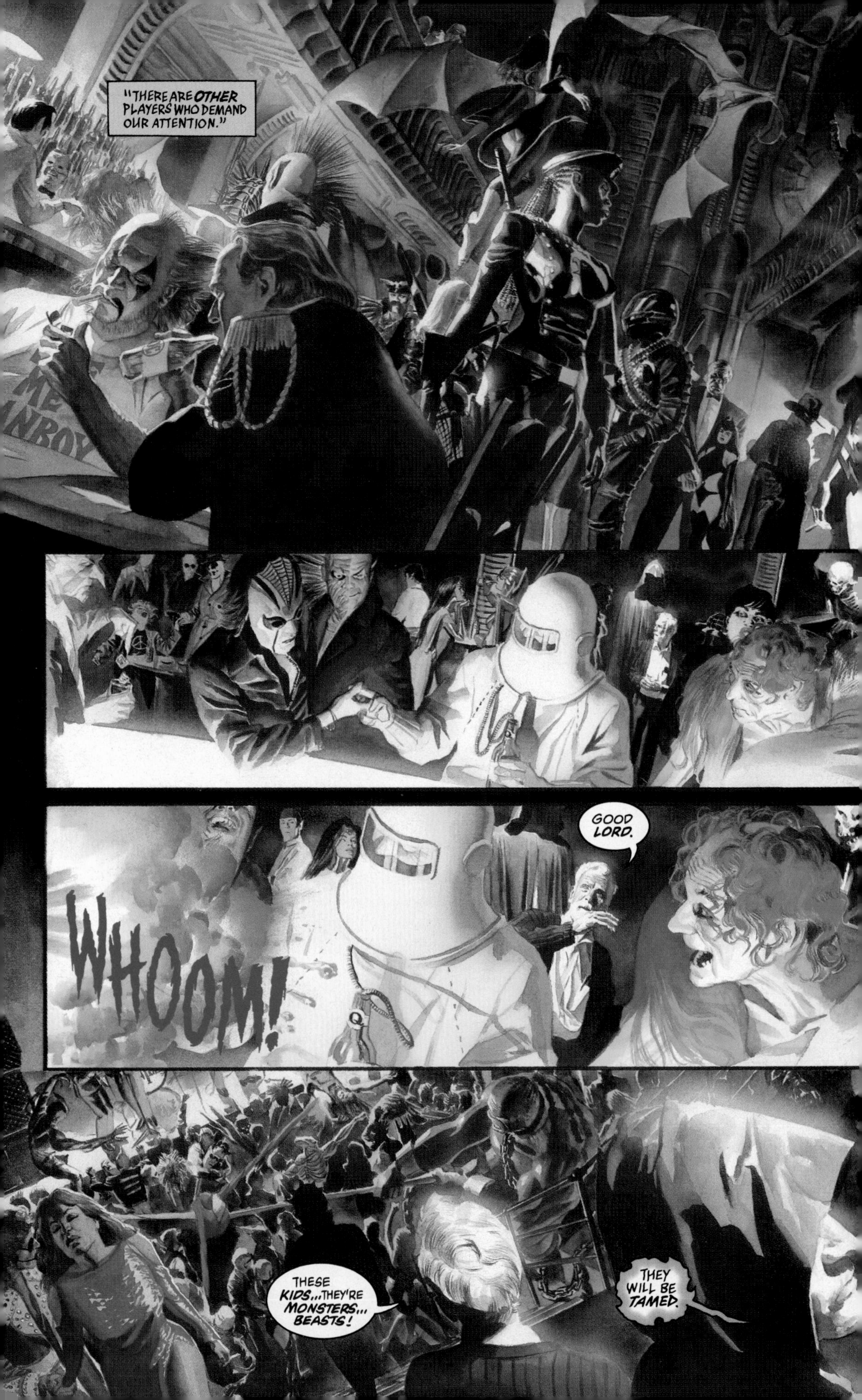
"THERE ARE OTHER PLAYERS WHO DEMAND OUR ATTENTION."
WHOOM!
GOOD LORD.
THESE KIDS...THEY'RE MONSTERS... BEASTS!
THEY WILL BE TAMED.

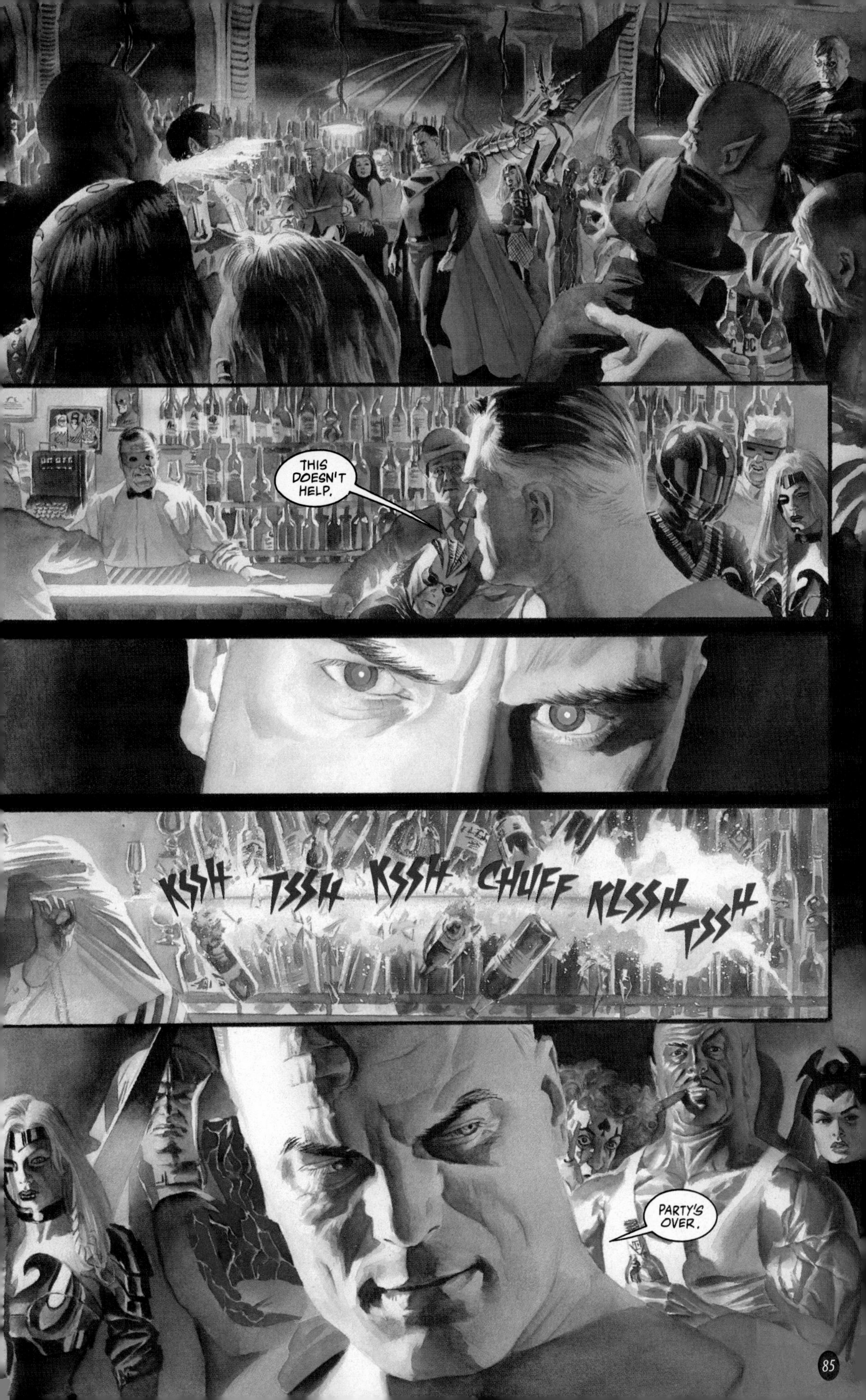
THIS DOESN'T HELP.
KSSH TSSH KSSH CHUFF KLSSH TSSH
PARTY'S OVER.

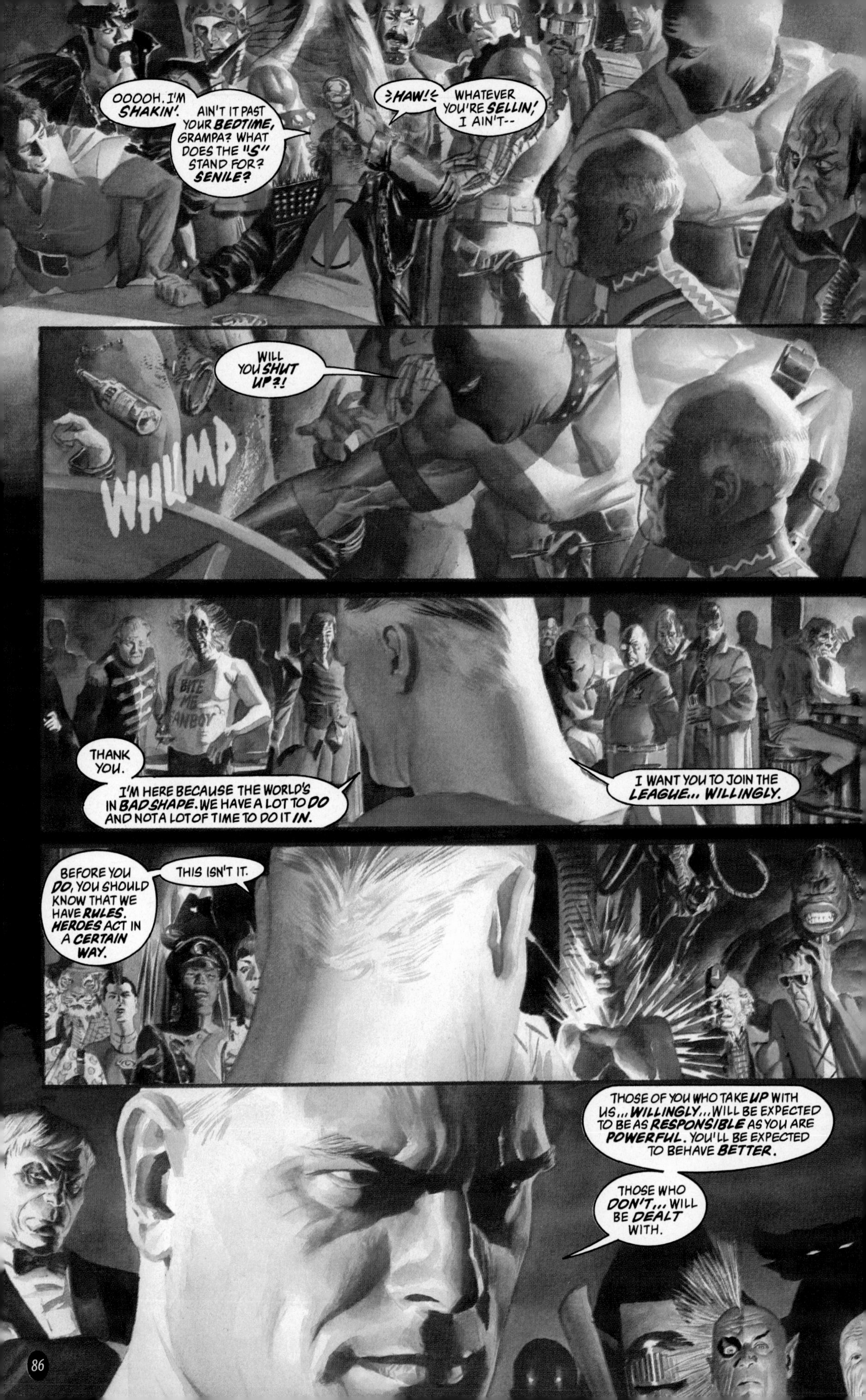
OOOOH. I'M SHAKIN'.
AIN'T IT PAST YOUR BEDTIME, GRAMPA? WHAT DOES THE "S" STAND FOR? SENILE?
>HAW!<
WHATEVER YOU'RE SELLIN', I AIN'T--
WILL YOU SHUT UP?!
WHUMP
THANK YOU.
I'M HERE BECAUSE THE WORLD'S IN BAD SHAPE. WE HAVE A LOT TO DO AND NOT A LOT OF TIME TO DO IT IN.
I WANT YOU TO JOIN THE LEAGUE... WILLINGLY.
BEFORE YOU DO, YOU SHOULD KNOW THAT WE HAVE RULES. HEROES ACT IN A CERTAIN WAY.
THIS ISN'T IT.
THOSE OF YOU WHO TAKE UP WITH US... WILLINGLY... WILL BE EXPECTED TO BE AS RESPONSIBLE AS YOU ARE POWERFUL. YOU'LL BE EXPECTED TO BEHAVE BETTER.
THOSE WHO DON'T... WILL BE DEALT WITH.

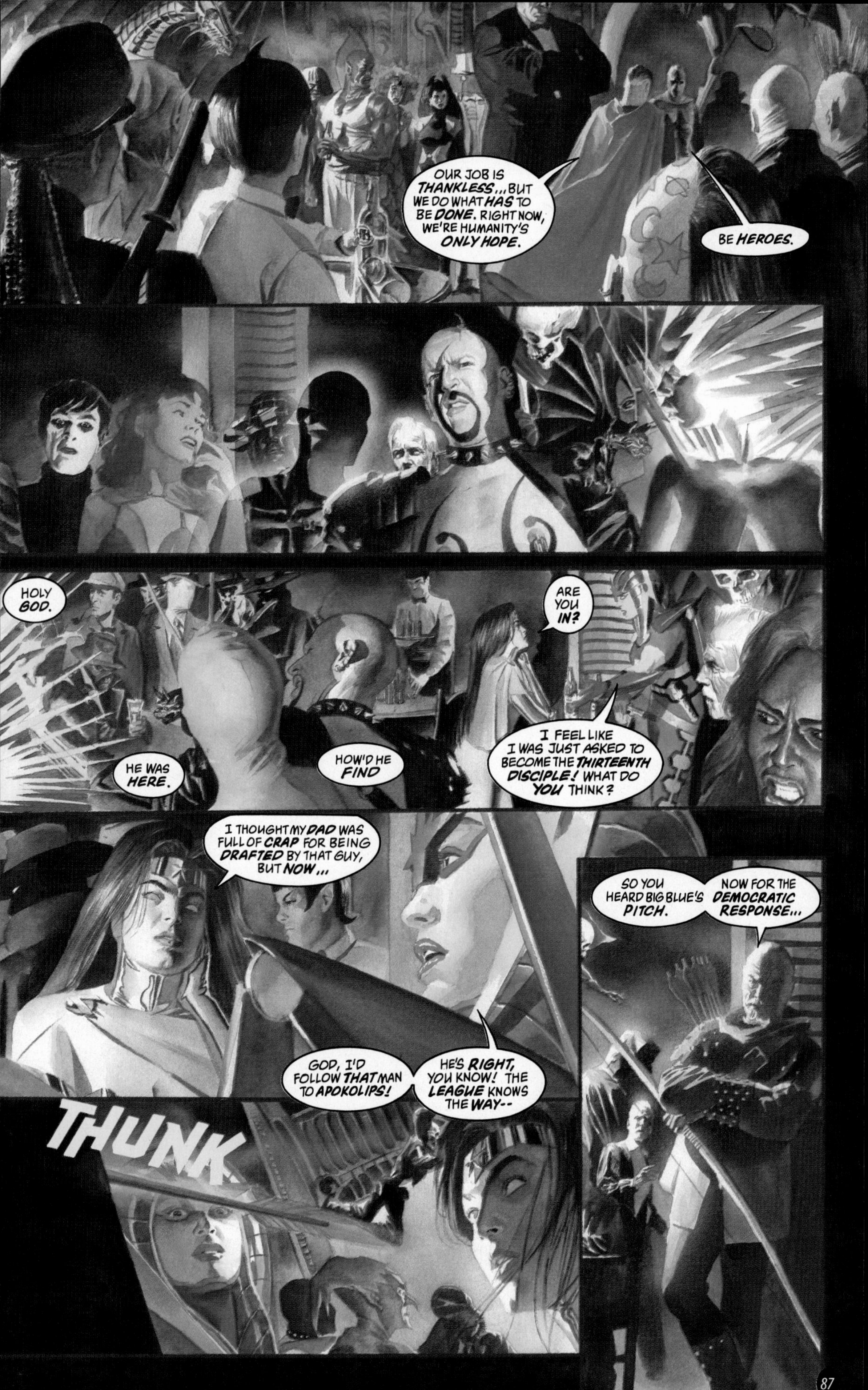
OUR JOB IS THANKLESS... BUT WE DO WHAT HAS TO BE DONE. RIGHT NOW, WE'RE HUMANITY'S ONLY HOPE.
BE HEROES.
HOLY GOD.
ARE YOU IN?
HE WAS HERE.
HOW'D HE FIND
I FEEL LIKE I WAS JUST ASKED TO BECOME THE THIRTEENTH DISCIPLE! WHAT DO YOU THINK?
I THOUGHT MY DAD WAS FULL OF CRAP FOR BEING DRAFTED BY THAT GUY, BUT NOW...
SO YOU HEARD BIG BLUE'S PITCH.
NOW FOR THE DEMOCRATIC RESPONSE...
GOD, I'D FOLLOW THAT MAN TO APOKOLIPS!
HE'S RIGHT, YOU KNOW! THE LEAGUE KNOWS THE WAY--
THUNK

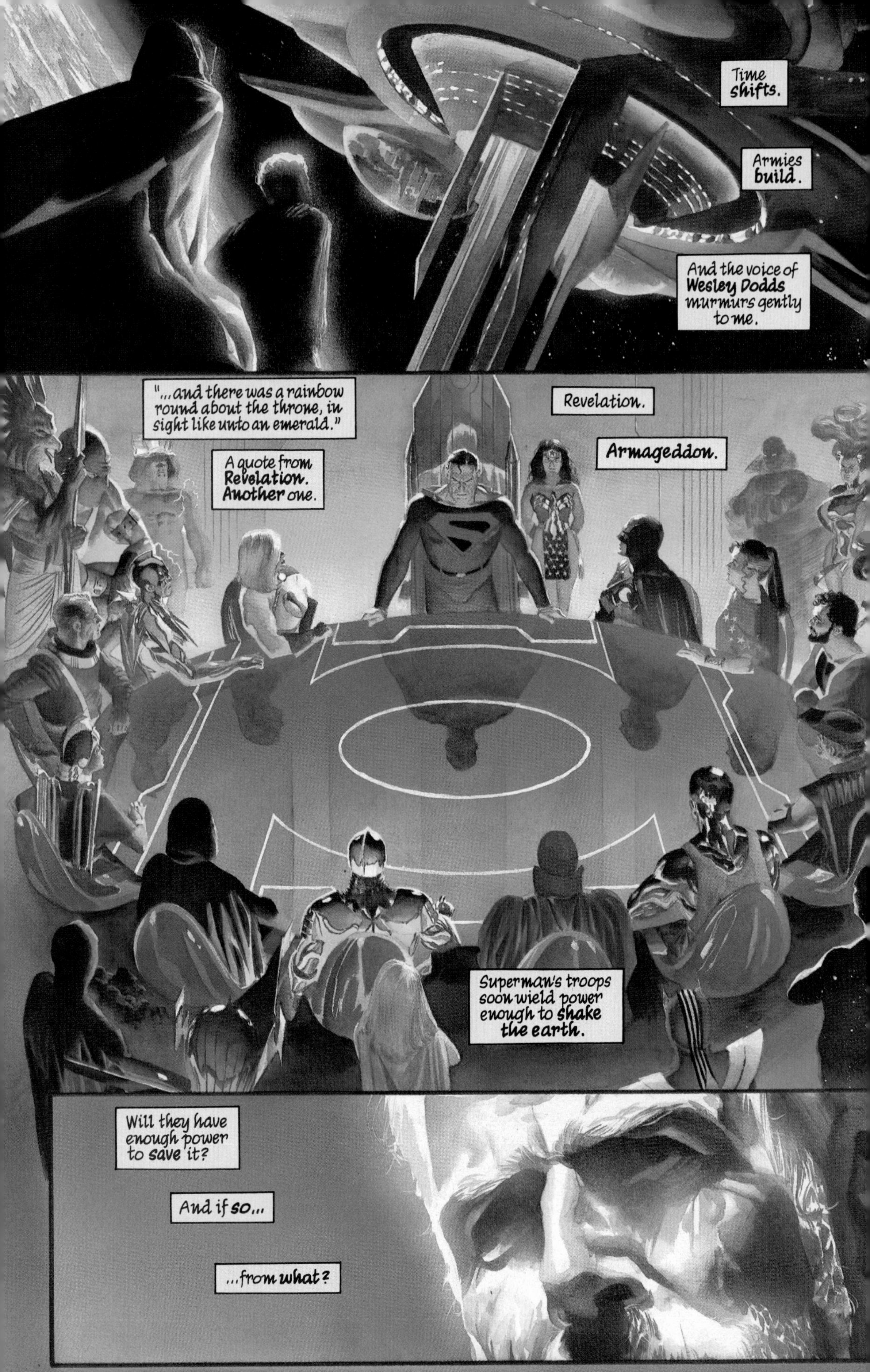
Time shifts.
Armies build.
And the voice of Wesley Dodds murmurs gently to me.
"...and there was a rainbow round about the throne, in sight like unto an emerald."
A quote from Revelation. Another one.
Revelation.
Armageddon.
Superman's troops soon wield power enough to shake the earth.
Will they have enough power to save it?
And if so...
...from what?

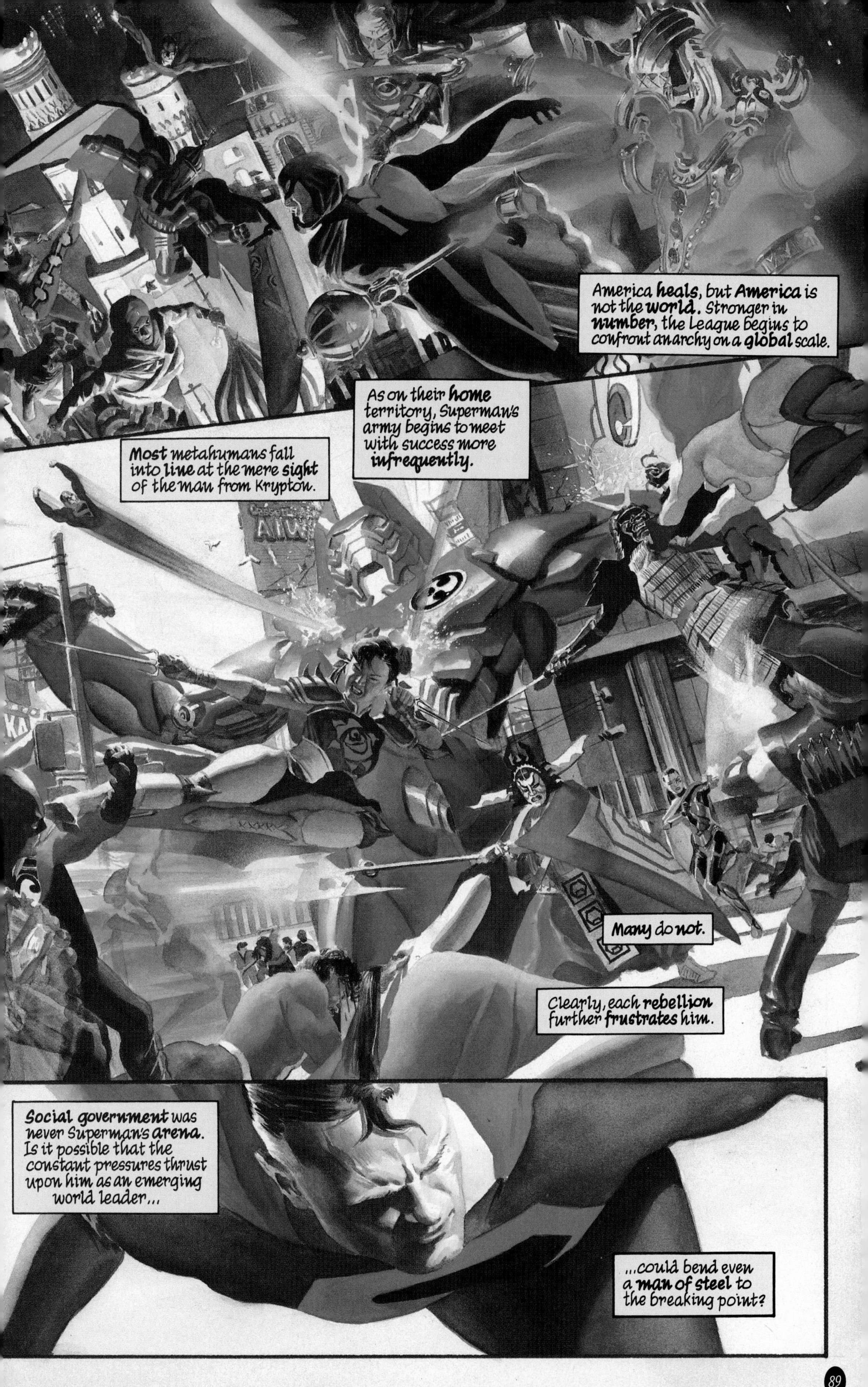
America **heals**, but **America** is not the **world**. Stronger in **number**, the League begins to confront anarchy on a **global** scale.
As on their **home** territory, Superman's army begins to meet with success more **infrequently**.
Most metahumans fall into **line** at the mere **sight** of the man from Krypton.
Many do **not**.
Clearly, each **rebellion** further **frustrates** him.
Social government was never Superman's **arena**. Is it possible that the constant pressures thrust upon him as an emerging world leader...
...could bend even a **man of steel** to the breaking point?

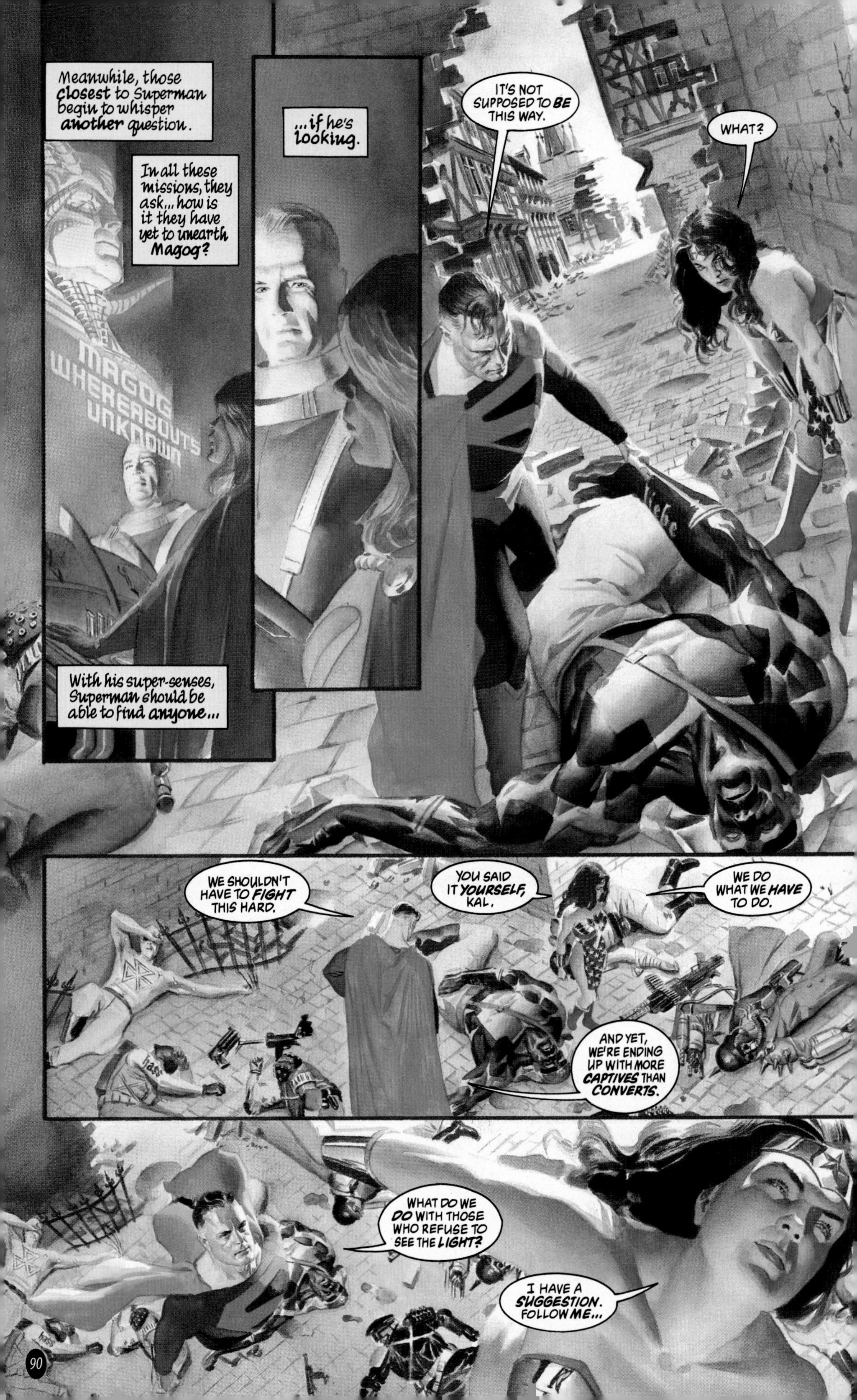
Meanwhile, those closest to Superman begin to whisper another question.
In all these missions, they ask... how is it they have yet to unearth Magog?
MAGOG WHEREABOUTS UNKNOWN
With his super-senses, Superman should be able to find anyone...
...if he's looking.
IT'S NOT SUPPOSED TO BE THIS WAY.
WHAT?
WE SHOULDN'T HAVE TO FIGHT THIS HARD.
YOU SAID IT YOURSELF, KAL.
WE DO WHAT WE HAVE TO DO.
AND YET, WE'RE ENDING UP WITH MORE CAPTIVES THAN CONVERTS.
WHAT DO WE DO WITH THOSE WHO REFUSE TO SEE THE LIGHT?
I HAVE A SUGGESTION. FOLLOW ME...

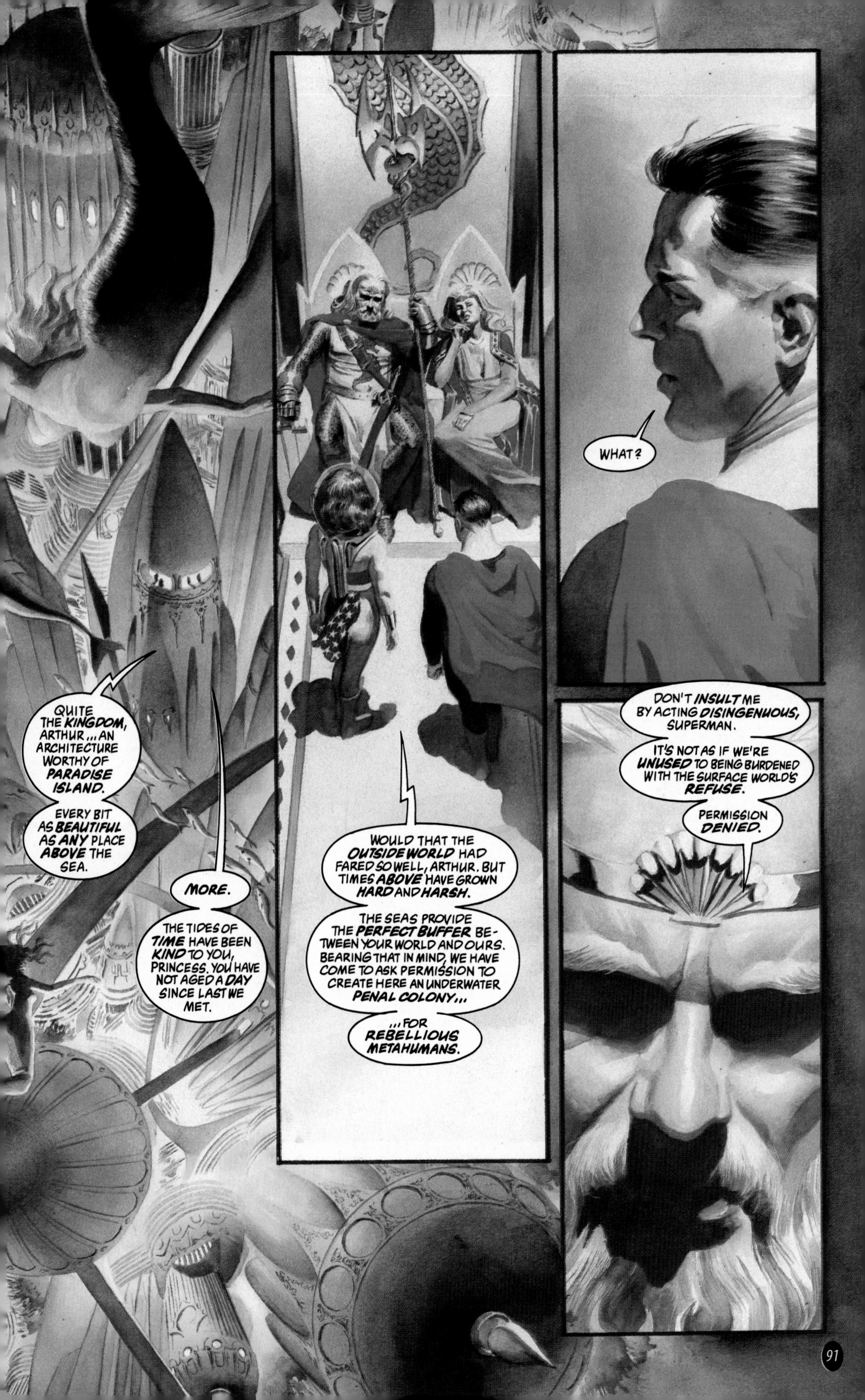
QUITE THE KINGDOM, ARTHUR... AN ARCHITECTURE WORTHY OF PARADISE ISLAND.
EVERY BIT AS BEAUTIFUL AS ANY PLACE ABOVE THE SEA.
MORE.
THE TIDES OF TIME HAVE BEEN KIND TO YOU, PRINCESS. YOU HAVE NOT AGED A DAY SINCE LAST WE MET.
WOULD THAT THE OUTSIDE WORLD HAD FARED SO WELL, ARTHUR. BUT TIMES ABOVE HAVE GROWN HARD AND HARSH.
THE SEAS PROVIDE THE PERFECT BUFFER BETWEEN YOUR WORLD AND OURS. BEARING THAT IN MIND, WE HAVE COME TO ASK PERMISSION TO CREATE HERE AN UNDERWATER PENAL COLONY...
...FOR REBELLIOUS METAHUMANS.
WHAT?
DON'T INSULT ME BY ACTING DISINGENUOUS, SUPERMAN.
IT'S NOT AS IF WE'RE UNUSED TO BEING BURDENED WITH THE SURFACE WORLD'S REFUSE.
PERMISSION DENIED.

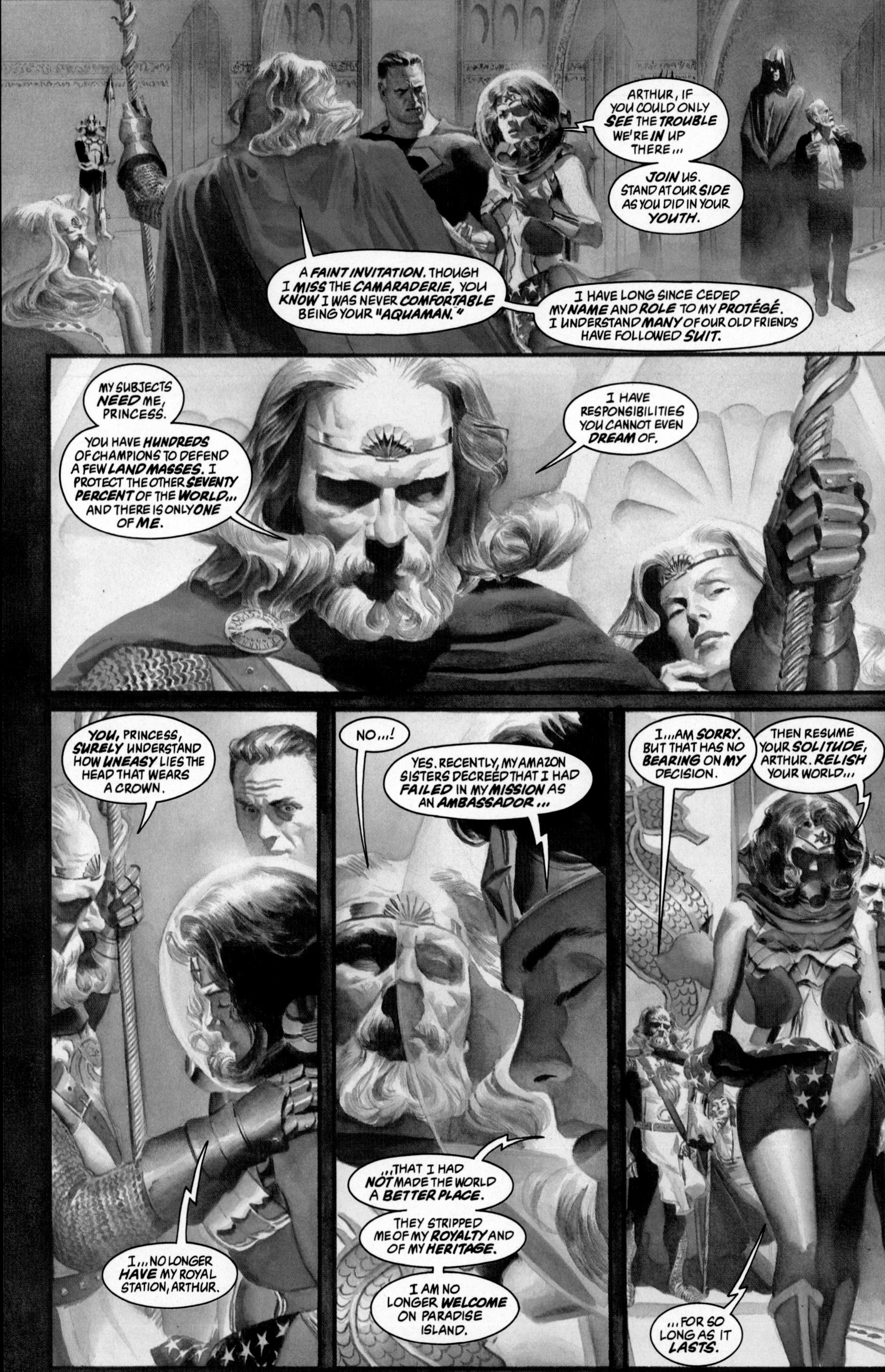
ARTHUR, IF YOU COULD ONLY SEE THE TROUBLE WE'RE IN UP THERE...
JOIN US. STAND AT OUR SIDE AS YOU DID IN YOUR YOUTH.
A FAINT INVITATION. THOUGH I MISS THE CAMARADERIE, YOU KNOW I WAS NEVER COMFORTABLE BEING YOUR "AQUAMAN."
I HAVE LONG SINCE CEDED MY NAME AND ROLE TO MY PROTÉGÉ. I UNDERSTAND MANY OF OUR OLD FRIENDS HAVE FOLLOWED SUIT.
MY SUBJECTS NEED ME, PRINCESS.
YOU HAVE HUNDREDS OF CHAMPIONS TO DEFEND A FEW LAND MASSES. I PROTECT THE OTHER SEVENTY PERCENT OF THE WORLD... AND THERE IS ONLY ONE OF ME.
I HAVE RESPONSIBILITIES YOU CANNOT EVEN DREAM OF.
YOU, PRINCESS, SURELY UNDERSTAND HOW UNEASY LIES THE HEAD THAT WEARS A CROWN.
I... NO LONGER HAVE MY ROYAL STATION, ARTHUR.
NO...!
YES. RECENTLY, MY AMAZON SISTERS DECREED THAT I HAD FAILED IN MY MISSION AS AN AMBASSADOR...
...THAT I HAD NOT MADE THE WORLD A BETTER PLACE.
THEY STRIPPED ME OF MY ROYALTY AND OF MY HERITAGE.
I AM NO LONGER WELCOME ON PARADISE ISLAND.
I... AM SORRY. BUT THAT HAS NO BEARING ON MY DECISION.
THEN RESUME YOUR SOLITUDE, ARTHUR. RELISH YOUR WORLD...
...FOR SO LONG AS IT LASTS.

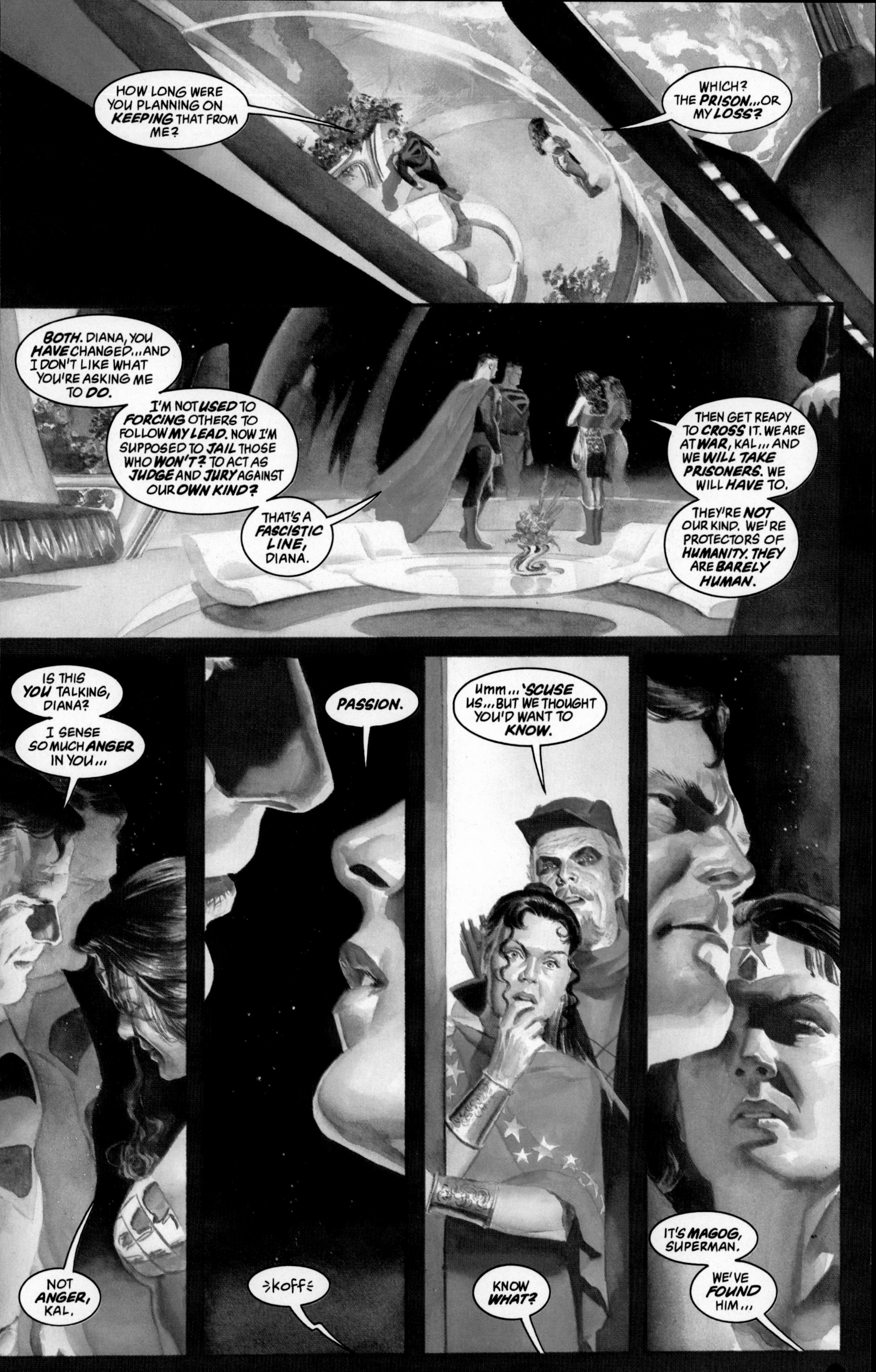

HOW LONG WERE YOU PLANNING ON KEEPING THAT FROM ME?
WHICH? THE PRISON...OR MY LOSS?
BOTH. DIANA, YOU HAVE CHANGED...AND I DON'T LIKE WHAT YOU'RE ASKING ME TO DO.
I'M NOT USED TO FORCING OTHERS TO FOLLOW MY LEAD. NOW I'M SUPPOSED TO JAIL THOSE WHO WON'T? TO ACT AS JUDGE AND JURY AGAINST OUR OWN KIND?
THAT'S A FASCISTIC LINE, DIANA.
THEN GET READY TO CROSS IT. WE ARE AT WAR, KAL... AND WE WILL TAKE PRISONERS. WE WILL HAVE TO.
THEY'RE NOT OUR KIND. WE'RE PROTECTORS OF HUMANITY. THEY ARE BARELY HUMAN.
IS THIS YOU TALKING, DIANA?
I SENSE SO MUCH ANGER IN YOU...
NOT ANGER, KAL.
PASSION.
KOFF
UMM... 'SCUSE US... BUT WE THOUGHT YOU'D WANT TO KNOW.
KNOW WHAT?
IT'S MAGOG, SUPERMAN.
WE'VE FOUND HIM...

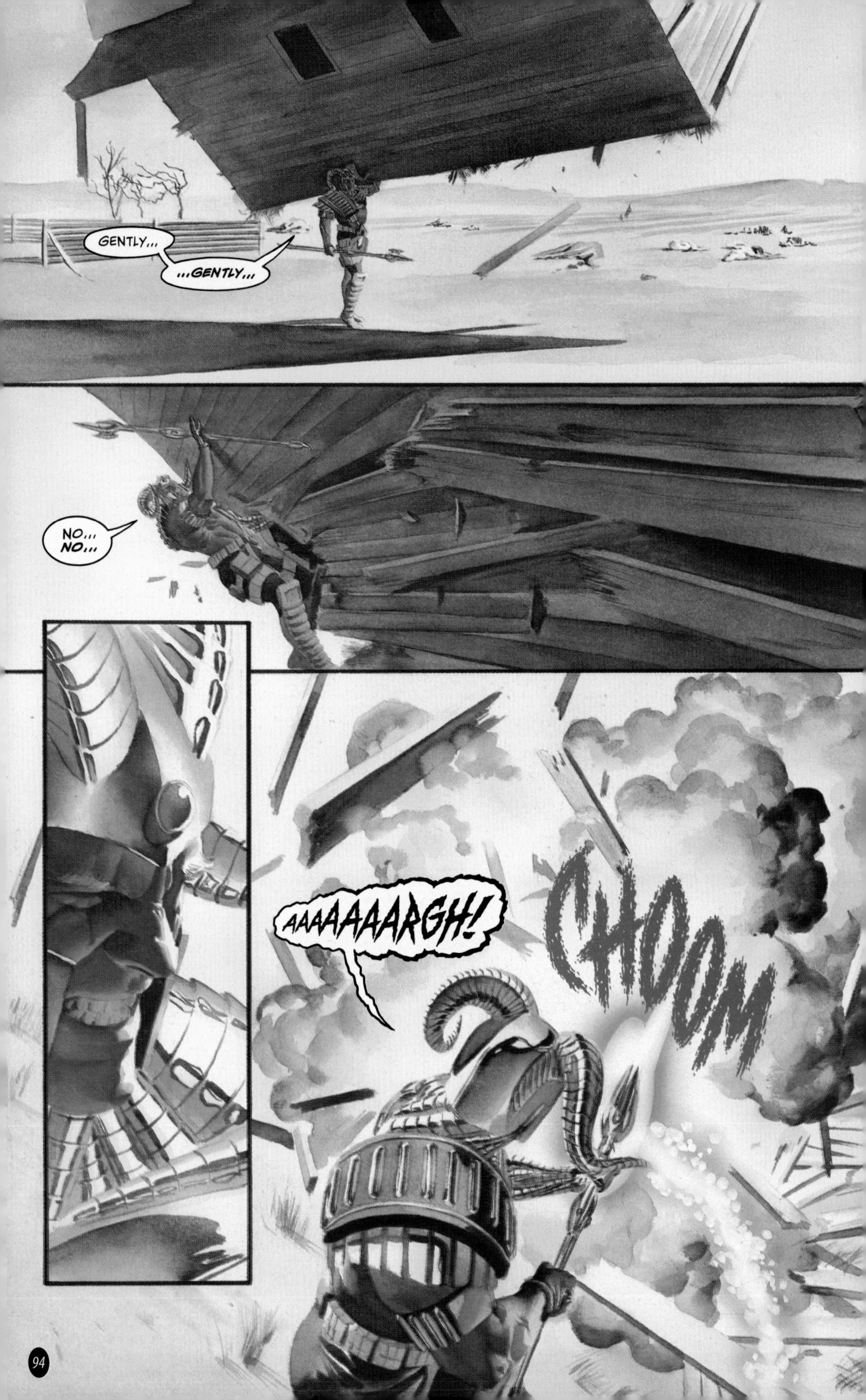
GENTLY...
...GENTLY...
NO...
NO...
AAAAAAAARGH!
CHOOM

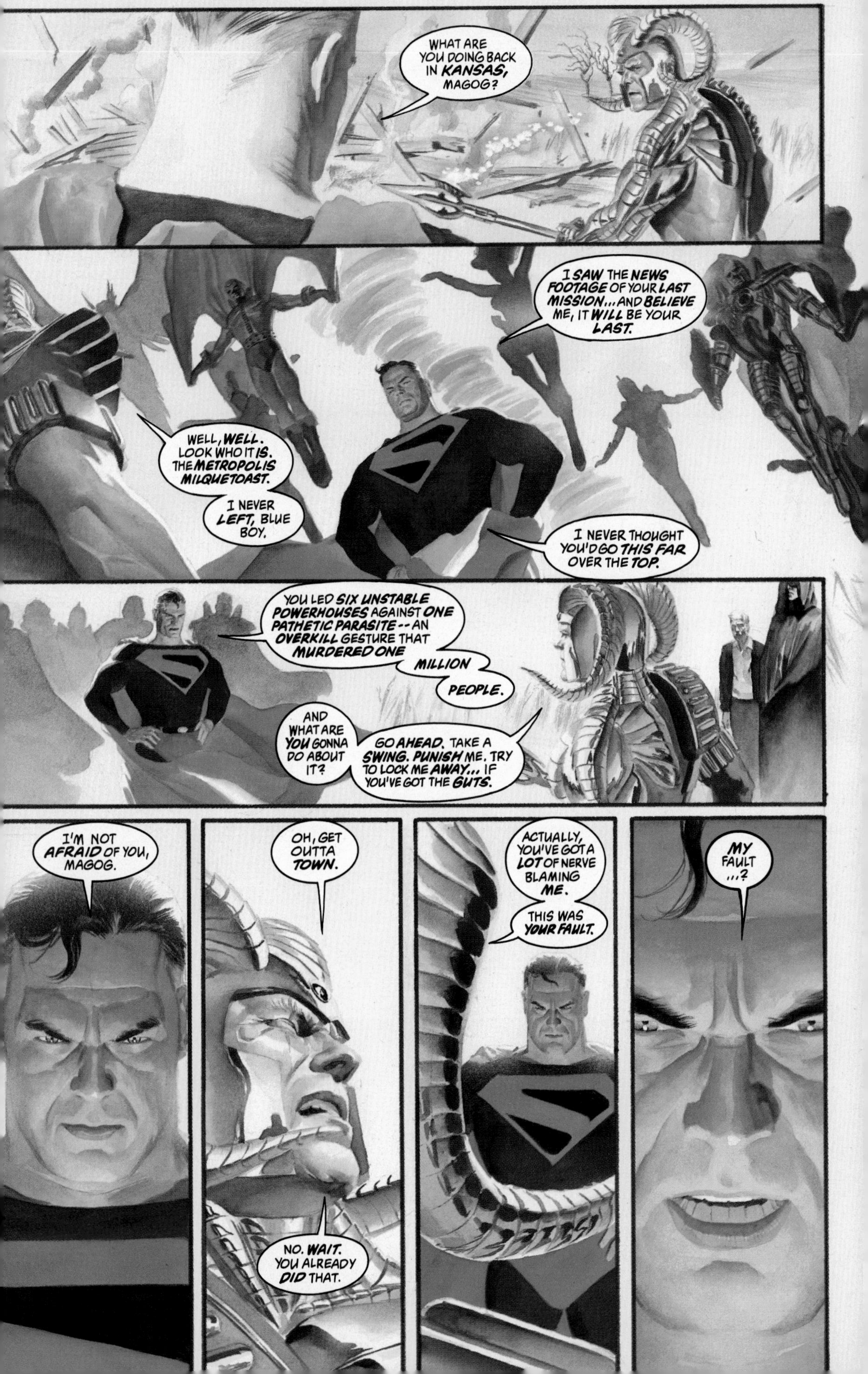
WHAT ARE YOU DOING BACK IN KANSAS, MAGOG?
I SAW THE NEWS FOOTAGE OF YOUR LAST MISSION... AND BELIEVE ME, IT WILL BE YOUR LAST.
WELL, WELL. LOOK WHO IT IS. THE METROPOLIS MILQUETOAST.
I NEVER LEFT, BLUE BOY.
I NEVER THOUGHT YOU'D GO THIS FAR OVER THE TOP.
YOU LED SIX UNSTABLE POWERHOUSES AGAINST ONE PATHETIC PARASITE -- AN OVERKILL GESTURE THAT MURDERED ONE
MILLION
PEOPLE.
AND WHAT ARE YOU GONNA DO ABOUT IT?
GO AHEAD. TAKE A SWING. PUNISH ME. TRY TO LOCK ME AWAY... IF YOU'VE GOT THE GUTS.
I'M NOT AFRAID OF YOU, MAGOG.
OH, GET OUTTA TOWN.
NO. WAIT. YOU ALREADY DID THAT.
ACTUALLY, YOU'VE GOT A LOT OF NERVE BLAMING ME.
THIS WAS YOUR FAULT.
MY FAULT ...?

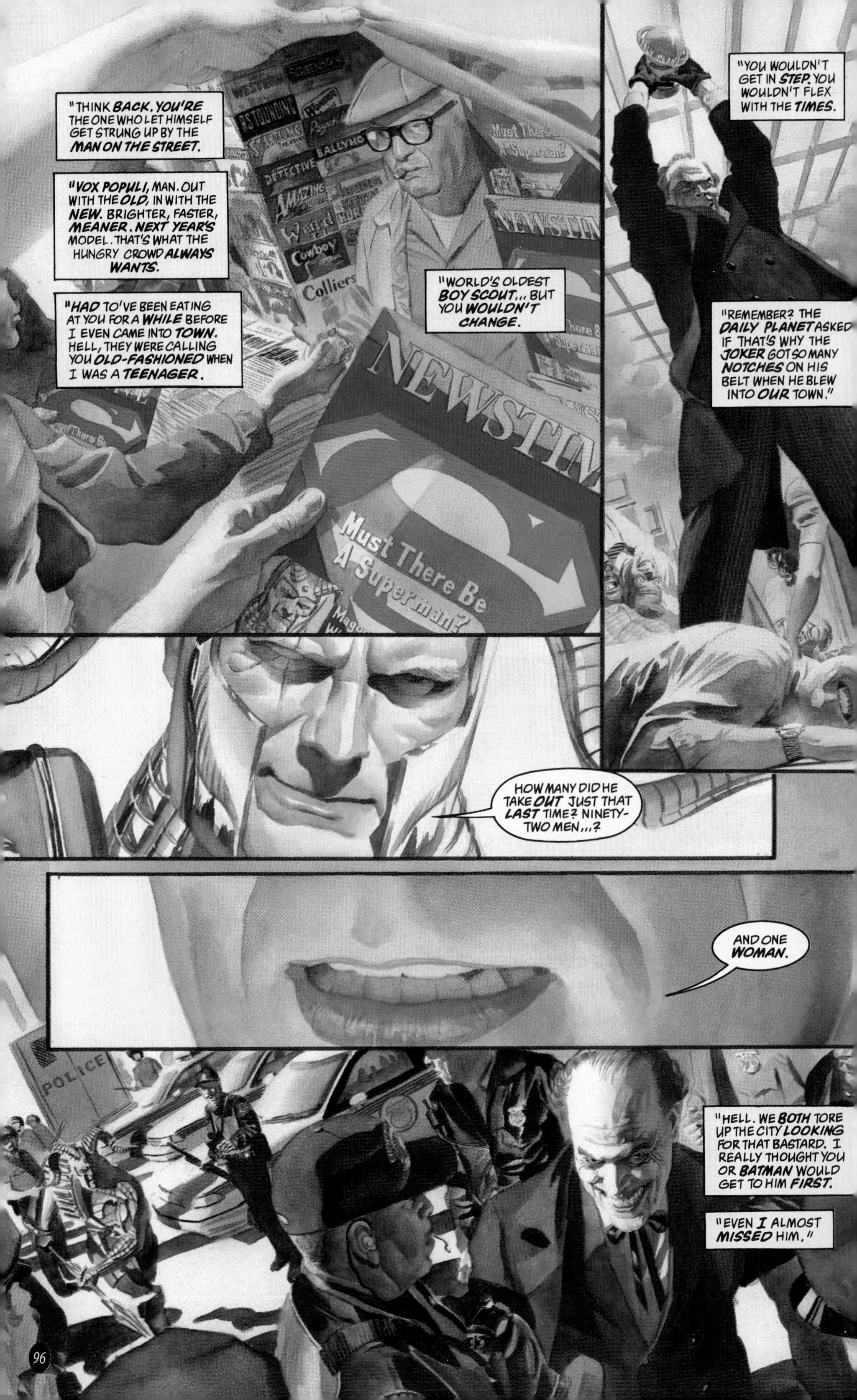
"THINK BACK. YOU'RE THE ONE WHO LET HIMSELF GET STRUNG UP BY THE MAN ON THE STREET.
"VOX POPULI, MAN. OUT WITH THE OLD, IN WITH THE NEW. BRIGHTER, FASTER, MEANER. NEXT YEAR'S MODEL. THAT'S WHAT THE HUNGRY CROWD ALWAYS WANTS.
"HAD TO'VE BEEN EATING AT YOU FOR A WHILE BEFORE I EVEN CAME INTO TOWN. HELL, THEY WERE CALLING YOU OLD-FASHIONED WHEN I WAS A TEENAGER.
"WORLD'S OLDEST BOY SCOUT... BUT YOU WOULDN'T CHANGE.
"YOU WOULDN'T GET IN STEP. YOU WOULDN'T FLEX WITH THE TIMES.
"REMEMBER? THE DAILY PLANET ASKED IF THAT'S WHY THE JOKER GOT SO MANY NOTCHES ON HIS BELT WHEN HE BLEW INTO OUR TOWN."
HOW MANY DID HE TAKE OUT JUST THAT LAST TIME? NINETY-TWO MEN...?
AND ONE WOMAN.
"HELL. WE BOTH TORE UP THE CITY LOOKING FOR THAT BASTARD. I REALLY THOUGHT YOU OR BATMAN WOULD GET TO HIM FIRST.
"EVEN I ALMOST MISSED HIM."

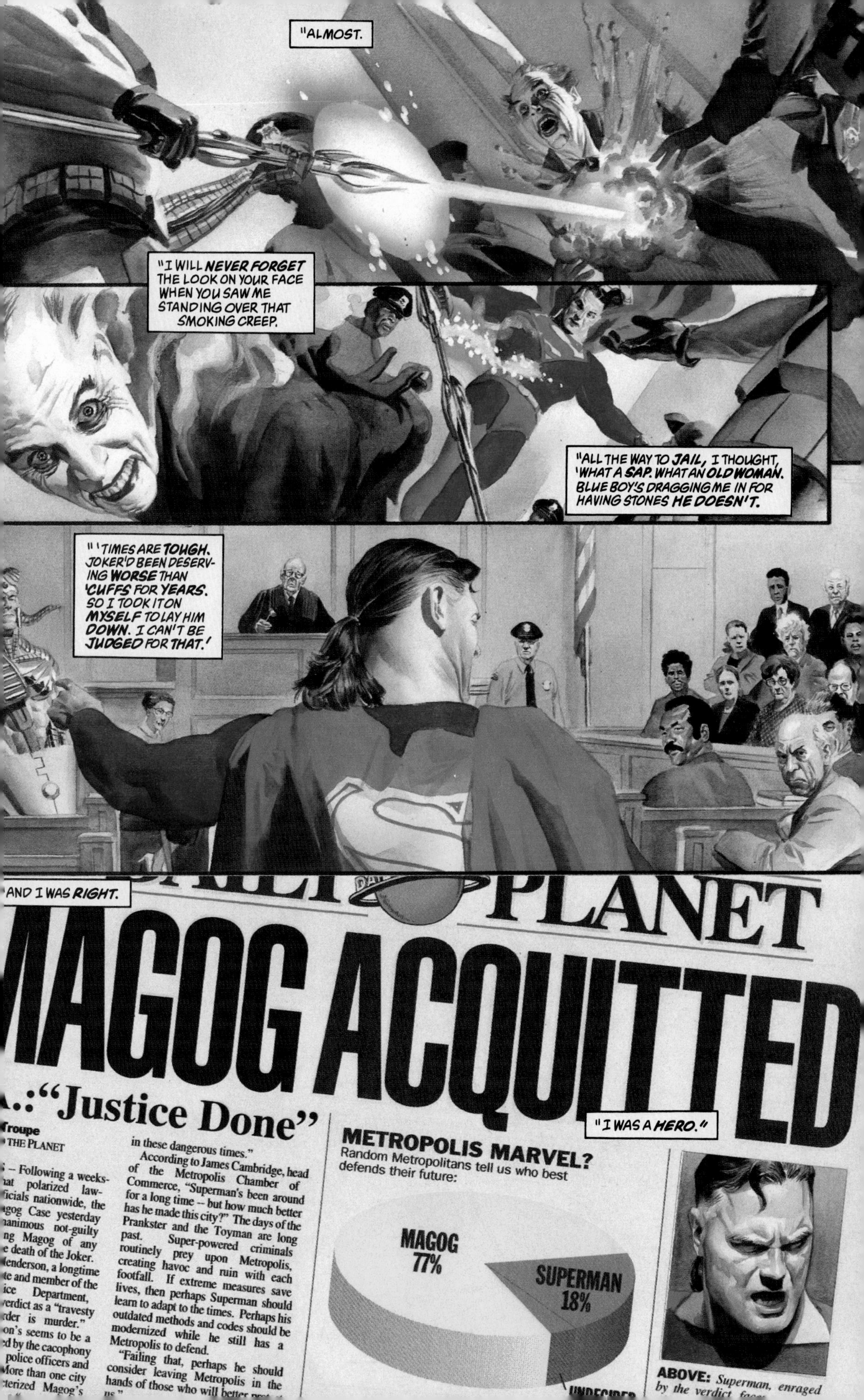

"ALMOST.
"I WILL NEVER FORGET THE LOOK ON YOUR FACE WHEN YOU SAW ME STANDING OVER THAT SMOKING CREEP.
"ALL THE WAY TO JAIL, I THOUGHT, 'WHAT A SAP. WHAT AN OLD WOMAN. BLUE BOY'S DRAGGING ME IN FOR HAVING STONES HE DOESN'T.
"'TIMES ARE TOUGH. JOKER'D BEEN DESERVING WORSE THAN 'CUFFS FOR YEARS. SO I TOOK IT ON MYSELF TO LAY HIM DOWN. I CAN'T BE JUDGED FOR THAT.'
AND I WAS RIGHT.
PLANET
MAGOG ACQUITTED
"Justice Done"
THE PLANET
– Following a weeks-
polarized law-
ficials nationwide, the
gog Case yesterday
nanimous not-guilty
ng Magog of any
e death of the Joker.
enderson, a longtime
te and member of the
ice Department,
verdict as a "travesty
rder is murder."
on's seems to be a
d by the cacophony
police officers and
More than one city
cterized Magog's
in these dangerous times."
According to James Cambridge, head of the Metropolis Chamber of Commerce, "Superman's been around for a long time -- but how much better has he made this city?" The days of the Prankster and the Toyman are long past. Super-powered criminals routinely prey upon Metropolis, creating havoc and ruin with each footfall. If extreme measures save lives, then perhaps Superman should learn to adapt to the times. Perhaps his outdated methods and codes should be modernized while he still has a Metropolis to defend.
"Failing that, perhaps he should consider leaving Metropolis in the hands of those who will better
"I WAS A HERO."
METROPOLIS MARVEL?
Random Metropolitans tell us who best defends their future:
MAGOG 77%
SUPERMAN 18%
ABOVE: Superman, enraged by the verdict

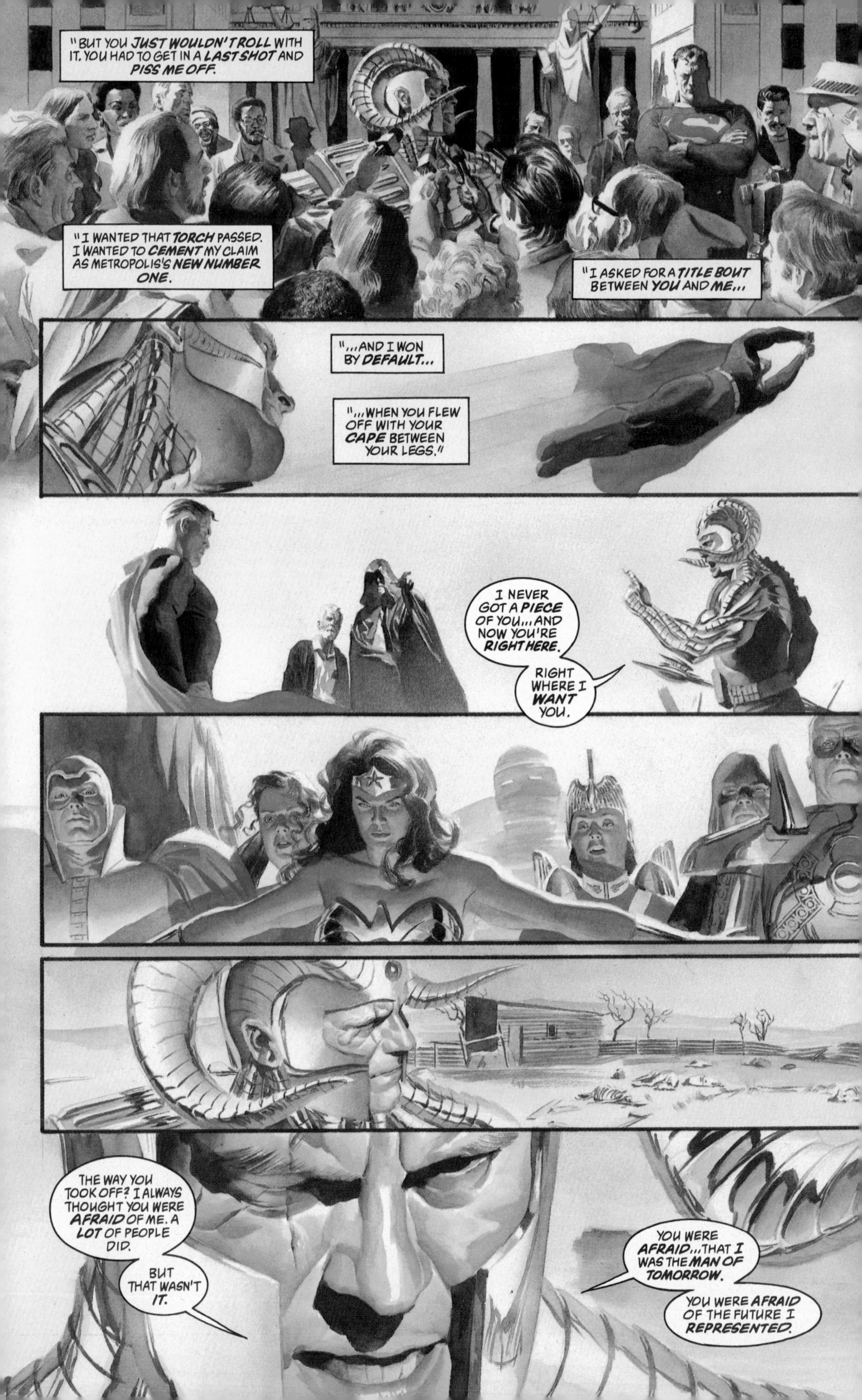
"BUT YOU JUST WOULDN'T ROLL WITH IT. YOU HAD TO GET IN A LAST SHOT AND PISS ME OFF.
"I WANTED THAT TORCH PASSED. I WANTED TO CEMENT MY CLAIM AS METROPOLIS'S NEW NUMBER ONE.
"I ASKED FOR A TITLE BOUT BETWEEN YOU AND ME...
"...AND I WON BY DEFAULT...
"...WHEN YOU FLEW OFF WITH YOUR CAPE BETWEEN YOUR LEGS."
I NEVER GOT A PIECE OF YOU... AND NOW YOU'RE RIGHT HERE.
RIGHT WHERE I WANT YOU.
THE WAY YOU TOOK OFF? I ALWAYS THOUGHT YOU WERE AFRAID OF ME. A LOT OF PEOPLE DID.
BUT THAT WASN'T IT.
YOU WERE AFRAID... THAT I WAS THE MAN OF TOMORROW.
YOU WERE AFRAID OF THE FUTURE I REPRESENTED.

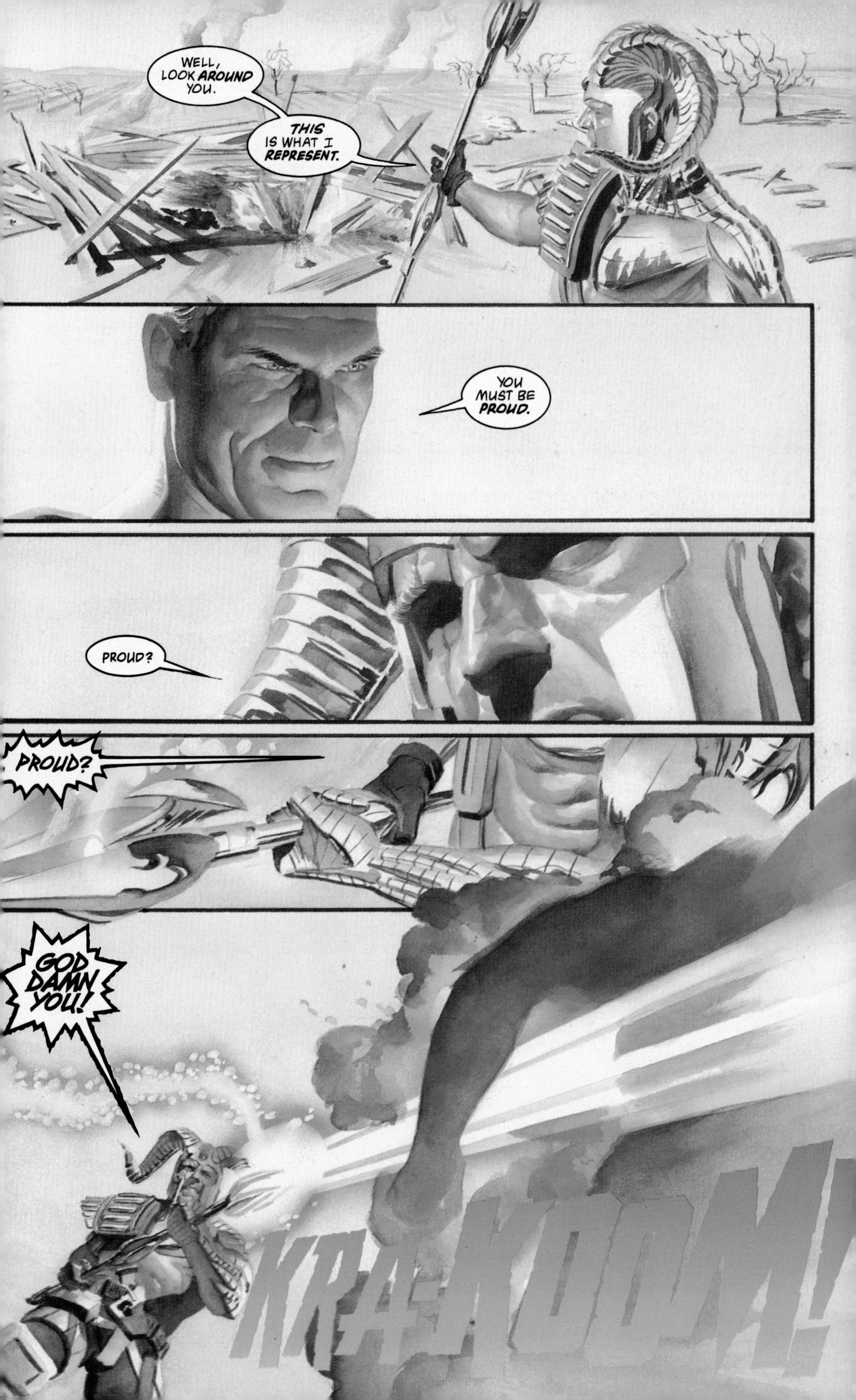
WELL, LOOK AROUND YOU.
THIS IS WHAT I REPRESENT.
YOU MUST BE PROUD.
PROUD?
PROUD?
GOD DAMN YOU!
KRA-KOOM!

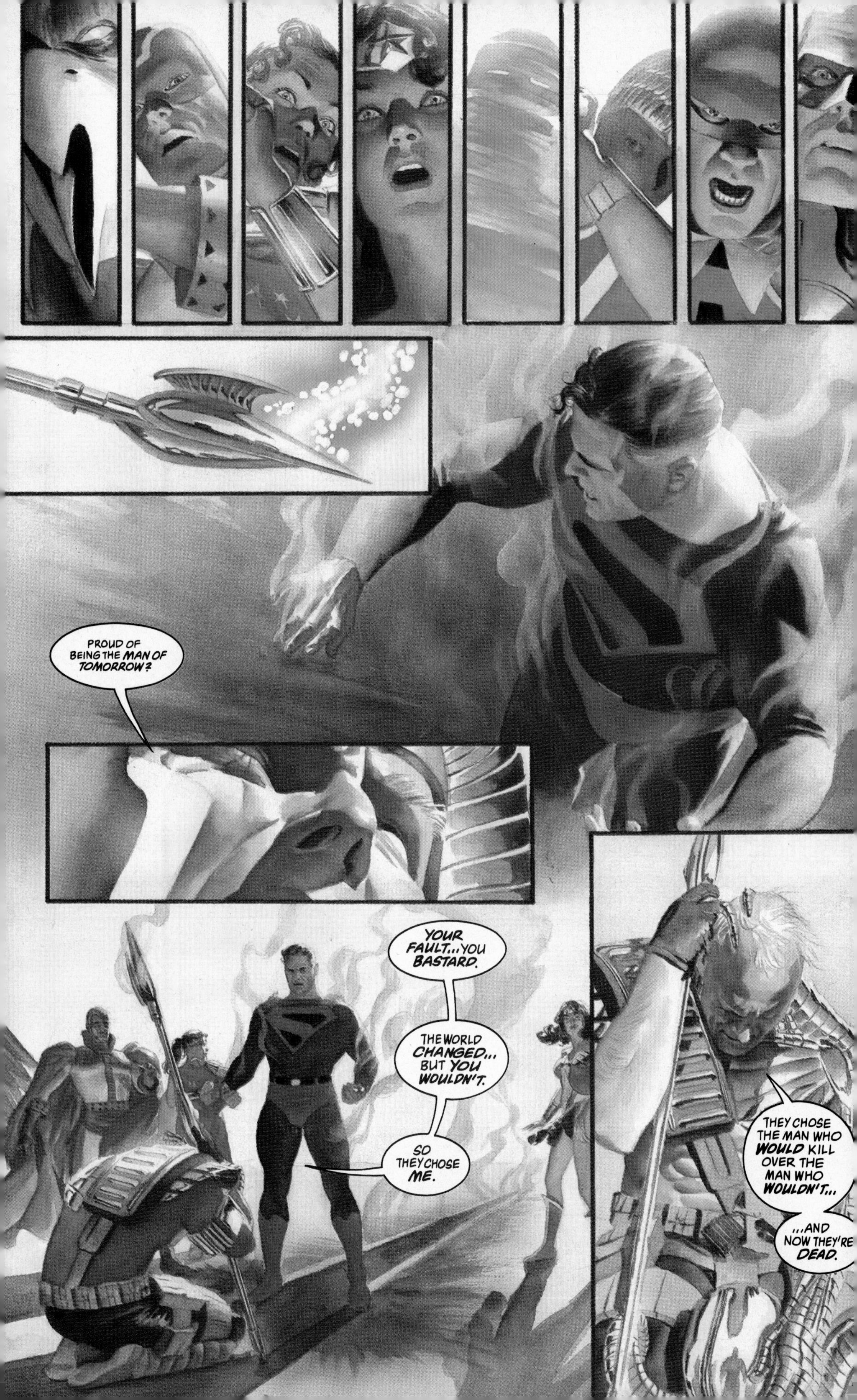

PROUD OF BEING THE MAN OF TOMORROW?
YOUR FAULT...YOU BASTARD.
THE WORLD CHANGED... BUT YOU WOULDN'T.
SO THEY CHOSE ME.
THEY CHOSE THE MAN WHO WOULD KILL OVER THE MAN WHO WOULDN'T...
...AND NOW THEY'RE DEAD.

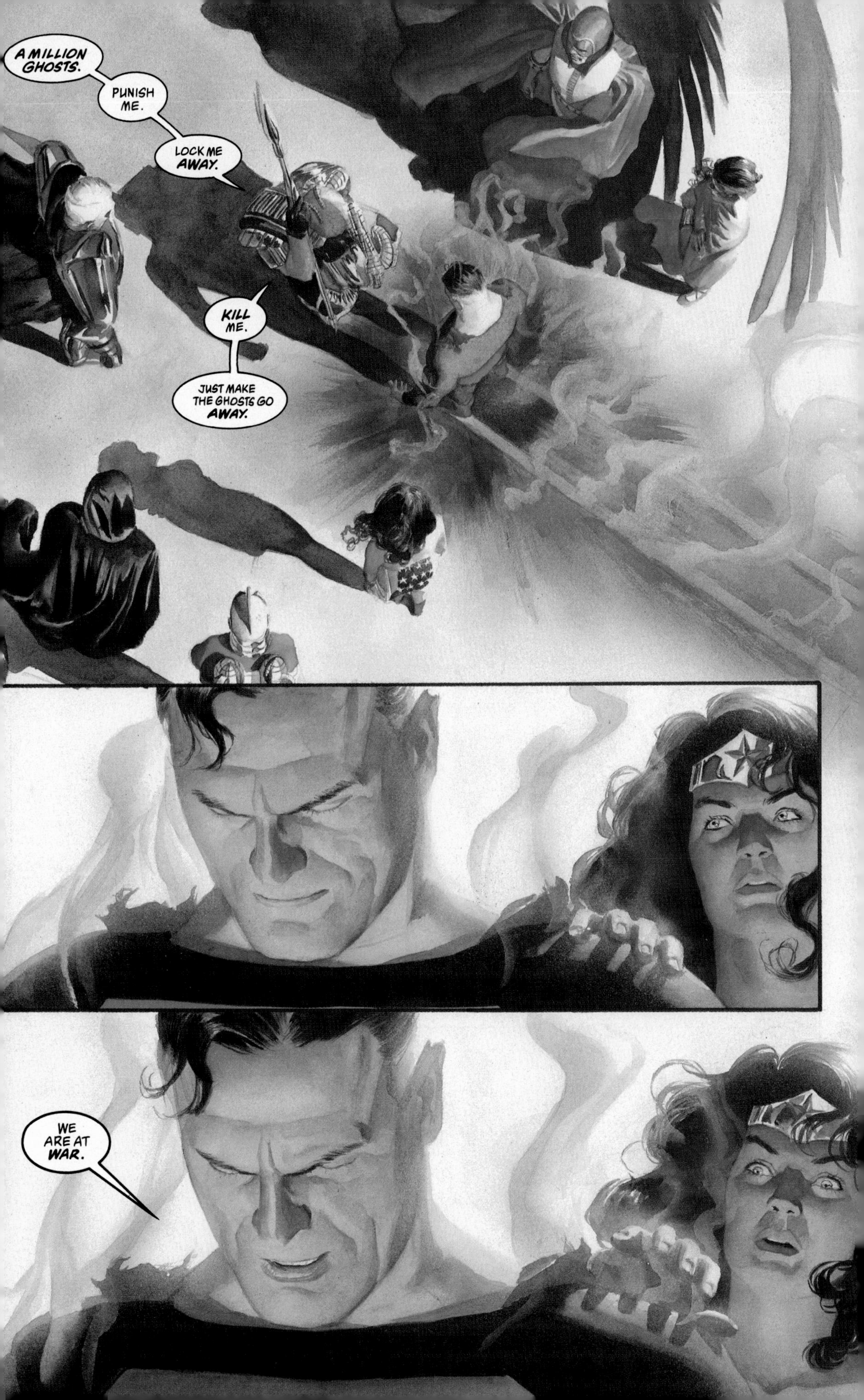
A MILLION GHOSTS.
PUNISH ME.
LOCK ME AWAY.
KILL ME.
JUST MAKE THE GHOSTS GO AWAY.
WE ARE AT WAR.

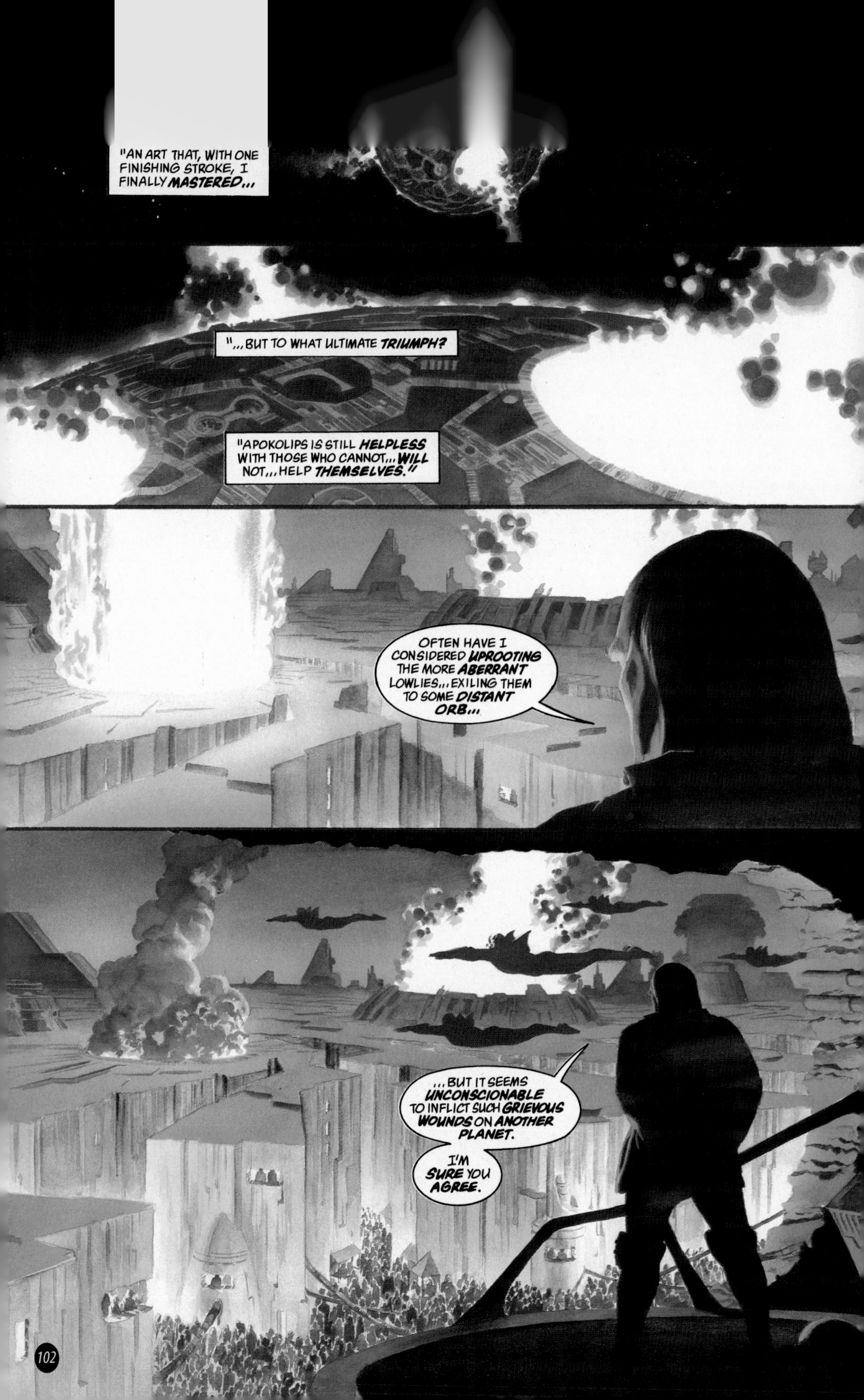
"AN ART THAT, WITH ONE FINISHING STROKE, I FINALLY MASTERED...
"...BUT TO WHAT ULTIMATE TRIUMPH?
"APOKOLIPS IS STILL HELPLESS WITH THOSE WHO CANNOT... WILL NOT... HELP THEMSELVES."
OFTEN HAVE I CONSIDERED UPROOTING THE MORE ABERRANT LOWLIES... EXILING THEM TO SOME DISTANT ORB...
...BUT IT SEEMS UNCONSCIONABLE TO INFLICT SUCH GRIEVOUS WOUNDS ON ANOTHER PLANET.
I'M SURE YOU AGREE.

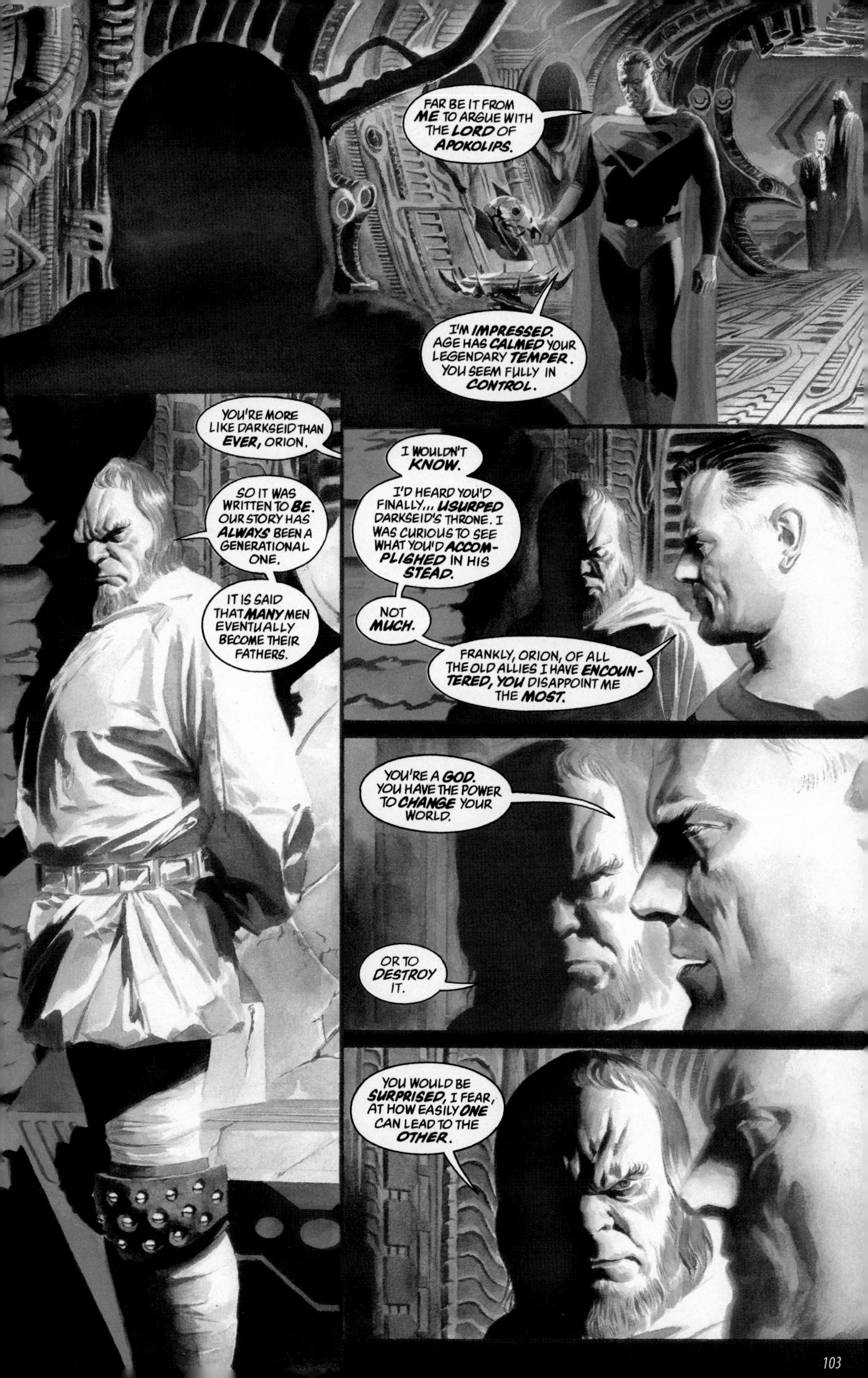

FAR BE IT FROM ME TO ARGUE WITH THE LORD OF APOKOLIPS.
I'M IMPRESSED. AGE HAS CALMED YOUR LEGENDARY TEMPER. YOU SEEM FULLY IN CONTROL.
YOU'RE MORE LIKE DARKSEID THAN EVER, ORION.
SO IT WAS WRITTEN TO BE. OUR STORY HAS ALWAYS BEEN A GENERATIONAL ONE.
IT IS SAID THAT MANY MEN EVENTUALLY BECOME THEIR FATHERS.
I WOULDN'T KNOW.
I'D HEARD YOU'D FINALLY... USURPED DARKSEID'S THRONE. I WAS CURIOUS TO SEE WHAT YOU'D ACCOMPLISHED IN HIS STEAD.
NOT MUCH.
FRANKLY, ORION, OF ALL THE OLD ALLIES I HAVE ENCOUNTERED, YOU DISAPPOINT ME THE MOST.
YOU'RE A GOD. YOU HAVE THE POWER TO CHANGE YOUR WORLD.
OR TO DESTROY IT.
YOU WOULD BE SURPRISED, I FEAR, AT HOW EASILY ONE CAN LEAD TO THE OTHER.

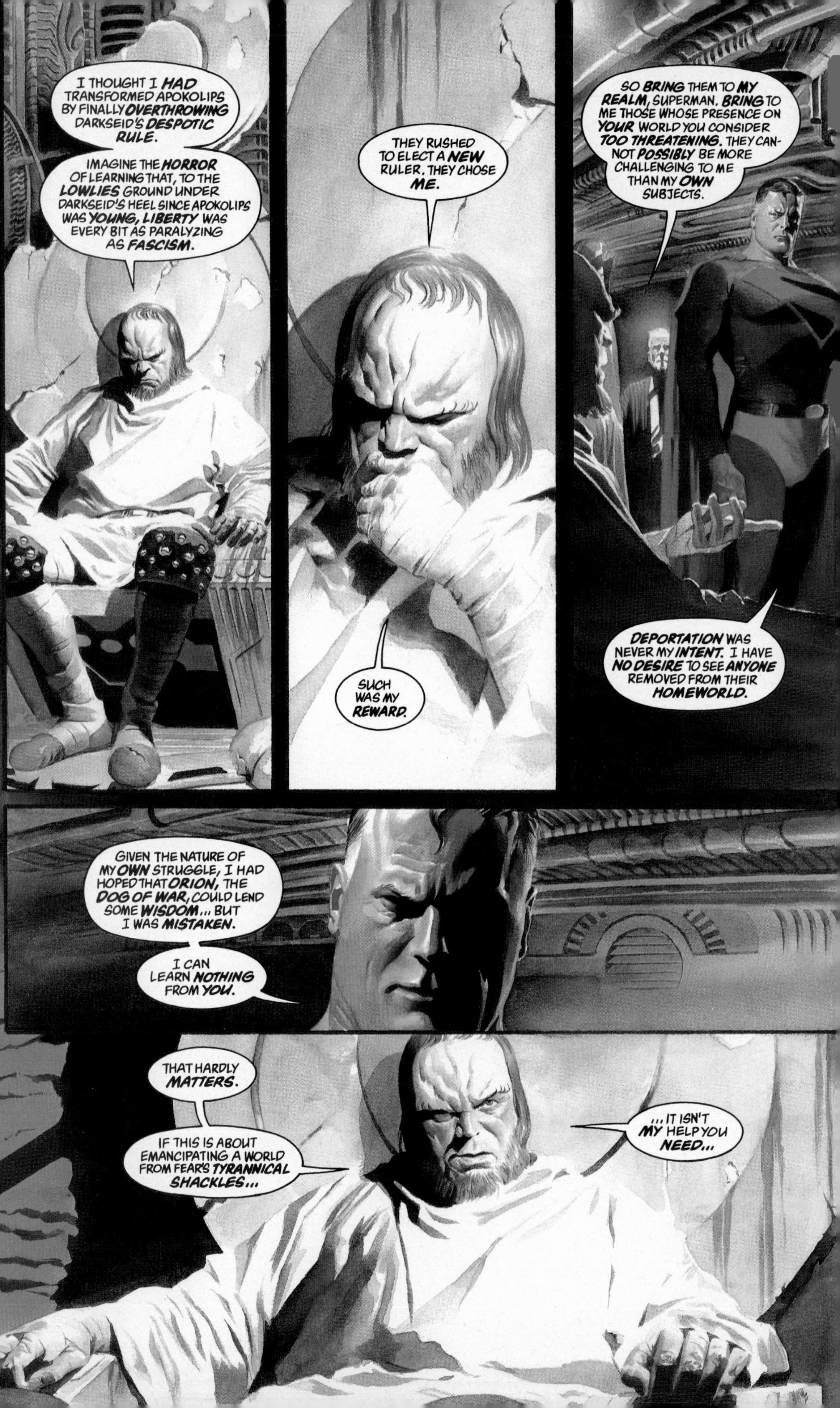
I THOUGHT I HAD TRANSFORMED APOKOLIPS BY FINALLY OVERTHROWING DARKSEID'S DESPOTIC RULE.
IMAGINE THE HORROR OF LEARNING THAT, TO THE LOWLIES GROUND UNDER DARKSEID'S HEEL SINCE APOKOLIPS WAS YOUNG, LIBERTY WAS EVERY BIT AS PARALYZING AS FASCISM.
THEY RUSHED TO ELECT A NEW RULER. THEY CHOSE ME.
SUCH WAS MY REWARD.
SO BRING THEM TO MY REALM, SUPERMAN. BRING TO ME THOSE WHOSE PRESENCE ON YOUR WORLD YOU CONSIDER TOO THREATENING. THEY CANNOT POSSIBLY BE MORE CHALLENGING TO ME THAN MY OWN SUBJECTS.
DEPORTATION WAS NEVER MY INTENT. I HAVE NO DESIRE TO SEE ANYONE REMOVED FROM THEIR HOMEWORLD.
GIVEN THE NATURE OF MY OWN STRUGGLE, I HAD HOPED THAT ORION, THE DOG OF WAR, COULD LEND SOME WISDOM... BUT I WAS MISTAKEN.
I CAN LEARN NOTHING FROM YOU.
THAT HARDLY MATTERS.
IF THIS IS ABOUT EMANCIPATING A WORLD FROM FEAR'S TYRANNICAL SHACKLES...
...IT ISN'T MY HELP YOU NEED...

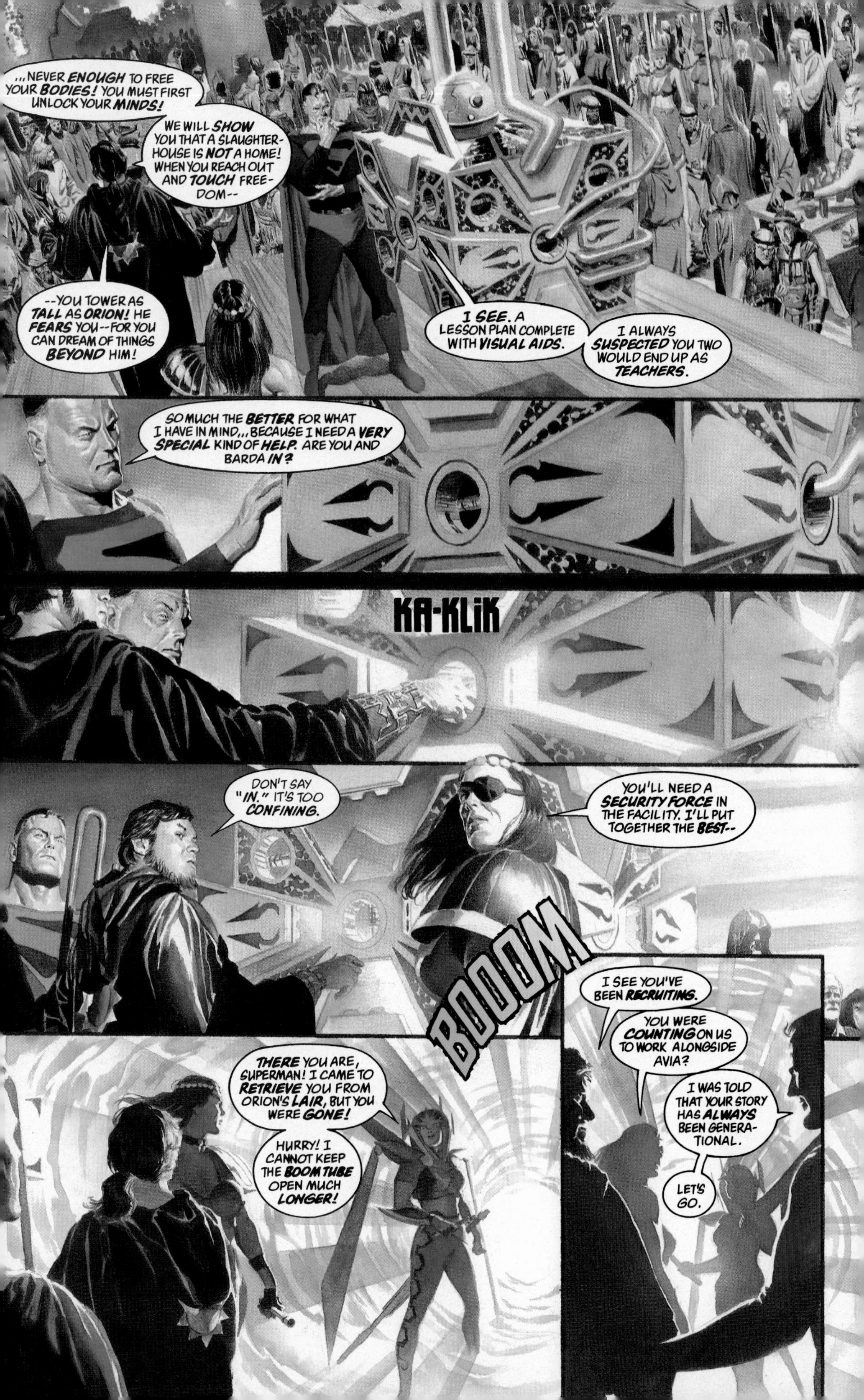
...NEVER ENOUGH TO FREE YOUR BODIES! YOU MUST FIRST UNLOCK YOUR MINDS!
WE WILL SHOW YOU THAT A SLAUGHTER-HOUSE IS NOT A HOME! WHEN YOU REACH OUT AND TOUCH FREE-DOM--
--YOU TOWER AS TALL AS ORION! HE FEARS YOU--FOR YOU CAN DREAM OF THINGS BEYOND HIM!
I SEE. A LESSON PLAN COMPLETE WITH VISUAL AIDS.
I ALWAYS SUSPECTED YOU TWO WOULD END UP AS TEACHERS.
SO MUCH THE BETTER FOR WHAT I HAVE IN MIND... BECAUSE I NEED A VERY SPECIAL KIND OF HELP. ARE YOU AND BARDA IN?
KA-KLIK
DON'T SAY "IN." IT'S TOO CONFINING.
YOU'LL NEED A SECURITY FORCE IN THE FACILITY. I'LL PUT TOGETHER THE BEST--
BOOOM
THERE YOU ARE, SUPERMAN! I CAME TO RETRIEVE YOU FROM ORION'S LAIR, BUT YOU WERE GONE!
HURRY! I CANNOT KEEP THE BOOM TUBE OPEN MUCH LONGER!
I SEE YOU'VE BEEN RECRUITING.
YOU WERE COUNTING ON US TO WORK ALONGSIDE AVIA?
I WAS TOLD THAT YOUR STORY HAS ALWAYS BEEN GENERA-TIONAL.
LET'S GO.

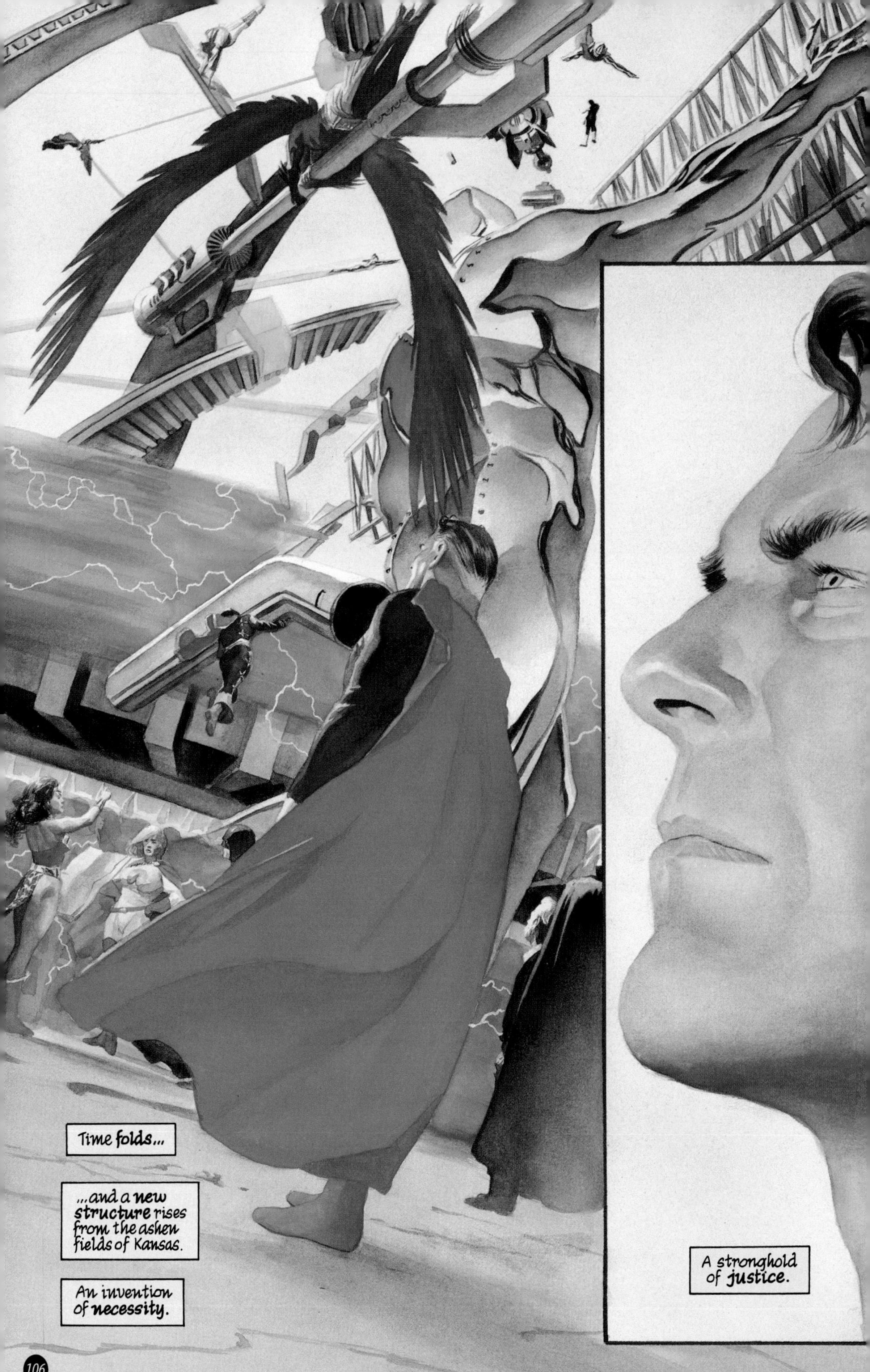

Time **folds**...
...and a **new structure** rises from the ashen fields of Kansas.
An invention of **necessity**.
A stronghold of **justice**.

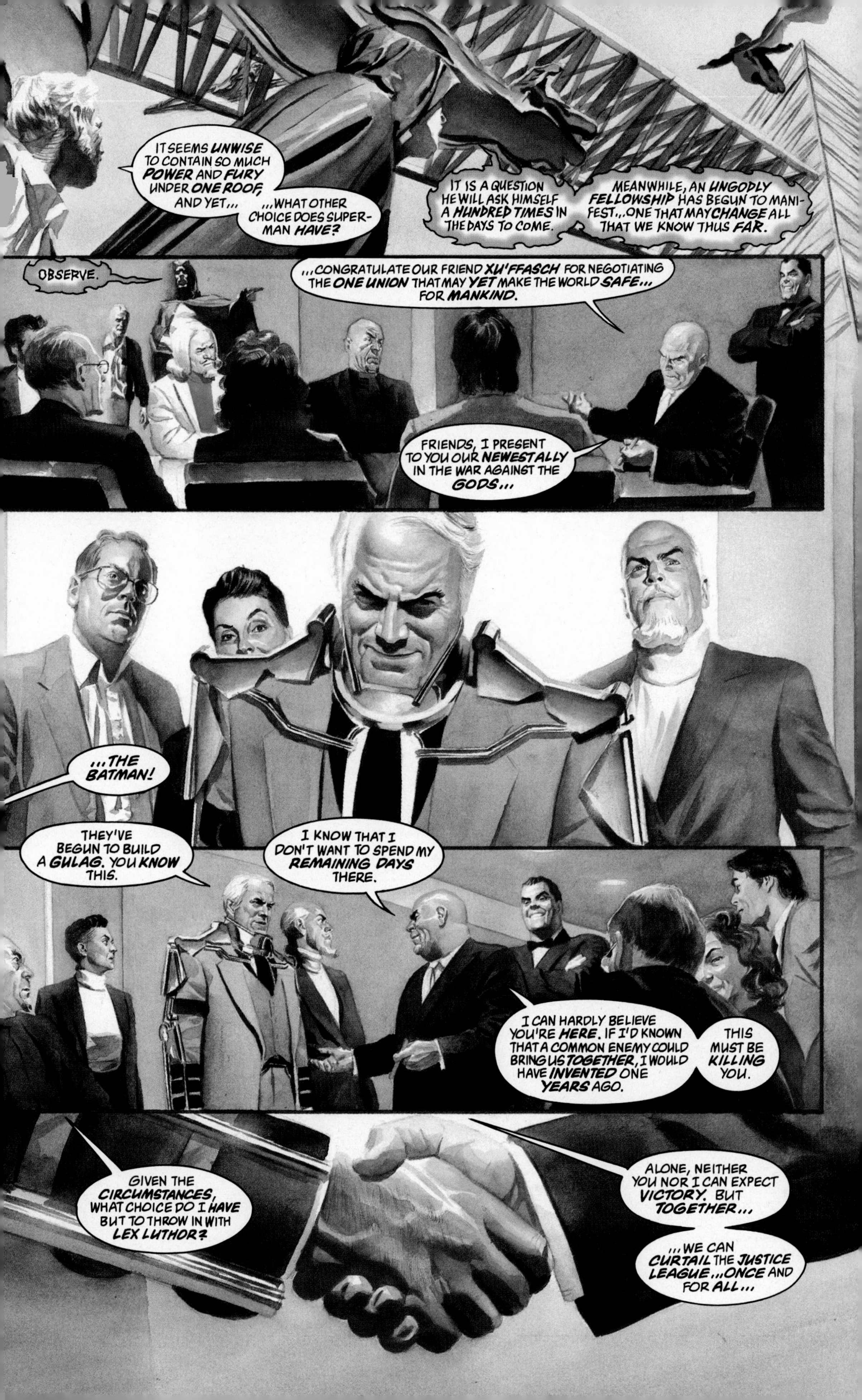

IT SEEMS UNWISE TO CONTAIN SO MUCH POWER AND FURY UNDER ONE ROOF, AND YET...
...WHAT OTHER CHOICE DOES SUPER-MAN HAVE?
IT IS A QUESTION HE WILL ASK HIMSELF A HUNDRED TIMES IN THE DAYS TO COME.
MEANWHILE, AN UNGODLY FELLOWSHIP HAS BEGUN TO MANI-FEST...ONE THAT MAY CHANGE ALL THAT WE KNOW THUS FAR.
OBSERVE.
...CONGRATULATE OUR FRIEND XU'FFASCH FOR NEGOTIATING THE ONE UNION THAT MAY YET MAKE THE WORLD SAFE... FOR MANKIND.
FRIENDS, I PRESENT TO YOU OUR NEWEST ALLY IN THE WAR AGAINST THE GODS...
...THE BATMAN!
THEY'VE BEGUN TO BUILD A GULAG. YOU KNOW THIS.
I KNOW THAT I DON'T WANT TO SPEND MY REMAINING DAYS THERE.
I CAN HARDLY BELIEVE YOU'RE HERE. IF I'D KNOWN THAT A COMMON ENEMY COULD BRING US TOGETHER, I WOULD HAVE INVENTED ONE YEARS AGO.
THIS MUST BE KILLING YOU.
GIVEN THE CIRCUMSTANCES, WHAT CHOICE DO I HAVE BUT TO THROW IN WITH LEX LUTHOR?
ALONE, NEITHER YOU NOR I CAN EXPECT VICTORY. BUT TOGETHER...
...WE CAN CURTAIL THE JUSTICE LEAGUE...ONCE AND FOR ALL...

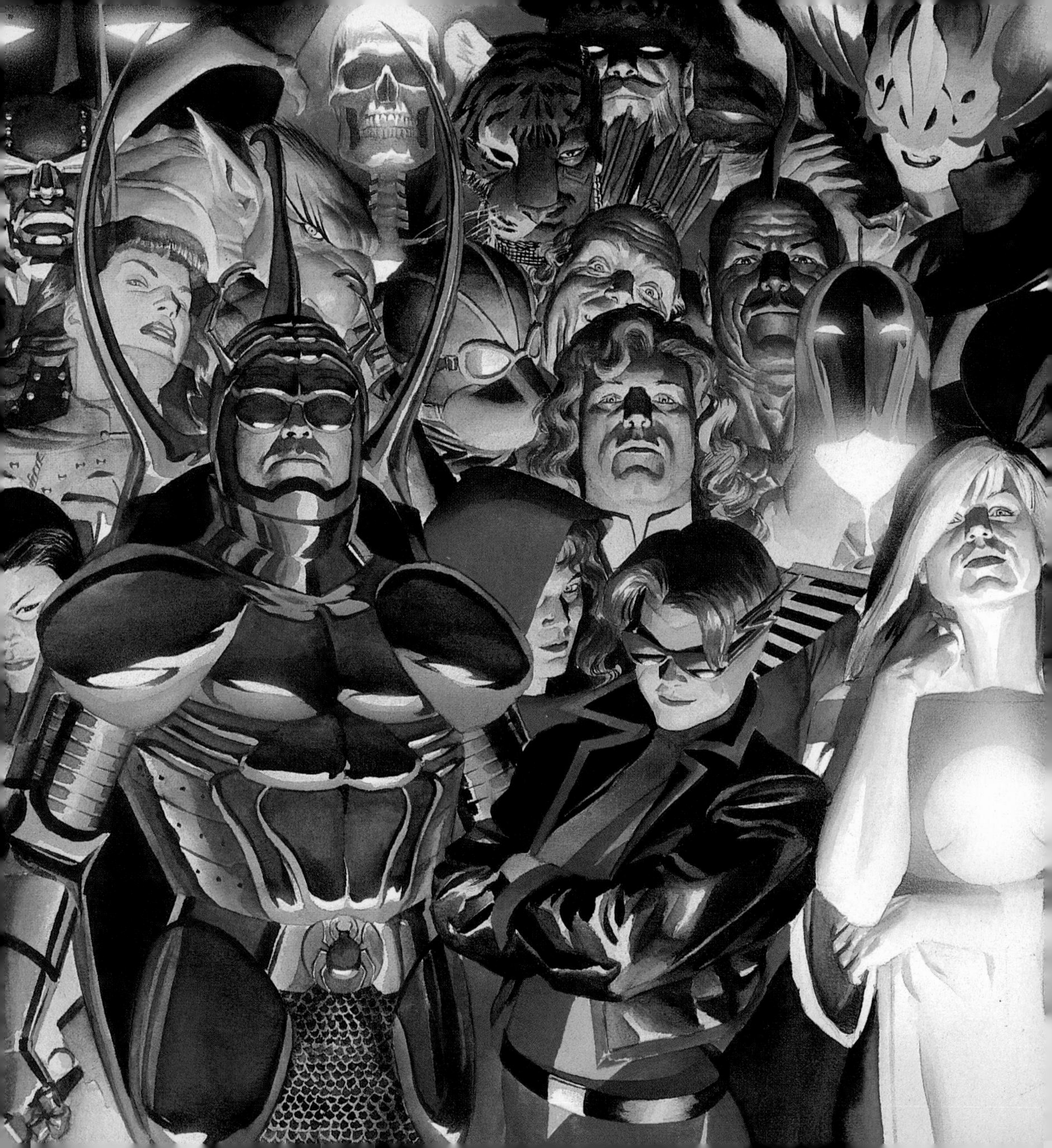

CHAPTER THREE

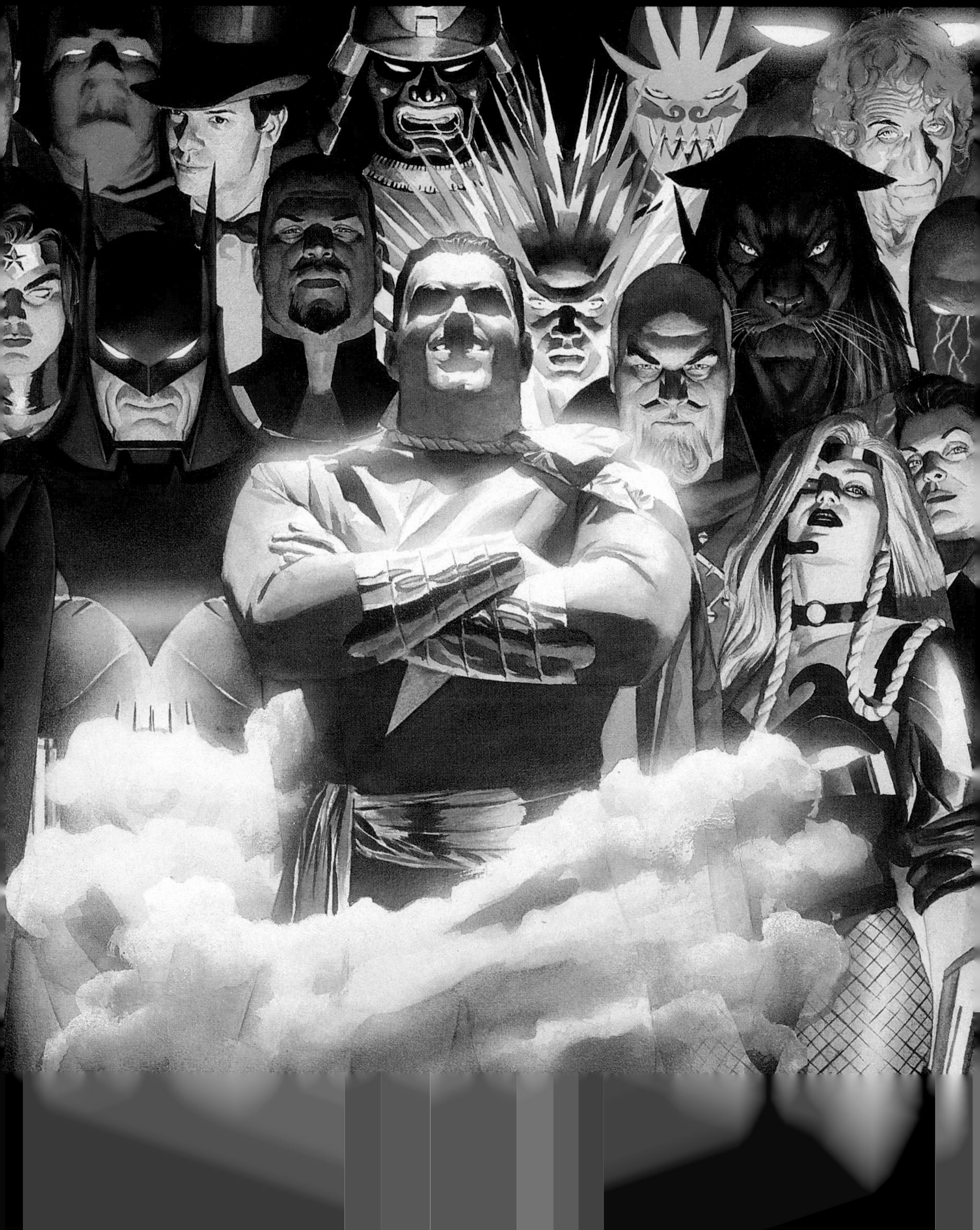

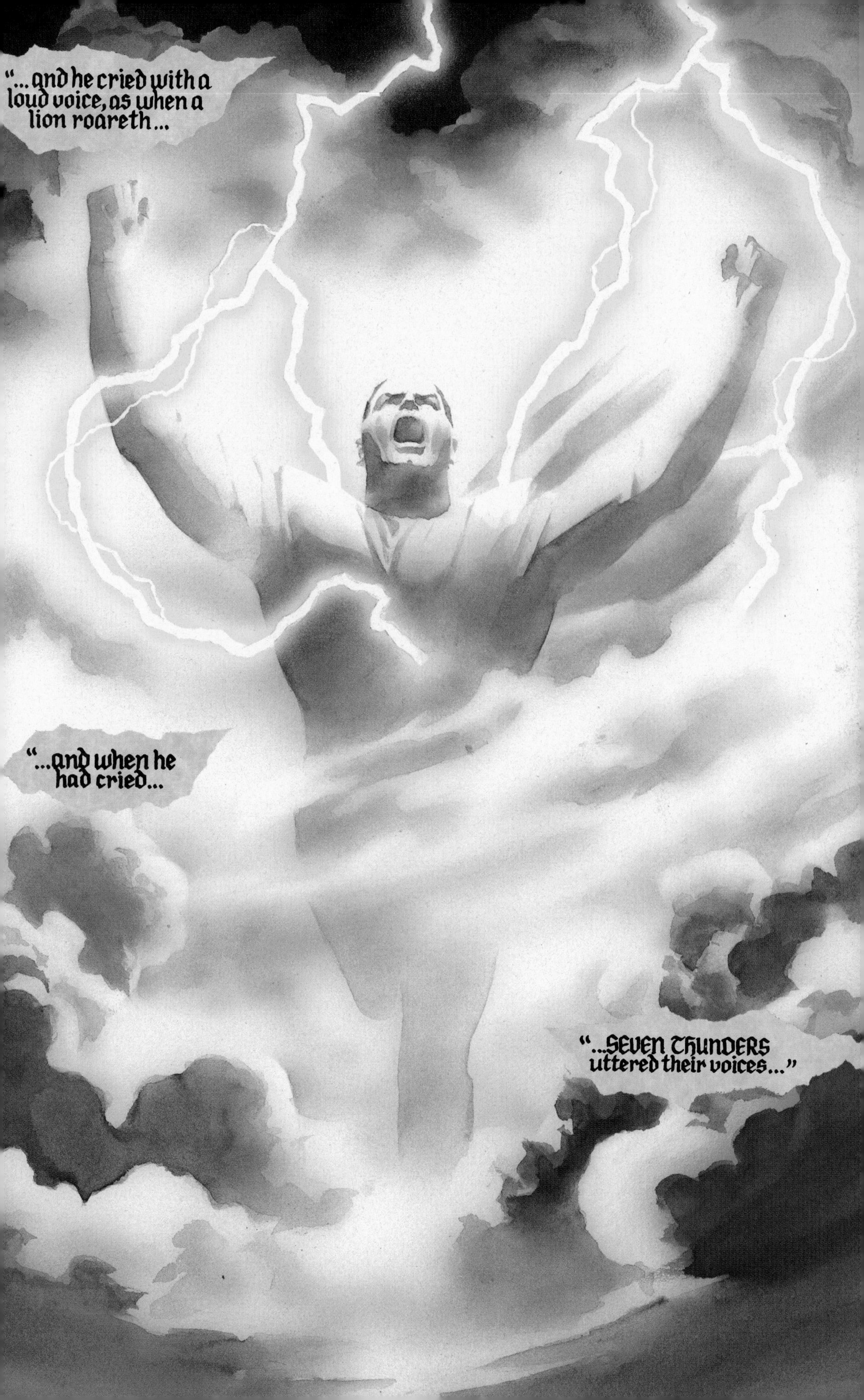
"...and he cried with a loud voice, as when a lion roareth...
"...and when he had cried...
"...SEVEN THUNDERS uttered their voices..."

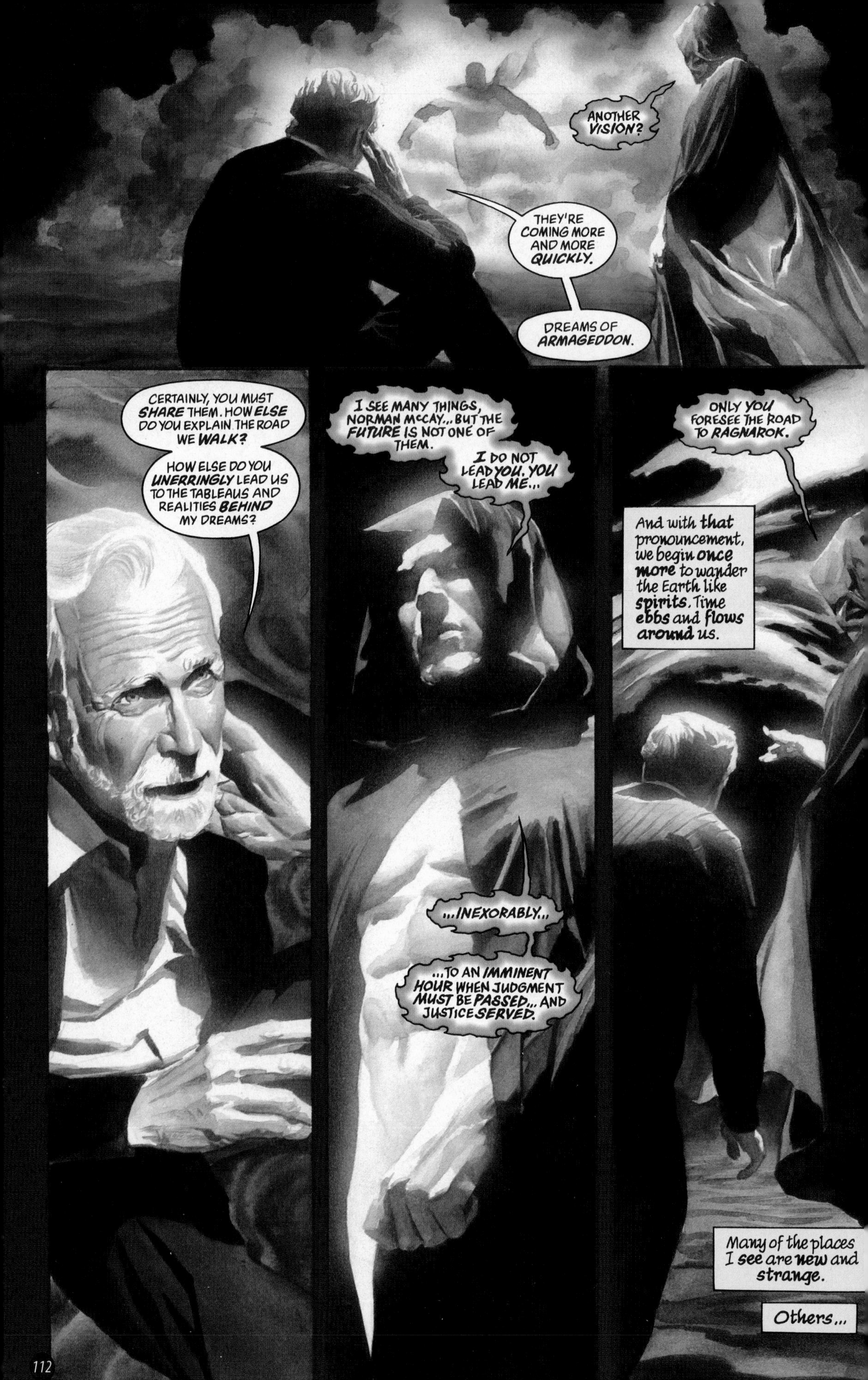
ANOTHER VISION?
THEY'RE COMING MORE AND MORE QUICKLY.
DREAMS OF ARMAGEDDON.
CERTAINLY, YOU MUST SHARE THEM. HOW ELSE DO YOU EXPLAIN THE ROAD WE WALK?
HOW ELSE DO YOU UNERRINGLY LEAD US TO THE TABLEAUS AND REALITIES BEHIND MY DREAMS?
I SEE MANY THINGS, NORMAN McCAY... BUT THE FUTURE IS NOT ONE OF THEM.
I DO NOT LEAD YOU. YOU LEAD ME...
...INEXORABLY...
...TO AN IMMINENT HOUR WHEN JUDGMENT MUST BE PASSED... AND JUSTICE SERVED.
ONLY YOU FORESEE THE ROAD TO RAGNAROK.
And with that pronouncement, we begin once more to wander the Earth like spirits. Time ebbs and flows around us.
Many of the places I see are new and strange.
Others...

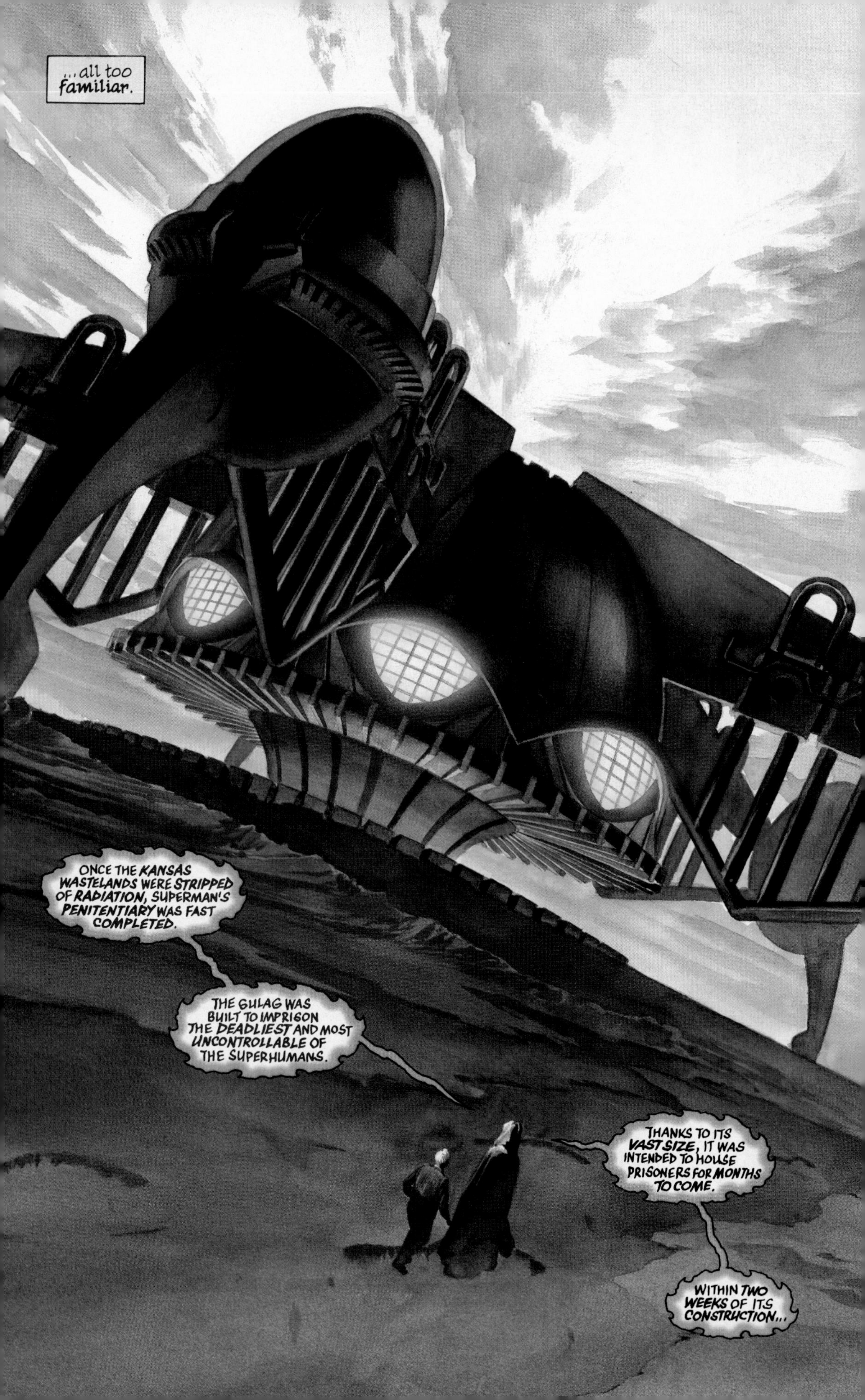
...all too familiar.
ONCE THE KANSAS WASTELANDS WERE STRIPPED OF RADIATION, SUPERMAN'S PENITENTIARY WAS FAST COMPLETED.
THE GULAG WAS BUILT TO IMPRISON THE DEADLIEST AND MOST UNCONTROLLABLE OF THE SUPERHUMANS.
THANKS TO ITS VAST SIZE, IT WAS INTENDED TO HOUSE PRISONERS FOR MONTHS TO COME.
WITHIN TWO WEEKS OF ITS CONSTRUCTION...

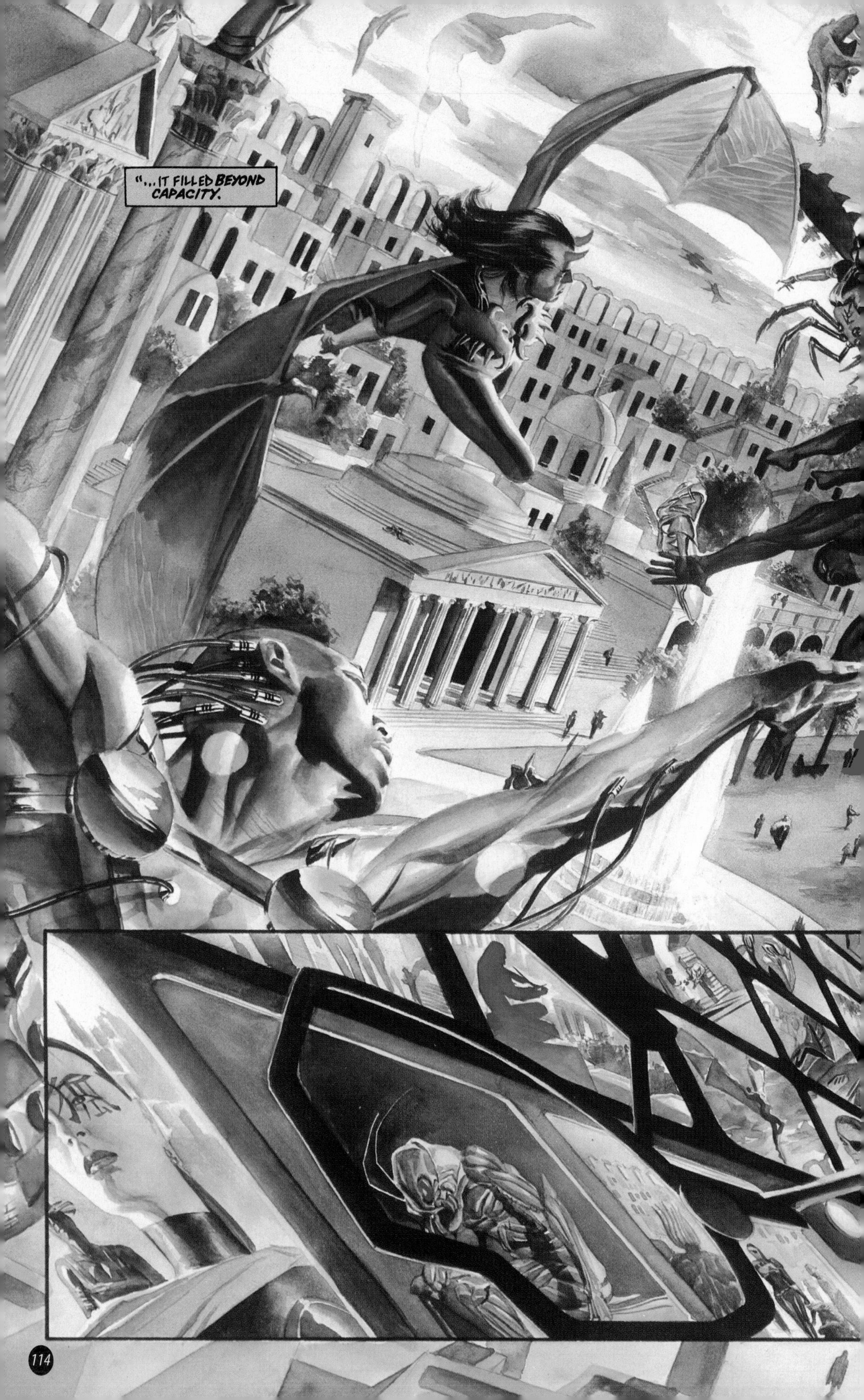
"...IT FILLED BEYOND CAPACITY.

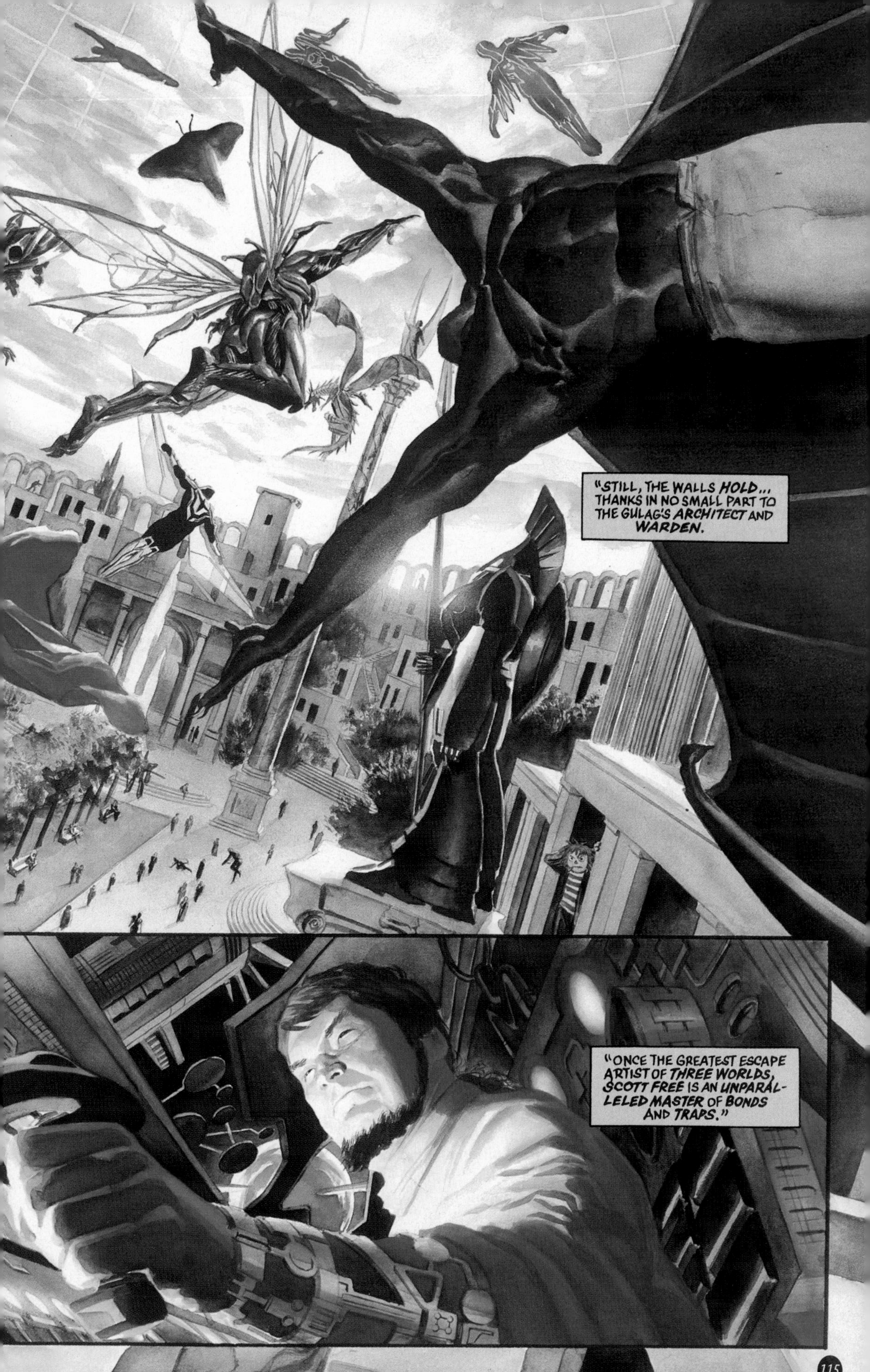
"STILL, THE WALLS HOLD... THANKS IN NO SMALL PART TO THE GULAG'S ARCHITECT AND WARDEN.
"ONCE THE GREATEST ESCAPE ARTIST OF THREE WORLDS, SCOTT FREE IS AN UNPARALLELED MASTER OF BONDS AND TRAPS."

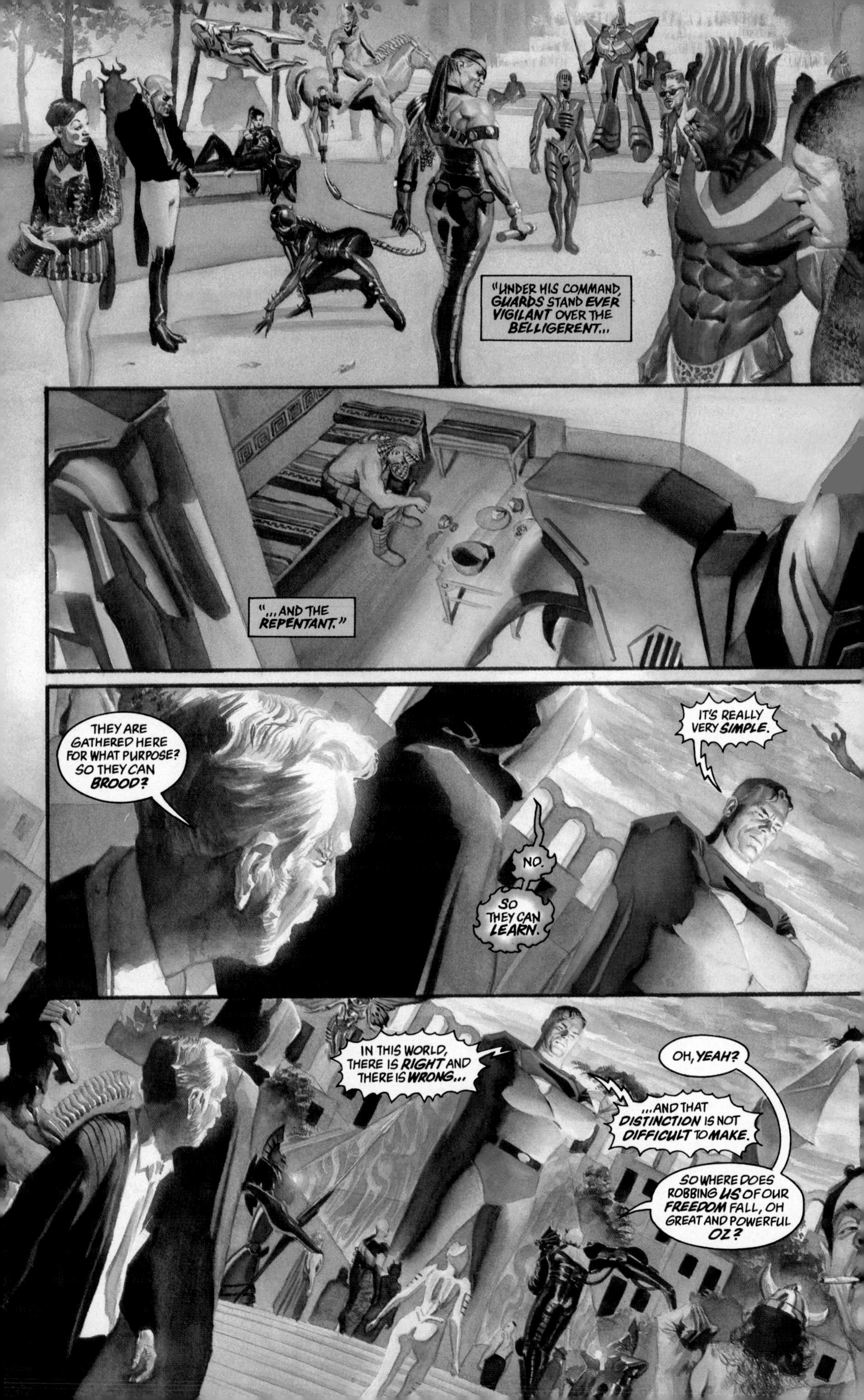
"UNDER HIS COMMAND, GUARDS STAND EVER VIGILANT OVER THE BELLIGERENT...
"...AND THE REPENTANT."
THEY ARE GATHERED HERE FOR WHAT PURPOSE? SO THEY CAN BROOD?
IT'S REALLY VERY SIMPLE.
NO.
SO THEY CAN LEARN.
IN THIS WORLD, THERE IS RIGHT AND THERE IS WRONG...
...AND THAT DISTINCTION IS NOT DIFFICULT TO MAKE.
OH, YEAH?
SO WHERE DOES ROBBING US OF OUR FREEDOM FALL, OH GREAT AND POWERFUL OZ?

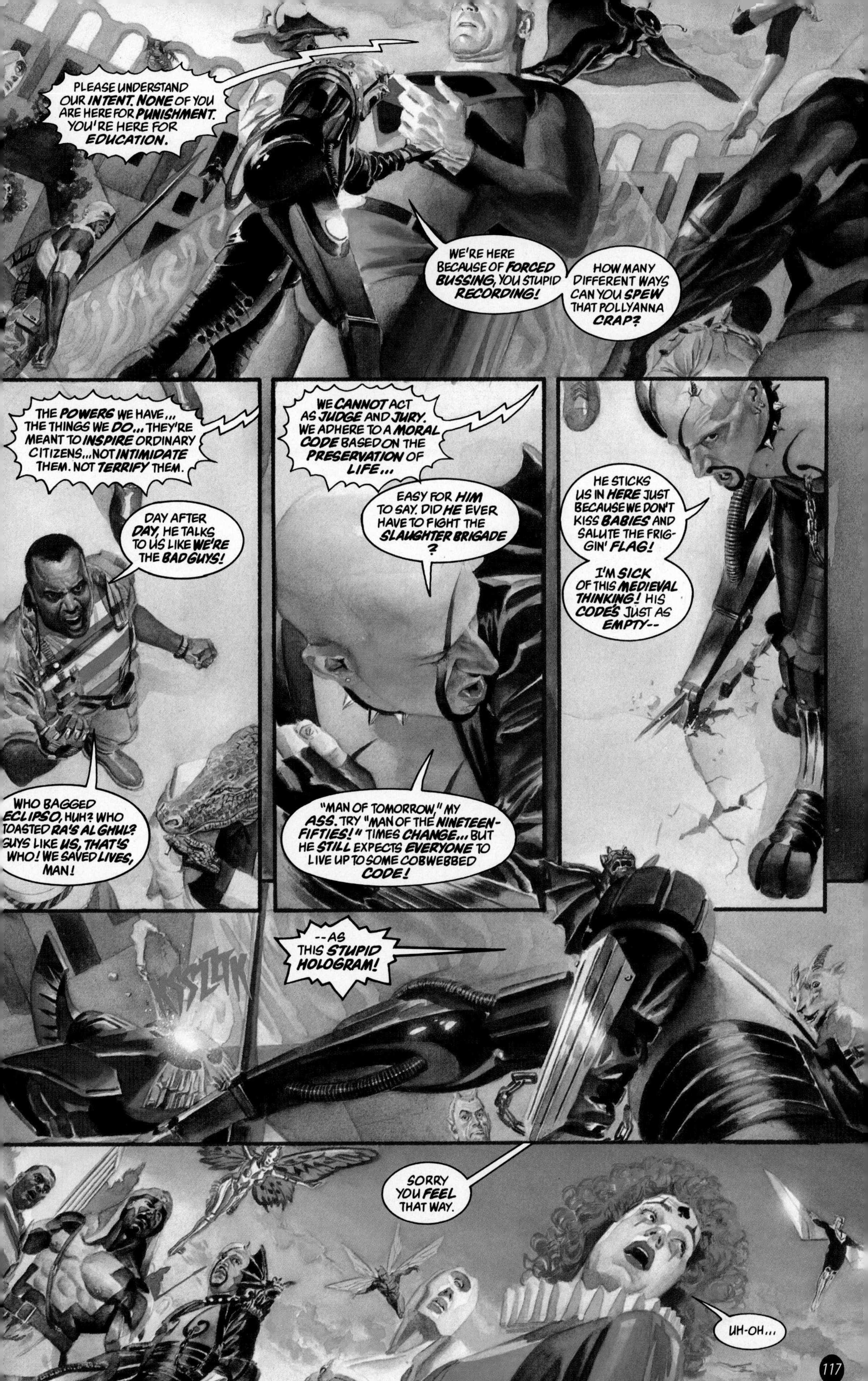
PLEASE UNDERSTAND OUR INTENT. NONE OF YOU ARE HERE FOR PUNISHMENT. YOU'RE HERE FOR EDUCATION.
WE'RE HERE BECAUSE OF FORCED BUSSING, YOU STUPID RECORDING!
HOW MANY DIFFERENT WAYS CAN YOU SPEW THAT POLLYANNA CRAP?
THE POWERS WE HAVE... THE THINGS WE DO... THEY'RE MEANT TO INSPIRE ORDINARY CITIZENS... NOT INTIMIDATE THEM. NOT TERRIFY THEM.
DAY AFTER DAY, HE TALKS TO US LIKE WE'RE THE BAD GUYS!
WHO BAGGED ECLIPSO, HUH? WHO TOASTED RA'S AL GHUL? GUYS LIKE US, THAT'S WHO! WE SAVED LIVES, MAN!
WE CANNOT ACT AS JUDGE AND JURY. WE ADHERE TO A MORAL CODE BASED ON THE PRESERVATION OF LIFE...
EASY FOR HIM TO SAY. DID HE EVER HAVE TO FIGHT THE SLAUGHTER BRIGADE?
"MAN OF TOMORROW," MY ASS. TRY "MAN OF THE NINETEEN-FIFTIES!" TIMES CHANGE... BUT HE STILL EXPECTS EVERYONE TO LIVE UP TO SOME COBWEBBED CODE!
HE STICKS US IN HERE JUST BECAUSE WE DON'T KISS BABIES AND SALUTE THE FRIG-GIN' FLAG!
I'M SICK OF THIS MEDIEVAL THINKING! HIS CODE'S JUST AS EMPTY--
--AS THIS STUPID HOLOGRAM!
KSSZZK
SORRY YOU FEEL THAT WAY.
UH-OH...

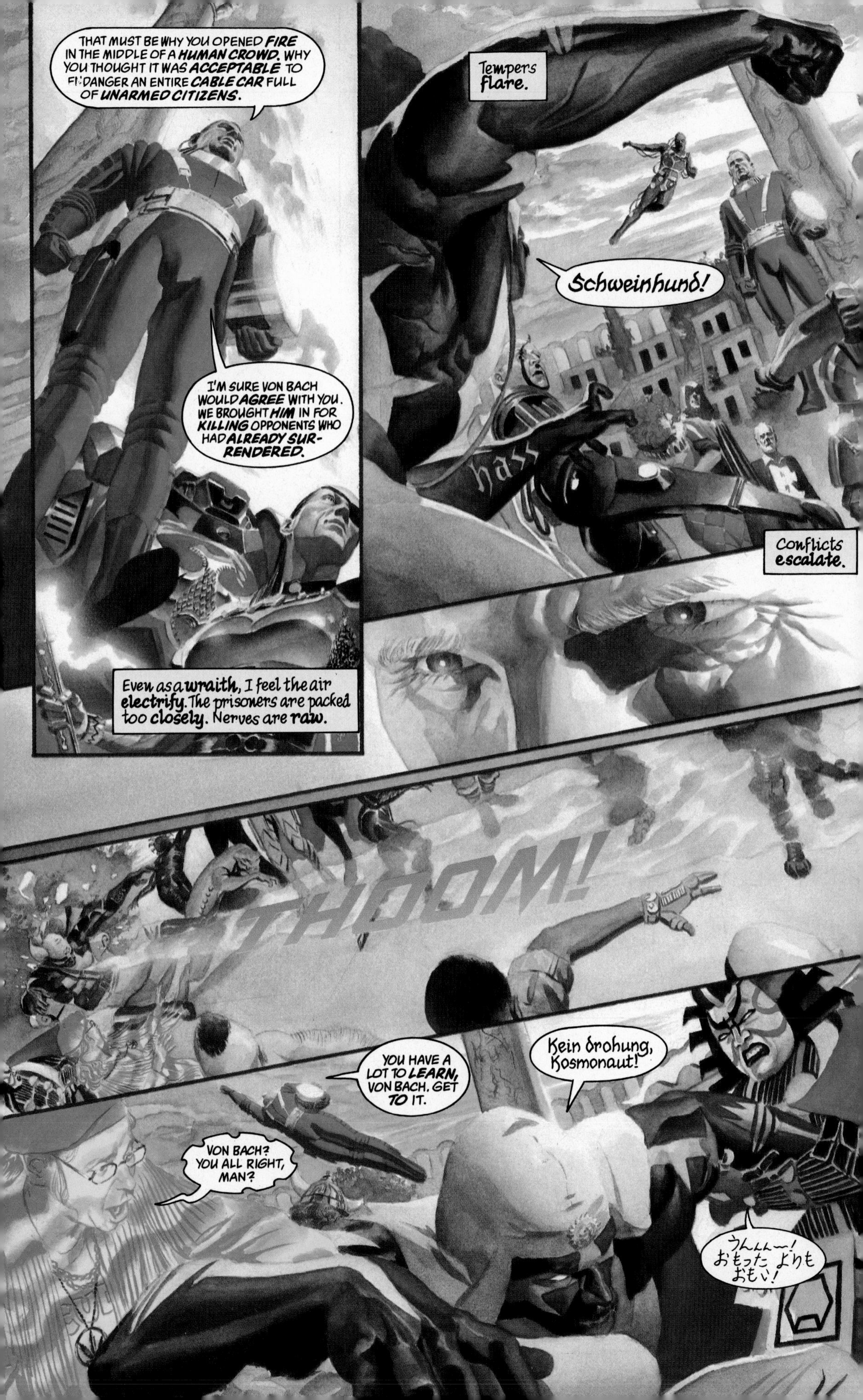
THAT MUST BE WHY YOU OPENED FIRE IN THE MIDDLE OF A HUMAN CROWD. WHY YOU THOUGHT IT WAS ACCEPTABLE TO ENDANGER AN ENTIRE CABLE CAR FULL OF UNARMED CITIZENS.
I'M SURE VON BACH WOULD AGREE WITH YOU. WE BROUGHT HIM IN FOR KILLING OPPONENTS WHO HAD ALREADY SURRENDERED.
Even as a wraith, I feel the air electrify. The prisoners are packed too closely. Nerves are raw.
Tempers flare.
Schweinhund!
hass
Conflicts escalate.
THOOM!
YOU HAVE A LOT TO LEARN, VON BACH. GET TO IT.
Kein drohung, Kosmonaut!
VON BACH? YOU ALL RIGHT, MAN?
うんんん〜！
おもったよりも
おもい！

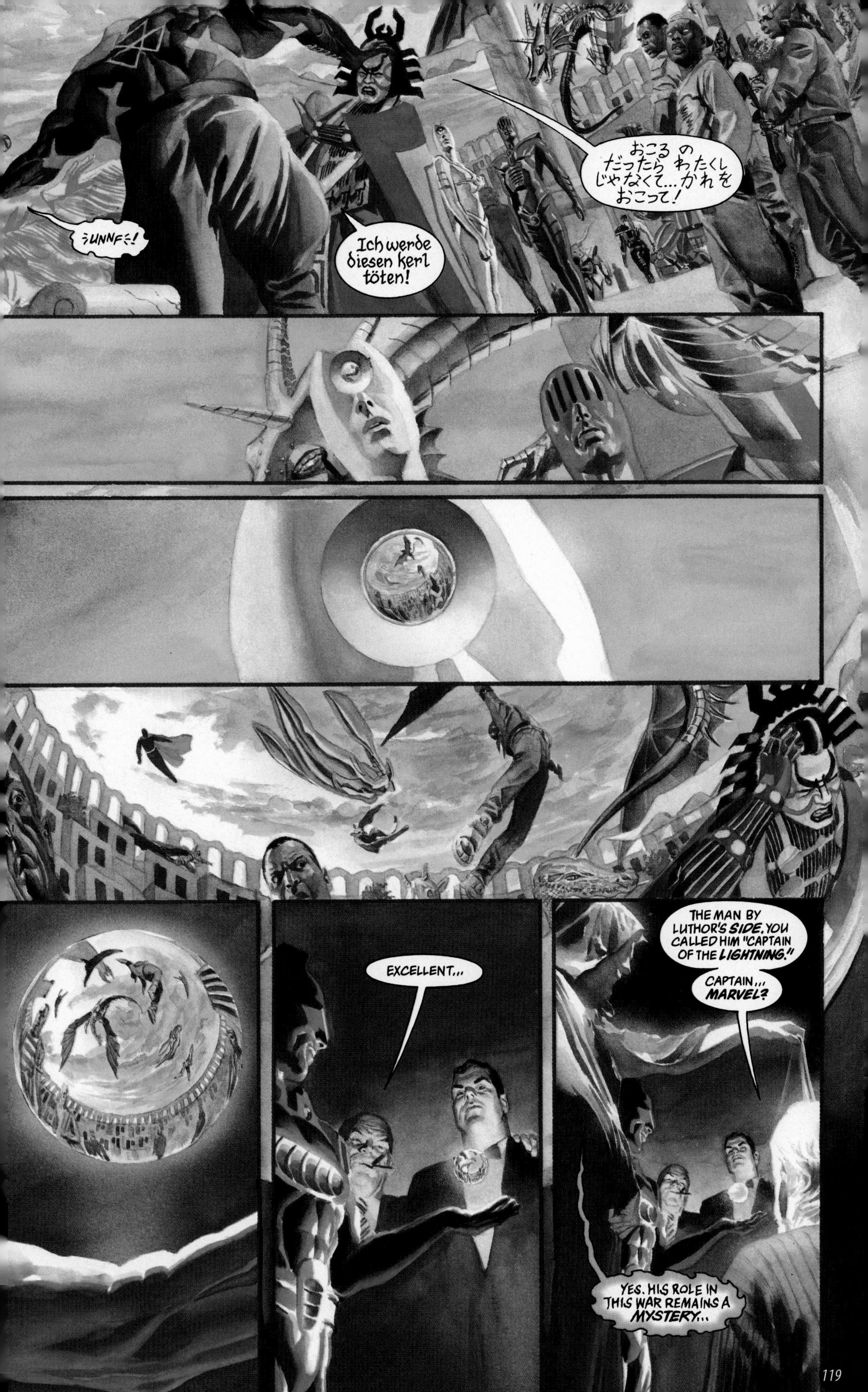
UNNF!
Ich werde diesen Kerl töten!
おこる の
だったら わたくし
じゃなくて…かれを
おこって!
EXCELLENT...
THE MAN BY LUTHOR'S SIDE. YOU CALLED HIM "CAPTAIN OF THE LIGHTNING."
CAPTAIN... MARVEL?
YES. HIS ROLE IN THIS WAR REMAINS A MYSTERY...

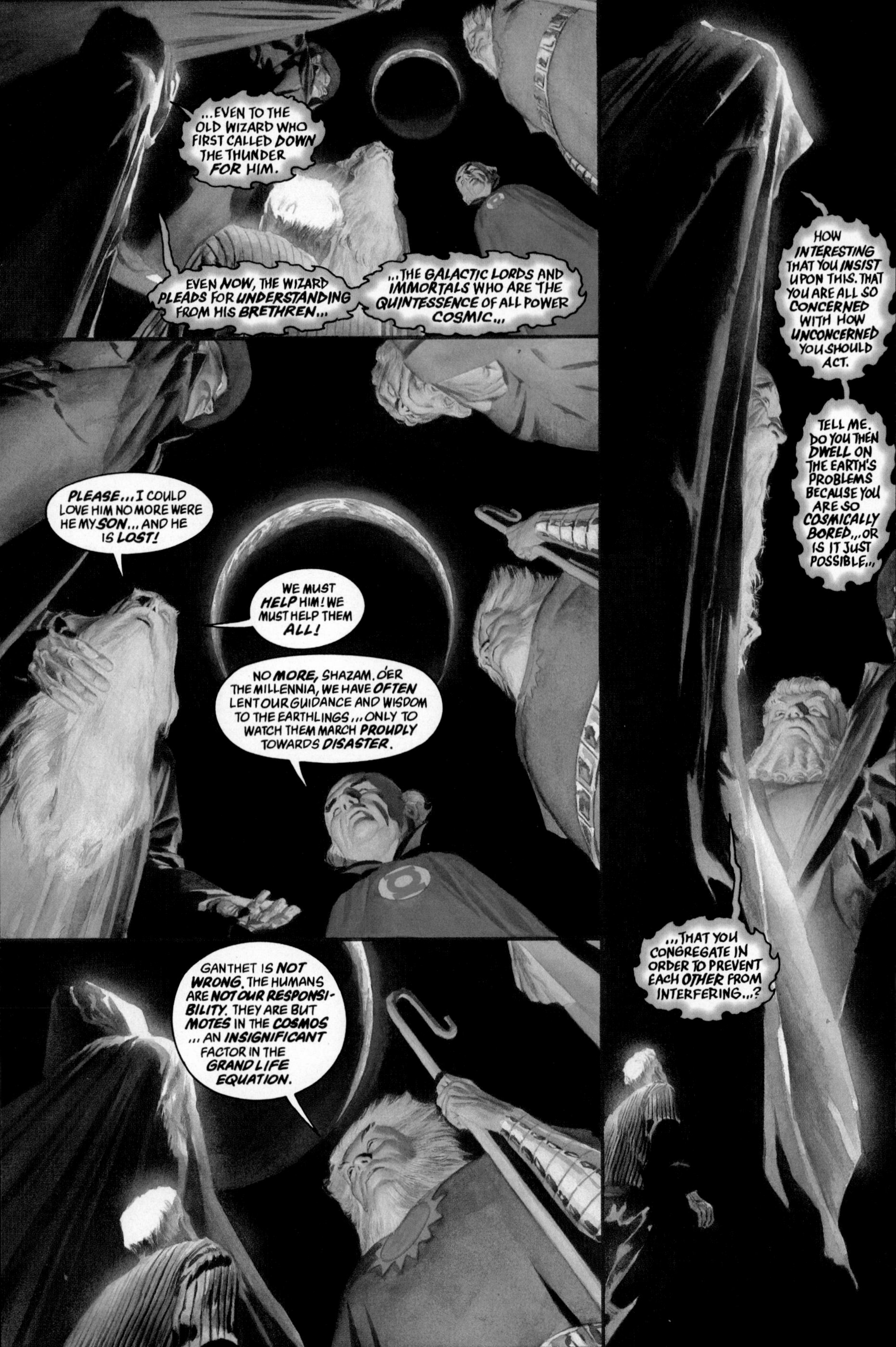
...EVEN TO THE OLD WIZARD WHO FIRST CALLED DOWN THE THUNDER FOR HIM.
EVEN NOW, THE WIZARD PLEADS FOR UNDERSTANDING FROM HIS BRETHREN...
...THE GALACTIC LORDS AND IMMORTALS WHO ARE THE QUINTESSENCE OF ALL POWER COSMIC...
PLEASE... I COULD LOVE HIM NO MORE WERE HE MY SON... AND HE IS LOST!
WE MUST HELP HIM! WE MUST HELP THEM ALL!
NO MORE, SHAZAM. O'ER THE MILLENNIA, WE HAVE OFTEN LENT OUR GUIDANCE AND WISDOM TO THE EARTHLINGS... ONLY TO WATCH THEM MARCH PROUDLY TOWARDS DISASTER.
GANTHET IS NOT WRONG. THE HUMANS ARE NOT OUR RESPONSI-BILITY. THEY ARE BUT MOTES IN THE COSMOS ...AN INSIGNIFICANT FACTOR IN THE GRAND LIFE EQUATION.
HOW INTERESTING THAT YOU INSIST UPON THIS. THAT YOU ARE ALL SO CONCERNED WITH HOW UNCONCERNED YOU SHOULD ACT.
TELL ME. DO YOU THEN DWELL ON THE EARTH'S PROBLEMS BECAUSE YOU ARE SO COSMICALLY BORED... OR IS IT JUST POSSIBLE...
...THAT YOU CONGREGATE IN ORDER TO PREVENT EACH OTHER FROM INTERFERING...?

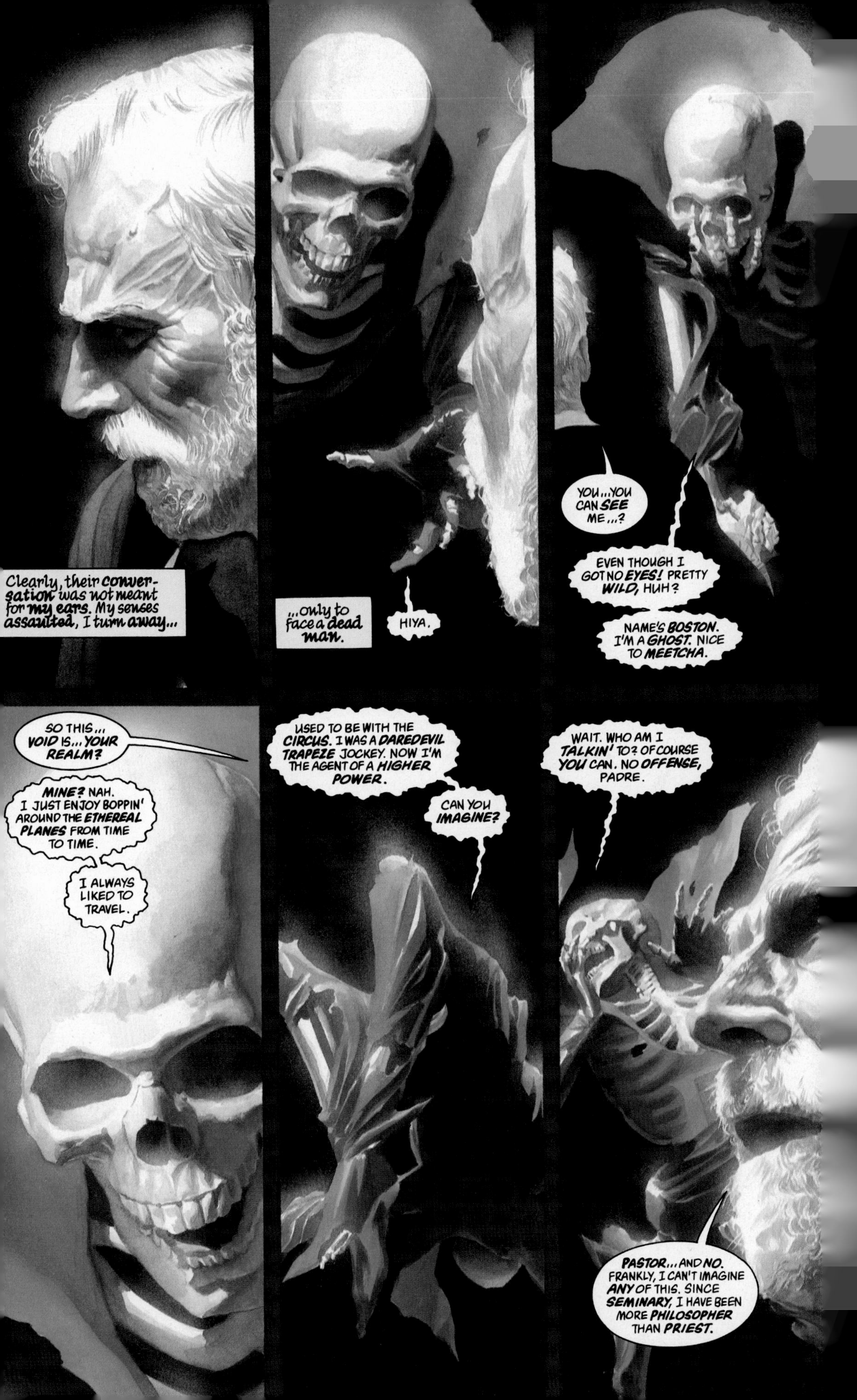
Clearly, their conversation was not meant for my ears. My senses assaulted, I turn away...
...only to face a dead man.
HIYA.
YOU...YOU CAN SEE ME...?
EVEN THOUGH I GOT NO EYES! PRETTY WILD, HUH?
NAME'S BOSTON. I'M A GHOST. NICE TO MEETCHA.
SO THIS... VOID IS... YOUR REALM?
MINE? NAH. I JUST ENJOY BOPPIN' AROUND THE ETHEREAL PLANES FROM TIME TO TIME.
I ALWAYS LIKED TO TRAVEL.
USED TO BE WITH THE CIRCUS. I WAS A DAREDEVIL TRAPEZE JOCKEY. NOW I'M THE AGENT OF A HIGHER POWER.
CAN YOU IMAGINE?
WAIT. WHO AM I TALKIN' TO? OF COURSE YOU CAN. NO OFFENSE, PADRE.
PASTOR... AND NO. FRANKLY, I CAN'T IMAGINE ANY OF THIS. SINCE SEMINARY, I HAVE BEEN MORE PHILOSOPHER THAN PRIEST.

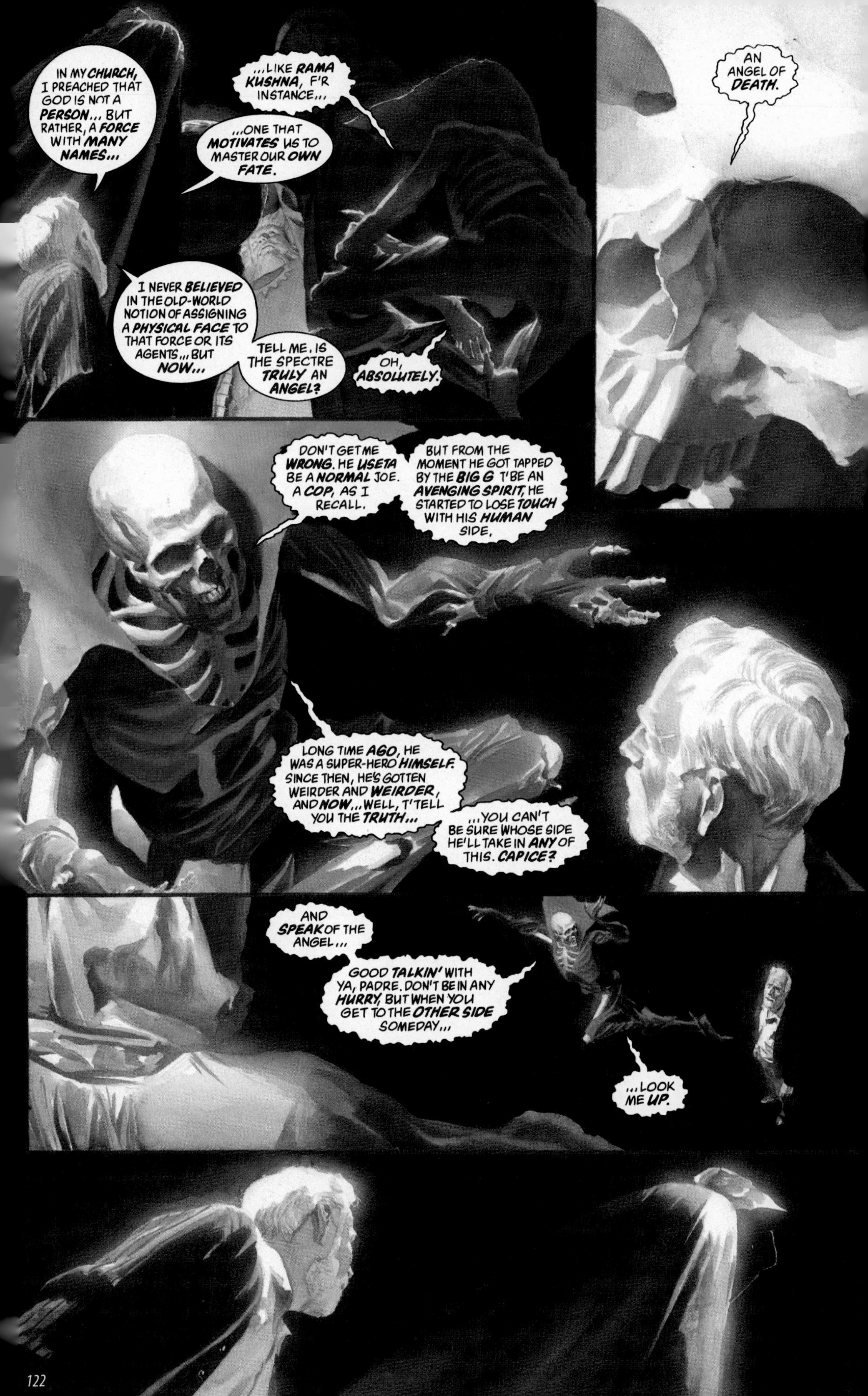

IN MY CHURCH, I PREACHED THAT GOD IS NOT A PERSON... BUT RATHER, A FORCE WITH MANY NAMES...
...LIKE RAMA KUSHNA, F'R INSTANCE...
...ONE THAT MOTIVATES US TO MASTER OUR OWN FATE.
AN ANGEL OF DEATH.
I NEVER BELIEVED IN THE OLD-WORLD NOTION OF ASSIGNING A PHYSICAL FACE TO THAT FORCE OR ITS AGENTS... BUT NOW...
TELL ME. IS THE SPECTRE TRULY AN ANGEL?
OH, ABSOLUTELY.
DON'T GET ME WRONG. HE USETA BE A NORMAL JOE. A COP, AS I RECALL.
BUT FROM THE MOMENT HE GOT TAPPED BY THE BIG G T'BE AN AVENGING SPIRIT, HE STARTED TO LOSE TOUCH WITH HIS HUMAN SIDE.
LONG TIME AGO, HE WAS A SUPER-HERO HIMSELF. SINCE THEN, HE'S GOTTEN WEIRDER AND WEIRDER, AND NOW... WELL, T'TELL YOU THE TRUTH...
...YOU CAN'T BE SURE WHOSE SIDE HE'LL TAKE IN ANY OF THIS. CAPICE?
AND SPEAK OF THE ANGEL...
GOOD TALKIN' WITH YA, PADRE. DON'T BE IN ANY HURRY, BUT WHEN YOU GET TO THE OTHER SIDE SOMEDAY...
...LOOK ME UP.

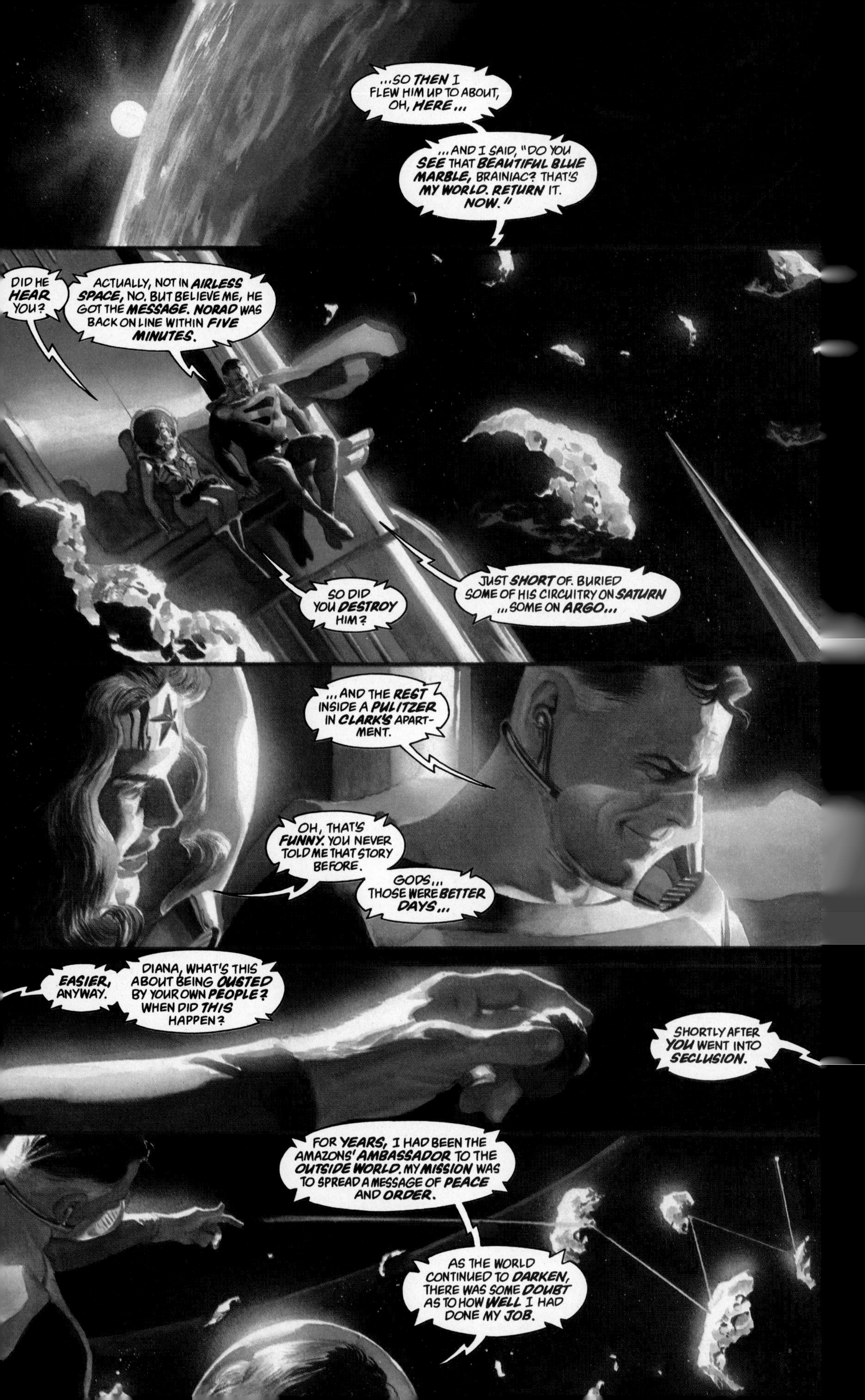

...SO THEN I FLEW HIM UP TO ABOUT, OH, HERE...
...AND I SAID, "DO YOU SEE THAT BEAUTIFUL BLUE MARBLE, BRAINIAC? THAT'S MY WORLD. RETURN IT. NOW."
DID HE HEAR YOU?
ACTUALLY, NOT IN AIRLESS SPACE, NO. BUT BELIEVE ME, HE GOT THE MESSAGE. NORAD WAS BACK ON LINE WITHIN FIVE MINUTES.
SO DID YOU DESTROY HIM?
JUST SHORT OF. BURIED SOME OF HIS CIRCUITRY ON SATURN ...SOME ON ARGO...
...AND THE REST INSIDE A PULITZER IN CLARK'S APARTMENT.
OH, THAT'S FUNNY. YOU NEVER TOLD ME THAT STORY BEFORE.
GODS... THOSE WERE BETTER DAYS...
EASIER, ANYWAY.
DIANA, WHAT'S THIS ABOUT BEING OUSTED BY YOUR OWN PEOPLE? WHEN DID THIS HAPPEN?
SHORTLY AFTER YOU WENT INTO SECLUSION.
FOR YEARS, I HAD BEEN THE AMAZONS' AMBASSADOR TO THE OUTSIDE WORLD. MY MISSION WAS TO SPREAD A MESSAGE OF PEACE AND ORDER.
AS THE WORLD CONTINUED TO DARKEN, THERE WAS SOME DOUBT AS TO HOW WELL I HAD DONE MY JOB.

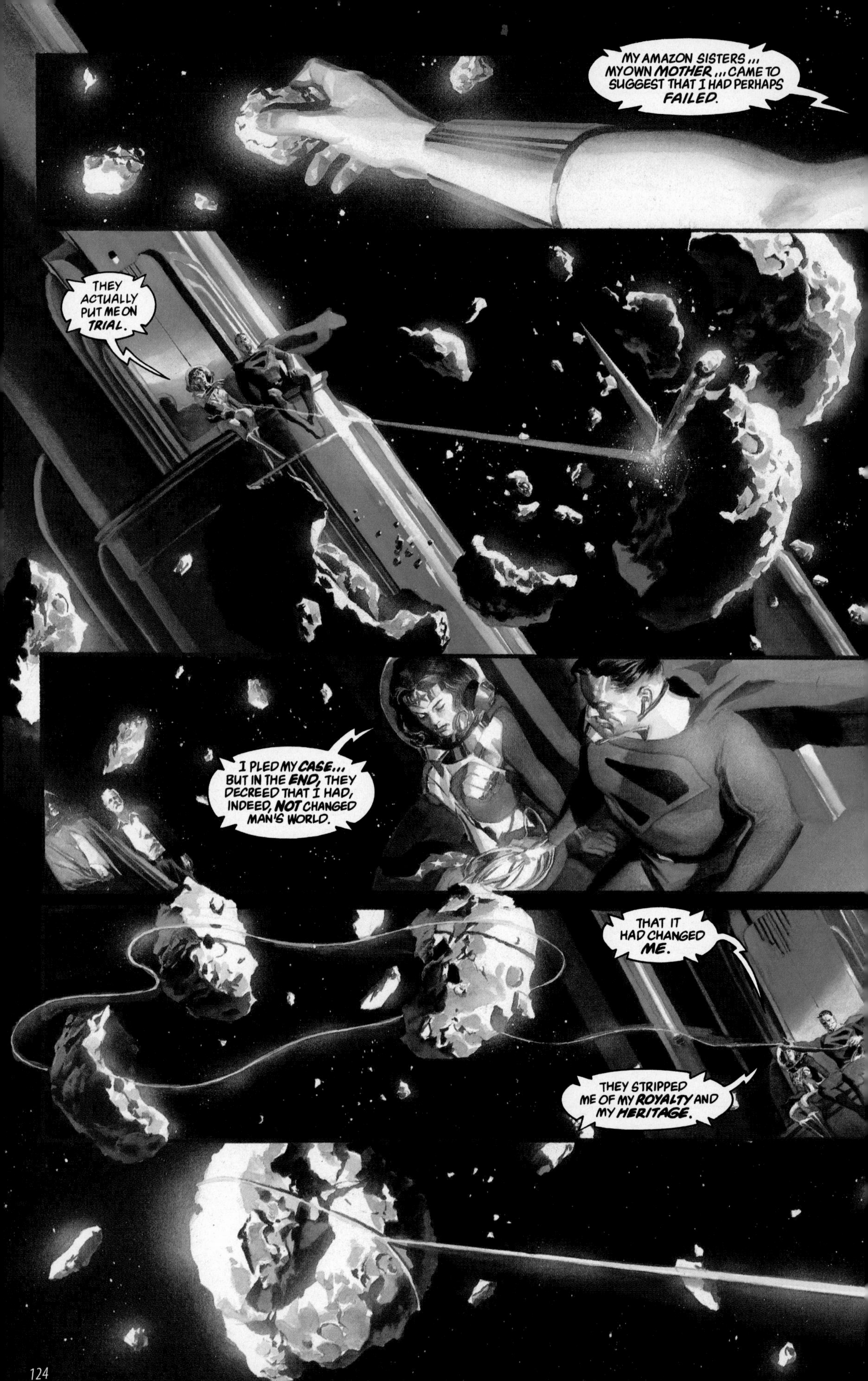
MY AMAZON SISTERS... MY OWN MOTHER... CAME TO SUGGEST THAT I HAD PERHAPS FAILED.
THEY ACTUALLY PUT ME ON TRIAL.
I PLED MY CASE... BUT IN THE END, THEY DECREED THAT I HAD, INDEED, NOT CHANGED MAN'S WORLD.
THAT IT HAD CHANGED ME.
THEY STRIPPED ME OF MY ROYALTY AND MY HERITAGE.

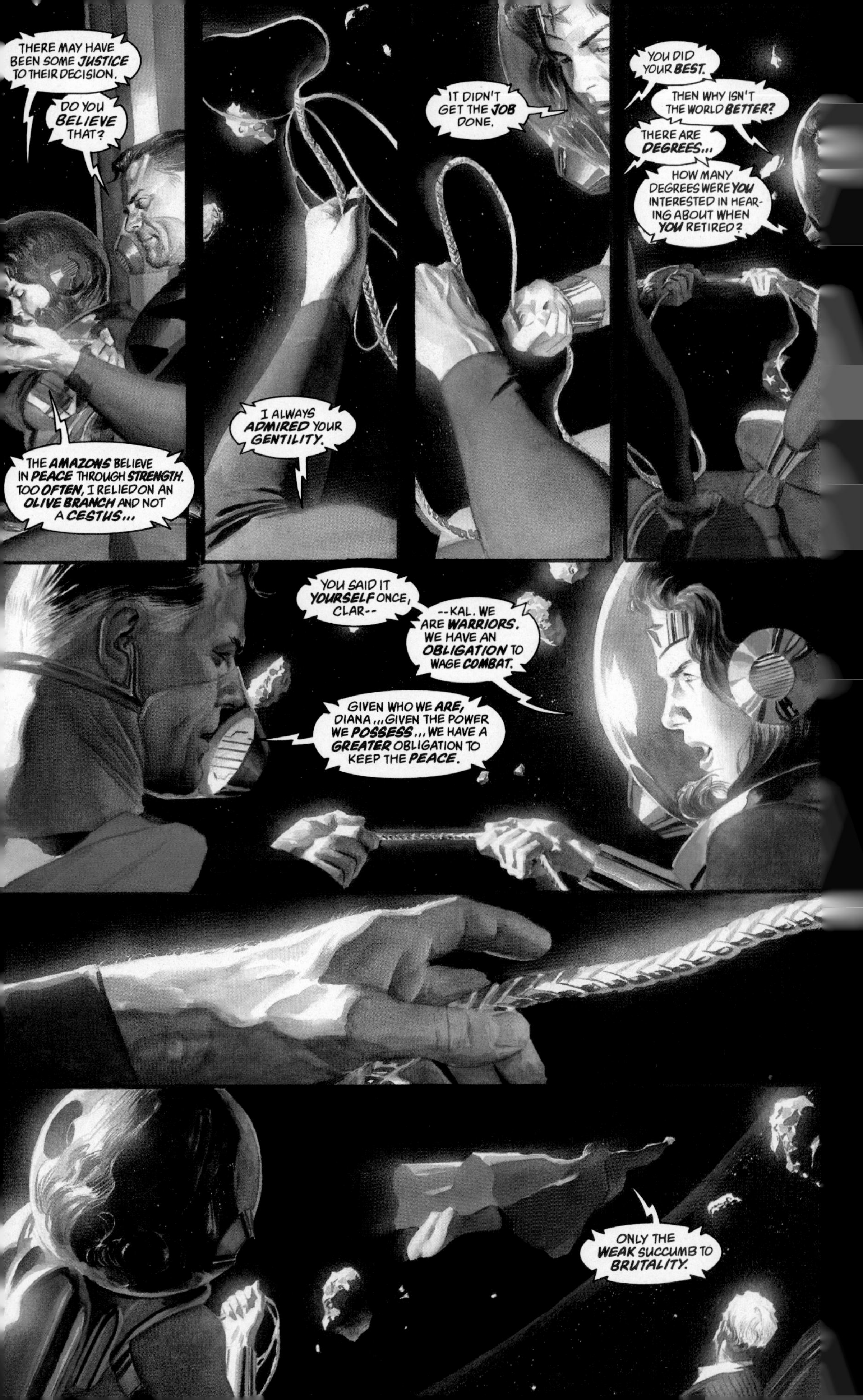
THERE MAY HAVE BEEN SOME JUSTICE TO THEIR DECISION.
DO YOU BELIEVE THAT?
THE AMAZONS BELIEVE IN PEACE THROUGH STRENGTH. TOO OFTEN, I RELIED ON AN OLIVE BRANCH AND NOT A CESTUS...
I ALWAYS ADMIRED YOUR GENTILITY.
IT DIDN'T GET THE JOB DONE.
YOU DID YOUR BEST.
THEN WHY ISN'T THE WORLD BETTER?
THERE ARE DEGREES...
HOW MANY DEGREES WERE YOU INTERESTED IN HEARING ABOUT WHEN YOU RETIRED?
YOU SAID IT YOURSELF ONCE, CLAR--
--KAL. WE ARE WARRIORS. WE HAVE AN OBLIGATION TO WAGE COMBAT.
GIVEN WHO WE ARE, DIANA... GIVEN THE POWER WE POSSESS... WE HAVE A GREATER OBLIGATION TO KEEP THE PEACE.
ONLY THE WEAK SUCCUMB TO BRUTALITY.

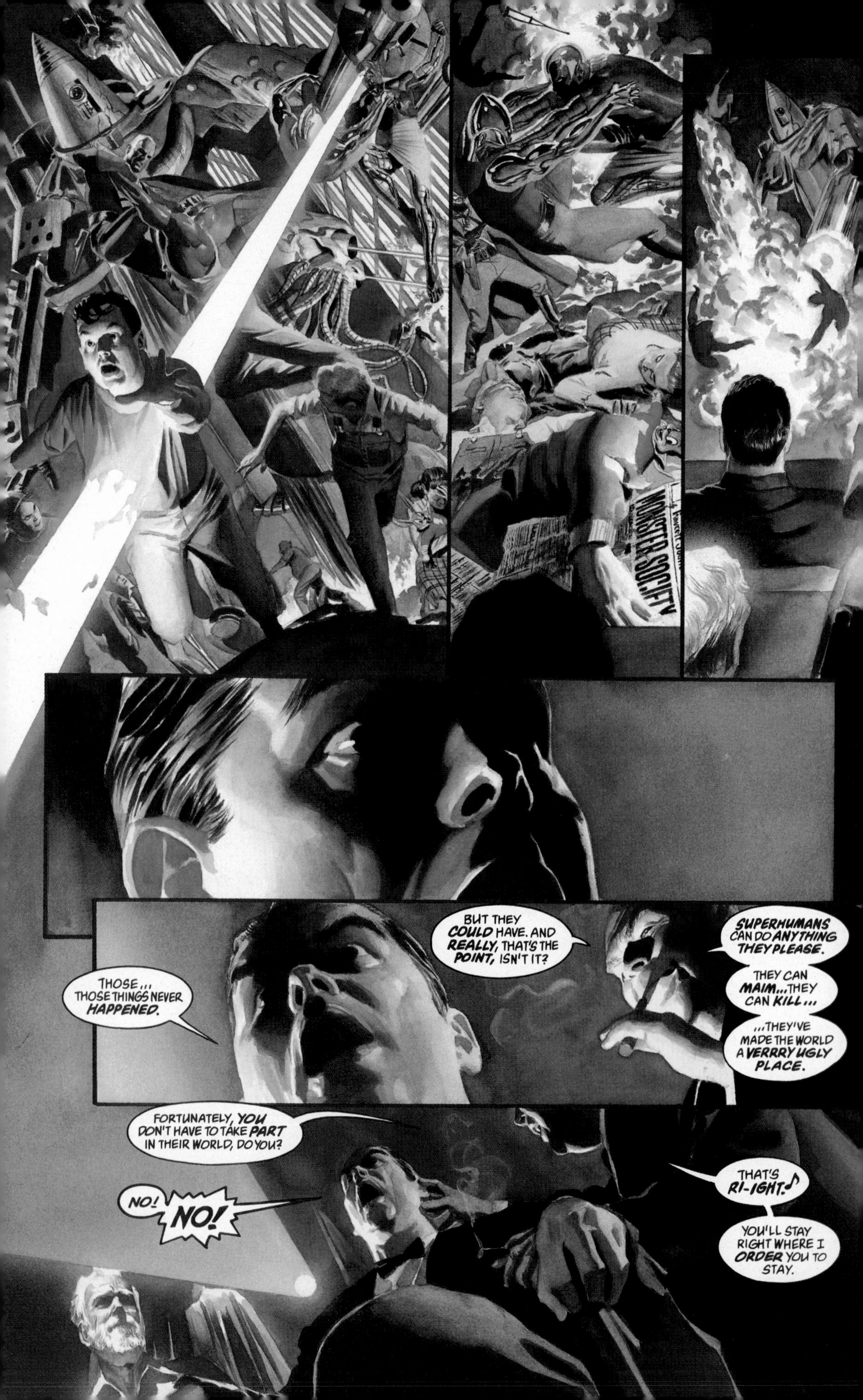
MONSTER SOCIETY
THOSE... THOSE THINGS NEVER HAPPENED.
BUT THEY COULD HAVE. AND REALLY, THAT'S THE POINT, ISN'T IT?
SUPERHUMANS CAN DO ANYTHING THEY PLEASE.
THEY CAN MAIM... THEY CAN KILL...
...THEY'VE MADE THE WORLD A VERRRY UGLY PLACE.
FORTUNATELY, YOU DON'T HAVE TO TAKE PART IN THEIR WORLD, DO YOU?
NO! NO!
THAT'S RI-IGHT.♪
YOU'LL STAY RIGHT WHERE I ORDER YOU TO STAY.

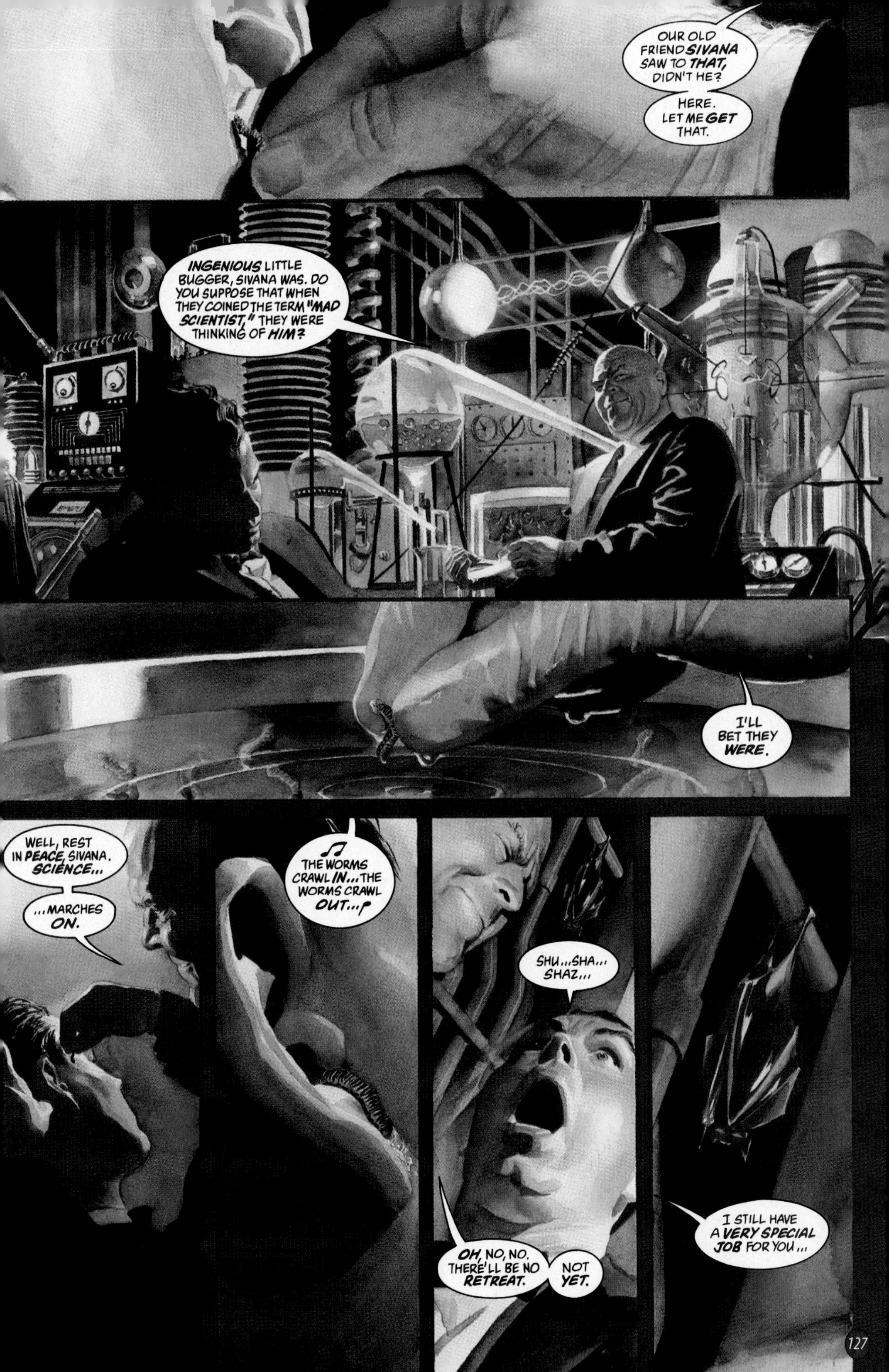
OUR OLD FRIEND SIVANA SAW TO THAT, DIDN'T HE?
HERE. LET ME GET THAT.
INGENIOUS LITTLE BUGGER, SIVANA WAS. DO YOU SUPPOSE THAT WHEN THEY COINED THE TERM "MAD SCIENTIST," THEY WERE THINKING OF HIM?
I'LL BET THEY WERE.
WELL, REST IN PEACE, SIVANA. SCIENCE...
...MARCHES ON.
THE WORMS CRAWL IN... THE WORMS CRAWL OUT...
SHU...SHA... SHAZ...
OH, NO, NO. THERE'LL BE NO RETREAT.
NOT YET.
I STILL HAVE A VERY SPECIAL JOB FOR YOU...

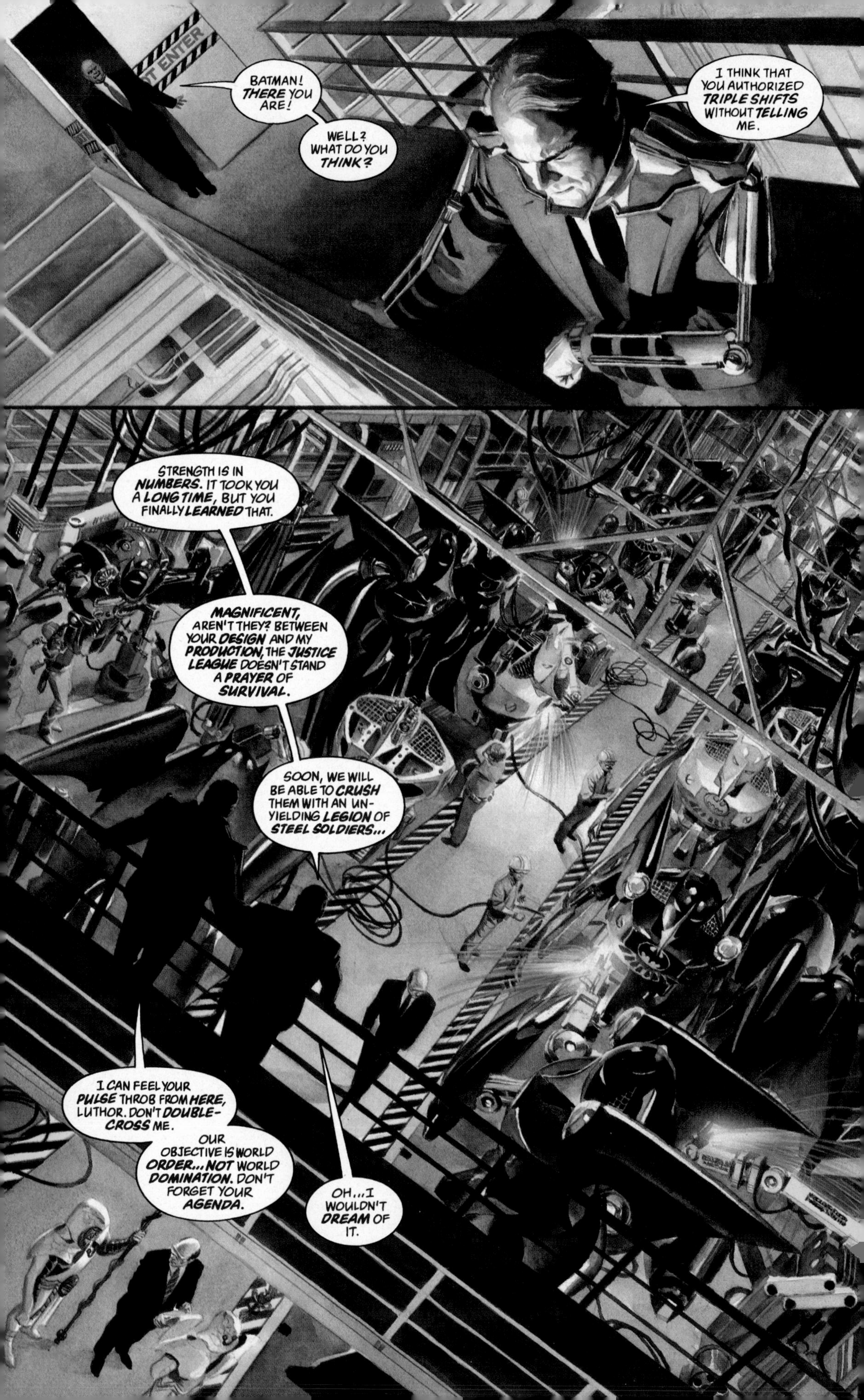
BATMAN! THERE YOU ARE!
WELL? WHAT DO YOU THINK?
I THINK THAT YOU AUTHORIZED TRIPLE SHIFTS WITHOUT TELLING ME.
STRENGTH IS IN NUMBERS. IT TOOK YOU A LONG TIME, BUT YOU FINALLY LEARNED THAT.
MAGNIFICENT, AREN'T THEY? BETWEEN YOUR DESIGN AND MY PRODUCTION, THE JUSTICE LEAGUE DOESN'T STAND A PRAYER OF SURVIVAL.
SOON, WE WILL BE ABLE TO CRUSH THEM WITH AN UNYIELDING LEGION OF STEEL SOLDIERS...
I CAN FEEL YOUR PULSE THROB FROM HERE, LUTHOR. DON'T DOUBLE-CROSS ME.
OUR OBJECTIVE IS WORLD ORDER... NOT WORLD DOMINATION. DON'T FORGET YOUR AGENDA.
OH... I WOULDN'T DREAM OF IT.

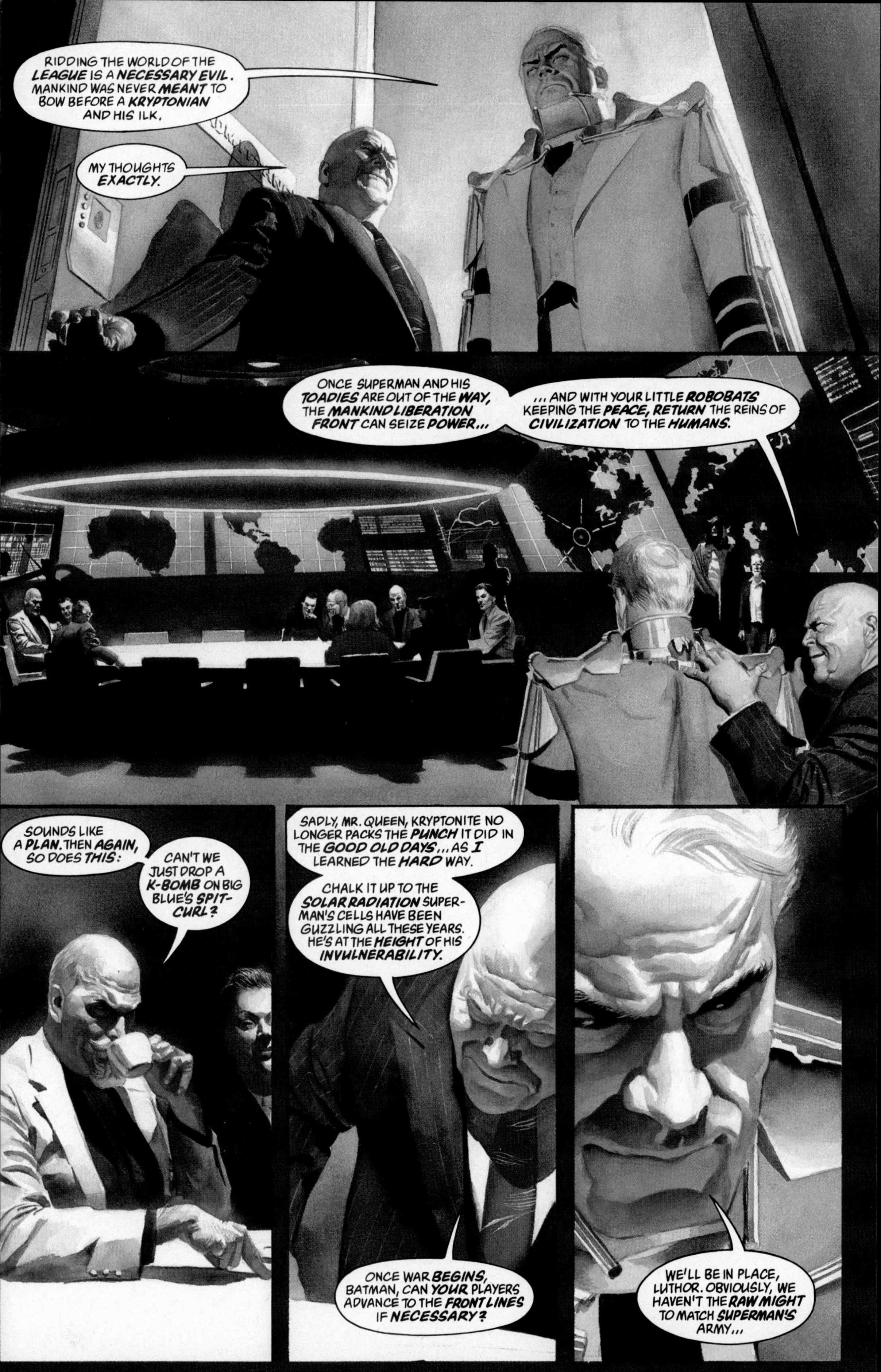

RIDDING THE WORLD OF THE LEAGUE IS A NECESSARY EVIL. MANKIND WAS NEVER MEANT TO BOW BEFORE A KRYPTONIAN AND HIS ILK.
MY THOUGHTS EXACTLY.
ONCE SUPERMAN AND HIS TOADIES ARE OUT OF THE WAY, THE MANKIND LIBERATION FRONT CAN SEIZE POWER...
...AND WITH YOUR LITTLE ROBOBATS KEEPING THE PEACE, RETURN THE REINS OF CIVILIZATION TO THE HUMANS.
SOUNDS LIKE A PLAN. THEN AGAIN, SO DOES THIS:
CAN'T WE JUST DROP A K-BOMB ON BIG BLUE'S SPIT-CURL?
SADLY, MR. QUEEN, KRYPTONITE NO LONGER PACKS THE PUNCH IT DID IN THE GOOD OLD DAYS... AS I LEARNED THE HARD WAY.
CHALK IT UP TO THE SOLAR RADIATION SUPERMAN'S CELLS HAVE BEEN GUZZLING ALL THESE YEARS. HE'S AT THE HEIGHT OF HIS INVULNERABILITY.
ONCE WAR BEGINS, BATMAN, CAN YOUR PLAYERS ADVANCE TO THE FRONT LINES IF NECESSARY?
WE'LL BE IN PLACE, LUTHOR. OBVIOUSLY, WE HAVEN'T THE RAW MIGHT TO MATCH SUPERMAN'S ARMY...

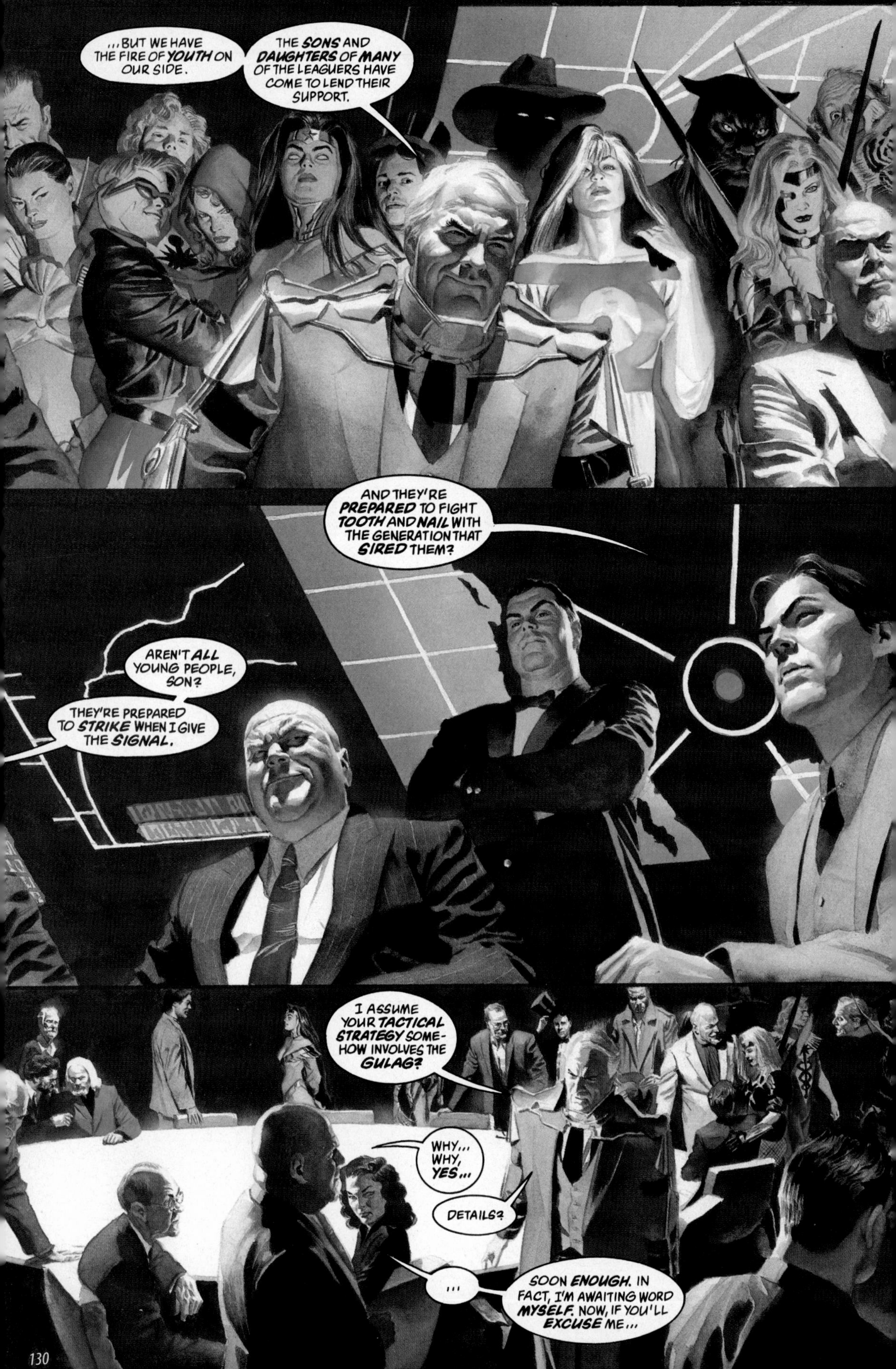
...BUT WE HAVE THE FIRE OF YOUTH ON OUR SIDE.
THE SONS AND DAUGHTERS OF MANY OF THE LEAGUERS HAVE COME TO LEND THEIR SUPPORT.
AND THEY'RE PREPARED TO FIGHT TOOTH AND NAIL WITH THE GENERATION THAT SIRED THEM?
AREN'T ALL YOUNG PEOPLE, SON?
THEY'RE PREPARED TO STRIKE WHEN I GIVE THE SIGNAL.
I ASSUME YOUR TACTICAL STRATEGY SOME-HOW INVOLVES THE GULAG?
WHY... WHY, YES...
DETAILS?
...
SOON ENOUGH. IN FACT, I'M AWAITING WORD MYSELF. NOW, IF YOU'LL EXCUSE ME...

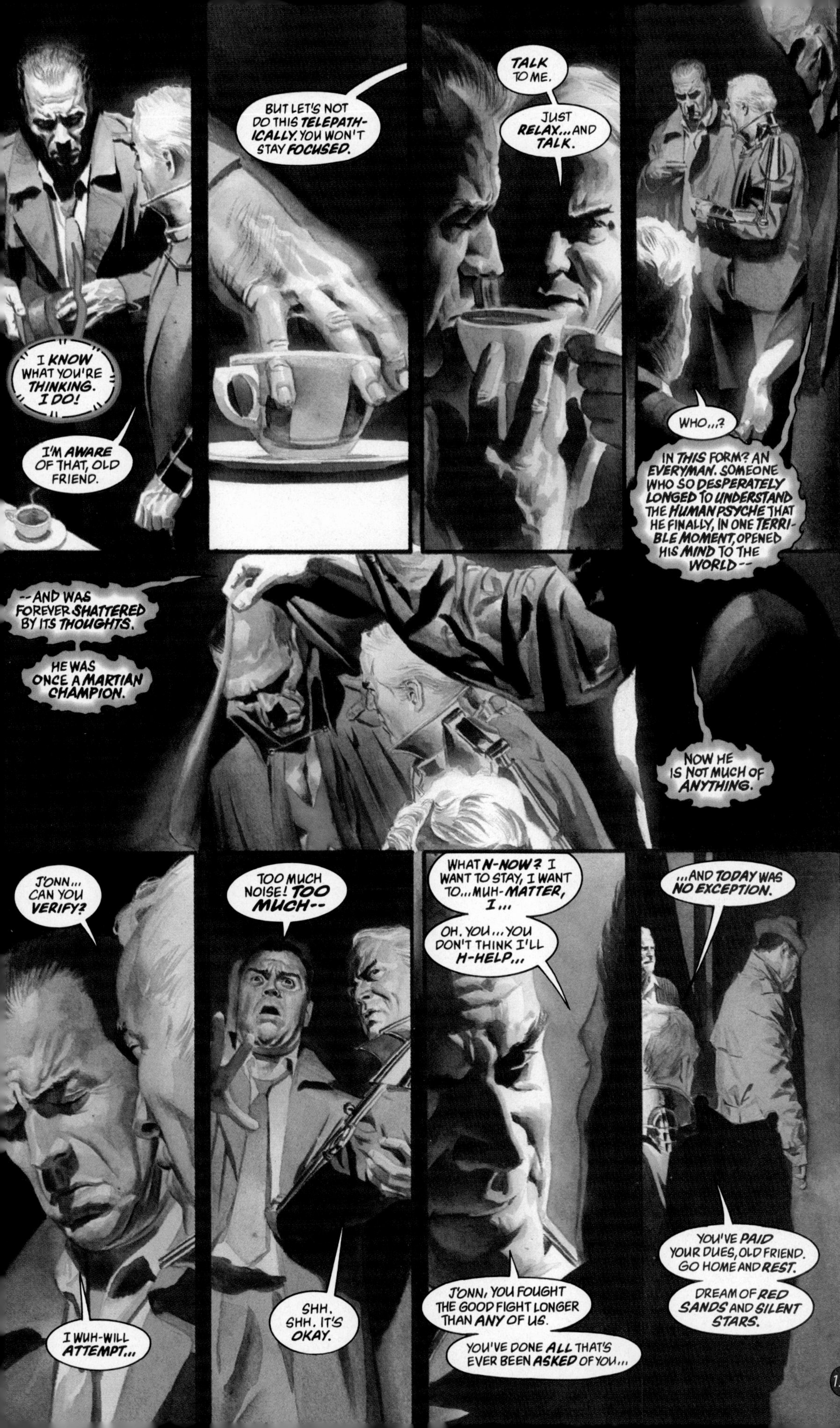
I KNOW WHAT YOU'RE THINKING. I DO!
I'M AWARE OF THAT, OLD FRIEND.
BUT LET'S NOT DO THIS TELEPATHICALLY. YOU WON'T STAY FOCUSED.
TALK TO ME.
JUST RELAX... AND TALK.
WHO...?
IN THIS FORM? AN EVERYMAN. SOMEONE WHO SO DESPERATELY LONGED TO UNDERSTAND THE HUMAN PSYCHE THAT HE FINALLY, IN ONE TERRIBLE MOMENT, OPENED HIS MIND TO THE WORLD--
--AND WAS FOREVER SHATTERED BY ITS THOUGHTS.
HE WAS ONCE A MARTIAN CHAMPION.
NOW HE IS NOT MUCH OF ANYTHING.
J'ONN... CAN YOU VERIFY?
I WUH-WILL ATTEMPT...
TOO MUCH NOISE! TOO MUCH--
SHH. SHH. IT'S OKAY.
WHAT N-NOW? I WANT TO STAY, I WANT TO... MUH-MATTER, I...
OH. YOU... YOU DON'T THINK I'LL H-HELP...
J'ONN, YOU FOUGHT THE GOOD FIGHT LONGER THAN ANY OF US.
YOU'VE DONE ALL THAT'S EVER BEEN ASKED OF YOU...
...AND TODAY WAS NO EXCEPTION.
YOU'VE PAID YOUR DUES, OLD FRIEND. GO HOME AND REST.
DREAM OF RED SANDS AND SILENT STARS.

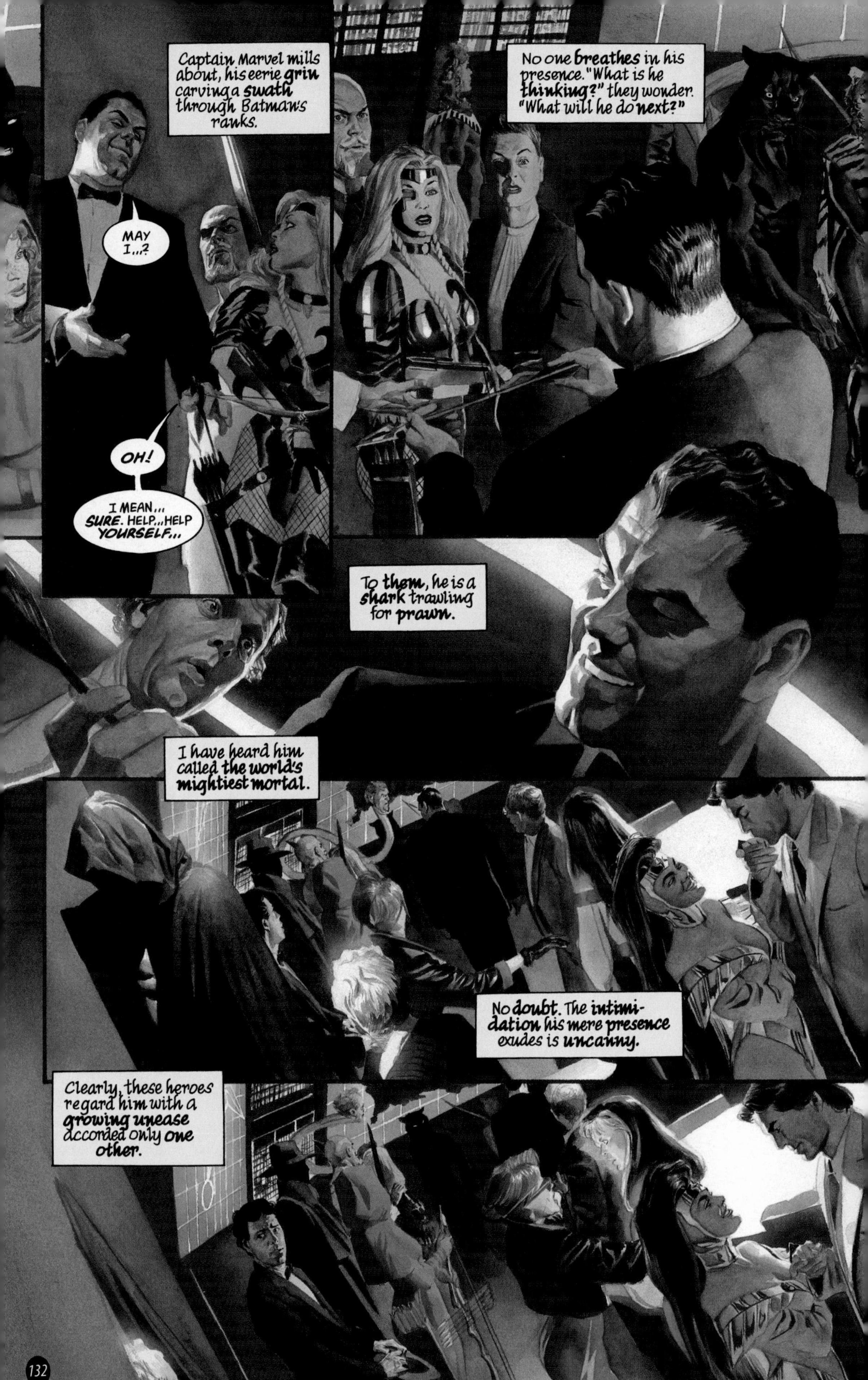

Captain Marvel mills about, his eerie grin carving a swath through Batman's ranks.
MAY I...?
OH!
I MEAN... SURE. HELP...HELP YOURSELF...
No one breathes in his presence. "What is he thinking?" they wonder. "What will he do next?"
To them, he is a shark trawling for prawn.
I have heard him called the world's mightiest mortal.
No doubt. The intimidation his mere presence exudes is uncanny.
Clearly, these heroes regard him with a growing unease accorded only one other.

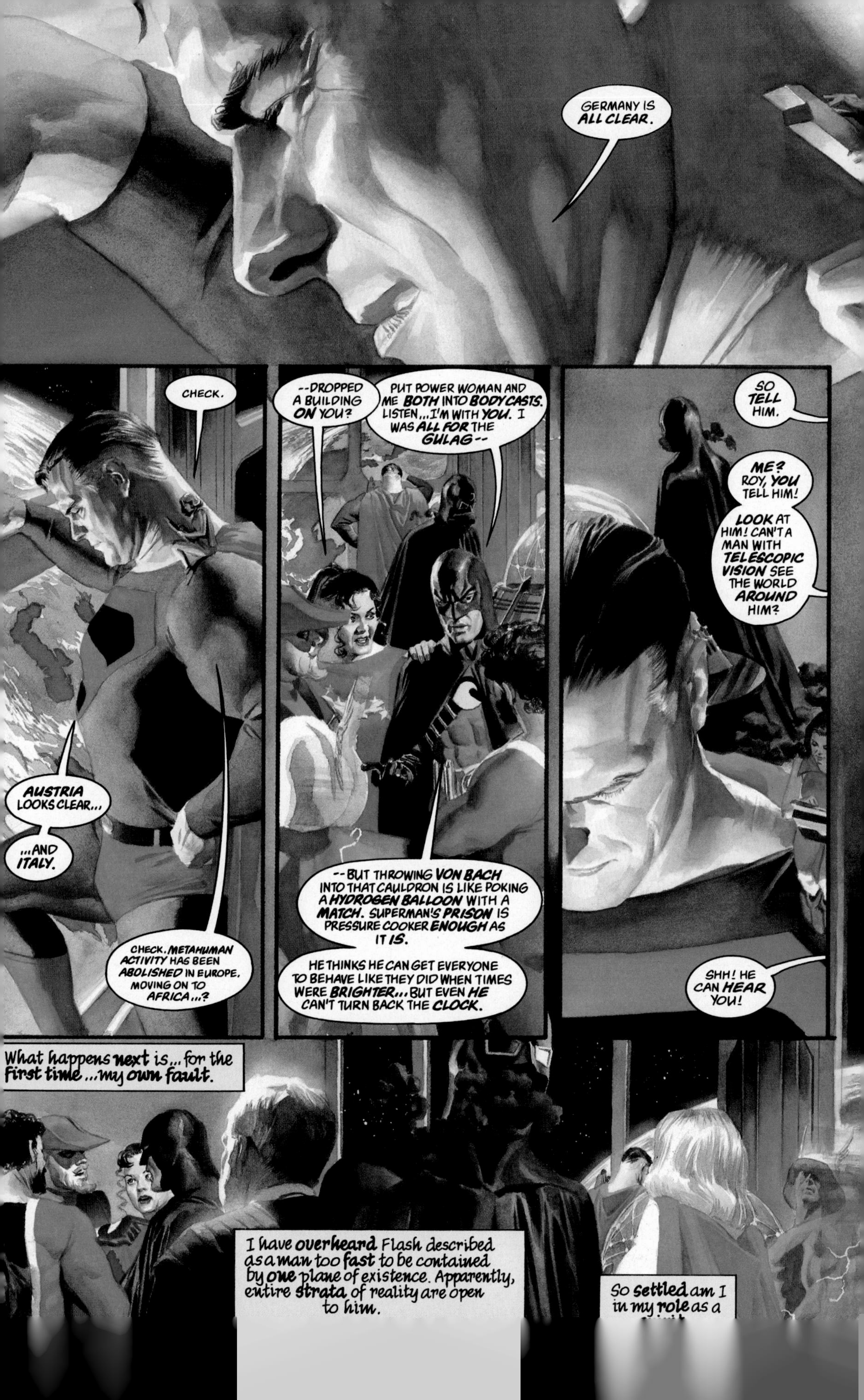
GERMANY IS ALL CLEAR.
CHECK.
AUSTRIA LOOKS CLEAR...
...AND ITALY.
CHECK. METAHUMAN ACTIVITY HAS BEEN ABOLISHED IN EUROPE. MOVING ON TO AFRICA...?
--DROPPED A BUILDING ON YOU?
PUT POWER WOMAN AND ME BOTH INTO BODY CASTS. LISTEN... I'M WITH YOU. I WAS ALL FOR THE GULAG--
--BUT THROWING VON BACH INTO THAT CAULDRON IS LIKE POKING A HYDROGEN BALLOON WITH A MATCH. SUPERMAN'S PRISON IS PRESSURE COOKER ENOUGH AS IT IS.
HE THINKS HE CAN GET EVERYONE TO BEHAVE LIKE THEY DID WHEN TIMES WERE BRIGHTER... BUT EVEN HE CAN'T TURN BACK THE CLOCK.
SO TELL HIM.
ME? ROY, YOU TELL HIM!
LOOK AT HIM! CAN'T A MAN WITH TELESCOPIC VISION SEE THE WORLD AROUND HIM?
SHH! HE CAN HEAR YOU!
What happens next is... for the first time... my own fault.
I have overheard Flash described as a man too fast to be contained by one plane of existence. Apparently, entire strata of reality are open to him.
So settled am I in my role as a

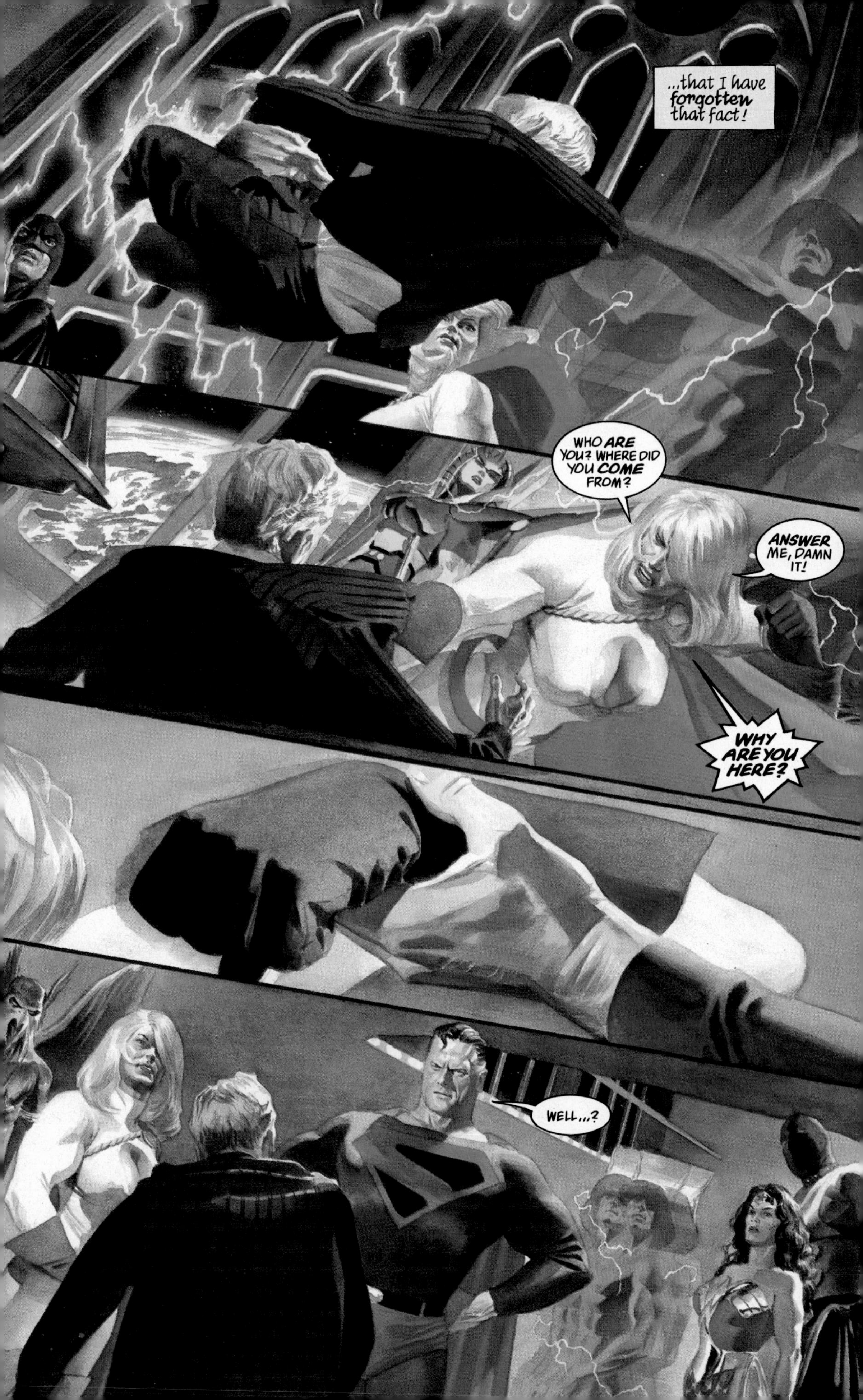
...that I have forgotten that fact!
WHO ARE YOU? WHERE DID YOU COME FROM?
ANSWER ME, DAMN IT!
WHY ARE YOU HERE?
WELL...?

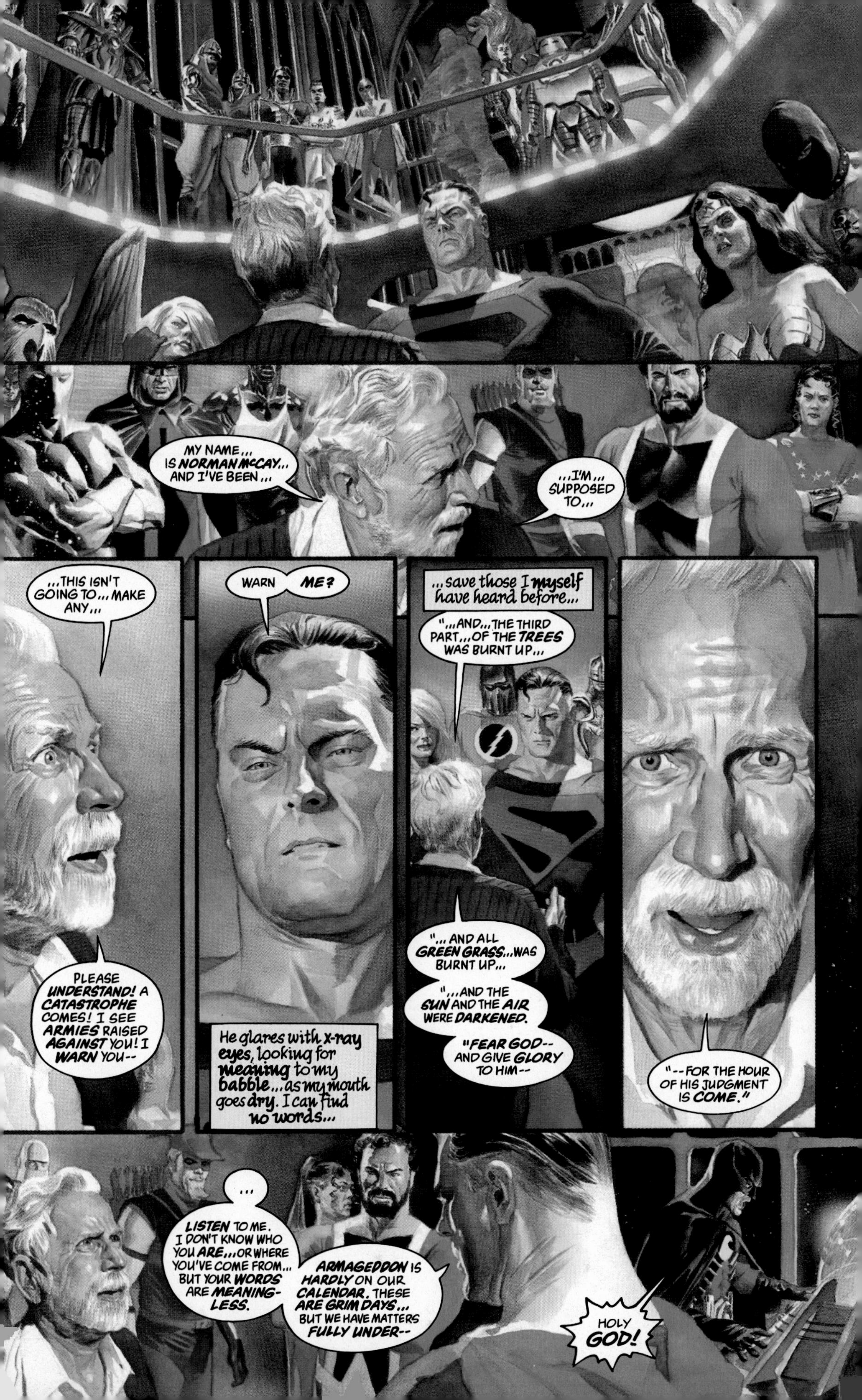
MY NAME... IS NORMAN McCAY... AND I'VE BEEN...
...I'M... SUPPOSED TO...
...THIS ISN'T GOING TO... MAKE ANY...
PLEASE UNDERSTAND! A CATASTROPHE COMES! I SEE ARMIES RAISED AGAINST YOU! I WARN YOU--
WARN
ME?
He glares with x-ray eyes, looking for meaning to my babble... as my mouth goes dry. I can find no words...
...save those I myself have heard before...
"...AND... THE THIRD PART... OF THE TREES WAS BURNT UP...
"...AND ALL GREEN GRASS...WAS BURNT UP...
"...AND THE SUN AND THE AIR WERE DARKENED.
"FEAR GOD-- AND GIVE GLORY TO HIM--
"--FOR THE HOUR OF HIS JUDGMENT IS COME."
...
LISTEN TO ME. I DON'T KNOW WHO YOU ARE...OR WHERE YOU'VE COME FROM... BUT YOUR WORDS ARE MEANING-LESS.
ARMAGEDDON IS HARDLY ON OUR CALENDAR. THESE ARE GRIM DAYS... BUT WE HAVE MATTERS FULLY UNDER--
HOLY GOD!

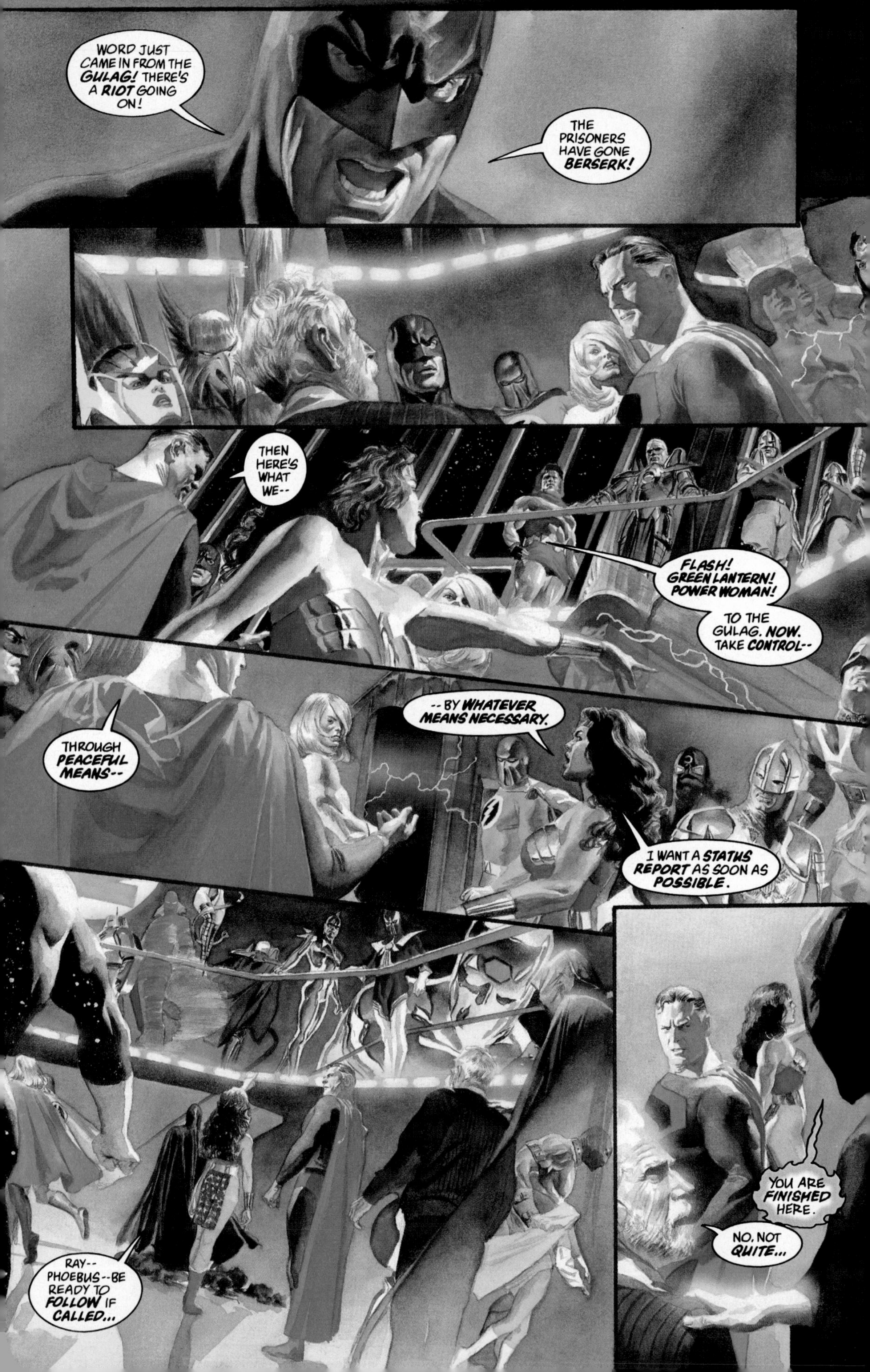
WORD JUST CAME IN FROM THE GULAG! THERE'S A RIOT GOING ON!
THE PRISONERS HAVE GONE BERSERK!
THEN HERE'S WHAT WE--
FLASH! GREEN LANTERN! POWER WOMAN!
TO THE GULAG. NOW. TAKE CONTROL--
THROUGH PEACEFUL MEANS--
--BY WHATEVER MEANS NECESSARY.
I WANT A STATUS REPORT AS SOON AS POSSIBLE.
RAY--PHOEBUS--BE READY TO FOLLOW IF CALLED...
YOU ARE FINISHED HERE.
NO, NOT QUITE...

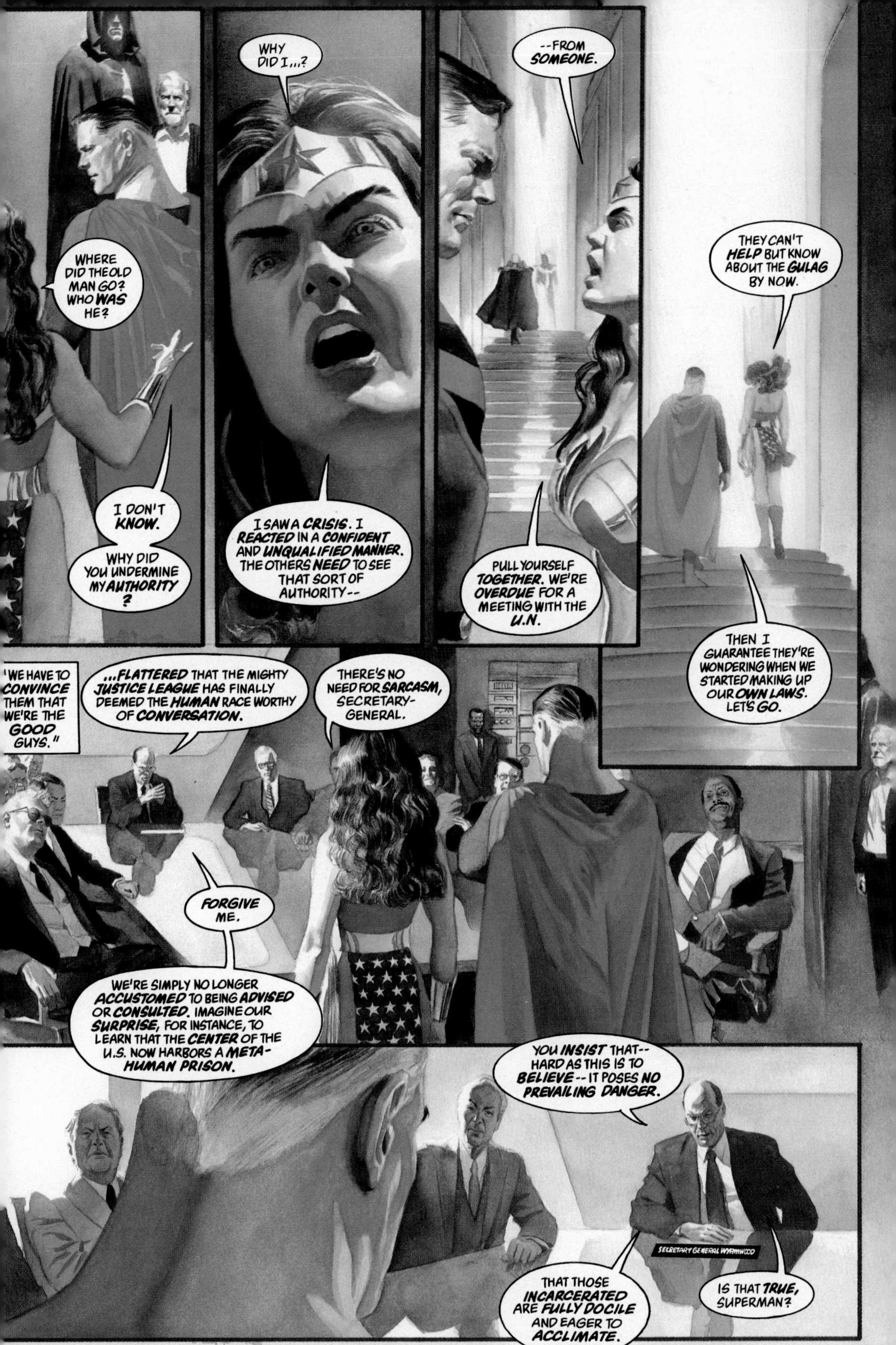
WHERE DID THE OLD MAN GO? WHO WAS HE?
I DON'T KNOW.
WHY DID YOU UNDERMINE MY AUTHORITY?
WHY DID I...?
I SAW A CRISIS. I REACTED IN A CONFIDENT AND UNQUALIFIED MANNER. THE OTHERS NEED TO SEE THAT SORT OF AUTHORITY--
--FROM SOMEONE.
PULL YOURSELF TOGETHER. WE'RE OVERDUE FOR A MEETING WITH THE U.N.
THEY CAN'T HELP BUT KNOW ABOUT THE GULAG BY NOW.
THEN I GUARANTEE THEY'RE WONDERING WHEN WE STARTED MAKING UP OUR OWN LAWS. LET'S GO.
'WE HAVE TO CONVINCE THEM THAT WE'RE THE GOOD GUYS."
...FLATTERED THAT THE MIGHTY JUSTICE LEAGUE HAS FINALLY DEEMED THE HUMAN RACE WORTHY OF CONVERSATION.
THERE'S NO NEED FOR SARCASM, SECRETARY-GENERAL.
FORGIVE ME.
WE'RE SIMPLY NO LONGER ACCUSTOMED TO BEING ADVISED OR CONSULTED. IMAGINE OUR SURPRISE, FOR INSTANCE, TO LEARN THAT THE CENTER OF THE U.S. NOW HARBORS A META-HUMAN PRISON.
YOU INSIST THAT-- HARD AS THIS IS TO BELIEVE-- IT POSES NO PREVAILING DANGER.
SECRETARY GENERAL WYRMWOOD
THAT THOSE INCARCERATED ARE FULLY DOCILE AND EAGER TO ACCLIMATE.
IS THAT TRUE, SUPERMAN?

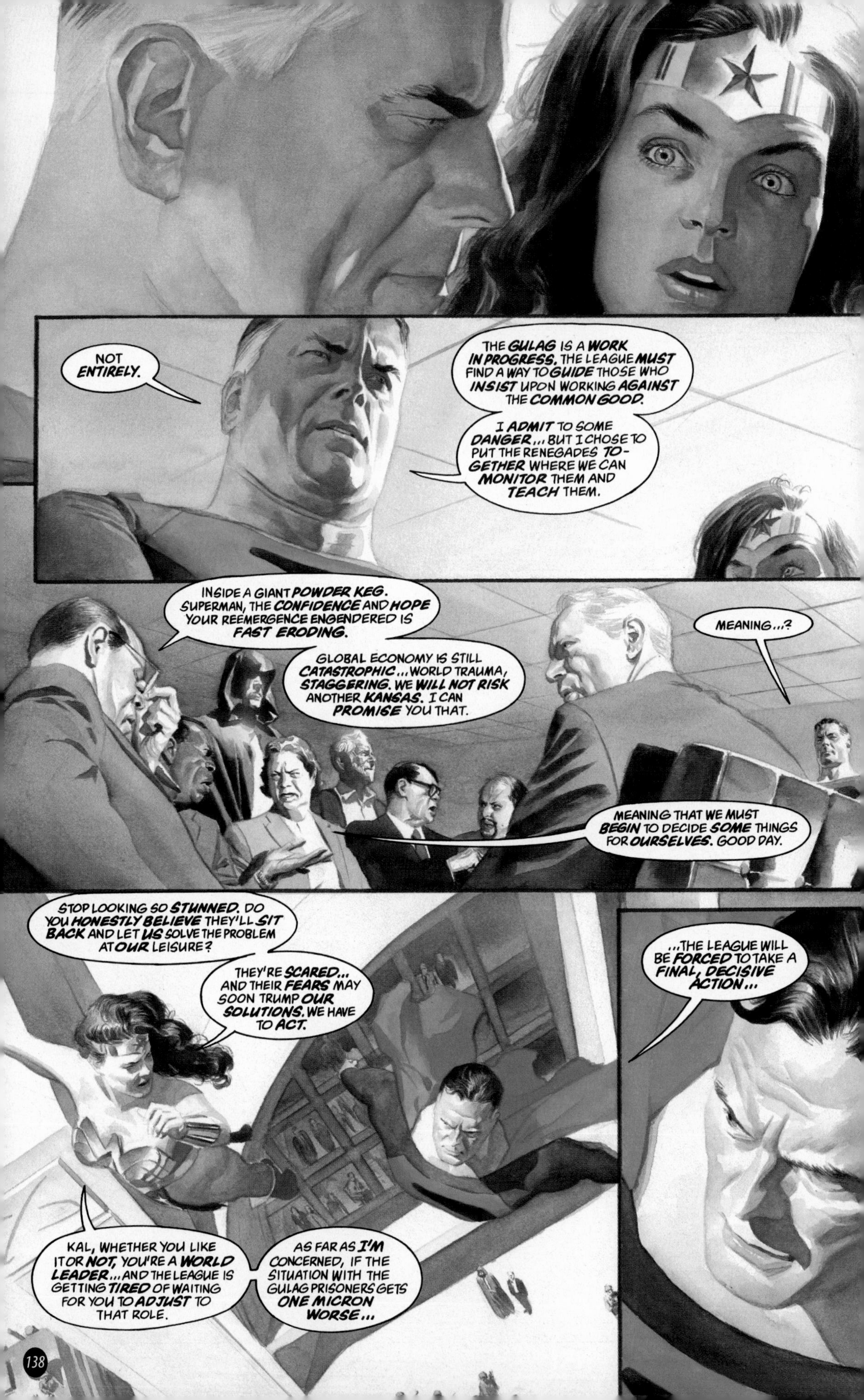
NOT ENTIRELY.
THE GULAG IS A WORK IN PROGRESS. THE LEAGUE MUST FIND A WAY TO GUIDE THOSE WHO INSIST UPON WORKING AGAINST THE COMMON GOOD.
I ADMIT TO SOME DANGER... BUT I CHOSE TO PUT THE RENEGADES TO-GETHER WHERE WE CAN MONITOR THEM AND TEACH THEM.
INSIDE A GIANT POWDER KEG. SUPERMAN, THE CONFIDENCE AND HOPE YOUR REEMERGENCE ENGENDERED IS FAST ERODING.
GLOBAL ECONOMY IS STILL CATASTROPHIC... WORLD TRAUMA, STAGGERING. WE WILL NOT RISK ANOTHER KANSAS. I CAN PROMISE YOU THAT.
MEANING...?
MEANING THAT WE MUST BEGIN TO DECIDE SOME THINGS FOR OURSELVES. GOOD DAY.
STOP LOOKING SO STUNNED. DO YOU HONESTLY BELIEVE THEY'LL SIT BACK AND LET US SOLVE THE PROBLEM AT OUR LEISURE?
THEY'RE SCARED... AND THEIR FEARS MAY SOON TRUMP OUR SOLUTIONS. WE HAVE TO ACT.
KAL, WHETHER YOU LIKE IT OR NOT, YOU'RE A WORLD LEADER... AND THE LEAGUE IS GETTING TIRED OF WAITING FOR YOU TO ADJUST TO THAT ROLE.
AS FAR AS I'M CONCERNED, IF THE SITUATION WITH THE GULAG PRISONERS GETS ONE MICRON WORSE...
...THE LEAGUE WILL BE FORCED TO TAKE A FINAL, DECISIVE ACTION...

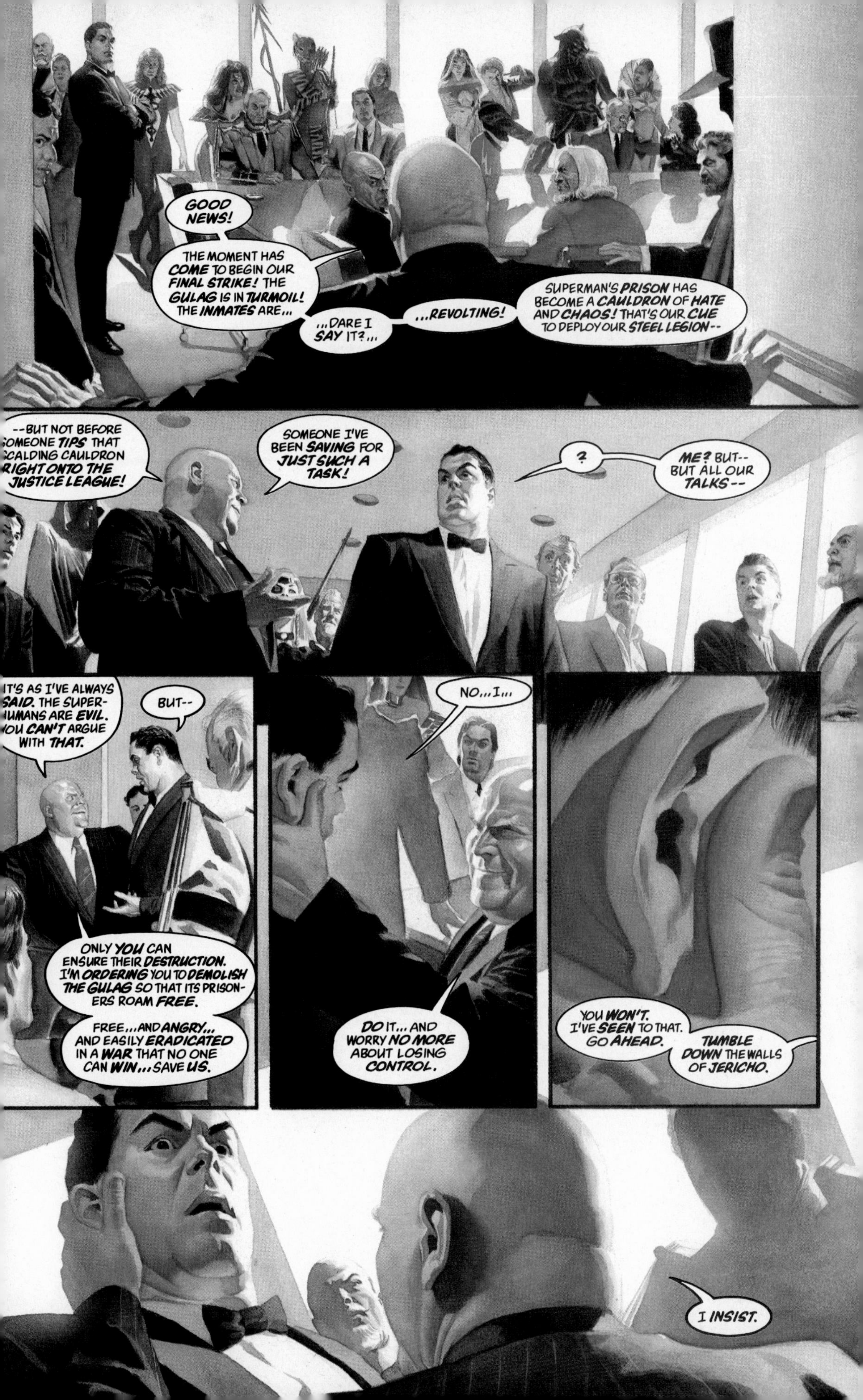

GOOD NEWS!
THE MOMENT HAS COME TO BEGIN OUR FINAL STRIKE! THE GULAG IS IN TURMOIL! THE INMATES ARE...
...DARE I SAY IT?...
...REVOLTING!
SUPERMAN'S PRISON HAS BECOME A CAULDRON OF HATE AND CHAOS! THAT'S OUR CUE TO DEPLOY OUR STEEL LEGION--
--BUT NOT BEFORE SOMEONE TIPS THAT SCALDING CAULDRON RIGHT ONTO THE JUSTICE LEAGUE!
SOMEONE I'VE BEEN SAVING FOR JUST SUCH A TASK!
?
ME? BUT-- BUT ALL OUR TALKS--
IT'S AS I'VE ALWAYS SAID. THE SUPER-HUMANS ARE EVIL. YOU CAN'T ARGUE WITH THAT.
BUT--
ONLY YOU CAN ENSURE THEIR DESTRUCTION. I'M ORDERING YOU TO DEMOLISH THE GULAG SO THAT ITS PRISON-ERS ROAM FREE.
FREE...AND ANGRY... AND EASILY ERADICATED IN A WAR THAT NO ONE CAN WIN...SAVE US.
NO...I...
DO IT...AND WORRY NO MORE ABOUT LOSING CONTROL.
YOU WON'T. I'VE SEEN TO THAT. GO AHEAD.
TUMBLE DOWN THE WALLS OF JERICHO.
I INSIST.

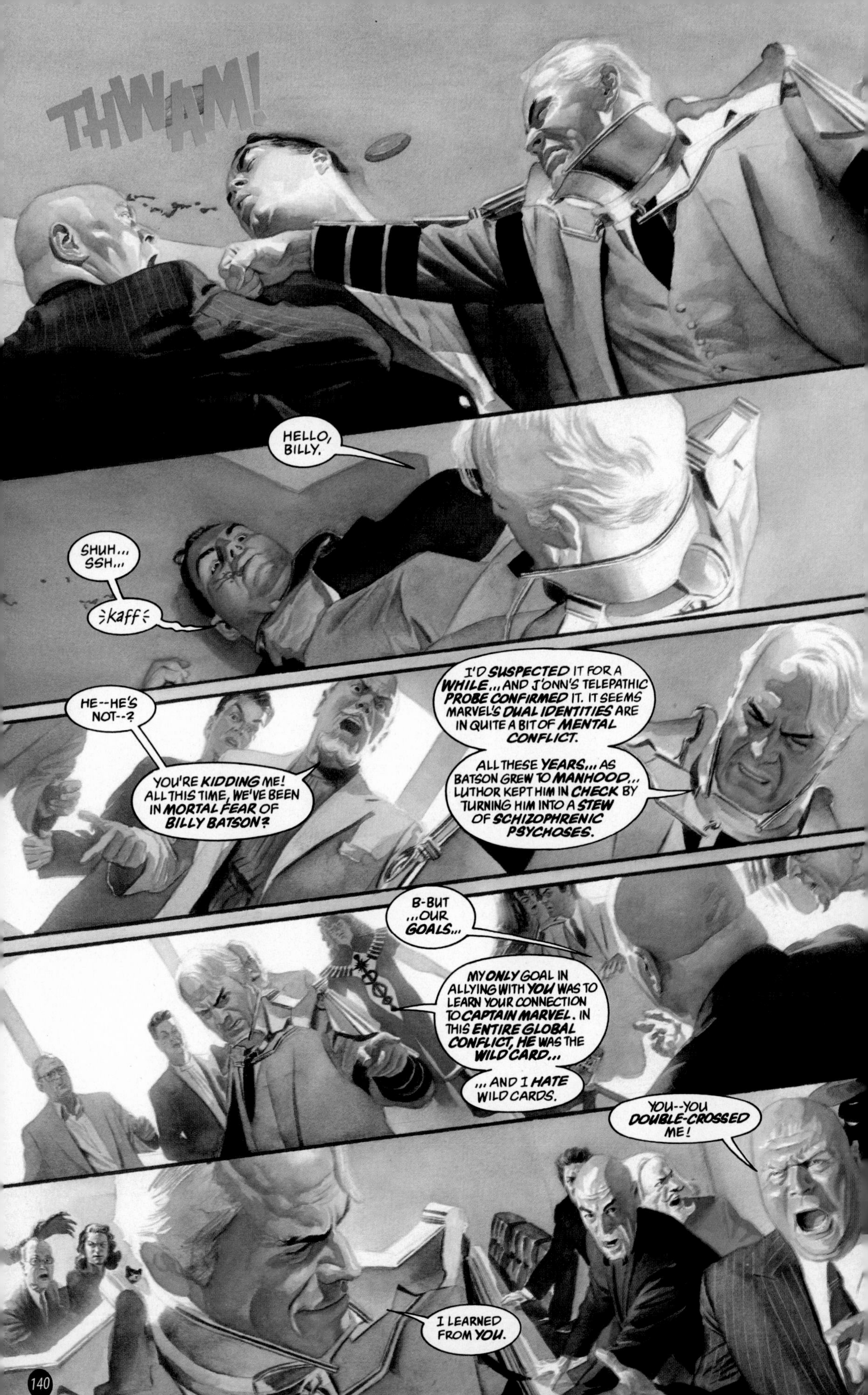
THWAM!
HELLO, BILLY.
SHUH... SSH...
kaff
HE--HE'S NOT--?
YOU'RE KIDDING ME! ALL THIS TIME, WE'VE BEEN IN MORTAL FEAR OF BILLY BATSON?
I'D SUSPECTED IT FOR A WHILE... AND J'ONN'S TELEPATHIC PROBE CONFIRMED IT. IT SEEMS MARVEL'S DUAL IDENTITIES ARE IN QUITE A BIT OF MENTAL CONFLICT.
ALL THESE YEARS... AS BATSON GREW TO MANHOOD... LUTHOR KEPT HIM IN CHECK BY TURNING HIM INTO A STEW OF SCHIZOPHRENIC PSYCHOSES.
B-BUT ...OUR GOALS...
MY ONLY GOAL IN ALLYING WITH YOU WAS TO LEARN YOUR CONNECTION TO CAPTAIN MARVEL. IN THIS ENTIRE GLOBAL CONFLICT, HE WAS THE WILD CARD...
...AND I HATE WILD CARDS.
YOU--YOU DOUBLE-CROSSED ME!
I LEARNED FROM YOU.

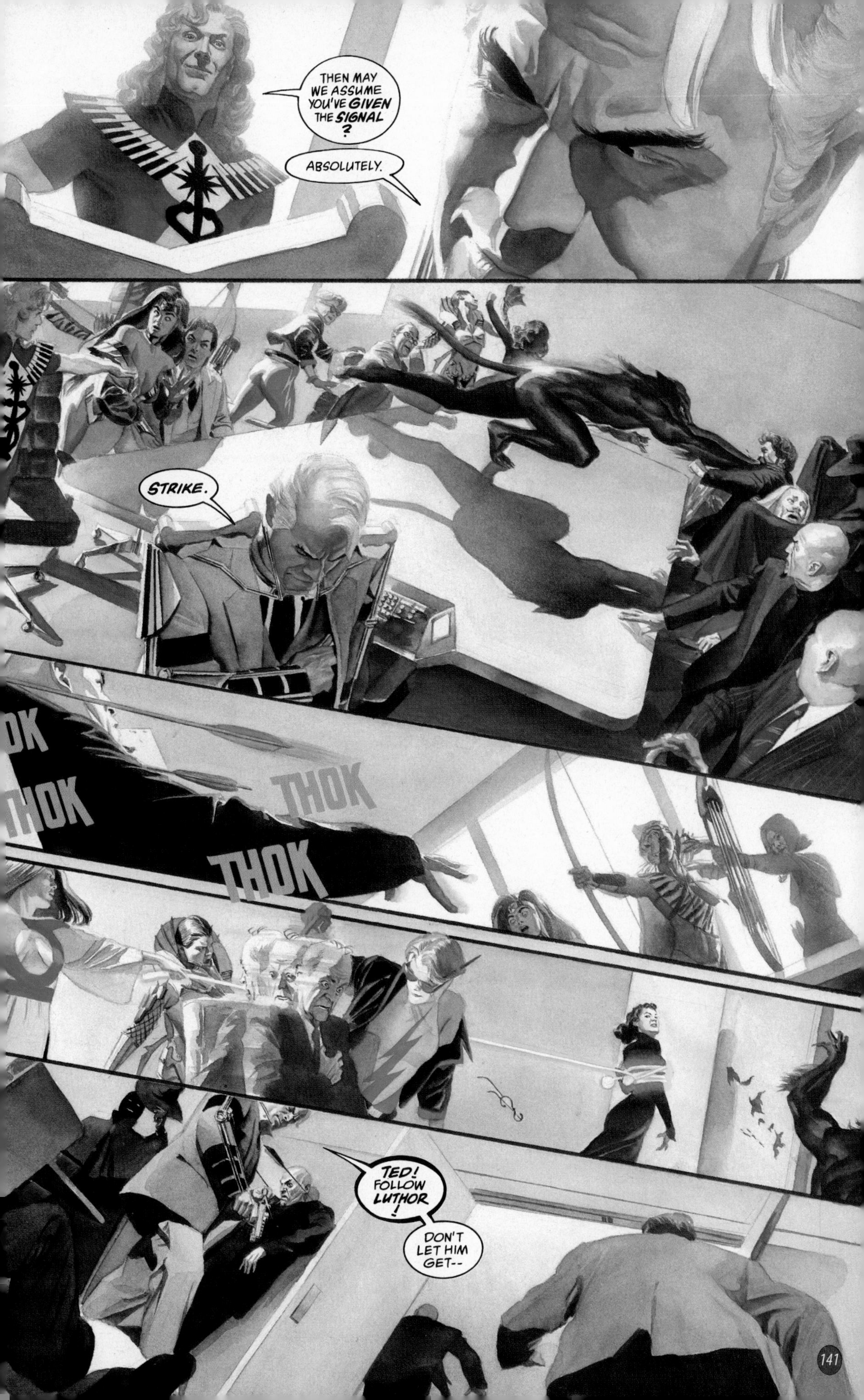

THEN MAY WE ASSUME YOU'VE GIVEN THE SIGNAL ?
ABSOLUTELY.
STRIKE.
THOK
THOK
THOK
THOK
TED! FOLLOW LUTHOR !
DON'T LET HIM GET--

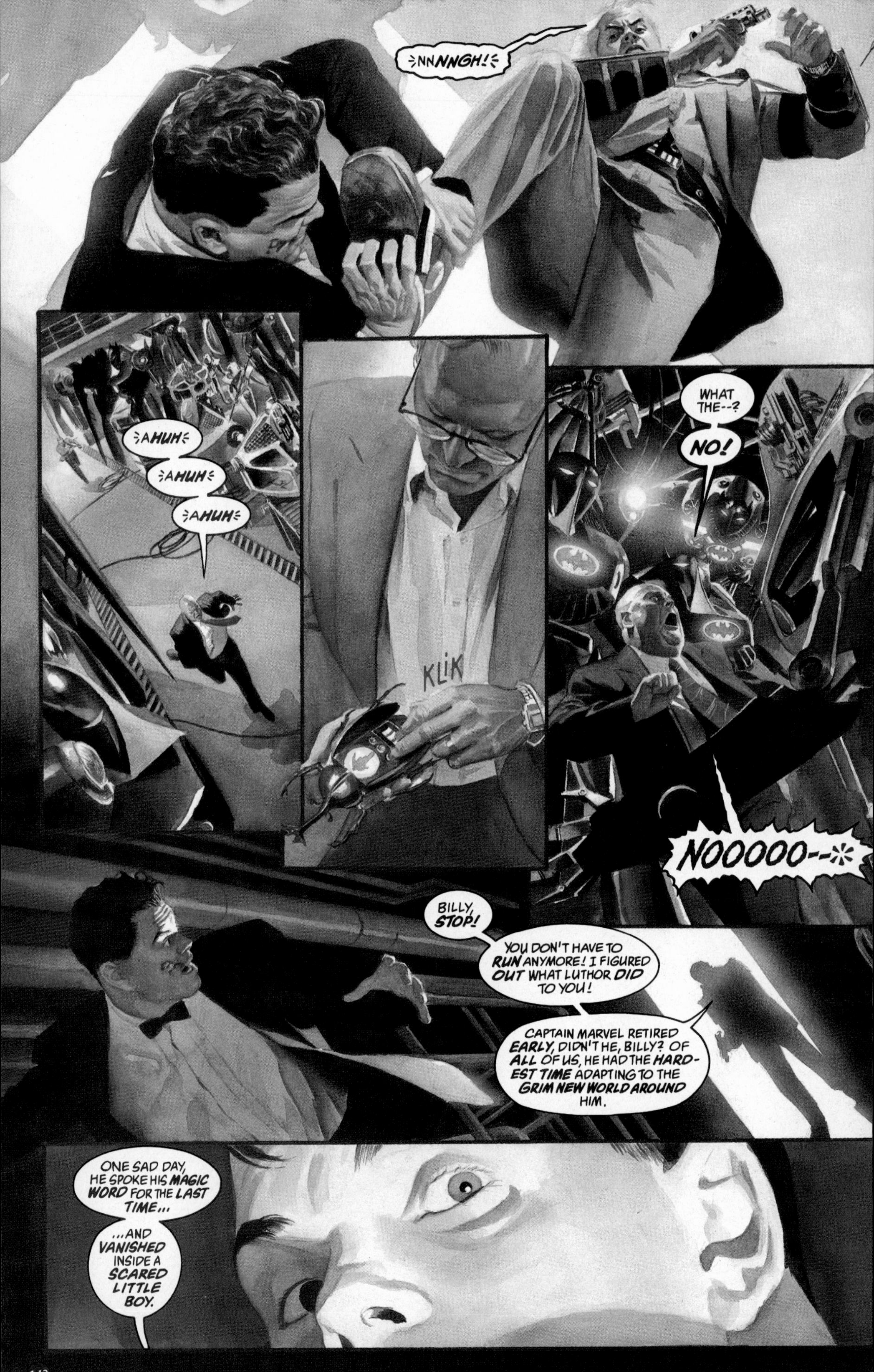
NNNNGH!
AHUH
AHUH
AHUH
KLIK
WHAT THE--?
NO!
NOOOOO--
BILLY, STOP!
YOU DON'T HAVE TO RUN ANYMORE! I FIGURED OUT WHAT LUTHOR DID TO YOU!
CAPTAIN MARVEL RETIRED EARLY, DIDN'T HE, BILLY? OF ALL OF US, HE HAD THE HARD-EST TIME ADAPTING TO THE GRIM NEW WORLD AROUND HIM.
ONE SAD DAY, HE SPOKE HIS MAGIC WORD FOR THE LAST TIME...
...AND VANISHED INSIDE A SCARED LITTLE BOY.

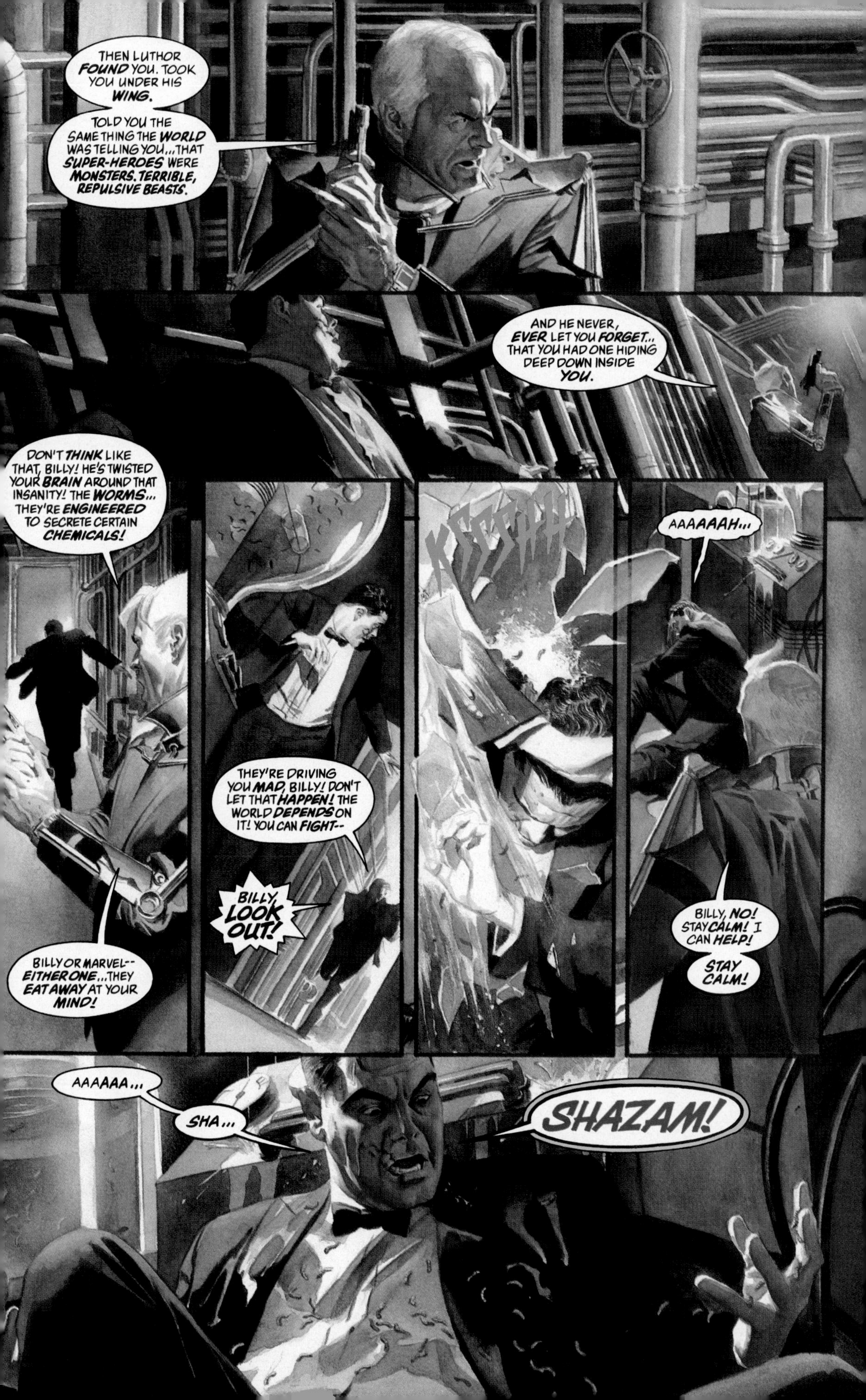

THEN LUTHOR FOUND YOU. TOOK YOU UNDER HIS WING.
TOLD YOU THE SAME THING THE WORLD WAS TELLING YOU...THAT SUPER-HEROES WERE MONSTERS. TERRIBLE, REPULSIVE BEASTS.
AND HE NEVER, EVER LET YOU FORGET... THAT YOU HAD ONE HIDING DEEP DOWN INSIDE YOU.
DON'T THINK LIKE THAT, BILLY! HE'S TWISTED YOUR BRAIN AROUND THAT INSANITY! THE WORMS... THEY'RE ENGINEERED TO SECRETE CERTAIN CHEMICALS!
BILLY OR MARVEL-- EITHER ONE... THEY EAT AWAY AT YOUR MIND!
THEY'RE DRIVING YOU MAD, BILLY! DON'T LET THAT HAPPEN! THE WORLD DEPENDS ON IT! YOU CAN FIGHT--
BILLY, LOOK OUT!
KRSSHH
AAAAAAH...
BILLY, NO! STAY CALM! I CAN HELP!
STAY CALM!
AAAAAA...
SHA...
SHAZAM!

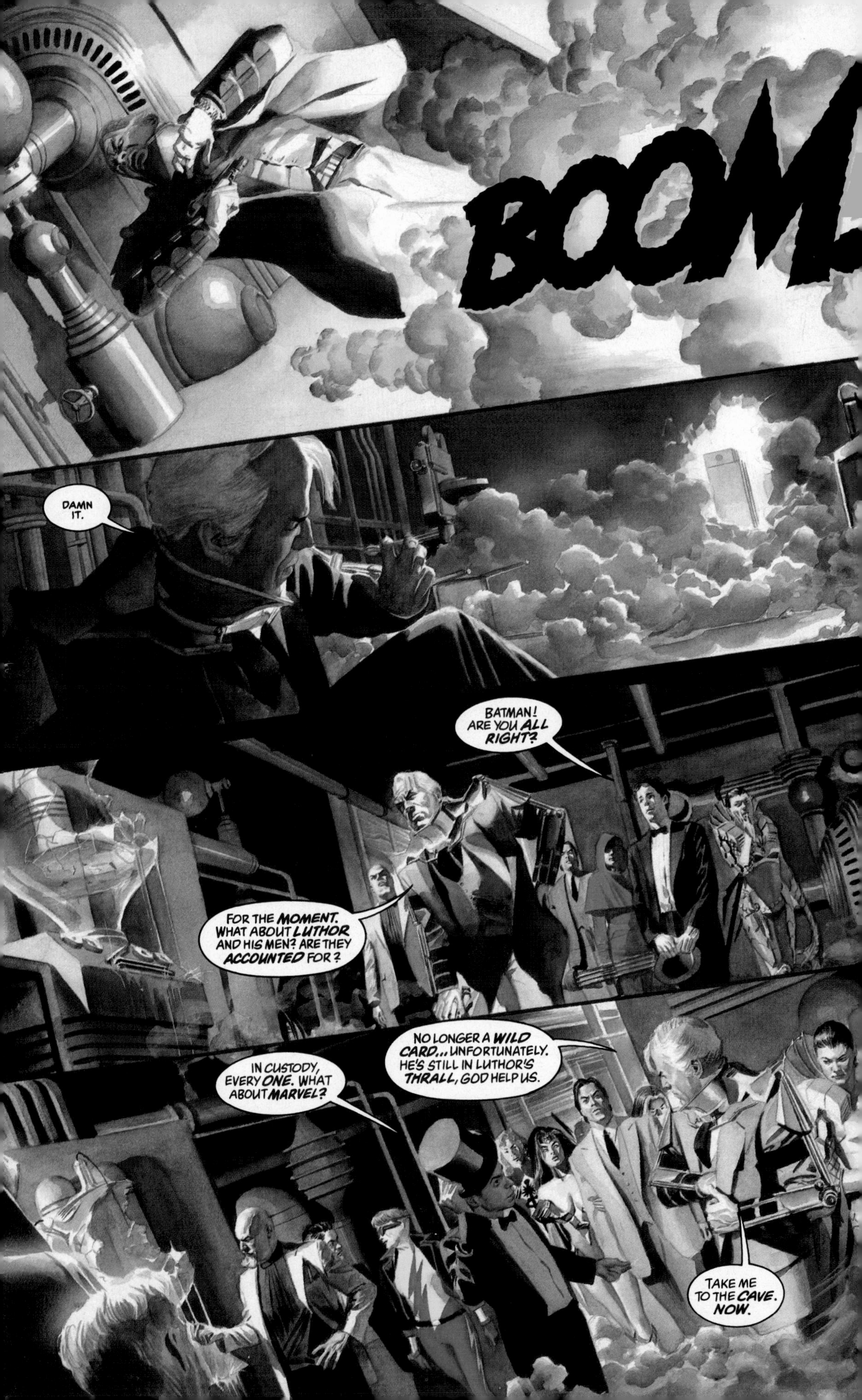
BOOM!
DAMN IT.
BATMAN! ARE YOU ALL RIGHT?
FOR THE MOMENT. WHAT ABOUT LUTHOR AND HIS MEN? ARE THEY ACCOUNTED FOR?
IN CUSTODY, EVERY ONE. WHAT ABOUT MARVEL?
NO LONGER A WILD CARD... UNFORTUNATELY. HE'S STILL IN LUTHOR'S THRALL, GOD HELP US.
TAKE ME TO THE CAVE. NOW.

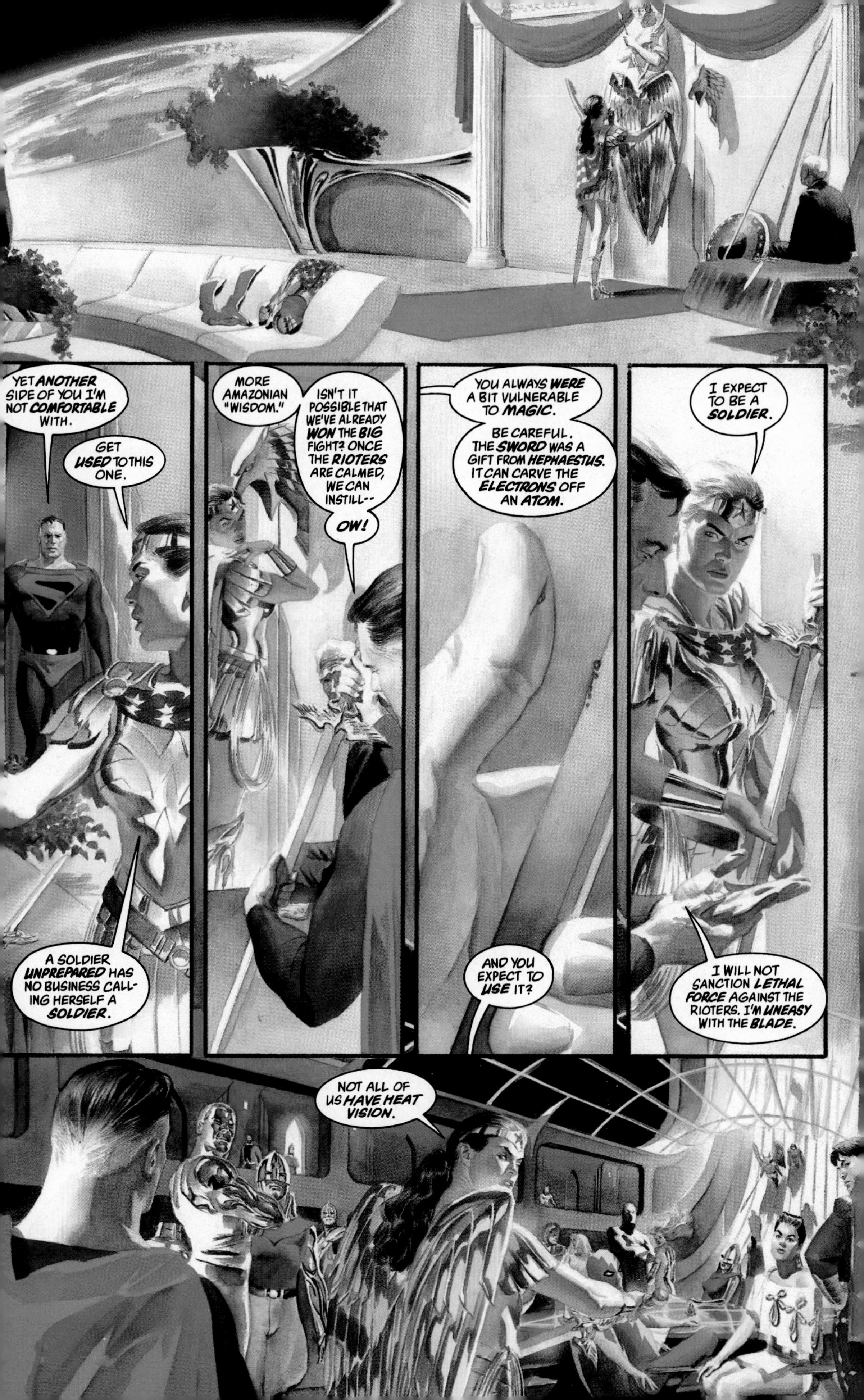
YET ANOTHER SIDE OF YOU I'M NOT COMFORTABLE WITH.
GET USED TO THIS ONE.
A SOLDIER UNPREPARED HAS NO BUSINESS CALLING HERSELF A SOLDIER.
MORE AMAZONIAN "WISDOM."
ISN'T IT POSSIBLE THAT WE'VE ALREADY WON THE BIG FIGHT? ONCE THE RIOTERS ARE CALMED, WE CAN INSTILL--
OW!
YOU ALWAYS WERE A BIT VULNERABLE TO MAGIC.
BE CAREFUL. THE SWORD WAS A GIFT FROM HEPHAESTUS. IT CAN CARVE THE ELECTRONS OFF AN ATOM.
AND YOU EXPECT TO USE IT?
I EXPECT TO BE A SOLDIER.
I WILL NOT SANCTION LETHAL FORCE AGAINST THE RIOTERS. I'M UNEASY WITH THE BLADE.
NOT ALL OF US HAVE HEAT VISION.

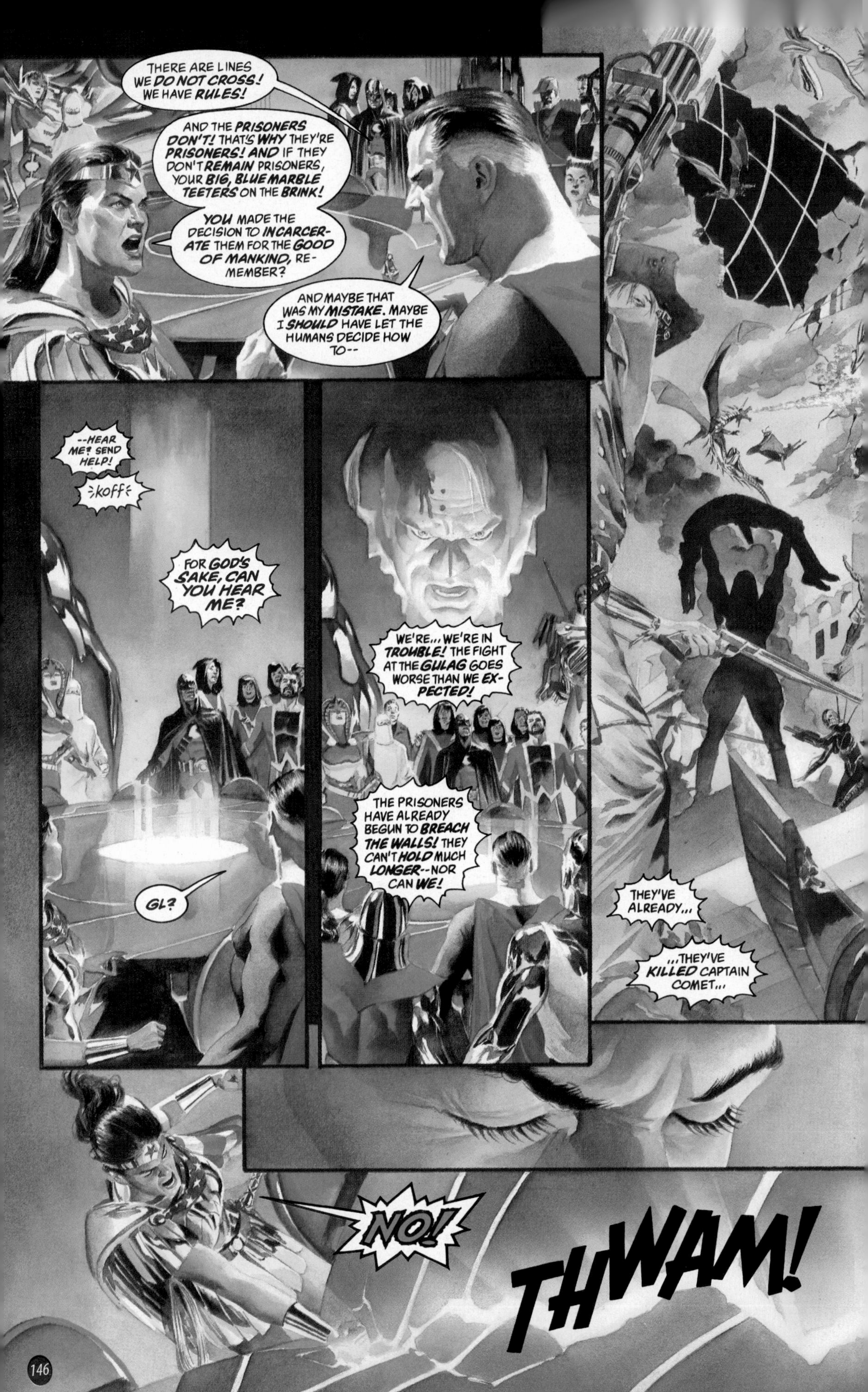

THERE ARE LINES WE DO NOT CROSS! WE HAVE RULES!
AND THE PRISONERS DON'T! THAT'S WHY THEY'RE PRISONERS! AND IF THEY DON'T REMAIN PRISONERS, YOUR BIG, BLUE MARBLE TEETERS ON THE BRINK!
YOU MADE THE DECISION TO INCARCERATE THEM FOR THE GOOD OF MANKIND, REMEMBER?
AND MAYBE THAT WAS MY MISTAKE. MAYBE I SHOULD HAVE LET THE HUMANS DECIDE HOW TO--
--HEAR ME? SEND HELP!
koff
FOR GOD'S SAKE, CAN YOU HEAR ME?
GL?
WE'RE... WE'RE IN TROUBLE! THE FIGHT AT THE GULAG GOES WORSE THAN WE EXPECTED!
THE PRISONERS HAVE ALREADY BEGUN TO BREACH THE WALLS! THEY CAN'T HOLD MUCH LONGER--NOR CAN WE!
THEY'VE ALREADY...
...THEY'VE KILLED CAPTAIN COMET...
NO!
THWAM!

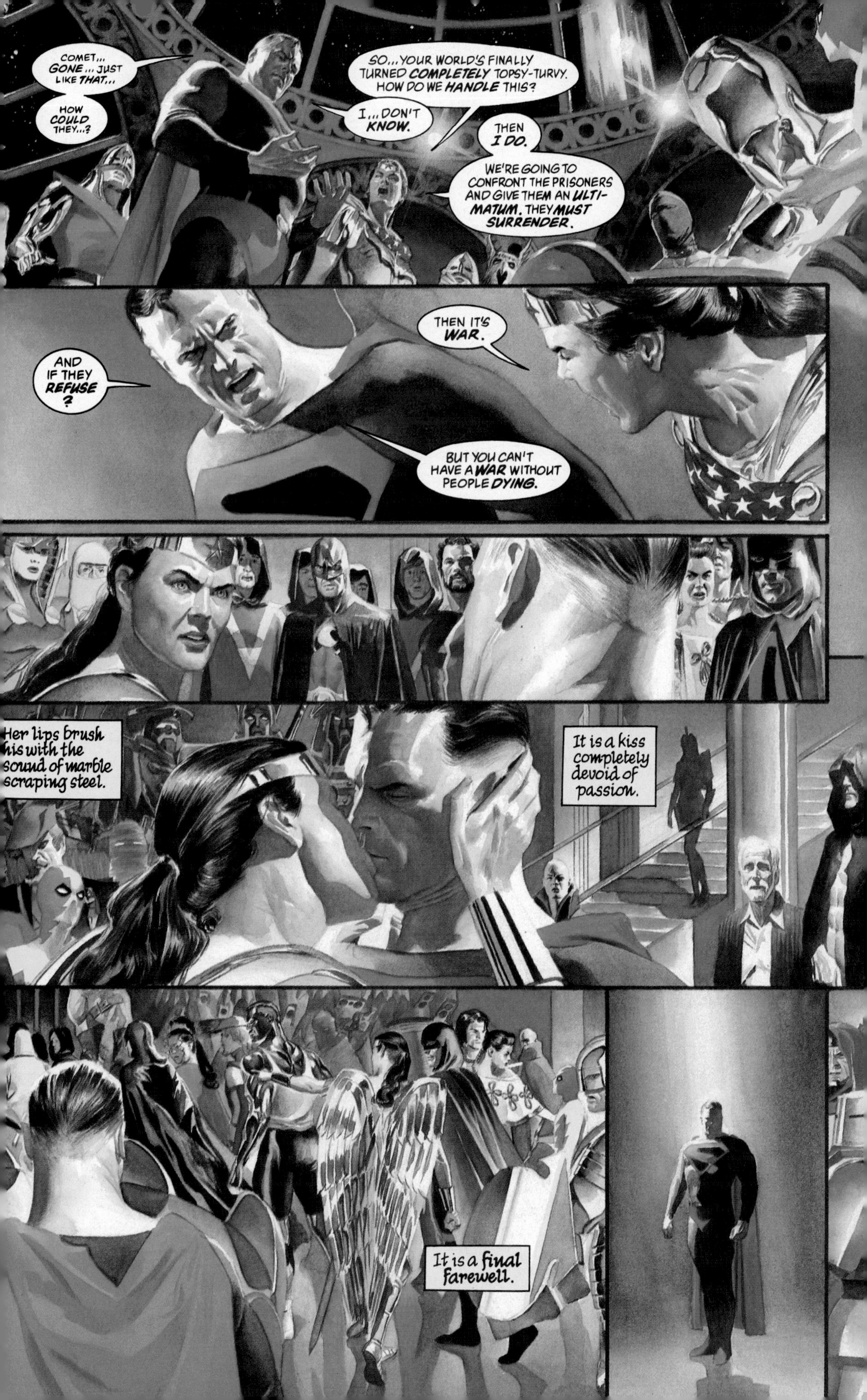
COMET... GONE... JUST LIKE THAT...
HOW COULD THEY...?
SO... YOUR WORLD'S FINALLY TURNED COMPLETELY TOPSY-TURVY. HOW DO WE HANDLE THIS?
I... DON'T KNOW.
THEN I DO.
WE'RE GOING TO CONFRONT THE PRISONERS AND GIVE THEM AN ULTI-MATUM. THEY MUST SURRENDER.
AND IF THEY REFUSE?
THEN IT'S WAR.
BUT YOU CAN'T HAVE A WAR WITHOUT PEOPLE DYING.
Her lips brush his with the sound of marble scraping steel.
It is a kiss completely devoid of passion.
It is a final farewell.

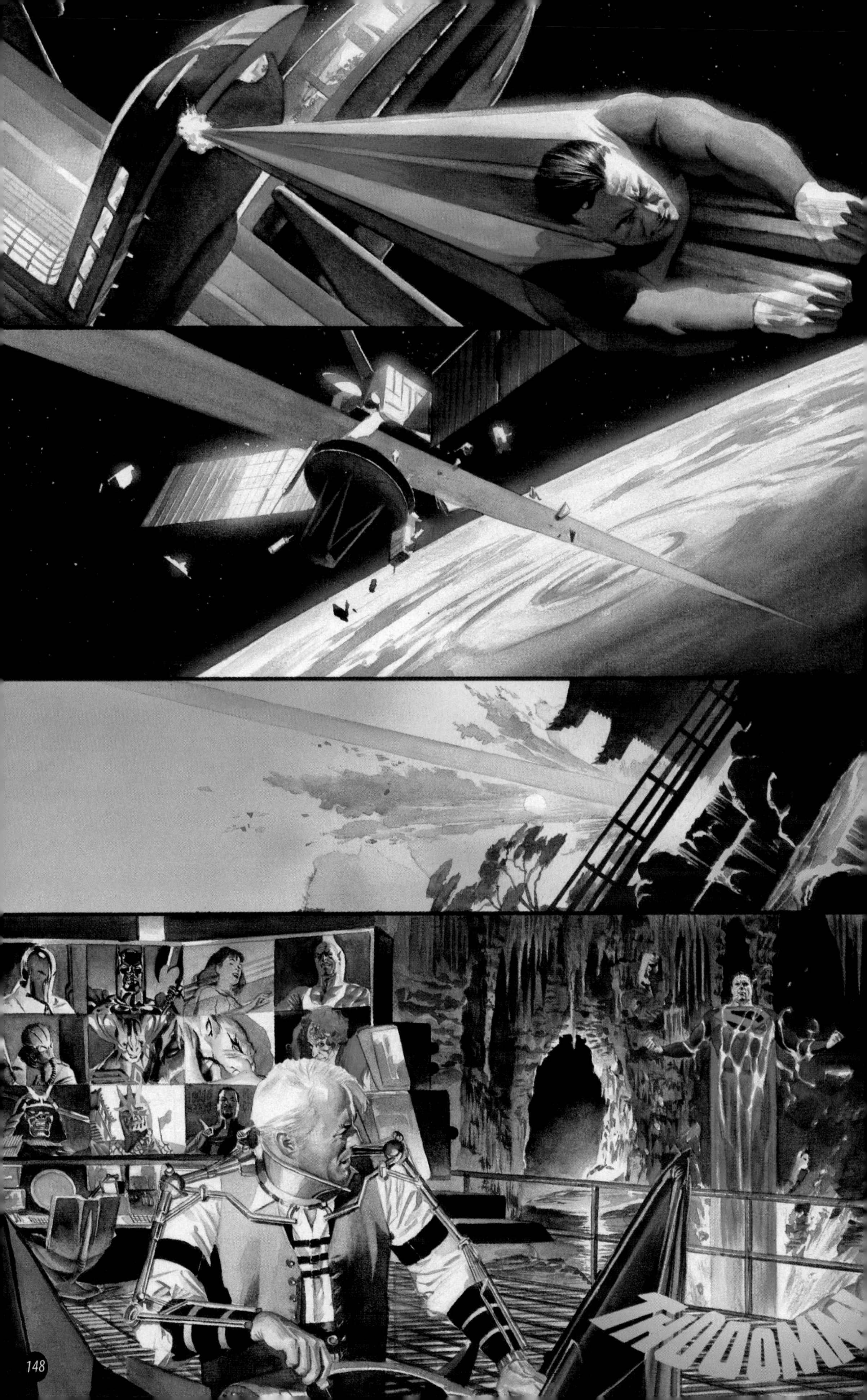
THOOOMM

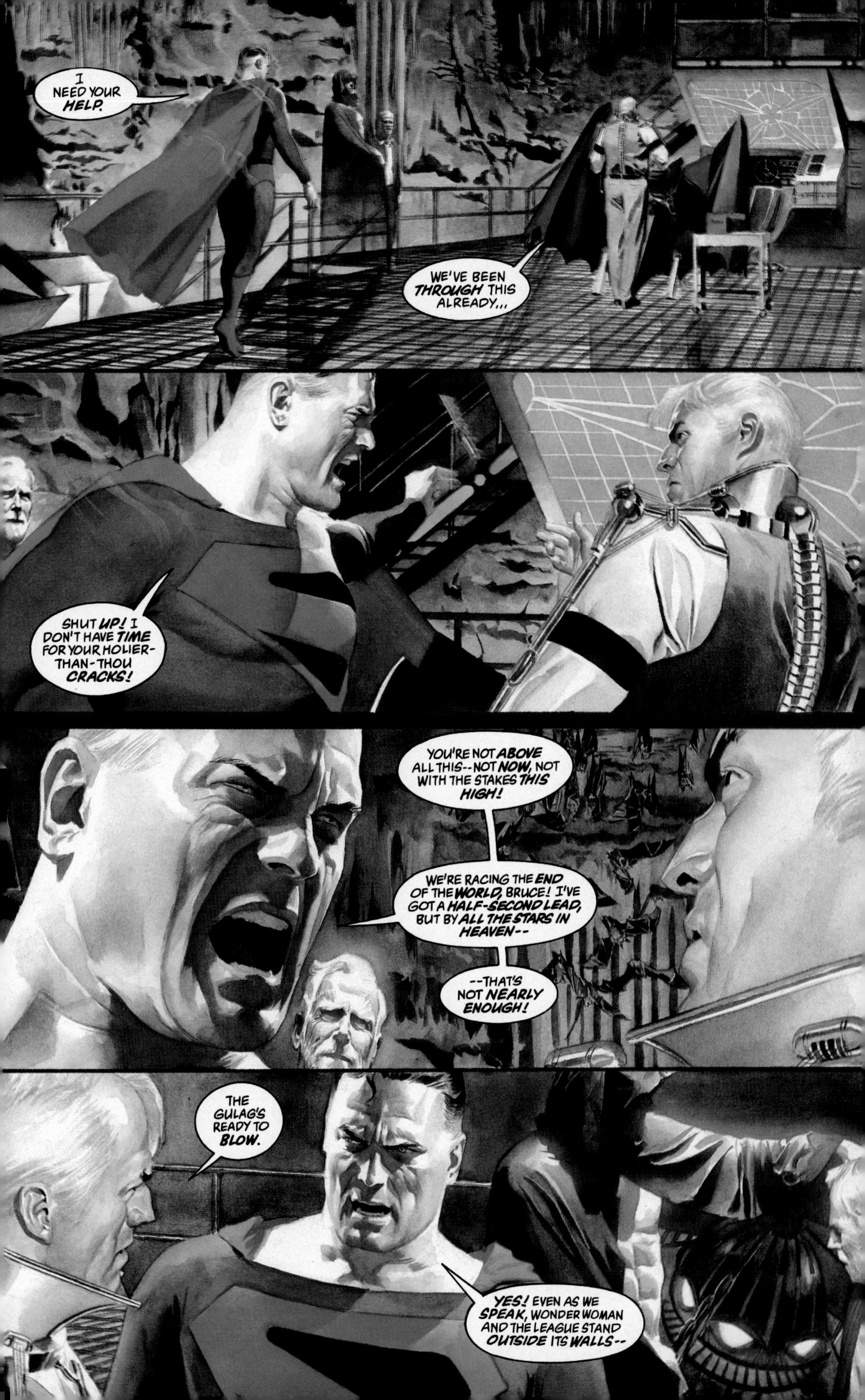
I NEED YOUR HELP.
WE'VE BEEN THROUGH THIS ALREADY...
SHUT UP! I DON'T HAVE TIME FOR YOUR HOLIER-THAN-THOU CRACKS!
YOU'RE NOT ABOVE ALL THIS--NOT NOW, NOT WITH THE STAKES THIS HIGH!
WE'RE RACING THE END OF THE WORLD, BRUCE! I'VE GOT A HALF-SECOND LEAD, BUT BY ALL THE STARS IN HEAVEN--
--THAT'S NOT NEARLY ENOUGH!
THE GULAG'S READY TO BLOW.
YES! EVEN AS WE SPEAK, WONDER WOMAN AND THE LEAGUE STAND OUTSIDE ITS WALLS--

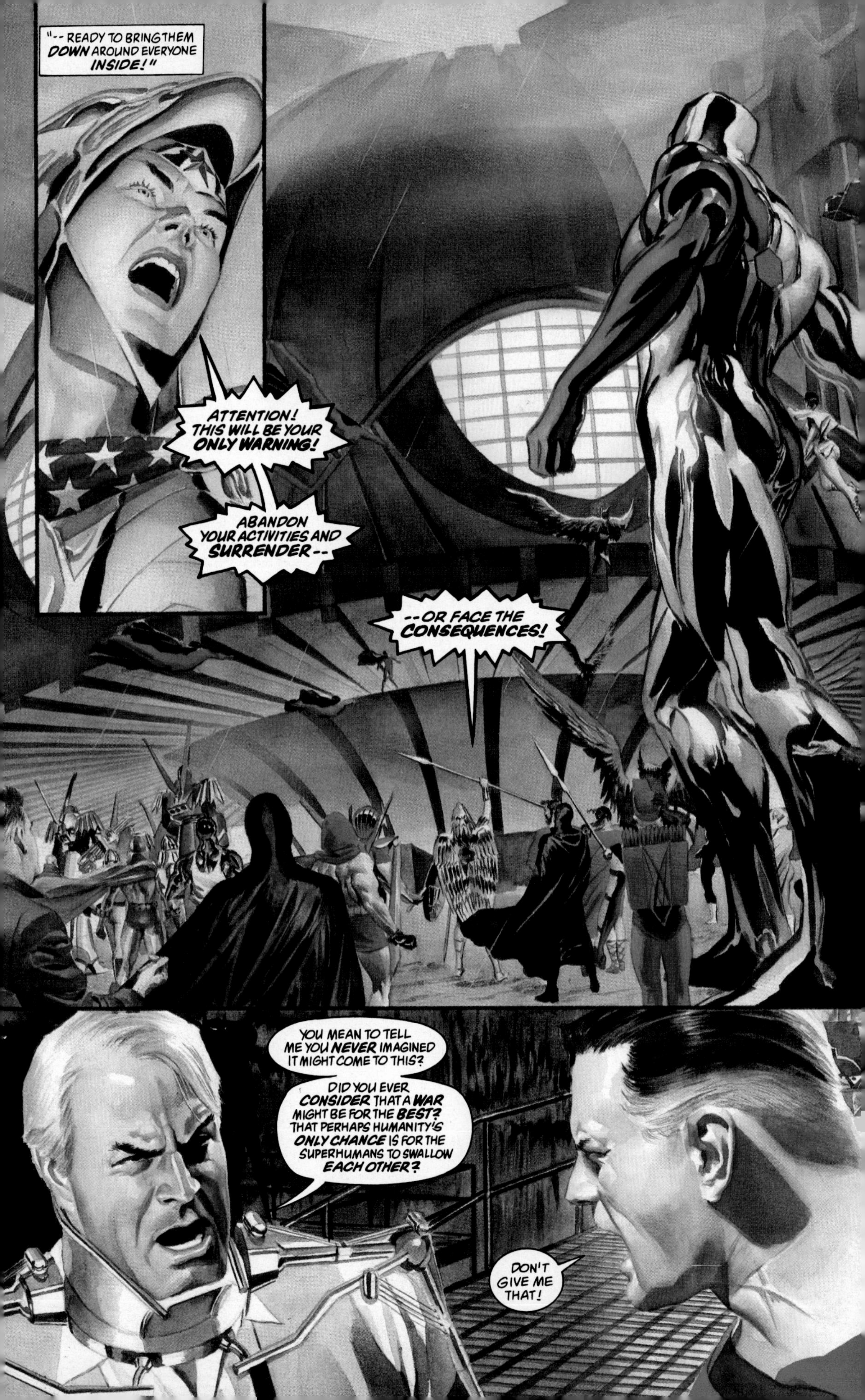
"-- READY TO BRING THEM DOWN AROUND EVERYONE INSIDE!"
ATTENTION! THIS WILL BE YOUR ONLY WARNING!
ABANDON YOUR ACTIVITIES AND SURRENDER--
--OR FACE THE CONSEQUENCES!
YOU MEAN TO TELL ME YOU NEVER IMAGINED IT MIGHT COME TO THIS?
DID YOU EVER CONSIDER THAT A WAR MIGHT BE FOR THE BEST? THAT PERHAPS HUMANITY'S ONLY CHANCE IS FOR THE SUPERHUMANS TO SWALLOW EACH OTHER?
DON'T GIVE ME THAT!

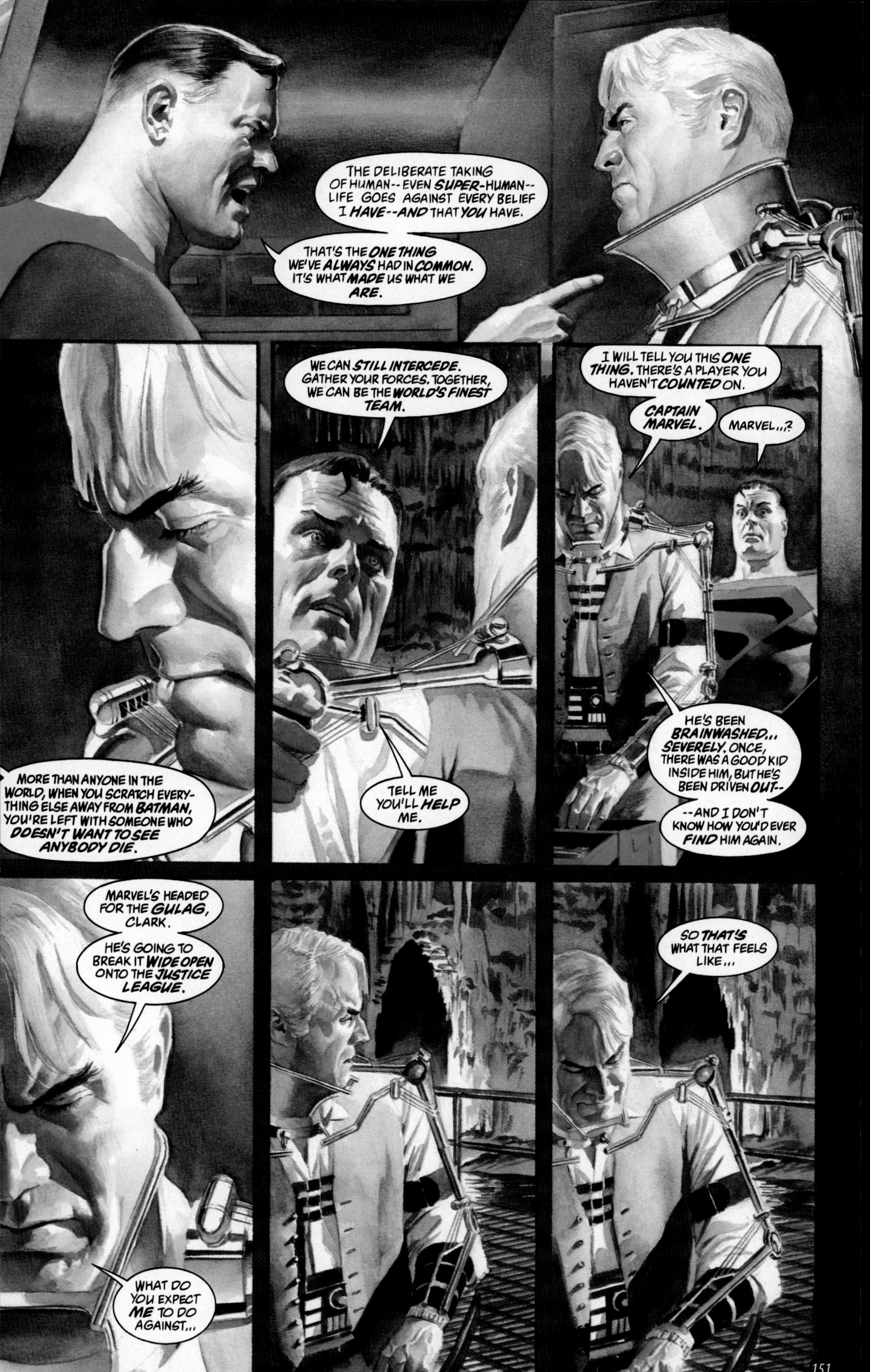
THE DELIBERATE TAKING OF HUMAN-- EVEN SUPER-HUMAN-- LIFE GOES AGAINST EVERY BELIEF I HAVE--AND THAT YOU HAVE.
THAT'S THE ONE THING WE'VE ALWAYS HAD IN COMMON. IT'S WHAT MADE US WHAT WE ARE.
MORE THAN ANYONE IN THE WORLD, WHEN YOU SCRATCH EVERY-THING ELSE AWAY FROM BATMAN, YOU'RE LEFT WITH SOMEONE WHO DOESN'T WANT TO SEE ANYBODY DIE.
WE CAN STILL INTERCEDE. GATHER YOUR FORCES. TOGETHER, WE CAN BE THE WORLD'S FINEST TEAM.
TELL ME YOU'LL HELP ME.
I WILL TELL YOU THIS ONE THING. THERE'S A PLAYER YOU HAVEN'T COUNTED ON.
CAPTAIN MARVEL.
MARVEL...?
HE'S BEEN BRAINWASHED... SEVERELY. ONCE, THERE WAS A GOOD KID INSIDE HIM, BUT HE'S BEEN DRIVEN OUT--
--AND I DON'T KNOW HOW YOU'D EVER FIND HIM AGAIN.
MARVEL'S HEADED FOR THE GULAG, CLARK.
HE'S GOING TO BREAK IT WIDE OPEN ONTO THE JUSTICE LEAGUE.
WHAT DO YOU EXPECT ME TO DO AGAINST...
SO THAT'S WHAT THAT FEELS LIKE...

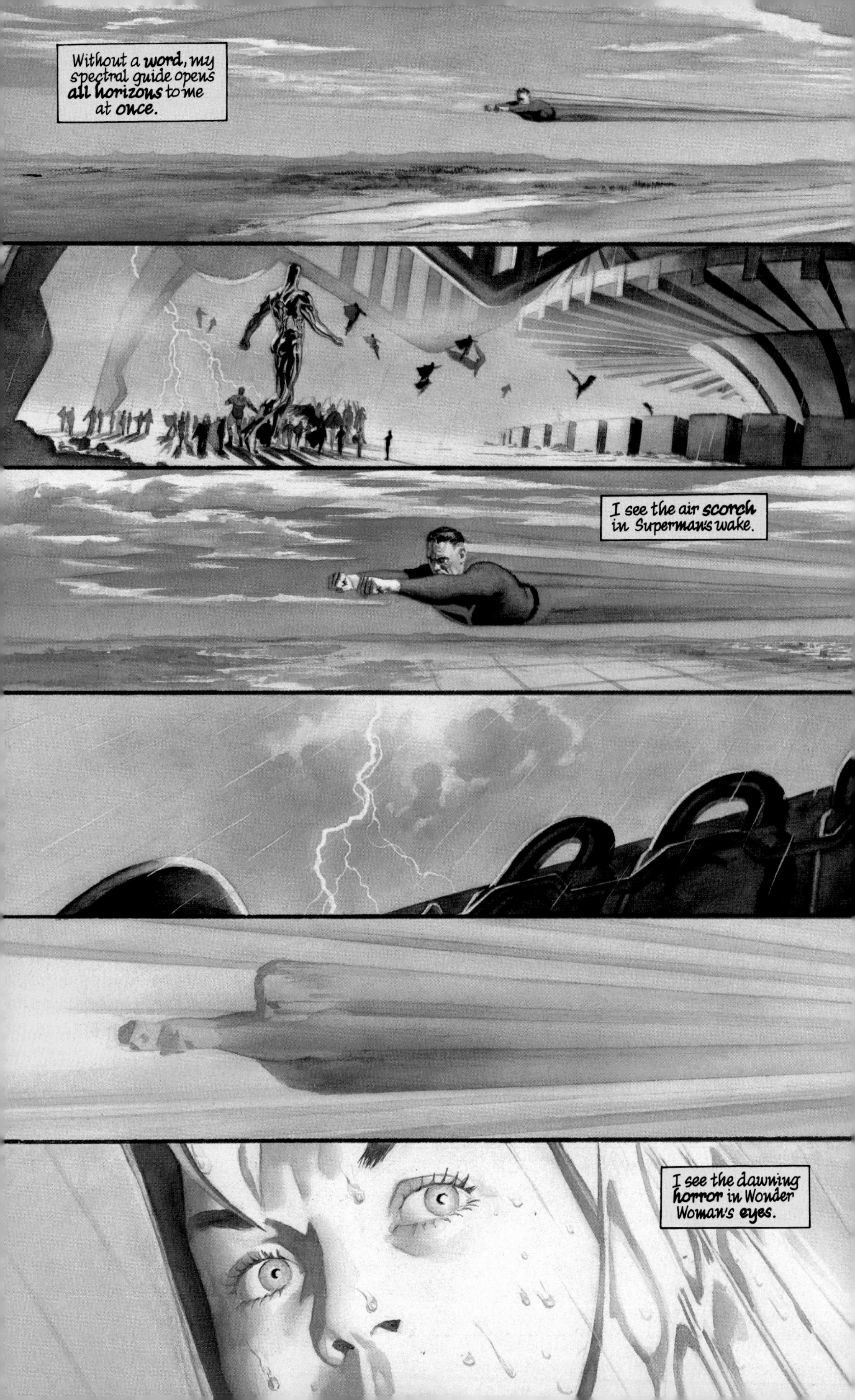
Without a word, my spectral guide opens all horizons to me at once.
I see the air scorch in Superman's wake.
I see the dawning horror in Wonder Woman's eyes.

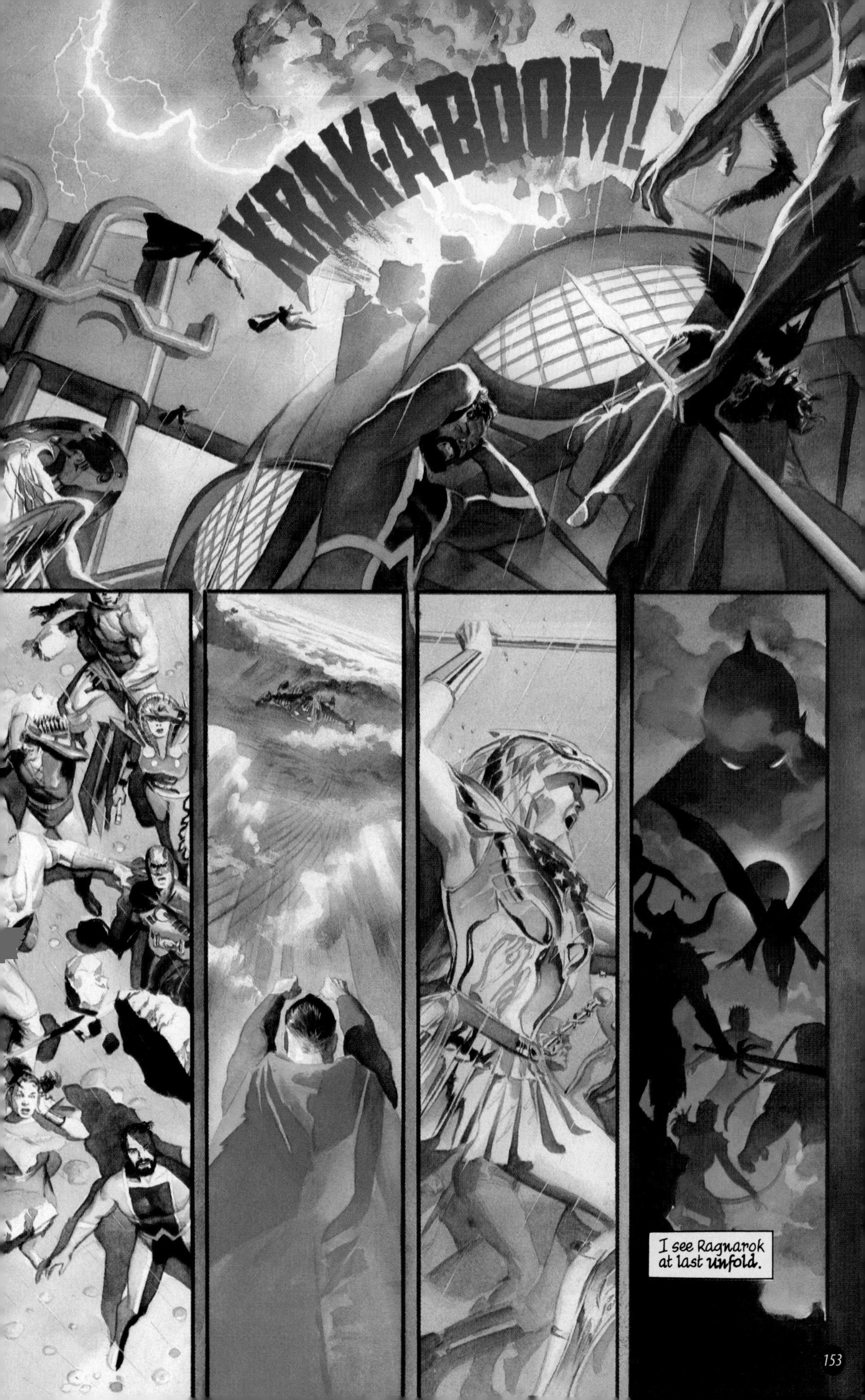
KRAKA-BOOM!
I see Ragnarok at last unfold.

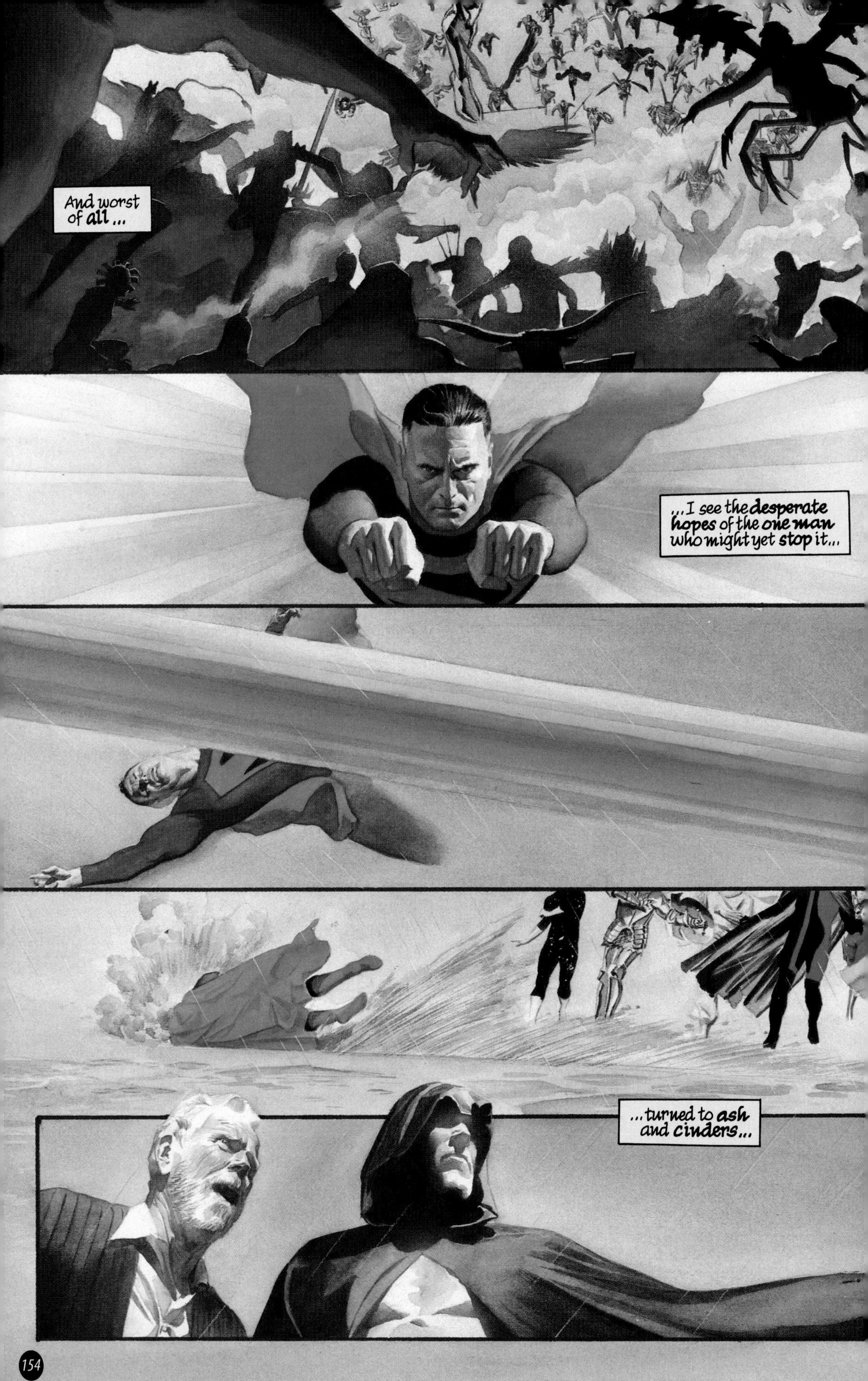

And worst of all...
...I see the desperate hopes of the one man who might yet stop it...
...turned to ash and cinders...

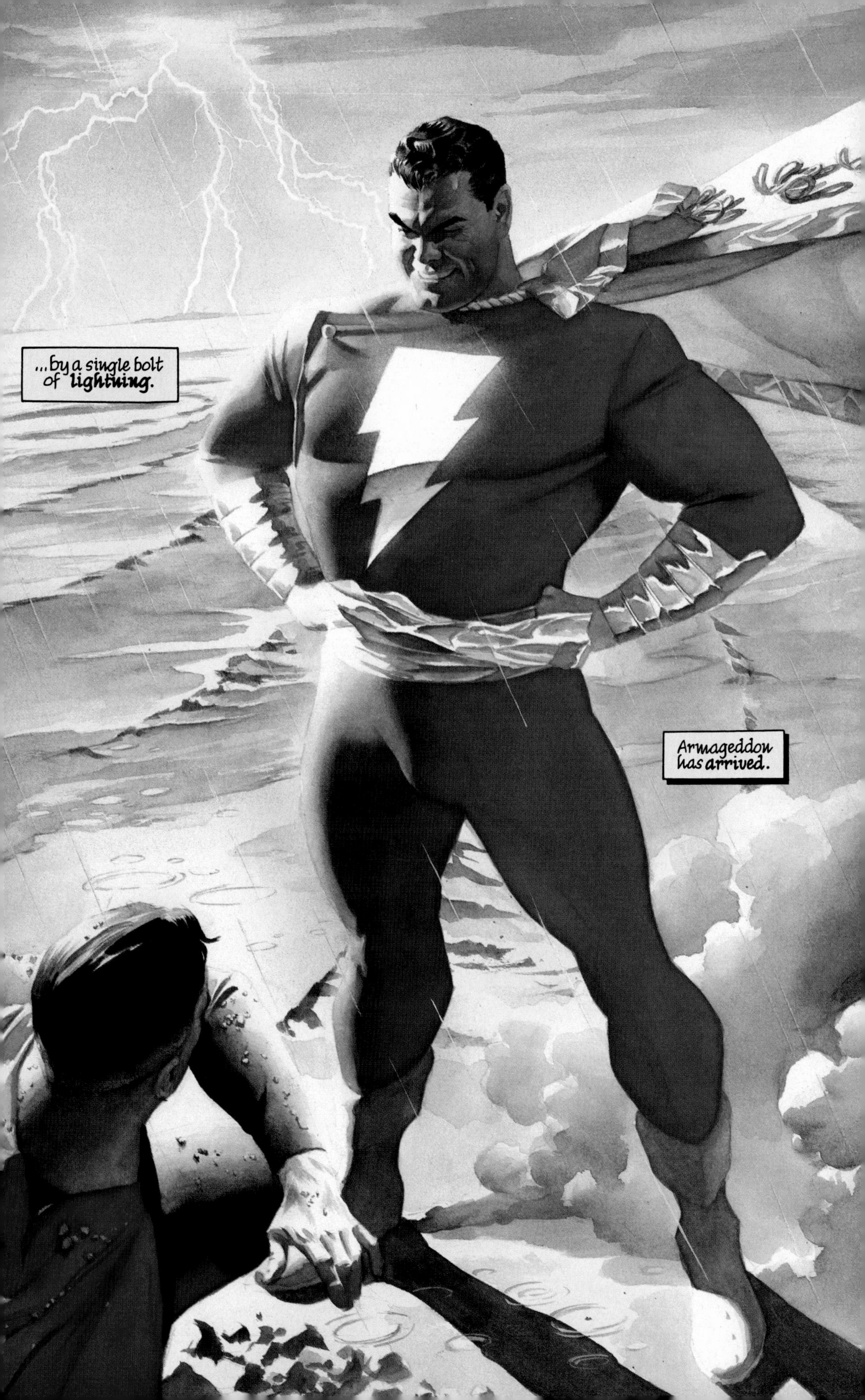
...by a single bolt of lightning.
Armageddon has arrived.

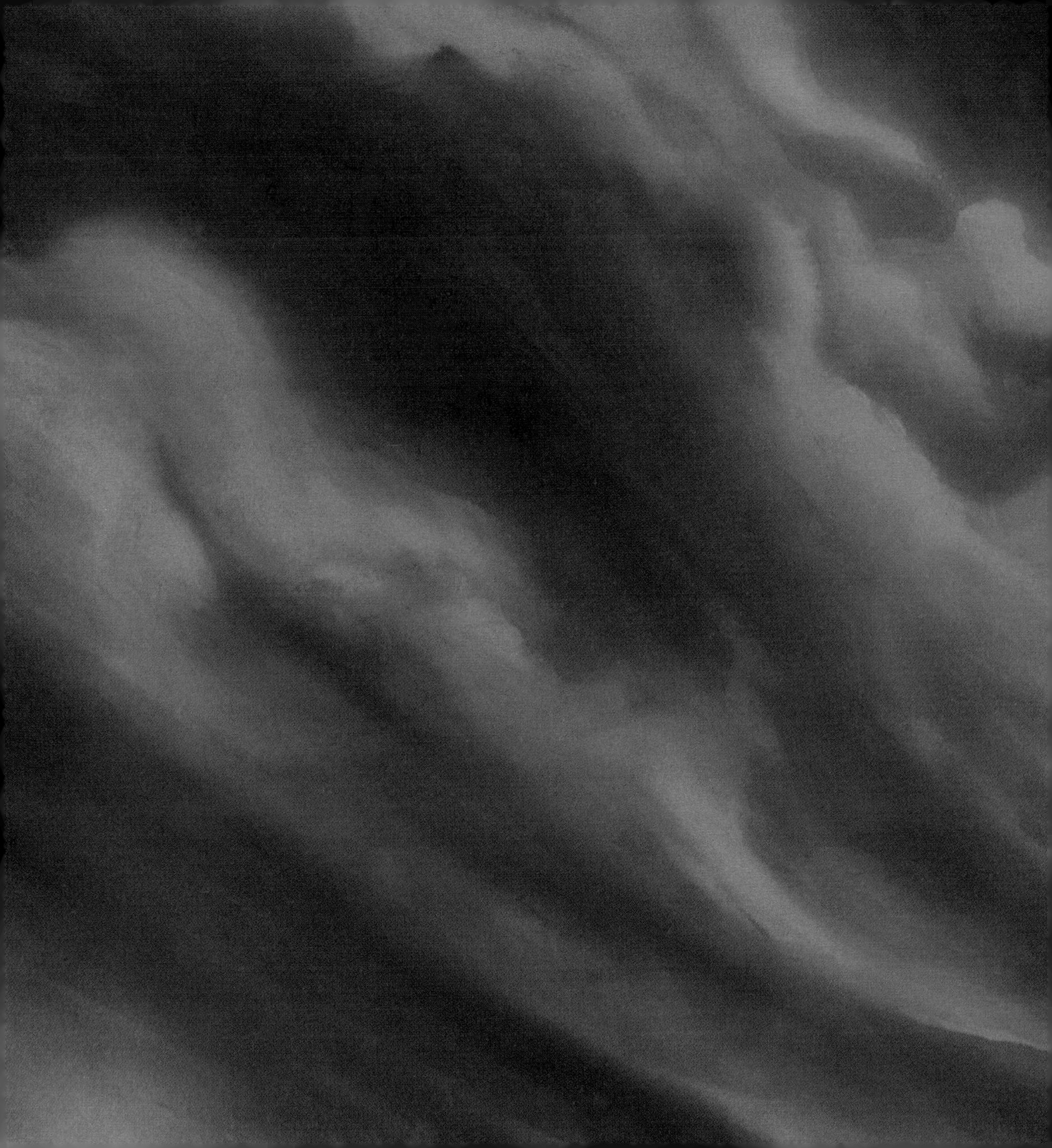

CHAPTER FOUR

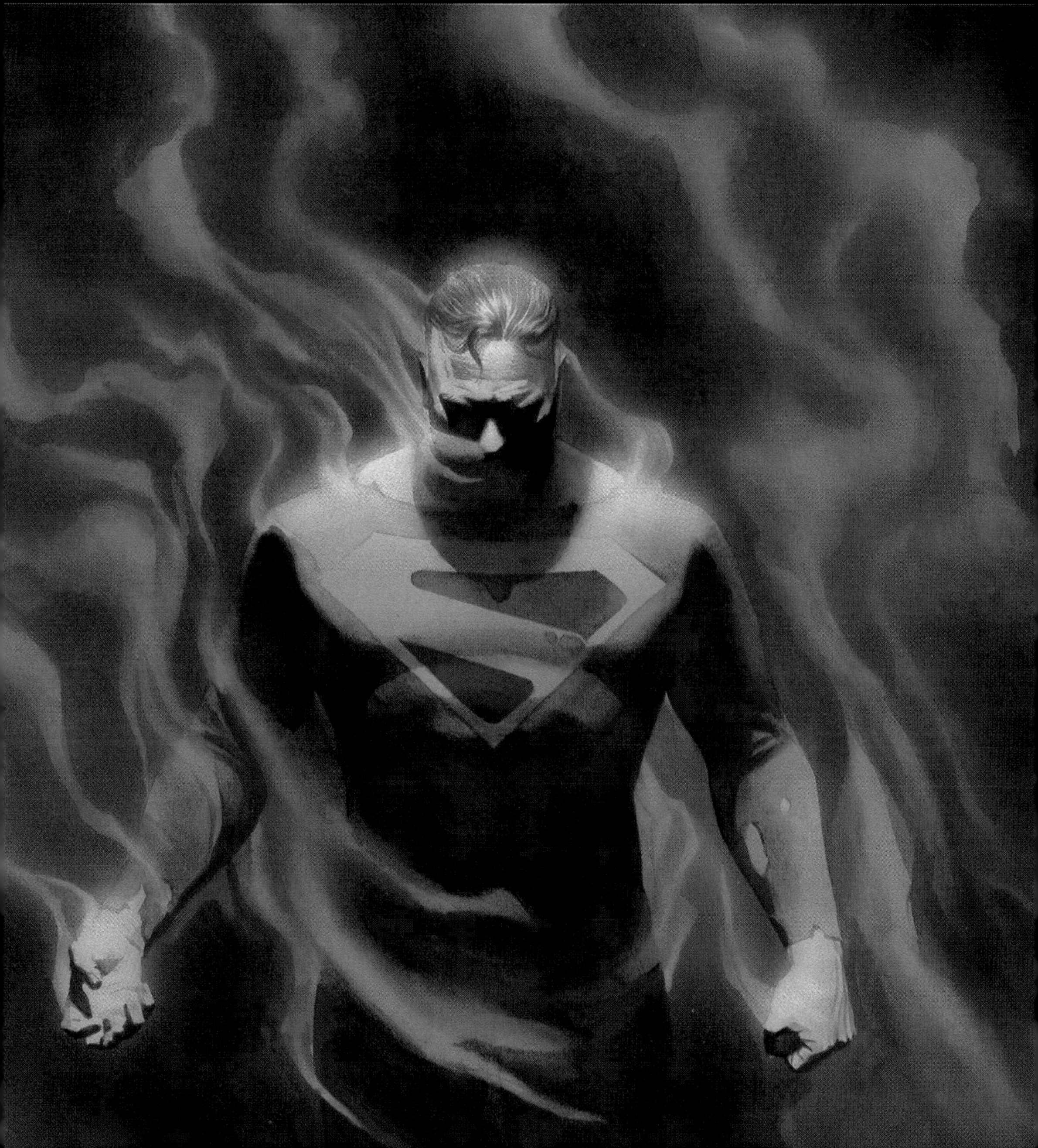

Never-Ending Battle

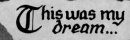

There were voices... and thunderings, and lightnings...

"...and an earthquake."

This was my dream...

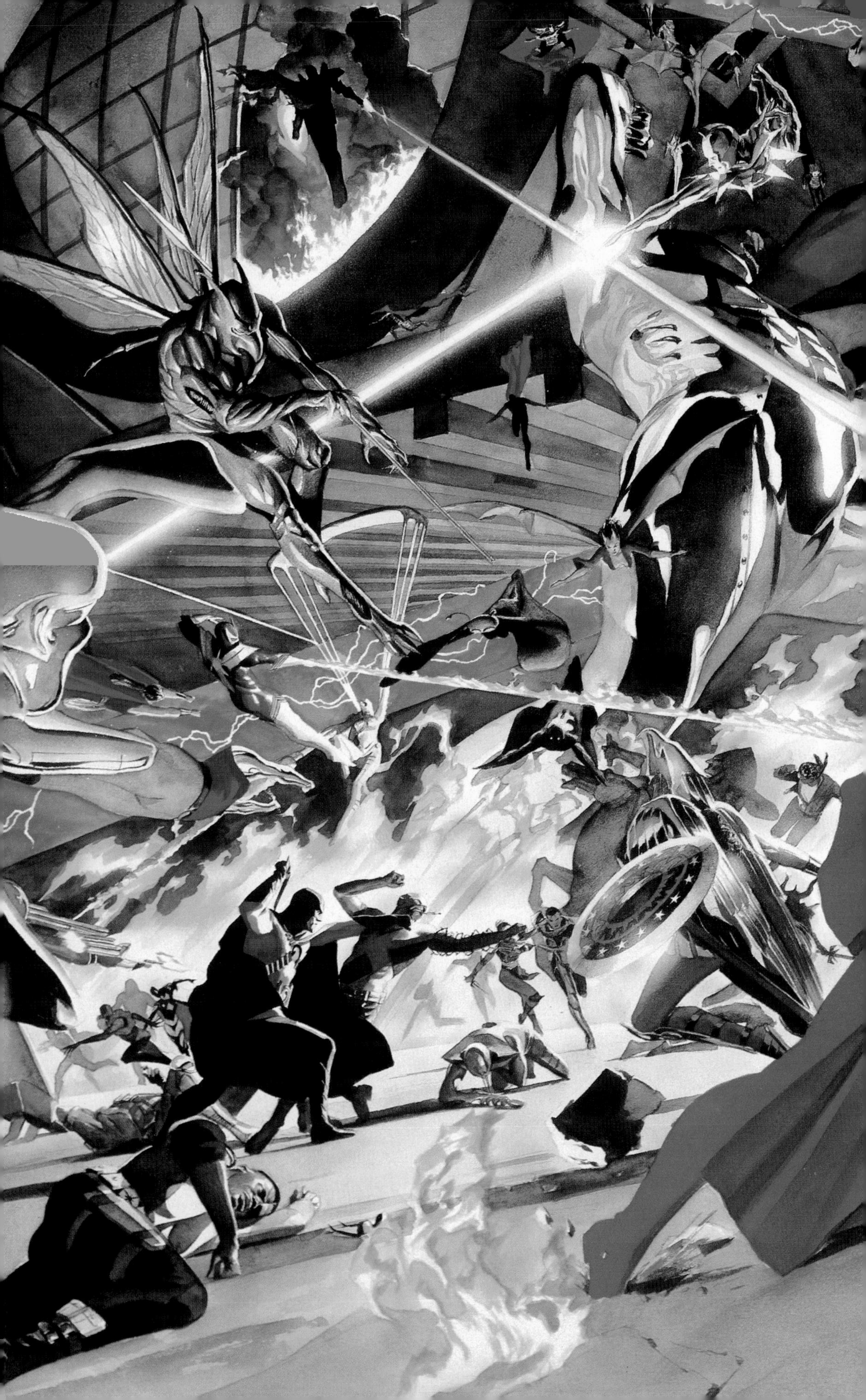

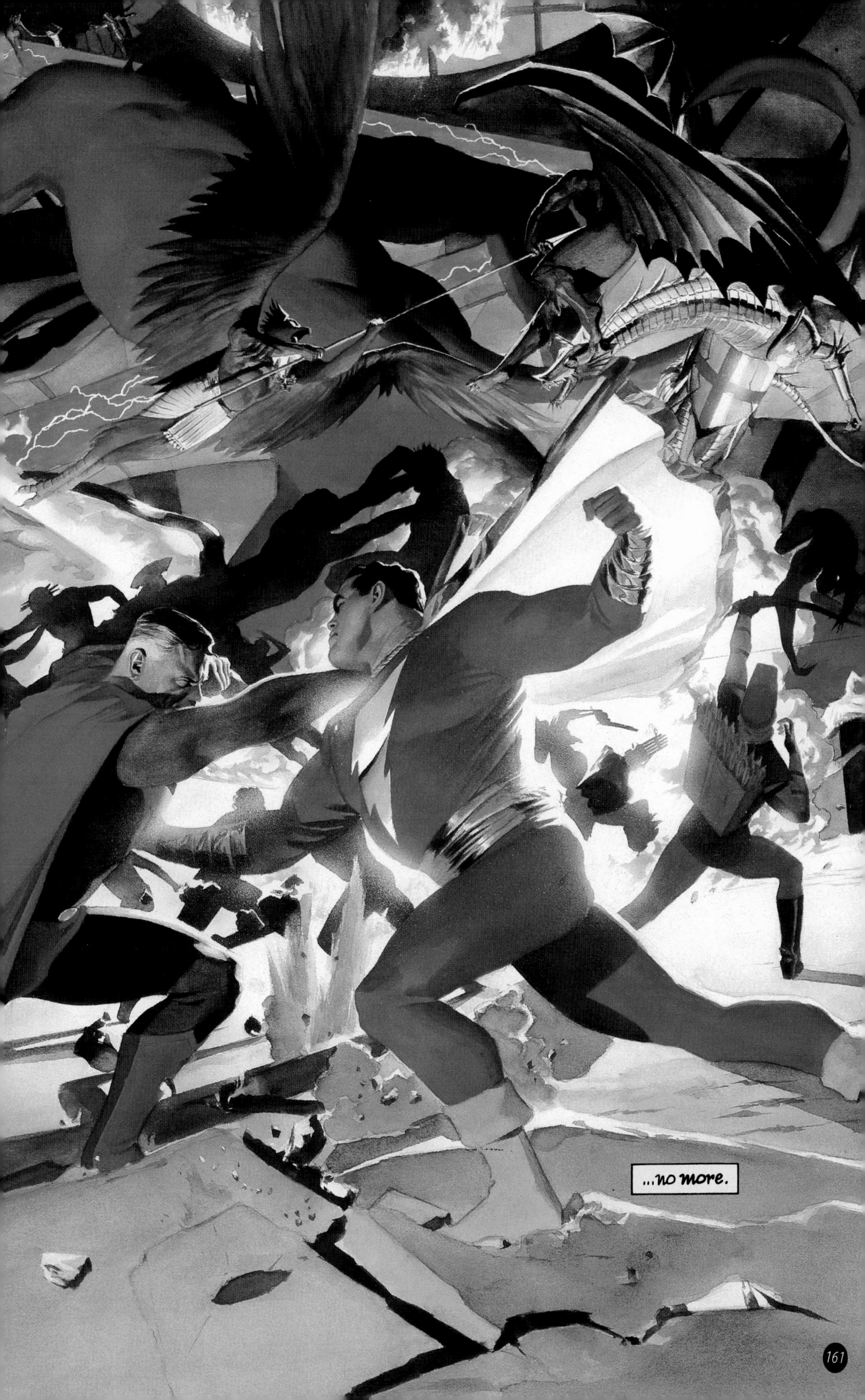
...no more.

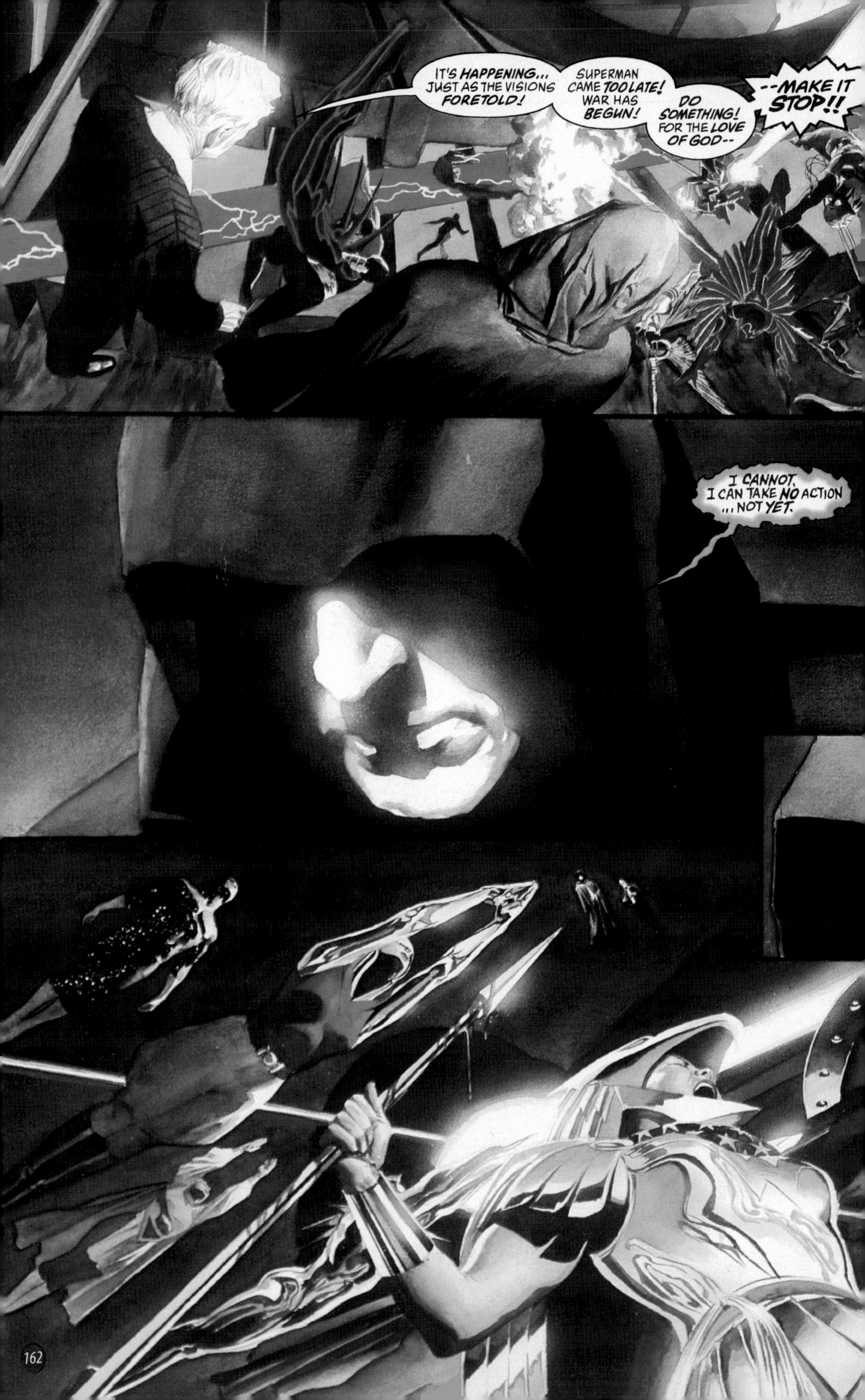
IT'S HAPPENING... JUST AS THE VISIONS FORETOLD!
SUPERMAN CAME TOO LATE! WAR HAS BEGUN!
DO SOMETHING! FOR THE LOVE OF GOD--
--MAKE IT STOP!!
I CANNOT. I CAN TAKE NO ACTION ... NOT YET.

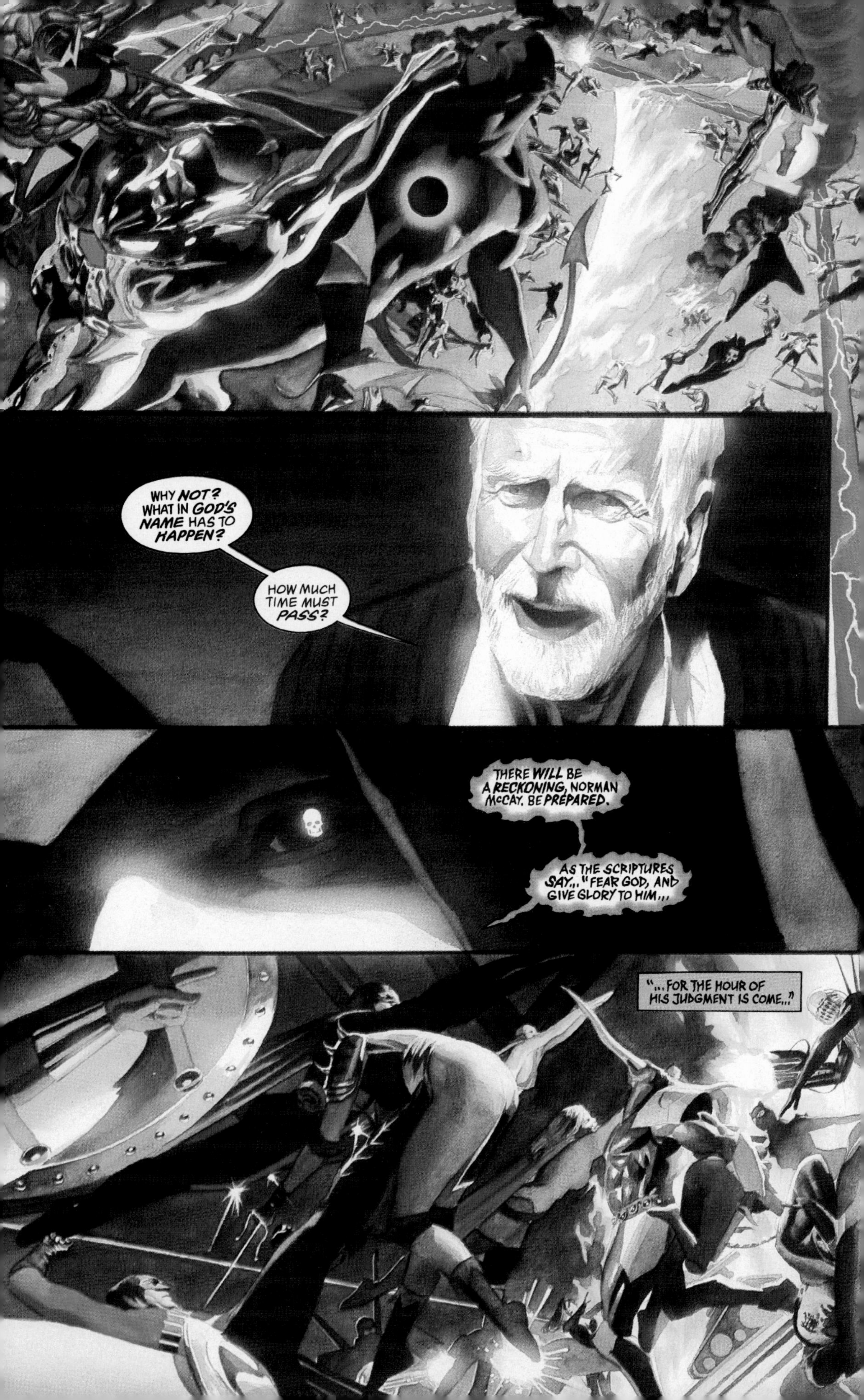
WHY NOT? WHAT IN GOD'S NAME HAS TO HAPPEN?
HOW MUCH TIME MUST PASS?
THERE WILL BE A RECKONING, NORMAN McCAY. BE PREPARED.
AS THE SCRIPTURES SAY... "FEAR GOD, AND GIVE GLORY TO HIM...
"...FOR THE HOUR OF HIS JUDGMENT IS COME..."

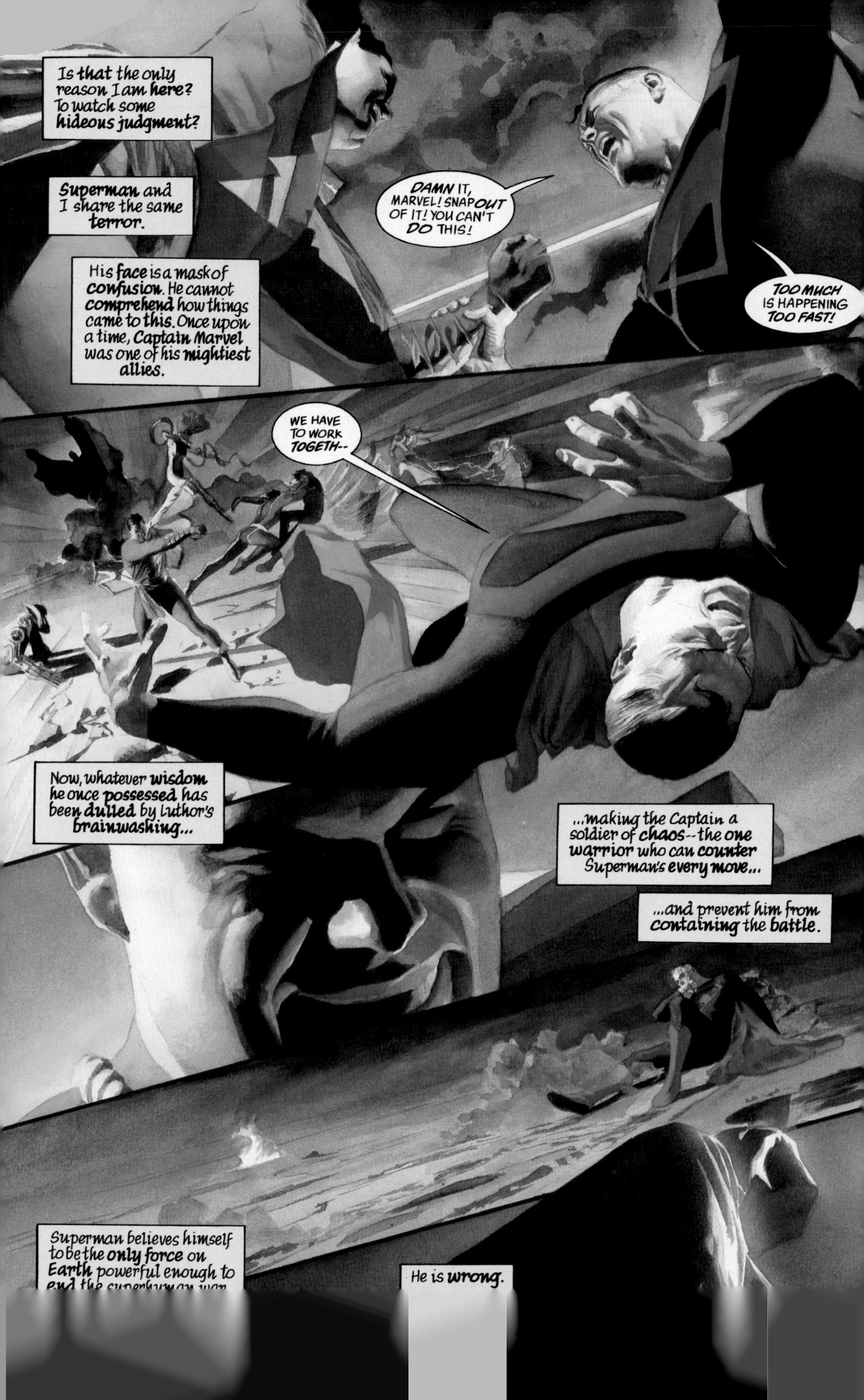
Is that the only reason I am here? To watch some hideous judgment?
Superman and I share the same terror.
His face is a mask of confusion. He cannot comprehend how things came to this. Once upon a time, Captain Marvel was one of his mightiest allies.
DAMN IT, MARVEL! SNAP OUT OF IT! YOU CAN'T DO THIS!
TOO MUCH IS HAPPENING TOO FAST!
WE HAVE TO WORK TOGETH--
Now, whatever wisdom he once possessed has been dulled by Luthor's brainwashing...
...making the Captain a soldier of chaos--the one warrior who can counter Superman's every move...
...and prevent him from containing the battle.
Superman believes himself to be the only force on Earth powerful enough to
He is wrong.

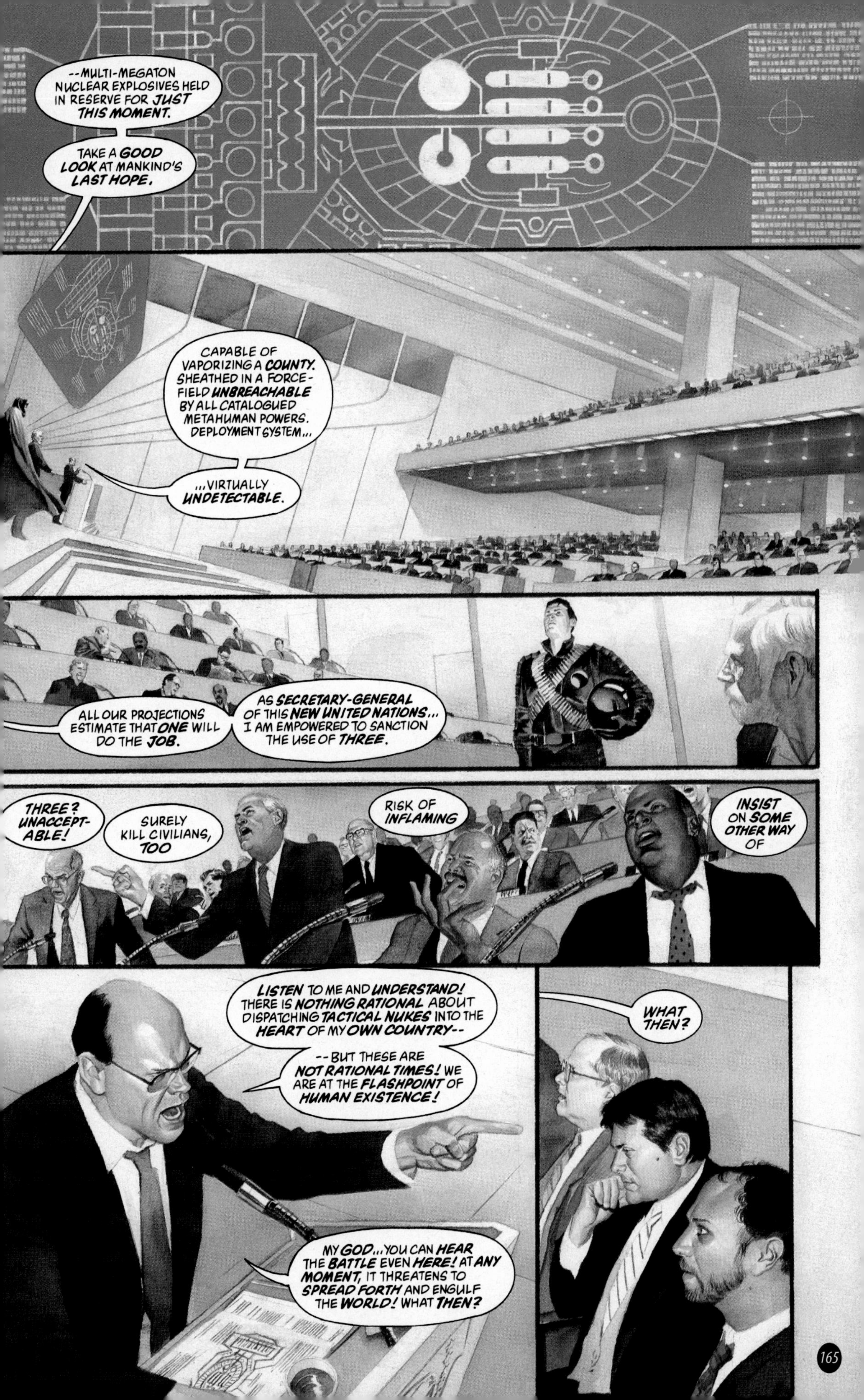
--MULTI-MEGATON NUCLEAR EXPLOSIVES HELD IN RESERVE FOR JUST THIS MOMENT.
TAKE A GOOD LOOK AT MANKIND'S LAST HOPE.
CAPABLE OF VAPORIZING A COUNTY. SHEATHED IN A FORCE-FIELD UNBREACHABLE BY ALL CATALOGUED METAHUMAN POWERS. DEPLOYMENT SYSTEM...
...VIRTUALLY UNDETECTABLE.
ALL OUR PROJECTIONS ESTIMATE THAT ONE WILL DO THE JOB.
AS SECRETARY-GENERAL OF THIS NEW UNITED NATIONS... I AM EMPOWERED TO SANCTION THE USE OF THREE.
THREE? UNACCEPT-ABLE!
SURELY KILL CIVILIANS, TOO
RISK OF INFLAMING
INSIST ON SOME OTHER WAY OF
LISTEN TO ME AND UNDERSTAND! THERE IS NOTHING RATIONAL ABOUT DISPATCHING TACTICAL NUKES INTO THE HEART OF MY OWN COUNTRY--
--BUT THESE ARE NOT RATIONAL TIMES! WE ARE AT THE FLASHPOINT OF HUMAN EXISTENCE!
MY GOD... YOU CAN HEAR THE BATTLE EVEN HERE! AT ANY MOMENT, IT THREATENS TO SPREAD FORTH AND ENGULF THE WORLD! WHAT THEN?
WHAT THEN?

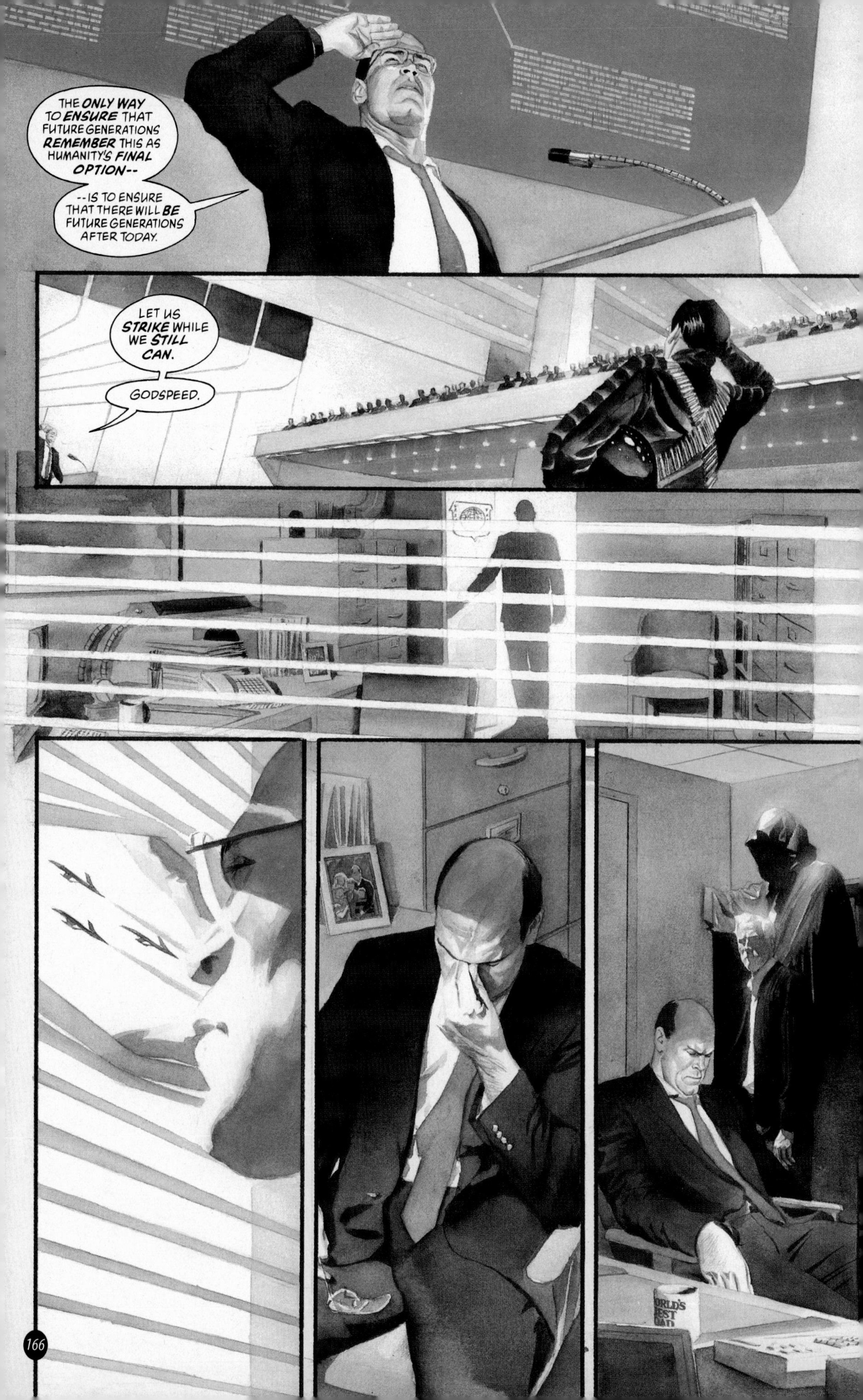
THE ONLY WAY TO ENSURE THAT FUTURE GENERATIONS REMEMBER THIS AS HUMANITY'S FINAL OPTION--
--IS TO ENSURE THAT THERE WILL BE FUTURE GENERATIONS AFTER TODAY.
LET US STRIKE WHILE WE STILL CAN.
GODSPEED.

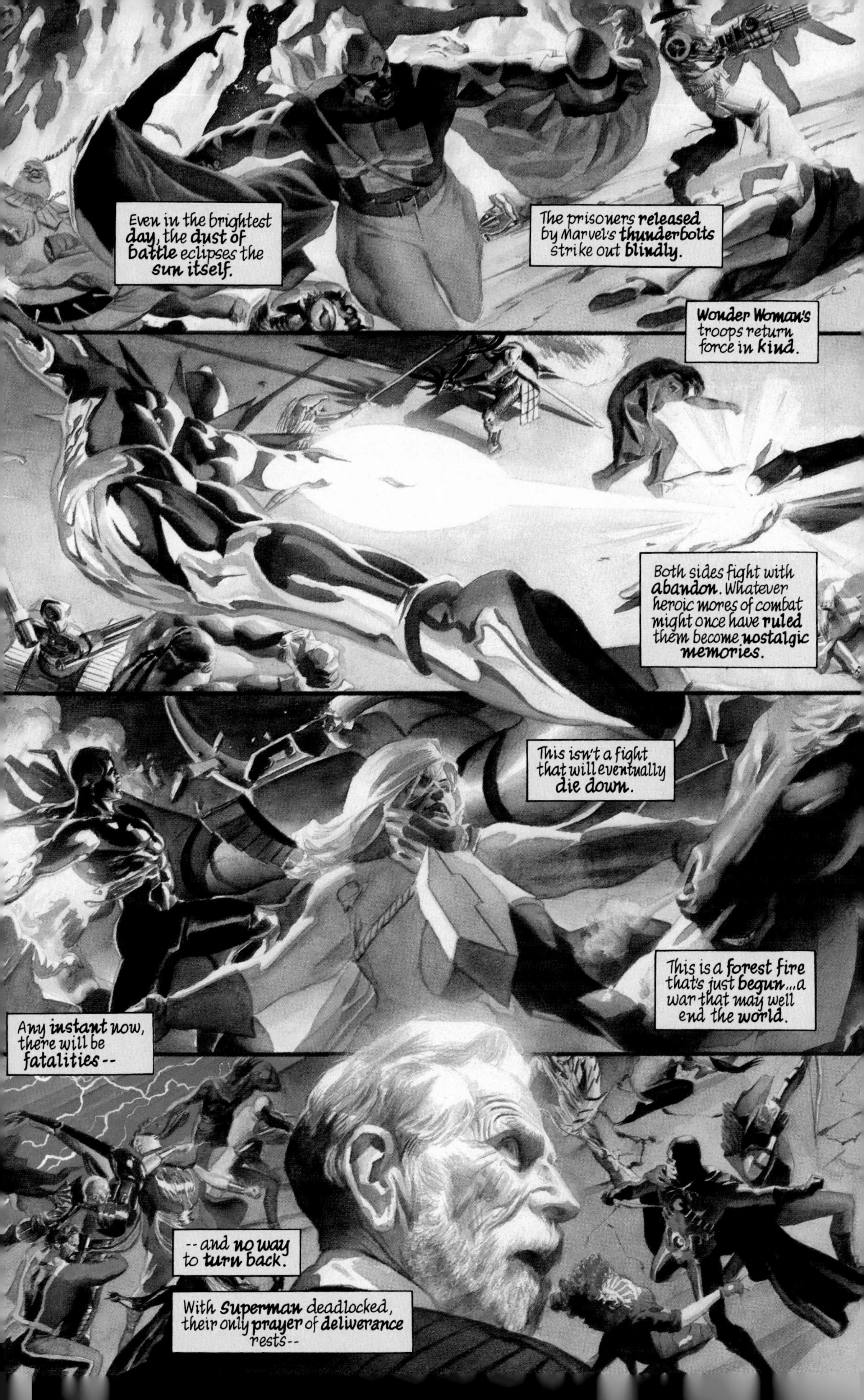

Even in the brightest day, the dust of battle eclipses the sun itself.
The prisoners released by Marvel's thunderbolts strike out blindly.
Wonder Woman's troops return force in kind.
Both sides fight with abandon. Whatever heroic mores of combat might once have ruled them become nostalgic memories.
This isn't a fight that will eventually die down.
This is a forest fire that's just begun...a war that may well end the world.
Any instant now, there will be fatalities--
--and no way to turn back.
With Superman deadlocked, their only prayer of deliverance rests--

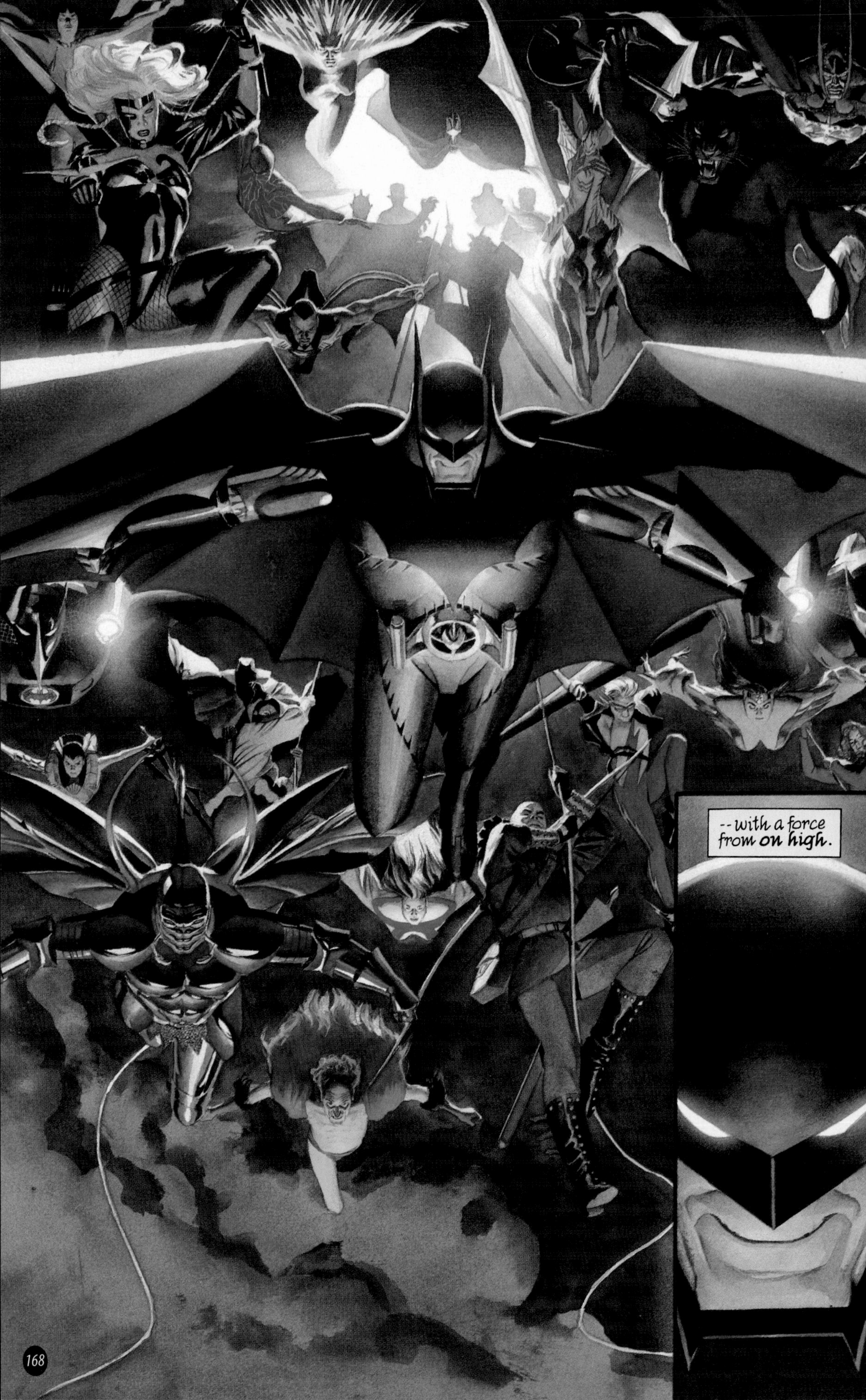
--with a force from on high.

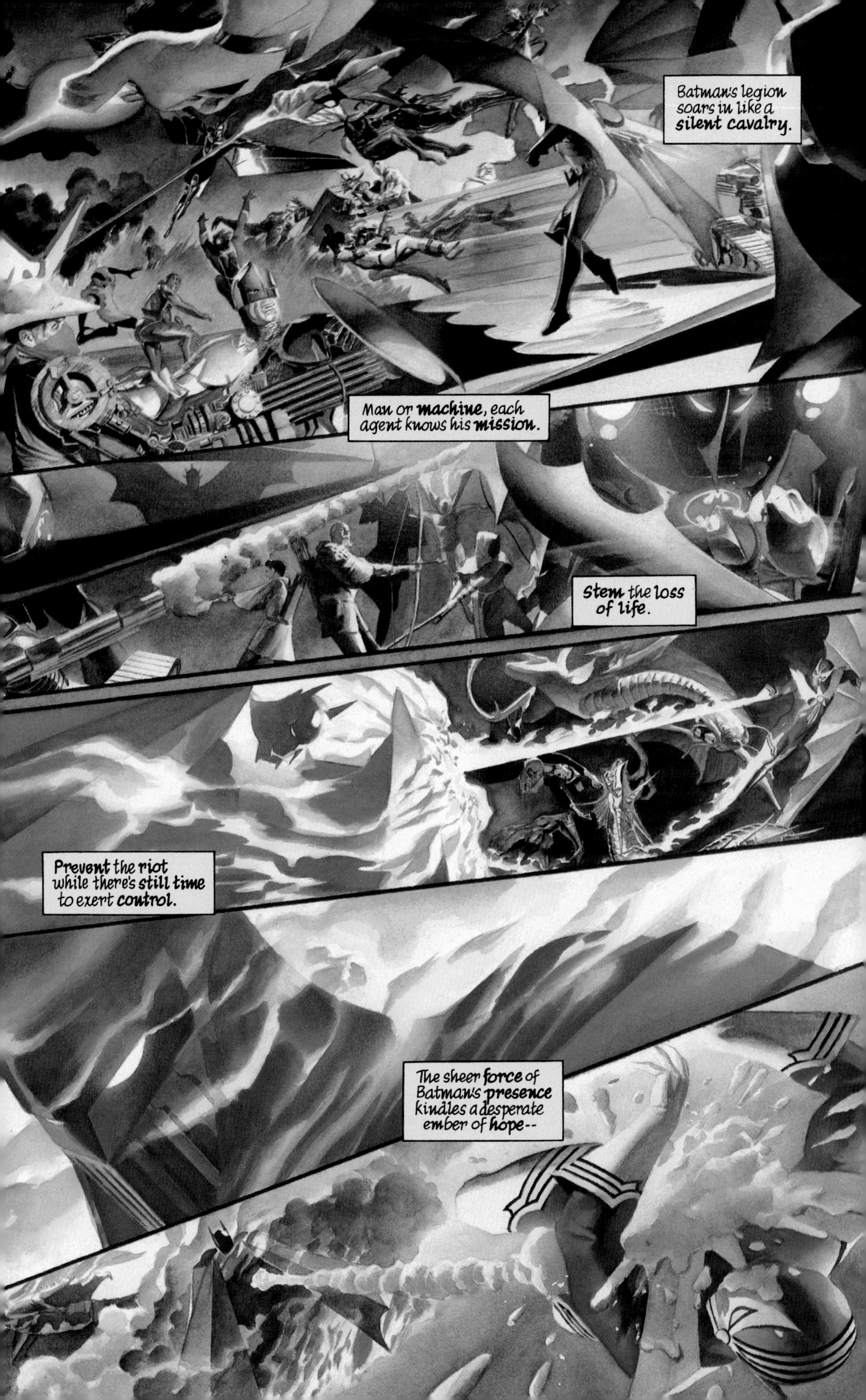
Batman's legion soars in like a silent cavalry.
Man or machine, each agent knows his mission.
Stem the loss of life.
Prevent the riot while there's still time to exert control.
The sheer force of Batman's presence kindles a desperate ember of hope--

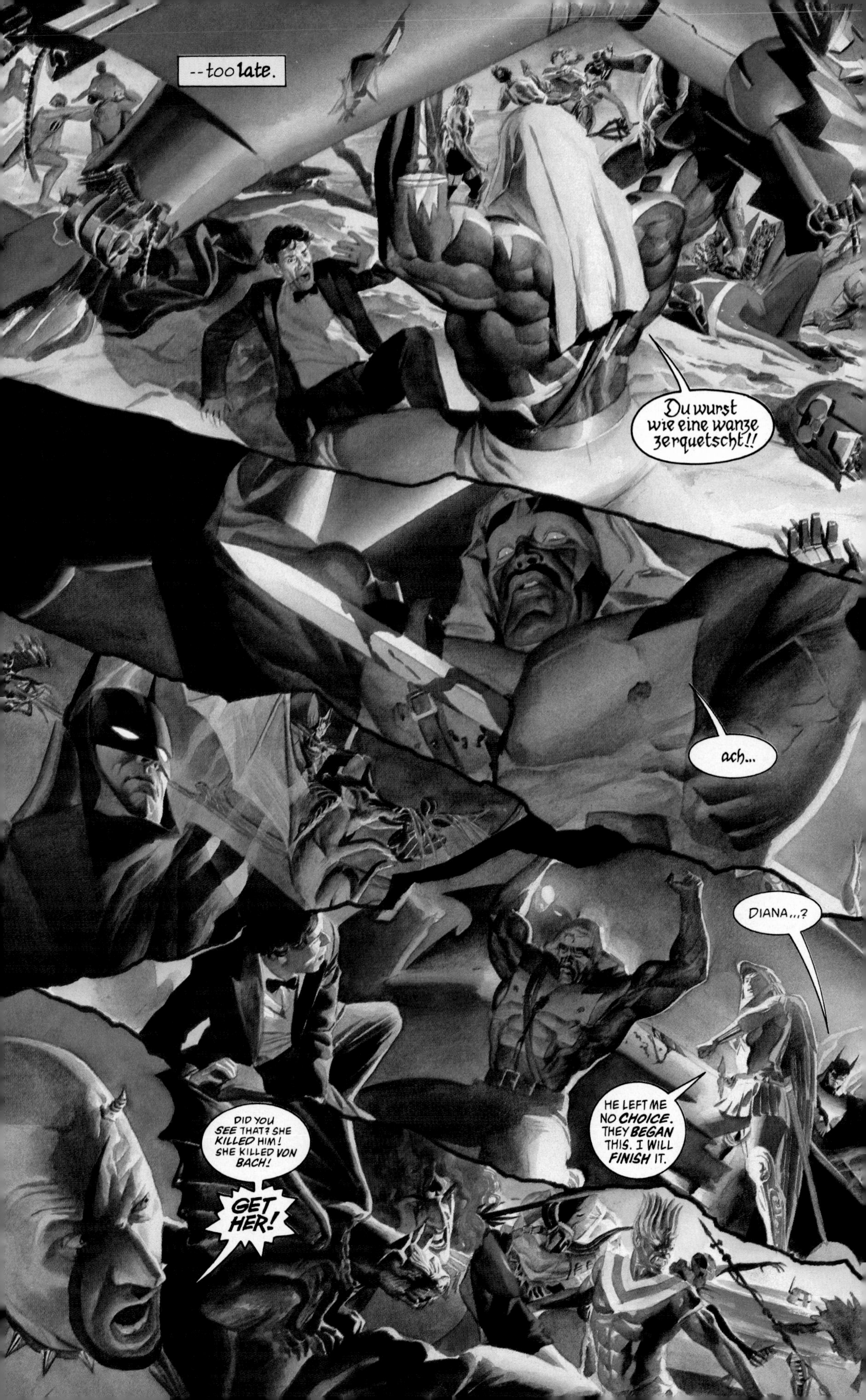
--too late.
Du wurst wie eine wanze zerquetscht!!
ach...
DIANA...?
HE LEFT ME NO CHOICE. THEY BEGAN THIS. I WILL FINISH IT.
DID YOU SEE THAT? SHE KILLED HIM! SHE KILLED VON BACH!
GET HER!

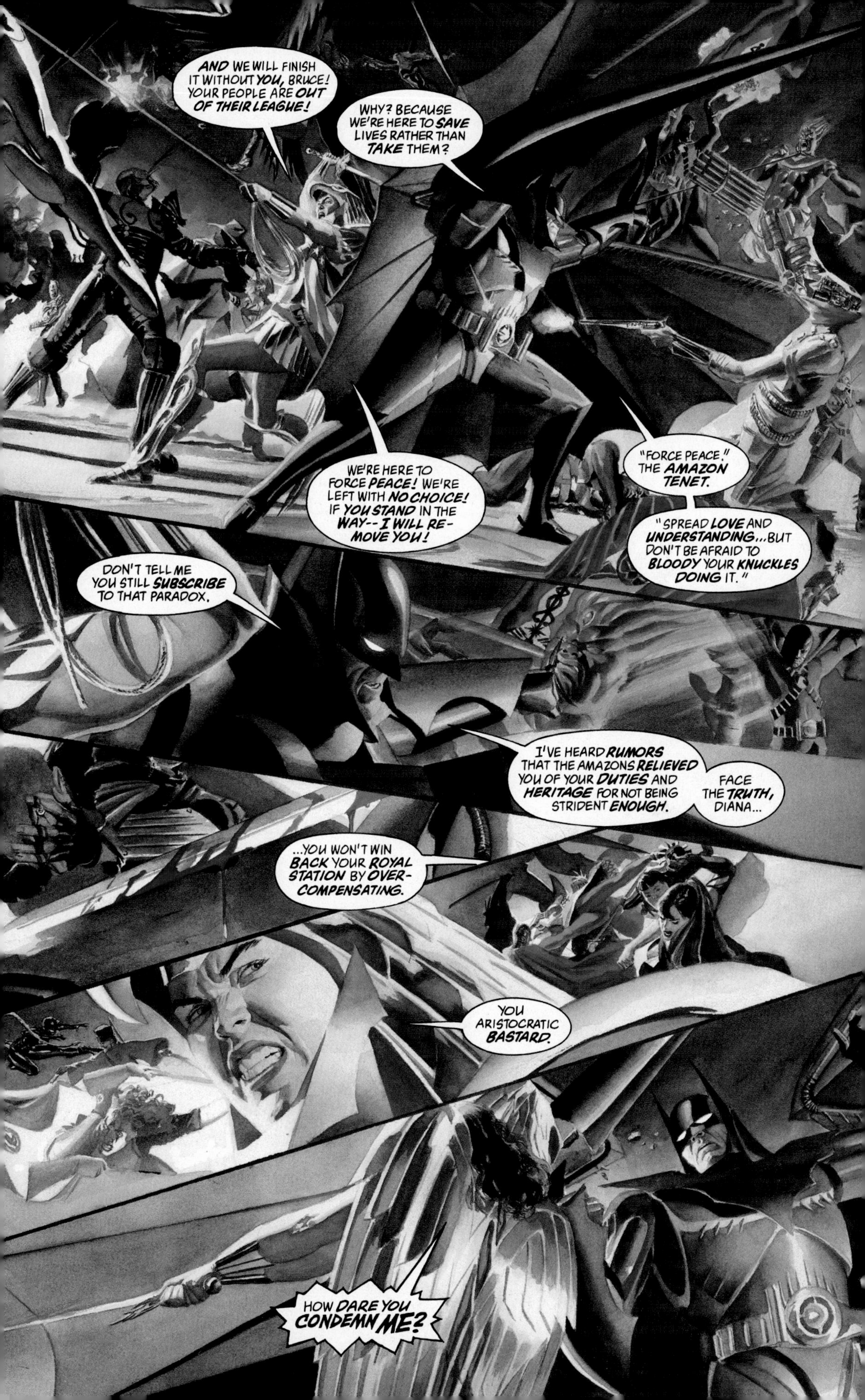
AND WE WILL FINISH IT WITHOUT YOU, BRUCE! YOUR PEOPLE ARE OUT OF THEIR LEAGUE!
WHY? BECAUSE WE'RE HERE TO SAVE LIVES RATHER THAN TAKE THEM?
WE'RE HERE TO FORCE PEACE! WE'RE LEFT WITH NO CHOICE! IF YOU STAND IN THE WAY-- I WILL REMOVE YOU!
"FORCE PEACE." THE AMAZON TENET.
"SPREAD LOVE AND UNDERSTANDING... BUT DON'T BE AFRAID TO BLOODY YOUR KNUCKLES DOING IT."
DON'T TELL ME YOU STILL SUBSCRIBE TO THAT PARADOX.
I'VE HEARD RUMORS THAT THE AMAZONS RELIEVED YOU OF YOUR DUTIES AND HERITAGE FOR NOT BEING STRIDENT ENOUGH.
FACE THE TRUTH, DIANA...
...YOU WON'T WIN BACK YOUR ROYAL STATION BY OVER-COMPENSATING.
YOU ARISTOCRATIC BASTARD.
HOW DARE YOU CONDEMN ME?

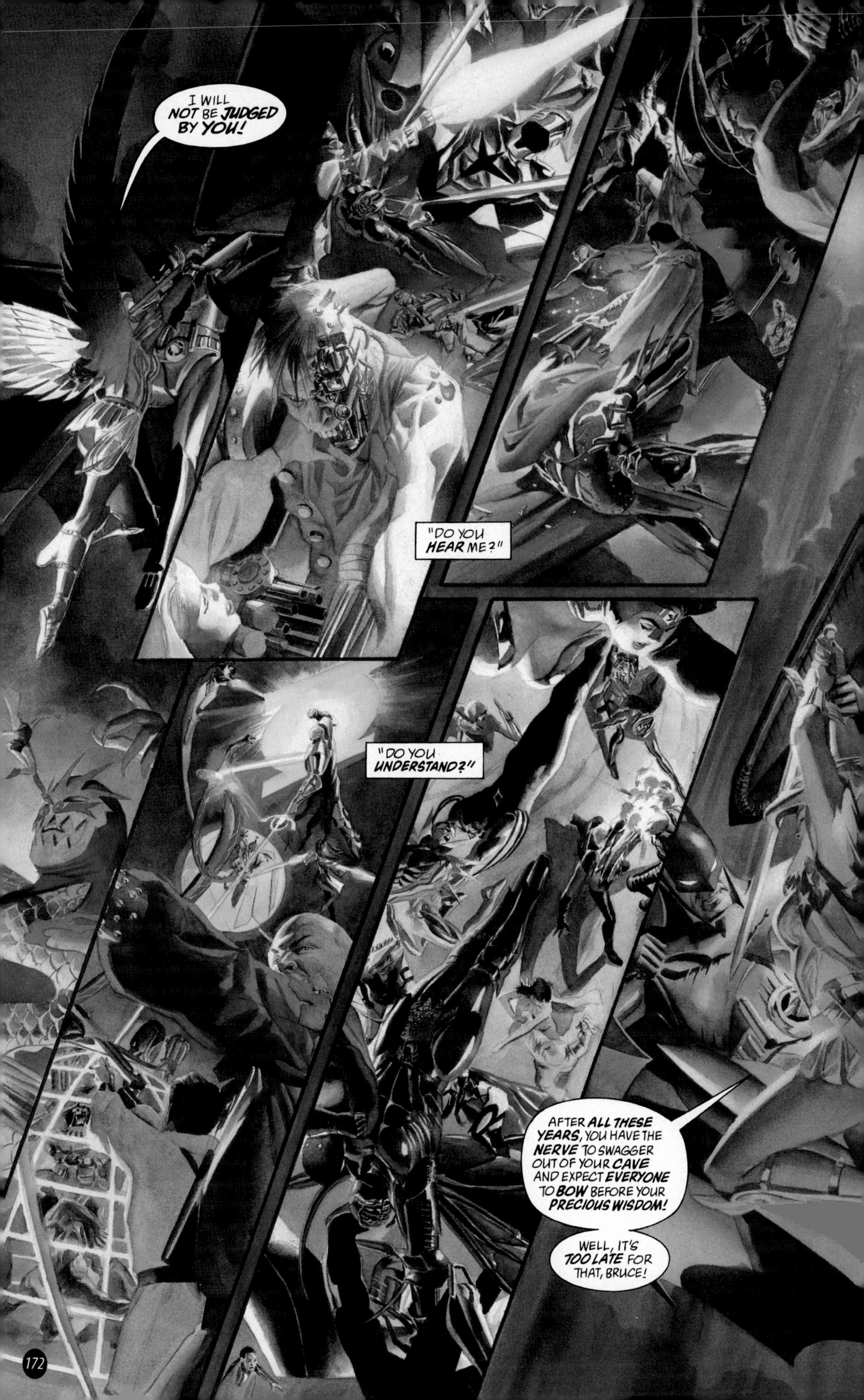
I WILL NOT BE JUDGED BY YOU!
"DO YOU HEAR ME?"
"DO YOU UNDERSTAND?"
AFTER ALL THESE YEARS, YOU HAVE THE NERVE TO SWAGGER OUT OF YOUR CAVE AND EXPECT EVERYONE TO BOW BEFORE YOUR PRECIOUS WISDOM!
WELL, IT'S TOO LATE FOR THAT, BRUCE!

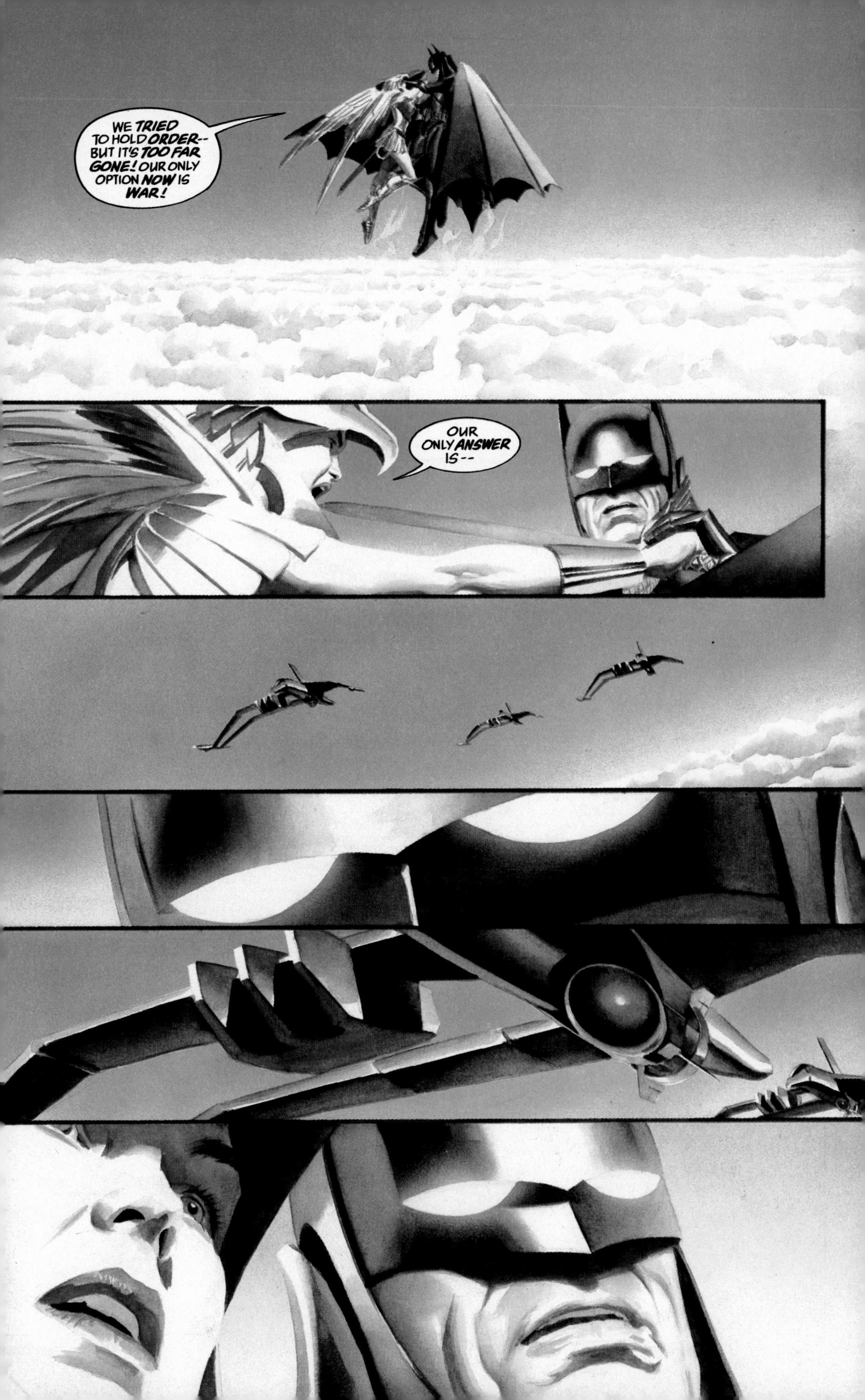
WE TRIED TO HOLD ORDER-- BUT IT'S TOO FAR GONE! OUR ONLY OPTION NOW IS WAR!
OUR ONLY ANSWER IS--

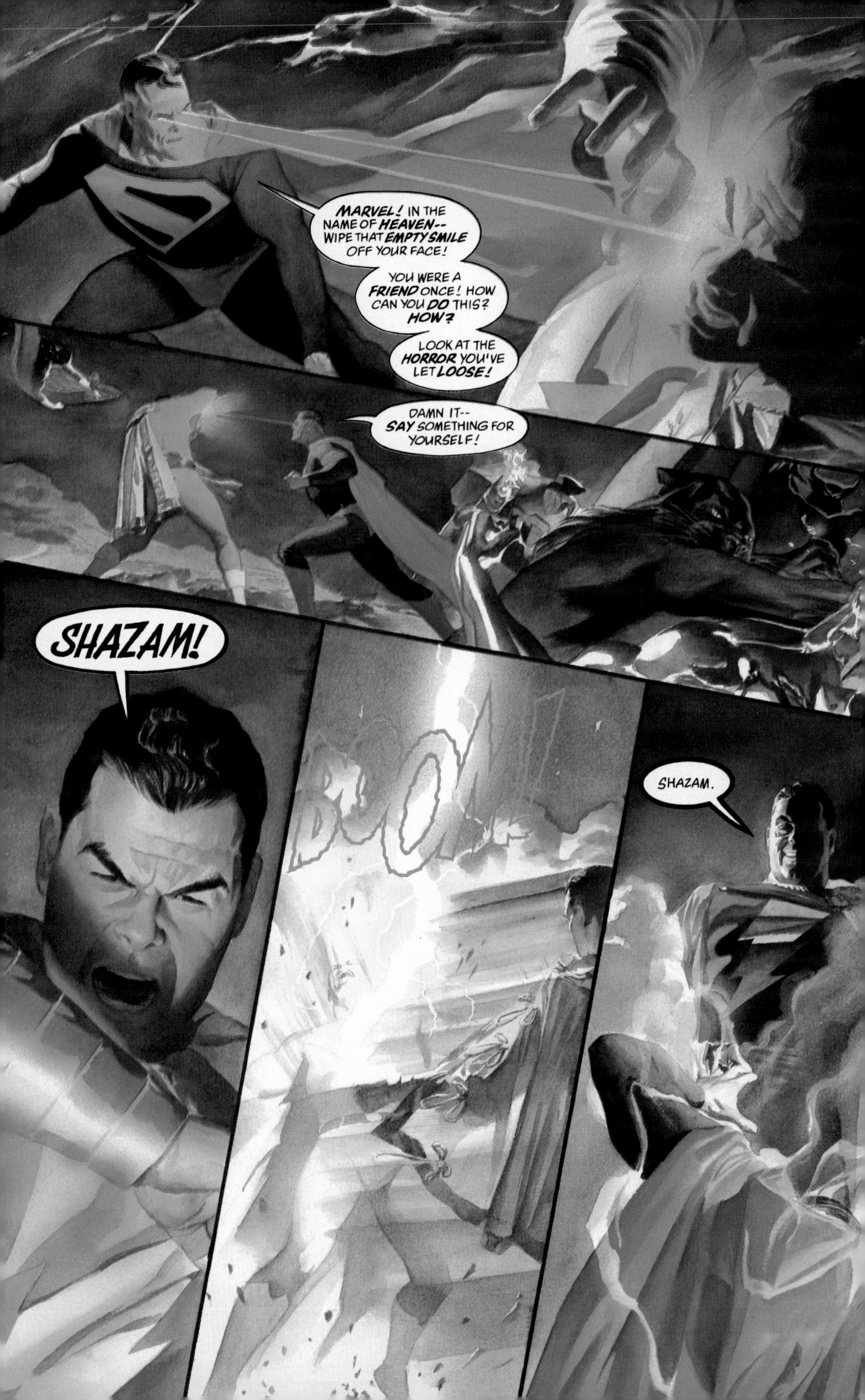
MARVEL! IN THE NAME OF HEAVEN-- WIPE THAT EMPTY SMILE OFF YOUR FACE!
YOU WERE A FRIEND ONCE! HOW CAN YOU DO THIS? HOW?
LOOK AT THE HORROR YOU'VE LET LOOSE!
DAMN IT-- SAY SOMETHING FOR YOURSELF!
SHAZAM!
BOOM!
SHAZAM.

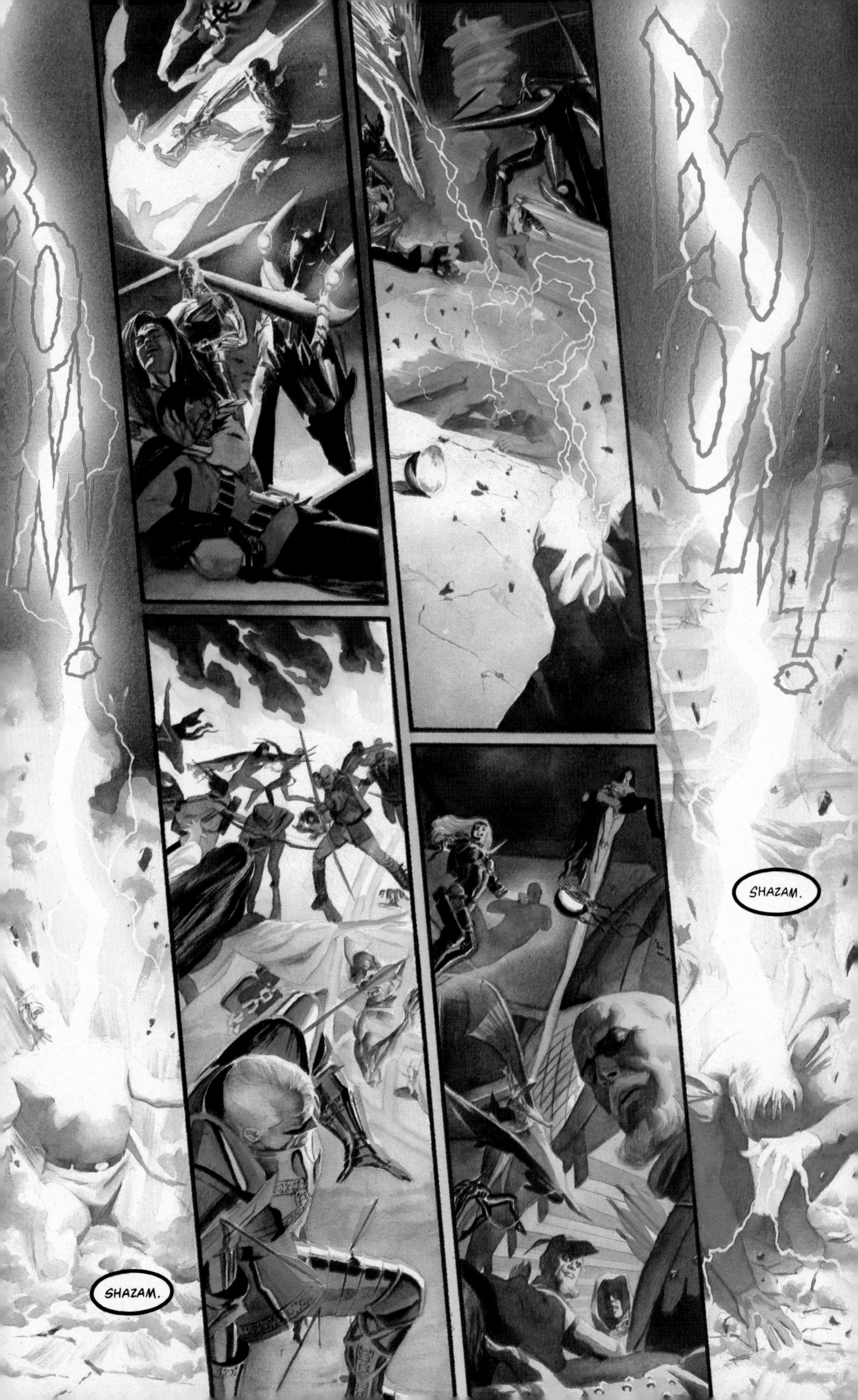
BOOM!
BOOM!
SHAZAM.
SHAZAM.

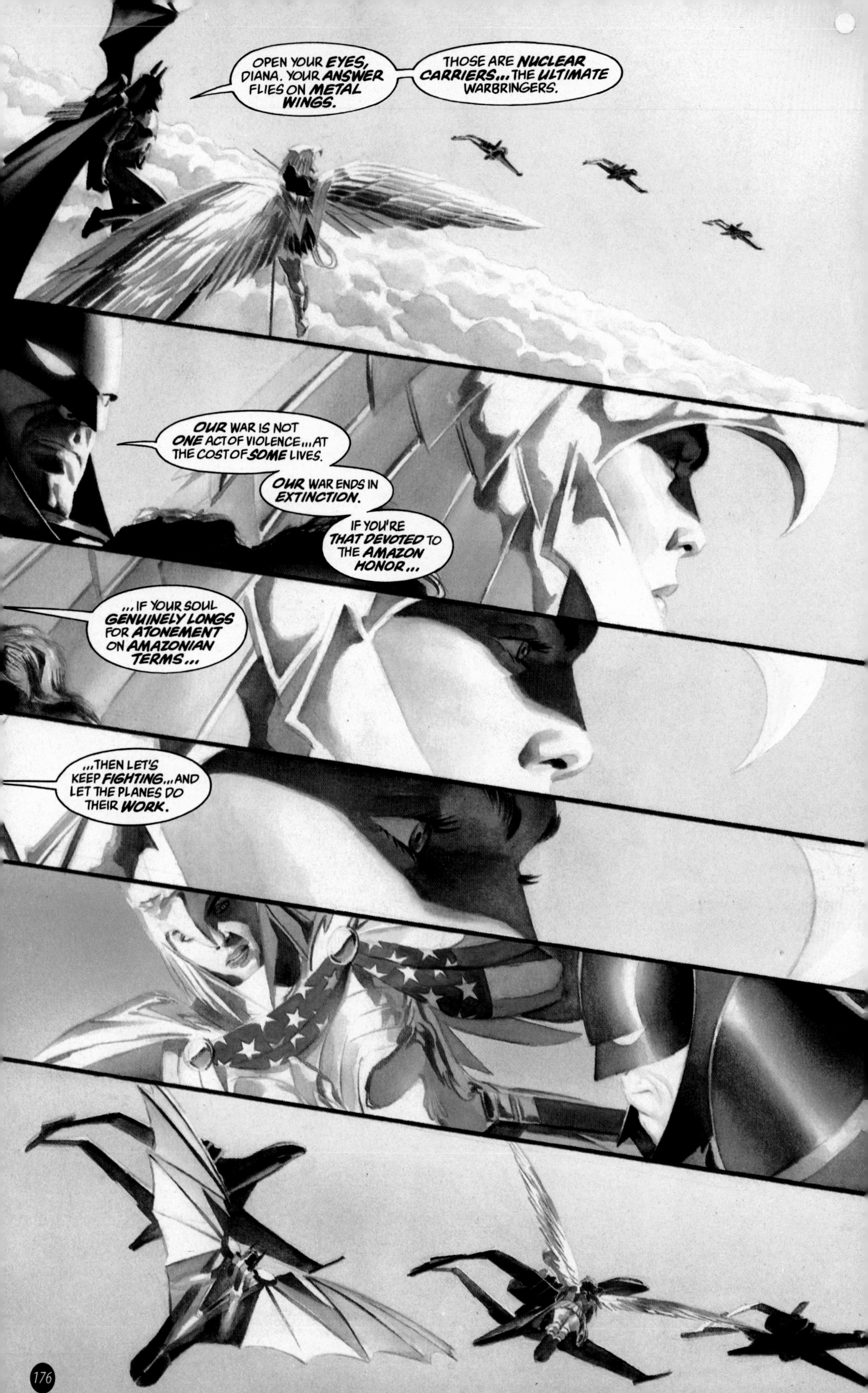

OPEN YOUR EYES, DIANA. YOUR ANSWER FLIES ON METAL WINGS.
THOSE ARE NUCLEAR CARRIERS... THE ULTIMATE WARBRINGERS.
OUR WAR IS NOT ONE ACT OF VIOLENCE... AT THE COST OF SOME LIVES.
OUR WAR ENDS IN EXTINCTION.
IF YOU'RE THAT DEVOTED TO THE AMAZON HONOR...
...IF YOUR SOUL GENUINELY LONGS FOR ATONEMENT ON AMAZONIAN TERMS...
...THEN LET'S KEEP FIGHTING... AND LET THE PLANES DO THEIR WORK.

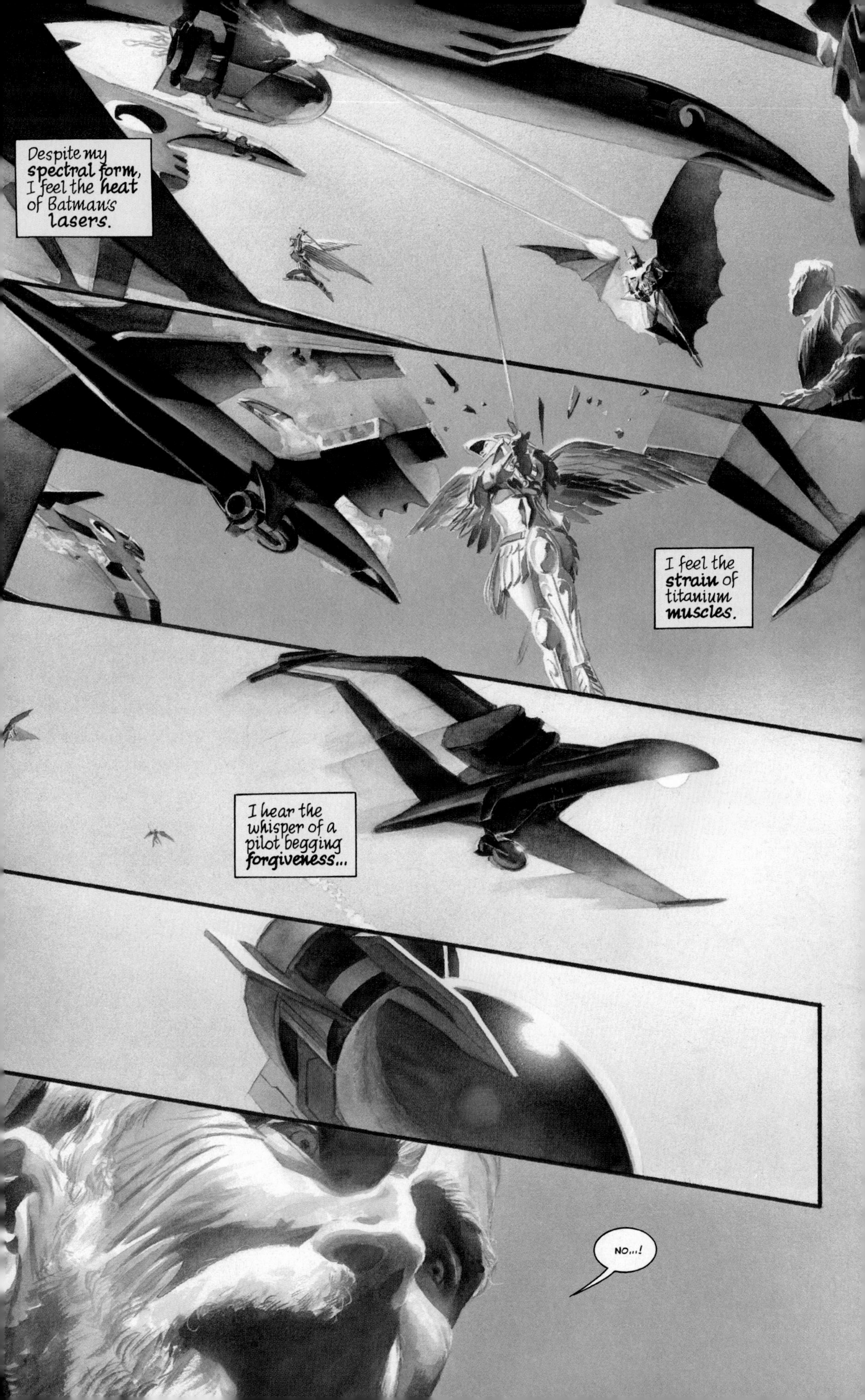
Despite my spectral form, I feel the heat of Batman's lasers.
I feel the strain of titanium muscles.
I hear the whisper of a pilot begging forgiveness...
NO...!

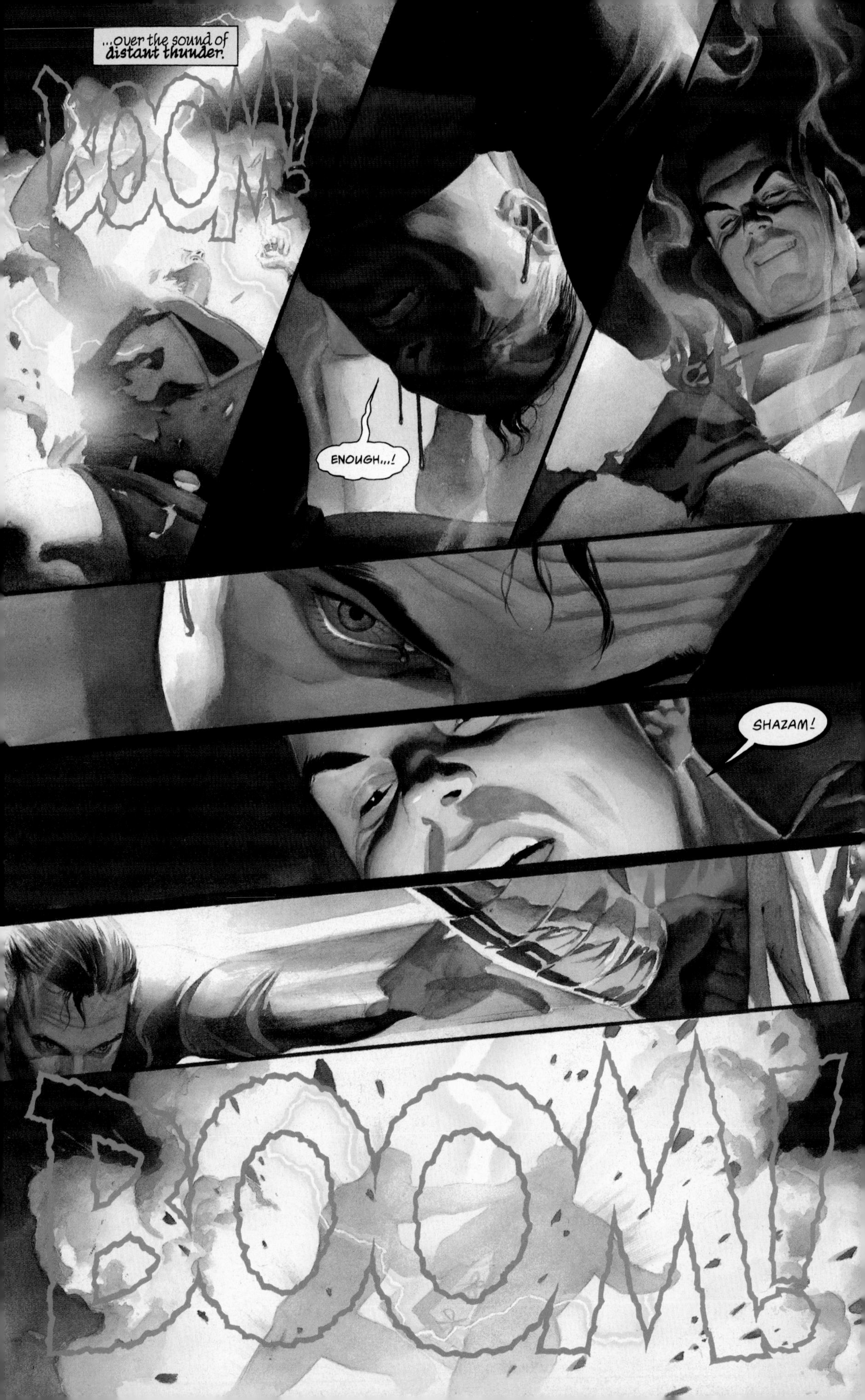
...over the sound of distant thunder.
BOOM!
ENOUGH...!
SHAZAM!
BOOM!

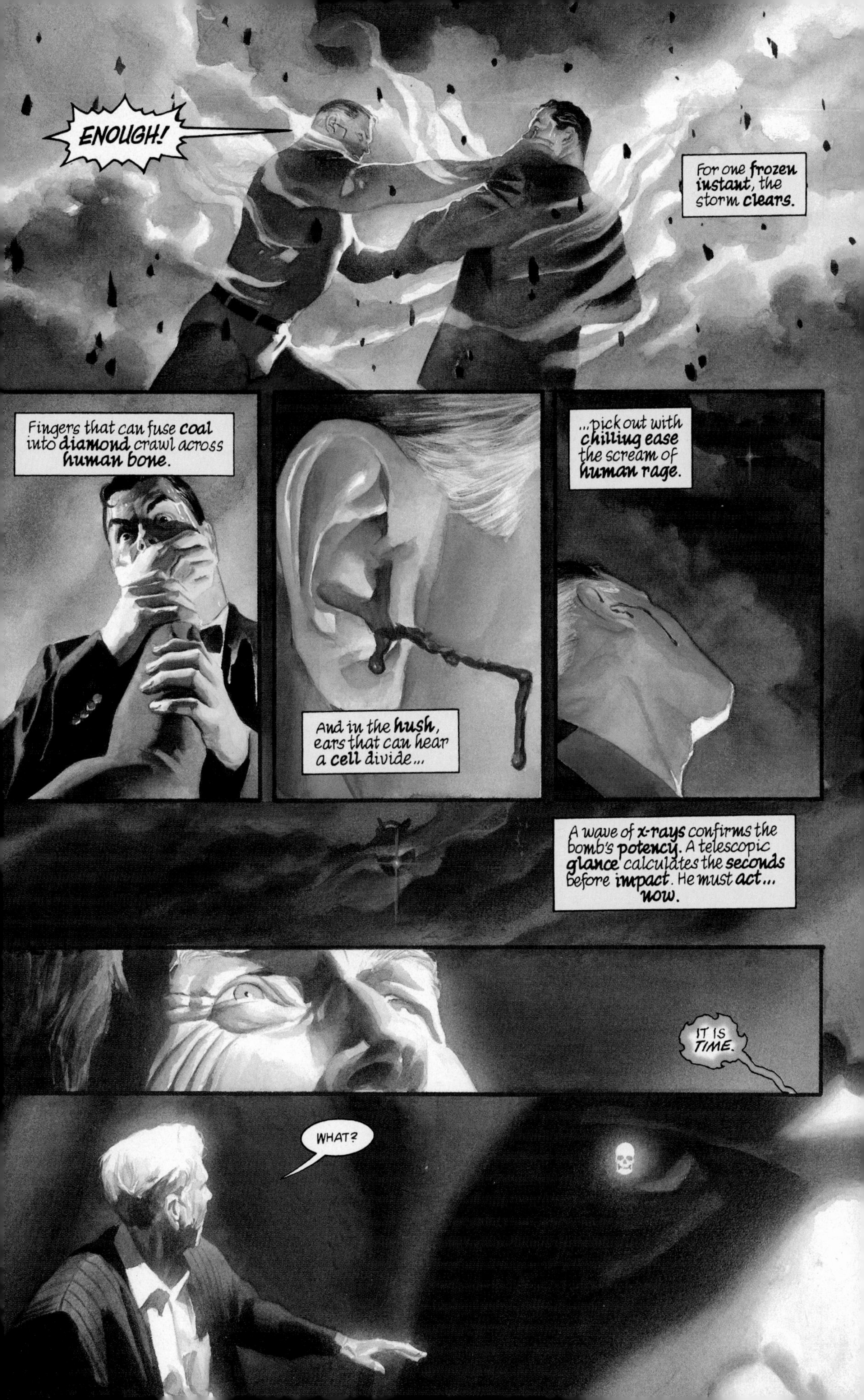
ENOUGH!
For one frozen instant, the storm clears.
Fingers that can fuse coal into diamond crawl across human bone.
And in the hush, ears that can hear a cell divide...
...pick out with chilling ease the scream of human rage.
A wave of x-rays confirms the bomb's potency. A telescopic glance calculates the seconds before impact. He must act... now.
IT IS TIME.
WHAT?

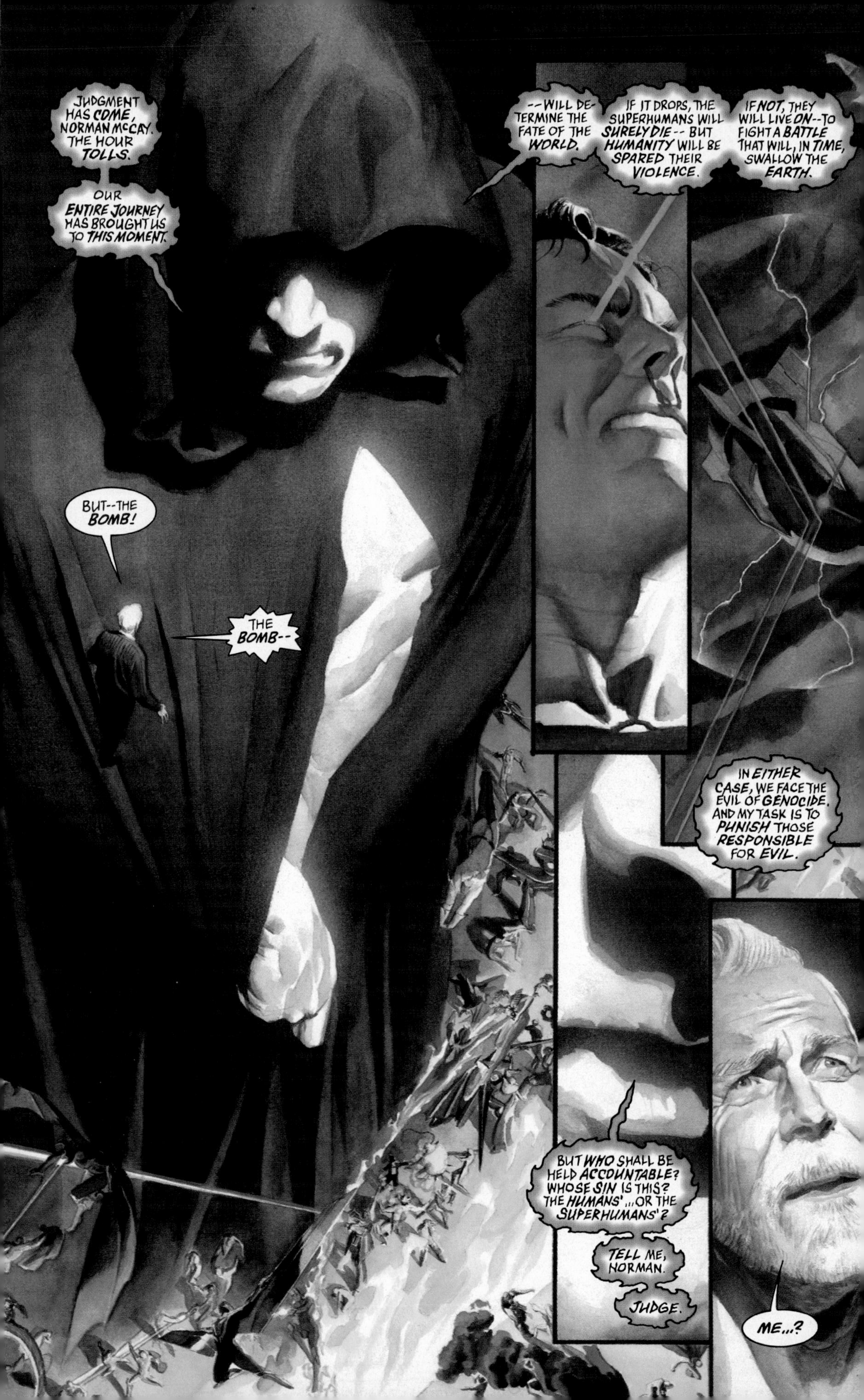
JUDGMENT HAS COME, NORMAN McCAY. THE HOUR TOLLS.
OUR ENTIRE JOURNEY HAS BROUGHT US TO THIS MOMENT.
--WILL DETERMINE THE FATE OF THE WORLD.
IF IT DROPS, THE SUPERHUMANS WILL SURELY DIE -- BUT HUMANITY WILL BE SPARED THEIR VIOLENCE.
IF NOT, THEY WILL LIVE ON--TO FIGHT A BATTLE THAT WILL, IN TIME, SWALLOW THE EARTH.
BUT--THE BOMB!
THE BOMB--
IN EITHER CASE, WE FACE THE EVIL OF GENOCIDE. AND MY TASK IS TO PUNISH THOSE RESPONSIBLE FOR EVIL.
BUT WHO SHALL BE HELD ACCOUNTABLE? WHOSE SIN IS THIS? THE HUMANS'...OR THE SUPERHUMANS'?
TELL ME, NORMAN.
JUDGE.
ME...?

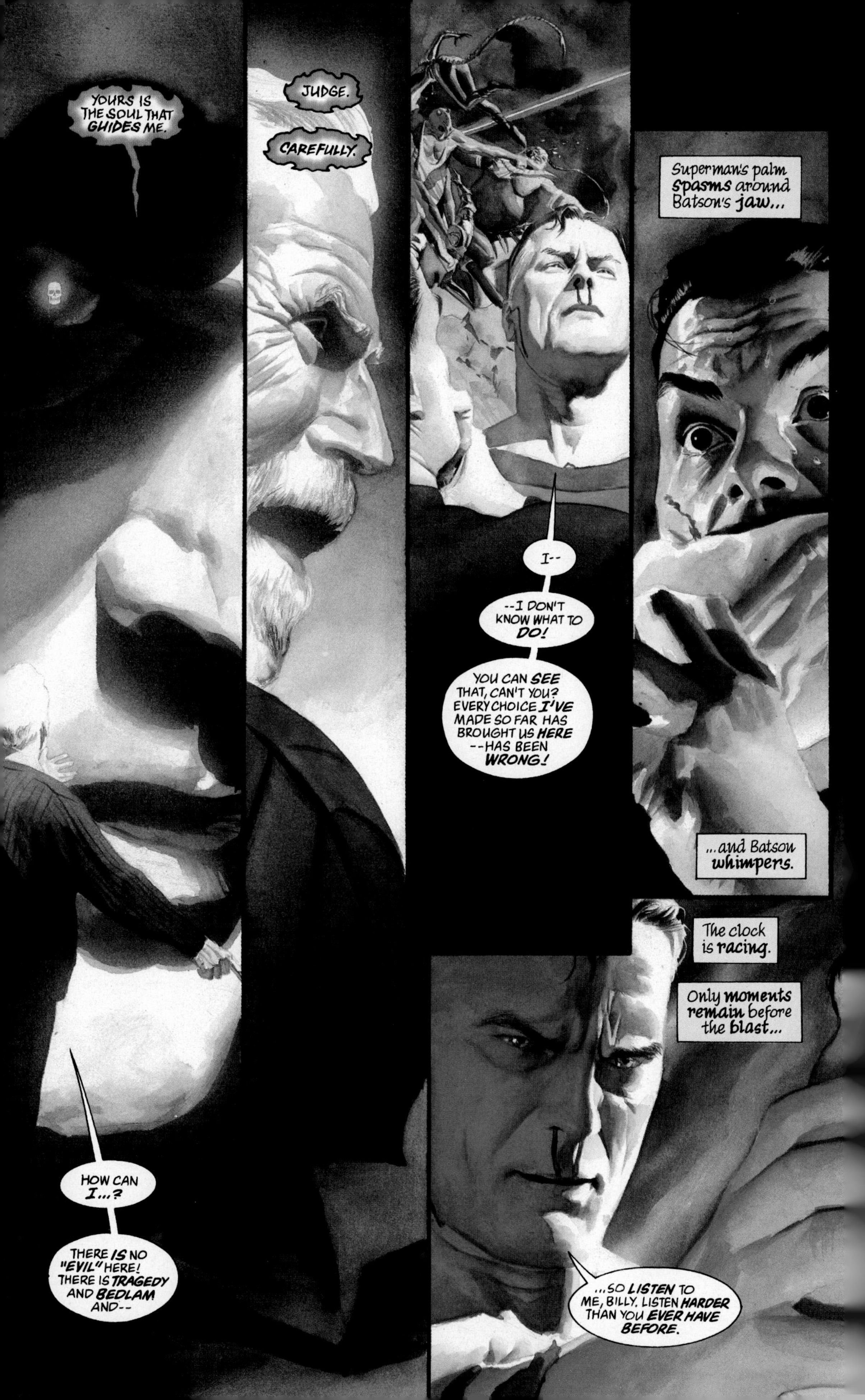
YOURS IS THE SOUL THAT GUIDES ME.
HOW CAN I...?
THERE IS NO "EVIL" HERE! THERE IS TRAGEDY AND BEDLAM AND--
JUDGE.
CAREFULLY.
I--
--I DON'T KNOW WHAT TO DO!
YOU CAN SEE THAT, CAN'T YOU? EVERY CHOICE I'VE MADE SO FAR HAS BROUGHT US HERE --HAS BEEN WRONG!
Superman's palm spasms around Batson's jaw...
...and Batson whimpers.
The clock is racing.
Only moments remain before the blast...
...SO LISTEN TO ME, BILLY. LISTEN HARDER THAN YOU EVER HAVE BEFORE.

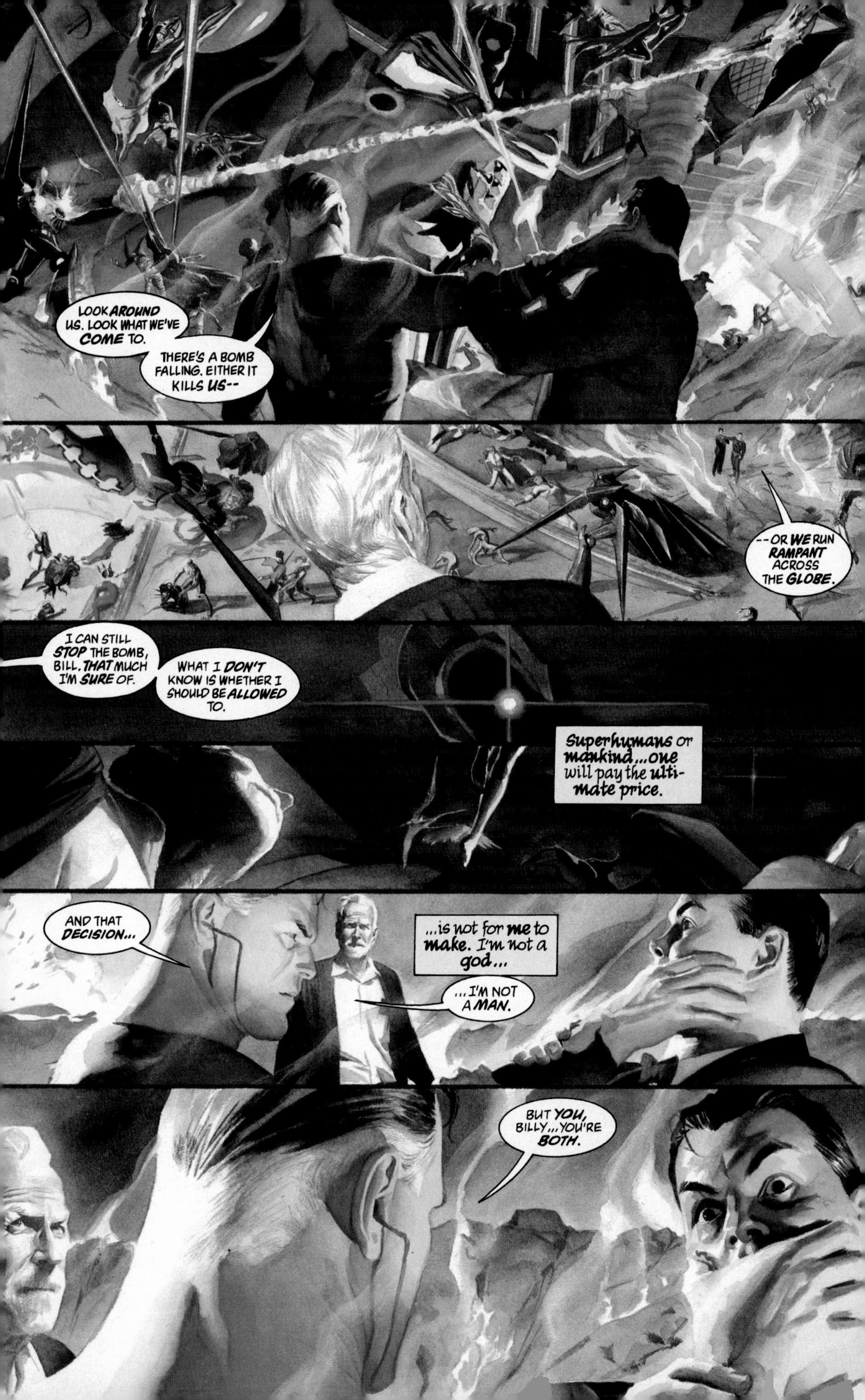
LOOK AROUND US. LOOK WHAT WE'VE COME TO.
THERE'S A BOMB FALLING. EITHER IT KILLS US--
--OR WE RUN RAMPANT ACROSS THE GLOBE.
I CAN STILL STOP THE BOMB, BILL. THAT MUCH I'M SURE OF.
WHAT I DON'T KNOW IS WHETHER I SHOULD BE ALLOWED TO.
Superhumans or mankind...one will pay the ultimate price.
AND THAT DECISION...
...is not for me to make. I'm not a god...
...I'M NOT A MAN.
BUT YOU, BILLY... YOU'RE BOTH.

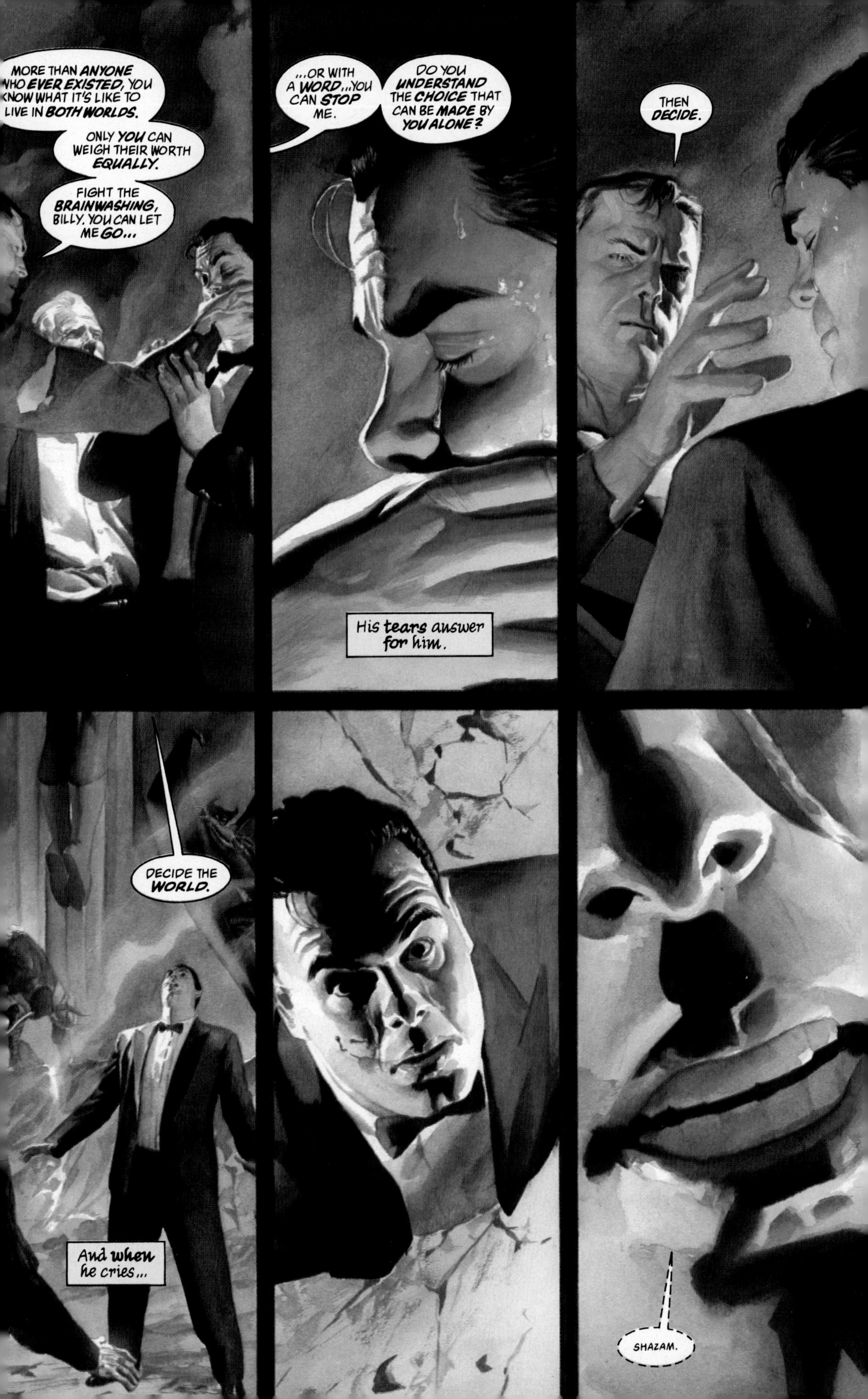

MORE THAN ANYONE WHO EVER EXISTED, YOU KNOW WHAT IT'S LIKE TO LIVE IN BOTH WORLDS.
ONLY YOU CAN WEIGH THEIR WORTH EQUALLY.
FIGHT THE BRAINWASHING, BILLY. YOU CAN LET ME GO...
...OR WITH A WORD...YOU CAN STOP ME.
DO YOU UNDERSTAND THE CHOICE THAT CAN BE MADE BY YOU ALONE?
His tears answer for him.
THEN DECIDE.
DECIDE THE WORLD.
And when he cries...
SHAZAM.

...seven thunders utter their voices.

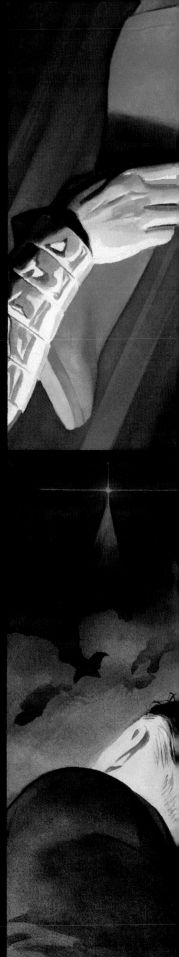

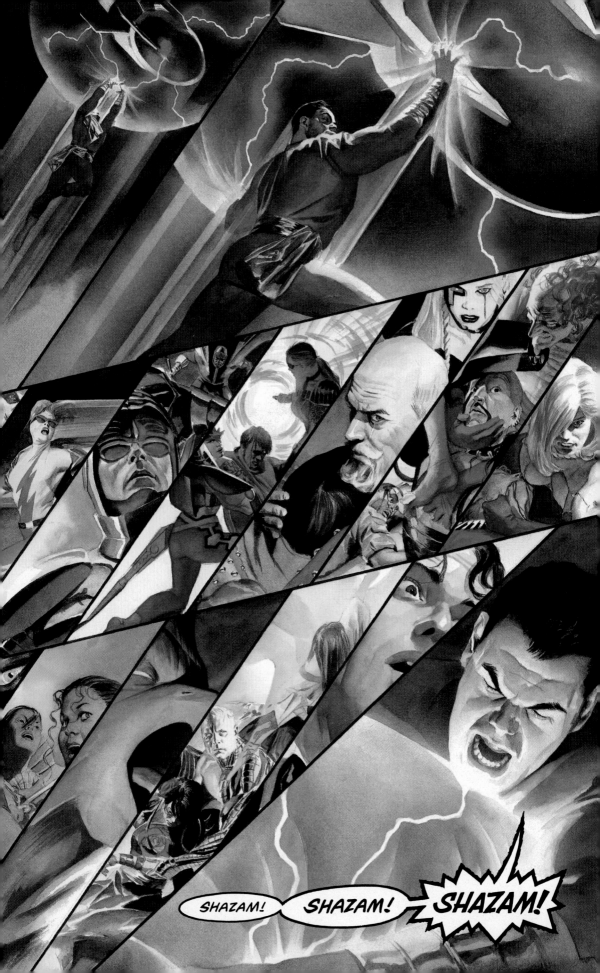

SHAZAM! SHAZAM! SHAZAM!

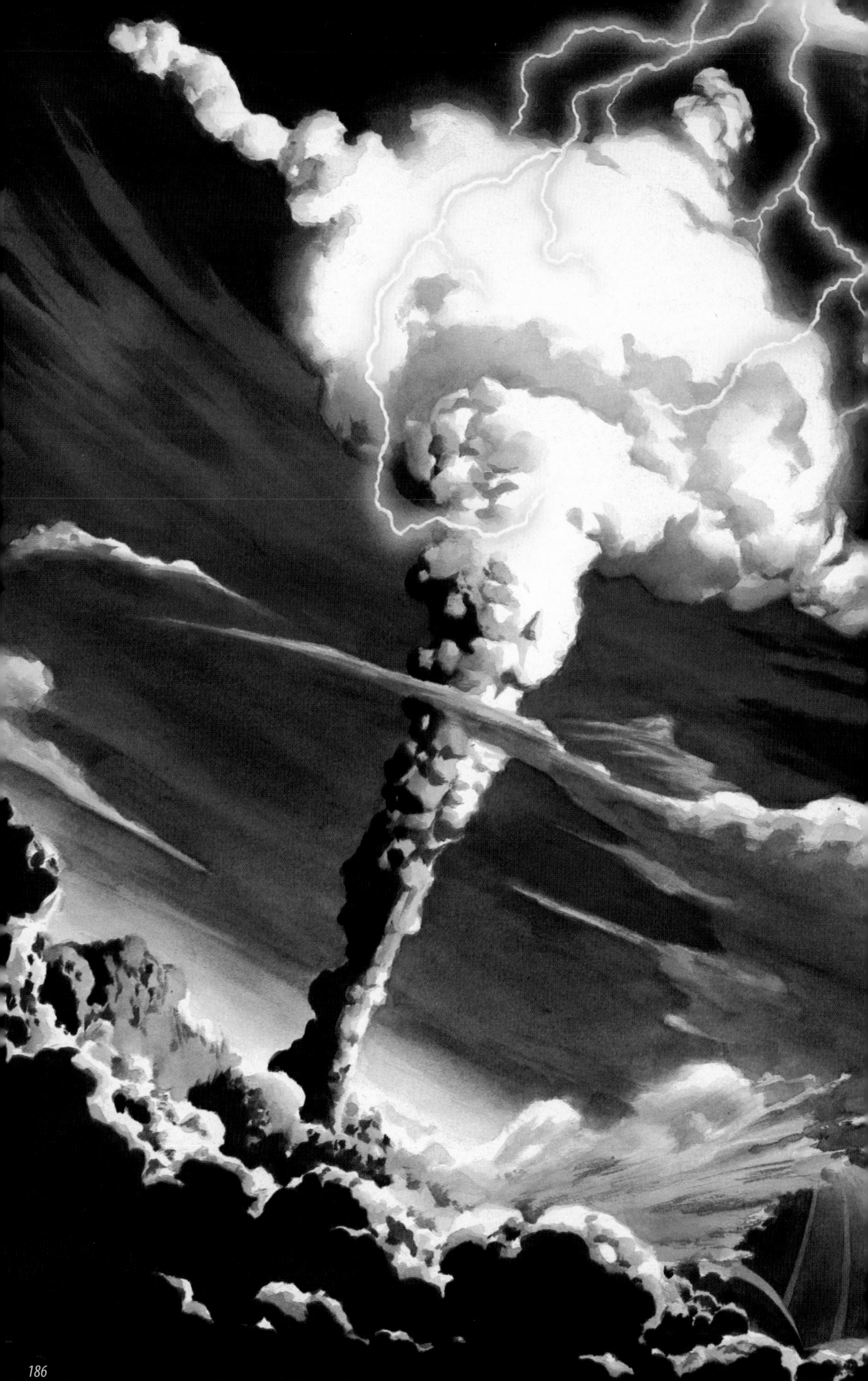

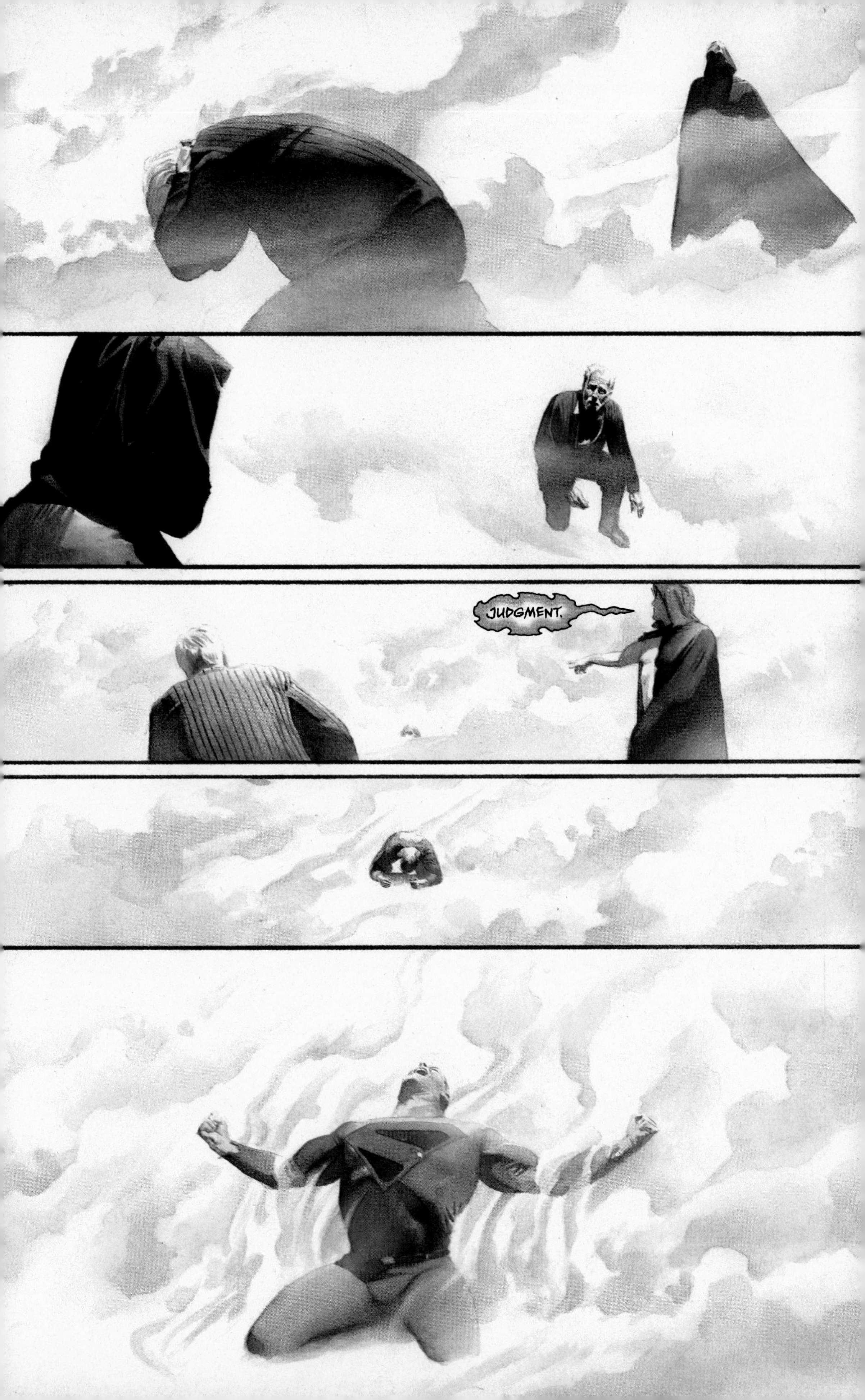
JUDGMENT.

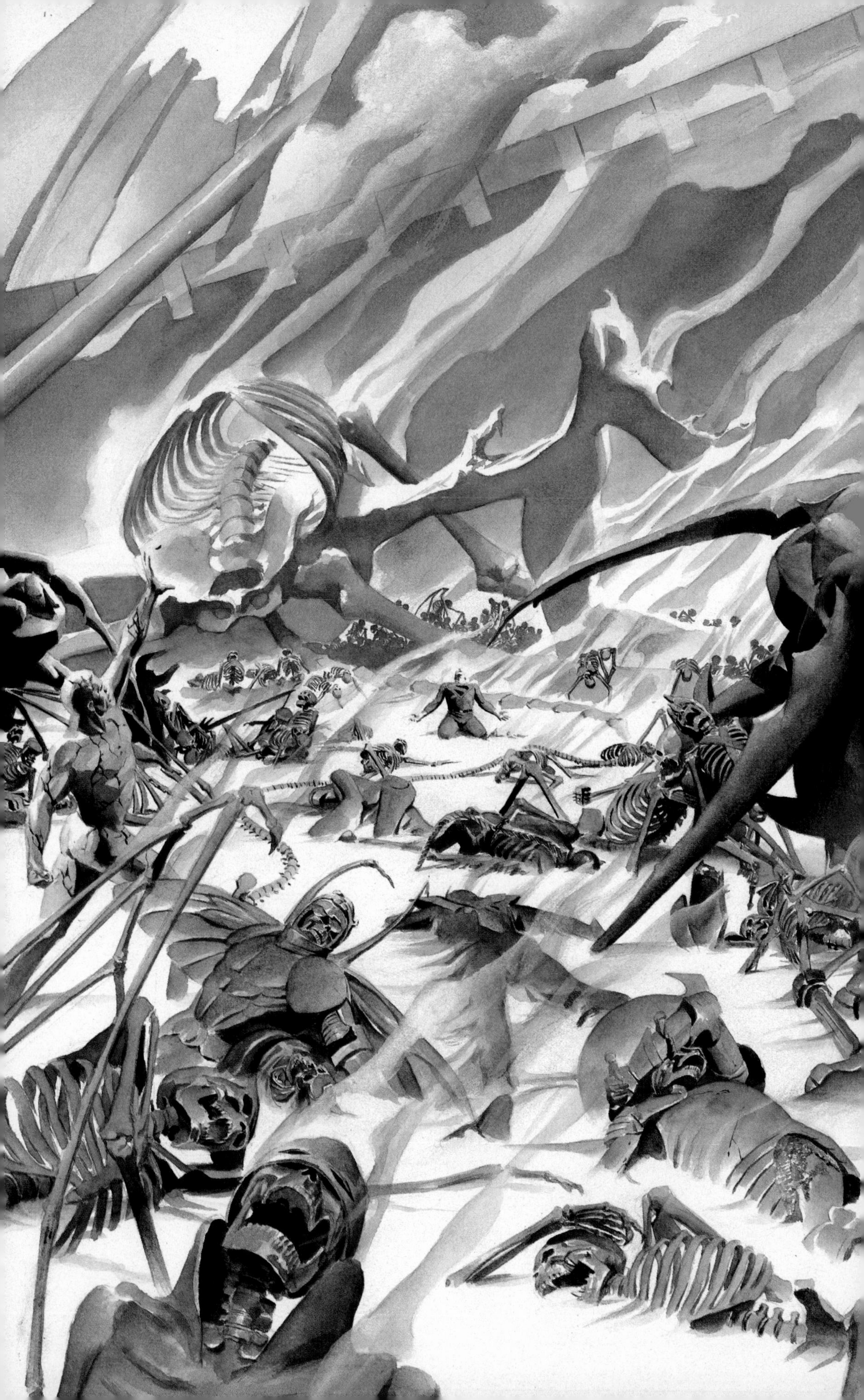

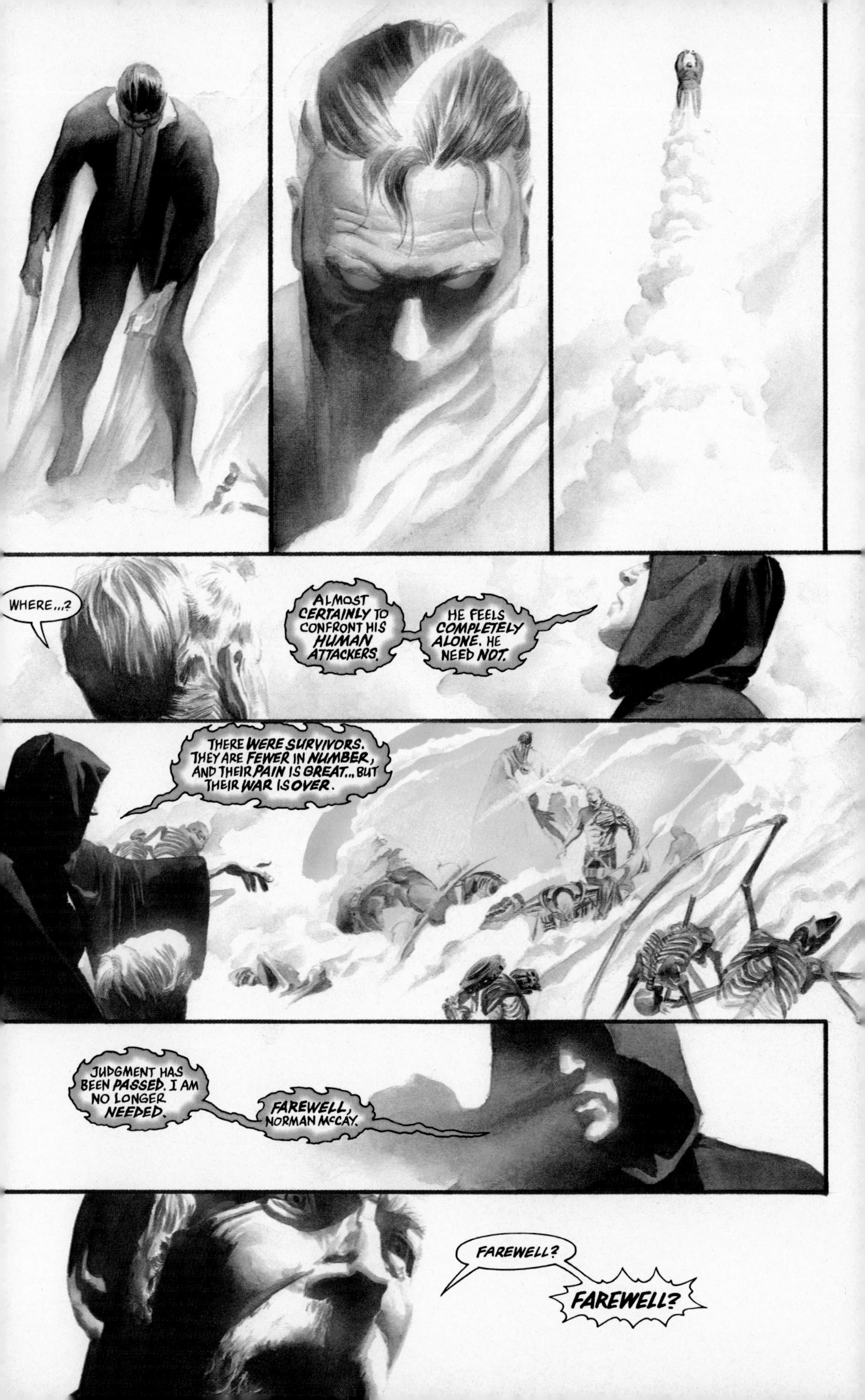
WHERE...?
ALMOST CERTAINLY TO CONFRONT HIS HUMAN ATTACKERS.
HE FEELS COMPLETELY ALONE. HE NEED NOT.
THERE WERE SURVIVORS. THEY ARE FEWER IN NUMBER, AND THEIR PAIN IS GREAT... BUT THEIR WAR IS OVER.
JUDGMENT HAS BEEN PASSED. I AM NO LONGER NEEDED.
FAREWELL, NORMAN McCAY.
FAREWELL?
FAREWELL?

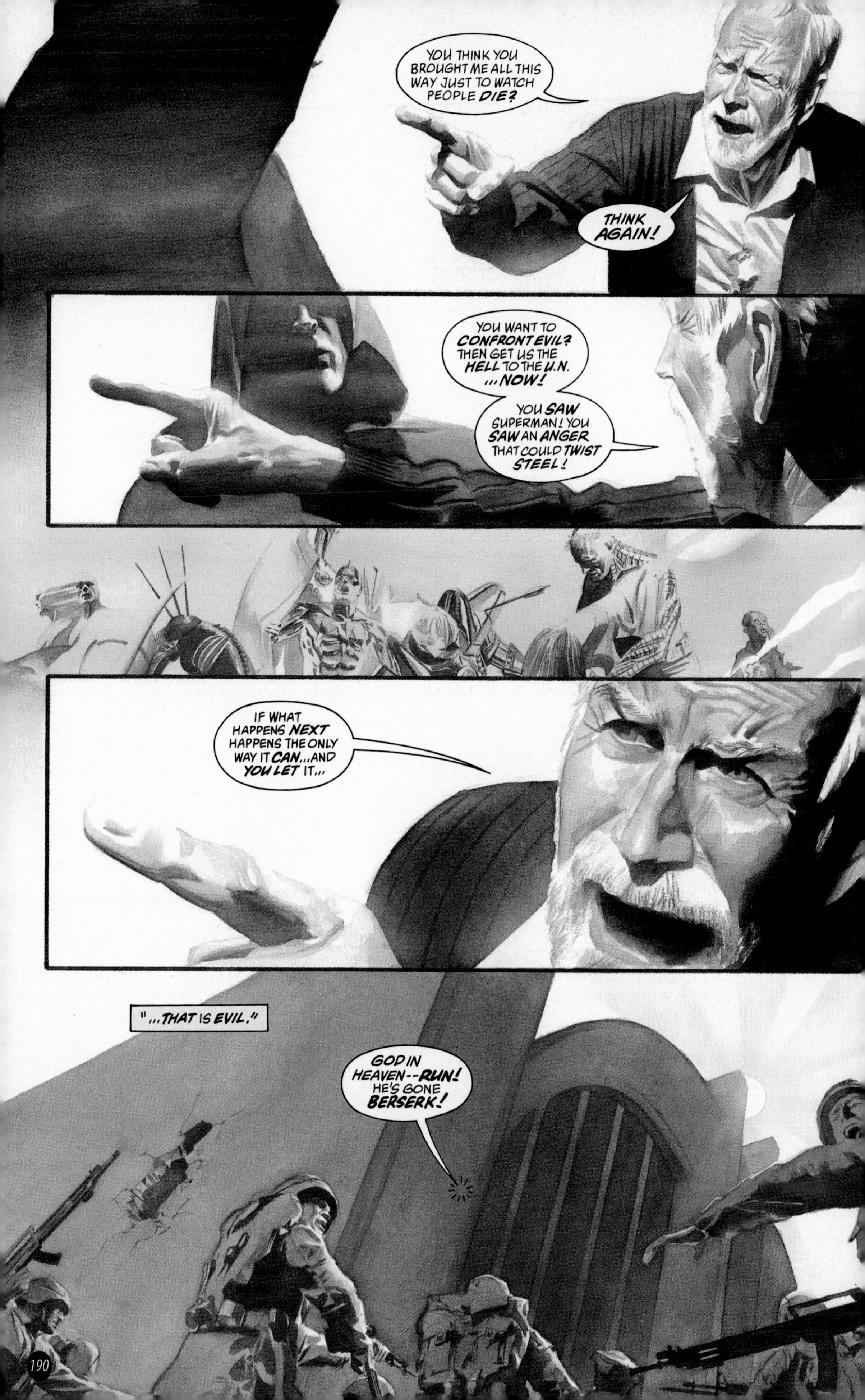
YOU THINK YOU BROUGHT ME ALL THIS WAY JUST TO WATCH PEOPLE DIE?
THINK AGAIN!
YOU WANT TO CONFRONT EVIL? THEN GET US THE HELL TO THE U.N. ...NOW!
YOU SAW SUPERMAN! YOU SAW AN ANGER THAT COULD TWIST STEEL!
IF WHAT HAPPENS NEXT HAPPENS THE ONLY WAY IT CAN...AND YOU LET IT...
"...THAT IS EVIL."
GOD IN HEAVEN--RUN! HE'S GONE BERSERK!

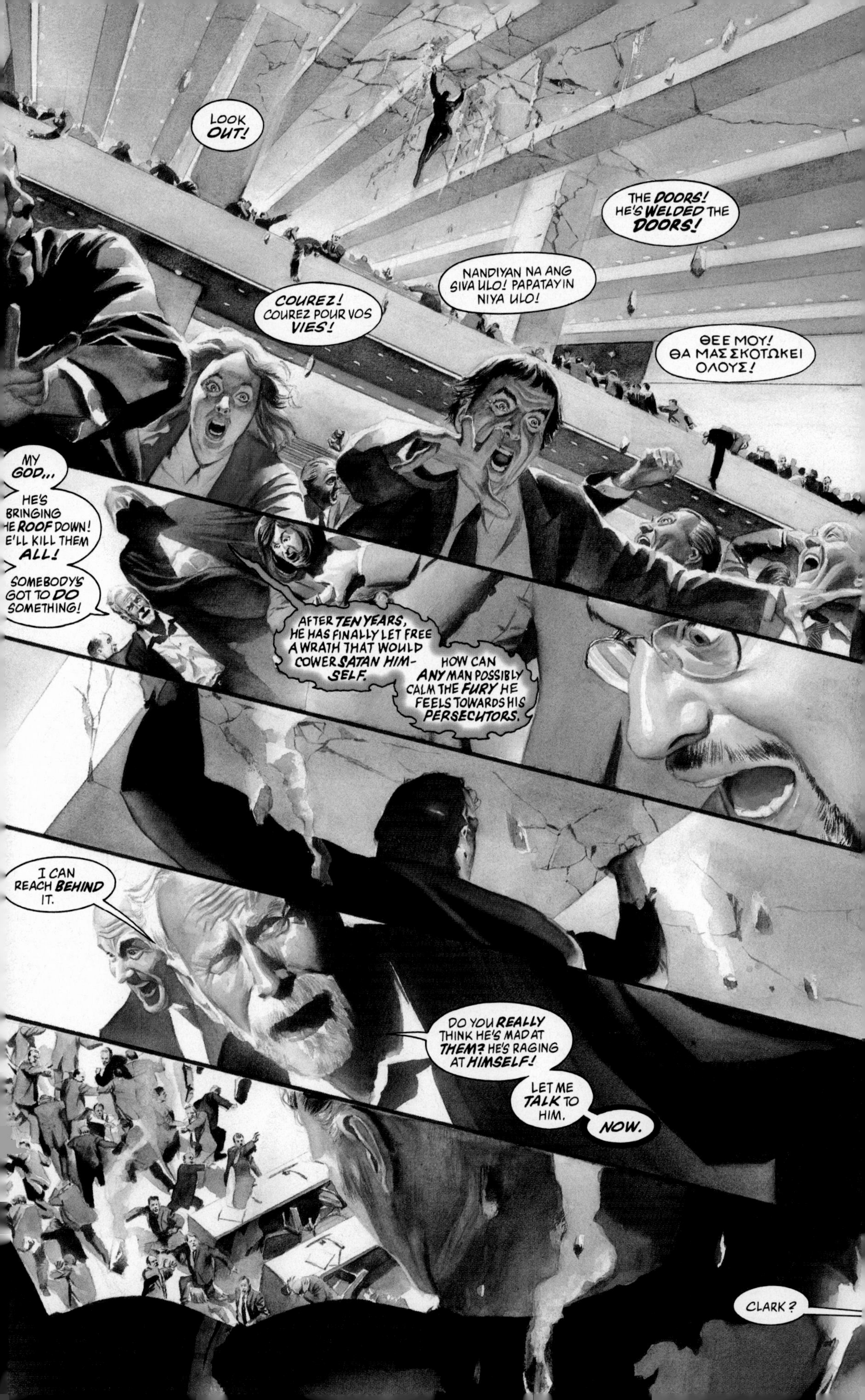
LOOK OUT!
THE DOORS! HE'S WELDED THE DOORS!
NANDIYAN NA ANG SIVA ULO! PAPATAYIN NIYA ULO!
COUREZ! COUREZ POUR VOS VIES!
ΘΕΕ ΜΟΥ! ΘΑ ΜΑΣ ΣΚΟΤΩΚΕΙ ΟΛΟΥΣ!
MY GOD...
HE'S BRINGING HE ROOF DOWN! E'LL KILL THEM ALL!
SOMEBODY'S GOT TO DO SOMETHING!
AFTER TEN YEARS, HE HAS FINALLY LET FREE A WRATH THAT WOULD COWER SATAN HIMSELF.
HOW CAN ANY MAN POSSIBLY CALM THE FURY HE FEELS TOWARDS HIS PERSECUTORS.
I CAN REACH BEHIND IT.
DO YOU REALLY THINK HE'S MAD AT THEM? HE'S RAGING AT HIMSELF!
LET ME TALK TO HIM.
NOW.
CLARK?

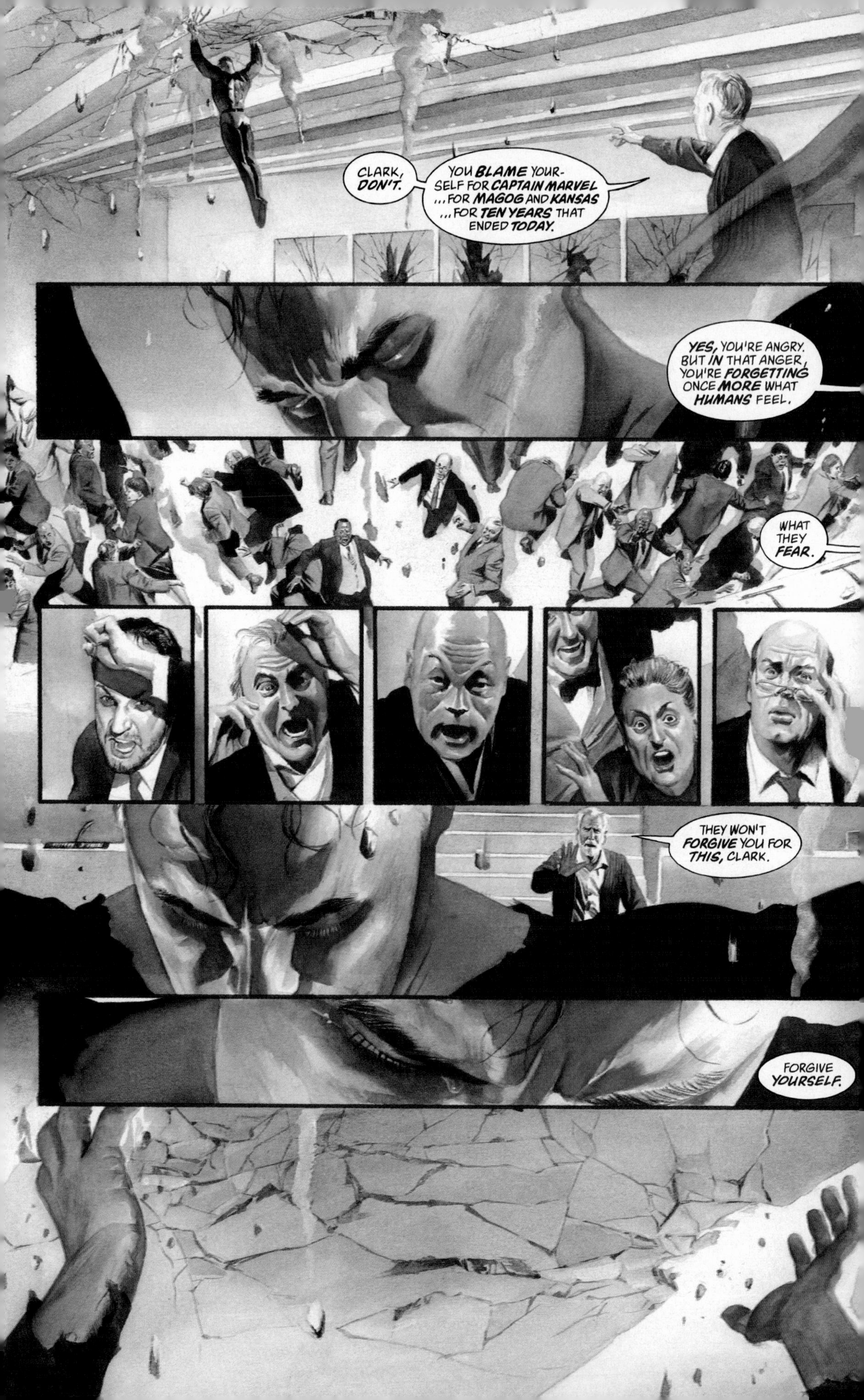
CLARK, DON'T.
YOU BLAME YOURSELF FOR CAPTAIN MARVEL ...FOR MAGOG AND KANSAS ...FOR TEN YEARS THAT ENDED TODAY.
YES, YOU'RE ANGRY. BUT IN THAT ANGER, YOU'RE FORGETTING ONCE MORE WHAT HUMANS FEEL.
WHAT THEY FEAR.
THEY WON'T FORGIVE YOU FOR THIS, CLARK.
FORGIVE YOURSELF.

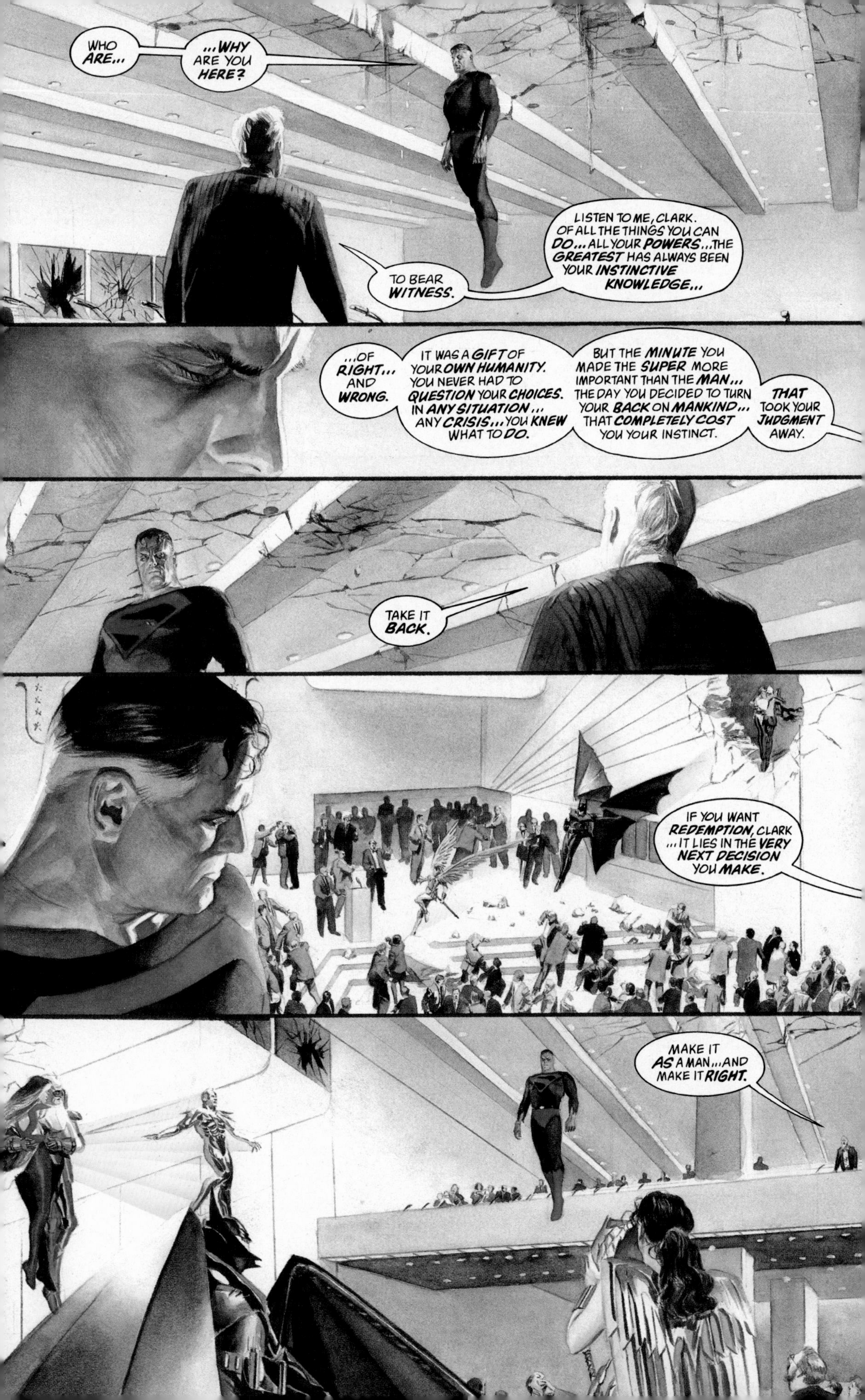
WHO ARE...
...WHY ARE YOU HERE?
TO BEAR WITNESS.
LISTEN TO ME, CLARK. OF ALL THE THINGS YOU CAN DO... ALL YOUR POWERS... THE GREATEST HAS ALWAYS BEEN YOUR INSTINCTIVE KNOWLEDGE...
...OF RIGHT... AND WRONG.
IT WAS A GIFT OF YOUR OWN HUMANITY. YOU NEVER HAD TO QUESTION YOUR CHOICES. IN ANY SITUATION... ANY CRISIS... YOU KNEW WHAT TO DO.
BUT THE MINUTE YOU MADE THE SUPER MORE IMPORTANT THAN THE MAN... THE DAY YOU DECIDED TO TURN YOUR BACK ON MANKIND... THAT COMPLETELY COST YOU YOUR INSTINCT.
THAT TOOK YOUR JUDGMENT AWAY.
TAKE IT BACK.
IF YOU WANT REDEMPTION, CLARK ...IT LIES IN THE VERY NEXT DECISION YOU MAKE.
MAKE IT AS A MAN... AND MAKE IT RIGHT.

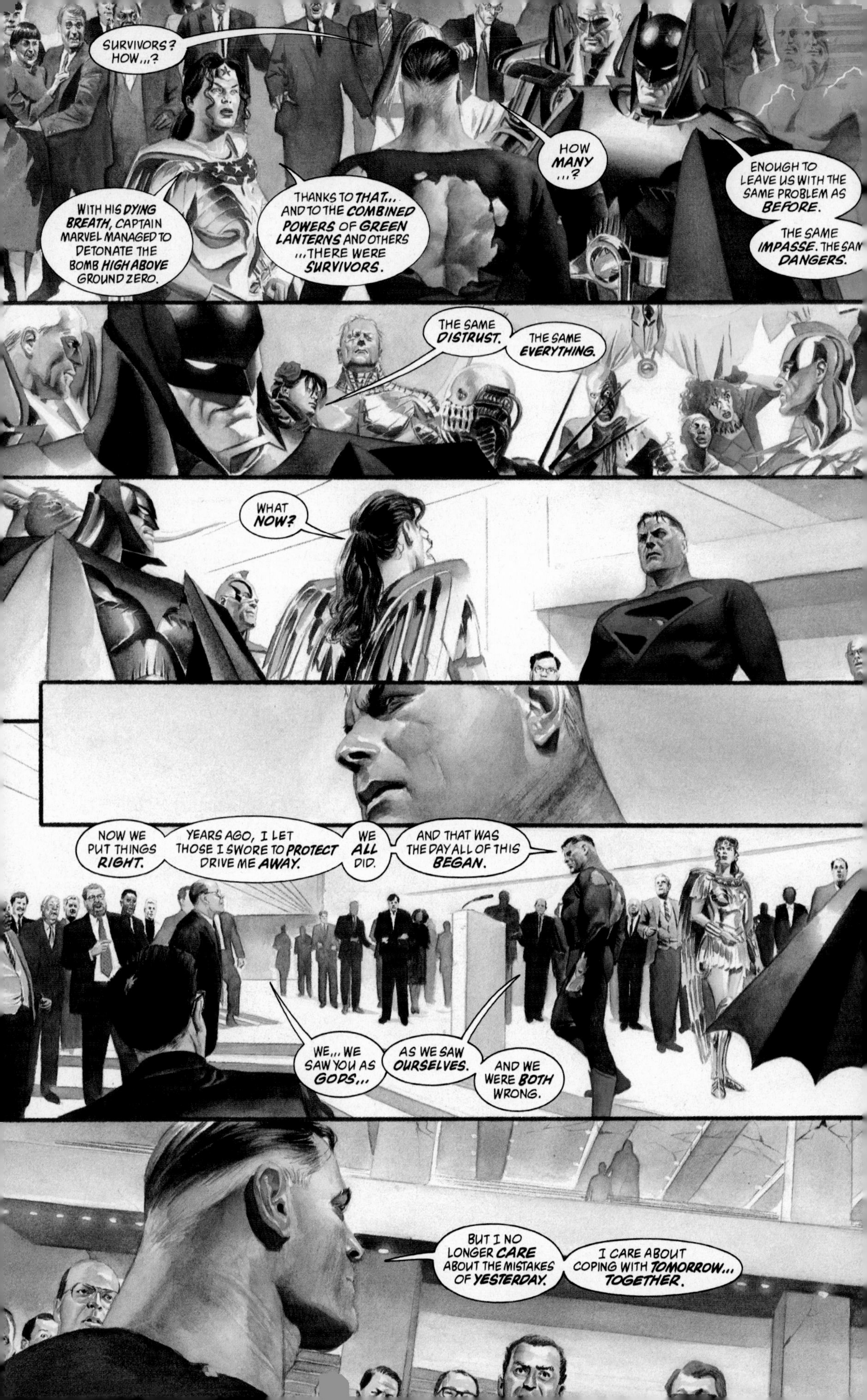
SURVIVORS? HOW...?
WITH HIS DYING BREATH, CAPTAIN MARVEL MANAGED TO DETONATE THE BOMB HIGH ABOVE GROUND ZERO.
THANKS TO THAT... AND TO THE COMBINED POWERS OF GREEN LANTERNS AND OTHERS ...THERE WERE SURVIVORS.
HOW MANY ...?
ENOUGH TO LEAVE US WITH THE SAME PROBLEM AS BEFORE.
THE SAME IMPASSE. THE SAN DANGERS.
THE SAME DISTRUST.
THE SAME EVERYTHING.
WHAT NOW?
NOW WE PUT THINGS RIGHT.
YEARS AGO, I LET THOSE I SWORE TO PROTECT DRIVE ME AWAY.
WE ALL DID.
AND THAT WAS THE DAY ALL OF THIS BEGAN.
WE... WE SAW YOU AS GODS...
AS WE SAW OURSELVES.
AND WE WERE BOTH WRONG.
BUT I NO LONGER CARE ABOUT THE MISTAKES OF YESTERDAY.
I CARE ABOUT COPING WITH TOMORROW... TOGETHER.

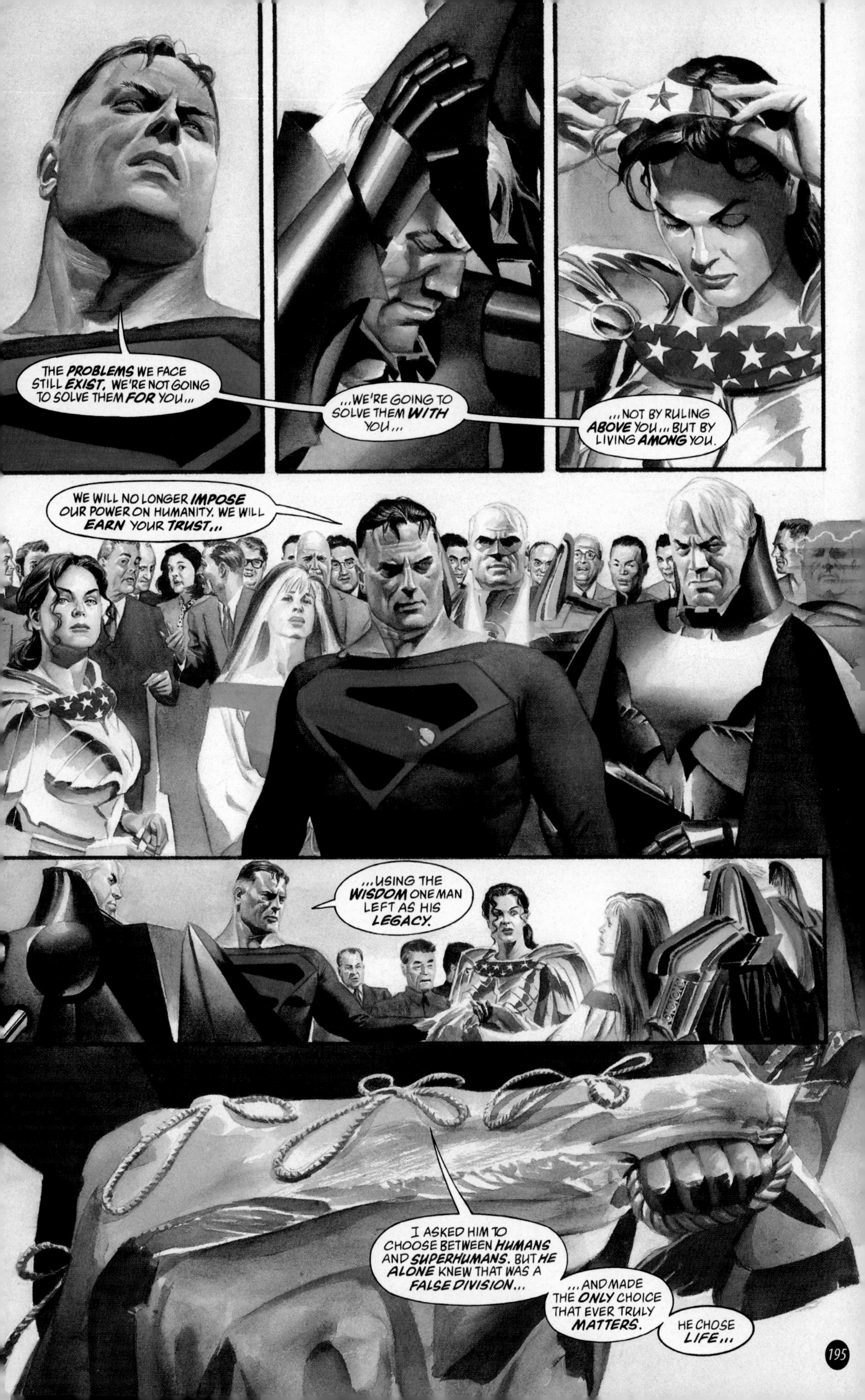

THE PROBLEMS WE FACE STILL EXIST. WE'RE NOT GOING TO SOLVE THEM FOR YOU...
...WE'RE GOING TO SOLVE THEM WITH YOU...
...NOT BY RULING ABOVE YOU... BUT BY LIVING AMONG YOU.
WE WILL NO LONGER IMPOSE OUR POWER ON HUMANITY. WE WILL EARN YOUR TRUST...
...USING THE WISDOM ONE MAN LEFT AS HIS LEGACY.
I ASKED HIM TO CHOOSE BETWEEN HUMANS AND SUPERHUMANS. BUT HE ALONE KNEW THAT WAS A FALSE DIVISION...
...AND MADE THE ONLY CHOICE THAT EVER TRULY MATTERS.
HE CHOSE LIFE...

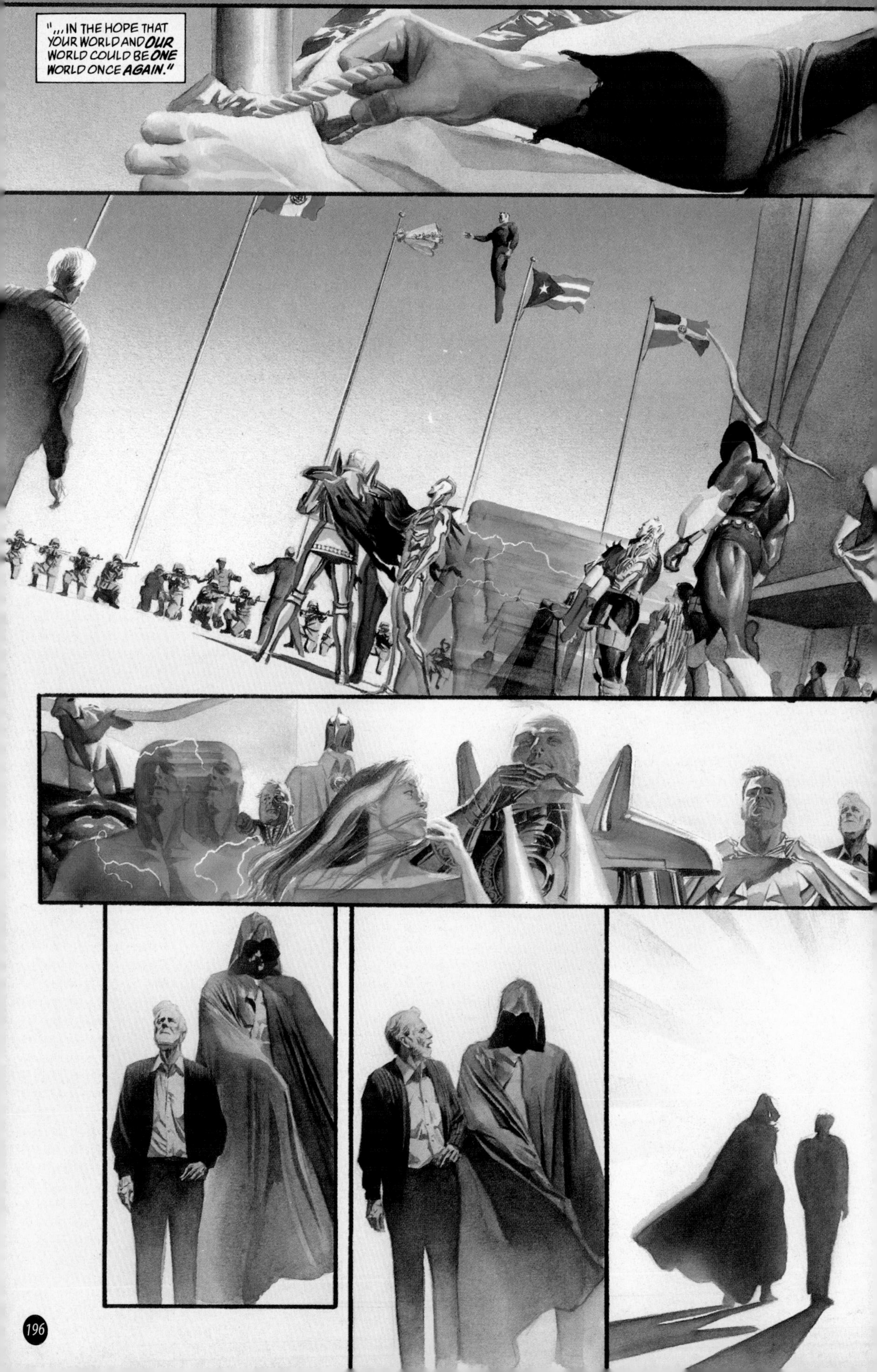
"...IN THE HOPE THAT YOUR WORLD AND OUR WORLD COULD BE ONE WORLD ONCE AGAIN."

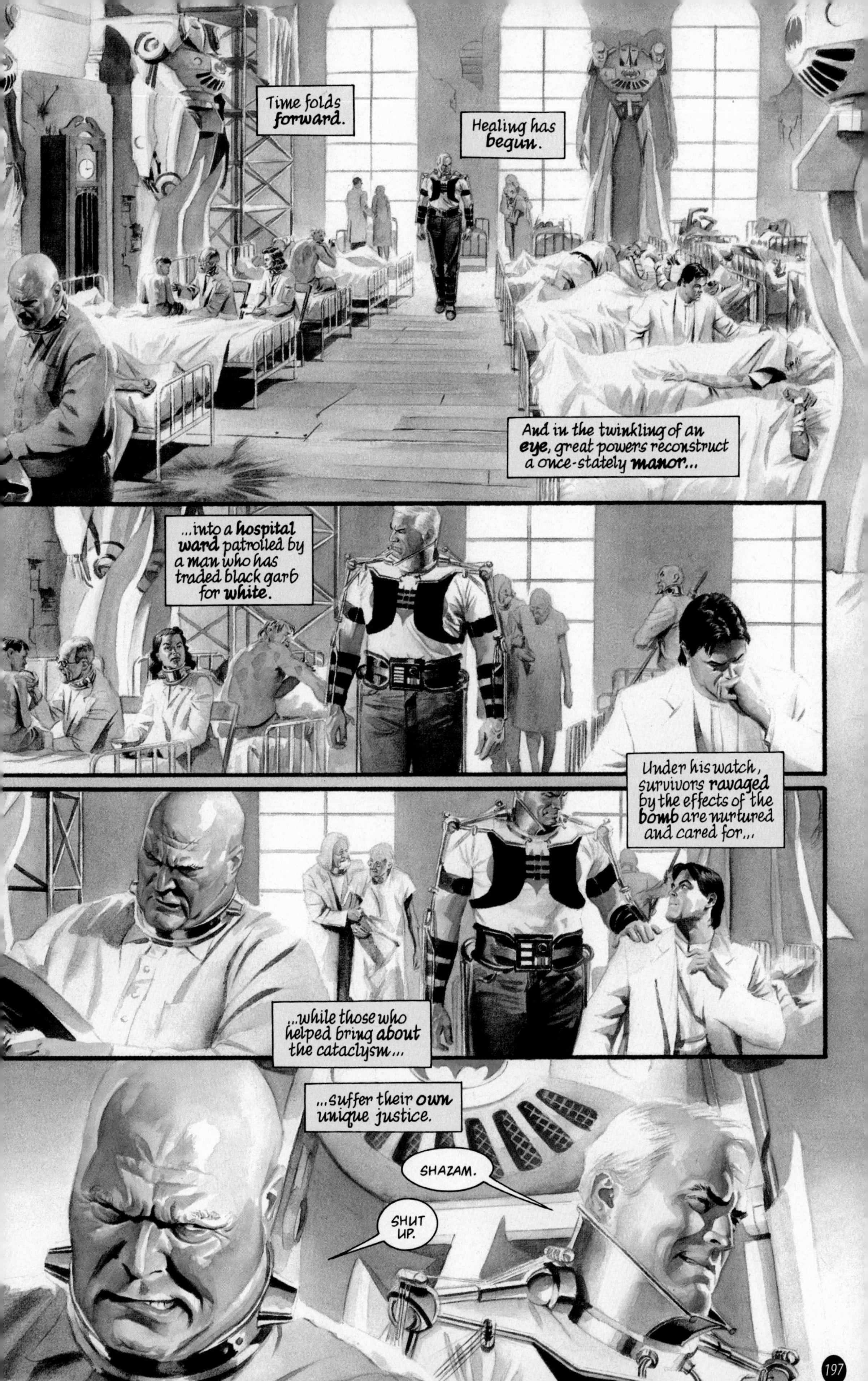

Time folds forward.
Healing has begun.
And in the twinkling of an eye, great powers reconstruct a once-stately manor...
...into a hospital ward patrolled by a man who has traded black garb for white.
Under his watch, survivors ravaged by the effects of the bomb are nurtured and cared for...
...while those who helped bring about the cataclysm...
...suffer their own unique justice.
SHAZAM.
SHUT UP.

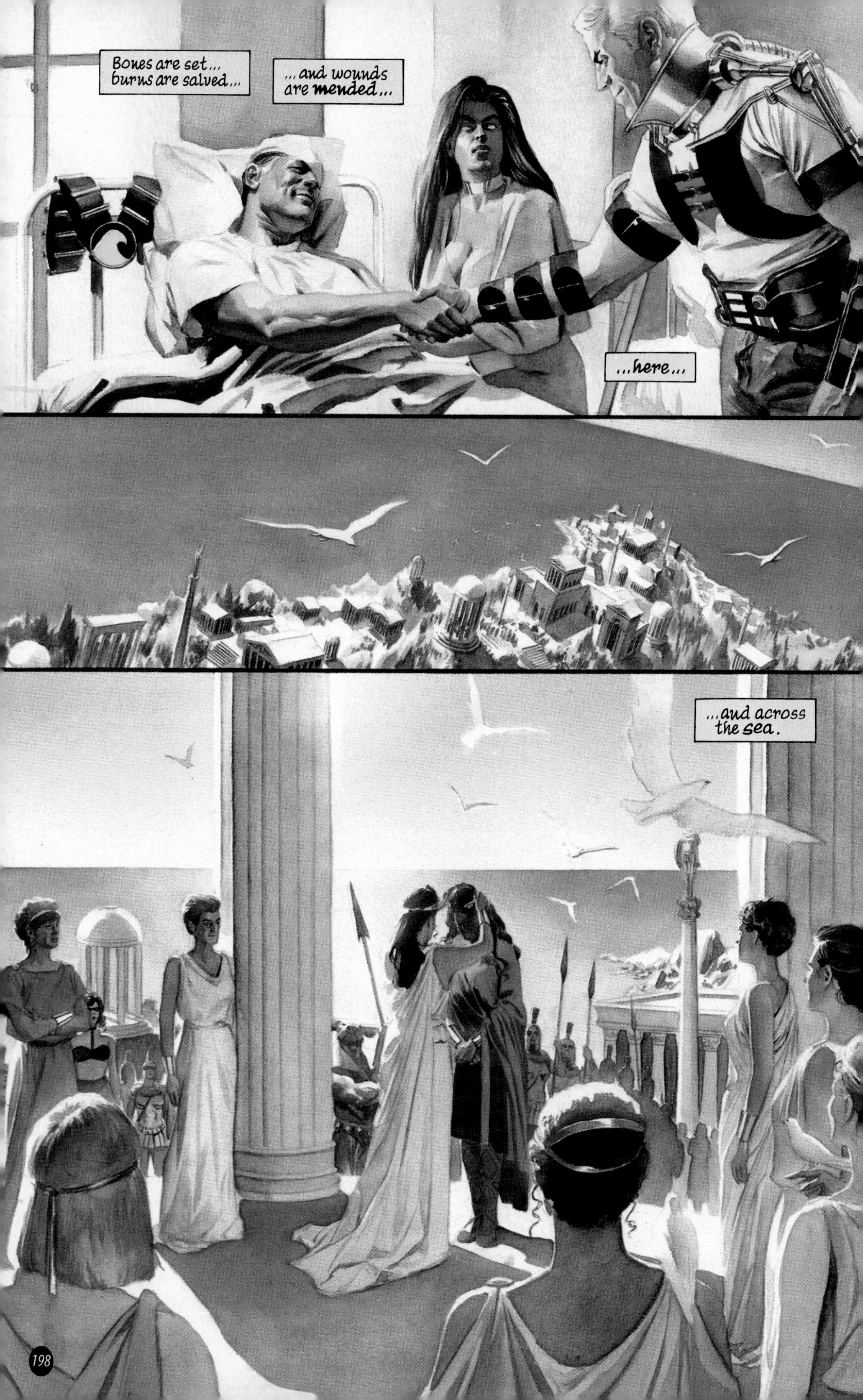
Bones are set... burns are salved...
...and wounds are **mended**...
...here...
...and across the **sea**.

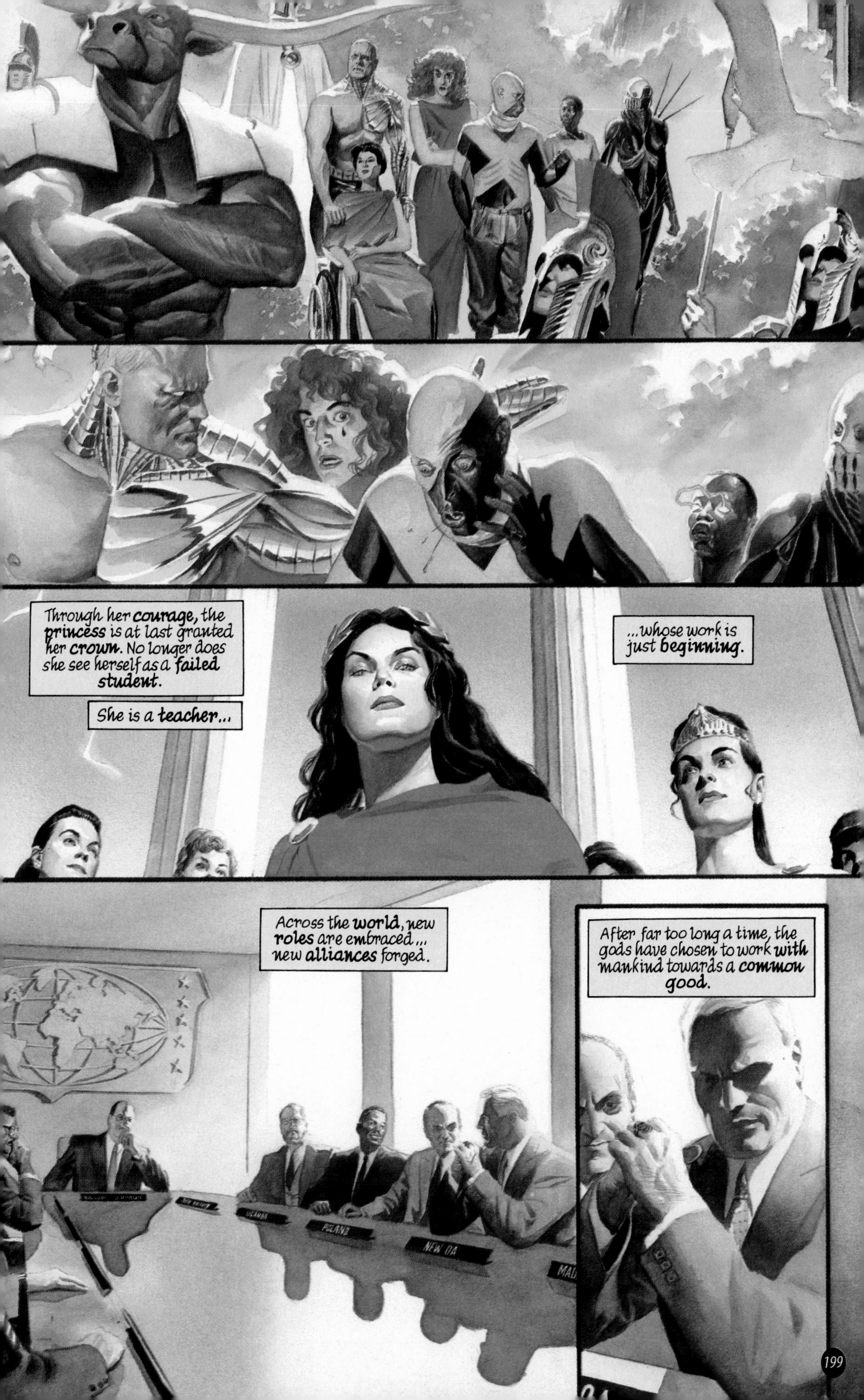
Through her **courage,** the **princess** is at last granted her **crown.** No longer does she see herself as a **failed student.**
She is a **teacher...**
...whose work is just **beginning.**
Across the **world,** new **roles** are embraced... new **alliances** forged.
POLAND
After far too long a time, the gods have chosen to work **with** mankind towards a **common good.**

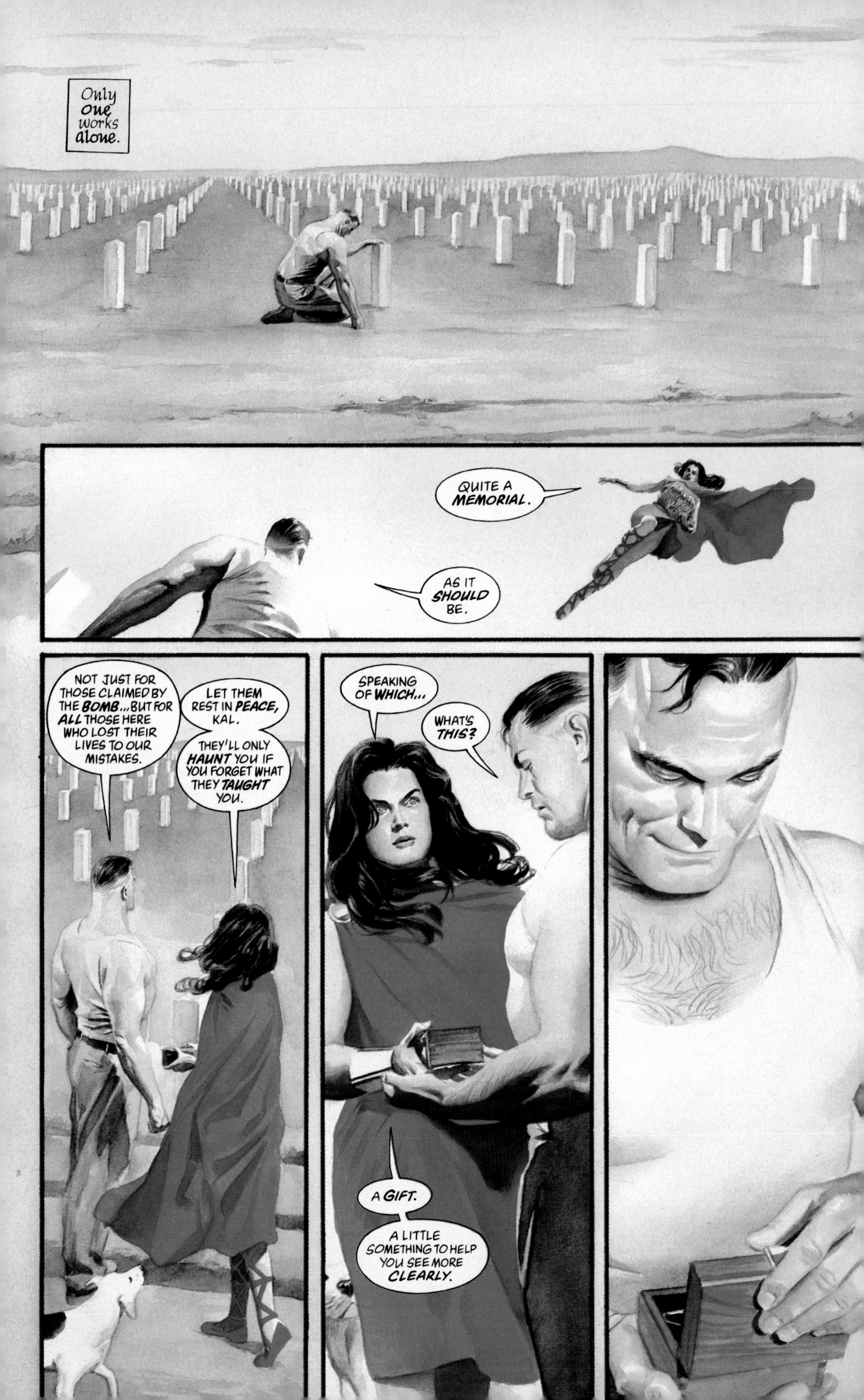
Only one works alone.
QUITE A MEMORIAL.
AS IT SHOULD BE.
NOT JUST FOR THOSE CLAIMED BY THE BOMB...BUT FOR ALL THOSE HERE WHO LOST THEIR LIVES TO OUR MISTAKES.
LET THEM REST IN PEACE, KAL.
THEY'LL ONLY HAUNT YOU IF YOU FORGET WHAT THEY TAUGHT YOU.
SPEAKING OF WHICH...
WHAT'S THIS?
A GIFT.
A LITTLE SOMETHING TO HELP YOU SEE MORE CLEARLY.

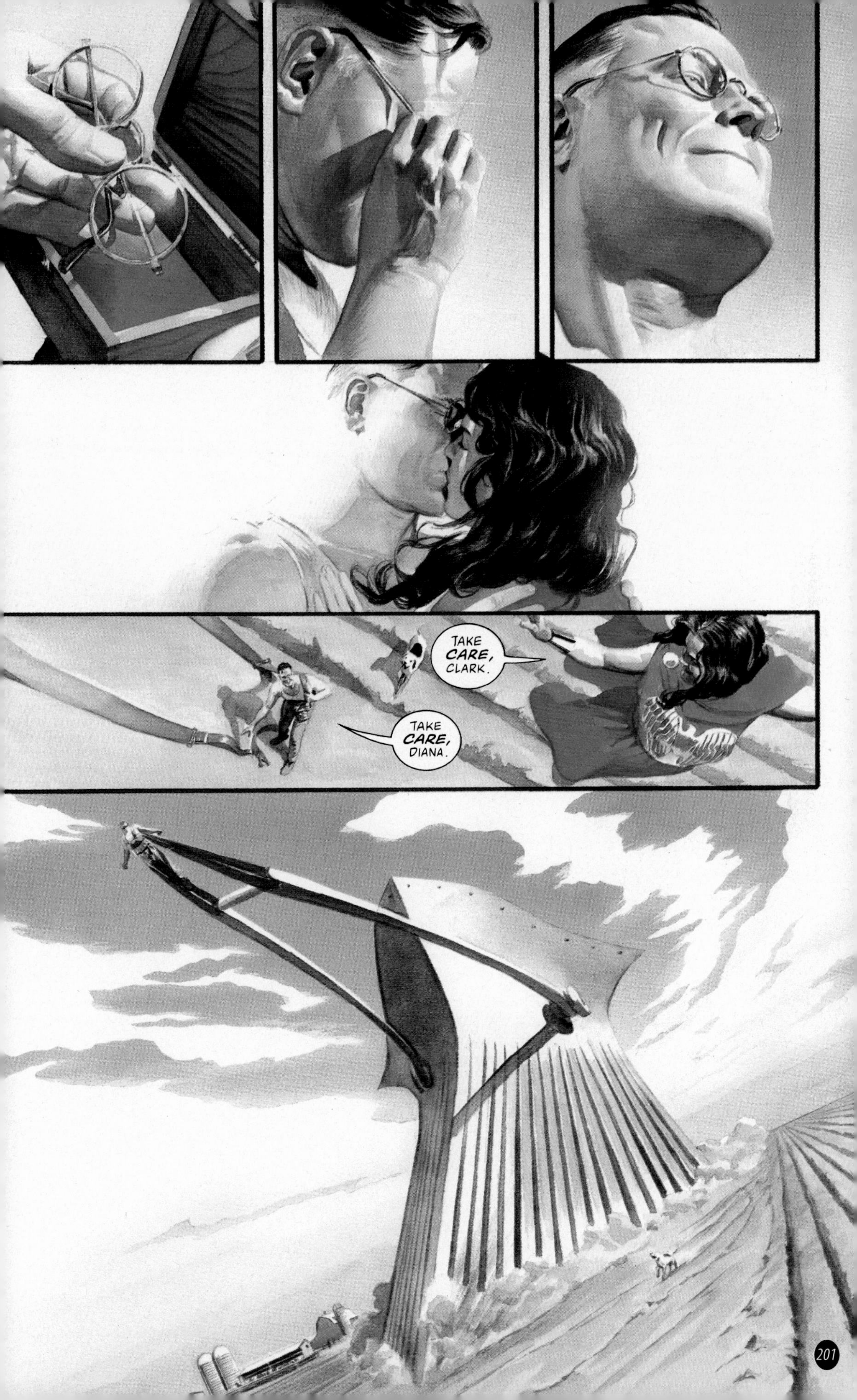
TAKE CARE, CLARK.
TAKE CARE, DIANA.

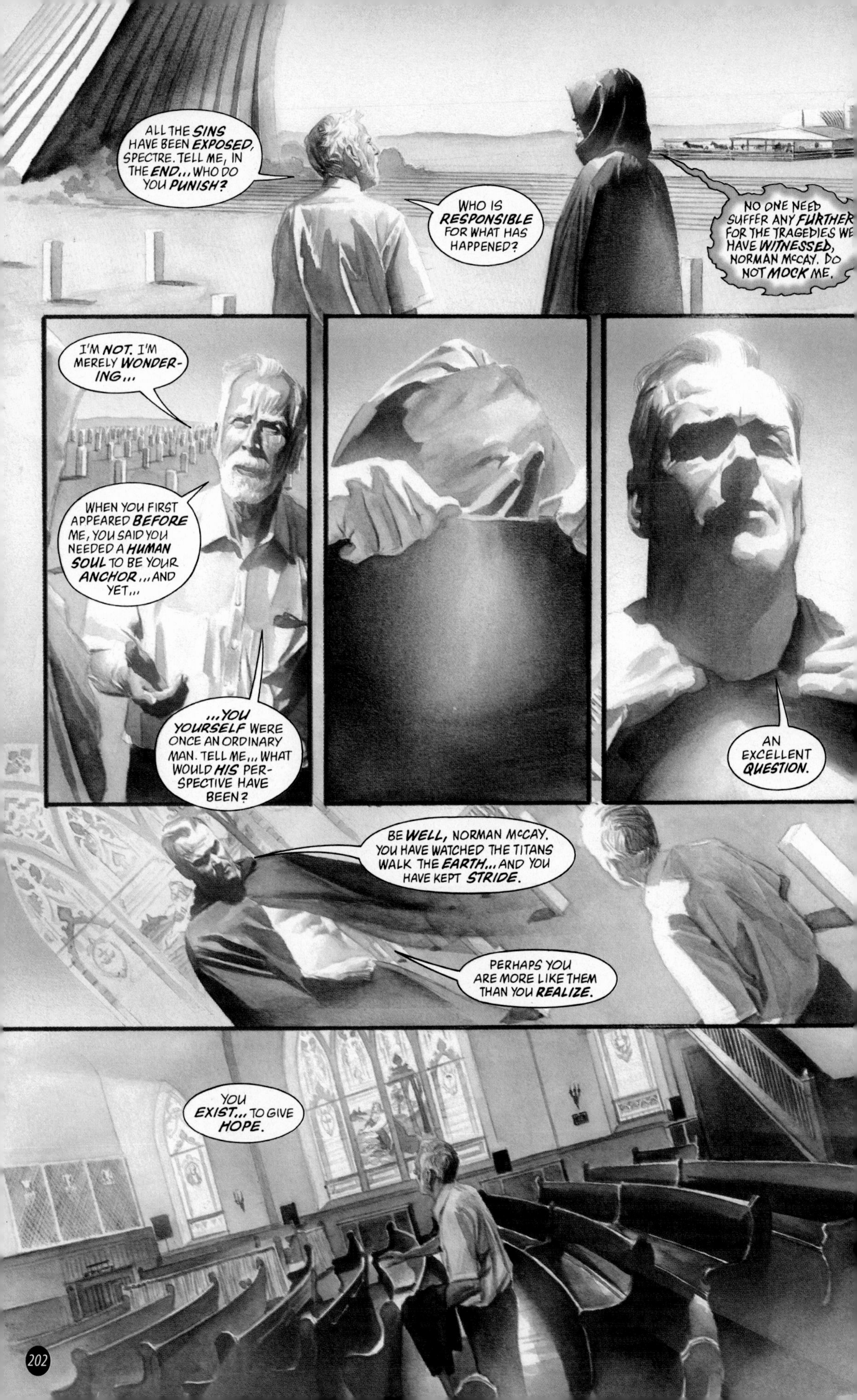

ALL THE SINS HAVE BEEN EXPOSED, SPECTRE. TELL ME, IN THE END... WHO DO YOU PUNISH?
WHO IS RESPONSIBLE FOR WHAT HAS HAPPENED?
NO ONE NEED SUFFER ANY FURTHER FOR THE TRAGEDIES WE HAVE WITNESSED, NORMAN McCAY. DO NOT MOCK ME.
I'M NOT. I'M MERELY WONDER-ING...
WHEN YOU FIRST APPEARED BEFORE ME, YOU SAID YOU NEEDED A HUMAN SOUL TO BE YOUR ANCHOR... AND YET...
...YOU YOURSELF WERE ONCE AN ORDINARY MAN. TELL ME... WHAT WOULD HIS PER-SPECTIVE HAVE BEEN?
AN EXCELLENT QUESTION.
BE WELL, NORMAN McCAY. YOU HAVE WATCHED THE TITANS WALK THE EARTH... AND YOU HAVE KEPT STRIDE.
PERHAPS YOU ARE MORE LIKE THEM THAN YOU REALIZE.
YOU EXIST... TO GIVE HOPE.

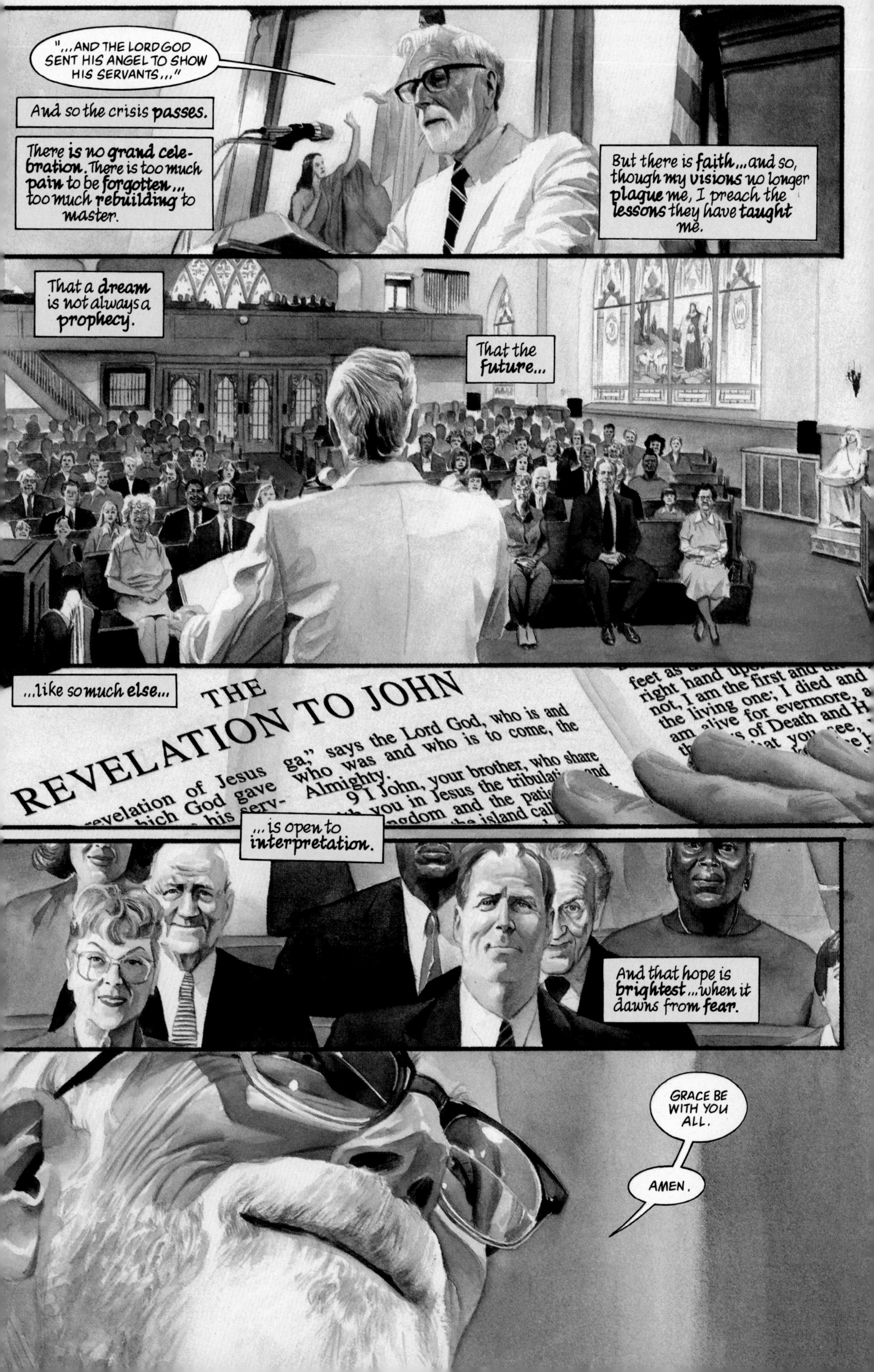
"...AND THE LORD GOD SENT HIS ANGEL TO SHOW HIS SERVANTS..."
And so the crisis passes.
There is no grand celebration. There is too much pain to be forgotten... too much rebuilding to master.
But there is faith...and so, though my visions no longer plague me, I preach the lessons they have taught me.
That a dream is not always a prophecy.
That the future...
...like so much else...
THE REVELATION TO JOHN
...is open to interpretation.
And that hope is brightest...when it dawns from fear.
GRACE BE WITH YOU ALL.
AMEN.

ONE YEAR LATER..

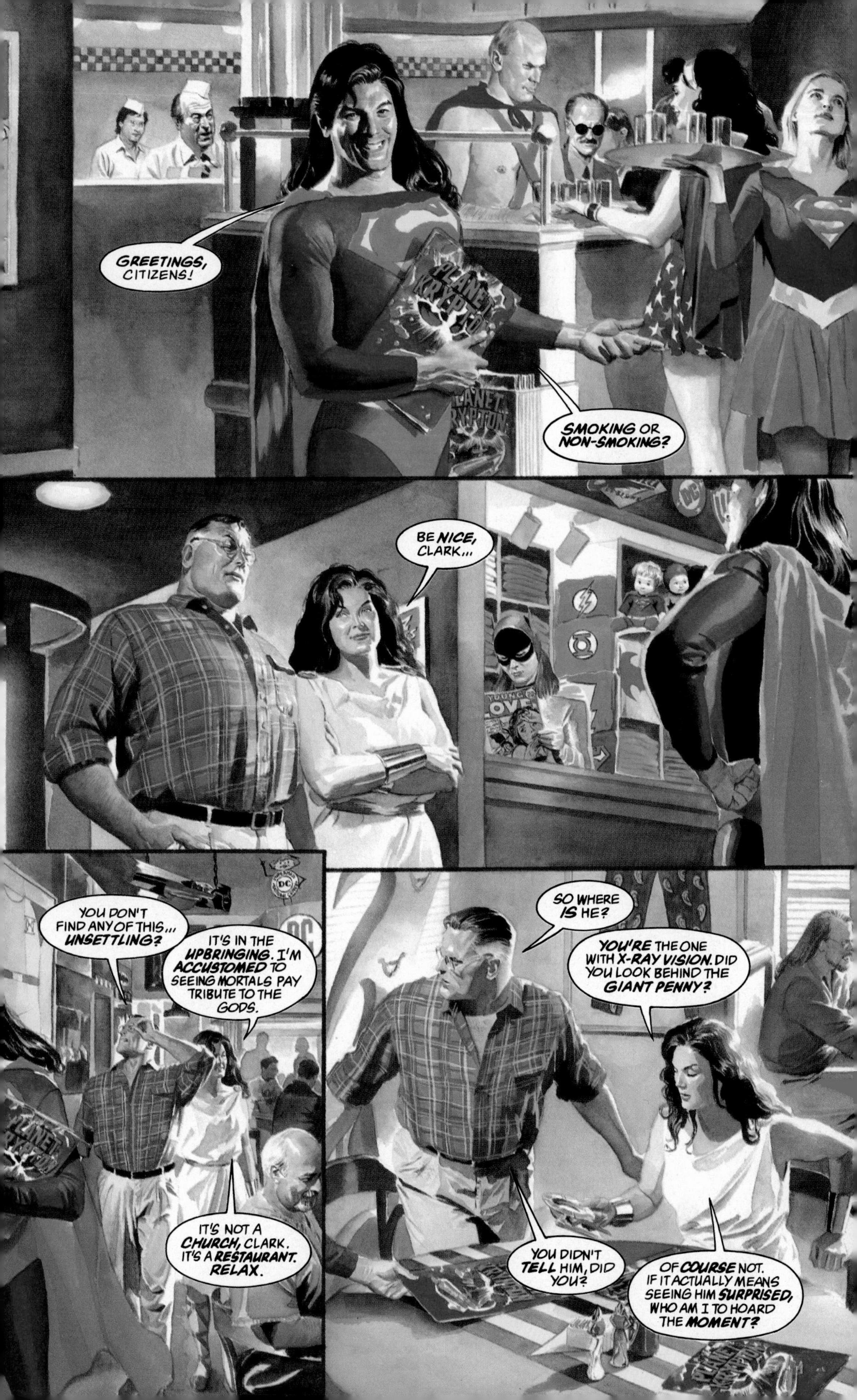
GREETINGS, CITIZENS!
SMOKING OR NON-SMOKING?
BE NICE, CLARK...
YOU DON'T FIND ANY OF THIS... UNSETTLING?
IT'S IN THE UPBRINGING. I'M ACCUSTOMED TO SEEING MORTALS PAY TRIBUTE TO THE GODS.
IT'S NOT A CHURCH, CLARK. IT'S A RESTAURANT. RELAX.
SO WHERE IS HE?
YOU'RE THE ONE WITH X-RAY VISION. DID YOU LOOK BEHIND THE GIANT PENNY?
YOU DIDN'T TELL HIM, DID YOU?
OF COURSE NOT. IF IT ACTUALLY MEANS SEEING HIM SURPRISED, WHO AM I TO HOARD THE MOMENT?

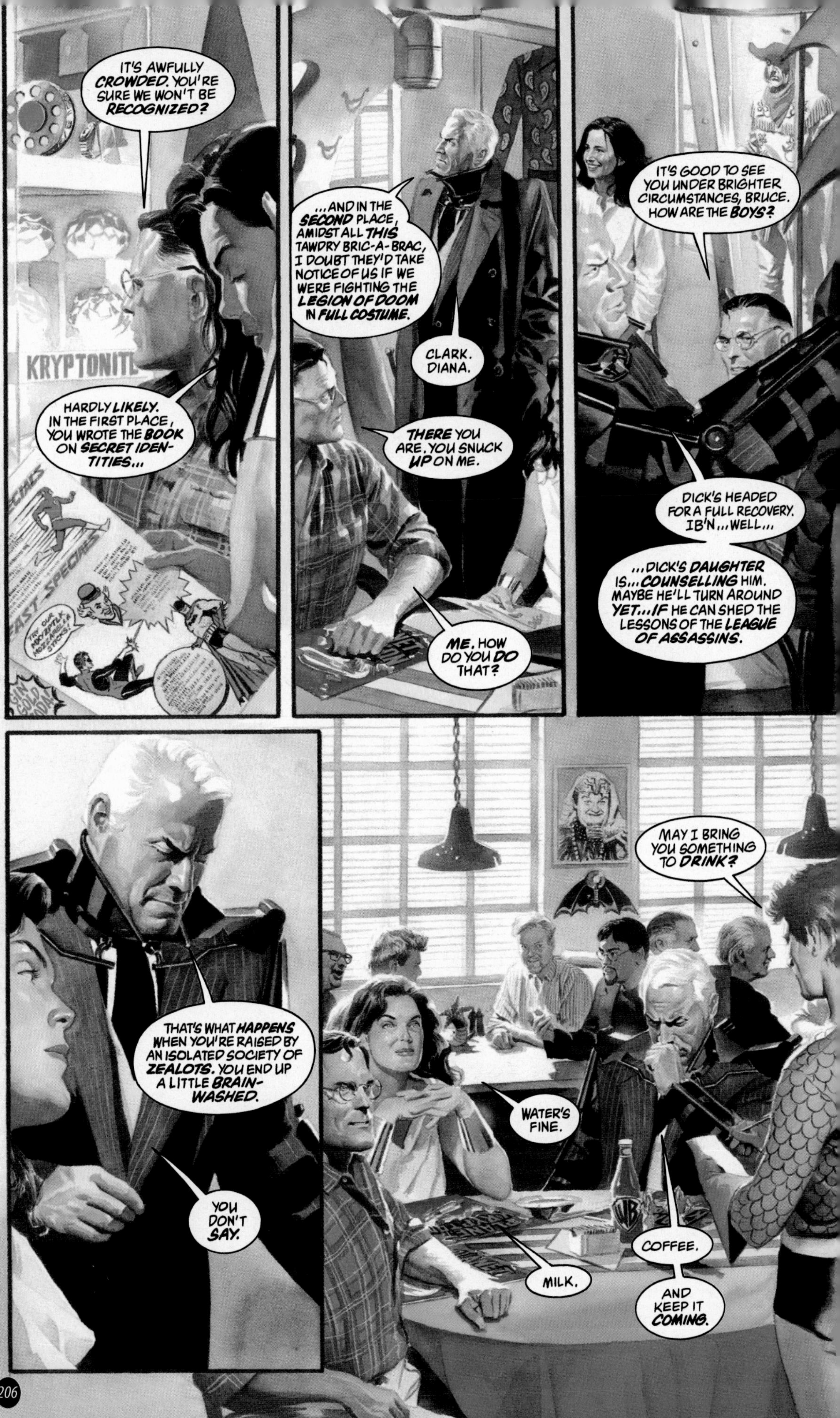
IT'S AWFULLY CROWDED. YOU'RE SURE WE WON'T BE RECOGNIZED?
KRYPTONITE
HARDLY LIKELY. IN THE FIRST PLACE, YOU WROTE THE BOOK ON SECRET IDENTITIES...
...AND IN THE SECOND PLACE, AMIDST ALL THIS TAWDRY BRIC-A-BRAC, I DOUBT THEY'D TAKE NOTICE OF US IF WE WERE FIGHTING THE LEGION OF DOOM IN FULL COSTUME.
CLARK. DIANA.
THERE YOU ARE. YOU SNUCK UP ON ME.
ME. HOW DO YOU DO THAT?
IT'S GOOD TO SEE YOU UNDER BRIGHTER CIRCUMSTANCES, BRUCE. HOW ARE THE BOYS?
DICK'S HEADED FOR A FULL RECOVERY. IB'N...WELL...
...DICK'S DAUGHTER IS...COUNSELLING HIM. MAYBE HE'LL TURN AROUND YET...IF HE CAN SHED THE LESSONS OF THE LEAGUE OF ASSASSINS.
THAT'S WHAT HAPPENS WHEN YOU'RE RAISED BY AN ISOLATED SOCIETY OF ZEALOTS. YOU END UP A LITTLE BRAIN-WASHED.
YOU DON'T SAY.
MAY I BRING YOU SOMETHING TO DRINK?
WATER'S FINE.
MILK.
COFFEE.
AND KEEP IT COMING.

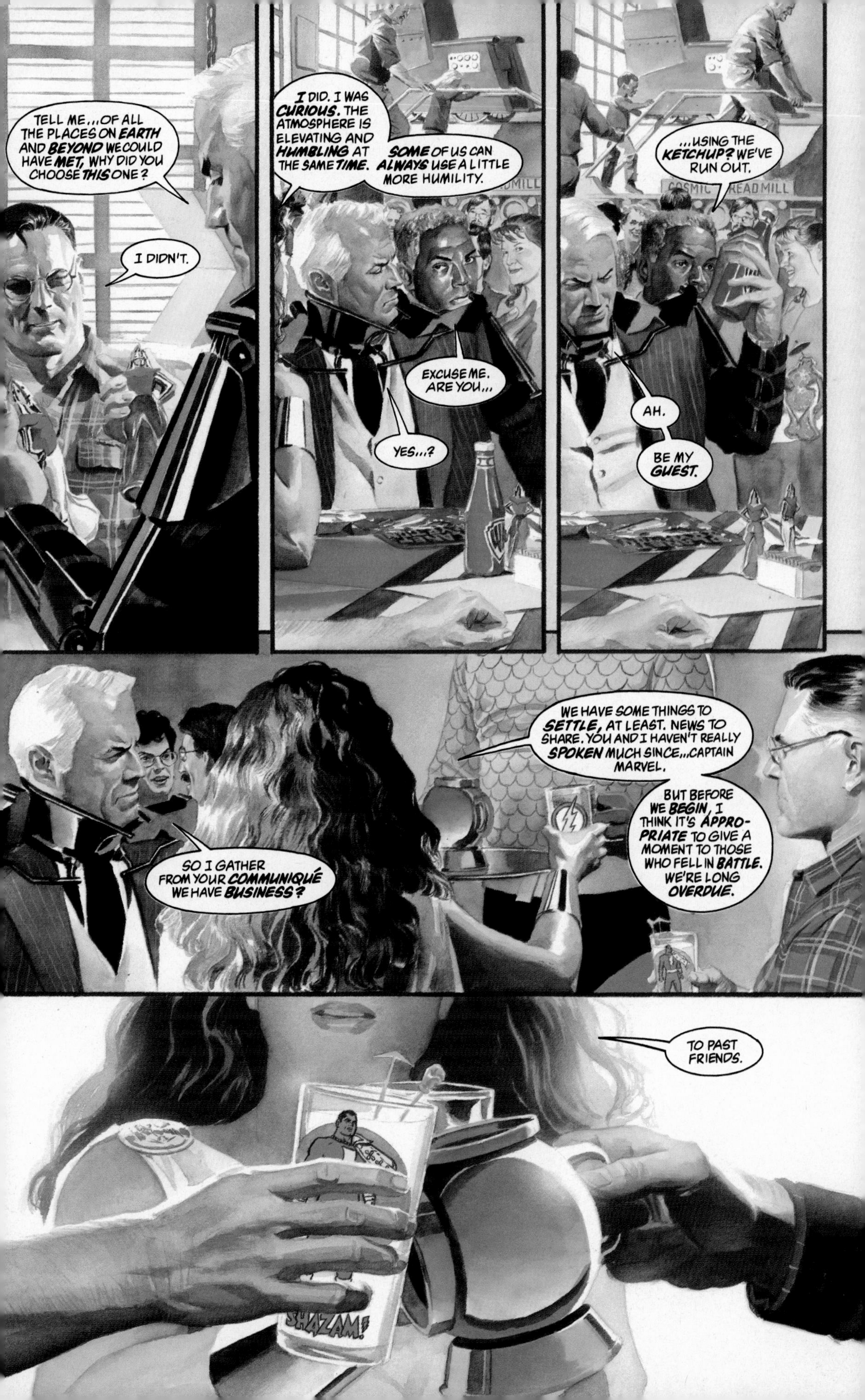
TELL ME...OF ALL THE PLACES ON EARTH AND BEYOND WE COULD HAVE MET, WHY DID YOU CHOOSE THIS ONE?
I DIDN'T.
I DID. I WAS CURIOUS. THE ATMOSPHERE IS ELEVATING AND HUMBLING AT THE SAME TIME.
SOME OF US CAN ALWAYS USE A LITTLE MORE HUMILITY.
EXCUSE ME. ARE YOU...
YES...?
...USING THE KETCHUP? WE'VE RUN OUT.
COSMIC TREADMILL
AH.
BE MY GUEST.
SO I GATHER FROM YOUR COMMUNIQUÉ WE HAVE BUSINESS?
WE HAVE SOME THINGS TO SETTLE, AT LEAST. NEWS TO SHARE. YOU AND I HAVEN'T REALLY SPOKEN MUCH SINCE...CAPTAIN MARVEL.
BUT BEFORE WE BEGIN, I THINK IT'S APPROPRIATE TO GIVE A MOMENT TO THOSE WHO FELL IN BATTLE. WE'RE LONG OVERDUE.
TO PAST FRIENDS.
SHAZAM!

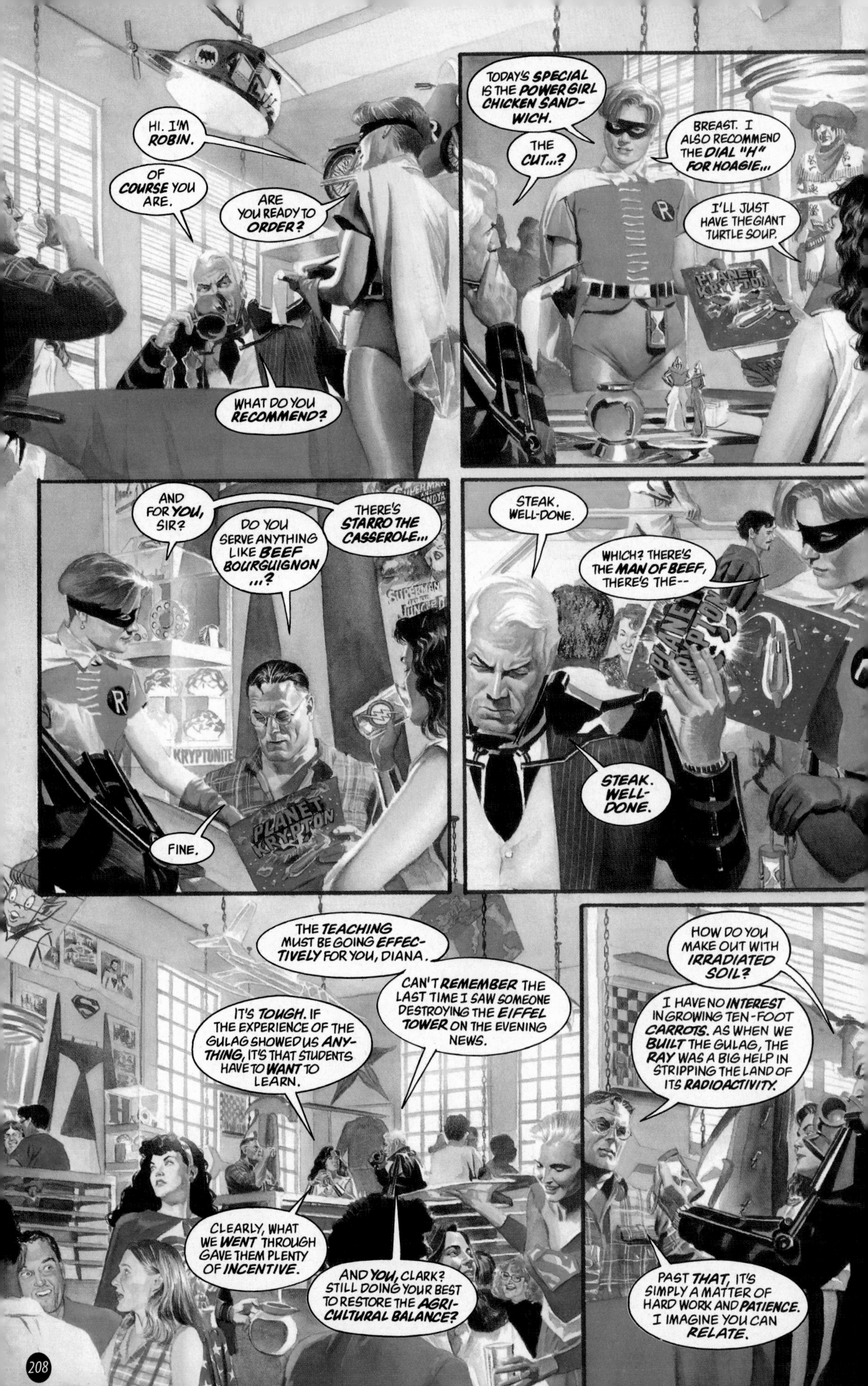
HI. I'M ROBIN.
OF COURSE YOU ARE.
ARE YOU READY TO ORDER?
WHAT DO YOU RECOMMEND?
TODAY'S SPECIAL IS THE POWER GIRL CHICKEN SAND-WICH.
THE CUT...?
BREAST. I ALSO RECOMMEND THE DIAL "H" FOR HOAGIE...
I'LL JUST HAVE THE GIANT TURTLE SOUP.
PLANET KRYPTON
AND FOR YOU, SIR?
THERE'S STARRO THE CASSEROLE...
DO YOU SERVE ANYTHING LIKE BEEF BOURGUIGNON ...?
KRYPTONITE
FINE.
PLANET KRYPTON
STEAK. WELL-DONE.
WHICH? THERE'S THE MAN OF BEEF, THERE'S THE--
STEAK. WELL-DONE.
THE TEACHING MUST BE GOING EFFEC-TIVELY FOR YOU, DIANA.
CAN'T REMEMBER THE LAST TIME I SAW SOMEONE DESTROYING THE EIFFEL TOWER ON THE EVENING NEWS.
IT'S TOUGH. IF THE EXPERIENCE OF THE GULAG SHOWED US ANY-THING, IT'S THAT STUDENTS HAVE TO WANT TO LEARN.
CLEARLY, WHAT WE WENT THROUGH GAVE THEM PLENTY OF INCENTIVE.
AND YOU, CLARK? STILL DOING YOUR BEST TO RESTORE THE AGRI-CULTURAL BALANCE?
HOW DO YOU MAKE OUT WITH IRRADIATED SOIL?
I HAVE NO INTEREST IN GROWING TEN-FOOT CARROTS. AS WHEN WE BUILT THE GULAG, THE RAY WAS A BIG HELP IN STRIPPING THE LAND OF ITS RADIOACTIVITY.
PAST THAT, IT'S SIMPLY A MATTER OF HARD WORK AND PATIENCE. I IMAGINE YOU CAN RELATE.

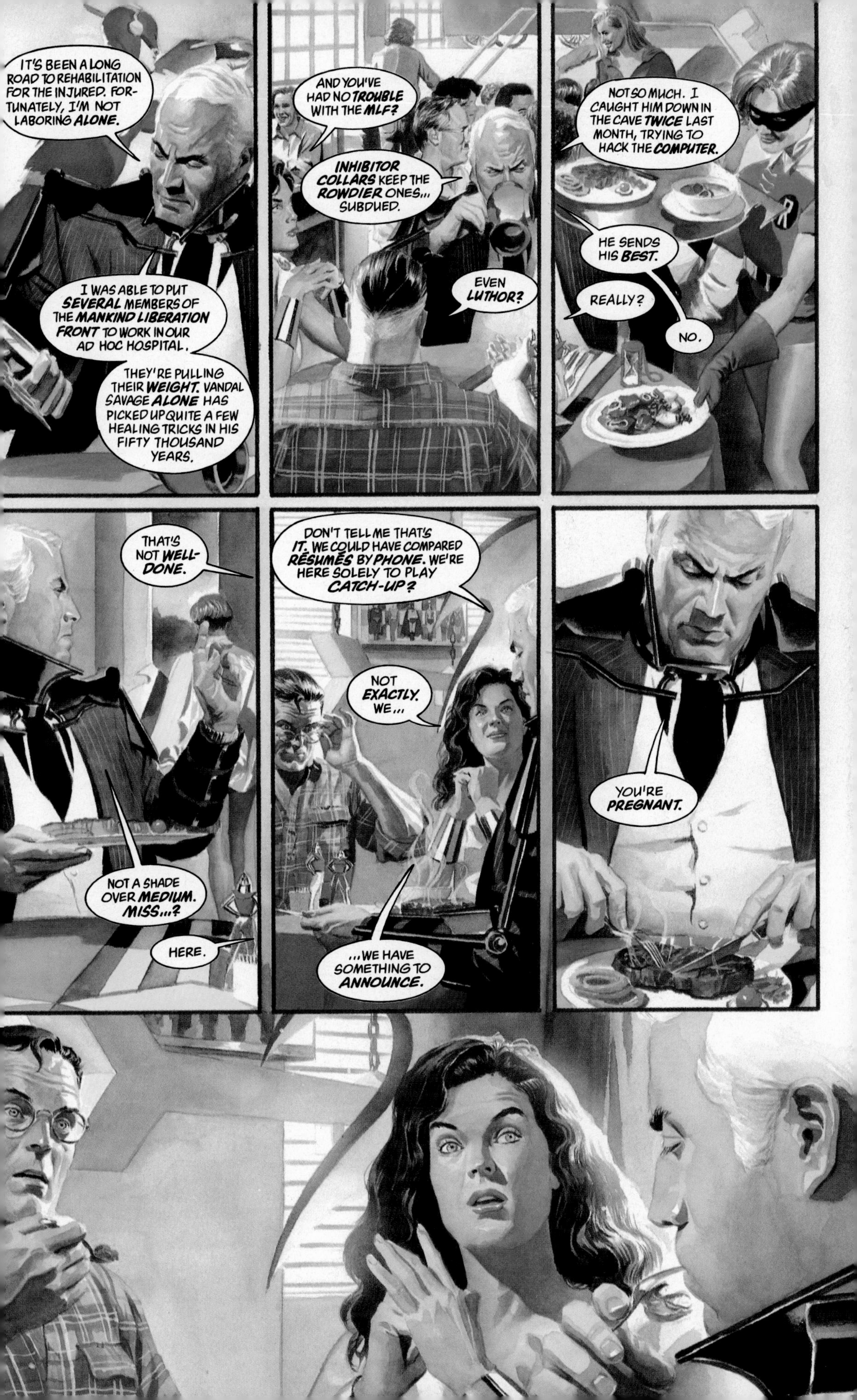
IT'S BEEN A LONG ROAD TO REHABILITATION FOR THE INJURED. FORTUNATELY, I'M NOT LABORING ALONE.
I WAS ABLE TO PUT SEVERAL MEMBERS OF THE MANKIND LIBERATION FRONT TO WORK IN OUR AD HOC HOSPITAL.
THEY'RE PULLING THEIR WEIGHT. VANDAL SAVAGE ALONE HAS PICKED UP QUITE A FEW HEALING TRICKS IN HIS FIFTY THOUSAND YEARS.
AND YOU'VE HAD NO TROUBLE WITH THE MLF?
INHIBITOR COLLARS KEEP THE ROWDIER ONES... SUBDUED.
EVEN LUTHOR?
NOT SO MUCH. I CAUGHT HIM DOWN IN THE CAVE TWICE LAST MONTH, TRYING TO HACK THE COMPUTER.
HE SENDS HIS BEST.
REALLY?
NO.
THAT'S NOT WELL-DONE.
NOT A SHADE OVER MEDIUM. MISS...?
HERE.
DON'T TELL ME THAT'S IT. WE COULD HAVE COMPARED RÉSUMÉS BY PHONE. WE'RE HERE SOLELY TO PLAY CATCH-UP?
NOT EXACTLY. WE...
...WE HAVE SOMETHING TO ANNOUNCE.
YOU'RE PREGNANT.

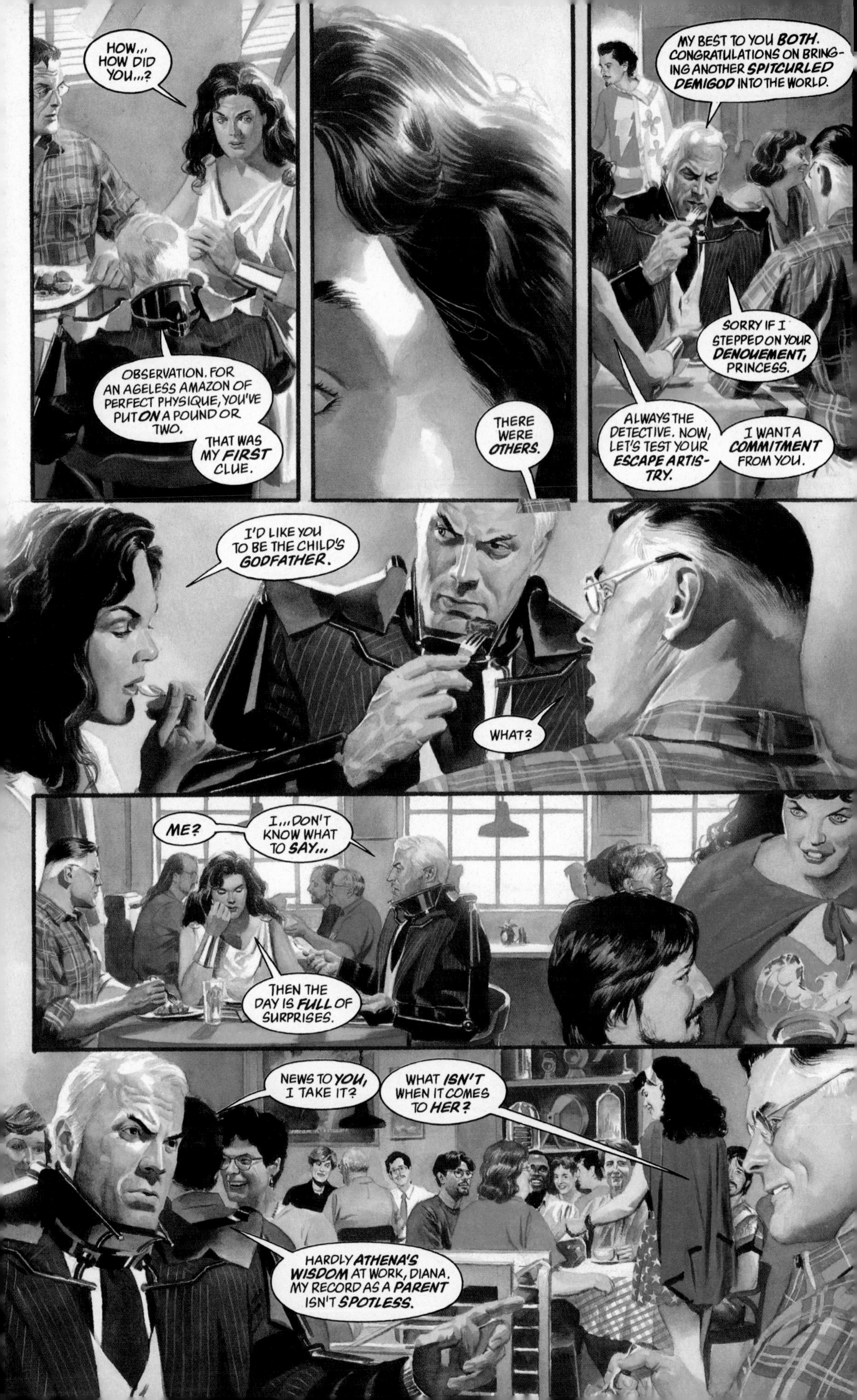
HOW... HOW DID YOU...?
OBSERVATION. FOR AN AGELESS AMAZON OF PERFECT PHYSIQUE, YOU'VE PUT ON A POUND OR TWO.
THAT WAS MY FIRST CLUE.
THERE WERE OTHERS.
MY BEST TO YOU BOTH. CONGRATULATIONS ON BRINGING ANOTHER SPITCURLED DEMIGOD INTO THE WORLD.
SORRY IF I STEPPED ON YOUR DENOUEMENT, PRINCESS.
ALWAYS THE DETECTIVE. NOW, LET'S TEST YOUR ESCAPE ARTISTRY.
I WANT A COMMITMENT FROM YOU.
I'D LIKE YOU TO BE THE CHILD'S GODFATHER.
WHAT?
ME?
I... DON'T KNOW WHAT TO SAY...
THEN THE DAY IS FULL OF SURPRISES.
NEWS TO YOU, I TAKE IT?
WHAT ISN'T WHEN IT COMES TO HER?
HARDLY ATHENA'S WISDOM AT WORK, DIANA. MY RECORD AS A PARENT ISN'T SPOTLESS.

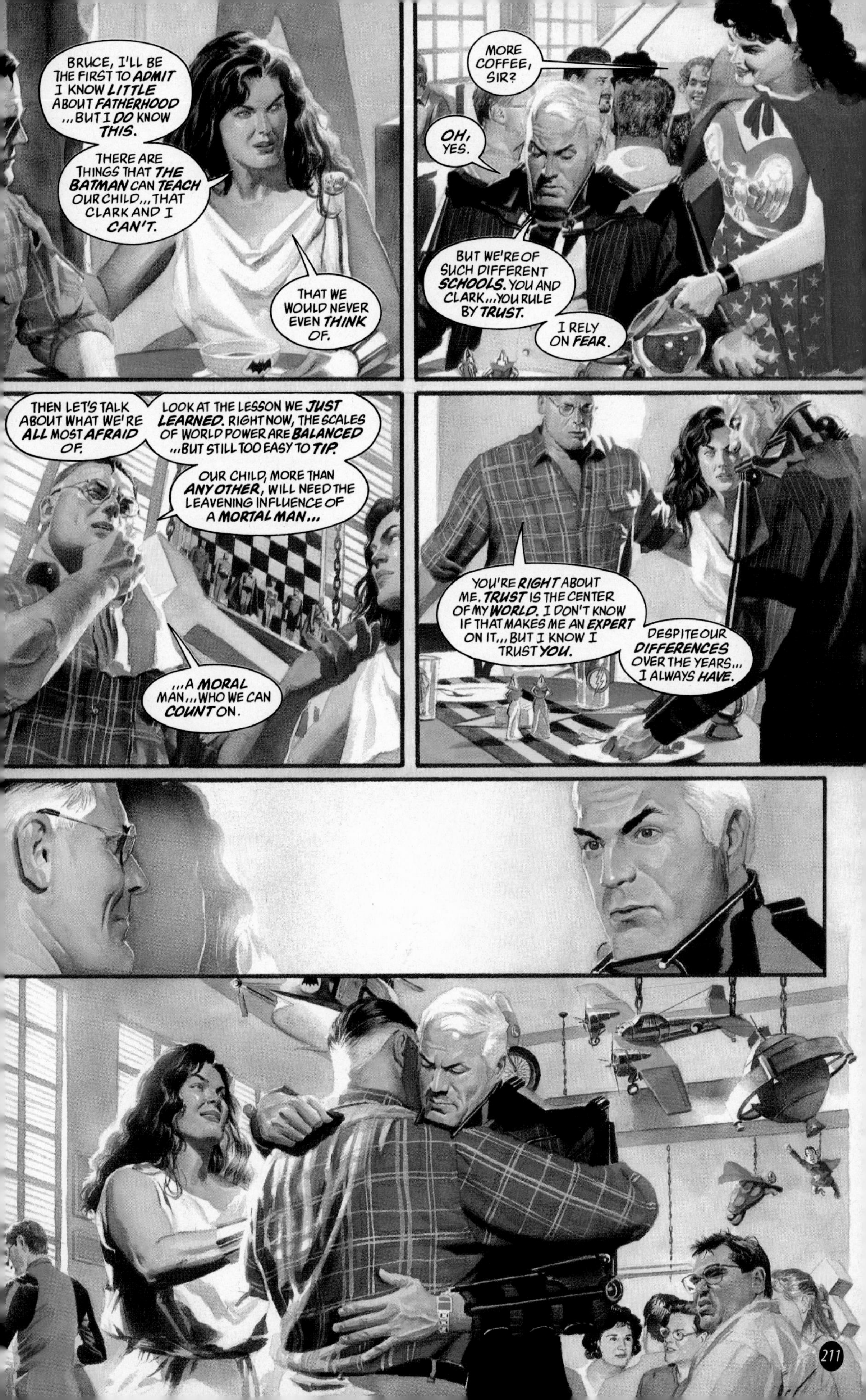

BRUCE, I'LL BE THE FIRST TO ADMIT I KNOW LITTLE ABOUT FATHERHOOD ...BUT I DO KNOW THIS.
THERE ARE THINGS THAT THE BATMAN CAN TEACH OUR CHILD... THAT CLARK AND I CAN'T.
THAT WE WOULD NEVER EVEN THINK OF.
MORE COFFEE, SIR?
OH, YES.
BUT WE'RE OF SUCH DIFFERENT SCHOOLS. YOU AND CLARK... YOU RULE BY TRUST.
I RELY ON FEAR.
THEN LET'S TALK ABOUT WHAT WE'RE ALL MOST AFRAID OF.
LOOK AT THE LESSON WE JUST LEARNED. RIGHT NOW, THE SCALES OF WORLD POWER ARE BALANCED ...BUT STILL TOO EASY TO TIP.
OUR CHILD, MORE THAN ANY OTHER, WILL NEED THE LEAVENING INFLUENCE OF A MORTAL MAN...
...A MORAL MAN... WHO WE CAN COUNT ON.
YOU'RE RIGHT ABOUT ME. TRUST IS THE CENTER OF MY WORLD. I DON'T KNOW IF THAT MAKES ME AN EXPERT ON IT... BUT I KNOW I TRUST YOU.
DESPITE OUR DIFFERENCES OVER THE YEARS... I ALWAYS HAVE.

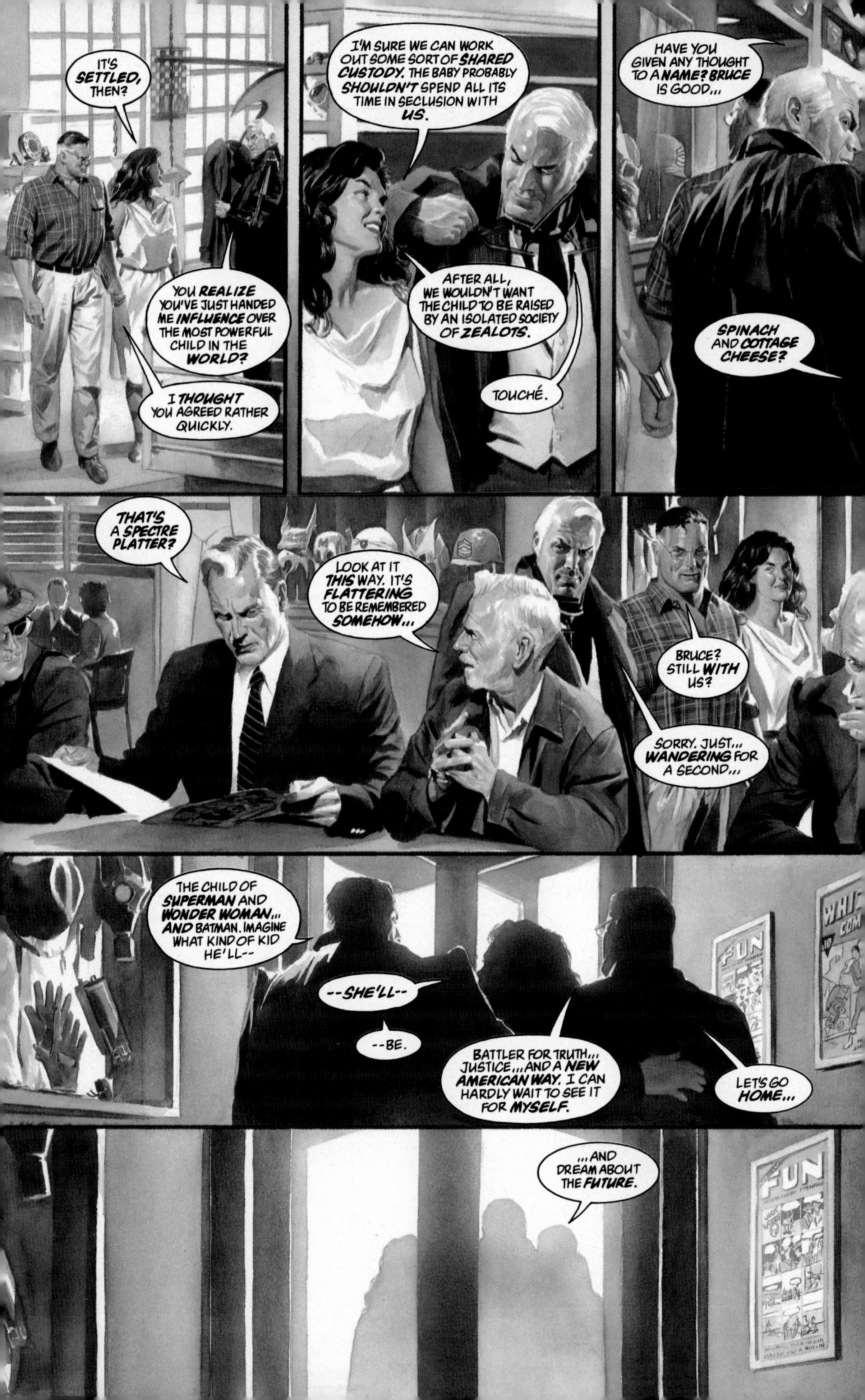
IT'S SETTLED, THEN?
YOU REALIZE YOU'VE JUST HANDED ME INFLUENCE OVER THE MOST POWERFUL CHILD IN THE WORLD?
I THOUGHT YOU AGREED RATHER QUICKLY.
I'M SURE WE CAN WORK OUT SOME SORT OF SHARED CUSTODY. THE BABY PROBABLY SHOULDN'T SPEND ALL ITS TIME IN SECLUSION WITH US.
AFTER ALL, WE WOULDN'T WANT THE CHILD TO BE RAISED BY AN ISOLATED SOCIETY OF ZEALOTS.
TOUCHÉ.
HAVE YOU GIVEN ANY THOUGHT TO A NAME? BRUCE IS GOOD...
SPINACH AND COTTAGE CHEESE?
THAT'S A SPECTRE PLATTER?
LOOK AT IT THIS WAY. IT'S FLATTERING TO BE REMEMBERED SOMEHOW...
BRUCE? STILL WITH US?
SORRY. JUST... WANDERING FOR A SECOND...
THE CHILD OF SUPERMAN AND WONDER WOMAN... AND BATMAN. IMAGINE WHAT KIND OF KID HE'LL--
--SHE'LL--
--BE.
BATTLER FOR TRUTH... JUSTICE... AND A NEW AMERICAN WAY. I CAN HARDLY WAIT TO SEE IT FOR MYSELF.
LET'S GO HOME...
...AND DREAM ABOUT THE FUTURE.

APOCRYPHA

Cool and dispassionate, the Spectre is aware that a Great Evil is about to be visited upon the world. He's not been graced with specifics — despite his tremendous powers, he's not clairvoyant — but he does know that it involves a coming clash between the superhumans. As God's Terrible, Swift Sword, the Spectre is using Norman McCay — an eminently human point of view — to judge the exact nature of that evil and how it will be punished. However, the Spectre cannot take any sort of judgmental action unless he witnesses an evil being committed — which is why he requires Norman to guide their journey.

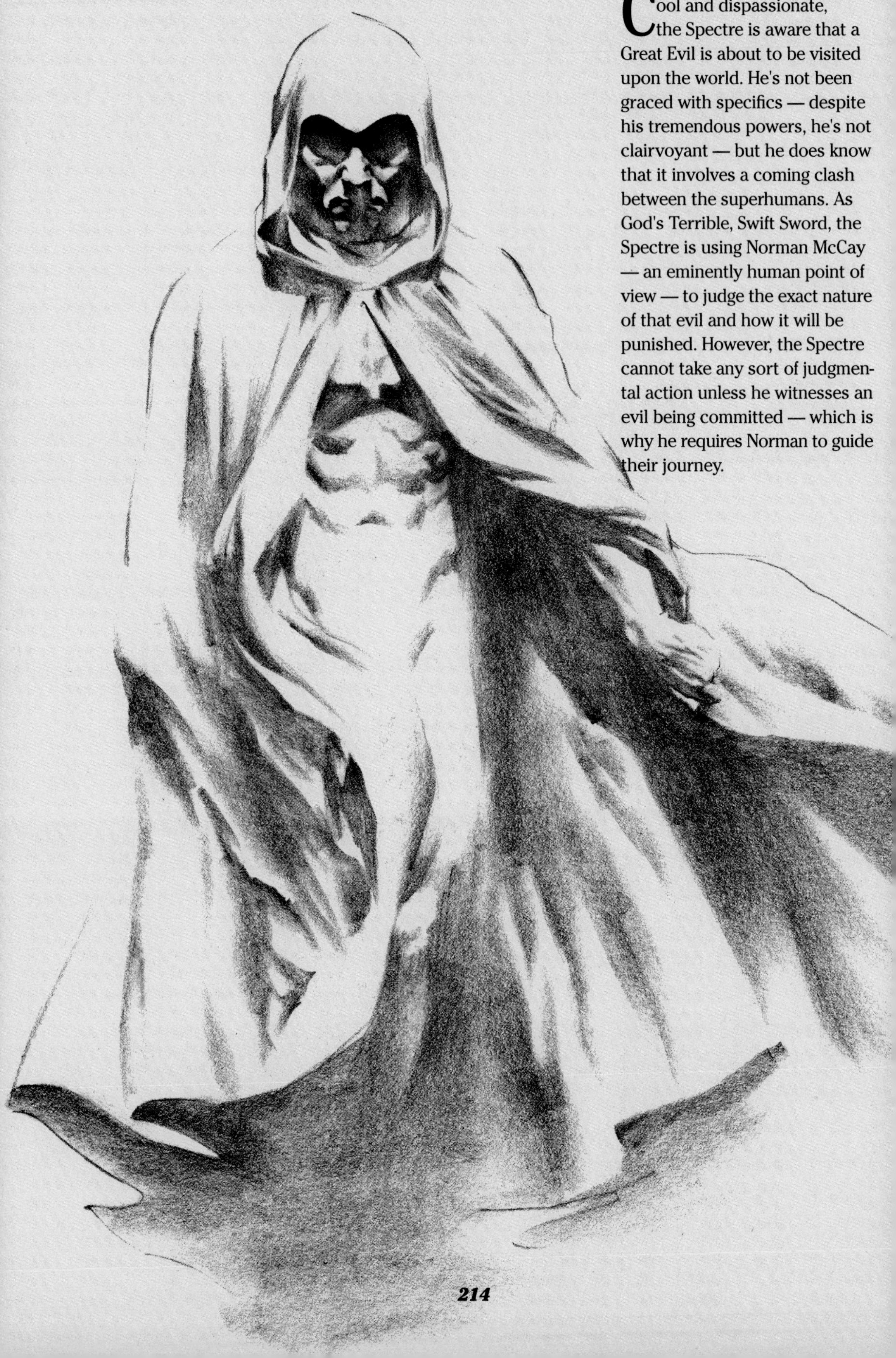

NORMAN McCAY

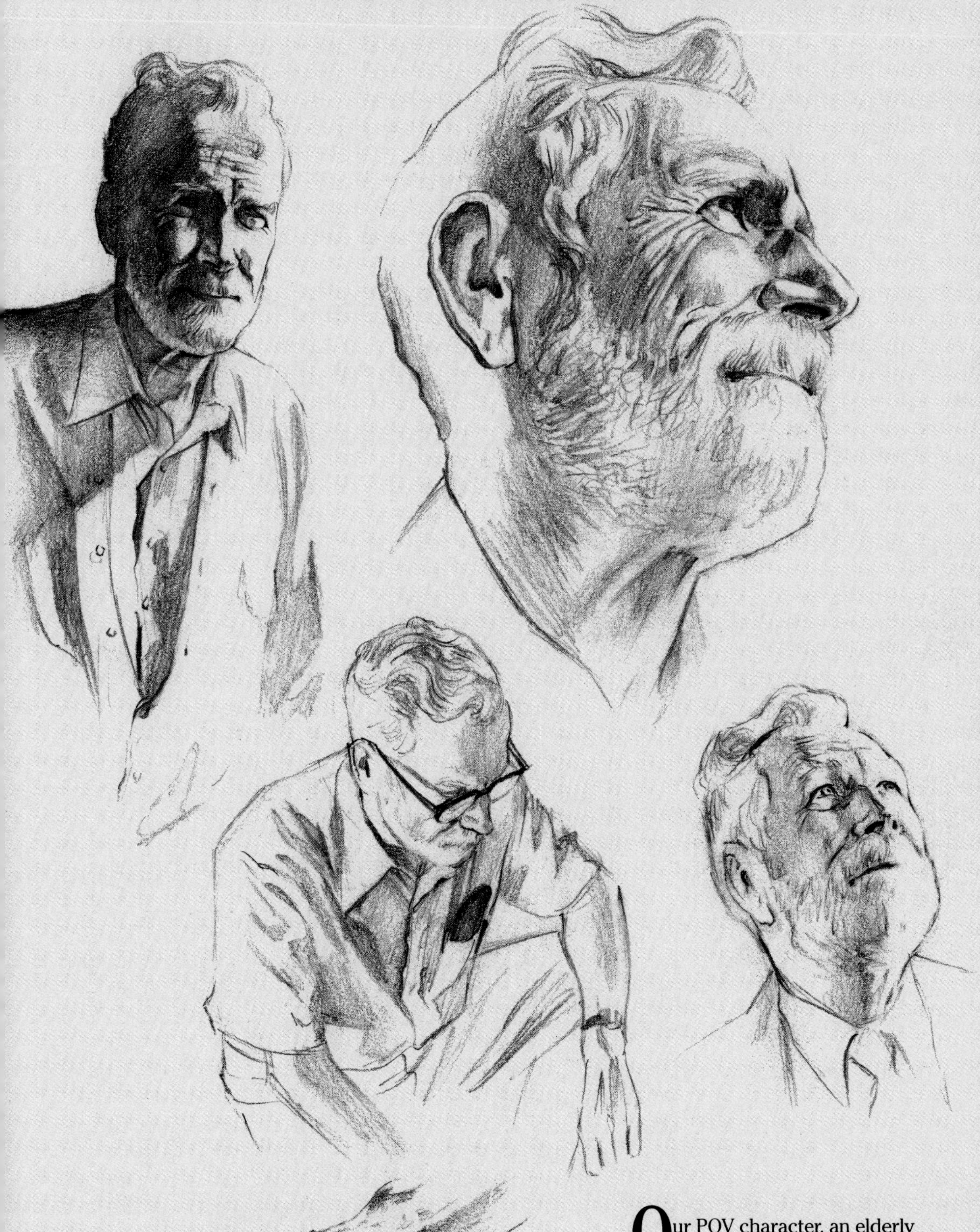

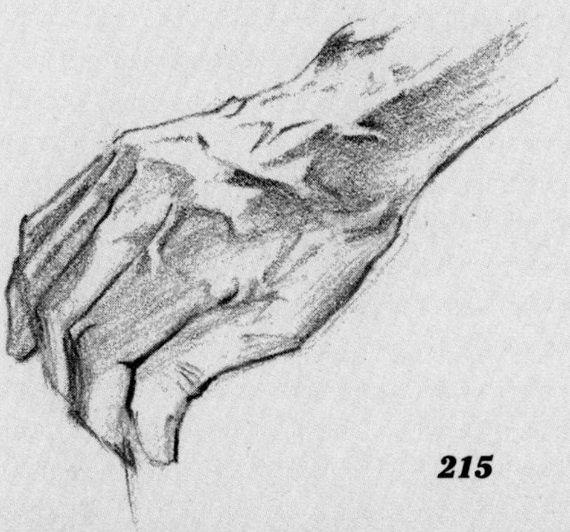

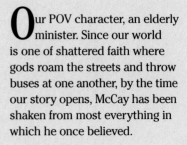

Our POV character, an elderly minister. Since our world is one of shattered faith where gods roam the streets and throw buses at one another, by the time our story opens, McCay has been shaken from most everything in which he once believed.

SUPERMAN

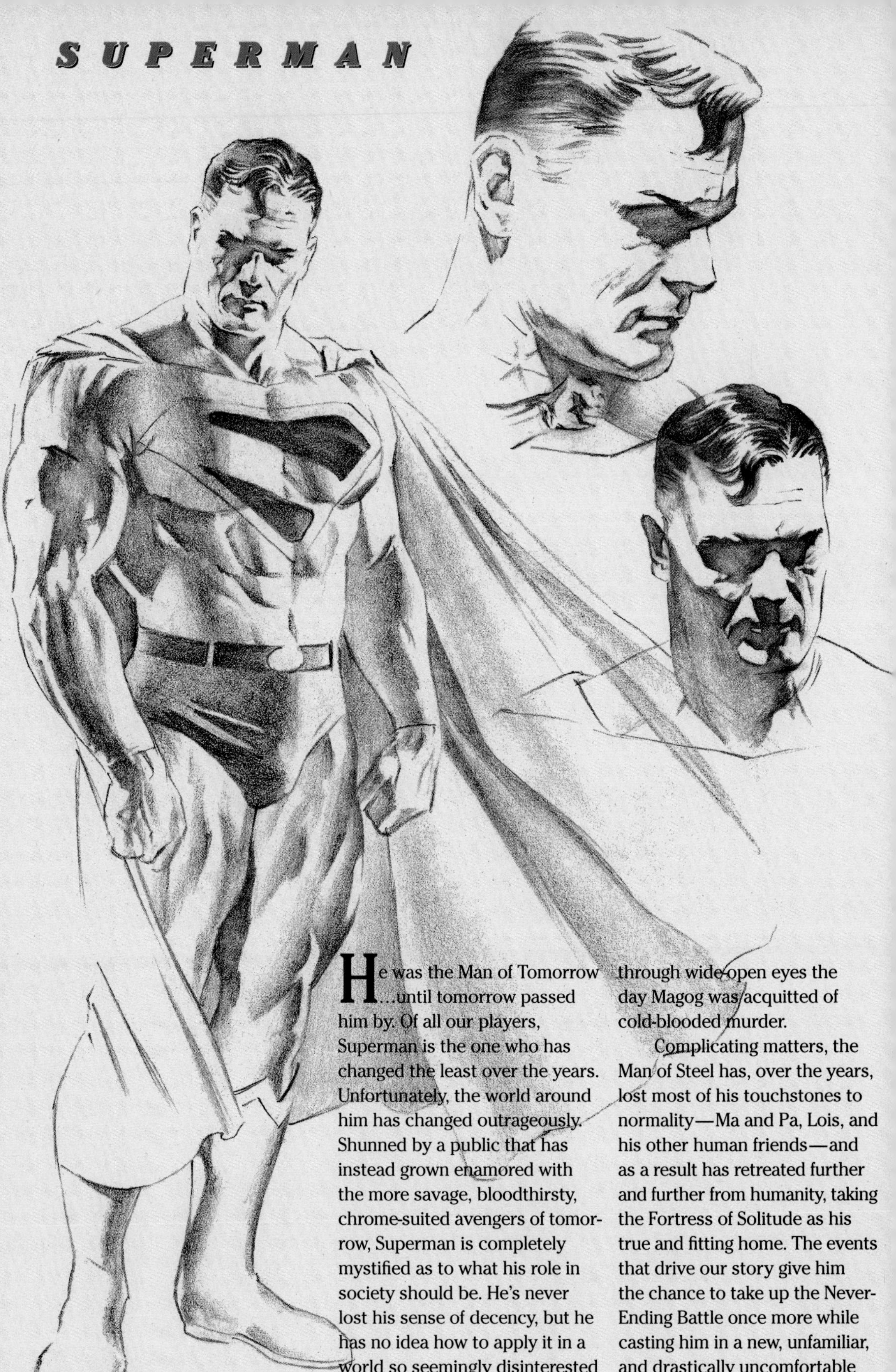

He was the Man of Tomorrow ...until tomorrow passed him by. Of all our players, Superman is the one who has changed the least over the years. Unfortunately, the world around him has changed outrageously. Shunned by a public that has instead grown enamored with the more savage, bloodthirsty, chrome-suited avengers of tomorrow, Superman is completely mystified as to what his role in society should be. He's never lost his sense of decency, but he has no idea how to apply it in a world so seemingly disinterested in decency—the world he saw through wide-open eyes the day Magog was acquitted of cold-blooded murder.

Complicating matters, the Man of Steel has, over the years, lost most of his touchstones to normality—Ma and Pa, Lois, and his other human friends—and as a result has retreated further and further from humanity, taking the Fortress of Solitude as his true and fitting home. The events that drive our story give him the chance to take up the Never-Ending Battle once more while casting him in a new, unfamiliar, and drastically uncomfortable light—that of a world leader.

She is much the same character she has always been—but she is coping (not well) with the realization that she has not well served her gods-given mission as an ambassador and teacher of peace but as an Amazon warrior. As our crisis builds, she will naturally seek deliverance through military strategy and final combat.

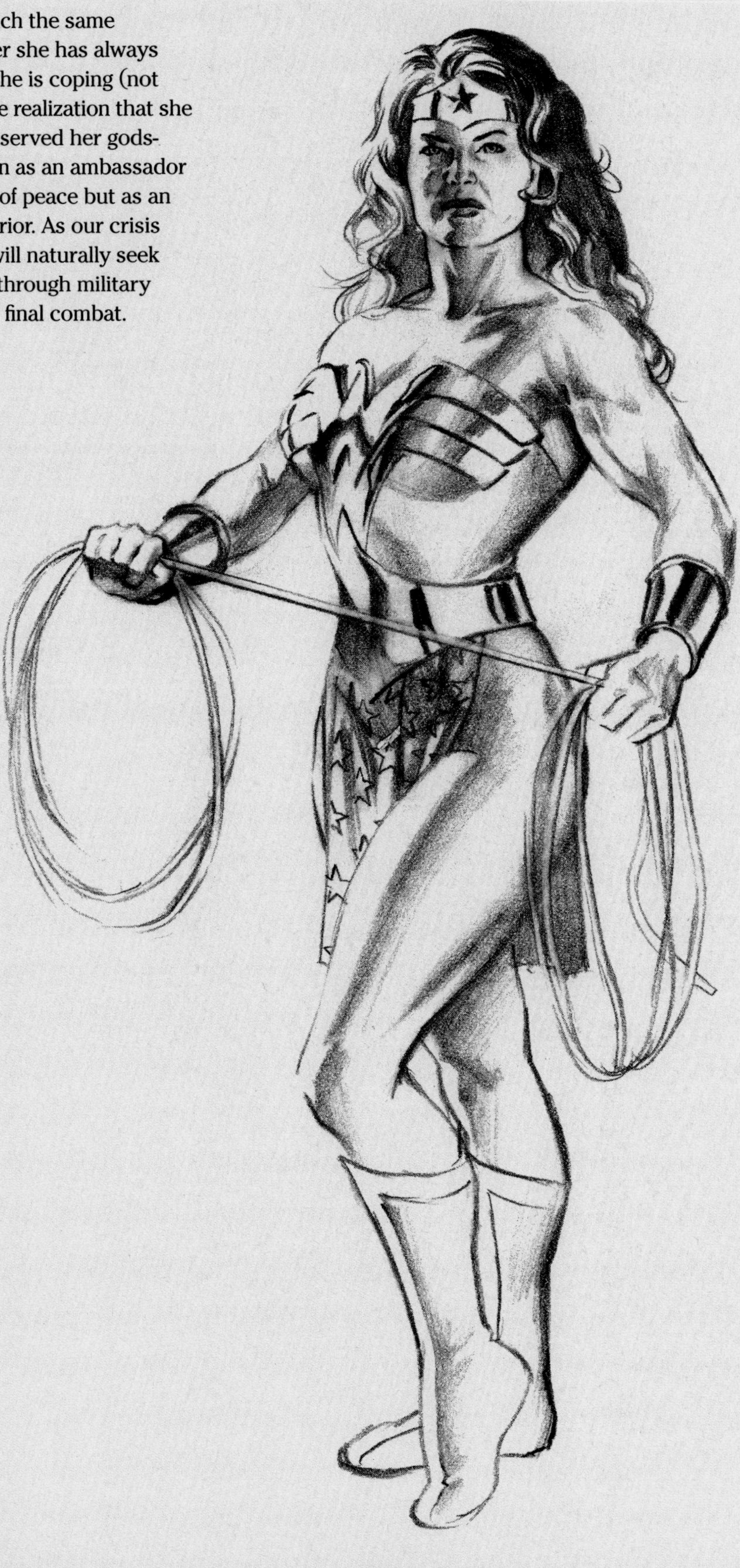

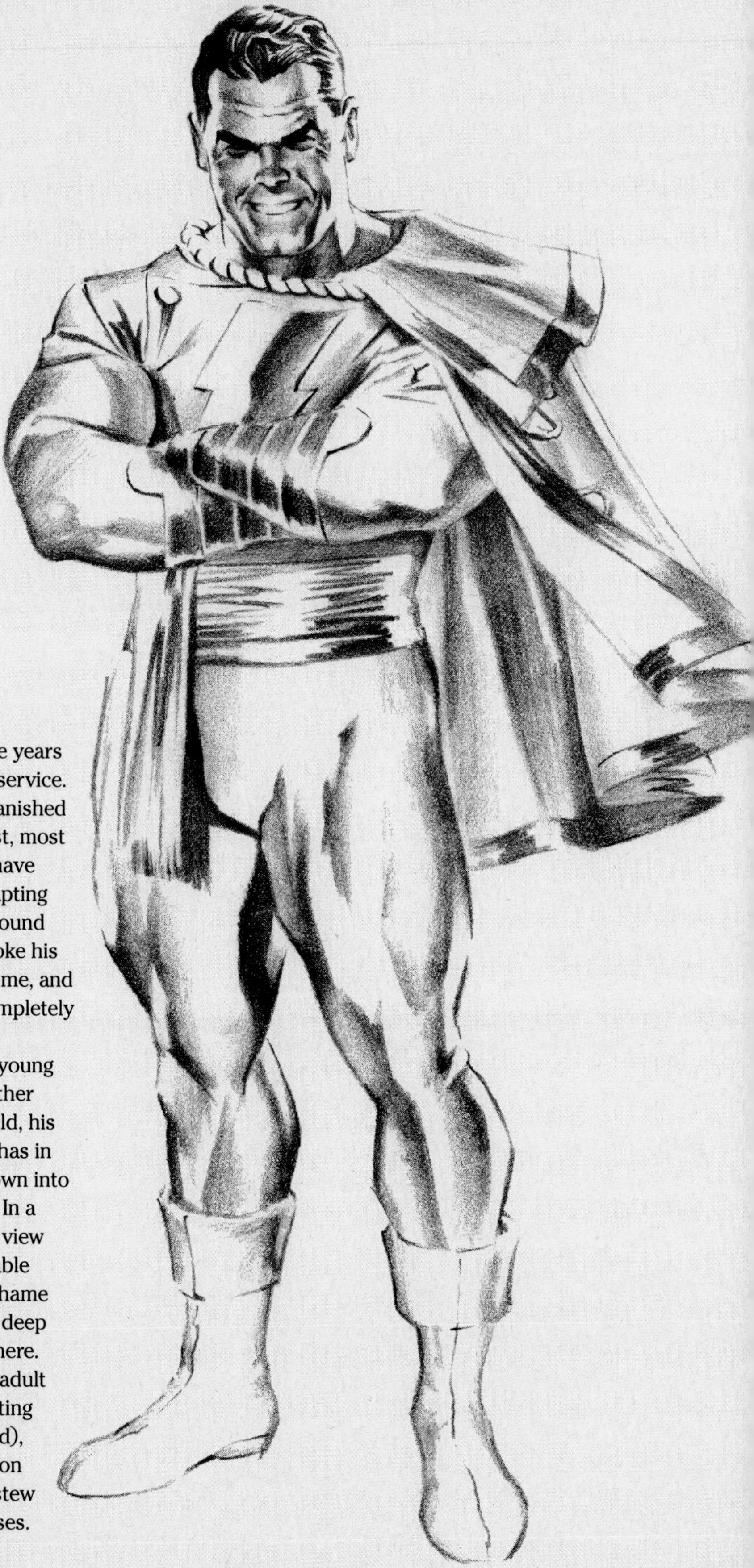

Like most of his peers, Captain Marvel chose years ago to retire from public service. In point of fact, Marvel vanished early; as one of the purest, most noble heroes, he would have had the hardest time adapting to the grim new world around him. One day, Marvel spoke his magic word for the last time, and Billy Batson's life was completely his own again.

Unfortunately, given young Billy's immaturity and rather naive outlook on the world, his attitude towards Marvel has in the intervening years grown into something quite twisted. In a society that has come to view super-heroes as undesirable monsters, Billy's secret shame is that he has one hiding deep down inside him somewhere. By the time we meet the adult Billy (grown into the spitting image of the Marvel of old), he'll be a leading champion of human rights…and a stew of schizophrenic psychoses.

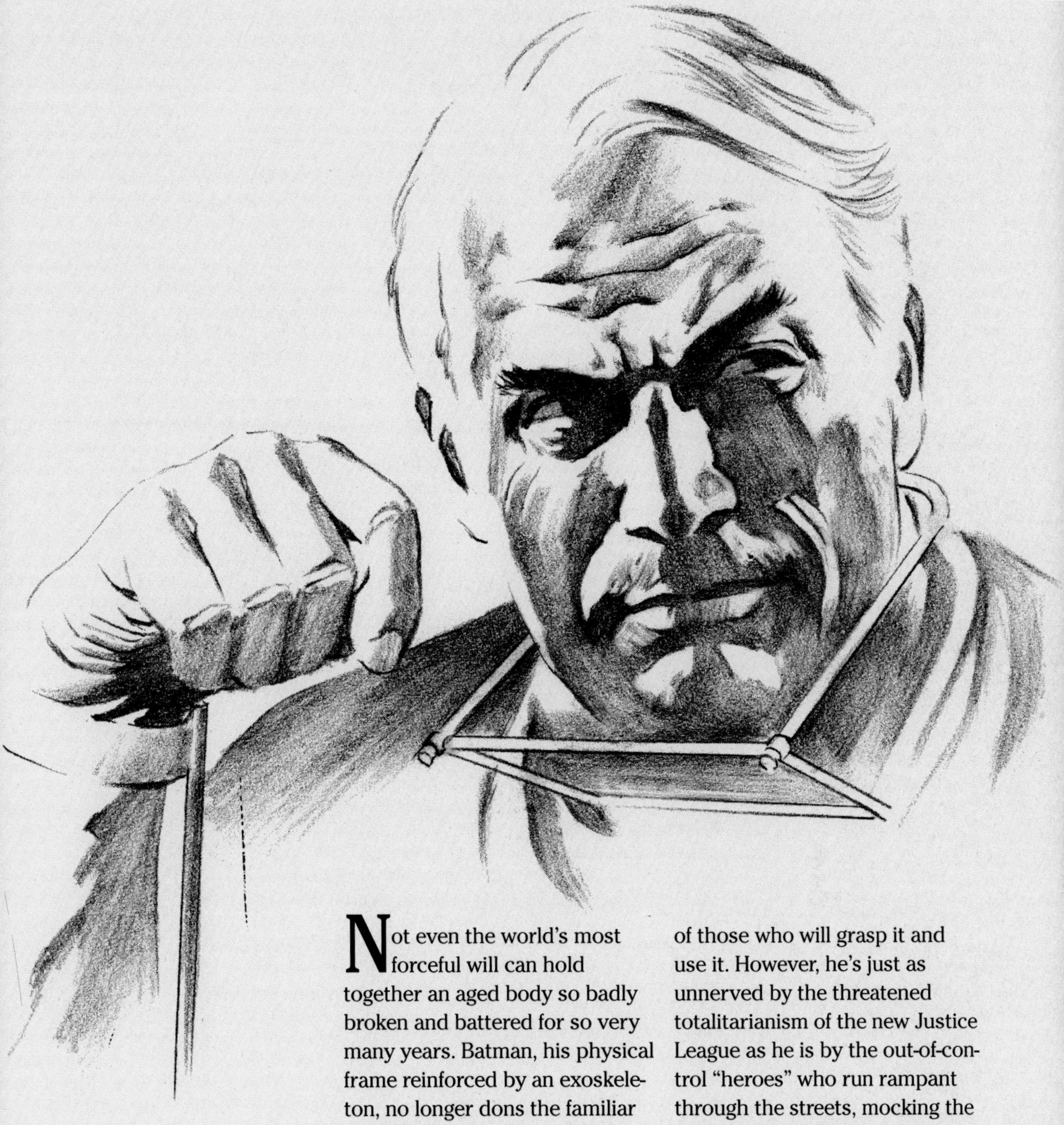

Not even the world's most forceful will can hold together an aged body so badly broken and battered for so very many years. Batman, his physical frame reinforced by an exoskeleton, no longer dons the familiar cape and cowl. Now—out of costume but having long ago abandoned his foppish Bruce Wayne persona—he holes up night and day in his Batcave, remotely monitoring his robotic Bat-Knights, using them (with tremendous success) to maintain order in Gotham City. Batman—the aristocrat—believes (as billionaires are wont to do) that a measure of power and rule rightfully belongs in the hands of those who will grasp it and use it. However, he's just as unnerved by the threatened totalitarianism of the new Justice League as he is by the out-of-control "heroes" who run rampant through the streets, mocking the standards that Batman once set. When it comes to dealing with the threat of the "new breed" of heroes, Batman—as always—has his own ideas. Like Luthor, he's convinced that a steady, concentrated, methodical approach to the problem will win him the world...but unlike Luthor, Batman is spurred on instead to fast, hard-strike action by the reemergence of the League.

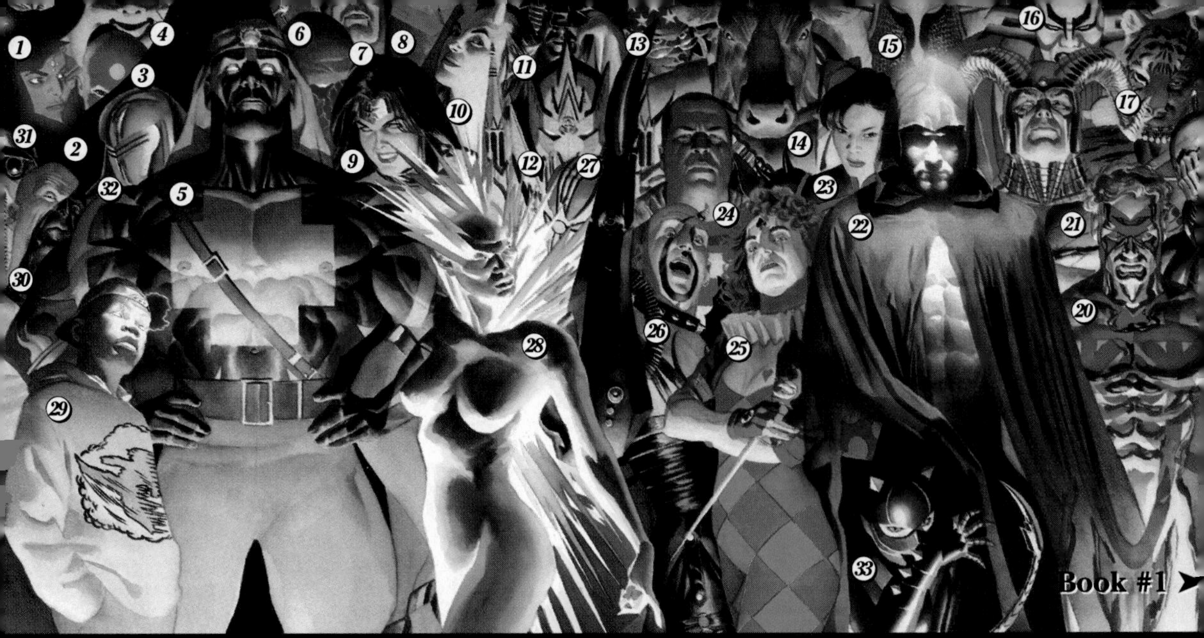
Book #1

1. Original Red Tornado - *Ma Hunkel armored with more than a pot for a helmet*
2. Hawkman - *combining the spirit of the old with the otherworldly flesh of the new*
3. Lady Marvel - *formerly Mary Marvel, caretaker of the Power of Shazam*
4. King Marvel - *formerly Captain Marvel Jr., caretaker of the Power of Shazam*
5. Aleea Strange - *half-human, half-alien daughter of Adam Strange and Alanna Strange*
6. Human Bomb - *still the same combustible hero of old*
7. Midnight - *a spirit manifesting itself as a living smoke cloud*
8. The Whiz - *son of Lady and King Marvel, and natural inheritor of the Power of Shazam*
9. Captain Comet - *Silver Age icon and one-time epitome of human perfection*
10. Bulletman II - *modern steel-coated human bullet*
11. Brainiac's Daughter - *the living computer's human progeny, and ancestor of Brainiac 5*
12. Bulletgirl II - *modern steel-coated human bullet*
13. Robotman III - *Victor Stone, formerly Cyborg, now an organism made of liquid metal*
14. Starman VIII - *formerly Star Boy, from the 30th Century*
15. Golden Guardian III - *second body cloned from the original Golden Age shield-bearer, the Guardian*
16. Powerman - *robot minion of Superman*
17. Hourman III - *current inheritor of the mantle with none of the time limits implied by the name*
18. Sandman IV - *formerly Sandy the Golden Boy, for whom the sands of time have stood still*
19. Red Tornado III - *fire-haired, wind-manipulating successor to the throne*
20. Living Doll - *daughter of Doll Man and Doll Girl*
21. Tornado - *re-formed spirit of the Tornado Champion*
22. Avia - *Big Barda and Mister Miracle's mega-rod-bearing daughter*
23. Atlas - *legendary demigod figure*
24. Atom-Smasher - *formerly Nuklon, godson of the original Atom*
25. Donna Troy - *formerly Wonder Girl, Troia, and Darkstar, now an Amazonian champion*
26. The Ray II - *son of the original, and Lord of Light*
27. Wonder Woman - *former Amazonian princess and now Superman's second-in-command*
28. Red Robin - *formerly Nightwing, Dick Grayson, the original Robin, is following in his mentor's footsteps again*
29. Norman McCay - *a preacher an the Spectre's human anchor*
30. Red Arrow - *formerly Speedy, the Arsenal, now following more closely th methods of his mentor, Green Arrow.*
31. Superman - *reluctant leader of the superhumans and still the greates hero of any age*
32. Aquaman II - *formerly Aqualac now inheritor of his mentor's mantle*
33. Power Woman - *formerly Powe Girl, and still a major superhuman wrecking machine*
34. The Flash - *emanating from the Speed Force, the future Flash may hold all the spirits of the previous incarnations*
35. The Green Lantern - *merging his lantern into himself, he is the most powerful champion of that name*

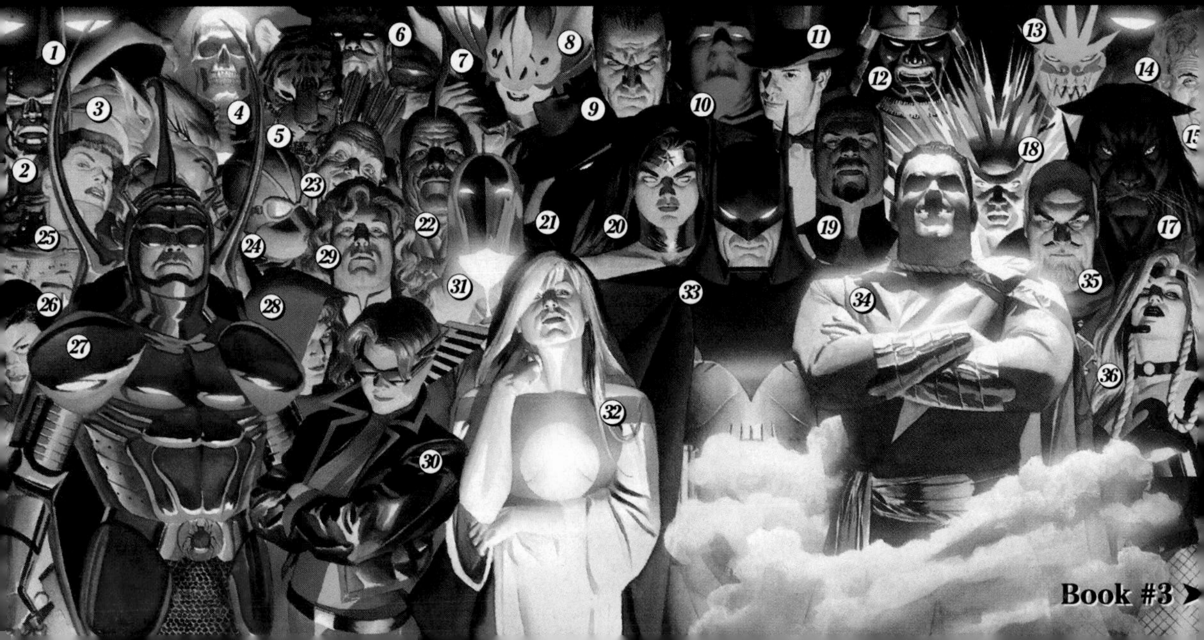
Book #3

Blue Devil II - a true magi...
mon from the netherworld
Shiva the Destroyer - r-armed defender of India, sed on the Hindu god
Judomaster II - female inheritor he mantle
Buddha - sumo-sized scourge China
Von Bach - Yugoslavian uld-be dictator
Nuculoid - pliable nuclear-powered o
Mr. Terrific II - overequipped date of the old version, with little derstanding of "fair play"
Tusk - elephant-shaped man-o-war
Nightstar - half-human, half-alien ughter of the late Starfire and the mer Nightwing

10. Demon Damsel - *would-be Legion member*
11. Pinwheel - *blade-laden, leather-clad master of pain*
12. Cathedral - *holy terror of the underworld*
13. Stars - *modern Star-Spangled Kid with cosmic rod*
14. Manotaur - *classical Greek myth armed for the future*
15. Black Mongul - *Mongolian shadow of death*
16. Kabuki Kommando - *the Fourth World's Japanese champion*
17. Huntress III - *warrior queen of the African jungle*
18. N-I-L-8 - *a sentient armory with one deadly purpose*
19. Trix (after Matrix) - *a morphing biomechanism*

20. Captain Atom - *human nuclear reactor and symbol of the atomic age*
21. Magog - *gold-plated superhuman idol of the new age*
22. Spectre - *the wandering spirit of God's vengeance*
23. Tokyo Rose - *Japanese martial arts assassin*
24. Stripes - *modern Stripesy armed to the teeth*
25. Joker's Daughter II/ Harlequin - *one of many to follow the Joker's chaotic style*
26. 666 - *tattooed, self-mutilated man-machine of destruction*
27. Phoebus - *Earth's new champion fire elemental (after Firestorm)*
28. Lightning - *Black Lightning's metahuman daughter*
29. Thunder - *a new Johnny Thunder with the mischievous spirit of Thunderbolt*

30. Swastika - *American militia man and anarchist*
31. Germ-Man - *poison-gas-spewing master of biological warfare*
32. Stealth II - *cloaked one-woman war machine*
33. Catwoman II - *armored meta-human, successor to Selina Kyle*

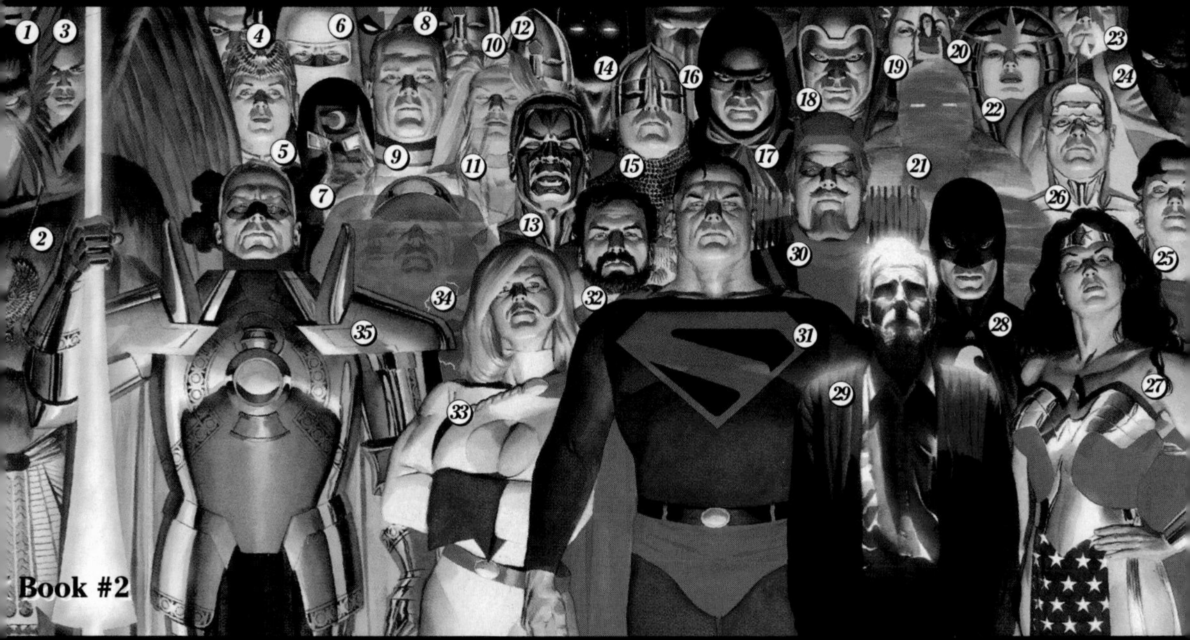

Book #2

A Bat-Knight - *one of Batman's* ot sentinels
Steel - *has switched his devotion* m Superman to Batman
Menagerie - *formerly Changeling,* l now only able to create the shapes maginary beasts
Deadman - *still dead and loving it*
Huntress III - *warrior queen of* African jungle
Cossack - *champion of Russia,* m the Batmen of many nations
Ace II - *otherworldly bat-hound,* l Batwoman's steed
Batwoman II - *Batman admirer* m the Fourth World
John Jones - *former Manhunter* m Mars, now a shell of his former self
. Mysteryman - *one of Batman's* ow crimefighters
. Zatara II - *son of the late Zatanna,* l grandson of the original Zatara

12. Samurai - *champion of Japan, from the Batmen of many nations*
13. Dragon - *champion of China, from the Batmen of many nations*
14. A Bat-Knight - *another of Batman's robot sentinels*
15. Creeper - *aging, wretched screwball superhero*
16. Nuculoid - *pliable nuclear-powered hero*
17. Wildcat III - *a man-panther with the original's spirit*
18. Lightning- *Black Lightning's metahuman daughter*
19. Condor - *current inheritor of the Black Condor mantle*
20. Nightstar - *half-human, half-alien daughter of the late Starfire and the former Nightwing*
21. Obsidian - *son of Alan Scott, the original Green Lantern, and Ross and Thorne, and still the Prince of Shadows*

22. Mr. Scarlet - *blue-collar bruiser, with bright red skin*
23. Ralph Dibny - *formerly the Elongated Man, now just stretched out*
24. Spy Smasher - *independent operative in the post-cold war world*
25. Phantom Lady II - *a literal phantom of the original*
26. Tula - *seafaring malcontent and daughter of Aquaman II*
27. Blue Beetle - *his high-tech suit of armor possibly incorporates the original scarab's power*
28. Red Hood - *daughter of Red Arrow and the mercenary Cheshire*
29. Darkstar - *son of Donna Troy and inheritor of her Darkstar role*
30. Flash IV - *Wally West's daughter, and currently the most human bearer of the name*
31. Fate V - *the Helmet of Nabu, a talisman that no longer needs a human host*

32. Green Lantern VI/Jade - *daughter of Alan Scott, the original Green Lantern, and Ross and Thorne, and a living battery of the Lantern's power*
33. Batman - *a master strategist, and still the world's greatest detective*
34. Captain Marvel - *a lost soul, but still the world's mightiest mortal*
35. Oliver Queen - *formerly Green Arrow, now married to longtime love Dinah Lance, Black Canary II*
36. Black Canary III - *daughter of Oliver and Dinah Queen, and the Golden Age Black Canary's granddaughter*
37. Dinah Queen - *formerly Black Canary II*

EVOLUTION

The Development of the Orion Pages

An example of one of the many photo references used by the artist.

Make no mistake. This is not, in its strictest sense, "director's cut" material. These aren't rediscovered "missing pages" that somehow got lost behind Alex's filing cabinet one Tuesday. They do, however, comprise a sequence Alex had envisioned painting from very early on: Orion on Apokolips, having usurped his father Darkseid's throne. Alex never lost the desire to paint this image, not even after (striking though it might be) we could find no room for it within the strict page count of the original monthly series. The elbow room of an expanded collected edition, however, gave Alex the opportunity to indulge himself—and you. But what to make of this after-the-fact sequence? We didn't even know where to put it within the narrative until using Orion suggested Orion's brother-of-sorts, Mr. Miracle, Super-Escape Artist. How could we use him? Well...who better to design an inescapable gulag? Would Superman think of that? Not necessarily...but Orion would suggest it if Superman were to come to Apokolips asking to use the planet as a prison, a dumping ground. Still, the Last Son of Krypton would never suggest uprooting natives from their homeworld. However, given where we were in the story just before gulag construction began, Superman would absolutely consult with Orion, the ultimate Dog of War. In fact, their conversation would allow us a chance to touch upon something missing from our original series: Superman's inability to comprehend the dark potential of his own power...

Mark Waid

KINGDOM COME/New Orion Sequence/Ms. Page 2

PAGE TWO

PANEL ONE: LOOKING PAST ORION TOWARDS SUPERMAN. BIG PANEL, LOTS OF ROOM FOR CONTRAST BETWEEN THE BRIGHT, COLORFUL, SHINING MAN OF STEEL AND THE DISMAL ROOM AROUND HIM. IN FACT, DOES IT WORK TO HAVE ANOTHER "WINDOW" BEHIND SUPERMAN SO WE CAN CONTRAST HIM TO MORE OF THE OUTSIDE TERRAIN?

1 SUPERMAN: Far be it for ME to argue with the LORD of APOKOLIPS.

2 SUPERMAN: I'm IMPRESSED. Age has CALMED your legendary TEMPER. You seem fully in CONTROL.

PANEL TWO: OUR FIRST FULL SHOT OF ORION.

3 SUPER/off: You're more like Darkseid than EVER, Orion.

PANEL THREE: ORION, SUPERMAN. SUPERMAN LOOKS OUT THE WINDOW.

4 ORION: So it was written to BE. Our story has ALWAYS been a generational one.

5 ORION: It is said that MANY men eventually become their fathers.

6 SUPERMAN: I wouldn't KNOW.

7 SUPERMAN: I'd heard you'd finally...USURPED Darkseid's throne. I was curious to see what you'd ACCOMPLISHED in his STEAD.

PANEL FOUR: SUPERMAN, SLIGHTLY PAINED, LOOKS OUT OVER THE RUINS OF APOKOLIPS.

8 SUPERMAN: Not MUCH.

9 SUPERMAN: Frankly, Orion, of all the old allies I have ENCOUNTERED, YOU disappoint me the MOST.

10 SUPERMAN: You're a GOD. You have the power to CHANGE your world.

11 ORION/off: Or to DESTROY it.

PANEL FIVE: LOOKING PAST ORION AS HE STARES INTENTLY TOWARDS SUPERMAN, WHO CONTINUES TO LOOK OUT THE WINDOW.

12 ORION: You would be SURPRISED, I fear, at how easily ONE can lead to the OTHER.

Each page of *Kingdom Come* went through various stages of production and development. The first stage (not pictured here) was the preliminary outline. This summarized an entire sequence from the story. Consulting with the editors, Dan Raspler and Peter Tomasi, Mark then wrote a detailed script which paced the story by breaking down the contents of

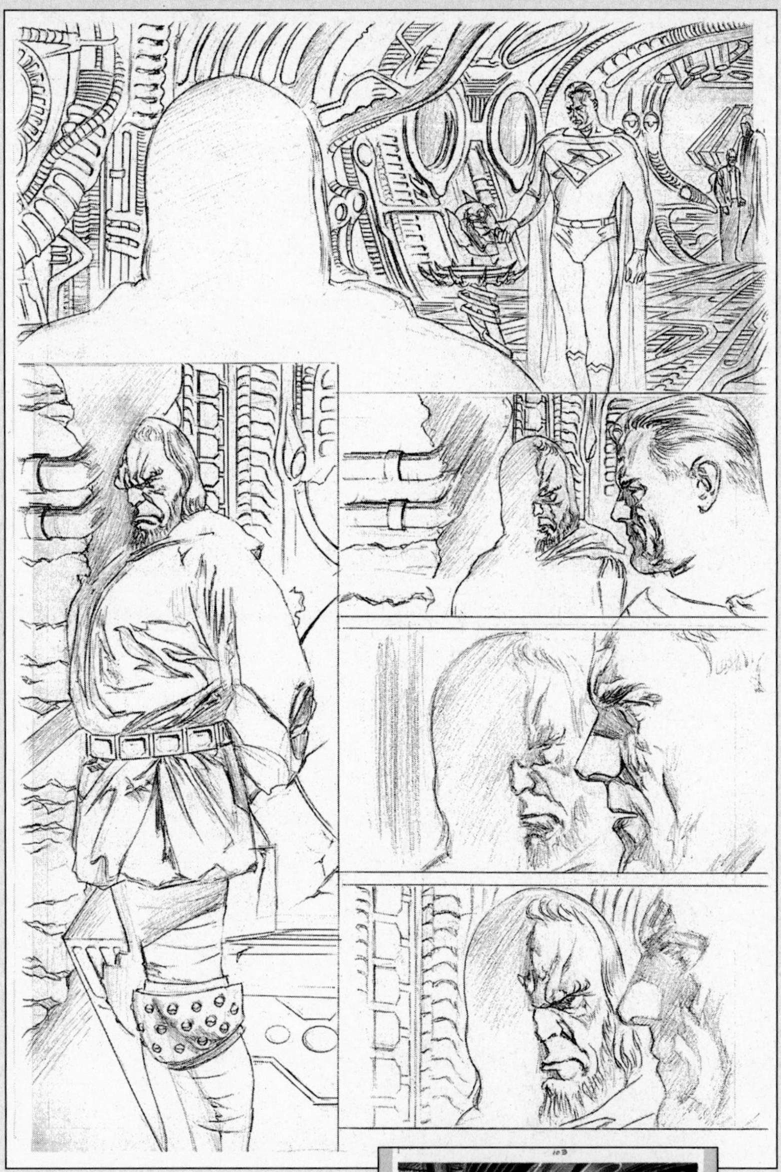

Pencil Artwork
(actual size: 11 1/8" x 17 1/2")

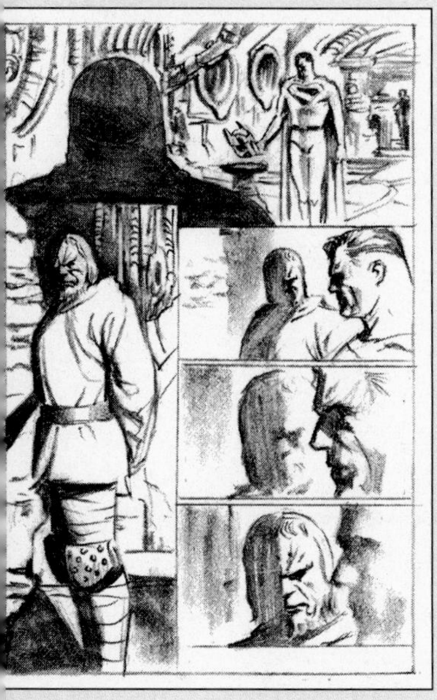

Thumbnail Rough
(actual size: 3 1/8" x 4 15/16")

each page. The dialogue as well as the setup for each and every panel were presented in text for Alex to then visually represent.

Before producing full-size artwork, Alex drew small thumbnail roughs which allowed him to work out compositional problems. This provided an opportunity for all involved to check the pacing of the story prior to producing the actual finished art.

Once all notes, modifications, and approvals were received, the thumbnail images were transferred onto oversize boards that eventually became the finished artwork. Copies of the pencilled art were made in order for Peter Tomasi to map out the placement of the word balloons. (Note the differences between the script and the art, which necessitated a reorganization of the placement of the word balloons within the various panels.) The balloon placements were then sent to Todd Klein, the letterer, so he could create and letter the word balloons from the script. In most cases, lettering is done directly on the art board. For *Kingdom Come*, as with most painted books, the finished lettering was placed on an acetate overlay.

Alex then rendered the images with gouache paints. First, he did a monochromatic black & white stage to fully detail all the forms, and then he layered over the color transparently. Some opaque painting and airbrushed lighting effects were also used. The lettering and painted art were then combined and sent to the separator to produce the finished comic page.

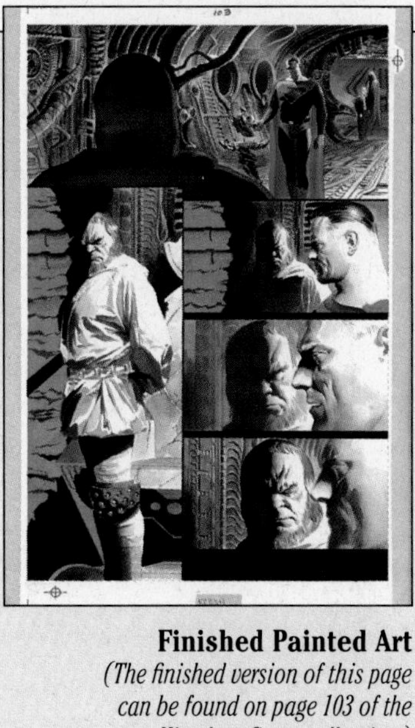

Finished Painted Art
(The finished version of this page can be found on page 103 of the Kingdom Come collection.)

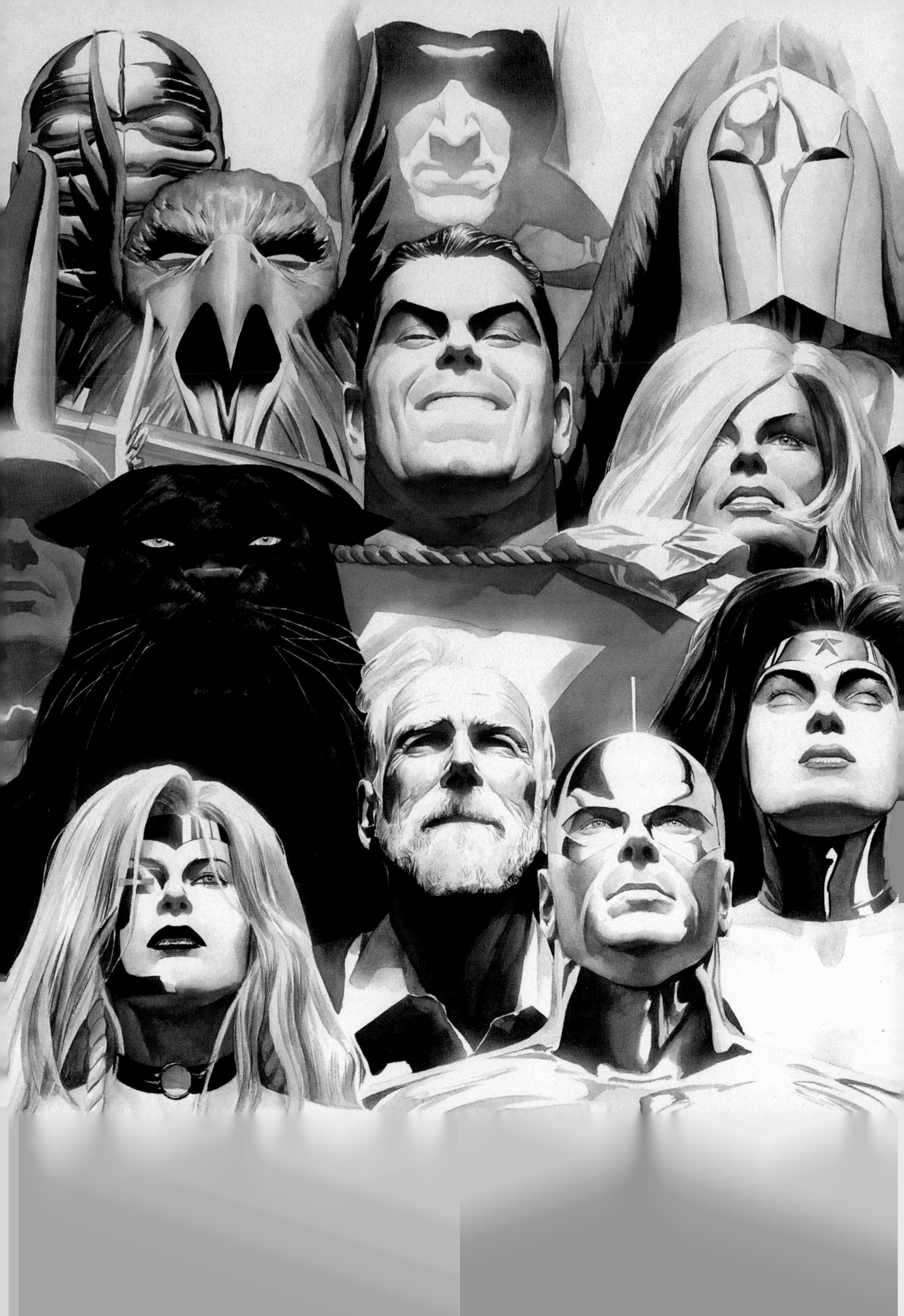

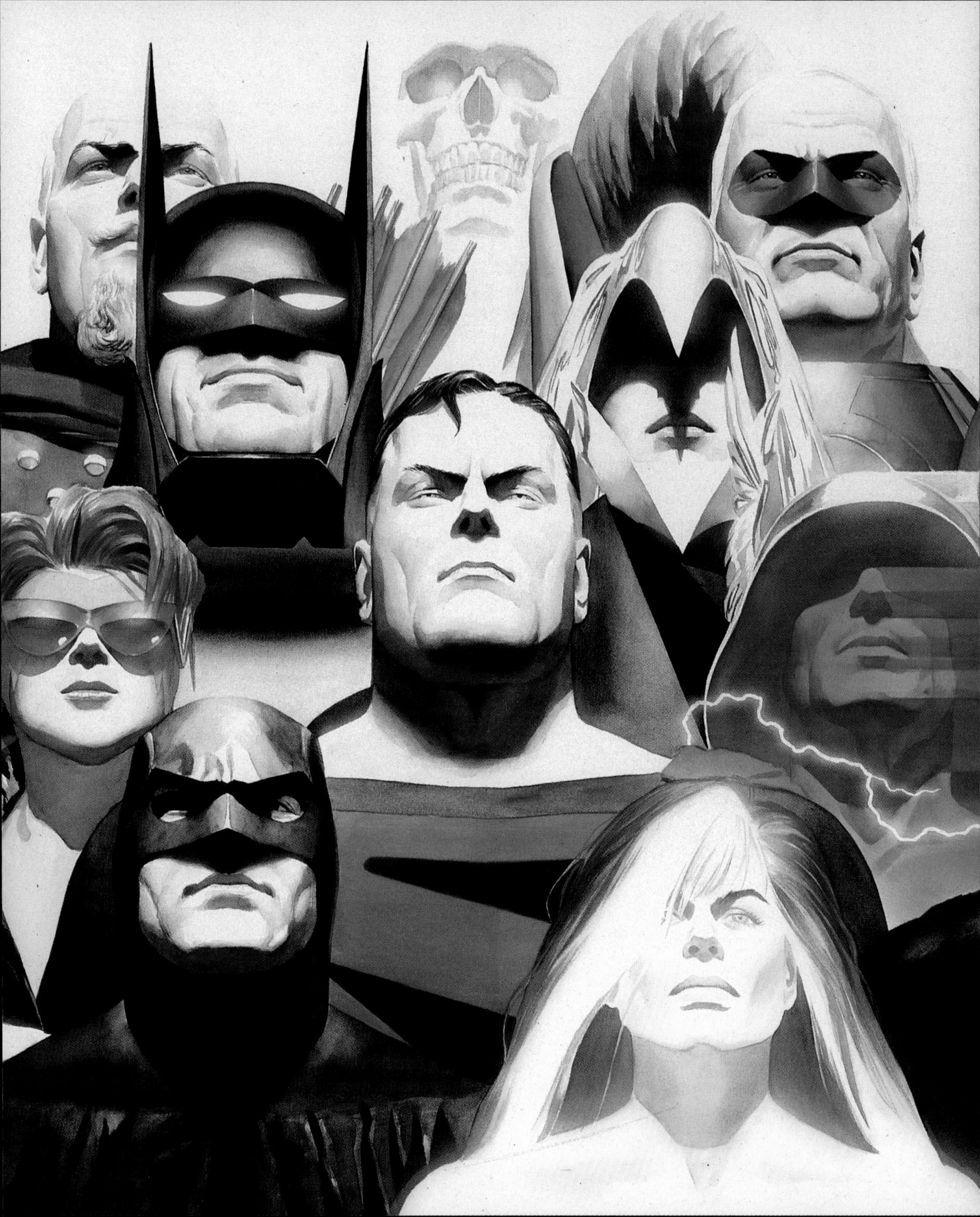

Artwork created specifically for use as a wraparound screenprinted T-shirt design produced by DC Comics.

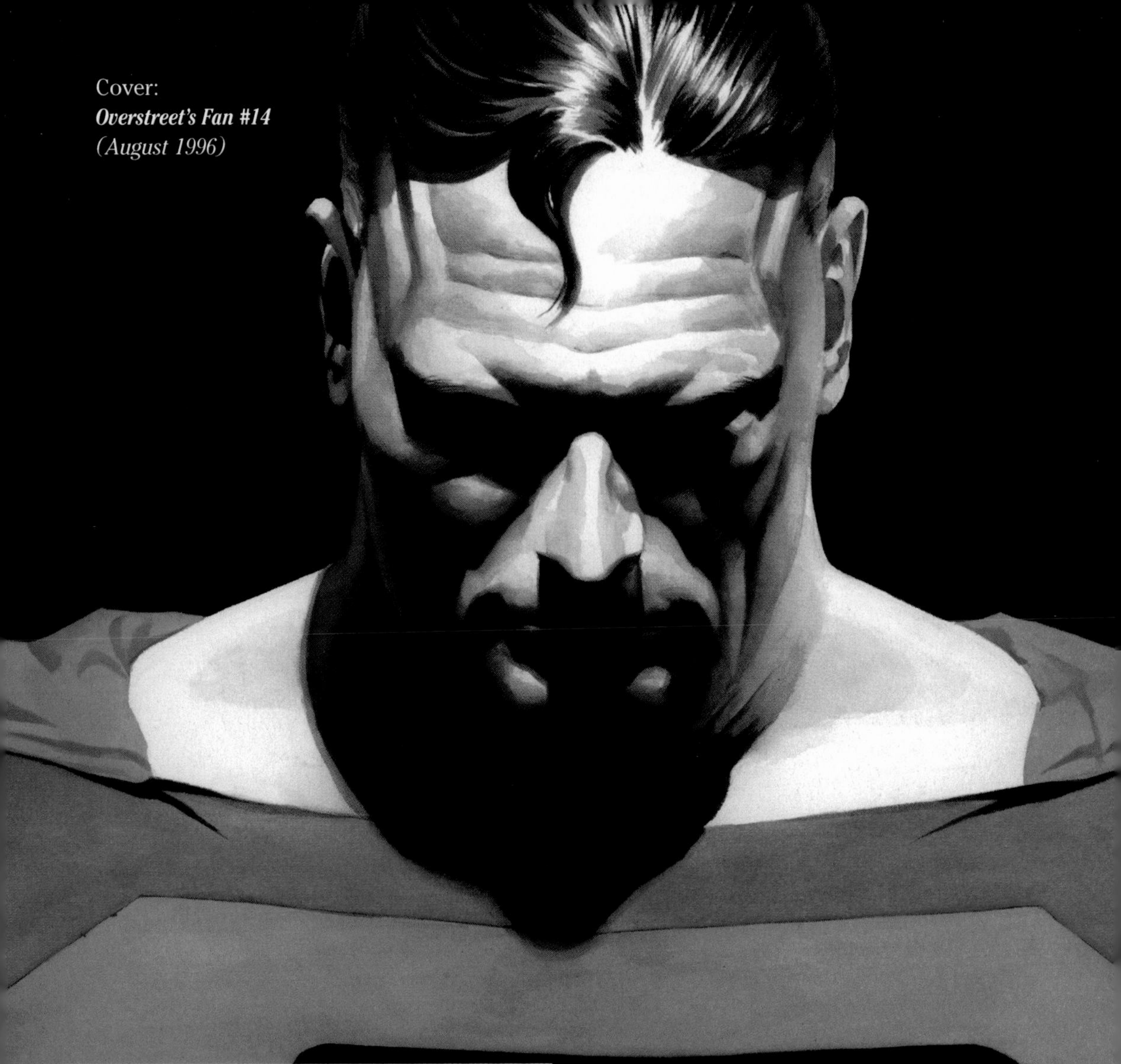

Cover:
Overstreet's Fan #14
(August 1996)

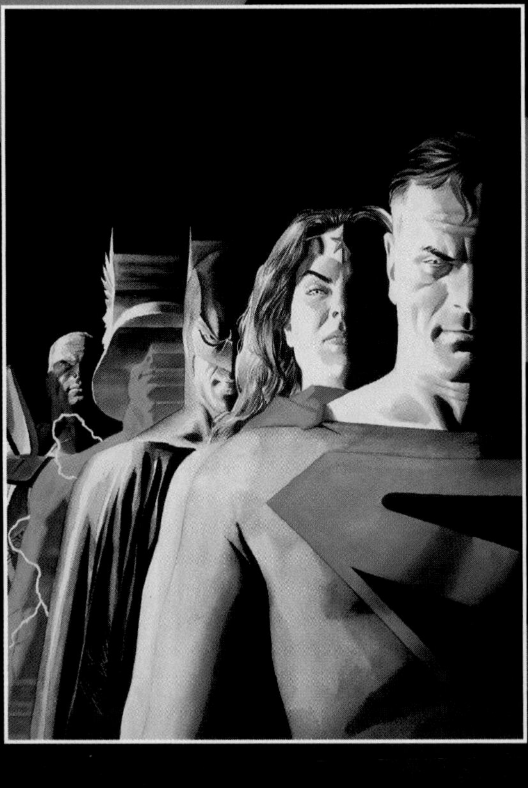

Art for:
Wizard #57 Cover
(May 1996)

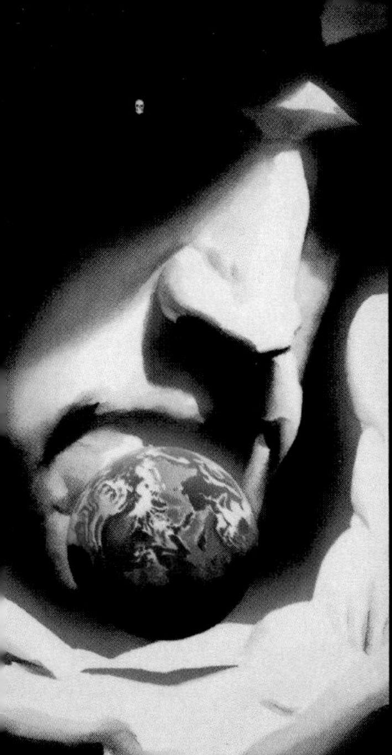
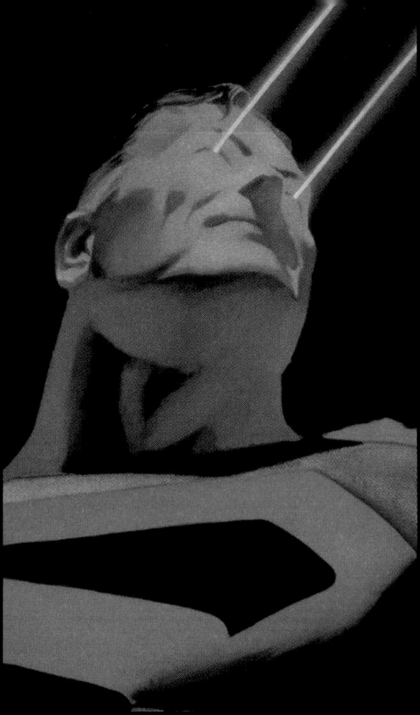
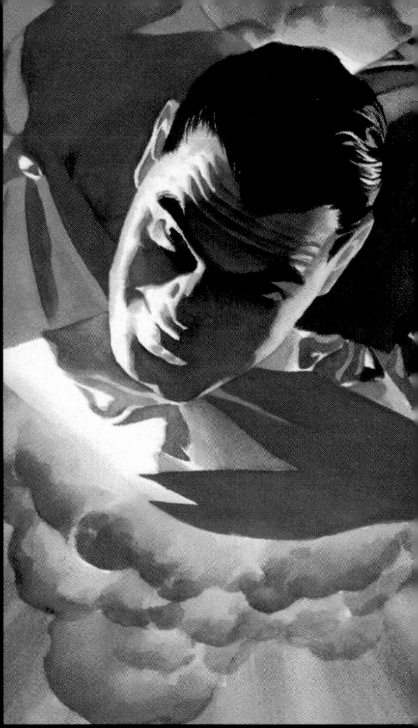

New artwork created for six bonus Creator Collection cards that were part of the *Kingdom Come* trading card set produced by Fleer/SkyBox. 12,000 boxes of these cards were produced for sale.

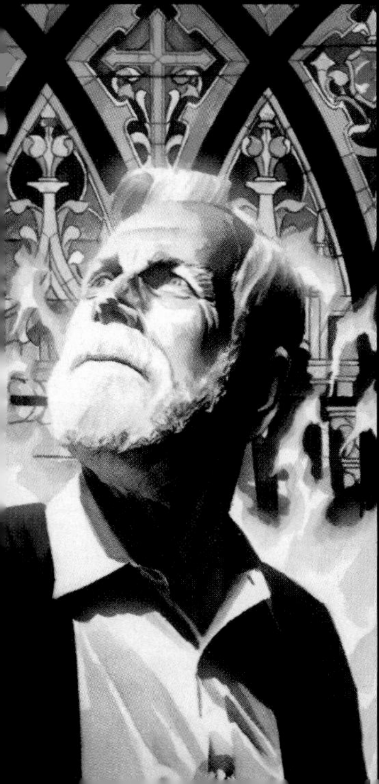
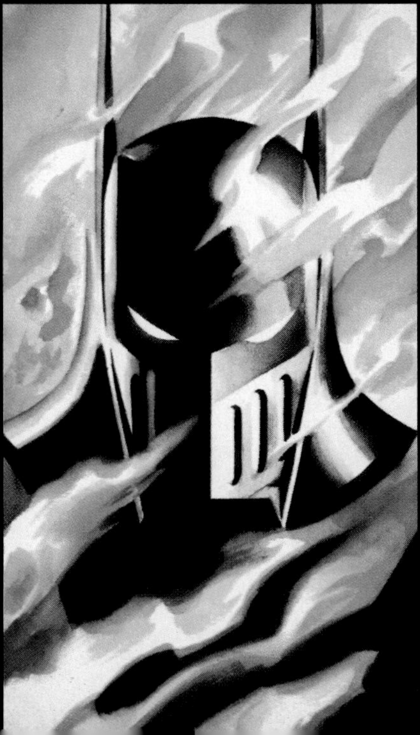
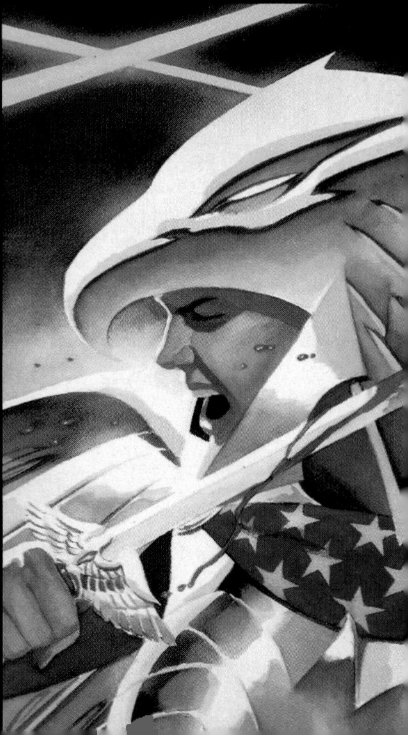

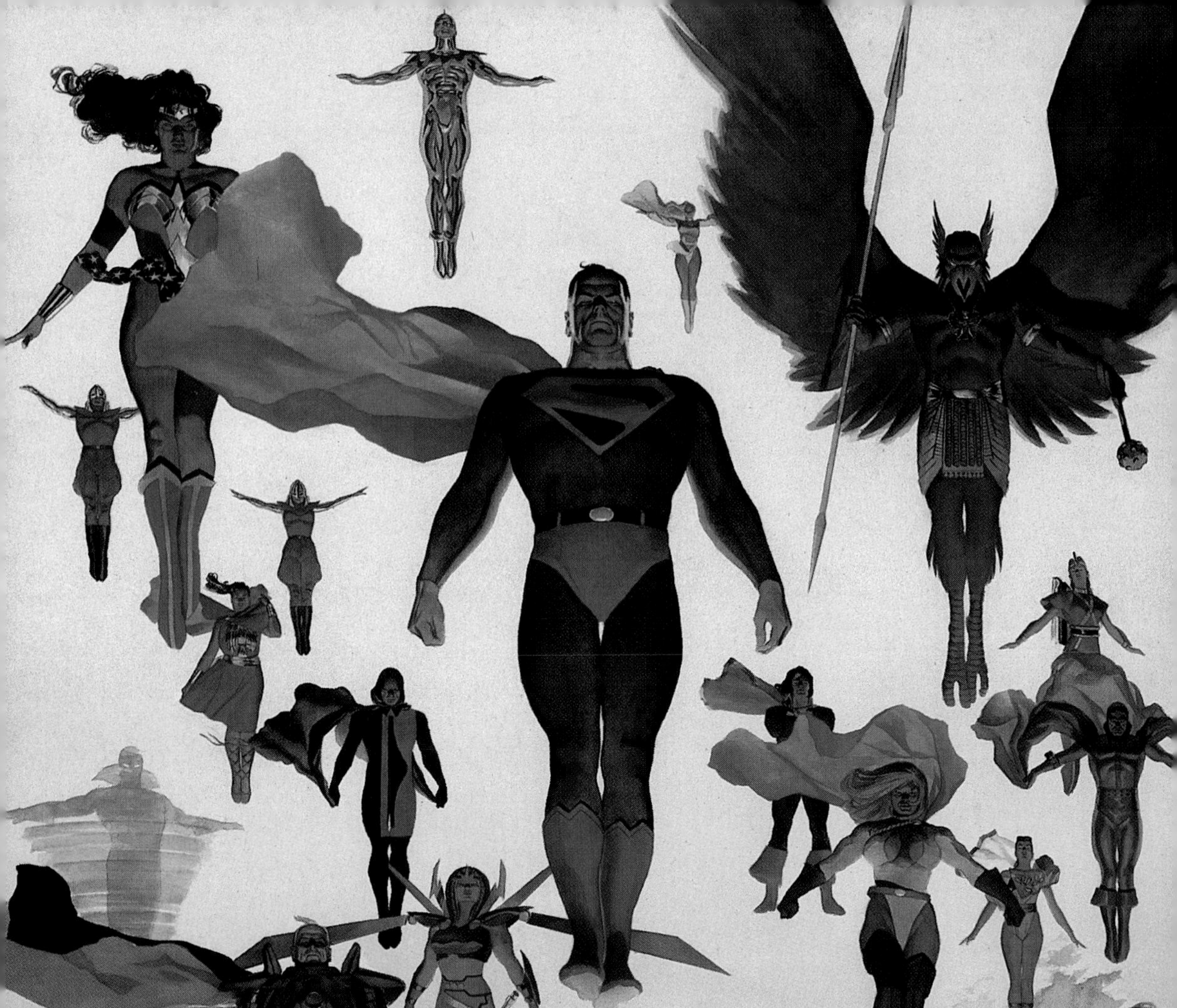

Artwork created for use on the first retail poster released by DC Comics. Poster measures *22"x 34"*. Second retail *Kingdom Come* poster (not shown) pictures the covers from the first three issues.

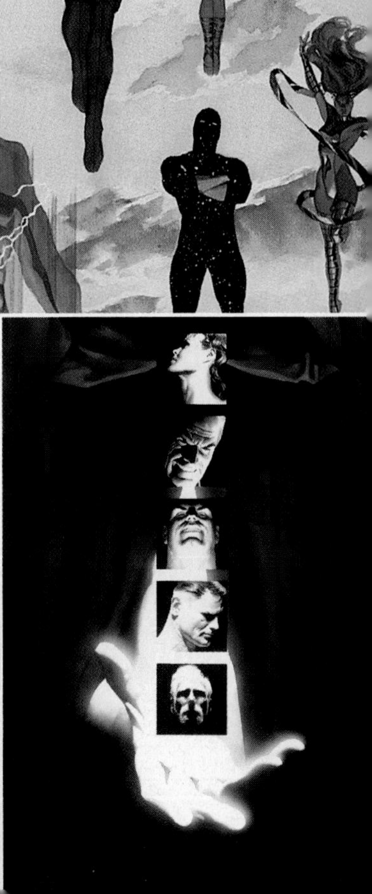

Artwork that was created for advance promotions for the series. Promotional poster issued by DC Comics measured *24"x 38"* and the text read *"The dreamer. The thunder. The bat. The eagle. The angel. Whose will be done? Kingdom Come."*

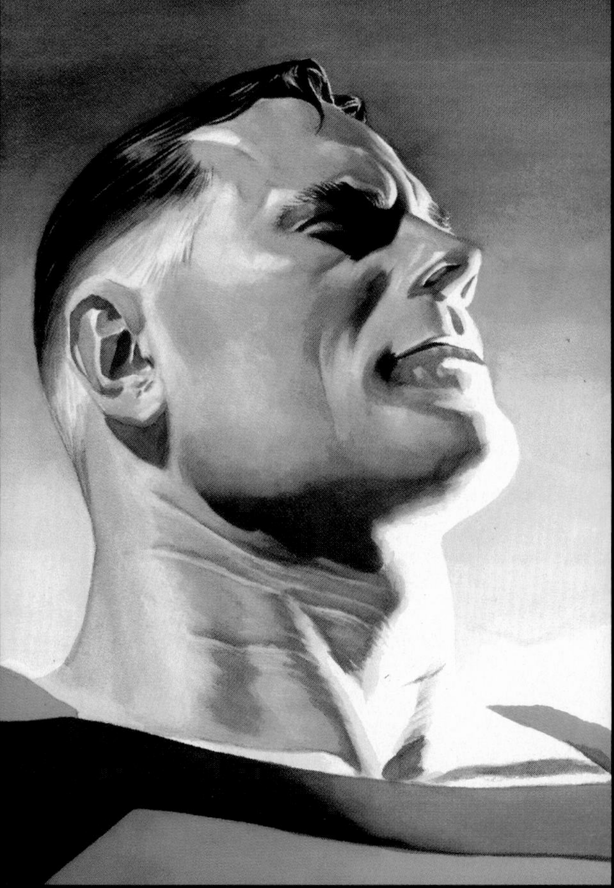

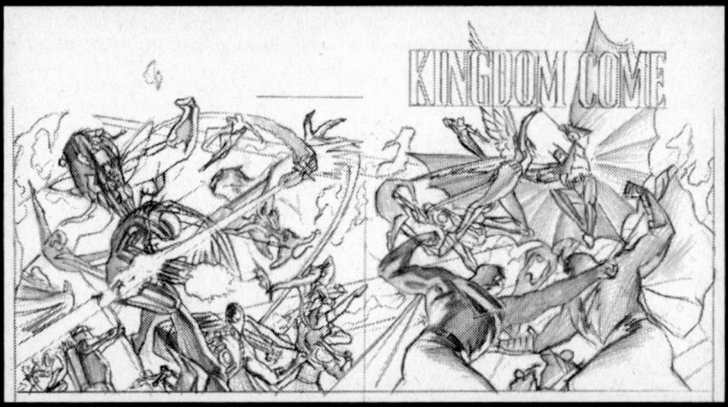
KINGDOM COME

Proposed cover rough for softcover edition of the *Kingdom Come* collection from DC Comics.

Color art from the cover of *Kingdom Come: Revelations* which was part of the *Deluxe Kingdom Come* limited-edition package produced by Graphitti Designs for DC Comics.

Final wraparound color artwork (without copy), of the Warner/Aspect *Kingdom Come* novelization by Elliot S. Maggin. Eight new pieces of art (four color and four black and white), were created for inclusion in this book as well as the cover pictured here.

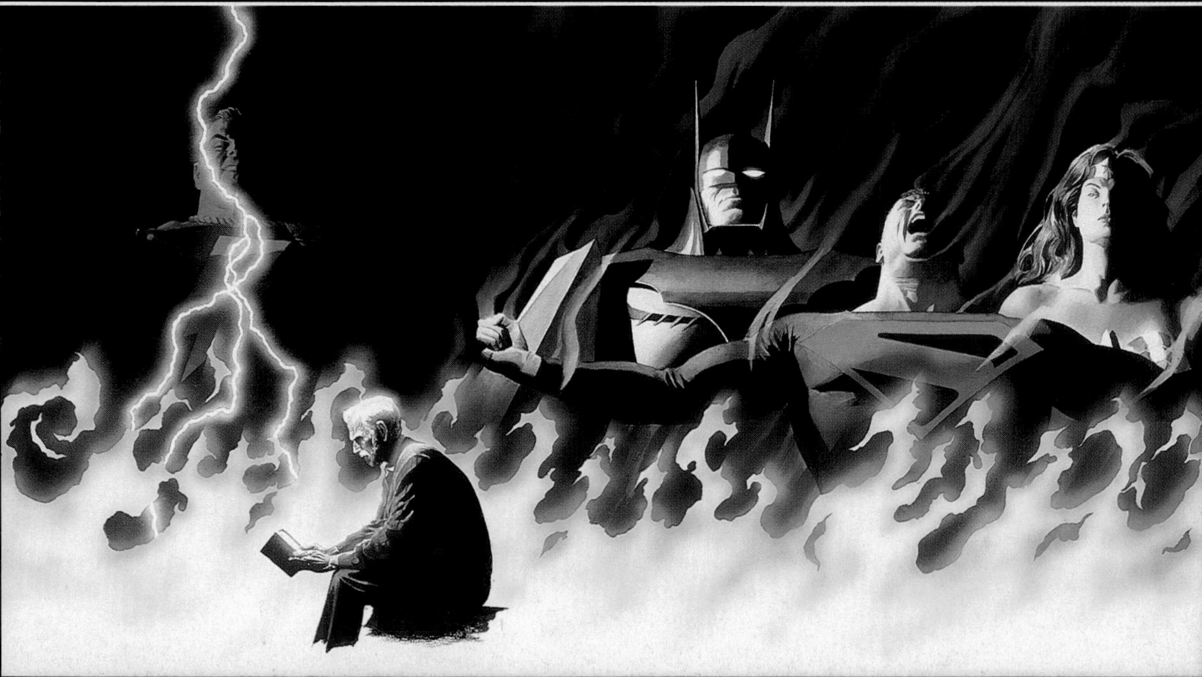

The two most important

people responsible for

this project's existence

(and mine), are my folks,

Clark and Lynette. Clark

Norman Ross is certainly

the real-life basis for

Norman McCay and was

kind enough to model

for this project, helping

to make my tribute to

his profession and good

character possible.

Lynette Ross is the artist

who passed her gift on

to me. My very career is

a testament to her.

Alex Ross

FOR VANITY'S SAKE, I wish to show off my friends as to who played who with respect to the physical presence and personality they lent to my work. Their charity to model for me has been my greatest treasure.

Frank Kasy	Clark/Superman, Magog
Matt Paoletti	Bruce/Batman, John Jones
Lisa Beaderstadt	Diana/Wonder Woman, Big Barda
Sal Abbinanti	Bill/Captain Marvel
Ron Bogacki	Lex Luthor
Kenn Kooi	Red Robin/Ibn al Xu'ffasch
Jennifer van Winkle	Nightstar
Mark Braun	Ted/Blue Beetle
Kamilla Herr	Selina Kyle
Barry Crain	Edward Nigma
Jim Wisnewski	Vandal Savage, King
Mark Kolodny	Zatara II
Steve Darnall	Ralph Dibny
Jill Thompson	Joker's Daughter
Brian Azzarello	666
Tony Akins	Stars & Stripes, Condor
Scott Beaderstadt	Orion, Scott Free, Highfather, Zeus
Lindsay Ross	Captain Atom
Mike Spooner	Wesley Dodds

**Karen Kooi   Holly Blessen   Sung Koo   Terry LaBan
Alex Wald   Ken Sanzel   Laura Strohl   Ruth Morrison
Aldrin Aw   Angel Medina   Maureen McTigue
Heidi MacDonald   David Vinson   Jason Liebig   Bob Kahan
Chantal d'Aulnis   Mike Carlin   Amy Schmetterling
Rob Simpson   Steve Korté   Scott Sonneborn   Scott Nybakken
Rich Markow   Nick Bertozzi   Laurie Kerr   Maura Healy**

...and to the many others who unbeknownst to them found their way onto these pages.

ACKNOWLEDGMENTS

I've said this before, but it bears repeating: without the ideas and advice of Brian Augustyn, Tom Peyer, and Len Strazewski, the end result of the last three years' effort would not be *Kingdom Come*, but rather a handful of ill-sorted puzzle pieces that I would still be unsuccessfully trying to force-fit together.

Thanks are also due Dan Raspler and his assistant, Peter Tomasi, both of whom spent many a late night working editorial miracles, and to letterer Todd Klein, who graced us with work above and beyond the excellence of which he is routinely capable.

The two men, however, who will never know how much I owe them are Elliot S. Maggin and Christopher Reeve, who twice upon a time taught me who Superman really was…and who he could be. Together, they gave me one of the best friends I have ever had.

Mark Waid

My thanks also to Dan and Pete for their toil and sweat and for making my job all the easier with their great efficiency and frequent communication.

I am indebted to Sung Koo, James Robinson, Steve Darnall and Ruth Morrison for creative input.

The artists who lightened my load for character and prop design include David Williams, Tony Akins, Barry Crain, Dave Johnson, John Olimb, Aldrin Aw and Andrew Kudelka.

Costume props were provided by Lemen Yuen and David Williams. German and Japanese text was translated by Jennifer van Winkle and Alex Wald.

Thanks to Ken and Laura Sanzel of Four Color Images for enhancing the credibility of *Kingdom Come* and my work by mounting a successful gallery show of the artwork.

Thanks to Gethesmane Church for posing as itself.

Alex Ross

GRAPHIC NOVELS

ENEMY ACE: WAR IDYLL
George Pratt

**THE FLASH: LIFE STORY OF
THE FLASH**
M. Waid/B. Augustyn/G. Kane/
J. Staton/T. Palmer

GREEN LANTERN: FEAR ITSELF
Ron Marz/Brad Parker

THE POWER OF SHAZAM!
Jerry Ordway

WONDER WOMAN: AMAZONIA
William Messner-Loebs/
Phil Winslade

COLLECTIONS

**THE GREATEST 1950s
STORIES EVER TOLD**
Various writers and artists

**THE GREATEST TEAM-UP
STORIES EVER TOLD**
Various writers and artists

AQUAMAN: TIME AND TIDE
Peter David/Kirk Jarvinen/
Brad Vancata

DC ONE MILLION
Various writers and artists

THE FINAL NIGHT
K. Kesel/S. Immonen/
J. Marzan/various

THE FLASH: BORN TO RUN
M. Waid/T. Peyer/G. LaRocque/
H. Ramos/various

**GREEN LANTERN:
A NEW DAWN**
R. Marz/D. Banks/R. Tanghal/
various

**GREEN LANTERN: BAPTISM
OF FIRE**
Ron Marz/Darryl Banks/
various

**GREEN LANTERN: EMERALD
KNIGHTS**
Ron Marz/Darryl Banks/
various

HAWK & DOVE
Karl and Barbara Kesel/
Rob Liefeld

HITMAN
Garth Ennis/John McCrea

HITMAN: LOCAL HEROES
G. Ennis/J. McCrea/
C. Ezquerra/S. Pugh

**HITMAN: TEN THOUSAND
BULLETS**
Garth Ennis/John McCrea

IMPULSE: RECKLESS YOUTH
Mark Waid/various

JACK KIRBY'S FOREVER PEOPLE
Jack Kirby/various

JACK KIRBY'S NEW GODS
Jack Kirby/various

JACK KIRBY'S MISTER MIRACLE
Jack Kirby/various

**JUSTICE LEAGUE: A NEW
BEGINNING**
K. Giffen/J.M. DeMatteis/
K. Maguire/various

**JUSTICE LEAGUE:
A MIDSUMMER'S NIGHTMARE**
M. Waid/F. Nicieza/J. Johnson/
D. Robertson/various

JLA: AMERICAN DREAMS
G. Morrison/H. Porter/J. Dell/
various

JLA: JUSTICE FOR ALL
G. Morrison/M. Waid/H. Porter/
J. Dell/various

**JUSTICE LEAGUE OF AMERICA:
THE NAIL**
Alan Davis/Mark Farmer

JLA: NEW WORLD ORDER
Grant Morrison/
Howard Porter/John Dell

JLA: ROCK OF AGES
G. Morrison/H. Porter/J. Dell/
various

JLA: STRENGTH IN NUMBERS
G. Morrison/M. Waid/H. Porter/
J. Dell/various

**JLA: WORLD WITHOUT
GROWN-UPS**
T. Dezago/T. Nauck/H. Ramos/
M. McKone/various

**JLA/TITANS: THE TECHNIS
IMPERATIVE**
D. Grayson/P. Jimenez/
P. Pelletier/various

JLA: YEAR ONE
M. Waid/B. Augustyn/
B. Kitson/various

KINGDOM COME
Mark Waid/Alex Ross

**LEGENDS: THE COLLECTED
EDITION**
J. Ostrander/L. Wein/J. Byrne/
K. Kesel

LOBO'S GREATEST HITS
Various writers and artists

LOBO: THE LAST CZARNIAN
Keith Giffen/Alan Grant/
Simon Bisley

LOBO'S BACK'S BACK
K. Giffen/A. Grant/S. Bisley/
C. Alamy

**MANHUNTER: THE SPECIAL
EDITION**
Archie Goodwin/Walter Simonson

**THE RAY: IN A BLAZE OF
POWER**
Jack C. Harris/Joe Quesada/
Art Nichols

**THE SPECTRE: CRIMES AND
PUNISHMENTS**
John Ostrander/Tom Mandrake

**STARMAN: SINS OF THE
FATHER**
James Robinson/Tony Harris/
Wade von Grawbadger

STARMAN: NIGHT AND DAY
James Robinson/Tony Harris/
Wade von Grawbadger

STARMAN: TIMES PAST
J. Robinson/O. Jimenez/
L. Weeks/various

**STARMAN: A WICKED
INCLINATION...**
J. Robinson/T. Harris/
W. von Grawbadger/various

UNDERWORLD UNLEASHED
M. Waid/H. Porter/
P. Jimenez/various

**WONDER WOMAN:
THE CONTEST**
William Messner-Loebs/
Mike Deodato, Jr.

**WONDER WOMAN:
SECOND GENESIS**
John Byrne

WONDER WOMAN: LIFELINES
John Byrne

**DC/MARVEL: CROSSOVER
CLASSICS II**
Various writers and artists

**DC VERSUS MARVEL/
MARVEL VERSUS DC**
R. Marz/P. David/D. Jurgens/
C. Castellini/various

**THE AMALGAM AGE
OF COMICS:
THE DC COMICS COLLECTION**
Various writers and artists

**RETURN TO THE AMALGAM
AGE OF COMICS:
THE DC COMICS COLLECTION**
Various writers and artists

OTHER COLLECTIONS
OF INTEREST

CAMELOT 3000
Mike W. Barr/Brian Bolland/
various

RONIN
Frank Miller

WATCHMEN
Alan Moore/Dave Gibbons

ARCHIVE EDITIONS

**THE FLASH ARCHIVES
Volume 1**
(FLASH COMICS 104, SHOWCASE
4, 8, 13, 14, THE FLASH 105-108)
J. Broome/C. Infantino/J. Giella/
various
**THE FLASH ARCHIVES
Volume 2**
(THE FLASH 109-116)
J.Broome/C. Infantino/J. Giella/
various

**GREEN LANTERN ARCHIVES
Volume 1**
(SHOWCASE 22-23,
GREEN LANTERN 1-5)
**GREEN LANTERN ARCHIVES
Volume 2**
(GREEN LANTERN 6-13)
All by J. Broome/G. Kane/
J. Giella/various

SHAZAM ARCHIVES Volume 1
(WHIZ COMICS 2-15)
SHAZAM ARCHIVES Volume 2
(SPECIAL EDITION COMICS 1,
CAPTAIN MARVEL ADVENTURES 1,
WHIZ COMICS 15-20)
All by B. Parker/C.C. Beck/
J. Simon/J. Kirby/various

**THE NEW TEEN TITANS
Volume 1**
(DC COMICS PRESENTS 26,
THE NEW TITANS 1-8)
Marv Wolfman/George Pérez/
various

**TO FIND MORE COLLECTED EDITIONS AND MONTHLY COMIC BOOKS FROM DC COMICS,
CALL 1-888-COMIC BOOK FOR THE NEAREST COMICS SHOP OR GO TO YOUR LOCAL BOOK STORE.**

Visit us at www.dccomics.com